P9-EFG-068

Children's Understanding

The Development
of Mental Models

Children's Understanding

The Development
of Mental Models

Graeme S. Halford
The University of Queensland, Australia

LEA LAWRENCE ERLBAUM ASSOCIATES, PUBLISHERS
1993   Hillsdale, New Jersey   Hove and London

Lawrence Erlbaum Associates, Inc., Publishers
365 Broadway
Hillsdale, New Jersey 07642

Library of Congress Cataloging-in-Publication Data

Halford, Graeme S.
   Children's understanding : the development of mental models /
Graeme S. Halford.
      p.   cm.
   Includes bibliographical references (p.   ) and index.
   ISBN 0-89859-970-9 (cloth). — ISBN 0-8058-1233-4 (pbk.)
   1. Cognitive learning. 2. Comprehension in children. 3. Mental
representation. 4. Inference. I. Title.
LB1062.H24 1993
370.15′2—dc20   92-20953
                                                               CIP

Books published by Lawrence Erlbaum Associates are printed on acid-free
paper, and their bindings are chosen for strength and durability.

Printed in the United States of America
10 9 8 7 6 5 4 3 2 1

For all who helped,
beginning with my parents.

Contents

PART IV DOMAIN-SPECIFIC PROCESSES AND CONCEPTS

PART V CONCLUSIONS

PREFACE

This book presents a theory of cognitive development that gives a central role to children's understanding. One reason for this is that the concepts children understand have a strong influence on the strategies, skills, and competencies they can develop. Furthermore, understanding is no longer a nebulous concept but one that can be rigorously and usefully explicated. This is one of the ways that recent developments in cognition and cognitive science have fundamentally changed the way we view cognitive development; others include the insights cognitive science has provided into the nature of human reasoning, such as the significant role played by memory retrieval processes and analogy. Our conception of what develops has been influenced by research into acquisition of strategies, rules, knowledge of regularities in the world, and the processes entailed in coding and organizing knowledge.

Contemporary models of learning are much more relevant to cognitive development than traditional models, and I have tried to integrate this new contribution into the theory of cognitive development. I have had a longstanding interest in the problems of conceptual complexity and processing capacity, and have drawn on the extensive cognitive science literature on these topics to define their implications for cognitive development more precisely. In this respect, I have found the new Parallel Distributed Processing (PDP), Connectionist, Neutral Net models especially useful, because they have led me to fundamentally new explanations for processing capacity limitations. This has also provided a new basis for phenomena that have been attributed to cognitive developmental stages. The result has been a new synthesis of processes entailed in cognitive development, and one that I personally have found very exciting. I hope I have conveyed something of that excitement in this book.

The book is intended primarily for graduates and senior undergraduates in psychology, education, and cognitive science. It has implications for education, especially in mathematics and science, but the orientation is to defining the underlying psychological processes, rather than to specifying teaching techniques. Further work is therefore required before application in the classroom.

Much of the argument has a mathematical basis, but I have tried to present the math in a way that requires a minimum of specialized mathematical knowledge. The details of the mathematical treatments are provided in appendices, footnotes, or in other published works that are cited where relevant. Empirical work is presented in summary form, and the full details can be obtained from published works.

One of the most pleasant aspects of writing a book is to recall those people who have contributed so generously to the development of ideas through their extremely competent criticisms and suggestions as well as their support and encouragement. In this respect I have been particularly fortunate to have had a long association with John Bain, whose knowledge of cognition is unusual in its depth and profundity, and who has been so selfless and supportive as a research collaborator. He deserves great credit for sharpening and developing my understanding of many concepts of cognition that have come to take a central role in my theory of cognitive development. There have been many other people also with whom I have been very fortunate to collaborate, and who have contributed in a similar way. These include Murray Maybery, Bill Wilson, Julie Stewart, Sue Smith, Janet Wiles, Michael Humphreys, Matthew McDonald, Barbara Hodkin, Cathy Brown, Mark Bahr, Elizabeth Leitch, Campbell Dickson, Jian Guo, Ross Gayler, Mavis Kelly, Rosemary Baker, Craig Shaw, Susan Robinson, and Susan Buntine.

Another major debt is to the people whose contributions to the literature have provided inspiration for, as well as the building blocks of, this work, and who are acknowledged of course in the citations. However there are some with whom I have been fortunate to enjoy a special relationship from which I have derived great intellectual stimulation, as well as support and encouragement. These are too numerous to mention exhaustively, but I would like to express my special appreciation to John Flavell, Bob Siegler, Dedre Gentner, Robbie Case, Pat Cheng, Keith Holyoak, Rochel Gelman, Donald Broadbent, Alan Baddeley, Lyn Reder, John Anderson, David Klahr, and Jacqueline Goodnow. The deficiencies that remain despite the best efforts of my friends and collaborators will be recognizably mine.

My most special acknowledgement of all goes to my wife, Lyn English, whose support, love, and enthusiasm gave me the resources I needed to do this work.

—*Graeme S. Halford*

Biographical Sketch

Graeme Sydney Halford

Graeme Sydney Halford was born on November 11, 1937, in Sydney, Australia. He was educated at Dubbo High School and Barker College, Hornsby. He obtained a Bachelor of Arts with Honours in 1962, and a Master of Arts with Honours in 1965, from the University of New England. He was given his first lecturing appointment at the University of Newcastle, New South Wales. He obtained a PhD from the University of Newcastle in 1969. Later he became a senior lecturer at the University of Newcastle, an associate professor at Queens University, Kingston, Canada, and a senior lecturer, then reader, at the University of Queensland. He was awarded a personal chair at the University of Queensland in 1989. He conducts research on cognitive development and adult cognitive processes, and is especially interested in the role of learning and information processing limitations in shaping children's cognitions. He has published approximately 80 technical works, including the book, *The Development of Thought*, and articles in Cognitive Psychology, Child Development, and other prestigious journals. He is a Fellow of the American Psychological Society, a Fellow of the Australian Psychological Society, and a Fellow of Academy of the Social Sciences in Australia. He is currently working on a Parallel Distributed Processing model of analogical reasoning, and is very interested in exploring the implications of the model for processing capacity limitations in adults and children. He is a member of the National Committee for Psychology of the Australian Academy of Science. Professor Halford's main recreation is yachting, but also enjoys theatre and ballet and is interested in the graphic arts.

INTRODUCTION

1

THE NATURE OF UNDERSTANDING

One of the most notable things about children is that they are very organized, intelligent, and adaptive. They have the ability to acquire a prodigious amount of information about their world and to represent and interpret that information in a way that not only makes sense but equips them to solve a huge, and largely unpredictable, array of problems. This book is about how children acquire information, how they represent it, and how they use it to build problem-solving skills. With this information I hope to explain why children understand things the way they do and how they use that understanding in solving problems.

Although the book is concerned with basic processes in cognitive development, understanding is emphasized because it confers a certain cognitive autonomy on the child. To the extent that children understand something, they can devise their own way of representing it and dealing with it. They can also devise new ways of dealing with changed circumstances they might meet in the future. Furthermore they can use their understanding as a basis for acquiring further information. In effect, understanding is one of the most valuable acquisitions a child or anyone else can make. Furthermore the processes entailed in understanding constitute a major challenge for contemporary cognitive science.

This book is concerned with children's understanding of concepts and with the way that understanding is used for such processes as making inferences, developing problem-solving strategies, organizing memory, and aiding learning. It will be argued that understanding plays a crucial role in cognitive development, but it needs to be considered in relation to other basic processes such as learning, memory, and development of capacity.

The term *understanding* can apply to an extremely wide range of activities, including language comprehension, reading, problem solving, and memory. It would obviously not be possible to cover all these topics in one book, even were it desirable to do so. Instead, I examine the basic processes entailed in understanding and the role they play in cognitive development.

The controversy concerning the utility of understanding as a topic for scientific enquiry that once existed between gestalt psychologists on the one hand and learning theorists on the other has now passed us by and has been replaced by a new consensus. Although gestalt psychologists considered understanding important and emphasized representations, "seeing" the problem, and insight as basic factors in thought (Humphrey, 1951), psychologists working within the learning theory tradition regarded such notions as unscientific and subjective. Thus, Bugelski (1964) contended that "understanding does not contribute anything but a feeling of satisfaction" (p. 204). Since that time, and especially in the last decade, there seems to be growing recognition that understanding plays an important role in learning and thinking, especially with respect to the acquisition and use of mathematical, scientific, and technological concepts (Gentner & Stevens, 1983; Resnick, 1983b).

There are several reasons for the growth of interest in understanding as a topic of scientific enquiry. One has been the development of cognitive models that give a rigorous definition of what it means to understand something. For example, Simon and Hayes (1976) developed a program called UNDERSTAND that could interpret natural language descriptions of a problem and create an appropriate representation or problem space. Another influence was the work of Gelman and Gallistel (1978), which indicated that children's counting was not based solely on the exercise of mechanical skills but reflected understanding of counting principles. Then Greeno, Riley, and Gelman (1984) produced a computer simulation model of the constraint exercised by elementary number concepts on counting strategies. This meant that not only could understanding be defined rigorously but the way it influenced actual performance could be modeled in detail.

The importance of understanding has also been clearly seen in research on mathematical and scientific education. It has been found that children's errors in arithmetic are often based on faulty understanding or, more frequently, on failure to apply the understanding they have (Resnick & Omanson, 1987). It has also been found useful to analyze what is entailed in mathematicians' understanding of their discipline (Michener, 1978). Investigation of high school and college students' performance on problems in physics has shown that misunderstandings persist even after courses are successfully completed (McCloskey, 1983). This has led to increased interest in ways of promoting understanding and guiding children to develop rational justification for their problem-solving strategies (Resnick, 1983b).

Research on cognitive development, particularly within the Piagetian context, has frequently revolved around the question of what children understand. It has often been a matter of contention as to whether, for example, preschool children genuinely understand concepts like conservation and classification or whether their apparent successes are based on mechanical application of rules. I have reviewed this issue elsewhere (Halford, 1982, 1989), but in this book I try to show that a better definition of understanding can sharpen long-standing issues in cognitive development and lead to new insights. It is more useful to specify the mental model that a child has of a concept than to categorize the child as understanding or not understanding that concept.

UNDERSTANDING AND MENTAL MODELS

Understanding entails mental models, and the growth of interest in understanding was reflected in two books both using the title *Mental Models*, both published in the same year (Gentner & Stevens, 1983; Johnson-Laird, 1983). This interest is largely due to our realization that the type of mental models that we have profoundly influences the expectations we have about the world, the way we go about solving problems, and the way we acquire new knowledge.

To set the stage for our argument, we briefly consider some examples of the way mental models influence our ability to solve problems. Figure 1.1 shows a gestalt area problem that originated with Wertheimer and was discussed by Humphrey (1951). The figure ABCD is a square, and AP = CQ. The problem is to find the area of the square ABCD plus the parallelogram, APCQ. According to Gestalt psychology, the essential step is to see that the problem may be represented as two triangles, PDC and AQB. The sum of these two triangles equals the required area, so the solution is PD × AB, or an equivalent. The striking thing about this problem is how much easier it is once the right mental model is adopted. The restructuring of the original problem representation into the much more advantageous representation based on the sum of two triangles is an example of what the gestalt psychologists called "insight." Another example of the way mental models can facilitate or inhibit problem solving occurs in the well-known problem about the car and the bird. A car makes a journey from Town A to Town B, 100 miles apart, and travels at 25 miles per hour. At the moment the car leaves A, a bird leaves B, flies towards the car at 50 miles per hour and, on reaching the car, returns to B. Then it flies out to meet the car again, returns to B, and so on until the car reaches B. How far does the bird fly?

Attempts to solve the problem by calculating the time of each out-and-return journey, then summing the times, leads to a very complex series, with cumbersome calculations. A better "mental model" is to say that since the

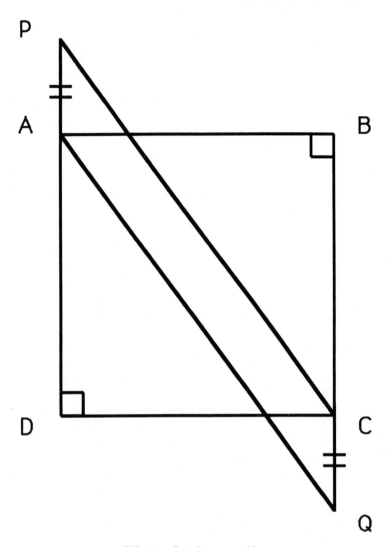

FIG. 1.1. Gestalt area problem.

car will take 4 hours to travel from A to B, and the bird flies at 50 miles per hour, then the bird flies 200 miles.

The importance of mental models, as we noted, has been highlighted in the context of scientific education. A problem investigated by McCloskey (1983) is illustrated in Fig. 1.2. Students are asked to say where a bomb will land after it is dropped from an aircraft, ignoring air resistance. The correct solution is that the bomb will travel a parabolic path, striking the ground directly beneath the aircraft. Some of the incorrect solutions offered by students are shown. These errors are found to occur because of naive mental models about motion. Some students believe, even after completing courses on mechanics, that an object moves because it receives an "impetus" to move, and that the impetus is lost over time. In this case the bomb receives the impetus to move from the plane, and when it leaves the plane it loses the impetus. This leads to a variety of incorrect solutions, such as that the bomb falls between the release point and the point that the plane has reached by the time bomb hits the ground, that the bomb falls straight down, or even that the bomb falls behind the point where it was released. Empirical study showed that even some students who had passed their examinations in the subject did not understand the basic principles of Newtonian mechanics exemplified in this problem.

Our final example of the importance of mental models concerns a classic finding in the field of cognitive development. The paradigm was one that was developed by Bryant and Trabasso (1971) to assess young children's ability to make transitive inferences (e.g., $a < b$, $b < c$, therefore $a < c$). It entailed training children with relative lengths of pairs of colored sticks, so that for example the red stick was shorter than the blue stick. The sticks formed an ascending series, with Stick 1 the shortest and Stick 5 the longest. Having been trained on the adjacent pairs, $1 < 2$, $2 < 3$, $3 < 4$, $4 < 5$ (and the inverses $2 > 1$, etc.), children were tested on all possible pairs. Performance on the pair $2 < 4$ was regarded as the test of ability to make transitive inferences, because it requires the inference $2 < 3$, $3 < 4$, therefore $2 < 4$.

Trabasso, Riley, and Wilson (1975) increased the length of the series, so there was a fifth pair such that $5 < 6$. This raises the interesting possibility of comparing one- and two-step transitive inferences. Comparison of 2 with 4, or 3 with 5 entails a one-step inference; for example, $2 < 3$, $3 < 4$, therefore $2 < 4$. Comparison of 2 with 5 entails a two-step inference; $2 < 3$, $3 < 4$, therefore $2 < 4$, then $4 < 5$, therefore $2 < 5$. The more complex sequence of steps required for the two-step inference makes it appear virtually

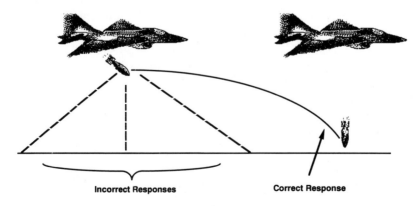

Incorrect Responses   **Correct Response**

FIG. 1.2. Problem concerning laws of motion.

certain that it would be more difficult, producing longer decision times and more errors. Empirical results were the opposite of this, the two-step inference actually being faster and more accurate.

The reason for this result is now very well known. Study of serial position effects showed that both children and adults performed this task by constructing an ordered array. That is, they encoded the premises as an image, or a verbally rehearsed string, with the elements in the order 1, 2, 3, 4, 5, (6). Thus the mental model that people used was not based on making inferences from separate premises, $2 < 3$, and $3 < 4$ and so on, but on accessing an integrated array representation. Once the problem elements are assembled into the array, any comparison could be made easily by accessing the array; we only have to examine the array to see that $2 < 3, 3 < 4, \ldots 2 < 5$ and so on. Moreover, the further the elements in the array are separated, the clearer the difference between them. This is an example of the symbolic distance effect; the more different two mental symbols are, the more easily they are distinguished. This explains why the two-step inference, $2 < 5$ is easier than one-step inferences $2 < 4$ or $3 < 5$.

The very extensive literature on transitive inference has been the subject of a number of reviews (Breslow, 1981; Halford, 1982; Thayer & Collyer, 1978; Trabasso, 1975, 1977). This program of research illustrates how the knowledge of the mental model that is used for a task clarifies the nature of the person's performance. We could argue endlessly over whether children of a particular age should be categorized as understanding transitivity on the basis of this evidence. It is more useful to know what mental processes they employ in performing the task. Their performance on this and related tasks can then be predicted. This is not to argue that there are no important age differences in the task. On the contrary, in many of the concepts we examine, including transitivity, there are very significant age differences, and they represent some very important principles. However these principles can be recognized more clearly by defining precisely the mental models used rather than by categorizing children according to some arbitrarily defined mastery criterion.

I also want to illustrate an argument that is taken up in a number of contexts later in this book. It is that analysis of understanding can often explain why tasks are difficult. Understanding of transitive inference entails constructing an ordered set of premise elements; in this case the set of sticks in the order 1, 2, 3, 4, 5, (6). The construction of this ordered set representation is responsible for part of the difficulty of transitive inference. To see why this is so, consider the problem "Peter is happier than Tom, Bill is happier than Peter, who is the happiest?" Most of us experience some slight feeling of effort in solving the problem. I suggest the reason is that both premises have to be processed jointly in order to construct the correct order. From the first premise we know that (for example) Peter belongs in Position 1 or 2, but we do not know which. From the second premise we know that Peter is in Position 2 or 3, but again we would not know which from the second premise alone. Only by considering both premises jointly can we determine the position of Peter uniquely. A similar argument applies for Tom and Bill. Both premises must be processed jointly to determine the correct ordinal position of any element in the problem.

Tasks like this that require relations to be considered jointly in order to construct an appropriate mental model are difficult, both for children and adults. I suggest that whereas our information processing capacity is prodigious, even virtually unlimited in some respects, we have quite restricted capacity for this type of performance. In fact it is not hard to put even adult processing capacity under a strain with this type of problem. To illustrate, consider this problem:

Wendy is taller than Mark.

Bill is taller than Jenny.

Jenny is taller than Wendy.

What is the correct order of height?

Most people find this a moderately effortful task, and success rates as low as 50% have been obtained on problems of this form with adults (Foos, Smith, Sabol, & Mynatt, 1976). The source of the difficulty is to be found in the amount of information that has to be stored and processed in a single step, when the third premise (Jenny is taller than Wendy) is processed. Analysis of these storage and processing loads sheds a lot of light on difficulties experienced in cognitive tasks. This example also illustrates another theme of this book. The difficulties that children experience with tasks like transitive inference are not unique to children but affect adults also, because they reflect fundamental properties of human cognitive architecture. They just affect children more, for reasons that we will explore later. One purpose of this book is to define, explain, and suggest ways of overcoming, such limitations.

NATURE OF UNDERSTANDING

The term *understanding* has been used very widely and rather loosely, with the result that it is not possible to find a definition that would satisfy all uses. However, some essential properties of understanding can be specified. These are:

1. Representation. To understand a concept entails having an internal, cognitive representation or mental model that reflects the structure of that concept. The representation defines the workspace for problem solving and decision making with respect to the concept. Simon and Hayes (1976) pointed out that to understand a task is to have an internal representation of the problem space, together with a set of operators for moving from one situation to another within the problem space. Holland, Holyoak, Nisbett, and Thagard (1986) defined *understanding* as having a mental model of a situation. In an earlier book (Halford, 1982) I argued that understanding means having a representation that is structurally isomorphic to the problem. Despite their different orientations, there is some consensus among the theorists that understanding means having an internal representation or mental model that corresponds to a concept, task, or phenomenon.

Representations are discussed in detail in chapter 2, but for the moment we should note that there is no restriction on the mode of representations, so it can be analog or analytic and may consist of images or propositions. The choice of representation probably depends on individual differences and task demands. The important thing is that the structure of the mental model must correspond to the structure of the concept, phenomenon, or task that is represented. There need not necessarily be any literal similarity between the representation and its referent, and they may even have no individual features in common. However there must be some type of structural correspondence. We illustrate this concept later in this chapter, and a formal definition of structural correspondence is given in Appendix 2.A.

2. Generality. The mental models that serve as a basis for understanding must have a certain degree of generality, in the sense that they must be transferable from one situation to another. Thus a representation that provides an understanding of transitivity must be capable of representing a variety of problem forms, not just one problem. Ability to transfer should therefore be a criterion of understanding, and the mechanisms that mediate transfer are considered in chapters 4 and 6.

3. Generativity. Representations that provide a basis for understanding must be generative so that predictions or inferences can be made from them that go "beyond the information given" (Bruner, 1957, p. 67). One use of mental models is to predict the environment, and models can be considered valid to the extent that predictions generated from them correspond to the environment. Mental models can also be useful in recall tasks, because they permit aspects of a situation to be predicted, reducing the amount of information that must be recalled. They can also assist learning, because once a mental model of a situation has been constructed it can be used to predict new aspects of the situation, reducing the effort required.

4. Guidance of skills. Understanding should guide the development of problem-solving strategies and skills. Greeno, Riley, and Gelman (1984), and VanLehn and Brown (1980) presented sophisticated models of the way understanding number constrains the development of counting strategies. Halford, Smith, Maybery, Stewart, and Dickson (1991) presented a model of the way understanding of the concept of order constrains the development of transitive inference strategies in children. Ability to develop appropriate strategies should be a criterion of understanding. It seems entirely reasonable that if one understands a concept it should be possible to devise at least some actions that are appropriate to it.

This is not to imply however that understanding is used whenever a task is being performed. Understanding can be used to develop strategies for new tasks, or for old tasks in new contexts, where no appropriate strategy is available. Alternatively, a new strategy might be developed to replace an inefficient strategy. However, understanding need not be employed for tasks for which effective strategies already exist. Understanding tends to impose high processing loads and, therefore, will not be used where less demanding, more automatic processes suffice. Furthermore, understanding is not the only mechanism involved in strategy selection and development. There are also associative strategy-selection mechanisms that operate without representations of the problem (Siegler, 1989a, 1989b). Where these mechanisms suffice they will tend to be preferred, because they impose smaller processing loads and understanding will tend to be used only where associative processes are inadequate. Understanding is therefore important in development because it permits adaptation to major changes or enables new concepts to be applied.

5. Organization of information. Understanding should lead to organization of knowledge, so that relations between representations are recognized and kept consistent. To take a simple example, understanding the concept of an ordered set will entail recognition that the second item is the successor to the first, but also that the third is the successor to the second, and so on. It would probably also entail recognition that the same relation, that of succession, exists between the first and second and between the second and third elements, and so on. Furthermore, it would be recognized that "predecessor" is the opposite of "successor," so if the second element is the successor to the first, the first is the predecessor of the second, and so on. This is an example of organization within a simple representation, but relations between this and other representations should also be recognized. For example, the correspondence between different instances of ordered sets should be recognized, so the natural numbers {1, 2, 3, , , ,} are recognized as being ordered. The particular kind of organization will depend of course on the subject matter. Michener (1978) sketched the kind of organization of knowledge required to understand mathematics, and showed how it depends on such things as reference examples and concepts of known generality.

Organization of knowledge can assist memory search and thereby aid recall (Somerville & Wellman, 1979), and it can guide the search for new inputs (Gelman & Greeno, 1989). It should facilitate learning by making the material to be learned more predictable, thereby reducing the learning effort required.

UNDERSTANDING AND REASONING

Now we illustrate the process of understanding with respect to a specific task. We use the concept of transitivity for this purpose for several reasons. The first is that it entails all the basic processes involved in reasoning, including comprehension of instructions and premises; representation, transformation, and integration of representations; and production of an inference from the representation. Furthermore these processes occur in the context of a task that is simple enough to be tractable to detailed empirical analysis. Another reason is that there has been very extensive research on the topic with both children and adults (Breslow, 1981; Halford, 1982; Thayer & Collyer, 1978; Trabasso, 1975, 1977). Furthermore this research has led to more consensus about the nature of the underlying mechanisms than is true of some other cognitive concepts such as quantity or class. There are a number of models of these processes that have been well substantiated empirically and that integrate contributions from earlier theories (Foos, Smith, Sabol, & Mynatt, 1976; Halford, Smith, Maybery, Stewart, & Dickson, 1991; Halford et al., 1992; Sternberg, 1980a, 1980b). These features make transitive inference a useful reference task.

A simple transitive inference problem might entail the premises that Bill is happier than Peter, and Peter is happier than Tom. This obviously implies (to us) that Bill is happier than Tom. It also implies that the order of happiness is Bill, Peter, Tom. We know all this because we "understand" both the concept of transitivity and what it means to place people in order with respect to happiness. I would like to consider what this understanding entails and how it is utilized to solve the problem.

This understanding must entail some kind of representation. Most people could probably choose from a variety of mental models for this situation, but it would be consistent with the data of Trabasso, Riley, and Wilson (1975), to assume that Bill, Peter, and Tom are mentally arranged from left-to-right in order of happiness, as shown in Fig. 1.3. The inference, Bill is happier than Tom, can be simply read off from the representation. The concept of arranging things in left–right or top–bottom order is what Cheng and Holyoak (1985) called a "pragmatic reasoning schema," that is, an abstract knowledge structure induced from ordinary life experience. It can be used as a kind of template, or prototypical ordered set, to structure the premises. Its use entails analogical reasoning, defined by Gentner (1983) as a mapping from one structure, the base or source, to another structure, the target. In this case the left–right (top–down) schema serves as the source, and the premise information is the target.

In terms of the structure-mapping theory of analogy (Gentner, 1983), the problem elements are assigned to, or "mapped into," the three positions left, middle, and right, as shown in Fig. 1.3. It is then clear how there is a struc-

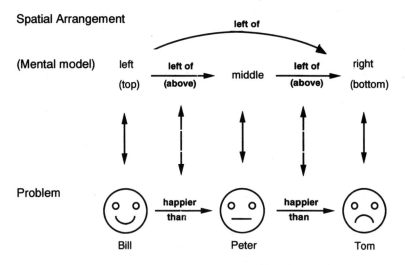

FIG. 1.3. Mapping of transitive-inference problem into a schema.

tural correspondence between the spatial arrangement and the problem. The left position corresponds to Bill, the middle to Peter, and the right to Tom. Furthermore, the relation "left of" consistently corresponds to the relation "happier than." Therefore this task entails recognizing a relationship between two representations, the left–right (top–down) schema and the premises. Once the premise information has been organized as an ordered set, the left–right schema can be ignored, and only the string of premise elements and the relation (in this case "happier than") need be retained.

The transitive inference process, as it has been explicated through empirical work and theory construction in the last three decades, depends primarily on organizing the premise elements as an ordered set. The template for this ordering comes from a common ordering schema, the left–right or top–bottom arrangement. This schema is really used as an analog for the purpose of structuring the premise information. Understanding a transitive inference problem entails constructing a mental model of it in this way. An inference is then made from this mental model.

The process I have just described illustrates the point that much of human reasoning is largely analogical in character. Therefore, I consider briefly the nature of analogies in the next section.

Analogies and Reasoning

According to Gentner (1983), an analogy consists of a source or base (Gentner used the latter term, but the former seems now to be more common, so I will adopt it), and a target. The analogy is constructed by mapping the source into the target. In the simple analogy, "man is to house as dog is to ?," "man is to house" is the source and "dog is to ?" is the target. Man is mapped into dog, house into "?", and the relation "lives in" in the source is mapped into the corresponding relation in the target. In this case the corresponding relations in source and target happen to be the same relation, but this is not always true, a matter we discuss in chapter 2.

To solve this simple problem, the source is mapped into the target, then the relation "lives in" is applied to "dog," and the solution "kennel" is generated. That is, the structural correspondence between source and target is used to generate the answer in a way that has a lot in common with the transitive inference solution given above.

The same kind of reasoning can be used for categorical syllogisms. Consider the problem: P implies Q; not Q, therefore not P. Is this valid? One way for a nonlogician to solve this problem is to use a familiar example as a mental model, generate the answer from the model, then map it into the problem. One might say; rain implies clouds; no clouds, therefore no rain. This everyday phenomenon is isomorphic to the problem, and can serve as a mental model of it. Then since we know that there can be no rain when there is no cloud, we recognize the inference as valid, and conclude that the categorical syllogism is valid. I am not suggesting that such reasoning is infallible, and indeed it is known to be subject to certain sources of error, such as using inappropriate analogs. I am suggesting that analogy is a natural reasoning process, and that syllogistic reasoning can be performed by using a familiar situation as a mental model. The syllogism is mapped into the mental model, then the mapping rules are used to generate a solution.

Alternative Representations

Individuals may vary a great deal in the way they would construct mental models. For example, some people might prefer the left–right schema, whereas others might use top–down. The choice of mental model may vary widely, but the principles entailed in the reasoning process are still quite consistent. The most important one that we have enunciated so far is that the mental model has to bear some structural similarity to the problem.

Young children might not be familiar with left–right or top–down ordering schemas, because both are culturally induced. A mental model that they might be expected to use is shown in Fig. 1.4. The model consists of three toy blocks, one large, one medium, one small. Children presumably have plenty of experience playing with different-sized blocks, and at least occasionally place them in order, even if only accidentally, and notice the kind

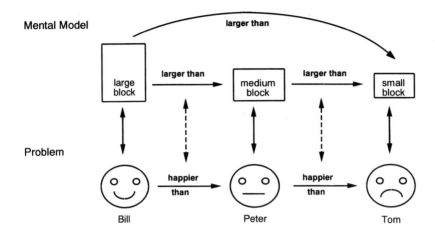

FIG. 1.4. Alternate schema for transitive-inference problem.

of series, or "staircase" that they form. Such an experience could conceivably be used as a mental model for a transitive inference or ordering task. In effect, the blocks are used as an analog of the ordered set entailed in the transitive inference. In terms of Gentner's (1983) structure-mapping theory of analogy, the staircase of blocks in Fig. 1.4 would be the source, and the transitive inference problem would be the target. Each element in the source is mapped or assigned to an element in the target in such a way that there is structural correspondence between the two. Source and target correspond to mental model and problem situation respectively, but we retain the latter terms because they are more suitable for situations other than analogies.

Another way to represent a transitive inference problem is in the form of a rule. A mathematically sophisticated person might understand a transitivity rule of the form $(a > b)$, $(b > c) \rightarrow (a > c)$, or (aRb), $(bRc) \rightarrow (aRc)$, where R is a transitive relation. That is, if a is more than b, and b is more than c, then a is more than c. As Fig. 1.5 shows, the use of the rule to solve the transitive inference problem is not different in principle from the use of the concrete analog, in that the premise information can be mapped into the rule, which serves as a source. There are some differences, in that rule-based reasoning might be more precise and less prone to errors such as choosing bad analogs. However it is still necessary in many cases to recognize the structural correspondence between the rule and the problem presented. In this example, all elements and relations in the mental model are mapped into elements and relations in the problem in such a way that mental model and problem correspond.

Mental Model (known rule)

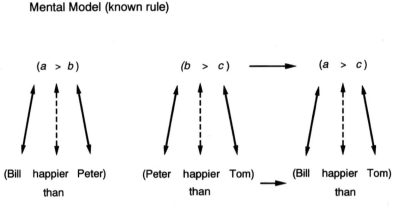

FIG. 1.5.   Rule-based schema for transitive-inference problem.

UNDERSTANDING AND COGNITIVE DEVELOPMENT

The purpose of this section is to sketch the role of understanding in the overall picture of cognitive development. The theory per se is not presented here because it requires more extended treatment, but I try to give the flavor of the argument in order to provide an advanced organizer for the remainder of the book.

The overall scheme for cognitive development is very broadly sketched in Fig. 1.6. The two major classes of determining factors are the *environment* and *innate structures,* transmitted through heredity. I will not take a position on the question of whether individual differences in cognition have an hereditary component, but it must be true that the cognitive equipment that we inherit as a species plays a role in cognitive development. Furthermore, there is evidence that there are innate constraints on the kinds of things we are disposed to learn (Gelman, 1990; Keil, 1990). Given certain cognitive equipment, cognition develops through interaction with the environment. Many of the concepts that children acquire are instantiated in the environment. For example, the concept of quantity relates to quantities of objects and materials that are experienced in the everyday world. The conservation principle, that quantities are invariant over certain transformations such as rearrangement, is a phenomenon that corresponds to common experience. The environment is richly structured, with many regularities, and detection of this structure and regularity is a major component of cognitive development. The structure and regularity are often overlaid with a lot of "noise" or irregularity, but there are learning mechanisms that permit this to be filtered out. Furthermore the detection of some regularities requires cultural support. For example, conservation depends on culturally based measurement and comparison operations. Cognitive development does not proceed solely by spon-

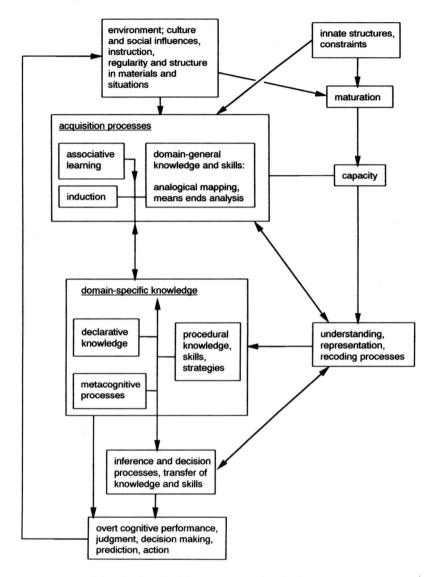

FIG. 1.6. Sketch of factors in cognitive development.

taneous exploration but is aided by social influences and instruction. However, the child is an active builder of cognitions rather than a passive recipient of information, and a child's knowledge is not a gift from his or her mentors.

Innate structures and constraints operate through maturation, which has several aspects, not all of which are purely neurological. For example, the extra mobility that comes *inter alia* from limb development promotes acquisition of the object concept in infants. Factors such as myelination increase speed of processing and may also increase efficiency and resistance to interference between competing activities.

One very controversial question is whether the capacity to store and process information increases with maturation. This question is taken up in detail in chapter 3, but for the time being I simply want to leave open the possibility of an age-related increase in capacity mediating some aspects of cognitive development.

The last decade of research on cognitive development has given new emphasis to the importance of knowledge (Chi & Ceci, 1987). Knowledge depends on interaction with the environment, but it is not sufficient to draw attention either to the role of knowledge per se or to the environmental influences that shape it. It is also necessary to consider the acquisition processes that lead to knowledge. Therefore I devote considerable space to associative learning and induction mechanisms that are relevant to knowledge acquisition in cognitive development. However, there are also domain-general skills, including analogical mapping and means–end analysis, that are important to the acquisition of knowledge and strategies, and their role in cognitive development needs to be explored.

Domain-specific knowledge is not necessarily confined to one domain, but it is not general to all domains. That is, it encompasses knowledge that belongs to one or more domains, but not to all domains. It is therefore distinguished from knowledge that can be applied to any domain, which includes abilities such as analogical reasoning and means–end analysis, discussed above.

There are a number of distinctions that can be drawn between types of domain-specific knowledge. It is usual to distinguish declarative knowledge ("knowing that") from procedural knowledge ("knowing how"). Some types of knowledge seem to fall into both categories; for example, stopping at a red traffic light entails declarative knowledge in the sense that we know it is a rule and procedural knowledge in that we we perform the action. However other types of knowledge seem to belong more clearly in one category. For example, some people might know about certain mathematical concepts but lack the skills for operating with them. Alternatively, we all possess skills such as walking and riding bicycles that we cannot adequately explain or describe. In this case we have procedural knowledge without the corresponding declarative knowledge. There are also cases where one type of knowledge is used to build the other. For example, a child's concept of number (declarative knowledge) might be used to develop appropriate counting strategies (procedural knowledge; Greeno et al., 1984). Declarative knowledge is normally regarded as stored in semantic memory, which is a long-term store that holds what are roughly the equivalent of facts (e.g., one's name, number relation), and is distinguished from episodic memory, which holds context-specific knowledge such as what we ate for breakfast this morning.

It is usual to assume there is a memory for skills, strategies, and other kinds of procedural knowledge. These categories are convenient and are often situationally defined, but they do not necessarily imply the existence of distinct physiological stores. Indeed, it is quite possible that can all be explained in terms of a single set of mnemonic processes (Humphreys, Bain, & Pike, 1989).

Another category is *metacognitive knowledge,* which is knowledge about one's own cognitions. This includes such things as knowing how many items one can remember, how to select or develop strategies for classes of tasks, and how to monitor one's own cognitive activities.

Understanding draws on, and contributes to, all of these processes, as indicated in Fig. 1.6. The knowledge base is used to create representations, which are the basis of understanding. Representations can be drawn from knowledge of the current situation, or they can be transferred from other situations, a process that is essentially analogical. However, it is important that representations are dynamic rather than static, and recoding and reorganization of information is an important component of understanding. I also argue that both children and adults have limited capacity to represent information, and this factor has some important consequences for the way problems are solved.

Understanding, or the ability to represent concepts and situations in a way that is general, generative, connected to other representations, and able to guide skill development, is important in reasoning, inference, and the development and transfer of skills. These processes also draw on domain knowledge. *Overt cognitive performance,* which includes the decisions and judgments we make and the predictions and actions we take, can arise out of reasoning and inference, or it can occur in more automatic fashion by direct retrieval of domain knowledge. Finally, overt cognitive performance influences a person's environment and thereby indirectly affects the underlying cognitive processes. In the chapters that follow I examine all the processes in Fig. 1.6 in detail, and consider how they contribute to the process of cognitive development as a whole.

OUTLINE OF THE BOOK

Part II, comprising chapters 2–5, deals with general processes. Chapter 2 is devoted to a more detailed consideration of mental models and representations. We also consider related concepts such as schemas, the representation of information in perception, and compare representations with analogies. We consider representational systems including semantic networks, condition-action rules, and parallel distributed processes. Then we define four different levels of complexity in representations. Techniques for diagnosing cognitive representations are also considered.

The nature of cognitive processing capacity is considered in chapter 3. Criteria for deciding whether a specific task is capacity limited are outlined, and techniques for measuring processing capacity are considered. It is argued that there is no general purpose pool of capacity, but a number of mechanisms specialized for certain modalities and functions, together with channels for transmitting information from one mechanism to another. The theory of parallel distributed processing is applied to the capacity question, and an explanation for the traditional finding that capacity is limited to a fixed number of chunks regardless of size is presented. The same concepts are used to offer an explanation for the paradox that whereas overall storage capacity does not appear to increase with age, ability to process structure does.

Learning mechanisms are discussed in chapter 4, and it is proposed that cognitive development requires no specialized transition processes, but mechanisms that apply in other contexts can account for cognitive growth. Associative learning processes that lead to representations are considered, together with induction mechanisms by which children can learn the regularities in their environment. The theory of skill acquisition is outlined, and a computer simulation model of strategy development in transitive inference is examined in detail. It is also suggested that analogies play an important role in acquisition of complex cognitive concepts.

Analogies, which are one of the most important domain-general processes, are considered in detail in chapter 5. Theories of analogical reasoning, including computer simulation models, are examined, and their implications for developmental issues are assessed. Children's ability to perform analogical reasoning, and the factors that influence this performance are considered. The costs and benefits of using analogies for reasoning, learning, and transfer are assessed. A structure mapping analysis of humor is also presented.

Part III is devoted to a theory of cognitive development. The theory of the book is outlined in detail in chapter 6, drawing on the material presented in chapters 2–5. The processes by which understanding develops, and the role it plays in cognitive development, are examined.

Part IV is concerned with domain-specific concepts and processes. Processes involved in making deductive and inductive inferences are considered in chapter 7. It is argued, following work by Johnson-Laird (1983) and Cheng and Holyoak (1985), that most deductive inferences depend on content-specific processes that are essentially analogical. This argument is applied to relational syllogisms, such as transitivity, and to categorical syllogisms. Inductive inferences and hypothesis testing are also examined.

The mental models that are entailed in classification and in quantitative concepts related to counting, arithmetic, algebra, and elementary calculus are considered in chapter 8. The learning processes that lead to acquisition of concepts, and the structure mapping processes entailed in their application, are considered. Structure mapping analysis shows why some tasks that have been perennially troublesome to students cause difficulty because of the structural complexity that is inherent in them, and ways of handling this problem will be suggested. Processes by which children come to understand variables are also considered. Finally it is argued that understanding of conservation is a reflection of the whole set of rules that comprise the concept of quantity. Adoption of the conservation rule, in preference to a nonconservation rule, is very hard to explain by itself, but it can be explained by postulating that the conservation rule receives support from other rules that comprise the concept of quantity.

In chapter 9 children's performance on the balance scale is examined, and six types of rules are analyzed into four levels of conceptual complexity. Given the ages at which children can use these representations, as discussed in chapter 6, it is argued that some rules should be understood earlier than present evidence indicates. Then the mental models involved in a variety of problems from Newtonian Mechanics are analyzed, and the reasons for difficulties and misconceptions are analyzed. Misconceptions persist partly because they correspond to rules that are supported by everyday experience, but also because the distinction between the misconception and the valid concept requires some complex structures to be represented. Children's understanding of the apparent–real distinction and their concept of mind are examined in relation to structure-mapping theory.

Part V, comprising chapter 10, brings the argument together. It suggests that although overall capacity does not increase with age, the structural complexity of representations does increase. This explains some of the phenomena that have been attributed to stages of development. However, capacity for more complex representations does not automatically lead to acquistion of new concepts. Cognitive development is experience driven, and learning and induction mechanisms are important in providing a store of information that provides the "raw material" of cognitive processes. Cognitive skills are developed from this same store of information, but this process also depends on experience. Basic reasoning mechanisms, especially analogy, are shown to account for many of the characteristics of children's reasoning.

GENERAL PROCESSES

2

MENTAL MODELS
AND REPRESENTATIONS

The idea that human reasoning depends on mental models has arisen from two main sources. The first is disillusionment with the idea that human reasoning can be described in terms of psycho-logic or mental logic. It now appears that those aspects of thought that Piaget once conceptualized in terms of psychologic are probably better treated in terms of mental models and the operations on them (Halford, 1992). Piaget's empirical work has held up better than is often supposed, as I have argued extensively elsewhere (Halford, 1989), and many of his theoretical conceptions, including structure, schema, and assimilation, have reappeared in contemporary cognitive psychology (Halford, 1992). However the concept of psycho-logic has encountered a number of difficulties. One problem has been that it has proved very difficult to define a psycho-logic that convincingly captures the nature of human reasoning in anything more than a very approximate or restricted sense. Such attempts were made not only by Piaget (e.g., Piaget, 1947-1950, 1957) but also by Osherson (1974a, 1974b, 1975, 1976) and Braine (1978) but, despite their sophistication, these formulations have not led to any consensus about the nature of human reasoning.

Furthermore there is considerable evidence that at least some human reasoning depends on processes other than psycho-logic. Evidence by Henle (1962) and Luria (1976) found that people tended to judge the validity of syllogisms by the factual accuracy of the premises and conclusions, rather than by whether the argument conformed to the rules of logic. The intrusion of world knowledge can be mitigated by inducing children to adopt a play or fantasy orientation (Dias & Harris, 1988, 1990; English, submitted) but it is nevertheless true that decisions are based at least partly on world knowledge rather than logic. Furthermore Tversky and Kahneman (1973) showed that natural reasoning mechanisms depend heavily on retrieval of information from memory, rather than on the application of logical rules. Johnson-Laird (1983, chapter 2) reviewed the argument that human reasoning depends on mental logic, and concluded that there was no decisive evidence to corroborate that claim.

The other source for the idea that human reasoning depends on mental models is research on understanding of scientific and technological concepts. A sample of the work of McCloskey on this question is considered in chapter 1. It was found that even students who had passed examinations in mechanics understood the concept of motion in a way that was experience-based rather than logical. It seems that the way such concepts are represented mentally differs in important respects from the corresponding canonical scientific theories. It was in an attempt to define the nature of this understanding that the theory of mental models was developed.

The concept of mental models has achieved wide currency in the adult cognition literature but has been less readily accepted in the field of cognitive development. One possible reason for this is the influential role of competing approaches, of which three seem to be most significant. The first is the Piagetian orientation towards psycho-logic, which, at least to its adherents, seems to make the concept of mental models unnecessary. The second is the approach that seeks to promote earlier acquisition of concepts. Finally, there is the computational approach, which has depended on one or other computer metaphor, and mental models did not at first seem to fit well with the information processes employed in this context. One could speculate at length on the reason why mental models have not been more widely employed in cognitive developmental theorizing, but the important point is that it is probably an historical accident, and there is no sound reason why mental models should not be adopted more extensively as accounts of children's reasoning. The time certainly seems ripe to reinterpret some of the major issues in cognitive development in terms of mental models.

THE NATURE OF MENTAL MODELS

As with understanding, the term *mental models* has been so widely used that it is probably impossible to produce a definition that would fit every context. In a review of the literature, Rouse and Morris (1986) pointed out that in the skills and ergonomics literature the term has been used to refer to all the knowledge that a person brings to bear on a problem. They suggested a more concise definition: "Mental models are the mechanisms whereby humans generate descriptions of system purpose and form, explanation of system functioning and observed system states, and predictions of future system states"

(p. 360). However Johnson-Laird's (1983) concept of mental models seems still more restricted. He suggested that there are three kinds of representations: "propositional representations which are strings of symbols that correspond to natural language, mental models which are structural analogues of the world, and images which are the perceptual correlates of models from a particular point of view" (1983, p. 165).

Johnson-Laird's definition is probably closer to the way the term *mental models* has been used in theories of human reasoning, but it does not seem appropriate to regard mental models as one kind of representation. The reason is that if Johnson-Laird's categorization is mutually exclusive and exhaustive, this means that a process cannot be both imaginal or propositional and also be a mental model, but there seems to be no reason why this should be so. It seems quite likely that mental models can have images or propositions as components. This would be consistent with Johnson-Laird's suggestion that mental models are structural analogues, which is supported by Collins and Gentner (1987), who suggested that some mental models are representations from another domain that are used by analogy.

Rips (1986) pointed out a number of difficulties that arise if mental models are regarded as a unique class of representations. It would seem more appropriate to define mental models as a process that can draw on one or more types of representation. It seems possible to adopt a definition of mental models that is in keeping with the spirit of Johnson-Laird's approach and with the work of Gentner and Stevens (1983), but that avoids the implication that mental models cannot include propositional or imaginal representations. I propose that *mental models* are representations that are active while solving a particular problem and that provide the workspace for inference and mental operations. They may be influenced by, but do not include, background knowledge. Mental models may consist of any combination of propositional or imaginal representations.

It is typical of mental models that they are incomplete and approximate, rather than being true scientific theories, though this is not a necessary property, because a mental model that was complete and accurate would not be a contradiction. They also have a semantic component, and they reflect the knowledge, experience, and goals of the individual, even though not all this information is actively represented at any one time. This means that mental models can reflect multiple constraints, not all of which are incorporated into the mental model itself. Mental models can be retrieved from memory, where a particular representation has been associated with that situation in the past, they can be transferred from another situation and used by analogy, or they can be constructed out of components obtained from both of these sources. Analogies are mappings from one representation to another, so the fact that mental models comprise representations means they can be used in analogies. Therefore Johnson-Laird's idea that mental models are structural analogs is preserved in this definition.

REPRESENTATIONS

Given that understanding entails representations and that mental models are representations, it is essential to consider the nature of representations in some detail.

Recall from chapter 1 that representations are the workspace of thinking and understanding. Cognitive representations are internal, but they must bear a high degree of correspondence to the environment that they represent. Furthermore they must be able to constrain actions, strategies, and procedures used in problem solving. They must be usable to generate predictions about the environment, and they must aid learning and memory. In this chapter we explore these properties in greater detail, but first we need to define representations explicitly.

Properties of Representations

The theory of representations has been specified in a number of contexts, and all the treatments have a common core of agreement that we will extract. In the context of measurement theory, representations are defined by Suppes and Zinnes (1963) and Coombs, Dawes, and Tversky (1970) as a mapping from one system to another, such that every element in the representing system is mapped uniquely into an element in the represented system, and relations between elements in the representing system correspond to relations between the mapped elements in the represented system. For the formal definition, see Appendix 2.A.

Halford and Wilson (1980) defined a representation as a mapping from a symbol system to an environment system. The symbol system expresses the structure of a representation, whereas the environment system expresses the structure of the aspect of the world that is represented. A representation entails mapping representation elements into elements in the world so that any functions (relations, transformations) between representation elements correspond to functions (relations, transformations) between environment elements. To be valid, the representation had to be consistent, defined in terms of commutativity (see Appendix 2.A).

According to Palmer (1978), "to specify a representation completely one must state: (1) what the represented world is; (2) what the representing world is; (3) what aspects of the represented world are being modeled; (4) what aspects of the representing world are doing the modeling; and (5) what are the correspondences between the two worlds. A representation is really a *representational system* that includes all five aspects" (p. 262).

The most extensive theory of cognitive representation was developed by Holland, Holyoak, Nisbett, and Thagard (1986), who defined it as a quasi-homomorphism, or q-morphism, between a person's mental representation and the corresponding portion of the environment. It is a *homomorphism* because any element in the representation can be mapped to more than one element in the environment. Categorization is provided within the model by mapping representation elements to collections or categories of environment elements. It is called a *quasi-homomorphism* because of imperfections, which allows for the fact that realistic psychological representations will not be completely valid. Validity was defined by Holland et al. in terms of commutativity, as with the treatment of Halford and Wilson.

Despite different terminologies and emphases, all these treatments are basically in agreement that a representation comprises a representing structure that is in correspondence to a represented structure. We will develop this idea in order to specify the nature of cognitive representations and mental models.

A cognitive representation consists of an internal structure that mirrors the structure of a segment of the environment. To take a simple example, an ordered set, such as {Bill, Peter, Tom} ordered for happiness as in Fig. 1.3, is a structure. It consists of the elements Bill, Peter, and Tom, and the relation "happier than" between the elements Bill and Peter, between Peter and Tom, and between Bill and Tom. A set of elements linked by one or more relations, functions, or transformations constitutes a structure. Because the argument is the same for structures based on relations, functions, and transformations, we refer to relations only, unless there is a specific reason for mentioning the alternatives.

The representation is mapped into the segment of the environment being represented in such a way that relations in the representation correspond to relations in the environment. This is the *structural correspondence* property of representations, and it is illustrated in Fig. 2.1. Notice that in every case where there is an R in correspondence to R', the arguments of R are mapped into the arguments of R'; that is, a is mapped to a', b to b', and so on. A representation must also be *consistent*. This means that if a particular cognitive process represents a particular element in the environment on one occasion, it must do so on other occasions. There must be some mechanism to prevent cognitive processes from drifting from one aspect of the environment to another.[1] These two properties of consistency and structural cor-

---

[1]There is some disagreement as to whether mappings must be unique. Grossberg (1980) and Halford and Wilson (1980) assumed isomorphisms (unique mappings), whereas Holland et al. (1986) proposed a homomorphism with one-to-many mappings from representations to environment, thereby providing a categorization function. At the microstructure level mappings are probably isomorphisms, and the categorization function can be handled by superimposition of representations.

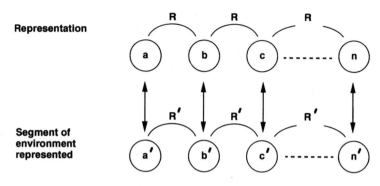

FIG. 2.1. Cognitive representation expressed as a mapping from a representation structure to an environment structure.

respondence are sufficient to establish that representations are valid. Representations need not resemble the aspects of the environment they represent, so representations are not "pictures in the head." Such a notion would have difficulties in any case. A picture in the head requires some sentient being, a "homunculus" to perceive it, but then the representations of the homunculus need to be perceived, which requires a further homunculus, and so on *ad infinitum*. There are a number of epistemological problems with the idea that we put a copy of the world in our heads, so it is important to recognize that the concept of representation does not entail the idea of a mental copy of the world. It only entails the idea that there is a set of cognitive processes that can be mapped into segments of the environment in such a way that the consistency and correspondence properties hold. These criteria can be maintained in quite a mechanistic way that does not entail any circularity.

The consistency and correspondence criteria are soft constraints that hold in an approximate rather than in an absolute sense. The correspondence property can sometimes conflict with the consistency property, in which case the representation that provides the best overall fit to all constraints is selected. Although some discrepancies between representations and the environment can be tolerated, it is essential that most of our stored representations of the environment represent it validly, and it would be dangerously maladaptive for it to be otherwise. Thus our internal representations of reality tell us that the sun rises in the morning and sets at night rather than the reverse, that being hit by a speeding car will be damaging, that profligate use of money leads to financial ruin, and so on.

This not to say that discrepant representations are not important to psychological theory. To take one example from the many available, Tversky and Kahneman (1973) showed that people judge relative frequency by availability. For example, if asked whether the letter "r" occurs more often as the first or the third letter of a word most people say, incorrectly, the first letter. The reason is that we judge the relative frequency of occurrence in each position by attempting to retrieve, from memory, examples of words beginning with r, and words with r as the third letter. Because the former are easier to retrieve (are more "available"), we say there are more of them. The errors produced by availability and similar strategies are theoretically significant because of the insights they give into natural reasoning processes. However it is a mistake to interpret the phenomenon as indicating that most such processes lead to errors. Most of the time they yield the right answer because frequency of events in the environment is positively correlated with their availability in memory. Thus the existence of what might be called "cognitive illusions," that is, situations where our natural cognitive mechanisms lead us astray, does not imply that most cognitive processes represent the environment incorrectly, any more than the existence of perceptual illusions indicates perceptual processes are normally nonveridical. Important exceptions notwithstanding, in general our cognitive processes must, and do, represent the environment correctly.

Types of Representations

It is possible to distinguish two major kinds of cognitive representation, imaginal and propositional. There is controversy about the status of images, some theorists (Kosslyn, 1981; Paivio, 1971) arguing that they entail similar processes to those that underlie perception. According to this view images are coherent and integrated, with relations between elements being preserved in much the same manner as they were in the original object or scene. Furthermore the image can be scanned and can undergo transformations such as rotation in much the same way as real scenes and objects. Images are also content-specific to a high degree, in that they represent particular objects or scenes, rather than abstractions.

The alternate view is that the content of images could be represented as propositions. A proposition is a unit of information that can have a truth value. For example, "cat" is not a proposition, because it cannot be true or false, but "cats climb trees" is a proposition because it can be true or false. *Propositional representations* are strings of cognitive symbols that can have a truth value. A proposition usually has two components, the *predicate,* which expresses some kind of action, relation, or state, and the *arguments,* which express the entities to which the predicate refers. For example the idea that cats climb trees can be expressed as climb(cats, trees), where the predicate is climb, and its arguments are "cats" and "trees." Different kinds of propositions can have different numbers of arguments. For example the proposition that a cat is fat, fat(cat) has one argument, "cat," but the proposition cats climb trees, climb(cats, trees) has two arguments, "cats" and "trees."

Images are analog representations, whereas propositions are analytic and are less tied to specific content. An image of a cat is relatively specific to a particular cat, in that it has a particular size, shape, possibly a specific color, and so on, whereas a proposition can represent a particular object, or a category of objects, or a variable that can assume a number of different values. For example, the proposition "animals can be pets," canbe(animals, pets), treats animals as a variable that can be instantiated as a dog, cat, horse, and so on.

Some theorists argue that images do not exist as a separate mode of representation (Anderson, 1978, 1979; Pylyshyn, 1973, 1981) but that the subjective experience of imagery corresponds to information that can be coded in propositional form. Johnson-Laird (1983) suggested that the issue might depend on the level of analysis that is employed. At some level it is possible that images and propositions are represented in a common code, but at higher or more "global" levels of analysis, they appear as different kinds of representations. The problem is that we do not yet know enough about the way information is coded in the nervous system to settle the matter, and there is quite impressive empirical evidence for representations that function in a way that is consistent with an imaginal code (Kosslyn, 1981; Paivio, 1971). Even though it might ultimately be possible to express imaginal representations in the same code as propositional representations, as argued by Anderson (1978, 1979), Fodor (1975), or Pylyshyn (1973), for most theoretical purposes it is still convenient to distinguish the two modes of representation.

Palmer (1978) argued that the essential difference between imaginal and analytic representations is that in the former representation of relations is intrinsic. To illustrate, consider the relation bigger-than(man, cat). In a picture or a visual image, the fact that the man is bigger than the cat is represented by the fact that the man is actually drawn bigger. The relation bigger than is inherent in the picture or image. By contrast, in the propositional representation, bigger-than(man, cat), there is nothing intrinsic to the expression "bigger-than" that allows it to represent the relation of size. The validity of the representation is based on linguistic convention, and is extrinsic to the representation itself.

Another issue is whether verbal processes can be distinguished as a distinct mode of representation. Subjectively, we often seem to express, and represent, ideas and situations in words, but it is hard to rule out the hypothesis that they are represented as propositions and translated into words. The idea is that input and output are in verbal form, but the information is retained in propositional form. There is evidence that the actual form of words is not retained, but the meaning is (Sachs, 1967), which supports the view that it is propositions rather than words that are represented. In the developmental area, Brainerd and Reyna (in press) argued that cognitive representations comprise the gist of the input, rather than a literal copy, which is consistent with the theory of propositional representations.

Whether conceptual development precedes language development or the reverse has been a long-standing issue in developmental psychology. The Sapir-Whorf hypothesis (Whorf, 1956) was that language was necessary to conceptual development. On the other hand Slobin (1972) pointed out that children often comprehend concepts they cannot express. He gave the example of a child who remarks, "Anything is not to break—just glasses and plates." The child has recognized the distinction between breakable and unbreakable objects, but has not learned the appropriate word. The generative property of language is used with great ingenuity to improvise forms for unfamiliar situations. I once knew a 3-year-old who pointed toward my car and said, "Your dragon Graeme." At first I could see nothing about my car that resembled a dragon, then I realized she was pointing towards the trailer that was behind the car—for draggin'. The important point for our purposes is that the concept must have been represented in some way before the process of generating a natural language form to express it can begin. Vygotsky (1934/1962) argued that thought and language have different phylogenetic and ontogenetic roots, but that they interact in a number of ways during development. This seems consistent with evidence such as that reported by Slobin, mentioned above. Thought does entail a representational system that is independent of the surface form of language in which it might from time to time be expressed. Indeed it may be logically necessary to have such a representational system to serve both thought and language (Fodor, 1975).

So far the discussion has been confined to internal, cognitive representations. However we also use external representations such as pencil and paper, books, computer screens, graphs, and concrete aids such as arithmetic blocks or an abacus. However the structure of the external representation must be mapped into an internal representation. Many such external representations are technically analogs, and their effective use requires that the criteria for good analogies be met, but there are a number of cases where this is not achieved. Some examples of this occur when concrete aids are used to teach mathematics, which will be discussed in chapters 5 and 8.

Complex cognitive processing probably necessitates multiple representations. Janvier (1987) and Kaput (1987) proposed that mathematics requires moving back and forth among several representational systems, both internal and external. A mathematician might use symbols on paper, graphs, images (visual, aural, and motor), and natural language. Success in mathematics can often depend on the ease with which a structure in one representation can be recognized in (mapped into) another. This exemplifies the fact that seeing correspondence between representations is an important cognitive function.

Palmer (1978) pointed out that many of the distinctions that have been made between the representational types are logically irrelevant to theories of cognitive functioning. He argued that the essential thing about a representation is the information it contains. He defined two representations as equivalent if they preserve the same information about the phenomena represented. To the extent that imagery and verbal or propositional representations contain the same information, they are equivalent, and the distinction between them loses relevance. This means that in a logical sense the code of a representation does not matter provided it contains the relevant information. This argument is particularly relevant to this book, because in the issues we examine the most important consideration is often the structure of the representation rather than the code.

Although the form of the representation may not matter in terms of strictly logical analysis, it can have important implications for the psychological processes that operate on the representations. One aspect concerns the resources required to maintain the representation. The resources required to maintain linguistic information may be different from those required for visual imagery, for example. Linguistic representations are held for short periods in what Baddeley (1990) called the articulatory loop, which consists of a short-term store that decays at a fixed rate (Schweickert & Boruff, 1986), being virtually obliterated after 2 seconds. Acoustic strings in short-term memory must be maintained by rehearsal, so the number of items that can be stored depends on the number that can be rehearsed in 2 seconds. This means that fewer longer items, or items that are slow to pronounce, can be stored (Baddeley, Thomson, & Buchanan, 1975; Standing, Bond, Smith, & Isely, 1980). Adults can usually store about seven digits, but only two or three 5-syllable words. However this limitation does not apply to information that is stored as visual images (Baddeley, Grant, Wight, & Thomson, 1975; Baddeley & Lieberman, 1980).

As Paivio (1971) demonstrated it is easier to produce analog, presumably imaginal, representations of concrete than of abstract concepts. Paivio had participants think of a picture or a sentence and relate a number of nouns, and the time to begin drawing the picture or writing the sentence was recorded. Where nouns were abstract, it took longer to represent them as drawings, but abstractness had less effect on verbal representations. Thus different representations are appropriate for different materials. Paivio also found that imaginal/pictorial representations were more advantageous for relating larger numbers of items. The advantage of visual imagery seems to be that it permits a lot of information to be integrated economically into one representation.

Representations and Perception

Perception is not the topic of this book, but there is an important issue as to whether perceptual representations should be considered distinct from conceptual representations. This issue has been debated for a considerable time without any real consensus emerging. Piaget (1950) always insisted that perception and thought were distinct, whereas Bryant (1974) tended to suggest that the perceptual–conceptual distinction may be unnecessary. I argued (Halford, 1982) that Bryant's claims for similarity of perceptual and reasoning processes only apply to restricted examples of reasoning. More recently Mandler (1988) argued cogently for the perceptual–conceptual distinction on the grounds that conceptual knowledge is accessible to consciousness, whereas most of the information that is utilized in perception is not accessible to consciousness. For example, size constancy means that an object appears roughly the same size irrespective of distance, at least over a reasonable range of distances. To achieve size-constancy, we take into account not only retinal size, but also distance. The essence of Mandler's argument is that we are not consciously aware of utilizing this information, and we do not consciously select the information used.

One result of this argument would be that metacognitive processes have limited effect on perception. We cannot, so to speak, choose our perceptions in the same way as we choose hypotheses when solving a problem. Perceptual processes tend to be more unconscious, and beyond our ability to control them in accordance with our strategies. We can of course choose where to look, and there are orienting reactions in other sense modalities, but in general perception is not under the control of our goals in the same way that conception tends to be. This was established through the failure of the directive state school of perception (Bruner & Postman, 1948; see also review by Allport, 1955), which attempted to claim that motives influence perception but failed to martial solid evidence for the claim. On a wet weekend we see the sky as grey, however blue we wish it to be. Conceptual processes also have limited influence on perception. There is a limit to "cognitive penetrability" (Pylyshyn, 1984; Rock, 1985), meaning that cognitive processes have limited influence on perception.

The perceptual–conceptual distinction will no doubt be debated for a long time to come, but I suggest the following grounds for differentiating perceptual from conceptual representations. First, perceptual representations are tied to the current perceptual input. "Top–down" processes, that is processes that take into account some cognitive knowledge, may influence perception, but perceptual representations appear to be more constrained by the current sensory input than occurs with conception. For example, if we are looking at a dog we can only "see" a dog; we cannot see a horse, an elephant, or a car. Conceptual representations do, however, have a high degree of mobility and transferability. One can, as illustrated in Fig. 1.4, use three squares ordered for area to represent the happiness relations between three people. Square size is not happiness, yet it can be used to represent degrees of happiness. Thus conceptual representations are more transferable across situations than percepts.

A second basis for differentiation is that conceptual representations are more accessible across space and time. It is possible to imagine what one's pet looks like even when on the opposite side of the world. It is also possible to recall a mathematical concept without external stimulation. Perception, however, does not break space and time barriers in this way. One sees what one is looking at now, not what one saw yesterday.

A third difference between perception and conception is in computational power. When even an infant views a scene, immensely complex computational processes are going on to give the infant a view of the scene that is consistent with all the incoming information, for example processes concerned with size, shape, and color constancies. These computations are considerably more complex than the inferences that most people can carry out in thought. Thus a 3-year-old who can parse the complex input of a three-dimensional percept without effort may be unable to perform a much simpler transitive inference problem, as we see in chapter 7. It is as though conception is less specialized, more transferable, than perception, but this generality is achieved at the cost of computational power.

This point is important because it implies that we cannot infer conceptual competence when the task can be performed by perceptual processes. To take a simple example; suppose we present a transitive inference problem in which a 3-foot green stick is shown to be longer than a 2-foot blue stick, which in turn is shown to be longer than a 1-foot red stick. Suppose we leave all three sticks visible and ask a child to infer which is longer, the green or the red stick. It is clear that no transitive inference is required, because one can literally see that the green stick is longer than the red stick (I have discussed the methodology of testing transitive inferences elsewhere; Halford, 1982).

Despite the clarity of the perceptual–conceptual distinction in cases like this, it is easy to lose sight of it when it becomes more subtle. For example, using information integration theory (Anderson, 1980), it has been shown that young children can integrate length and breadth information when judging areas. This seems at odds with the observation that sometimes they cannot integrate (say) time and distance information when judging velocity (Siegler & Richards, 1979; Wilkening, 1981). An important difference between the tasks is that when judging area, the figure whose area was being judged was actually visible. Participants could literally see the area. However the integration of time and distance normally needs to be made internally. In this respect therefore the two tasks are not comparable. Therefore, although I do not want to preempt the complex debate about the perceptual–conceptual distinction, it is necessary to the extent that we must not assume that a perceptual process and a conceptual process are the same, simply because of superficial similarities. It is likely that children can perform greater computational feats with perception than with conception, this being the price paid for the greater transferability of the latter.

Representations and Analogies

An analogy may be conceptualized as a mapping from one structure, the base or source, to another structure, the target (Gentner, 1983). The simple analogy in Fig. 2.2 illustrates this mapping process. The analogy is "human is to house as dog is to kennel," and it comprises a mapping from the source (or base), "human is to house," to the target, "dog is to kennel." Human is mapped into dog, and house into kennel, and the relation "lives in" between human and house corresponds to the same relation between dog and kennel. Thus there is a structural correspondence between source and target. In this respect analogies are similar to representations, because a representation is an internal structure that corresponds to a segment of the environment. However an analogy is not a mapping from a representation to the environment, but

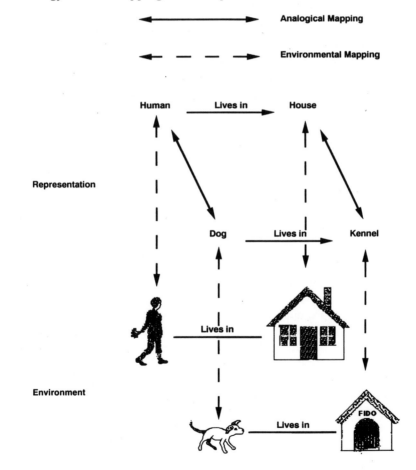

FIG. 2.2.   Analogy expressed as a mapping from one representation to another.

a mapping from one representation to another, as Holland et al. (1986) pointed out. In our current example, the source is a representation of the fact that a human lives in a house, and the target is a representation of the fact that a dog lives in a kennel. The analogy consists of a mapping from the source to the target. Both the analogical and representational mappings are shown in Fig. 2.2. Therefore the analogy is a mapping from the base representation to the target representation. Thus representations and analogies are both mappings from one structure to another, but with representations it is a mapping from a cognitive to an environmental structure, whereas with analogies it is a mapping from one cognitive structure to another.

KNOWLEDGE REPRESENTATION

The imaginal–propositional distinction was concerned with the code of representations, but there is another aspect that is concerned with the content of repesentations, and with the way that content is organized. A number of ways of conceptualizing the way information is represented in memory have been proposed. These include schemas, propositional networks, condition-action rules, and parallel distributed representations. We will consider these in turn.

Schemas

The concept of schema has long been employed in cognitive development theory by Piaget (1950), and in memory theory by Bartlett (1932), but for many decades it was avoided by most cognitive psychologists because of difficulty in defining its precise meaning. However there are now a number of systematic treatments of the concept (Bobrow & Norman, 1975; Minsky, 1975; Rumelhart & Ortony, 1977; Rumelhart, Smolensky, McClelland, & Hinton, 1986; Schank & Abelson, 1977).

A schema is a representation, but it represents a general category of things, situations, or phenomena, rather than specific instances. An example of a schema would be our notion of a room. The room schema does not refer to any specific room, but represents properties of rooms in general. Two other important properties of schemas are that they are flexible and generative. The room schema can represent a huge variety of rooms, even those with very unusual configurations of properties. A schema is generative in that it can be used to draw inferences; for example, if we are told someone is alone in a room containing a bed at 2 a.m., we can predict that they are likely to be sleeping.

It is useful to think of a schema as a set of constraints between variables.

Variables defining the room schema would be such things as floor area, number of windows, ceiling height, presence/absence of features such as sink, bath, oven, refrigerator, bed, fireplace, television, desk, and computer. The schema consists largely of the constraints between these variables. Thus if the floor area is huge, the room is more likely to be a ballroom than a bathroom. If the room contains a bed, it is unlikely to contain an oven, but if contains an oven, it is likely to contain a sink, and so on. Rumelhart et al. (1986) showed how the concept of schema can be modeled quite effectively using constraints between variables. According to this view schemas are not entities but are emergent phenomena arising from the interaction of multiple constraints.

Propositional Networks

Propositions can be linked together to form propositional networks, which can be conveniently represented as diagrams in which each proposition is represented by a node, and its links by arrows. This form of representation is treated in most standard texts on cognitive psychology or cognitive science (see, e.g., Best, 1989, pp. 249–255, or Stillings et al., 1987, pp. 21–30) and is discussed only briefly here. Each proposition is represented by a node, with a link to the relation expressed by that proposition, and a link to each argument. For example, the proposition "John likes dogs," likes (john, dog), would be expressed by a node, with a link to the relation "likes," and links to the arguments "John" and "dogs." Each proposition is represented by a node, and the nodes for different propositions are linked together to form networks. Propositional networks can represent concepts and the meanings of sentences. They have played an important role in a number of prominent theories of cognition, most notably in the ACT* theory of Anderson (1983). In this model, activation spreads in parallel throughout the network, so propositional networks function as associative networks. In ACT* propositional networks represent declarative knowledge, procedural knowledge being represented by production rules, or condition–action rules.

Condition–Action Rules

Condition–action rules are illustrated in Table 2.1 and have been found very useful in accounting for a wide variety of cognitive processes. Each rule has two major components, a condition and an action. The conditions specified in the condition side must be fulfilled for the action to occur. Condition–action rules have entered into many cognitive models in the form of production rules (Anderson, 1983, 1984; Klahr, 1984; Klahr & Wallace, 1976; Wallace, Klahr, & Bluff, 1987). Our concern here is with the basic logic of condition–

TABLE 2.1
Condition–Action Rules

Procedural Rules		
Condition		Action
If sum is: "3 + 4 = ?"	→	say answer "7"
If traffic light is red	→	stop
If weights on two sides of a beam balance are equal	→	say the beam will balance
Declarative Rules		
Condition		Assertion
If x is a cat	→	x will purr
If $(a > b)$ and $(b > c)$	→	$(a > c)$
If the brake is applied in a car	→	the car will stop

action rules, of which production rules may be considered a special case. Two kinds of condition–action rules are shown in Table 2.1, procedural and declarative. The way condition–action rules have traditionally been used corresponds to procedural rules. That is, the action side corresponds to something to be done, and the condition side specifies the circumstances in which it should be done. Models that distinguish procedural and declarative knowledge, such as Anderson's (1983) ACT* model, tend to represent procedural knowledge as production rules and declarative knowledge as semantic networks. However Holland et al. (1986) used condition–action rules to represent knowledge of the world. Although Holland et al. did not use the term *declarative rule*, the essence of their idea is incorporated into the declarative rules in Table 2.1, where we see a rule that if X is a cat, then X purrs. Holland et al. provided a very detailed account of the way predictive condition–action rules are learned through interaction with the environment. This process provides a model of induction because each rule represents accumulated experience with a particular regularity in the environment.

Procedural and declarative rules differ then on their action sides. Procedural rules specify something to do be done, either overtly or covertly. For example, they may specify an action such as stopping at a traffic light, a step in problem solving, or insertion (deletion) of an item in memory. The action may create a condition that triggers a further rule, thereby linking rules together into a strategy or procedure.

Declarative rules however make assertions about the world. It might be argued that making an assertion is an action, and therefore the declarative procedural distinction is unnecessary, at least when applied to condition–action rules. However the distinction is operationalized in terms of the factors that confirm the rules, and therefore control their acquisition. As we discuss in more detail in chapter 4, declarative rules are confirmed by events that correspond to their assertions, but procedural rules are confirmed if the outcome they produce is satisfactory. Consider, for example, a rule that says that if you go to a specified place in a kitchen, you will find a tin of sardines. You go there and find caviar. This does not confirm the assertion that sardines will be found, but it is a satisfactory outcome (assuming one likes caviar). This outcome would confirm a procedural rule, because it rewards you for going to the kitchen, but disconfirm a declarative rule, because it does not confirm the prediction that sardines will be found.

Much of a person's knowledge of the world can be expressed as declarative rules; that cars run on roads, cats purr, the sun rises in the East, 2 + 2 = 4, and so on. We all know a myriad declarative rules of this kind. Procedural rules underlie skills and strategies; for example, for the condition "2 + 2," the action is "4," and so on. In general, condition–action rules seem to capture an essential property of behavior that depends on responding to situations, either internal or external. Allport (1980b) argued that behavior is contingent on "calling patterns." That is, behavior is triggered by particular patterns of stimulation, either internal or external. When one action is triggered off it changes some aspect of the internal or external environment, and then the resulting new pattern activates another rule, thereby making a new action or assertion, which produces a further change in the environment, and so on. This recursive processing of rules seems to mirror quite well the way organisms behave, and models of this type, usually in the form of production rules, have yielded many successful computer simulations of cognitive processes (Anderson, 1983; Klahr & Wallace, 1976; Newell & Simon, 1972; Wallace et al., 1987). A further advantage of condition–action rules is that sophisticated and rigorous techniques now exist for analyzing the rules that are being used.

Holland et al. showed that condition–action rules conform to the definition of representations given earlier. The essence of the idea is illustrated in Fig. 2.3. The real-world fact that cats purr is expressed as a condition–action rule; the condition side is that something is a cat. The action side is the prediction that it purrs. The convention of using an arrow to link the condition to the action side is again employed. The mental model takes the form of a condition–action rule; if X is a cat $\rightarrow$ X purrs. This rule represents the environmental fact that cats are things that purr. The correspondence of the model to the environment is imprecise in this case, because all cats do not purr all of the time. Holland et al. (1986) accounted for this with the concept of the default hierarchy, which is illustrated in Table 2.2. It consists of a hierarchy of increasingly specific rules. The most specific rules are given priority, but if a more specific rule is not applicable, the system defaults to a more general rule. The most general rule in this example is that cats purr, but a more specific rule is that cats purr if they are domestic, and the most

Mental Model

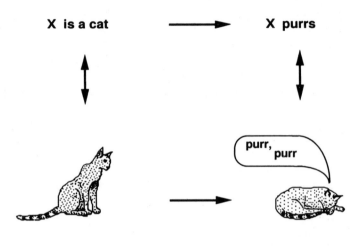

Environment

FIG. 2.3. Representation expressed as declarative condition–action rule.

specific rule (in our example) is that cats purr if they are domestic and are happy. If the condition side of the most specific rule matches the situation, that rule is activated. However if the available information is insuffiently detailed, then the most general rule is activated by default. This corresponds to the fact that, if we know something is a cat, domestic, and happy, we can make a fairly accurate prediction that it will purr. However if we only know that it is a cat, but do not know what sort of cat it is, or what state of contentment it is in, we might still predict that it will purr, but the prediction is less accurate.

TABLE 2.2
Default Hierarchy of Increasingly Specific Condition–Action Rules

C_1	If X is a cat	$\rightarrow$	X purrs
C_2	If X is a cat, and X is domestic	$\rightarrow$	X purrs
C_3	If X is a cat, and X is domestic, and X is happy	$\rightarrow$	X purrs

Holland et al. (1986) distinguished between synchronic and diachronic rules. Synchronic rules are those that apply in constant fashion, and are not time dependent. The rule 4 + 3 = 7 is not time dependent and is therefore synchronic. On the other hand the rule that if you apply the brake in a car it will stop is time dependent and is therefore a diachronic rule; applying the brake at Time *t1* will result in the car stopping at Time *t2*.

Contingencies

The notion that cognitive representations correspond to condition–action rules implies that the representations are explicit, in the sense that we are consciously aware of them. This is reasonable for some rules; for example, we are aware of knowing that cats purr. However it has been claimed that we know many environmental regularities of which we are not explicitly aware (Brooks, 1978; Karmiloff-Smith, 1986, 1987; Reber, 1989). It has also been suggested that basic learning mechanisms, such as Pavlovian conditioning, result in stored representations of environmental contingencies (Rescorla, 1988). Therefore it seems likely that many of our representations take the form of contingencies of which we are not consciously aware, and to which we do not have cognitive access, but that nevertheless influence our cognitive processes. These stored contingencies are laid down due to basic learning mechanisms. Furthermore they are well accounted for by parallel distributed processing models of cognition, to which we turn next.

Parallel Distributed Processes (PDP)

Parallel distributed processing (PDP) models of cognition use a different mode of representation than the other types of models that we have considered, and they also provide very powerful but very natural accounts of many basic cognitive phenomena. Therefore, we consider them in some detail, and I explore the implications of this type of representation for a number of issues in cognitive development.

In PDP models, information is represented not as nodes or elements but as large collections of features. One might think of a cat as a large collection of features such as legs, fur, tail, pointed ears, purrs, meows, and so on. In a parallel distributed process there are a large number of representational units that are sometimes identified with neural units, although Smolensky (1988) argued persuasively that PDP models are intermediate between neural models and traditional symbolic models of cognition. In PDP models each unit can be thought of as representing a single feature, so the representation is actually distributed over a large number of units.

The representation of a particular concept or element is achieved by a pattern of activation over all the neural units. A different element or concept can be represented by a different pattern of activation over the same neural units. In fact the same set of units can represent a large number of different concepts, each corresponding to a unique pattern of activation. Each pattern can be expressed as a set of activation values, or vector. There are a number of models of this type known as neural net models (Grossberg, 1980; McClelland & Rumelhart, 1986; Rumelhart & McClelland, 1986) but there have also been a number of models of memory storage and retrieval that work on similar lines (Anderson, 1973; McNicol & Stewart, 1980; Murdock, 1982, 1983). Grossberg (1980) argued that there must be feedback from the representation units to the input units to ensure that a particular pattern of activation always represents the same input. This mechanism achieves the consistency property of representations mentioned earlier.[2]

Learning in these models is achieved by varying the strengths of associative connections between the units. Each unit is connected to a very large number of other units, and these connections can be excitatory or inhibitory. Each learned association corresponds to a matrix of weights, representing the strengths of connections between two sets of units. An important property of learning in PDP systems is that multiple associations can be superimposed on the same set of weights. Each association is formed by making a small adjustment to a large set of weights, so that a large number of associations can be stored on the same set of connections without undue interference.

Readers who are not already familiar with PDP models and who wish to deepen their understanding will find a lucid account in Rumelhart and McClelland (1986). Chapter 1 can be read without any psychological or mathematical expertise. PDP has many properties that have important implications for cognitive development, and we discuss these properties next.

Emergent Properties of PDP.   Two properties that emerge from PDP are *automatic generalization* and *automatic discrimination*. These occur because if an input occurs that shares some but not all of the features of a particular pattern, the activation will reflect the degree of overlap. The more features two stimuli share the more overlap there will be in the patterns of activation that represent them. The strength of association to other patterns will in turn reflect this overlap in activation.

Contingency detection occurs because associations between regularly co-occurring features are continuously strengthened, whereas features that co-occur only occasionally tend to be only weakly associated. This means that

---

[2]The terms *Parallel Distributed Processing* and *Connectionist* are often used interchangeably, because PDP models are based on connections between units. However, a model can be connectionist but use local (node) rather than distributed representations. An example is the ACME model of Holyoak and Thagard (1989) discussed in chapter 5. Such a model is connectionist but not PDP.

contingencies between regularly co-occurring events can be "filtered out" from noise or irregularity in the environment. Much of cognitive development is a matter of detecting contingencies between phenomena in the environment, but there has been little attempt to explain this, apart from the sophisticated self-modifying production system model of Wallace et al. (1987). PDP models offer a promising way of accounting for this fundamentally important process.

Automatic averaging of patterns tends to occur in a similar way. If two patterns repeatedly co-occur but with random variations in each, the core or central tendencies of the two patterns will automatically become associated. The "noise," or random fluctuations, are filtered out. This gives representations a robustness that insulates them from minor variations in the environment.

Automatic averaging leads to one of the most important emergent properties of PDP, *prototype formation.* As the work of Rosch (1978) showed, natural categories tend to be built around prototypes; the natural category "dog" is built around a prototypical dog, one of around average size and with fairly normal "doglike" features. The prototype of a category is the instance that shares most features with other members of the same category and shares fewest features with members of other categories. Because of the way associations are superimposed in PDP, those features that are most frequently associated with a category tend to have the strongest excitatory connections to other features belonging to that category. This means that the central tendency or prototype of the category tends to be recognized automatically.

Patterns also tend to interact to a degree that reflects their featural overlap. Patterns with similar connections tend to support each other, whereas patterns with opposing sets of connections conflict with each other. This "crosstalk" is due to the influences that different associations have on the same set of weights. Because all associations are stored by modifying the weights of the same set of associative connections, they automatically influence each other.

Pattern completion. Recognition of partial patterns also occurs automatically with PDP. If an input occurs that corresponds to part of a pattern, the whole pattern tends to become active, due to excitatory connections between components of the same pattern and inhibitory connections to other patterns. Auto-associative connections tend to "clean-up" and clarify a pattern, removing random noise, so that familiar patterns can be recognized with clarity from incomplete or fuzzy information. This in turns leads to the property of *graceful degradation,* so that when overload or damage to the nervous system occurs, the system does not completely break down, because partial representations still contain most of the necessary information. However, representations become less distinct, because they are based on fewer units.

Graceful saturation means that when a set of neural units is overloaded with too much information, the result is not catastrophic breakdown, but loss of clarity. This is important to the understanding of capacity limitations.

PDP works by finding the best fit to multiple constraints. There is no "central executive" or other directing influence. Everything works by finding the representation that is most consistent with the input, either internal or external.

Schemas can also be handled very naturally by PDP processes (Rumelhart, Smolensky, McClelland, & Hinton, 1986). Recall that a schema can be thought of as a set of variables with constraints between them. Those constraints can be very naturally represented by PDP, and the concept that emerges is that a schema is the "best fit" to all the interacting constraints. This gives the concept of schema a great deal of flexibility, a property that is most necessary if it is to account for the variety of phenomena that are represented by schemas.

The emergent properties of PDP models have resulted in considerable success with basic cognitive processes such as perception, learning, and category formation. Rumelhart and McClelland (1986) produced a PDP model of the acquisition of the past-tense rule with English verbs, but the model has been criticized (Pinker & Mehler, 1988) on the grounds that it does not account for the abstract nature of grammatical rules. However Elman (1989) showed how grammatical categories can be learned, at least in principle, by a PDP mechanism. This controversy highlights an important issue concerning PDP models. This concerns the fact that PDP representations are always content-specific. Because acquisition of abstract concepts is an important aspect of cognitive development, the PDP approach cannot provide successful models in this area unless this problem can be handled.

PDP and Abstractions

One requirement to represent abstractions is to represent variables and predicates. Variables are abstractions that can take a number of values; for example, letters in an equation represent variables that can take a number of values depending on the other terms in the equation. However a category label like "animal" can be considered a variable, because it can be instantiated in a number of ways, such as dog, cat, horse, and so on.

A predicate can express an attribute or a relation. For example, the concept "large dog" can be expressed as large(dog), where the predicate "large" expresses the attribute, and its argument "dog" is the object having this attribute. Following Gentner (1983), we say that attributes are predicates having one argument, and relations are predicates having two or more arguments.

Both variables and predicates are abstractions in the sense that they represent general classes rather than specific instances. One problem has been how to represent them in PDP models. It is easy to express a variable or predicate as a set of activation values, normally expressed mathematically as a null vector. The problem however is to represent the binding of the variable to its value (a constant), or of the predicate to its arguments. To illustrate, consider the variable "size." We can represent size by a vector of activation values, but it must be possible to bind it to any of a number of values (constants), such as "large," "medium," and so on. This binding must be dynamic so that, for instance, "size" might be bound to "large" on one occasion, to "medium" on another occasion, and so on.

Two types of solutions have been proposed to this problem. Shastri (1988) proposed that the binding of a variable to a value can be achieved by synchronous activation of the patterns representing the variable and the value. This model was specifically designed to handle variable-constant bindings in language comprehension. Another solution, which appears to have more application in reasoning, was proposed by Smolensky (1990). The essence of this proposal is shown in Fig. 2.4. In Smolensky's (1990) approach to variable-constant bindings, there is one set of units whose activation pattern represents the variable, and another set that represents the constant. The binding of the variable to the constant is represented by a set of binding units, shown in the center of the figure. The pattern of activation of the binding

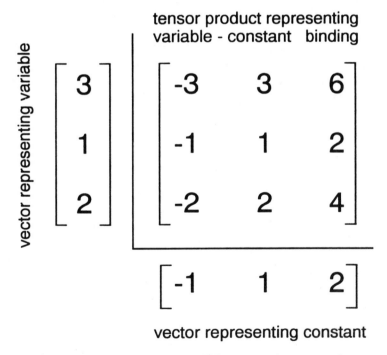

FIG. 2.4. Variable-constant binding in PDP representation, expressed as tensor product of two vectors.

units represents the particular combination of variable and constant that is bound. Each binding unit is connected to one unit in the variable representation and to one in the constant representation. The result is that the activations of the binding units are determined by the product of the activations of the variable and constant units, as shown in Fig. 2.4.

The variable and constants are each represented by vectors, and the activations of the binding units are collectively represented by the tensor product of these vectors. The way the tensor product is computed is illustrated in Fig. 2.4. Each tensor product unit is the product of the unit to which it corresponds in the variable and constant vectors. In an actual network, each tensor product unit would be connected to a unit in the variable vector and to a unit in the constant vector. Smolensky (1990) or Jordan (1986) can be consulted for a discussion of the mathematics of these representations, but for our purposes mathematical detail will not be required. It is sufficient to recognize that the activations of the binding units are a function of the products of the activations of the variable and binding units to which they are connected, and the tensor product is the set of activation values that arises from these products. This formulation provides for dynamic variable-constant binding, because which variable-constant pair is bound depends on the activations of the tensor product units. (Readers who want to consider the PDP model in detail should note that Fig. 2.4 is not a pattern associator, because the values in the body of the figure are activations, whereas in a pattern associator they are weights; see Rumelhart & McClelland, 1986, chapter 1).

Smolensky's approach to variable-constant binding was adapted to predicate-argument binding by Halford et al. (in press). In this case one vector represents the predicate, and there is another vector to represent each argument. An example is shown in Fig. 2.5. The predicate "larger than" is represented by one vector, and one argument "elephant" is represented by a second vector, whereas the second argument "dog" is represented by a third vector. There are therefore three vectors, one representing the predicate and one representing each of its arguments. As with the variable-constant binding in Fig. 2.4, the activations of the binding units are determined by the products of the inputs from the predicate and argument units to which each binding unit is connected. The activations of the bindings constitute the tensor product of the vectors and represent the binding of the predicate (larger than) to its arguments (elephant, dog). "Larger than" is a binary relation, and is therefore a two-place predicate (it has two arguments). Figure 2.6 shows the predicate-argument binding for a three-place predicate, arithmetic addition. Addition has three arguments, two addends and a sum. The predicate and its arguments are each represented by vectors of activations, and the binding is represented by the activations of the binding units in the center of the diagram (which are not shown for reasons of complexity). The binding represents the fact that $2 + 3 = 5$ under arithmetical addition. The way

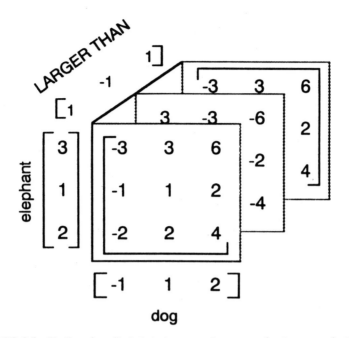

FIG. 2.5.   Binding of predicate to two arguments, expressed as tensor product of three vectors.

the concept of transitivity would be represented in this model is shown in Fig. 2.7. There is one vector representing the concept of transitivity, and one vector representing each argument, a, b, c. The figure illustrates the example "John is fairer than Peter, Peter is fairer than Tom." When John, Peter, and Tom are arranged in order of fairness, the representation comprises a ternary relation with John, Peter, Tom as arguments. The constituent binary relations can be recovered; for example, the relation "John is fairer than Peter" corresponds to the tensor product of vectors representing "fairer than," "John," and "Peter." Halford et al. (in press) showed how representations of this type can provide a basis for a PDP model of analogical reasoning. In fact representations of this kind have a number of important properties, including the fact that they provide a natural account of complexity and an explanation of capacity limitations. They will be very important to the argument of this book.

Whereas PDP models entail representations that are content specific, and special steps have to be taken to represent variables and predicates, condition–action rules (production rules) represent variables very readily. This is both a strength and a weakness, because although it is very convenient to the theorist to be able to represent variables easily, condition–action rules tend to conceal the problem of how variables are represented in cognitive processes. They therefore tend to obscure the fact that the achievement of

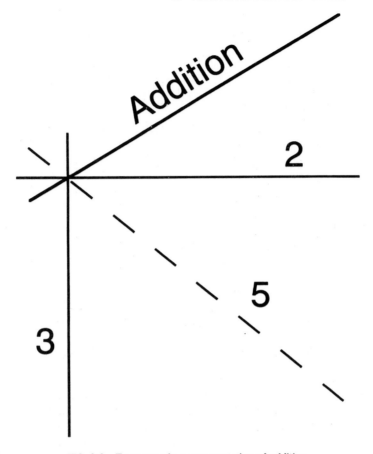

FIG. 2.6.   Tensor-product representation of addition.

abstractions is a major challenge to cognitive developmental theories. It would however be very useful if the best features of PDP models and production rules could be combined. Steps towards this have been taken (Touretzky & Hinton, 1988), although production rule models based on PDP representations are rather restricted in scope (this is true at the time of writing, but the field is moving rapidly). Although I do not want to prejudge some of the very complex issues concerning the relative merits of PDP and production rule models (or, more generally, PDP and symbolic models, see Smolensky, 1988), for the purposes of this book they are best regarded as two different levels of analysis. That is, production rules are more global, whereas PDP models are more fine grained. PDP models are very useful when one wants to consider the microstructure of cognition, but it would be impractical to represent every cognitive process in terms of PDP models at this time. Therefore both levels of analysis need to be employed.

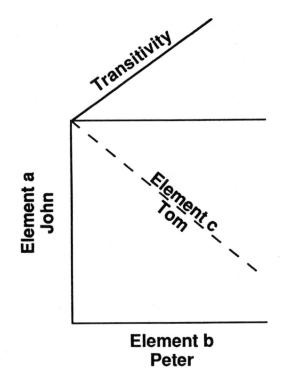

FIG. 2.7.   Tensor-product representation of transitivity.

Implicit and Explicit Knowledge

Research in a number of contexts has led to recognition of the need for more than one level of cognitive function. When reflecting on the merits and limitations of PDP models, Norman (1986) noted that "People do seem to have at least two modes of operation, one rapid, efficient, subconscious, the other slow, serial, conscious" (p. 542). The implication is that there are two modes of cognitive representation, an implicit mode in which performance is efficient and relatively effortless, but in which there is no cognitive access to the rules or knowledge employed, and an explicit mode in which performance may be more effortful and less efficient, but in which ability to access and manipulate the rules and knowledge used is greater. This distinction has been made in the context of learning by Reber (1989), with concepts by Brooks (1978), with skills by Hayes and Broadbent (1988), and in conceptual development in children by Karmiloff-Smith (1986). The developmental importance of the distinction lies partly in the fact that children who have achieved at the implicit level on a particular task cannot be assumed to have achieved at the explicit level. Considerably more cognitive effort may be required to make the transition from an implicit to an explicit mode of operation, and the transition is by no means inevitable in every case. Furthermore the oft-noted tendency for U-shaped development may sometimes be explained by a task being mastered first at the implicit level, then performance deteriorates until the explicit level is achieved.

Karmiloff-Smith (1986, 1987, 1990) argued that implicit knowledge consists of procedures for performing a task, without cognitive access to those procedures or the ability to link them to other knowledge. For example, a child may know how to say "a house" or "the house," without recognizing the common properties shared by "a" and "the." The child has efficiently functioning procedures for using "a" and "the" but does link them and does not have the concept of the article. Implicit knowledge is tantamount to performance without understanding.

Karmiloff-Smith argued that explicit knowledge comes about through *representational redescription*. This refers to the process of creating a higher level, explicit representation of knowledge that already exists in implicit form. The implicit knowledge continues to exist but becomes represented at a higher level that is linked to other cognitive processes. The representational redescription process occurs with all skills, is not stage related, and is not confined to children.

Karmiloff-Smith defined three levels of explicit knowledge. At the level of primary explicitation, the elements of the procedures involved in implicit knowledge become accessible to metaprocedural processes that can operate on them, define relationships between them, and link them to other representations. At the secondary explicitation level, the representations become consciously accessible. At the tertiary explicitation level it becomes possible to translate representations from one code to another. It is at this level that representations have a linguistically stateable form.

The theory has been illustrated by a task in which children are asked to draw (say) a house, then to draw a house that does not exist. By 4 to 5 years of age children have learned a procedure for drawing a house. However drawing a house that does not exist requires cognitive access to that procedure. It requires children to cognitively remove certain features (such as a door), and add other features (such as ears or a mouth). The ability to draw a house with genuinely novel features did not occur until about 11 years, which Karmiloff-Smith interpreted as showing that young children lack cognitive access to the drawing procedure. For 5-year-olds the concept of *house* is represented more implicitly than explicitly.

This theory and associated empirical work imply that skills can develop without understanding. Recall however that in chapter 1, I specified that understanding can constrain acquisition of new strategies. This implies that performance can develop with or without understanding. The reason is that there are both associative and metacognitive mechanisms for acquiring strategies and procedures. The latter depend on understanding, whereas the former do not. Therefore the view that undertanding emerges from performance, and the view that understanding constrains the (further) development of performance, are complementary rather than antagonistic. A similar conclusion was reached by Glaser and Bassock (1989) in a different context, after a review of the literature on learning and instruction.

Clark and Karmiloff-Smith (in press) contended that PDP models deal with implicit rather than explicit knowledge. They developed their argument with reference to the program NETtalk (Sejnowski & Rosenberg, 1986), which is based on PDP architecture and can transform text into speech but does not "understand" the language it is processing. It is not merely that NETtalk does not have any semantic interpretation of words, but that it does not, for example, represent the distinction between a vowel and a consonant, even though it is very competent to discriminate between the two. Clark and Karmiloff-Smith argue that a program like NETtalk can "negotiate" a problem domain without understanding that domain and without having any abstract representation of the concepts it uses, such as vowels and consonants.

A program such as NETtalk uses parallel distributed processing to transform strings of letters into phoneme representations, which can be converted into speech by a speech synthesizer. The letters are represented as sets of activation values on a large number of units. The phonemes are similarly represented as sets of activation values on another set of units. The connections between these two sets of units are initially set to random weights. The learning process entails gradually adjusting the connection weights so each letter string activates the right phoneme representation. Thus NETtalk learns to transform letter strings into phonemes.

In doing this it performs discriminations that are equivalent to (for example) the distinction between a vowel and a consonant. However, because the system has no representation of what a vowel is, it could not accept instructions to process vowels or consonants in a different way; for example, the instruction to map vowels into a different set of phonemes would have no meaning. The only way it could be achieved would be to retrain the system from the beginning. Furthermore if NETtalk were presented with a new problem that had only abstract or formal similarities to the task on which it had been trained, that problem too would have to be learned all over again. Thus NETtalk's learning is essentially content dependent, and it lacks the ability for abstraction or conceptualization. This is despite the fact that it can behave as if it had categories in some circumstances; for example, it might treat all vowels in a similar way. However it has no way of accessing its representation of what a vowel is, so this representation cannot be operated on by cognitive processes outside those that it has learned in this specific task. It is like Karmiloff-Smith's (1986) implicit knowledge; it can perform a task, but it has no cognitive access to the performance.

Research into parallel distributed processing has shown therefore that it is possible to have very powerful systems for performing a task, or finding one's way around in a domain, without having any cognitive access to the representations that are used, and without anything equivalent to understanding. The representations that are used cannot be related to anything outside that specific task, and they cannot be mapped into other tasks or other representations. The detailed account of implicit knowledge given by Clark and Karmiloff-Smith is very instructive in a developmental context because it provides a salutary demonstration of how much can be achieved without understanding, but it also gives us insight into the limitations of performance that is devoid of understanding. It also reminds us forcefully of the fallacy of attributing understanding solely on the basis of even very efficient performance, without further investigation.

What else is required for understanding? There are at least two further requirements. The first is the ability to transfer the knowledge to new tasks with the same relational structure but different content, that is, to isomorphic tasks. This is required in interproblem learning in the traditional learning set task, which has been employed with animals (Harlow, 1949) and children (Reese, 1963). Halford, Bain, and Maybery (under review) argued that this task entails analogical reasoning. Individual tasks can be learned without ability to transfer the basis of solution to isomorphic tasks with different contents, and transfer to isomorphs (interproblem learning, or learning set acquisition as it is often called) has been found to distinguish species at different phylogenetic levels (Bitterman, 1960). The second is the ability to reorganize the relational structure of a domain of knowledge, and relate it to other domains. An example would be to transform the formula for velocity, $V = s/t$ (velocity = distance/time) into alternatives such as $s = Vt$. This entails recognizing the correspondences between two different structures. Clark and Karmiloff-Smith (in press) suggested the possibility of second-order PDP models that are able to operate on first-order models, effectively constructing representations of the representations in the first-order models. They proposed that "second order connectionist (PDP) systems are those which are (a) able to treat their own representations as objects for further understanding and manipulation, (b) are able to do so independently of prompting by continued training inputs and (c) are able, as a result, to form structured representations of their own knowledge which can be manipulated, recombined and accessed by other computational processes" (Clark & Karmiloff-Smith, in press).

This definition of second-order PDP systems provides a useful blueprint for what it means to operate at an explicit level. I believe it provides a reasonably valid criterion for understanding, and I have incorporated it into the definition of understanding given in chapter 1. However the fact that PDP systems, which seem to give an impressive account of many aspects of human cognitive representations, have such difficulty handling explicit knowledge under-lines the cognitive achievement that it represents. We would be much better able to understand the developmental process if we knew what was required to extend first-order PDP systems into second-order systems. A PDP model of analogical reasoning would be an important step towards such second-order systems, and one such model is discussed in chapter 5.

ORIGINS OF MENTAL MODELS

Mental models are representations, so the existence of representations is a prerequisite for the development of mental models. There is now consider-able evidence that infants can employ representations at least by the age of about 3 months. In a series of ingenious studies, Baillargeon provided evi-dence that infants can represent a vanished object. In one particularly well-controlled study (Baillargeon, 1987b), 4-month-old infants were first habitu-ated to a screen that rotated through 180 degrees like a drawbridge. Then a box was placed behind the screen so that as the screen rotated it first oc-cluded the box then, in the impossible event condition, moved through the space the box should have occupied, the box having been surreptitiously re-moved. In the possible event condition, the screen stopped rotating at the point where it would have contacted the box. In the control condition the same two events were shown, but without the box. In the experimental con-dition, the infants looked reliably longer at the impossible event. No such effect occurred in the control condition, showing that it was the screen ap-parently moving through the space that should have been occupied by the box, rather than the particular type of movement used, that attracted the infant's attention.

This study indicates that the infants took some account of the existence of the box behind the screen. In other studies evidence was obtained that they also represented the height of the occluded object (Baillargeon & Graber, 1987), its specific location (Baillargeon, 1986, 1987a; Baillargeon, Spelke, & Wasserman, 1985), and even its compressibility (Baillargeon, 1987a, Experi-ment 2). These results suggest that infants had a representation of an object's features and position in space. The question is whether this representation amounts to understanding of the object and its relations to space and, more significantly for current purposes, whether it amounts to an accessible representational system.

Mandler (1988) argued that infants' representations are accessible because they can use symbolic gestures, they can make active comparisons between objects, they engage in voluntary imitation, and they are capable of active recall. To the extent that infants can do this, it indicates some degree of ac-cessibility. However it does not, of itself, show that infants can organize representations into coherent systems of the kind that are necessary for more than low levels of understanding. Therefore infants' ability to do this needs to be assessed.

One question concerns the inferences that can be made with their representations. I pointed out elsewhere (Halford, 1989) that if infants understand what is happening when a rotating screen moves through the space occupied by an occluded object, as in Baillargeon's studies, they should be able to infer that the object can no longer be there once the screen has moved through the space it had occupied. This could be tested by combining the retrieval and recovery techniques of LeCompte and Gratch (1972) or Ramsay and Campos (1978) with the impossible event demonstrations used by Baillargeon. That is, hide an attractive toy by rotating the screen so as to occlude it, then continue rotating the screen through the space the object should have occupied, then rotate the screen to the vertical position, so it is clear of the object but still occluding it. Infants should be able to infer that the object cannot still be there after the screen has moved through the space it occupied. They should therefore show more surprize on finding it still there, as compared with the possible event sequence in which the screen stops where it would be expected to contact the object. If they cannot make the inference, and as far as I know it remains to be tested, this would imply that they can represent the vanished object but have limited ability to make inferences about it.

The representations of occluded objects that infants have been shown to use in Baillargeon's studies relate to a spatial frame that is currently visible. The object is occluded, but the screen that hides it is still visible, and the situation is the same as when the object disappeared. Therefore infants' knowledge of the occluded object relates very much to a spatial frame that is here and now. It is possible that one of the things that develops is the ability to operate over greater spatiotemporal distances, which would give the concept of permanence greater robustness and stability.

The fact that these early representations are very restricted is illustrated by the *A*-not-*B* error, the tendency for 8- to 12-month-old infants who see an object hidden one or more times at Place A, then see it hidden at B, to search for it at A. Wellman, Cross, & Bartsch (1986) carried out a meta-analysis of research in the area, and have concluded that correct responses increase as a function of age, the number of hiding places, and the distinctiveness of the hiding places, and decrease as a function of delay.

Wellman et al. (1986) proposed that there are two modes of response to the problem, a direct-finding approach and an inferred-location approach. Direct finding is relatively primitive, and consists of an apparently automatic search for the object where it was seen to be hidden. The inferred-location approach is more reflective, and is analogous to predicting where a dog will be from observations of its movements. It depends on integrating object-movement information across trials. Notice that this approach explicitly relies on knowledge of movement-position constraint, and it can presumably mediate more powerful inferences and operate over greater spatio-temporal distances than the direct-finding approach. There seems to be some correspondence between the direct-finding and inferred-location dichotomy and the implicit/explicit distinction discussed in the last section.

Wellman et al. suggested that the variations in performance on the A-not-B task by 8-month-old children are due to a mixture of these two approaches. Direct finding is accurate, and is more likely to be employed with shorter delays, or if there are more hiding locations, thereby explaining the paradoxical finding that performance is better if there are more locations. Infants become more competent with the inferred-location approach as they grow older, and it permits correct performance at longer delays and in more complex tasks, such as when displacements are invisible. With 8-month-olds, however, it leads to errors, which explains why children of this age make errors on this task.

Comparison of Baillargeon's work with that of Wellman et al. suggests that much of the development that occurs over the first year might consist of ability to construct much more elaborate and powerful representations that can operate over greater spatiotemporal distances and mediate more complex inferences. The four-month-old infants investigated by Baillargeon can store information about an object that is occluded in the immediately visible spatial frame, but study of the Stage 4 error in 8- to 12-month-olds shows that even infants in this age range are still learning to make inferences over longer delays and about more complex sequences of events. Even relatively simple representations can guide behavior with respect to an immediately present spatial frame, but to guide behavior over greater spatiotemporal distances, a more elaborate representation that integrates more information is required. Such a representation must include information about the immediate situation and at least one other situation, either in the past or the future, together with transformations from one situation to another. Thus representations that take account of greater spatiotemporal distances necessarily integrate more information than representations of the immediate situation.

Recent research suggests that there may well be a physiological basis for this development. Goldman-Rakic (1987) reviewed evidence of delayed response and the A-not-B task in infants and monkeys and concluded that both might be a function of synaptic density in the prefrontal cortex, a structure that is also implicated in the same task by the work of Diamond (1988). Although the significance of these findings cannot be fully assessed at present (see also Fischer, 1987), they do support the behavioral evidence that understanding of the object concept is far from complete in 4- to 6-month-old infants.

The development of a more integrated conception of the object's position in space would tend to account for another phenomenon, the removal of conflict between different encodings of an object's position. Bremner (1978) suggested that 8-month-old infants might be in conflict over egocentric versus allocentric cues. If they have found a hidden object on (say) their left side, then are moved to the opposite side of the table, they are in conflict whether to search on their left (egocentric), or in the original location (allocentric). Bremner found the conflict could be overcome by making the locations more distinctive, thereby strengthening the allocentric cues, and McKenzie, Day, and Ihsen (1984) showed 6- to 8-month-old infants could be taught to ignore egocentric cues.

The fact that conflict occurs suggests that the representation employed is fragmented and consists of a number of restricted aspects that are not connected together in a coherent way. A more integrated representation would take into account not only the immediate situation but movements the child might make and the changes that result. It would integrate the child's movements with other spatial information so that egocentric and allocentric conceptions would not be in conflict.

To illustrate, saying that something is on my left is not in conflict with saying it is beside the window, because I know that if I swivel around in my chair, the object will be on my right, but still beside the window. The absence of conflict here is because an adult can represent space in a way that integrates successive situations into a coherent structure that permits operation over greater spatiotemporal distances and removes the conflict that arises from a succession of restricted representations of space that are largely independent of each other. The finding that younger infants are better at spatial localization in familiar surroundings, or where there are clearly defined landmarks (Acredolo, 1979; Keating, McKenzie, & Day, 1986), is also consistent with progressive integration, because such settings provide specific cues that can be used in isolation, whereas unfamiliar settings probably require judgments to be based on a wider sample of information.

Further evidence that one of the things that develops through infancy is ability to construct more elaborated representations that integrate more information comes from a hiding and recovery study by Haake and Somerville (1985). There were two conditions. In the object-present condition, infants were shown an object in the experimenter's hand, which was placed in a container, then withdrawn and the object was shown again, then the hand was placed in a second container, withdrawn and the infant was shown that the hand was empty. The object-absent condition was the same except that the infant was shown that the hand was empty when it was withdrawn from the first container. In the object present condition, the inference is that the object is in the second container, whereas in the object absent condition it must be in the first container. Haake and Somerville said that the logical search rule here is that the position of the object is defined by the point where it was last seen, and the path it traveled up to the point where it disappeared. This rule clearly requires integration of a number of pieces of information across both space and time, and it was not exhibited until 15–18 months of age. This supports my contention that early behavior with respect to objects and space reflects rather primitive, restricted representations that contain relatively small amounts of information. The representations of 18-month-olds integrate much more information, relating to two or more situations (or spatial frames), together with the transformations between situations.

The kind of evidence that does seem to indicate genuine understanding is provided by DeLoache (1987). Young children were shown a model toy hidden in a model room, then they tried to find the toy in a real room. Children of 2½ to 3 years were able to do this, although the younger children succeeded only in a second experiment where photographs were used instead of the model. This task entails constructing a representation of the model toy hidden in the model room, then mapping this representation into the real room situation. The representation need not be complex, and it could consist of a single relation, such as "behind the sofa." What seems to be important is the ability to transfer the representation to a new spatiotemporal frame, a new situation, then map it into that situation. This is a case of transfer between situations with the same relational structure, but different content, as discussed in the last section. It does suggest a genuinely accessible cognitive representation, albeit one of a simple kind, and it does not so far appear to have been demonstrated in infancy.

Research on infants' understanding of the object implies infants can represent vanished objects at least by 3–4 months, but that the representations are restricted to the immediate spatiotemporal frame, and the representational system lacks coherence, in the sense that individual representations are not connected together. The development of a reasonably complete understanding of the object-in-space extends over at least a good part of the first 2 years, as I have pointed out elsewhere (Halford, 1989). Given the definition of understanding adopted in chapter 1, this means that these early representations are important components of understanding, but that the process is far from complete. On the other hand, reasonably indisputable evidence for representations that are cognitively accessible has been obtained from 3-year-olds. There is probably little value in trying to locate the point in time when the capacity for understanding first exists. The conclusion that emerges most clearly from the evidence is that it is a gradual acquisition that has certainly begun by 3–4 months, and probably extends over a period of 2–3 years.

Dimensionality of Representations

A concept that has considerable importance in the argument of this book is the complexity metric based on the dimensionality of a concept, which is defined as the number of independent units of information required to represent the concept. This metric for complexity was first used for patterns by Leeuwenberg (1969) and was taken up by Restle (1970) and Simon (1972). It seems to have been first used to quantify complexity of concepts by Halford and Wilson (1980), who defined three different levels of mathematical structures. A fourth level was added by Halford (1987), and it will be the metric that includes these four levels that will be presented here. See Appendix 2.B for further treatment of the metric.

One-dimensional concepts are defined as predicates with one argument, or as unary relations. An example is category membership, such as CAT(Ferdinand), asserting that Ferdinand is a cat. Another is attribute–object bindings, such as RED(things), or LARGE(cat). One-dimensional concepts are also entailed in variable bindings, such as WEIGHT(100 grams). In the PDP model of Halford et al. (in press), one-dimensional concepts are represented by a tensor product of two vectors, one representing the predicate and one representing its argument, as shown in Figs. 2.4 and 2.8.

One-dimensional representations might be involved in an important way in the development of the object concept, because it arguably entails recognizing hiding place as a variable. The *A*-not-*B* error discussed earlier appears to reflect, at least in part, a tendency to form a fixed association between the object and its hiding place. Overcoming the *A*-not-*B* error entails recognizing that hiding place is a variable, because an object can be hidden now at one place, now at another. Representing this entails a dynamic binding of the variable hiding place to a specific location, and can be expressed as TOY-HIDING-PLACE(under-cloth). That is, there is a variable, TOY-HIDING-PLACE, which is bound to a particular location at any one time. This can be expressed by a tensor product of two vectors, one representing TOY-HIDING-PLACE, the other representing the current value, such as "under-cloth." This entails a rank-2 tensor product, as shown in Fig. 2.8.

Two-dimensional concepts are defined as predicates with two arguments, or as binary relations. An example is the binary relation LARGER-THAN(elephant, dog) discussed earlier. Two-dimensional concepts are represented by a tensor product of three vectors, one representing the predicate and two representing the arguments, as shown in Figs. 2.5 and 2.8.

Another example of a two-dimensional concept is a bivariate function, $x = f(y)$. Another example would be a unary operator, such as change sign; $x \rightarrow -x$. Binary relations, bivariate functions, and unary operators are all defined mathematically as sets of ordered pairs, and the detailed mathematical definitions are given by Halford and Wilson (1980), who discuss the similarities and differences.

Three-dimensional concepts are defined as predicates with three arguments, or as ternary relations. An example is a binary operation, such as arithmetic addition, which consists of the set of ordered 3-tuples of the form $\{ \ldots (2, 3 \rightarrow 5), \ldots (5, 1 \rightarrow 6) \ldots \}$. Bivariate functions, $x = f(y,z)$ are also examples.

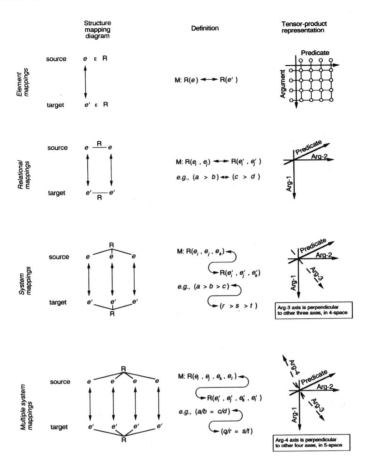

FIG. 2.8.   Four levels of structure mapping, with tensor-product representation.

All these structures are defined as sets or ordered 3-tuples (Halford & Wilson, 1980). Transitivity is a three-dimensional concept, because it can be expressed as a ternary relation, $R(a, b, c)$. The smallest structure that can instantiate transitivity consists of an ordered set of three elements. Class inclusion is also a ternary relation, because it comprises three classes, a superordinate, a subclass, and its complement. Therefore class inclusion is a three-dimensional concept. Three-dimensional concepts correspond to predicates with three arguments, and in the PDP model of Halford et al. (in press), three-dimensional concepts are represented by tensor products of four vectors, one representing the predicate, and three representing the arguments, as shown in Figs. 2.6, 2.7, and 2.8.

Four-dimensional concepts are defined as predicates with four arguments, or as quaternary relations. An example is a composition of binary operations, such as $a(b + c) = d$. Quaternary relations, and mathematical structures on which two binary operations are defined, such as rings and fields, are four-dimensional structures. In the PDP model of Halford et al. (in press), four-dimensional concepts are represented by tensor products of five vectors, one representing the predicate and four representing the arguments, as shown in Fig. 2.8.

It is usual to refer to predicates with 1, 2, 3, or 4 arguments as 1-, 2-, 3-, or 4-place predicates. A tensor product with two vectors is said to be rank 2, one with three vectors as rank 3, and so on. A concept of dimensionality N corresponds to an N-place predicate, and is represented by a tensor product of rank $N+1$.

Rules can also be categorized according to their dimensionality. Rules can be expressed as sets of ordered pairs, ordered 3-tuples, and so on. There are many examples of rules that consist of ordered pairs. Holland et al. (1986) talked of the rule that fast-moving objects slow down, a rule that corresponds to common experience because of the ubiquity of friction in the environment. This rule can be expressed as a transition function from the velocity of an object at $t1$ to the state of the object at $t2$. It is a bivariate function, and consists of all the ordered pairs of the form $\{. . . (Vt1, Vt2). . . \}$.

Scandura (1970) analyzed rules such as "to convert inches to feet, divide by 12." This rule can be expressed as a set of ordered pairs $\{(36, 3), (24, 2)$ . . . $(100, 8.3333) . . . (240, 20) . . . \}$. That is, it corresponds to the set of all ordered pairs in which the first member is the number of inches, and the second member is the number of feet. We might think of arithmetic addition as a rule, and it corresponds to the ordered 3-tuples, $\{. . (2, 1, 3), (5, 4, 9)$ . . .$\}$. The dimensionality of a rule is defined in the same way as the dimensionality of a predicate, by the number of arguments. Thus a rule that corresponds to a set of ordered pairs is two-dimensional, one that corresponds to a set of ordered 3-tuples is three-dimensional, and so on.

Recoding of Representations

Representations are not static, but change dynamically as learning, concept attainment, and problem solving proceed. This dynamic change process has not been extensively modeled, although the COPYCAT model of analogical reasoning (Mitchell & Hofstadter, 1990) provides a very interesting account of it. However, there is one aspect of recoding that is important to the argument of this book, and that is *conceptual chunking,* which is defined as converting a multidimensional representation into one dimension, or into fewer dimensions than the original.

This would mean that each of the tensor product representations shown in Fig. 2.8 could be reduced to a lower rank. There are great gains in efficiency from this process, but there are two limitations on it. The first is that structures can be "frozen," and alternatives are lost. The computational flexibility of the representation is also reduced. In effect, conceptual chunking converts representation of variables into representation of constants. This has the interesting implication that representation of constants is much less demanding than representation of variables. This tends to be borne out in many of the phenomena we will examine, where children can readily perform a task with a known content, but cannot transfer the principle to other contents in the same format. They can operate with constants, but not with variables.

The other limitation is that something of the structure must be known before a conceptual chunk can be defined. Therefore conceptual chunking is one of the main achievements of expertise. One characteristic of an expert is the ability to define conceptual chunks that represent concepts in a powerful and efficient way.

Mapping Representations

One important aspect of cognition is the ability to relate one representation to another. One process for doing this is *structure mapping*, which is the process underlying analogical reasoning, according to Gentner (1983). However, it is also important in a number of other contexts, such as transfer of training. Each value for the dimensionality of a representation gives rise to a specific level of structure mapping, and each level of structure mapping corresponds to an equivalence class of cognitive tasks. Therefore I will now outline the levels of structure mapping that correspond to the dimensionalities of representations. Concepts of dimensionality 1, 2, 3, or 4 correspond to element, relational, system, and multiple-system mappings, respectively. The levels of structure mapping, together with the dimensionality of the corresponding representations, are shown in Fig. 2.8. We will consider each level in turn.

Levels of Structure-Mapping

The basic idea of structure mapping was explained earlier. A structure mapping consists of a set of rules for assigning elements of Structure A to elements of Structure B in such a way that the relations (functions, transformations) of Structure A correspond to the relations (functions, transformations) of Structure B. The four levels of structure mapping correspond to four types of correspondence between two structures.

Element mappings assign elements of Structure A to elements of Structure B according to one of three criteria, similarity, convention, or prior

FIG. 2.9.   Element mapping. Reproduced from Halford (1987) by permission
of Elsevier Science Publishers (North Holland).

knowledge, the first two of which are illustrated in Fig. 2.9. According to
the similarity criterion, an element in Structure A can be mapped into an
element in Structure B to which it is similar. An image representing an object or event in the environment would be an example of a structure mapping based on similarity (see Fig. 2.9A). An image typically resembles the
thing it represents, so an image of a cat resembles a cat in some way. In this
case, Structure A is a representational structure, and Structure B is some kind
of structure in the environment. Alternatively, mappings may be based on
a convention linking an element in Structure A to an element in Structure
B. An example would be a word that is assigned to a referent by convention,
as illustrated in Fig. 2.9B. In this case also, a representational structure, linguistic in form, is mapped into a structure comprising a segment of the environment.

Relational mappings occur when elements in Structure A may be mapped
into elements in Structure B on the basis of similar relations between them.
This is illustrated in Fig. 2.10, where two sticks of different lengths are used
to represent the relation between a man and a boy. This mapping is not based
on similarity between a stick and the person it represents, but on the fact
that the relation between the sticks is similar to (at least) one relation between the man and the boy. That is, the size relation between the sticks is
similar to the size relation between man and boy.

Relational mappings are independent of element similarity and convention, so they have a greater degree of flexibility and abstractness than element mappings. The price that is paid for this is that elements must be mapped
in pairs. Whereas element mappings may be made considering one element
from each structure at a time, with relational mappings pairs of elements in

FIG. 2.10. Relational mapping. Reproduced from Halford (1987) by permission of Elsevier Science Publishers (North Holland).

Structure A must be mapped into pairs of elements in Structure B. This means that relational mappings entail a higher degree of structural complexity than element mappings.

System mappings are independent of both element and relational similarity, and convention, and are based purely on structural correspondence. This is illustrated in Fig. 2.11, where the representation of a transitive inference problem is shown as a structure mapping, similar to that in Fig. 1.3, discussed in chapter 1. In this case there is no resemblance between the elements of Structure A, the representation, and the elements of Structure B, the problem. That is, "top" does not resemble Tom, nor "middle" Bill, and so on. Nor is the mapping based on similarity between the relations in the two structures. That is, any resemblance between "above" and "happier than" is unneces-

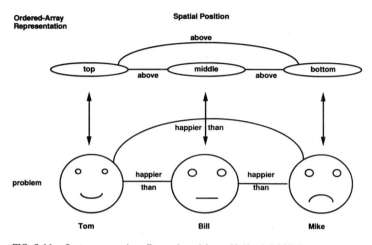

FIG. 2.11. System mapping. Reproduced from Halford (1987) by permission of Elsevier Science Publishers (North Holland).

sary to validate the mapping. The mapping is based on the fact that relations in Structure A consistently correspond to relations in Structure B. That is, "above" in Structure A consistently corresponds to "happier than" in Structure B, and to no other relation in Structure B. Wherever "above" occurs between two elements in Structure A, the relation "happier than" occurs between the elements into which they are mapped in Structure B. Therefore the correspondence between structures is consistent throughout, and the mapping conforms to the formal definition of correspondence in Appendix 2.A. By contrast, the system mapping in Fig. 2.12 is inconsistent and invalid. The

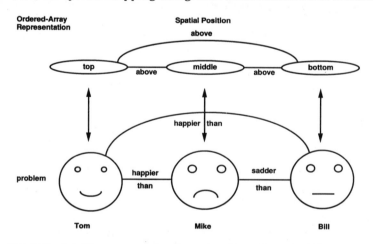

FIG. 2.12. Invalid system mapping. Reproduced from Halford (1987) by permission of Elsevier Science Publishers (North Holland).

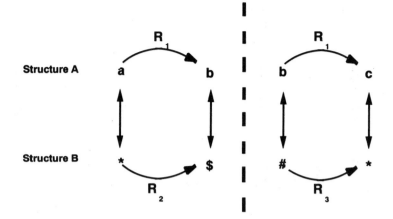

FIG. 2.13. Invalid system mapping divided into components.

inconsistency arises from the fact that "above" corresponds to "happier than" on two occasions, and to "sadder than" on the third occasion. System mappings have a higher degree of flexibility and abstractness than relational mappings. This is because they are independent of convention and similarity of elements and first-order relations. They depend on structural correspondence. The price paid for this is, once again, a higher processing load. System mappings require a set of at least three elements in Structure A to be mapped into at least three elements in Structure B. The reason is that the structural correspondence criterion is only meaningful if at least two binary relations, and three elements, in one structure are mapped into corresponding elements and relations in the other structure. This is illustrated in Fig. 2.13. This mapping, like that in Fig. 2.12, is invalid because correspondences are inconsistent. Element b is mapped into both $ and #, * is mapped into both a and c, $R1$ is mapped into both $R2$ and $R3$. The important point however is that this inconsistency is not apparent if only half the figure is examined. If we examine only the part of the figure on the left side of the vertical dotted line, no inconsistency is apparent. The same is true if we examine only the half of the figure on the right of the dotted line. The inconsistency is only apparent if we examine the whole figure. Therefore the structural correspondence rule, which is the basis of system mappings, depends on examining sets of three elements and two binary relations in each structure.

Multiple System Mappings

This level of mapping is similar to system mappings, except that ternary relations, and/or binary operations, are mapped instead of binary relations. The example in Fig. 2.14 shows a structure mapping representation of an

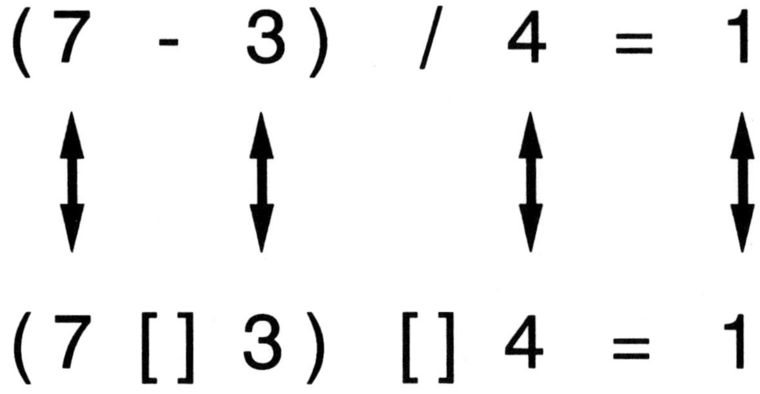

$$(7 \ - \ 3) \ / \ 4 \ = \ 1$$

$$\updownarrow \qquad \updownarrow \qquad\qquad \updownarrow \qquad\qquad \updownarrow$$

$$(7 \ [\ ] \ 3) \quad [\ ] \ 4 \ = \ 1$$

FIG. 2.14.   Multiple system mapping. Reproduced from Halford (1987) by permission of Elsevier Science Publishers (North Holland).

algebraic problem in which the task is to find two missing operations represented by the brackets [ ]. That is, given the equation:

$$(7 \ [\ ] \ 3) \ [\ ] \ 4 \ = \ 1$$

Find the missing operations. The problem is that both operations must be found before it can be confirmed that either of them is correct. It is not possible to find the first operation, then turn our attention to the second. The structure mapping to which this problem corresponds is shown in Fig. 2.14. Each structure comprises four elements and two binary operations, subtraction (addition) and division (multiplication). Each structure is a quaternary relation, and is four dimensional. The interpretation of the expression containing the missing operations is equivalent to a structure mapping, which indicates the correspondence between the two operations and expression contained in the problem. This structure mapping depends on structural correspondence but is more complex than system mappings. The reason for the added complexity is that it is a composition of two binary operations, rather than two binary relations. There is the operation $7 - 3 = 4$, and the operation $4 / 4 = 1$. Thus, whereas system mappings are a composition of two binary relations, such as "fairer than," a multiple system mapping is a composition of two binary operations, such as addition (subtraction) or multiplication (division). The greater complexity occurs because binary operations are three-dimensional concepts, whereas binary relations are two-dimensional concepts.

One theme of this chapter is that the representations people use have a major influence on the concepts they understand and the problems they can solve. This topic cannot be left however without considering empirical techniques for analyzing the representations that are used in cognitive processing. This is a large topic, which cannot be covered exhaustively, but some of the most important techniques are briefly described.

EMPIRICAL TECHNIQUES

Understanding cannot be equated with performance in any simple, one-to-one fashion, because performance can occur without understanding, as discussed earlier. It is essential however that there be some objective and rigorous techniques for analyzing the mental models that children have for particular concepts. Therefore the purpose of this section is to examine empirical techniques for diagnosing or analyzing the representations that are used in understanding and problem solving.

We will examine six techniques: protocol analysis, chronometric analysis (which includes componential analysis), multidimensional scaling, information integration theory, response pattern analysis, and experimental isolation of specific cognitive processes.

Protocol Analysis

The techniques of protocol analysis take many forms. Some of them depend on verbal accounts by participants of their problem-solving processes. These may be "think aloud" reports that are taken while problem solving is in process, they may be retrospective, or they may consist of responses to specific probe questions; for example, what subgoals did you use? What strategies did you use?

Ericsson and Simon (1984) argued that verbal reports are data like any other and may be either reliable or unreliable, just like latencies or error rates. The verbal–nonverbal dimension is orthogonal to the hard–soft dimension. These authors argued that verbal protocols can be just as useful and valid as any other data, if used with due regard for their limitations. For example, short-term memory limitations mean that introspective reports will only be valid descriptions of the most recent cognitive activity. Ericsson and Simon provided what amounts to a manual for verbal protocol analysis.

Protocol analysis can be as objective as any other diagnostic technique. To illustrate this, I refer to a study from the cognitive development literature in which children's problem-solving strategies were externalized in an ingenious and very objective manner.

Baylor and Gascon (1974) diagnosed weight-seriation strategies in children by giving them weights that differed by very small amounts and asking them to arrange them in order from heaviest to lightest by weighing them on a pan balance. The virtue of this technique is that every comparison made was externalized by overt weighing, and the weights had distinguishing features that were uncorrelated with their masses, but which permitted the sequence of decisions to be followed from a videotaped record. Thus, one of the protocols obtained, that for Line (aged 7;6) shows that she first weighs Items 6 and 7, finds that 7 > 6, so places them in the order 76, then weighs 1 and

3, finds 3 > 1, so adds them to the series yielding 7631, then weighs 2 and 4, finds 4 > 2, so adds 42 to the series yielding 763142, then adds 5 yielding 7631425, and stops. The inadequacy of the strategy is clearly revealed by this protocol, because the participant weighs each pair independently of the others, taking no account of the unknown relations between 6 and 3, or 1 and 4, and so on. The protocol clearly reveals therefore that this participant made no attempt to integrate the pairs.

Baylor & Gascon (1974) wrote computer programs to simulate the protocols, thereby providing a highly refined analysis of processes. Our concern here is with the fact that the strategy used by the participant was diagnosed objectively and accurately, and a detailed account of mental processes was provided.

Chronometric Analysis

Chronometric analysis is perhaps the most widely used experimental technique in cognitive psychology and figures prominently in classical studies by Posner and Boies (1971) and Paivio (1971), among others. Within cognitive development, Manis, Keating, and Morrison (1980) used a probe reaction-time task to investigate resource allocation by children to the Posner letter-match task. The highest load is expected to occur after presentation of the second letter because it is here that the two letters are compared, and a decision as to whether they are the same or different is made. Manis et al. found that the greatest increment in probe reaction time occurred at this point, and that this effect was greatest for the youngest children, indicating that their performance was most affected by the increased resource demands imposed by the comparison process.

Another sophisticated use of chronometric analysis was made by Hoving, Spencer, Robb, and Schulte (1978), who used the backward masking paradigm to determine the recognition threshold for visual stimuli and found that processing was actually faster for younger chilren. This last study is particularly notable for its ingenuity and rigorous control, but these and many other studies in the literature demonstrate that cognitive processes can be diagnosed by careful, systematic measurement of the duration of cognitive processes. The componential analysis used by Sternberg (1980a, 1980b; Sternberg & Rifkin, 1979) and discussed in chapters 5 and 7, is another example of chronometric analysis.

Multidimensional Scaling

Multidimensional scaling and cluster analysis were used by Miller and Gelman (1983) to investigate number understanding by children from kindergarten, Grades 3 and 6, and adults. Participants were required to judge the most similar and least similar pair of numbers from triads of numbers between 0 and 9. Multidimensional scaling and clustering solutions indicated that magnitude, probably defined by counting distance, was a major criterion of similarity for kindergarten children, but by Grade 6 criteria such as odd/even appeared as well.

Information Integration Theory

There is a review of information integration theory approaches to various issues in cognitive development by Anderson (1980). Basically the technique involves presenting stimuli that vary in two or more dimensions and having participants rate the stimuli on a linear scale. The ratings are then subjected to analysis of variance, and the main effects indicate which stimulus dimensions affect the ratings, and the presence or absence of interactions indicates whether the dimensions are combined additively or multiplicatively. For example, Anderson and Cuneo (1978) and Wilkening (1979) presented children with rectangles that varied in both height and width and found their judgments of area to be influenced by both these factors, as shown by significant main effects. However for 5-year-olds there was no interaction, and height and width were combined additively rather than multiplicatively to arrive at a judgment of area. Information integration theory has enabled objective and insightful answers to be provided to a number of long-standing problems such as how children use height and width information in conservation, or how they combine intention and damage in assessing guilt (Anderson, 1980).

Response Pattern Analysis

Response pattern analysis has been used in general cognitive psychology by Levine (1966), but it is best exemplified in the cognitive development area by the work of Gholson (1980) and Siegler (1976, 1981). In essence it entails defining a number of rules, strategies, or other processes, and testing on a set of tasks that vary in ways that are orthogonal to the variations among the strategies. Each mental process is then mapped into a unique pattern of responses across the test situations. Levine's (1966) methodology was designed to diagnose hypotheses in simple concept attainment situations. For an account of the procedure, see Halford (1982) or Liebert and Wicks-Nelson (1981). I briefly summarize the technique here.

Eight possible hypotheses were defined. In order to diagnose a participant's current hypothesis, the participant was presented with four "blank trials" in which he or she was asked to choose between pairs of stimuli. The pairs were constructed so that each hypothesis corresponded to a unique pattern of choices over the four pairs. Levine's method has two other characteristics that are important for our present concerns. The first is that there were only eight possible hypotheses but 16 possible response patterns in each set of four stimuli that were used for diagnosis. This means that guessing could be detected by the occurrence of response patterns that corresponded to no hypothesis. The second is that the hypotheses diagnosed on a set of blank trials should predict the response on the next feedback trial, thereby providing confirmatory evidence of the diagnosis. Three separate types of evidence, a response pattern that was consistent with a hypothesis, absence of evidence of guessing, and prediction of response on the next feedback trial, provided converging evidence for the diagnosis. Levine's technique has found considerable application for diagnosing hypothesis-testing processes in children (Gholson, 1980).

Siegler's rule assessment approach, like Levine's hypothesis procedure, depends on mapping rules into unique patterns of responses across a set of problems that are orthogonal to the set of mental processes, so both are appropriately called response pattern analyses. Siegler's approach has been applied to analysis of children's understanding of time, speed, and distance (Siegler & Richards, 1979); to the balance scale, proportionality, and conservation (Siegler, 1981); and to number (Siegler & Robinson, 1982).

Experimental Isolation of Critical Processes

In this approach a specific cognitive process is defined and a task is designed to measure it, together with specific control conditions that are designed to detect solution processes other than the one specified. An example is a study by Hill (reported by Suppes, 1965), who studied logical reasoning in children aged 6 and 8 years. Her reasoning tasks had the form: If that boy is John's brother, then he is 10 years old. That boy is not 10 years old. Is he John's brother? An important feature of the study was the use of baseline items such as: If that boy is not 10 years old, is he John's brother? Both tasks require many of the same cognitive processes (processing premises, interpreting the question, etc.), but they differ in that the reasoning task requires two premises to be integrated. This feature is therefore isolated by the use of the inference and control conditions. This study is therefore an example of the way that a specific cognitive process is first defined and then a test procedure designed to assess that specific process, with controls for alternative processes. In Hill's study alternative solution processes, such as guessing or answers based on empirical knowledge, are largely controlled by the baseline item.

Another example of the same approach is a study by Halford (1984) of transitive inferences. It was reasoned that the critical factor in transitive inferences is ability to integrate the premises; for example, given that $a > b$ and $b > c$, the critical performance is to integrate the premises to create the ordered triple abc. Halford presented two sets of premises that differed in that one contained a nonadjacent premise whereas the first did not. The two sets were $a > b, b > c, c > d, b > d, d > e$ and $a > b, b > c, c > d,$ $d > e, e > f$. Thus the two sets contained equal numbers of premises but the first contained a nonadjacent premise, $b > d$, which was absent from the second set. One task given to participants entailed first placing the pair bc in order, then adding d. The first step is equally easy in both conditions, because retrieval of the premise $b > c$ unequivocally indicates the order bc in both cases. Adding b is more difficult in the nonadjacent condition however because the premise $b > d$ indicates either of two alternative orders; bcd or bdc. Only by taking account of two premises $b > c$ and $c > d$ can this ambiguity be removed. In the nonadjacent condition however the only relevant premise is $c > d$, which unequivocally yields the order bcd. It was found that preschool children succeeded when the nonadjacent premise was absent, but failed when it was present, indicating that they could not take account of sufficient information to integrate two premises. However they performed the same task perfectly when it required only one premise to be considered. This interpretation was checked using other pairs of tasks that manipulated the number of premises that had to be considered in a single decision, with the same results.

The important point about both the Halford study and that of Hill is that tasks are not used as measures of global concepts, but a specific cognitive process was defined, and control procedures were adopted that embodied all other aspects of the task except that specific procedure. Thus failure, when it occurs, can be attributed to inability to perform that specific cognitive process. In this way much of the ambiguity of cognitive diagnosis can be removed.

SUMMARY

This chapter is concerned with the nature of mental models, and their role in understanding. The incentive to theorize about mental models came from difficulties with the notion of mental logic, and from research indicating that the way concepts are understood in real life called for a representational system that was incomplete and approximate, with an emphasis on semantic content. Mental models are defined as representations that are active while solving a particular problem, and provide the workspace for inference and mental operations. They may be influenced by, but do not include, background knowledge. Mental models may consist of any combination of propositional or imaginal representations.

A cognitive representation is an internal structure that mirrors a segment of the environment. The representation must be in structural correspondence to the environment and be consistent. Resemblance between the representation and the environment is not required, and representations are not "pictures in the head." There are imaginal and propositional representations, but the code of a representation is probably less important than the information it contains. Where representations contain the same information, which can be applied to a problem in the same way, they are equivalent. Complex reasoning entails multiple representation, and ability to map from one representation to another may be a major factor determining reasoning ability.

The perceptual–conceptual distinction is important to the theory of representations, because perceptual representations are more tied to current perceptual input, are less accessible across space and time, and have greater computational or inferential power than cognitive representations.

An analogy is a mapping from one mental structure to another, whereas a representation is a mapping from a mental structure to the environment. Because both entail structure mapping, it is regarded as the generic concept, and representations and analogies are specific cases.

Knowledge representations depends on a number of structures, including schemas, which represent a general category of things, situations, or phenomena. A *schema* can be conceptualized as a set of variables that have excitatory and inhibitory constraints to each other. Other knowledge representation structures are *propositional networks, condition–action rules*, and *contingencies*. Condition–action rules may be procedural or declarative; the former predict actions to be performed, the latter make assertions about the world.

Parallel distributed processing (PDP) models employ representations based on sets of activations over a large number of neural units, usually called vectors. PDP mechanisms have a number of useful emergent properties, including automatic discrimination and generalization, automatic averaging and prototype formation, and automatic regularity detection. PDP mechanisms tend to be content-specific, but variable-constant bindings and predicate arguments can be handled by tensor products of vectors.

A distinction is made between implicit and explicit representations, where the latter are cognitively accessible but the former are not. Evidence from infant studies suggests that representations are present at least by the age of 3–4 months, but that capacity for understanding is acquired gradually, and is probably extended over 2–3 years.

The dimensionality of representations is defined as the number of independent units of information required to specify the representation. It relates to the number of arguments in a predicate, N-dimensional representations being equivalent to N-place predicates. However an N-dimensional representation corresponds to a tensor product of rank $N+1$.

Four levels of structure mapping were defined:

Element mappings, in which an element in one structure is mapped into an element in the other structure on the basis of element similarity, prior learning, or convention. Structures at this level are unidimensional.

Relational mappings, in which a pair of elements and a binary relation between them in one structure is mapped into a pair of elements and a corresponding binary relation in the other structure. Structures at this level are two-dimensional.

System mappings, in which three elements and two binary relations, a binary operation, or a bivariate function, in one structure is mapped into three elements and two binary relations, a binary operation, or a bivariate function, in the other structure. Structures at this level are three-dimensional.

Multiple-system mappings, in which sets of four elements, and two binary operations or bivariate functions in one structure are mapped into sets of four elements, with two binary operations or bivariate functions, in the other structure. Structures at this level are four-dimensional.

Because there is no simple relationship between performance and understanding, techniques for assessing mental representations need to be considered. The main diagnostic techniques for this purpose are protocol analysis, chronometric analysis, componential analysis, multidimensional scaling, information integration theory, response pattern analysis, and experimental isolation of specific cognitive processes.

APPENDIX 2.A:
STRUCTURE AND STRUCTURE MAPPING

Structure

We will define a structure as a set of elements, with a set of functions, relations, or transformations defined on the elements. A structure mapping is a rule for assigning elements of one structure to elements of another in such a way that any functions, relations, or transformations between elements of the first structure correspond to functions, relations, or transformation in the second structure.

Structure Mapping

Suppose we have a representation comprising elements S_1 and S_2, with the relation R_s between them as shown in Fig. 2.15A. We also have a structure in the world comprising the elements E_1 and E_2, with the relation R_e between them. A structure mapping entails mapping S_1 into E_1, and S_2 into E_2 so that R_s corresponds to R_e.

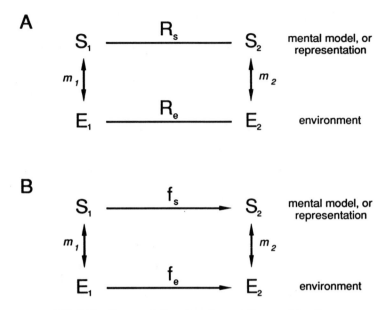

FIG. 2.15.   Representations based on relations and functions.

The criterion for validity of a relational structure mapping is provided by Suppes and Zinnies (1963) and Coombs, Dawes, and Tversky (1970), as part of their definition of a representation in measurement theory. The latter authors define a representation as follows:

A system $\alpha = \{A,R\}$ is said to be represented by another system $\beta = \{B,S\}$ if there exists a Function f from A into B (which assigns to each x in A a unique $f(x)$ in B) such that for all x,y in A

$$x \, R \, y \text{ implies } f(x)Sf(y). \tag{2}$$

Thus α is represented by β if there exists a correspondence f that maps A into B in such a way that if the relation R holds between some x and y in A then the relation S holds between $f(x)$ and $f(y)$ in B, where $f(x)$ and $f(y)$ are the images of x and y respectively (Coombs et al., 1970, p. 11).

Coombs et al.'s definition of a representation can be adopted as a definition of a valid structure mapping where the structures are based on relations. It can cover any case where two relational structures are placed in correspondence.

A structure mapping based on functions is valid if it is commutative, as Halford and Wilson (1980) and Holland et al. (1986) pointed out. The concept of a commutative diagram originated with category theory (Maclane, 1971) and is different from commutativity in arithmetic. The essence of it is shown in Fig. 2.15B.

Suppose we have a mental model consisting of two symbols, S_1 and S_2, and a function f_s between them. E_1 and E_2 are environmental, or world, states, events, or categories, and they have the function f_e between them. The vertical arrows, m_1 and m_2 represent mapping of the representation into the environmental categories. (Fig. 2.15B is upside down relative to the diagrams used by Holland et al., 1986, but is the same way up as Halford & Wilson's, 1980, diagrams.) Commutativity corresponds to the fact that the diagram is closed, and we arrive at the same result irrespective of the path taken. That is, if we apply f_s then m_2 we arrive at E_2, and if we first apply m_1, then f_e, we also arrive at E_2. Formally:

$$m_2 \ o \ f_s = f_e \ o \ m_1 \tag{1}$$

At this point it will be convenient to add a definition of correspondence that will apply to all the cases we will consider. *Correspondence between predicates:* A predicate P in Structure 1 is in correspondence to a predicate P' in Structure 2 if the arguments of P are mapped into P' and vice versa.

As Fig. 2.15 shows, validity criteria for structures based on functions are similar to those based on relations, and the two types of structures may be treated as equivalent for most of our purposes.

A transformation is a special case of a function; it is a function in which one set of elements is changed into another set. A transformation is really a way of interpreting a function, and the formal definitions are the same.

APPENDIX 2.B: THE DIMENSIONALITY METRIC

Elsewhere (Halford et al., in press) we discussed the dimensionality metric in the following terms. The essence of the dimensionality metric is that the complexity of a concept depends on its dimensionality, or the number of independent units of information required to define the concept. The units are of arbitrary size. This is related to the number of arguments in a predicate. A unary relation has only one argument, and therefore has only one dimension of variation. A binary relation has two arguments, and two dimensions of variation, because the values of the arguments can vary independently. Similarly, a ternary relation has three dimensions, and a quaternary relation four dimensions, and so on.

This idea might seem unusual if we are accustomed to thinking of arguments as lists that can be processed sequentially. However each argument in a relation defines a dimension of variation. The number of dimensions depends on the "-arity" of the relation. A unary relation on a Set S is a subset of S. A binary relation on S is a Subset S × S of ordered pairs of S. Similarly, a ternary relation on S is a Set S × S × S of ordered 3-tuples of S, and so on. Each argument can take a number of different values, so the number of arguments defines the number of dimensions of variation. Therefore the argument sets are not simply lists, but provide a measure of the degree of complexity in the structure.

The number of arguments defines the types of relationships that can exist within a structure. For example, a unary relation, $R(x)$; for example, BIG(dog), defines an attribute. Because it has a single dimension of variation, it is not possible to specify the way an attribute varies as a function of another attribute. This becomes possible with binary relations, $R(x, y)$; for example, BIG-GER(horse, dog). With ternary relations, $R(x, y, z)$, it is possible to define the way one attribute varies as a function of one other and how it varies as a function of two others, the latter not being possible with binary relations. As the "-arity" of a relation increases, so do the orders of interaction that are possible. This is a most important feature of predicates for our purposes, because in memory (Humphreys et al., 1989), in analogical reasoning (Halford et al., in press), and in the present context of cognitive development, we find it necessary to model the orders of interaction among the dimensions of a task.

Functions are a special case of relations; in functions mappings are unique. A zero-variate function, $f(\ ) = a$; for example, PRIME-MINISTER-IN-1990( ) = Hawke, has no argument and one dimension in the sense defined above. It is equivalent to a symbolic constant. Univariate functions have two arguments and two dimensions. A univariate function $f(a) = b$, is a set of ordered pairs (a,b) such that for each a there is precisely one b such that $(,b\epsilon f)$. In a similar way, bivariate functions, $f(a,b) = c$ have three arguments and three dimensions, and so on.

A unary operator has two arguments and is a special case of a univariate function; for example, the unary operator CHANGE SIGN comprises the set of ordered pairs $(x, -x)$. Binary operations have three arguments and have the same dimensionality as ternary relations and bivariate functions. (A binary operation on a Set A is a function from the Set A $\times$ A of ordered pairs of elements of A into A; that is, A $\times$ A $\to$ A. A bivariate function is defined as f:A $\times$ B $\to$ C.)

The number of arguments in quaternary relations corresponds to the number of arguments in trivariate functions and in compositions of binary operations. For example, the composition of binary operations of the form $a(b+c)$ = d is defined as the set of ordered 4-tuples $\{(3, 2, 4, 18) \ldots (2, 7, 3, 20) \ldots\}$.

The number of arguments is related to the dimensionality of a structure because it represents the number of independent terms required to define the structure, and the orders of interaction within the structure.

3

CAPACITY AND COMPLEXITY

It has long been a contentious question as to whether capacity to store and process information is a factor that changes with age. Several authors have placed the primary explanatory burden for cognitive development on some kind of information processing capacity or efficiency construct (Case, 1985; Chapman, 1987; Halford, 1982; McLaughlin, 1963; Pascual-Leone, 1970). Although these theories have generated considerable interest, they have never been without controversy. The idea that capacity changes with age has been seriously questioned (Chi, 1976; Schneider & Pressley, 1989). It has also been questioned as to whether capacity, or the closely related concept of resources, has any utility at all (Navon, 1984). In a more moderate vein, it has been pointed out that the concept has frequently been overextended. For example, Dempster (1981) pointed out that at one time it was regarded as self-evident that cognitive failures reflected capacity limitations. Such attributions made capacity virtually synonymous with performance. It appears that capacity is a potentially powerful concept, but one that has been fraught with difficulties. In this chapter I propose ways of solving some of these problems.

It is clear that capacity is certainly not the only thing that changes with age. We now know that children's memory performance is by no means a pure reflection of capacity, but is (also) a function of strategies and chunking (Kail, 1979; Schneider & Pressley, 1989), metacognitive knowledge (Flavell & Wellman, 1977), or domain-specific knowledge (Chi, 1978; Chi & Ceci, 1987). Children's reasoning is also known to be influenced by domain-specific knowledge and strategies (Carey, 1985).

The demonstrated importance of these factors has often been taken to imply that capacity limitations are an unnecessary construct. For example,

Schneider and Pressley (1989) stated that structural (capacity) changes can only be assumed if age differences cannot be explained by other factors. However, I believe this approach is inadequate, for two reasons. First, it means that capacity is always identified with the residual variance, and because it usually cannot be distinguished from measurement error, it is in danger of being overlooked. Second, it means that no attempt is made to understand the nature of capacity or to devise more direct ways of measuring it.

Apart from these specific objections, there seems to have been a pervasive reluctance to explore capacity explanations because they are seen as inherently pessimistic in the sense of implying limits to what children can achieve. Not only is this regarded as undesirable, but it seems to fly in the face of abundant evidence that apparent limitations can be overcome, either by more refined testing, or by training. However, I do not believe this is a cogent objection. First, I do not believe that desirability is a proper scientific criterion for evaluating a concept. However much we might hope that there are no limits to children's attainments, we must impartially evaluate the evidence. Furthermore, capacity limitations do not usually imply irremediable performance limits because there is almost always more than one way of performing a task. We are more likely to remediate failures if we understand their causes, because we then have a better chance of designing training or performance conditions to overcome them. If capacity limitations do affect performance, it is in our interest, both scientifically and practically, to explore them.

For all these reasons, I believe it is important to undertake a thorough examination of capacity, difficult though it is. It is obvious that capacity does not explain everything in cognitive development, and in the next chapter I argue that learning and induction mechanisms are of great importance. However, I am convinced that the full picture of cognitive development can never be clear until capacity is understood. Furthermore, a careful examination of the concept may lead to refinement of questions to be asked that might expedite progress. For example, because it is now clear that more than one capacity exists, it is possible that some capacities may increase over age while others remain constant, or even decrease. Thus the question, "Does capacity increase with age?" might itself cause confusion, because there may be no single answer. We cannot begin to assess these questions intelligently until the nature of capacity itself is understood. It turns out that there are several different concepts of capacity in the literature, so I outline them first, then proceed to the question of whether one or more capacities change with age.

As with most questions in cognitive development, it is essential to examine both the general cognition and cognitive development literature on capacity. The reason is that the solution to this problem might lie deeply in the nature of the underlying cognitive processes, and we have little chance of understanding it unless we take into account what general cognitive psychology has to offer. The concept of capacity has been addressed extensively in the adult cognition literature (Duncan, 1980; Hunt & Lansman, 1982; Kahneman, 1973; Navon, 1984; Navon & Gopher, 1979; Norman & Bobrow, 1975), yet apart from a review by Chapman (1987) and studies by Halford, Maybery, and Bain (1986) and Halford and Leitch (1989), there have been surprisingly few attempts to apply this literature to cognitive development.

Two different sets of distinctions need to be made. On the one hand, as I indicated earlier, there is evidence for a number of distinct capacities in human cognition. On the other hand, there are several concepts of capacity in the literature. The first set of disctinctions concern the nature of cognitive architecture and the number of capacities it contains. The second set of distinctions concern the concepts of capacity that theorists have constructed. It is important that architectural and conceptual distinctions not be confused. I will attend to the conceptual distinctions first, then proceed to the problems of cognitive architecture. The first concept of capacity to be considered is that of resource.

RESOURCES

The concept of resources implies that there is a type of mental energy that is in limited supply and the availability of which affects cognitive performance. There are several different concepts here that need to be kept distinct. For example, the terms resource and capacity are often used interchangeably, and both are often confused with the concept of task demand or load. However I believe the proper usages are as follows, and they will be adopted throughout this book:

> *Resource* is the mental energy that is available in a particular individual at a particular time, for a particular class of processes. It varies both across individuals and over time.

> *Capacity* refers to the maximum resources that an individual can make available. It corresponds to the "cognitive power" of an individual. It varies across individuals but is constant for one individual over time, apart from physiological changes such as maturation, aging, illness, drug states, and so on.

> *Demand* (or load) is not a property of persons, but of tasks. It represents the amount of mental effort that is required to perform a particular task.

The concept of resource developed out of attempts to account for people's ability to perform two tasks concurrently. Broadbent (1958) proposed that information passed through a limited capacity channel, which imposed restrictions on our ability to attend to incoming information. However, later research (Moray, 1959; Treisman, 1964) suggested that selective attention did not operate when information entered the system but at a later stage of processing. This led Moray (1967) to propose that there was a limited-capacity central processor. Kahneman (1973) proposed that there was a limited amount of attention that could be allocated to a task. However Kahneman also proposed that the amount of attentional resources could be increased by making greater effort, and that the allocation of resources could be switched from one task to another. The theory of capacity was developed into its modern form by Norman and Bobrow (1975), Navon and Gopher (1979), and Hunt and Lansman (1982). These later theories are essentially consistent in their basic tenets with the ideas of Kahneman.

The basic tenet of resource theory is that performance is a function of the resources allocated to it. This is expressed in the performance-resource function, illustrated in Fig. 3.1, according to which increased resources lead to improved performance. The resources available depend on the individual's capacity, and on the mental effort devoted to the task. The second basic tenet of capacity theory is that performance is a function of demand; that is, performance is worse for harder tasks that make greater information-processing demands. Demand affects the slope of the performance-resource function, as illustrated in Fig. 3.2. Where demand is low, a greater improvement in performance results from a given increase in resources.

The third basic tenet of resource theory is that as resources are reallocated from Task A to Task B, performance on Task A declines. This idea of the

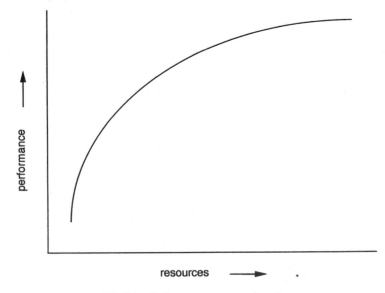

FIG. 3.1. Performance-resource function.

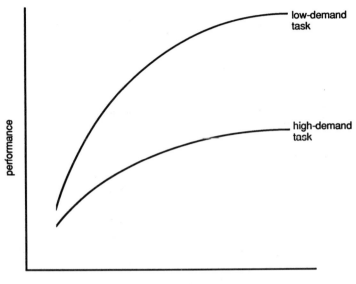

FIG. 3.2.   Performance-resource functions for high- and low-demand tasks.

tradeoff between performance on two concurrent tasks was expressed by Norman and Bobrow (1975) in the performance-operating characteristic, which is illustrated in Fig. 3.3. The performance-operating characteristic expresses the fact that, where two tasks are competing for a common resource, an increase in performance on one task will be obtained at the expense of a decrease in performance on the other. The essential idea is that resources are in complementary distribution, so that to the extent that they are used by one task, they become unavailable to another. Notice that the performance-operating characteristic has a downward slope only over the center portion of the figure. This is because no tradeoff is observed when the level of performance on either task is below a threshold value. The idea is that when the demand made by a task is very low, there will be sufficient capacity spare to permit optimal performance on the other task. Very low levels of performance on one task produce no deficit in the other, so there is no tradeoff.

Where there is a tradeoff, performance is said by Norman and Bobrow (1975) to be resource limited. Where there is no tradeoff, performance is said to be data limited. In the latter case the person has adequate capacity or resources for both tasks, and performance is only limited by availability of relevant information. Thus capacity theory accommodates the important point that many task failures are caused not by inadequate processing resources but by unavailability of the necessary information. Navon and Gopher (1979) developed the performance-operating characteristic model in much more de-

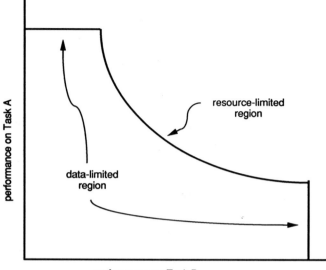

FIG. 3.3. Performance-operating characteristic.

tail and have likened it to the tradeoffs that occur when different activities compete for the same economic resource.

Measuring Processing Load

The tradeoff that occurs between two tasks when they compete for a common resource can be used to measure processing load. The usual procedure is to use a primary task that is performed concurrently with a secondary task. As Fig. 3.4 shows, performance on the secondary task tends to be poorer with a hard primary task. The easier the primary task (in the sense of lower demand), the more resources are available to the secondary task. Figure 3.4 has been drawn with hard primary tasks towards the left end of the abscissa, so resources will run in the same direction as in Figs. 3.1–3.3, but it should be noted that secondary task performance is a *decreasing* function of primary task difficulty. There are some precautions that must be observed when using this methodology. First, it is important that primary and secondary tasks do not depend on the same input and output processes. If, for example, both tasks required participants to press buttons to make their responses, the tradeoff might result from overloading motor control processes, rather than some central processing capacity that might be of interest. The safest procedure is to use different input and output modalities, as was done by Maybery et al. (1986). Transitive inference was the primary task, with visual premise

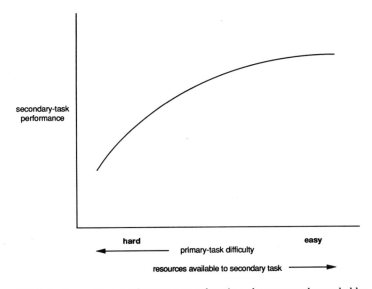

FIG. 3.4.   Second-task performance as a function of resources demanded by concurrent primary task.

presentation and manual button presses to indicate answers. The secondary task was to say "beep" to a tone. Thus the primary task was visual–manual and the secondary task was auditory–vocal. Even here, Maybery et al. carried out checks to ensure there was no conflict, such as might occur between vocal and manual responses.

A second precaution is to ensure that primary task difficulty remains constant, because otherwise secondary task performance may be affected by variations in primary task performance. Suppose, for example, that in Fig. 3.4, participants attempted to compensate for increased primary task difficulty by allocating more resources to the primary task but overreacted and raised their performance on the primary task. This would reduce resources available to the secondary task, but not because of primary task difficulty. Thus decline in secondary task performance might not reflect greater processing loads in the hard primary task but merely a reallocation of resources. A third precaution, as pointed out by Fisk, Derrick, and Schneider (1986) is to ensure that the secondary task remains sensitive to resources throughout the experiment. Should the resource demands of the secondary task decline due to developing automaticity, changes in strategies, or other factors, the tradeoff may cease to reflect the resource demands of the primary task.

Another problem is what Navon and Gopher (1979) called the *concurrence cost*, which is the extra load caused by coordinating two tasks. This means that a deficit in one task due to concurrent performance of the other, the *dual-task deficit*, might not be due solely to competition for resources, but might reflect the resources used by coordination. It is not clear, however, whether this applies to all task combinations. If the secondary task is probe reaction time (reaction to a signal that occurs at indeterminate times while performing the primary task), the secondary task and the coordination process are really identical. There is no sense in which tasks are coordinated, other than responding to the probe itself. It is not clear therefore that concurrence cost should impose interpretational difficulties in such a case. Also the easy-to-hard paradigm (Hunt & Lansman, 1982) can help disambiguate data based on the dual-task deficit, as we will see.

It is sometimes stated that if an easy and a hard primary task are used with an easy and a hard secondary task, then competition for a common resource will be reflected in an interaction of these two factors (Logan, 1979; Navon, 1984). Actually this prediction does not hold mathematically (Bain, Halford, Wilson, Maybery, & Kelly, in preparation). The form of the effect will depend on the shape of the performance-resource functions, as illustrated in Fig. 3.5. If the performance-resource functions for the secondary task are diverging, as shown in Fig. 3.5A, there will be a superadditive interaction, that is, one in which the effect of primary task difficulty will be greater on the easy secondary task. If the performance-resource functions converge as shown in Fig. 3.5B, there will be a subadditive interaction, in which primary task difficulty will have more effect on the hard secondary task. In the in-between case there will be no interaction, only main effects of primary and secondary task difficulty. Thus, an interaction is not necessary to demonstrate competition for a limited resource.

Measuring Capacity Limitations

We want to know whether children's ability to understand concepts is limited by their capacity, and so we need a methodology for addressing this question. The best way to distinguish capacity limitations from other factors that affect task difficulty is to use the trade-off that occurs when two tasks compete for a common resource. The measurement of capacity limitation amounts to assessing whether performance limitations are a function of the size of the resource pool available.

This logic was used by Hunt and Lansman (1982) to assess capacity limitations. Their easy-to-hard paradigm is summarized in Fig. 3.6. There is an easy and a hard version of the primary task. The easy version is performed jointly with a secondary task. The basic idea is that the larger an individual's capacity, the more resources he or she will have to spare while performing the easy primary task. These spare resources will be reflected in performance on the secondary task; that is, individuals with higher capacity will perform better on the secondary task. Thus, secondary task performance will be a measure of individual capacity.

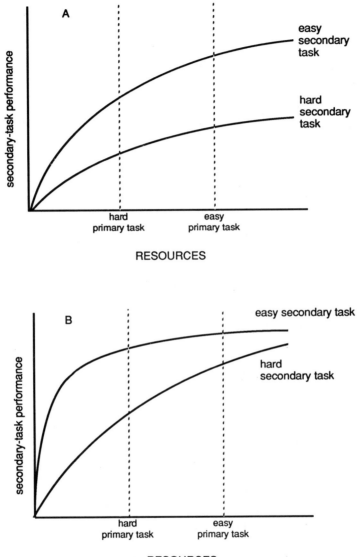

FIG. 3.5.   Forms of interaction between primary- and secondary-task difficulties.

We want to know whether the hard version of the primary task is capacity limited. That is, we want to know whether variations in performance on
it should be attributed to capacity differences between individuals. Because
secondary-task performance is a measure of capacity differences, if the hard
version of the primary task is capacity limited, performance on it should be
predicted by secondary-task performance.

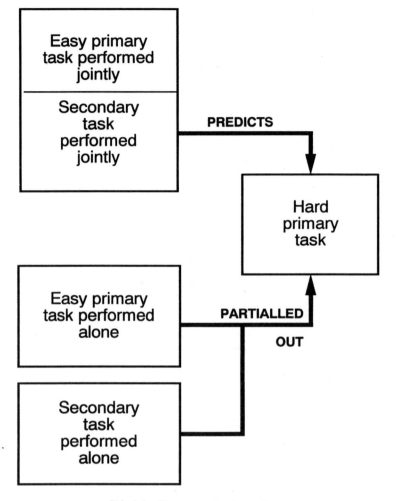

FIG. 3.6.   The easy-to-hard paradigm.

One problem is that any correlation between the secondary task and the hard primary task might reflect factors other than capacity. Hunt and Lansman (1982) overcame this problem by having both the easy version of the primary task, and the secondary task, performed alone. The correlation between these two tasks performed alone and the hard primary task is partialled out from the prediction of the hard primary task by the secondary task when performed jointly with the easy primary task (see Fig. 3.6). Partialling out these correlations effectively removes variance that the secondary task might share with the hard primary task for reasons other than capacity. For a more comprehensive treatment of the paradigm, see Hunt and Lansman (1982).

The easy-to-hard paradigm is not susceptible to a criticism made by Navon (1984) and Guttentag (1989) of the dual-task deficit approach to diagnosing capacity limitations. Navon (1984) argued that deficits resulting from dual-task situations might reflect, not competition for a common resource, but one task having a detrimental effect on the other. For example, one task might produce anxiety that adversely affects performance on the other task, or one task might produce an output that is a distracting stimulus for the other tasks. Consequently, the observation that performance is impaired when two tasks are performed concurrently, as compared with performance of either alone (the dual-task deficit), is not sufficient evidence of competition for a common resource. Navon argued that this places a severe limitation on the dual-task methodology to study capacity limitations. A similar argument was advanced by Brainerd and Reyna (1989) and Guttentag (1989).

These arguments do not apply to the easy-to-hard paradigm because the criterion, the hard primary task, is not performed jointly with another task. Therefore, performance on the hard primary task, and the variance it shares with the secondary task, cannot be attributed to one task interfering with the other. Therefore it appears that the easy-to-hard paradigm can be used to assess capacity limitations without danger of the artifacts described by Brainerd and Reyna (1989), Guttentag (1989), or Navon (1984). Given the potential of the easy-to-hard paradigm, it is curious that none of these authors cited it. The easy-to-hard paradigm was used as a converging operation by Halford, Maybery, and Bain (1986) in order to take into account the ambiguities that have been identified in the dual-task deficit methodology, but neither Guttentag (1989) nor Brainerd and Reyna (1989) made any comment on its use.

To summarize this section, the concept of resources was developed to account for the limited ability of human performers to process information. It takes into account the dual-task deficit and the relationship between performance and the amount of information processed at a given time within a task. Resources are a global concept in that they do not specify the relevant mechanism, which sometimes leads to dissatisfaction (Howe & Rabinowitz, 1990).[1] However, this is not a valid argument for dispensing with the concept. To use an analogy, the concept of electric current tells us how much work can be done by the electricity flowing down a particular conductor, but it does not specify the mechanism of conduction. It is a resource concept, and it is useful to supplement it with a mechanical theory of the behavior of electrons in a conductor. Notice however that doing this does not make the concept of current redundant. A theory of mechanism does not displace a resource concept, because the two are complementary. Therefore,

---

[1]Howe and Rabinowitz (1989) also seemed to want to argue against using resources as a panacea or as the sole explanation for cognitive development. This is not, and never has been, a feature of my position.

although it is highly desirable that we find the basis for capacity limitations, a question on which I will make a number of proposals, it does not follow that the resource concept should be abandoned. It has also been argued that dual-task deficits do not provide unequivocal evidence for resource competition, but there has been considerable danger of throwing out the baby with the bathwater. This is particularly so when critics who argue this way have ignored methodologies, such as the easy-to-hard paradigm, that appear to have the potential to remove this ambiguity.

Not only are resources not the sole factor in cognitive development, but limited resources are not the sole cause of task difficulty. Children and adults may make errors because the demands of a task exceed the resources they allocate to it, but this is far from being the only factor that influences either errors or solution times. Therefore, I will outline other sources of error. Given that errors can occur because of excessive processing loads, and for other reasons, it underlines the importance of being able to determine whether a particular performance is capacity limited. The theory of resources that I have outlined is useful for this purpose.

Difficulty, Complexity, and Processing Load

There are three main ways that a task can be made difficult independently of loads. These are: number of processing steps, knowledge, and availability of the relevant concepts, hypotheses, or strategies. Then there are memory storage loads, which must be distinguished from processing loads. Then there are factors that affect processing load but that are extrinsic to the task itself. Finally, there are intrinsic complexity factors that affect processing loads. We will consider all these in turn.

Number of Processing Steps.   Consider the following tasks:

$$22 + 7 + 5 = ?$$

$$7 + 4 + 9 + 3 + 6 + 5 = ?$$

They differ primarily in the number of steps they require. The second task will take longer, and there may be a slightly higher error rate, mainly because there is more opportunity for error when performing five additions than when performing two. On the other hand there is likely to be little, if any, difference in processing load. The level of effort at any given moment is likely to be little if at all higher when performing the second task than when performing the first. If we were to measure processing loads, we would probably find no detectable difference. If there were a difference, it would probably be due to "place-keeping"; that is, keeping track of where we are in the sequence. The loads imposed by the operations themselves would not differ between tasks.

Knowledge and Conceptual Sophistication. Tasks can be difficult because people lack the required knowledge. For example, a reasoning task that produces a high error rate is:

Premises:

If there is a circle in the box, there is a square in the box.

There is a square in the box.

Inference:

There is a circle in the box. (True/false?)

It is a common fallacy to answer that the inference, there is a circle in box, follows from the premises (the fallacy of affirmation of the consequent). One reason for this error is that people sometimes (mis)interpret the first premise as a double implication (biconditional) rather than as an implication (conditional); that is, they interpret "circle implies square" as "circle implies square and square implies circle" (Staudenmayer, 1975).

This type of difficulty is likely to increase error rates, but would not necessarily affect latency or processing load. Participants may well answer quickly, confidently, with no experience of effort, yet they answer incorrectly. The task does not impose an excessive processing load, it is simply that most people do not know enough about logic to realize that the task calls for implication rather than double implication. This type of error is due to domain knowledge more than processing load.

Carey (1985; Wiser & Carey, 1983) gave numerous examples of the way domain knowledge underlies the development of children's reasoning. The essence of her argument is that much of cognitive development consists of conceptual changes that show some parallels to the conceptual developments that occurred in the history of science. According to this view, which is considered in more detail in chapter 9, cognitive development has little to do with growth of memory or processing capacity but has to do with conceptual change. Although I agree that much of cognitive development depends on acquisition of knowledge and conceptual sophistication, my concern at present is to distinguish between limitations due to lack of knowledge or conceptual sophistication on the one hand and limitations due to capacity on the other.

Availability of the Correct Hypothesis. Some problems can be difficult because the correct hypothesis, even if known, may be difficult to retrieve from memory. Consider, for example, this analogy: bread : pain :: dog : ?.

This may be quite difficult, until it is realized that the "pain" is the French word for bread, in which case the solution "chien" (French word for dog) is very easily obtained. The fact that "pain" is an English word makes retrieval of the appropriate hypothesis particularly difficult. There is nothing structurally complex about this analogy. Its difficulty arises from the unlikely nature of the correct hypothesis and the consequent slowness to retrieve it from memory.

Instructions and other stimuli that communicate task demands are factors that can affect difficulty by affecting availability of the relevant concept or strategy. Such factors have had an important impact on procedures for diagnosing children's understanding of concepts. For example, Grieve and Garton (1981) argued that young children fail the class inclusion task, not because they are incapable of understanding hierarchical classification, but because they misinterpret the comparison they are expected to make. This hypothesis is discussed in detail in chapter 8, but for now I just want to note that the way task demands are communicated can influence availability of the correct hypothesis.

Short-Term Memory Storage Load. Some problems are difficult because of the information that must be retained in short-term memory for later use. A storage load, caused by retaining information for use later, is distinct from a processing load because the information is not actively constraining decision making while it is stored. Processing loads, on the other hand, are caused by information that is being actively processed to make a decision. A good example of a storage load occurs in mental arithmetic (Hitch, 1978). Try mentally adding 434 + 87. Strategies used by individuals vary considerably, but whatever strategy is used, information has to be stored in short-term memory.

If we start with the units column and add 4 + 7, we have to retain the units digit 1, and the carry digit, which has to be added into the tens column, yielding 3 + 8 + 1 = 12. Now we have to retain both the units and tens digits, plus the carry digit, while we add the carry digit to the hundreds column. If we also have to retain the augend and addend, the strain in short-term memory can be considerable.

Alternatively, some people round off either the augend or addend, then adjust the sum. For example, given 434 + 79, we might add 434 + 80, yielding 514, then subtract 1, yielding 513. This avoids the short-term memory load imposed by the carry digit and enables the units and tens digits to be added in one operation, again saving short-term memory load, but it incurs the penalty of an additional load due to the number that must be subtracted at the end. Either way, therefore, storage of intermediate results imposes a load on short-term memory.

Retention of the original problem data can also impose a load on short-term memory. This also occurs in mental arithmetic if the problem itself is not written down and must be retained in memory. However, the same problem can occur in reasoning tasks. For example, Bryant and Trabasso (1971) argued that young children failed to make transitive inferences, not because they did not understand the logic of transitivity, but because they failed to remember the premises.

Extrinsic Processing Loads. One way that extrinsic processing loads can be imposed is by reducing clarity of stimuli or task demands. Tasks will be harder if, for example, illumination is poor, if the stimuli are degraded, or if there is interference from other stimuli; for example, listening to speech with a tap running.

An interesting case of the stimulus-clarity factor occurs where the interfering stimulus is self-produced. This is particularly likely where two tasks are performed concurrently. Suppose, for example, that someone is performing an addition task while trying to avoid an electric shock. The anxiety caused by the possibility of shock may well interfere with the arithmetic task.

The stroop task is a good example of interference from competing stimuli. In the stroop task (Stroop, 1935) words are presented in colored inks, and participants are required to name the ink-color, ignoring the word-meanings. This is difficult if the words are themselves color names. Suppose the word "green" is printed in red ink; it is quite difficult to respond "red" because it is difficult to inhibit the processing of the graphic stimulus "green."

Intrinsic Processing Loads. Processing loads can be imposed because of a complexity factor that is intrinsic to the task itself. We will consider some examples before analyzing this type of load in detail.

Posner and Boies (1971) examined processing loads at different stages of the letter-match task. The task entails presenting two letters in succession, and participants press one of two buttons indicating whether the letters are the same or different. Probe reaction time was used as a measure of processing load (this entailed presenting an auditory stimulus, white noise, to which the participant had to respond as quickly as possible by pressing a button). Posner and Boies (1971) found the longest probe reaction times occurred after the second letter was presented, suggesting that this was the point where load was highest. This is reasonable because encoding the second letter and comparison with the first letter must both occur after the second letter is presented, whereas encoding alone occurs after the first letter is presented.[2]

An interesting point about comparison is that it necessarily requires two items to be considered in a single decision. Given a pair of letters like A B, we must consider both of them in parallel in order to compare them. It makes no sense to apply the comparison operation to A first, then to B. It is inherent

---

[2]This experiment was criticized by Allport (1980a) and McLeod (1977) because primary and secondary tasks used the same modality. If separate modalities are used, the pattern of secondary task latencies is different but still consistent with the proposition that the processing load is higher after the second letter is presented.

in the nature of comparison that we cannot compare less than two things. This is a structural constraint on processing loads. The load is imposed, not because of strategies or other psychological factors, but because of a structural complexity that is inherent in the task.

For another example, consider the following sentence that was investigated by Kimball (1973):

The boy that the girl that the man saw met slept.

Most people find this sentence rather difficult to parse, but why? It is quite short, and the domain knowledge required is certainly possessed by all of us. The reasons it is difficult are: (a) there are few semantic cues to sentence structure—boys, girls, and men all see, meet, and sleep, so there is no semantic basis for pairing subjects with verbs; (b) the center-embedded structure provides few syntactic cues that would assist in pairing subjects with verbs or verbs with objects; and (c) there are few function words that indicate clause boundaries.

The problem is, as Kimball (1973) showed, that no clause can be understood unless all of them are understood. This can be demonstrated by showing that the sentence is easy to understand if we insert constituent markers: (The boy (that the girl (that the man saw) met) slept). It is easy to understand the sentence now because the constituent markers enable us to parse one clause at a time. Without the constituent markers we could not do this, because of uncertainty as to which sets of words constituted a clause. The general principle is that parsing more than two constituents that have the status of sentences overloads working memory (Clark & Clark, 1977).

The structural complexity of these sentence-parsing tasks imposes a processing load, but, unlike the letter-match task, the complexity of the task can be reduced. It is easy, and quite normal, to construct sentences so that they do not impose such high processing loads. For example we might write: "The boy, who was met by the girl, who had been seen by the man, slept," or even: "The man saw the girl, who met the boy. The boy slept." These constructions permit constituents of the sentences to be parsed serially, with reduced processing load.

In these examples, processing load is related to the amount of information that has to be processed in parallel. In the letter-match task, comparison imposed a higher load than encoding because both letters had to be processed together in a single decision. In the sentence comprehension task the load is due to all major constituents having to be processed before the meaning of any of them is fully clear. In both tasks the load is due to the amount of information that has to be processed in parallel, or in a single decision.

To deal with this situation we need a way of relating load to task complexity. The first essential is a complexity metric. It turns out that two metrics have been developed that are applicable to conceptual complexity. One of these, based on the dimensionality of concepts, was introduced in chapter 2.

The other is based on the number of levels of embedding in a subroutine- or goal-hierarchy. We will consider these metrics in more detail.

Complexity Metrics

The first metric we consider is based on the number of levels of embeddedness of the subroutine or goal hierarchy, and the second is the dimensionality of a pattern, structure, or concept. The latter was mentioned in chapter 2. Now we relate it to complexity metrics and the concept of demand.

Embeddedness of the subroutine or goal hiearchy has been used by Egan and Greeno (1974) and Case (1985). It can be applied to tasks such as the Tower of Hanoi puzzle. (This entails three pegs, with a number of discs varying in size on the first peg. The aim is to transfer all discs to the third peg. Discs may be moved only one-at-a-time, and a larger disc cannot be placed on a smaller disc.) The task entails performing a sequence of steps, each to fulfil a goal. The top goal, to transfer all discs to peg three cannot be fulfilled immediately, so a subgoal is created. That cannot be fulfilled immediately either, so a further subgoal is created, and so on until a goal is set that can be fulfilled. This leads to a hierarchy of goals, each embedded within another. The more discs to be moved, the more levels of embedding there are. The number of levels of the goal hierarchy predicts task difficulty well.

Case's (1985) theory of cognitive development assesses complexity using an analysis that is essentially a goal hierarchy, but it is stated as a series of objectives. Case postulated four substages within each of the major stages: operational consolidation, operational coordination, bifocal coordination, and elaborated coordination. The lowest substage entails a single objective, the next substage entails two objectives, the next three, and the next four. A pointer must be retained for each objective, and the pointers are stored in short-term memory. Consequently the load on short-term storage space, another construct in Case's system, increases by one unit as the child progresses from one substage to the next.

Although levels of embedding is a useful metric, it has a number of defects. The first is that it is susceptible to alteration if the algorithm or procedure for performing the task is changed. That is, it is often possible to devise a different strategy that has a different number of levels. This results in a different complexity value for the task. The problem is that subroutine or goal hierarchies are not intrinsically constrained. That is, there is no structural feature of the task that is intrinsically associated with a specific number of levels in the hierarchy.

Another difficulty is that an embeddedness metric assumes that tasks are processed serially. However, parallel distributed processing conceptions of cognition (Rumelhart & McClelland, 1986), outlined in chapter 2, are difficult to reconcile with subroutine and goal hierarchies, and it has been commented that "subroutines . . . are probably not a good way to view the operation of the brain" (p. 135).

There is also the problem of deciding how much processing is performed at each step. The more processing done, in parallel, at each step, the less levels of embedding a subroutine hierarchy will contain and, by the placekeeping metric, the easier the task will be. However, as we saw earlier, tasks that require a lot of information to be processed in parallel are actually harder. For all these reasons an alternative metric is required.

Dimensionality.   A structural complexity metric has been developed for patterns based on the number of independent items of information that define it; that is, on its dimensionality (Leeuwenberg, 1969; Restle, 1970; Simon, 1972). The metric can be illustrated with a developmental study by Halford and MacDonald (1977). The problem was, as Olson (1970) found that young children find it difficult to copy diagonal patterns, one example of which is shown in Fig. 3.7. The difficulty turns out to be due to the fact that a diagonal is inherently more complex than a pattern with the same number of elements that runs up-and-down, or left-to-right across the page. The reason is that more instructions are required to generate the diagonal pattern. Suppose we have the first element in place. To locate the next element, we must supply the instruction; "up one place, right one place." The vertical pattern only requires "up one place," and the horizontal pattern "right one place." Halford and MacDonald showed that the difficulties experienced with the diagonal were shared by other patterns of equal structural complexity, such as the L-shaped pattern shown in Fig. 3.7. Thus the children's difficulty was caused by a degree of structural complexity that was inherent in the task. This difficulty is associated with the dimensionality of the patterns. A vertical or horizontal line is a one-dimensional pattern, whereas a diagonal or L-shaped pattern is two-dimensional. It is easier to quantify the complexity of a visual pattern because it is visible and its components can be observed directly. When dealing with concepts, the components have to be inferred, and this can often be a subtle process. The dimensionality of a concept depends on the number of independent components in its representation, but concepts, unlike percepts, can be recoded by a process that is under strategic control. The way a concept is represented depends on the cognitive operations that are being performed on it. We will illustrate this in the next section.

Factors that Determine Dimensionality of Concepts

Consider a concept such as "(nuclear) family," comprising subsets "parents" and "children." If we want to relate the family to something outside, such as neighborhood, we treat it as a whole and the concept has just one component. However if we want to examine the internal structure of the family,

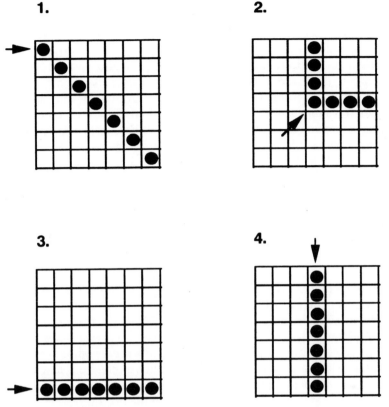

FIG. 3.7. One- and two-dimensional patterns. From Halford & McDonald (1977). Reprinted by permission of Chicago University Press.

it has three components, "parents," "children," and the "family" itself. Thus if we wanted to ask "are there more individuals in the family or in the parents," we would have to represent "family" with its subsets "parents" and "children" (the last is necessary to recognize that there are parts of family other than parents). Therefore, when treated as a whole, family entails a one-dimensional representation, but when treated in terms of its components, it entails a three-dimensional representation.

The dimensionality of representations was defined in chapter 2 in terms of two principles:

1. Only dimensions that constrain the current decision process are actively represented at a given point in time; and
2. aspects of a task that vary independently of each other must be represented as separate dimensions.

At the microstructural level, each dimension corresponds to a vector in a PDP representation.

A vector represents a set of items that all relate to one another in a fixed way within the current decision process. Thus, if we treat "family" as a whole and represent it as a single dimension and a single vector, then the structure of the family is taken as fixed, and no decisions are being made with respect to its components. We are not interested, for example, in what happens to family size as the number of children is increased. Relations between components of the family do not enter into the decision and are not separately represented. To take another example, consider the concept of speed, discussed in chapter 2. We can treat speed as a single dimension, provided we take the relations between its components as fixed. Its components, distance and time, are related by division, speed = distance/time. So long as this relationship is of no interest, speed can be processed as a single dimension. If however we wanted to consider variations in speed as a function of the distance run, or the time taken, then distance, time, and speed become separate dimensions and have to be represented as separate vectors.

Chunking reduces the dimensionality of a representation, as discussed in chapter 2. We can represent a family as being composed of parents and children. We then have three aspects, the family itself, the parents, and the children, together with the relations between them. There are three dimensions here; parents, children, and family. We can now represent, for example, the way family size varies as a function of number of children, number of parents, or both. Suppose, however, that our purpose is to relate families to other social groups, and that internal structure is of no interest. We can now represent family as a single dimension and can relate it to (say) neighborhoods, socio-economic groups, or other groups external to itself. We have switched from representing the internal structure of the family to representing its external structure. To reduce our processing load, we have chunked the representation of family from three dimensions to one.

Structure mapping requires the structures being mapped to be represented. Therefore the complexity of structure mapping depends on the dimensionality of the structures being mapped. Four levels of structure mapping are defined in chapter 2 and are related to the dimensionality of concepts. These can be summarized as follows. For element mappings, a single item in one structure is mapped into the other structure. The structure entailed in these mappings is one dimensional because it is defined by a single item of information such as a label. For relational mappings, a binary relation in one structure is mapped into a binary relation in the other structure. Binary relations are defined as sets of ordered pairs. They are two-dimensional because two independent items of information are used to define each relation. System mappings entail mapping ternary relations, binary operations, or trivariate functions from one structure to another. All these structures are defined as sets of ordered triples and are three dimensional. Multiple system mappings entail mapping compositions of the structures at the system mapping level. These compositions are defined on a minimum of four elements and are four-dimensional.

The next step is to show empirically that the dimensionality metric can predict processing load. Three empirical studies from our laboratory will be used for this purpose.

Complexity Metric and Processing Load

The first two studies we examine are concerned with transitivity. Analysis of the dimensionality of a task must be based on a model of the decisions to be made. Transitivity will be used because, as noted in chapter 1, there are detailed process models that enable us to make the kind of analysis required.

Consider two premises such as "Bill is taller than John; Bill is not as tall as Peter." After the premises are comprehended, they must be integrated into a three-term array: Peter, Bill, John. It is this integration of two two-term arrays into one three-term array that provides an illustration of structural complexity. To see why this is true, consider another transitive inference problem:

Mike is shorter than Jim. Bill is taller than Jim. Who is tallest?

In order to construct a three-term array, we must assign each name to an ordinal position; that is, we want to know who comes first, who second, and who third. To decide this we must consider both premises jointly. We cannot process one premise first, then discard it and go on to the second one. To see this, suppose we try to process the first premise in this way. We can conclude that Mike is in either the second or third position, but we cannot be sure which. From the second premise, considered alone, we could conclude that Bill is in either the first or second position, but again we cannot be sure which. Only by considering both premises can we conclude that Bill is in first position, Jim in second and Mike in third. No firm or unequivocal decisions can be made without considering both premises. Neither premise can be fully processed without considering the other. This means that premise integration has a certain degree of structural complexity. The PDP representation that is required for this situation was shown in chapter 2, Fig. 2.7, and an elaborated version is shown in Fig. 3.8. It comprises a vector representing the ternary relation, and a vector representing each of its arguments. Each of these components can be coded differently from the original input, and there is no suggestion that the premises are represented literally. However, because each of the arguments and the relation are free to vary independently, each must be represented by a separate vector.

The Rank 4 tensor product shown in Fig. 3.8 can be decomposed into three,

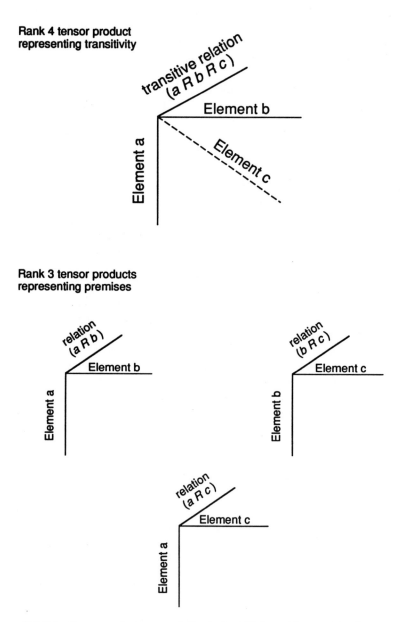

FIG. 3.8. Tensor-product representation for transitivity and for component relations.

Rank 3 tensor products, each representing a premise. The three-dimensional tensor product representing each premise comrises the relation and its two arguments. However, to represent the transitive inference, the four-dimensional tensor product is required. This follows from the principle that the information represented in the currently active mental model includes all the information that enters into the decision being made, and each component that is free to vary independently of the others must be represented by a separate vector.

It follows from this analysis that premise integration should impose a higher processing load than other phases of processing in transitive inference that do not entail this structural complexity. This prediction was tested by Maybery, Bain, and Halford (1986). Transitive inferences were presented to adult participants in a sentence-verification format, as shown in Fig. 3.9. The sentences were presented successively, then a target appeared, and participants were required to press one of two buttons, indicating whether the target was consistent with the premises. For example, in the problem in Fig. 3.9A the top-down order is JTN, so the target, with N above J, is inconsistent with the premises. Segmented presentation was used, so the first premise disappeared before the second was presented, which disappeared before the target appeared. The sequence of events in a trial was as shown in Fig. 3.10. Probe reaction time, saying "beep" to a tone, was used to assess information processing loads. Thus, the primary task was visual–manual and the secondary task was auditory–vocal, so different modalities were used as advised earlier in this chapter. Additional checks were carried out to ensure there was no conflict, such as might occur between vocal and manual responses. Premise integration occurs when the second premise is presented. Accordingly we would expect that processing load would be highest in that phase, and this should be reflected in longer probe reaction times for Probe 3. However in order to ensure that increased probe RT reflected the processing load imposed by premise integration and not some other factor, a control condition was used in which the premises could not be integrated, as shown in Fig. 3.9.[3]

---

[3]Howe and Rabinowitz (1990) argued that this procedure isolates empirical variables rather than theoretical processes. This claim appears to be based on extrapolation from another task they examined. However, there is nothing in their discussion to suggest that they have taken into account the extent and consistency of evidence showing that the theoretical processes identified in the transitive inference literature are well substantiated and can be reliably isolated by the empirical techniques used. See Maybery, Bain, and Halford (1986), and Maybery (1987). Their account of our argument is also inaccurate in many ways. For example, as the discussion above (which is elaborated on in chapter 7) makes clear, we do not assume that transitive inference is based on accurate, verbatim memory for the premises, as they claimed (Howe & Rabinowitz, 1990, p. 139). Furthermore, they claimed that I rely on a generic pool of resources (p. 139), despite my contention that there is more than one resource pool. They also claimed (p. 140) that I rely on span measures to assess processing capacity, which I do not (Halford, 1987; Halford, Maybery, & Bain, 1988). They also said that it is unclear why the conclusion does not impose a load (p. 140). This again misrepresents my position, because a conclusion does impose a load, but it

A. Transitive-inference task - requires system mapping

premises   J is above T

                  N is below T

target   N

                  J

                              (answer: false)

B. Control task - requires relational mapping

premises   R is above G

                  L is below S

target   L

                  S

                              (answer: false)

FIG. 3.9.   Sentence-verification format for *N*-term series tasks.

---

does not add to the peak load. The reason is that, as can be seen from the discussion above, transitive inference entails integrating the premises into a three-term array, and it is this that causes the peak load. Once the array is constructed, the conclusion can be read off from it. Thayer and Collyer pointed out as long ago as 1978 that once the array is constructed, reaching the conclusion is almost perceptual. Therefore the load it imposes will be small. Furthermore, whatever the magnitude of the load, it will not add to the premise integration load, because the latter is completed before the conclusion is read off. Finally, their claim that there are interpretational difficulties with the dual task methodology we used (p. 139) takes no account of the easy-to-hard paradigm that we used as a converging operation to handle this problem, as I pointed out earlier.

ready	clear screen	Premise 1	Premise 2	target	clear screen
		Q is below R	Q is above L	R L	
	Probe 1	Probe 2	Probe 3	Probe 4	Probe 5

FIG. 3.10. Probe positions for processing load study.

The results are shown in Fig. 3.11. It is clear that RT was increased for Probe 3, in the experimental condition only. Thus probe RT was longer in the only condition where premise integration occurred. This confirms that premise integration imposed a higher processing load than other aspects of the task. Other factors, such as processing of negatives, increased problem solution time had no effect on probe reaction time. Similarly, solution time for the transitive inference task decreased over trials, but the effect of premise integration on probe reaction time remained, illustrating the point that latencies and processing loads may vary independently.

The structure mapping required for premise integration is shown in Fig. 3.12. The structure mapping for processing of negatives is shown for comparison. With premise integration, two separate two-element mappings are combined to yield one mapping in which the three problem terms are assigned to the three positions, top, middle, bottom. Both premises must be

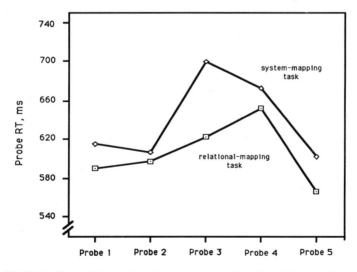

FIG. 3.11. Probe RTs as a function of probe position. From Maybery, Bain, & Halford (1986). Reproduced by permission of the American Psychological Association, Inc., copyright © (1986).

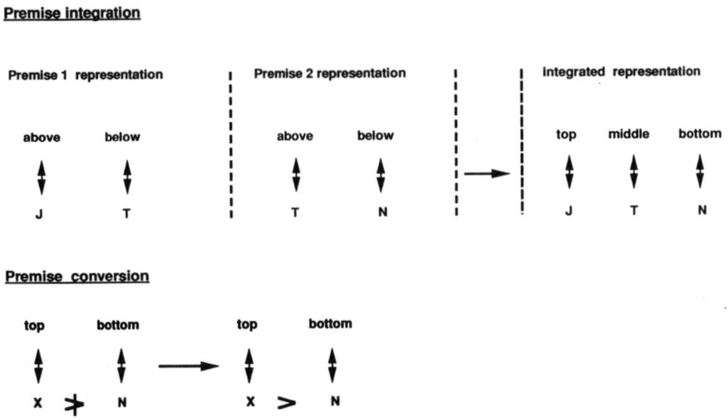

Premise integration

Premise 1 representation   Premise 2 representation   Integrated representation

above   below   above   below   top   middle   bottom

J   T   T   N   J   T   N

Premise conversion

top   bottom   top   bottom

X $\not>$ N   X $>$ N

FIG. 3.12. Structure-mapping representation of *N*-term series tasks.

integrated into a single mapping, and it is this that imposes the high processing load. Notice also that each integration produces a new ordered set, because the premise elements were not previously known to be in that order. If they were known to be in that order, the test for transitive inference is not valid. Insofar as an ordered set is a structure (by the definition in chapter 2), each transitive inference problem entails generating a new structure. Because of this the representation cannot be chunked into fewer dimensions. In converting a negation, a mapping with only two elements is converted to another mapping with two elements. In this case no more than one premise is ever considered in a single decision. This is why the processing load is less for converting a negation.

This study demonstrates that premise integration, a system mapping, imposes a higher processing load than conversion of a negation, a process that has been associated with a high processing load in previous theories, including that of Sternberg (1980a, 1980b). The load imposed by premise integration was first predicted by structure-mapping theory (Maybery et al., 1986). It has been confirmed using a rigorous methodology, and so the dimensionality metric associated with levels of structure mapping has received a degree of confirmation. The next study tested the prediction that young children's difficulty with transitive inference should be due to the load imposed by premise integration. This requires a capacity limitation study.

Capacity-Limitation Studies

The easy-to-hard paradigm of Hunt and Lansman (1982), discussed earlier, was used by Halford, Maybery, and Bain (1986) to test the hypothesis that children's transitive inferences are capacity limited. Three- to five-year-old children performed a three-term series (transitive inference) problem as the hard primary task. The easy primary task entailed verifying the truth of a single premise about the order of a pair of elements (two-term series task). The secondary task was to rehearse and recall a string of color names. As Fig. 3.13 shows, one of the concurrent tasks, the easy primary task, predicted performance on the hard primary task, with variance on the two tasks performed alone partialled out. This confirms that children's performance on the transitive inference task was capacity limited.

Loads and Multiple-System Mappings

The loads imposed by system and multiple-system mappings in the context of simple mathematical problems were tested using problems of the type shown below. The task is to find the missing operation(s), represented by the brackets:

$$(7 [\ ] 3)/4 = 1$$

$$(7 [\ ] 3) [\ ] 4 = 1$$

There is only one missing operation in the first problem, and it can easily be solved by multiplying both sides by 4, yielding $(7 [\ ] 3) = 4$, and then it is clear that the missing operation is subtraction. The second problem also has a unique solution, in that there is only one pair of operations that will fit. Taken one at a time, either operation would be as easy to find as in the first problem. The difficulty is that we must find both operations before we can be certain about either of them. That is, it is not possible to find the first operation, then turn our attention to the second. We must find the correct operations to fill both spaces in brackets before we can confirm either of them. Halford, Bain, and Maybery (1984a) found, using short-term memory recall as a secondary task, that the processing load is, in fact, higher for the problem where two operations must be found. This, then, is another example of a processing load imposed by structural complexity.

Notice that if the two-operation task were constructed in such a way that the operations could be found successively, dealing completely with one first then tackling the second, this increased processing load would not be expected. There would be an increase in solution time as compared with the single operation problem, but little or no increase in processing load.

This example further illustrates the point made earlier that the amount of information processed in parallel affects the processing load. In transitive inference, premise integration requires both premises to be processed jointly, in that neither can be fully interpreted without the other. This results in a high processing load, which has been confirmed by dual-task indicators. In this example, the second mathematics problem imposed a higher process-

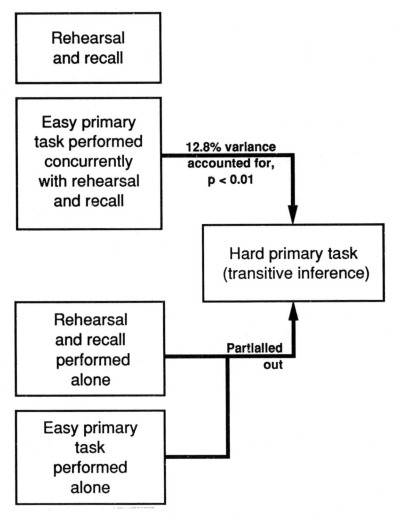

FIG. 3.13. Easy-to-hard paradigm applied to *N*-term series task.

ing load, because both operations had to be interpreted jointly. It was not possible to interpret either of them without the other. It would be possible to devise a serial hypothesis testing strategy, but it is implausible that participants test all hypotheses serially. It is far more likely that probable hypotheses are identified from a representation of the problem as a whole, then tested for confirmation. The identification of likely hypotheses entails processing both operations in parallel. Thus the amount of information that has to be processed in parallel affects processing load. This is captured by the dimensionality metric, but not by the embeddedness metric. With the latter, processing load depends on the number of subroutines successively executed. With the dimensionality metric, processing load depends on the number of dimensions, or independent units of information, that must be processed in parallel.

To summarize, the concept of resource entails the idea that performance is a function of the resources allocated (the performance-resource function, Fig. 3.1), that tasks vary in the demand they make on resources (the slopes of the performance-resource functions vary, Fig. 3.2), and that tasks that compete for a common, limited resource will show a tradeoff in performance (the performance-operating characteristic, Fig. 3.3). Secondary tasks can be used to assess resource demands of a primary task (Fig. 3.4). Interactions do not inevitably accompany competition for resources (Fig. 3.5), and interpretational difficulties with dual-task deficits can be alleviated using the easy-to-hard paradigm (Fig. 3.6). Demand for resource is not the only cause of task difficulty, and number of steps, knowledge required, availability of the correct hypothesis, and short-term memory storage load also affect solution times and errors. Consequently it is essential to know when task difficulty does reflect processing resources, and the easy-to-hard paradigm is useful for this purpose. The conceptual complexity metric based on the dimensionality of a concept, or the number of independent items of information required to represent it, is used to generate predictions concerning the information processing loads of transitive inference and certain algebraic tasks. These predictions are tested using secondary task indicators, with positive results. The concept of resources has been criticized because it includes no specification of mechanisms but, although a process theory is desirable, it complements rather than replaces a resource theory.

ALTERNATE CONCEPTS OF CAPACITY

We consider a number of concepts of capacity that have grown up outside the resource tradition. Short-term memory span has also been commonly associated with processing capacity but has not been defined in the manner of the resource concepts discussed above. We turn to it next.

Short-Term Memory Span

Short-term memory span, or related tasks such as backward-digit span, and the card-counting span task, have commonly been used as measures of processing capacity (Case, 1985; Chapman, 1987). I found this an attractive idea (Halford, 1982, chapter 10) until we performed a series of working-memory experiments, to be outlined later, that consistently failed to support it.

A number of influences were responsible for the notion that short-term memory span was equivalent to working memory. The influential memory model of Atkinson and Shiffrin (1968) has been widely interpreted as implying that short-term memory is the workspace of higher cognitive processes. Furthermore the tradition of using short-term memory span tests in intelligence test batteries has reinforced the supposition that there is a link between short-term memory and reasoning (Dempster, 1981; Humphreys, Lynch, Revelle, & Hall, 1983). However, there is evidence that short-term memory span possibly only reflects ability to maintain items in an acoustic buffer, and it may be more relevant to language processing than to concepts and reasoning per se.

Part of the evidence for this is that short-term memory span is sensitive to the word-length effect, that is, to the length of the items to be recalled. Baddeley, Thomson, and Buchanan (1975) found that span was less for long words than for short words. The effect was related to speed of articulation rather than to number of syllables, and span was equal to the number of words that could be rehearsed in approximately 2 seconds. Standing, Bond, Smith, and Isely (1980) found that rehearsal rate accounted for a high proportion of the variance in span, both across individuals and across materials. Case, Kurland, and Goldberg (1982) showed that it is possible to manipulate span by manipulating the rehearsal rate. Adults were tested on unfamiliar nonsense words, which they rehearsed at the same rate as 6-year-old children rehearsed familiar single-syllable words. Under these conditions adults' spans were reduced so they were the same as those of 6-year-olds.

It seems, therefore, that the size of short-term memory span largely reflects the efficiency of the articulatory loop, or phonological loop (Baddeley, 1990), which consists of a phonemic buffer in which information is maintained by rehearsal. The more efficient the rehearsal process, the more information that can be retained. This implies that short-term memory span tests measure the capacity of a system that is specialized for holding acoustically encoded information. It appears unlikely that it measures the capacity of the workspace that is involved in conceptualization and thinking.

This view is supported by Schweickert and Boruff (1986), who demonstrated that short-term memory span may be accounted for in terms of two parameters: decay rate and rehearsal rate. If items in the short-term memory buffer decay at a fixed rate, but are renewed by rehearsal, then the number of items that can be retained will be a function of rehearsal rate. Faster rehearsal will mean more items stored. Notice that this relationship is predicted to be a direct result of a simple decay model, and there is no implication of a trade-off between processing and storage, as in the model of Case (1985). Schweickert and Boruff (1986) suggested that this relationship might also apply to the central processor; that is, that the ability to process items will depend on the rate at which their activation decays and the rate at which they can be scanned. Given a fixed rate of decay, faster scanning will mean more items can be processed. According to this model, processing capacity will depend on scanning rate or processing rate. Schweickert and Boruff (1986) also offered the interesting speculation that the capacity of the central processor may be matched to the capacity of the short-term memory buffer. The reason would be that there is no utility in having more items in a buffer than the processor could use, and it would be most efficient to have a buffer large enough to supply all the information that the processor would require. This would explain two puzzling facts about memory span. On the one hand, it is known to be a good predictor of intellectual performance (Dempster, 1981; Humphreys et al., 1983), yet it does not appear to be the workspace of thinking. This paradox would be explained if short-term memory span and central processing occupy separate systems, but the capacities of those systems were matched.

Working Memory Studies

Even more cogent reasons for doubting that short-term memory is the workspace of thinking come from working-memory research. If short-term memory were the workspace of thinking, there should be a trade-off between reasoning and short-term recall, because the two tasks would be competing for the same short-term memory resource. This logic was used by Baddeley and Hitch (1974) to study the nature of working memory. They used a sentence verification task in which participants were shown a sentence such as "*A* precedes *B*," or "*A* is not preceded by *B*," followed by a display such as *AB*. Participants were required to press buttons indicating whether the sentence was true or false in relation to the display. (The correct response would be true in the two examples above.)

The participants were also required to hold a string of digits in short-term memory. If two digits were presented before the sentence verification task, and merely had to be recalled after it was completed, neither task interfered with the other. However if the digit preload was six items, or if participants were required to rehearse the digits while verifying the sentence (concurrent load condition), there was significant interference. Even then, however, participants still retained a sizeable number of items in short-term memory while performing the verification task.

Baddeley and Hitch (1974) interpreted these results as indicating that working memory is not a unitary system but has at least two components: a "central executive," which can be divided between processing and storage, and an "articulatory loop," which can hold phonemic information. It is only if the memory preload is large enough to overload the articulatory loop that the central executive would be devoted to storage, with consequent reduction of processing resources and impaired performance on cognitive tasks such as sentence verification. Baddeley, Grant, Wight, and Thomson (1975) and Baddeley and Lieberman (1980) added to this account by proposing that there is a further short-term memory system specialized for the processing of visuospatial information.

Klapp, Marshburn, and Lester (1983) have challenged the notion that short-term memory involves the working memory in which information is processed. The design of their Experiments 6 and 7 is summarized schematically in Fig. 3.14. They used a verification task, or a modified memory-scanning task, as their primary task. A memory preload, consisting of three, six, or nine letters, was presented prior to the verification task and had to be recalled after it. In the delay-before-task condition, there was a 5 s consolidation delay before the verification task. In the delay-after-task condition, this delay occurred after verification, to equalize the total retention interval. Interference between the verification and memory tasks occurred in the former, but not in the latter condition. Thus, if a few seconds elapsed between presentation of the memory preload and beginning of the sentence verification task, there was no interference. This result was not due to the preload not occupying short-term memory in the delay-before-task condition. In Experiment 8, Klapp et al. (1983) used the delay-before-task condition, but the primary task was retention and rehearsal of three digits, in place of the verification and scanning tasks used in Experiments 6 and 7. Interference did occur between the two memory tasks, indicating that the preload occupied the short-term memory system in the delay-before-task condition.

These results suggest that a memory preload does not interfere with cog-

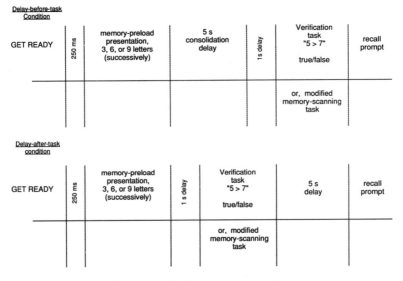

FIG. 3.14. Working-memory paradigm.

nitive processing if there is time to encode it before processing begins. When there was a 6.5-second gap between preload presentation and sentence verification, the preload could be encoded first and stored in some passive form while sentence verification was carried out, after which it would be retrieved and recalled. If, however, sentence verification began immediately on presentation of the memory preload, encoding of the preload would overlap with sentence verification, and interference would result. This interpretation is consistent with results obtained by Halford, Bain, and Maybery (1984b, Experiment 2). They used N-term series reasoning, which is more complex and presumably more demanding of resources than sentence verification. Their design is summarized in Fig. 3.15. Digits were presented continuously, at a rate of two per second beginning before the reasoning task was presented and continuing throughout it. A tone probe was used to tell participants which digits had to be encoded for subsequent recall. Participants were instructed to remember as many as possible of the six digits immediately preceding the tone. The probe could occur at any of the four positions shown in Fig. 3.15. If the tone occurred before the problem (Probe 1), digits could be encoded and stored before the problem began, as in the delay-before-task condition of Klapp et al. (1983). If the tone occurred during reasoning (Probe 2), participants would be obliged to encode the digits concurrently with the reasoning task. With Probe 3, encoding would begin immediately after response to the problem, and with Probe 4, 6–8 seconds after problem completion. Probe 4 is therefore the standard memory control condition. The timing of the recall prompt was adjusted so the total retention interval was constant.

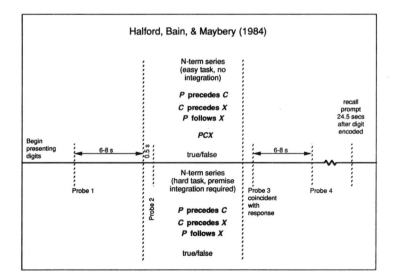

FIG. 3.15. Modified working-memory paradigm.

The N-term series problems occurred in a hard form, which required premise integration, or in an easy form, which did not. In the easy problems, each premise can be checked independently against the target (e.g., P precedes C can be checked against PC in the target, etc.). If all premises match the target, the correct answer is "true," "false" otherwise. In the easy task in Fig. 3.15, the answer is "false" because "P follows X" is not consistent with the target. In the hard task the first two premises must be integrated and checked to see if they are consistent with the third premise. In the example in Fig. 3.15, P precedes C must be integrated with C precedes X, and the resulting series PCX must be checked against the third premise, P follows X. It is inconsistent, so again the correct response would be "false."

Comparison of recall scores for Probe 1 and Probe 4 assesses displacement of information from STM due to N-term series reasoning. There was a small loss ($<$ 1 item), but it was no larger for the hard than for the easy reasoning task. The loss might have been due to lack of opportunity for rehearsal. If it had been due to processing load, if should have been greater with the hard primary task.

There was a greater reduction in recall if the memory items were encoded during reasoning (Probe 2), and this effect was greater for the hard reasoning task, indicating that it was due to the processing load imposed by the primary task. The implication is that reasoning interferes with encoding a memory load, but it is doubtful whether it interferes with mere retention of a short-term storage load.

The findings of Klapp et al. (1983) are consistent with the Halford et al. (1984b) study in showing that a process, encoding, interferes with reasoning more than storage of information does. Thus the trade-off is between one process and another, rather than between processing and storage.

This hypothesis is actually consistent with the findings of Baddeley and Hitch (1974). Recall that they found greater interference if the short-term memory load was actively rehearsed during sentence verification. Rehearsal, like encoding, is an active process. Thus Baddeley and Hitch's results also might reflect, at least in part, a trade-off between two active processes, rather than between processing and storage.

These results suggest that in studying working memory we are dealing with some kind of active process that has a large degree of independence from short-term memory storage processes. This suggestion is further reinforced by the finding of Brainerd and Kingma (1984), that transitive inference and premise retention are stochastically independent. This implies that there is only an indirect link between reasoning and storage, even when the information stored is relevant to the reasoning task.

All of this implies that the capacity of working memory cannot simply be identified with the capacity of any short-term storage system. The capacity of working memory reflects ability to encode, retrieve, transform, integrate, and otherwise manipulate information. However, this capacity for active processing of information seems at least partially independent of capacity to store information.

This is not to argue of course that storage is irrelevant to reasoning. Short-term memory stores must be used to retain results of earlier processing steps, ready for use in subsequent processing (Hitch, 1978), as we saw earlier. Furthermore, short-term memory probably also serves other functions, such as retention of a solution plan, placekeeping, pointers to relevant information, and so on. However the active processing that is responsible for the manipulative aspects of reasoning seems to be at least partially independent of short-term memory storage systems. Therefore it is not appropriate to identify short-term memory with the workspace of thinking or other higher cognitive processes. The next concept of processing capacity that I consider is related to short-term memory span but is more elaborate, and includes both short-term and working memory.

Total Processing Space

Case (1985) proposed that working memory has three components, total processing space, which is composed of operating space and short term storage space. Case argued that total processing space is constant from infancy to adulthood. However operating space, or the space required to carry out actual processing, is assumed to decrease with age due to increases in processing efficiency. It is assumed that there is a trade-off between processing and storage so that, as operating space decreases, more of the total processing space is left for storage. Case expressed this trade-off as:

Total Processing Space = Operating Space + Short Term Storage Space

The more processing efficiency increases, the less operating space is required for processing, so the more space that is left for storage functions. *Short-term storage* is defined as the proportion of the total processing space that is devoted to the maintenance and retrieval of recently activated schemes. Thus, short-term storage space is that component of capacity that is needed to maintain stored information. It increases with age, even though total processing space remains constant, because gains in processing efficiency reduce the operating space that must be devoted to processing.

This formulation is supported by a number of studies showing that processing speed predicts other aspects of performance. It is assumed that processing speed is a measure of efficiency so that faster processing implies more efficient processing, which should be accompanied by better performance. As we saw in an earlier section, short-term memory span is well predicted by rehearsal rate. Also, Case (1985) reported several more studies in which processing speed is linearly related to a number of cognitive tasks.

The linear correlation between processing speed and span, or between processing speed and other cognitive performance, is consistent with the hypothesis that capacity remains constant. Increases in performance with age can be attributed to increased processing efficiency, without postulating growth of capacity with age.

The strongest support for the processing–storage trade-off hypothesis comes from a set of four experiments by Case, Kurland, and Goldberg (1982). In Experiment 1, children aged 3–6 years were assessed for their word span, using a pool of seven words. Their rehearsal rate was assessed by measuring the time to articulate the words, from word presentation to onset of articulation. Both span and articulation rate increased with age and were significantly correlated ($r = .74$). This correlation remained significant when age was partialled out ($r = .35$). In the second experiment adults were tested for both span and articulation rate using nonsense words. Because the nonsense words were unfamiliar, they should be articulated more slowly. If span is dependent on rehearsal rate, rather than the reverse, or rather than both being dependent on some other factor, then experimental suppression of rehearsal rate should reduce span. The adults' rehearsal rate on the nonsense words was similar to that of the 6-year-olds on their familiar one-syllable words, and the adults' spans were also similar to the 6-year-olds. In fact, span was a linear function of rehearsal rate over both age and materials, a result that has been replicated in many contexts (see Baddeley, 1990, and Case, 1985, for reviews). This experiment establishes that the association between span and rehearsal rate is not merely a correlation, but span can be varied by manipulating rehearsal rate.

In their third experiment, Case, Kurland, and Goldberg (1982) used the card-counting span task, which requires children to count the number of dots on a card, then remember the count output. The number of cards for which they can do this constitutes the card-counting span. Counting rate was assessed, and card-counting span was found to be a function of counting rate. Again, a linear relationship was found between counting rate and span, and the correlation ($r = .69$) remained significant after age was partialled out ($r = .35$).

In their fourth experiment (Case et al., 1982), adults counted using nonsense numbers, which reduced their counting rate to that of 6-year-olds. Again, card-counting span was a linear function of counting rate, the adults' spans being reduced to that of 6-year-olds. Thus card-counting span, which depends more on processing than does memory span, was affected by manipulating processing rate.

Case's explanation for these data is that processing speed, as reflected in rehearsal, articulation, or counting rates, is a measure of processing efficiency. Processing efficiency increases with age, as evidenced by increased speed. As processing becomes more efficient, it requires less operating space, leaving more for storage. Case further postulated that total processing space remains constant over age. It follows that, when adults' processing efficiencies are reduced to those of 6-year-olds, their spans are correspondingly reduced, because both age groups have the same overall capacity.

The data of Case et al. (1982) are certainly consistent with this formulation, as are other findings of a linear association between processing speed and span. However the conclusion is not compelling. First, Case et al. (1982) scored span tasks without regard to order; that is, a response was scored correct if the items were recalled in any order, provided the last item was not recalled first. This means the associations between processing and span could be at least partly artifactual, because they might reflect guessing strategies. For example, children who were more numerate might count faster and be better able to guess the next item from those remaining. This seems particularly likely when it is remembered that they used pools of only 7 words in their memory span task, and 10 in their counting span task. Some participants had spans over 4, so guessing could account for a sizeable part of their responses.

Second, as Baddeley (1986) pointed out, and as we saw in the last section, it is possible to explain these results in terms of the articulatory loop, that is, by postulating that they are due to an auditory–articulatory storage system. The essence of the explanation would be that rehearsal of items refreshes their traces in an auditory store, which has a fixed decay rate. The faster items are rehearsed, the more traces can be refreshed before they decay. In card-counting span, faster counting would mean more count outputs would be rehearsed. If this is the explanation, it may mean that the association between rehearsal, or counting rate, and span has very little to do with capacity to reason or carry out other high-level cognitive tasks. It may reflect the operation of a relatively peripheral system that is rather specialized and concerned primarily with the storage of acoustic information, perhaps for language comprehension purposes.

The association between processing speed and span, impressive as it is, is not really direct evidence for the trade-off explanation for span. What is needed is a study in which retention of information is shown to be reduced by a processing load, along the lines of the working-memory studies discussed in the last section. According to Case's theory, the extent of the reduction should be greater if (a) the load is increased, with other factors held constant, and (b) if younger participants are used. The latter prediction follows because young participants are postulated to have lower processing efficiencies, which should cause them to use more operating space, leaving less short-term storage space.

Data concerning the first prediction are already available. Recall that working memory studies showed little tendency for cognitive processing to displace information from short-term memory. Furthermore, Halford et al.

(1984b, Experiment 1) varied the difficulty of an N-term series task in a way that has been shown (Maybery et al., 1986) to manipulate processing load. They found no significant reduction in recall of a short-term memory preload, irrespective of whether it was below, at, or above span. Even the fairly demanding task of solving N-term series problems did not displace information from short-term memory. Thus the first of the predictions that follow from the trade-off hypothesis does not appear to be confirmed.

Further negative evidence comes from an unpublished study by Halford and Maybery. In Experiment 1, 8- to 10-year-olds were presented with six words to remember, then asked to perform a processing task, then asked to recall the order of the words. The processing load was at one of two levels. At the easy level, it consisted of simply reading four pairs of numbers. At the difficult level, they were asked to subtract one number from another. The durations of the tasks were approximately equal. If short-term memory is the workspace of cognition, then the processing task should displace items from short-term memory. Furthermore the displacement should be greater for a high-load task such as subtraction, than for a low-load task such as reading digits. This effect did occur but was very small in magnitude. Most reductions in recall were shown to be due to interruption of rehearsal and to proactive interference. A replication of this experiment was performed using recall of digit strings as the preload, and N-term series with premise integration (high load) or without integration (low-load) as the primary task. Previous studies (Maybery et al., 1986; Halford et al., 1986) provide a manipulation check, showing that premise integration effectively manipulates processing load. However the higher load condition did not affect preload recall. The fact that processing load has little or no effect on retention of information in short-term memory confirms the working-memory studies discussed earlier, and casts doubt on the trade-off between operating space and short-term storage space.

In their second experiment, Halford & Maybery converted the card-counting span task, discussed earlier, to a dual-task paradigm. Children aged 5, 8, or 12 years were given a digit preload to remember, then counted dots on from one to four cards, then recalled the digit preload. If counting and preload retention share a common processing space, then card counting should displace the digit preload. Furthermore, if processing efficiency is less for younger children, they should use more operating space, and according to Case's (1985) formula (Total Processing Space = Operating Space + Short-Term Storage Space), they should show a greater loss. No evidence was found for an age effect on loss of the short-term memory preload as a function of card counting. These results call into question an account of cognitive development based on a single capacity that can be allocated to processing or maintenance of information in storage. This result was replicated in a further experiment using the same basic design but different tasks.

This line of experimentation was originally designed to elaborate my own theory, which linked processing capacity to short-term memory capacity, but our working-memory experiments showed this view to be untenable. It was then realized that Case's hypothesis that there is a simple trade-off between short-term storage space and processing space is also untenable, as the evidence outlined earlier shows.

The lack of interference between cognitive processing and storage of information in short-term memory led Baddeley and Hitch (1974) to propose that there are at least two systems, including a central executive and an articulatory loop. These authors did propose that the central executive could be flexibly allocated to processing or storage, but this was challenged by later studies (Halford et al., 1984b; Klapp et al., 1983). Even if true however, it does not imply that all of short-term memory capacity can be allocated to processing. Working-memory research has shown that at least some short-term memory processes are independent of processing space. Thus, a unitary model that postulates that there is one system that serves the functions of short-term memory storage and a workspace for cognitive processing does not appear to be tenable. The theory propounded by Case et al. (1982) and Case (1985) is explicitly a unitary process theory: "Operating space and short term storage space do not imply two different capacities . . . they imply one capacity that can be flexibly allocated to either of two functions" (Case, 1985, p. 290). Therefore Case's trade-off hypothesis requires modification to take into account evidence that more than one process is involved in short-term and working memory. Until this is done, one of Case's main tenets, that total capacity remains constant over age, is therefore subject to some doubt, as we later see.

On the other hand, the proposal that is probably the most important feature of Case's formulation, that processing efficiency is one of the main factors that increases with age, is probably sound. What is in doubt is the mechanism by which this occurs, and it cannot be simply attributed to a trade-off between short-term storage and processing. A more complex architecture is involved. Also, the identification of efficiency with speed, although it captures part of the truth, is probably not the whole story. I will suggest later that recoding of representations plays a major role in efficiency.

In order to study the capacity of working memory, we need to find a system that is more actively involved in cognitive processing than the short-term memory system. One possible candidate is primary memory, which we discuss next.

Primary Memory

William James (1890) said primary memory contains information that is still present in consciousness, but secondary memory is information of which we are not currently thinking. These definitions appear to be based on a distinction between active and passive memory: Primary memory is active, whereas secondary memory is passive. Short-term memory differs from primary memory in that it does not consist solely of information that is in an active state, because it also contains some information that is held in a rather passive form, as the research reviewed in the previous section showed. What is usually called short-term memory, therefore, would seem to overlap with both primary and secondary memory, because it contains some information that is in an active state and some that is in a passive state. Secondary memory holds information for periods varying from a few seconds to a lifetime, but its distinguishing feature is that the information is held in a passive state, in the sense that it is not being processed. Information in primary memory on the other hand is being processed in some way.

A way of operationalizing the distinction between primary and secondary memory was developed by Wickens, Moody, and Dow (1981) and Wickens, Moody, and Vidulich (1985). This was done using a rather complex paradigm based on a combination of Sternberg memory scanning, the Brown-Peterson paradigm, and the Wickens release from proactive interference procedure. The basic paradigm used by Wickens et al. (1981, 1985) is summarized in Fig. 3.16. The basic procedure is based on the memory-scanning paradigm. A memory set is presented followed by a probe, participants having to indicate whether the probe was in the memory set. For example, the memory set might consist of four words, and the probe would consist of a single word. Participants would have to say whether the probe word was in the memory set or not.

In the primary memory condition there is no intervening activity, so it is

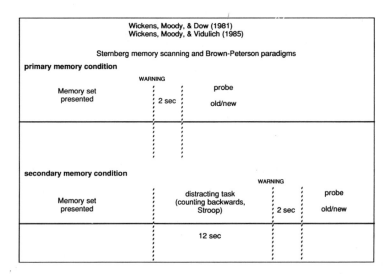

FIG. 3.16. Primary-memory paradigm.

expected that the memory set will remain active in primary memory. In the secondary memory condition, the procedure is the same except that a distracting task intervenes between memory-set presentation and probe. This activity should displace the memory-set items from primary into secondary memory.

The primary–secondary manipulation produced three effects: (a) The intercept of the memory-scanning function was approximately 100 ms greater in the secondary memory condition, presumably reflecting time to retrieve information from secondary memory; (b) negative probes produced longer RTs than positive probes for secondary memory; and (c) proactive interference was observed in secondary but not in primary memory.

Proactive interference was assessed by using three successive trials in the same semantic category, followed by a shift to a new category. The difference in RT between the first and third trial in a category is a measure of proactive interference.

Wickens et al. (1981, 1985) used this paradigm with sets of one, two, or four words. The effect of the primary–secondary manipulation is to force participants to retrieve the memory-set items in the secondary memory condition. In the primary memory condition, the memory set would remain active, and could be compared directly with the probe. The finding that the intercept of the memory-scanning function was approximately 100 ms greater in the secondary memory condition is consistent with time being spent retrieving information from secondary memory. Wickens et al. (1981) argued that proactive interference is a retrieval phenomenon, so it will not occur in the primary memory condition because retrieval is unnecessary.

For our present purposes the importance of the experiments by Wickens et al. is that they show how information that is being actively processed can be distinguished operationally from information that is in store but is not being processed. This opens the way for studies of processing capacity, as distinct from memory-storage capacity. To capitalize on the method of Wickens et al. (1981) it is not necessary to assume that active and passive information are held in different locations. As Halford, Maybery, and Bain (1988) noted, the active–passive distinction is quite compatible with parallel distributed storage models that contain only one store. There are a number of possibilities here. One is that what Wickens et al. called primary memory simply corresponds to the information that is currently active. That is, it corresponds to the current activation pattern on the neural units. Secondary memory, on the other hand, would correspond to information stored in the connections between units, but not currently active (recall the description of representation and storage in chapter 2).

Another possibility was outlined by Schneider and Detweiler (1987). This is, in PDP architecture, the connection weights between units may change at different rates. For short-term storage, weights change rapidly so information is quickly acquired but also quickly forgotten. For long-term storage, weights change slowly, so information is acquired and forgotten less rapidly. This suggestion seems capable of accounting for at least the majority of Wickens et al.'s findings. Slower weights would produce longer retrieval times, thereby accounting for Wickens et al.'s first finding. It accounts for less proactive interference in primary memory because fast weights, associated with short-term storage, are not susceptible to proactive interference, whereas slow weights are. The reason is that fast weights obliterate earlier traces rapidly, so they create less interference (recalling that successive acquisitions are superimposed on the same set of connections, see chapter 2). This accounts for Wickens et al.'s third finding. On the other hand there is more retroactive interference with fast weights, because new traces are established more quickly and interfere with older traces. This prediction does not appear to have been tested. The second finding, longer RTs for negative probes in secondary memory, may reflect longer retrieval times with slow weights, the effect being greater with negative probes because they are poorer retrieval cues, so the retrieval process requires more cycles.

The two-store model is challenged by some findings by Brannelly, Tehan, and Humphreys (1989). A second probe was presented for the same memory set after participants had responded to the first probe. According to Wickens et al.'s two-store model, information should be in active memory after the first probe, therefore the effects normally associated with secondary memory should not occur with the second probe. However, both the first and third of Wickens et al.'s findings were observed on the second probe. Yet, these findings are quite compatible with the fast and slow weights explanation, because the weights would be the same for both probes. Therefore the study by Brannelly et al. supports Schneider and Detweiler's (1987) suggestion. The important point for our purposes is still that active and passive memory can be distinguished, and the adoption of Wickens et al.'s technique does not entail committment to the two-store model. It is equally compatible with the (rather more sophisticated) fast and slow weights model.

Halford, Maybery, and Bain (1988) attempted to assess the capacity of primary memory by varying the set size and testing for proactive interference. The idea is that if the memory set size exceeds capacity to actively process information, some items will cease to be active. This will result in proactive interference when they are retrieved. With adults, Halford et al. found proactive interference with set sizes of six and greater, but not with set size four, consistent with Wickens et al. (1981, 1985). With 8- to 9-year-olds, proactive interference was found with set-size four, but not with set-size two. These results suggest the capacity of primary memory is between four and five items for adults, and between two and three items for 8- to 9-year-olds. This implies that active memory capacity increases with age. These findings will be added to others in the literature later in this chapter, when we consider the capacity of active memory further. First there is another concept of processing capacity to be examined.

Central Processing Space. Pascual-Leone (1970) defined a construct called central computing space or "M-space," which is postulated to be equivalent to the number of operational schemes that can be activated simultaneously. A large number of M-space tasks have been devised. One is the compound stimulus visual information task, in which children are trained to perform a response to each component of a multidimensional stimulus. For example, raise hand to a square, clap hands to red, and so on. When the multidimensional stimulus is presented, response is required to all attributes, so the child should raise hands, then clap hands, and so on, for the other attributes of the stimulus. The number of operational schemes that were activated simultaneously was estimated from the number of responses performed. Other tests included the digit placement test, the Cucui test, and the counting span test (Case, Kurland, & Daneman, 1979).

All these tasks require both processing and storage. For example, the counting span test requires counting (processing) and storage of the count outputs. In this sense they are measures of working memory as distinct from simple short-term memory, where items are recalled as presented. Case (1978) distinguished short-term memory from working memory on the basis that the latter requires transformation of the stimulus.

M-space tasks have been used successfully to predict performance on a variety of cognitive tasks (Bell & Kee, 1984; Gomez-Toussaint, 1976; Romberg & Collis, 1980). The methodology depends on first estimating the processing demands of the cognitive task by analyzing the number of operational schemes that must be activated simultaneously to perform it. The M-space task is then used to assess the number of schemes that participants of a given age can activate. The M-space measures are then used to predict performance on the cognitive task.

The correlation between the M-space measures and the cognitive performances it has been used to predict are usually in the range $r = .4 - .6$. This does yield a worthwhile prediction, but there is really no way of establishing that the correlation reflects information processing capacity. Most cognitive tasks correlate to about .4 or higher, so the correlations obtained between M-space and other cognitive tasks are not outside the range that might be obtained simply by using one task to predict another.

It is interesting to compare the M-space methodology with the easy-to-hard paradigm. The logic of the two paradigms is shown in Fig. 3.17. Figure 3.17A shows the easy-to-hard paradigm, in path-analysis notation. There are five tasks; the easy primary task performed alone (easya) and jointly (easyj), the hard primary task, the secondary task performed alone (secondarya) and jointly (secondaryj). There are three theoretical constructs: structural efficiency

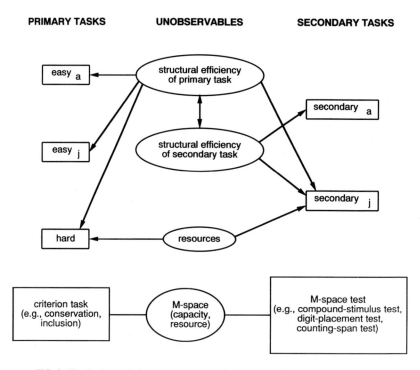

FIG. 3.17.   Path-analysis representation of easy-to-hard paradigm and M-space paradigm.

of the primary task, structural efficiency of the secondary task, and processing resources. As the path analysis diagram (adapted from Hunt & Lansman, 1982) shows, processing resources can be measured independently of the other constructs. The M-space task is shown in path-analysis notation in Fig. 3.17B, so as to compare it directly with the easy-to-hard paradigm. It can be seen that only one construct, which is notionally a type of processing resource, can be assessed. This construct cannot however be distinguished from any other factor that might influence performance. Consequently, M-space predictions might reflect features of tasks that are not related to capacity, such as strategies and coding processes.

By contrast, the easy-to-hard paradigm can distinguish resources from other factors. Therefore the easy-to-hard paradigm could be used as a converging operation to check whether M-space predictions do reflect capacity. Alternatively, correlations between the criterion task and other cognitive tasks could be partialled out. If the M-space tasks are consistently found to make predictions over and above those that can be made using another cognitive task as predictor, then there is some possibility that they reflect capacity. If, however, M-space tasks are found to account for no variance that cannot be accounted for using any of a variety of other cognitive tasks as predictors, then the claim that they measure processing capacity is doubtful. This check on the validity of M-space measures should be carried out.

Processing Speed

There is evidence from a number of different contexts that processing speed increases with age, and some theorists have attributed this change to increased processing resources, in accordance with the performance-resource function (Fig. 3.1). We saw earlier that the development of span can be largely attributed to increases in rehearsal rate (Case, 1985; Case et al., 1982). Elsewhere (Halford, 1982), I reviewed the literature on simple and choice reaction time, memory scanning, visual scanning, and letter comparison (in the Posner letter-match task) and concluded that there were age differences in speeds of all tasks. In an earlier review (Wickens, 1974), it was concluded that age differences in reaction time reflected central processing differences, a conclusion that seems to be reinforced by Kail (1986, 1990). Further evidence has accumulated that there is a general increase in processing speed with age and that processing resources might be implicated. Some of this evidence is summarized in Vernon (1987). The most relevant aspects will be considered here.

Inspection Time. The view that processing speed is related to processing resources is supported by the finding that inspection time is associated with both age and intelligence (Nettelbeck, 1987). The inspection time test normally entails presenting two vertical lines that are the same or that differ by a small amount. Participants are required to indicate whether they are the same or different. The display is presented briefly and is followed by a mask, which prevents further processing. The interval between presentation of the display and the mask, known as stimulus onset asynchrony, is gradually reduced to find the minimum interval at which near-perfect discrimination can just be achieved. This is a participant's inspection time. The measure is normally thought to be relatively free of higher cognitive processes, or response output processes, and to reflect a basic mental efficiency parameter. Therefore, the fact that it correlates with intelligence and cognitive development indicates that there is a basic processing speed factor that has an important role in intellectual functioning.

Global Processing Speed. Kail (1986) examined speed of processing as a function of age in two tasks, mental rotation and retrieval of names from memory. Kail reasoned that these tasks entail different mental processes and, therefore, if their development was a matter of domain-specific acquisition, they should have different growth functions. Furthermore, because domain-specific acquisitions are really learning functions, they would be hyperbolic, because this is the type of function most typical of learning. However, if development of processing speed was due to a central capacity, the growth function for both tasks should be the same and should be exponential. The functions that best fitted both data sets were the same and were exponential, in accordance with the central capacity hypothesis. These results were replicated and extended to visual search and mental addition, which again showed the same growth pattern (Kail, 1988).

A number of researchers have argued that if faster processing with age reflects a global change, the correlation between children's latencies and those of young adults should be constant at all ages and for all materials, and should be equal to one. This prediction, which is all the more interesting for being counter intuitive, has been confirmed in several studies, using tasks such as simple- and choice-reaction time, letter matching, matching of pictures and abstract patterns, and mental addition. Despite the widely varying mental processes used, impressive evidence has been obtained for a global processing speed factor that changes over age (Hale, 1990; Kail, 1986, 1988, 1991). Doubts were raised by Stigler, Nusbaum, and Chalip (1988) who demonstrated by simulation that the data obtained by Kail (1986) were consistent with a skill transfer model, which did not assume that capacity increased with age. However, Kail (1988) replied that transfer functions are consistently found to be domain specific, and therefore it is unlikely that global changes in processing speed across so many functions could reflect learning and transfer.

The most appropriate conclusion seems to be that there is a global processing speed factor that changes with age. Given the relationship between processing speed and intelligence, it seems quite plausible that global processing speed reflects resources available for intellectual tasks. It would therefore be very interesting to discover the mechanism responsible for this association.

A suggestion made by Schweickert and Boruff (1986), mentioned earlier, was that the central process might work in an analogous fashion to the articulatory loop. That is, information is maintained by some kind of cogitive rehearsal and is subject to decay. The amount of information that is effectively represented would depend on scanning rate, which would be a function of processing speed.

PDP models of information storage provide an alternative explanation that inverts the relationship between capacity and speed suggested by Schweickert and Boruff; that is, it suggests that the capacity of the representations might influence processing speed. The reason is that, in PDP models, as more stimuli are represented by a given set of units, the stimuli become less discriminable, and less discriminable representations require longer decision times. However, discriminability increases as the number of units increases. That is, more stimuli can be represented with clarity maintained if the number of units is increased. These relationships imply that there is a capacity limit to such representations, because if the number of stimuli represented on a given number of units is increased, eventually a point must be reached where the stimuli cannot be discriminated better than chance. Furthermore, the size of this capacity will be a function of the number of units that are available to represent the stimuli.

A similar set of relationships is found in distributed memory models (J. A. Anderson, 1973; Murdock, 1982, 1983; Pike, Dalgleish, & Wright, 1977). These models are reviewed by McNicol and Stewart (1980) and were designed to account for certain recognition and recall phenomena. One particular concern has been to account for the memory-scanning function (Sternberg, 1975), that is, the linear increase in response to a probe as a function of the number of items in the memory set. In these models each item is stored in memory as a set of features that are represented by neural units, so the representation is distributed over numerous units. The features for all items in a set are stored in a common memory location, so the representation is also parallel. The representation of a set of items is expressed mathematically as a vector, the elements of which represent the features. Recognition of a probe item (e.g., in the Sternberg scanning task) is accomplished by encoding the probe item also as a set of features, expressed in another vector, and correlating it with the storage vector.

It is characteristic of these models also that the discriminability of the items decreases as the number of items represented by a given set of units increases. The reason is that, as with the PDP models of McClelland and Rummelhart, the representation is both redundant and noisy, but this is consistent with what is known of neural functioning. The discriminability of the items can be expressed by the signal-to-noise ratio in signal detection theory. Anderson (1973) showed that, for his model, the signal-to-noise ratio $= N/K$, where N is the number of elements or units in a vector representing a set of items, and K is the number of items.

It has also been shown that recognition latency will increase as the signal-to-noise ratio decreases, if error rate is held constant. That is, the signal-to-noise ratio affects the speed–accuracy trade-off, so that lower signal-to-noise ratios are associated with longer latencies, higher errors, or both. Derivations of this kind have been shown to provide good predictions of the Sternberg memory-scanning function (McNicol & Stewart, 1980; Pike et al., 1977).

Extrapolating from this set of arguments leads to the prediction that processing rate will be faster for representations with larger capacity. For a given number of items, the larger the number of units available to represent them, the more discriminable they will be; that is, if we hold number of items k constant, the signal-to-noise ratio should increase as we increase N, the number of units representing the items. Because processing time is inversely related to the signal-to-noise ratio, processing time will decrease as the number of units in the representation increases. In this way we can predict that participants with larger capacities, in the sense of more units for representing information, will have shorter processing times. This explanation, like that of Schweickert and Boruff (1986), considered earlier, is speculative to some extent. Clearly there is an intriguing challenge for future research to discover the reason why there is a global increase in processing speed.

Number of Chunks

In a now-classic paper, Miller (1956) proposed that humans are limited to processing seven independent items of information (plus or minus two). The primary evidence came from the coincidence between digit span, which is about seven items for adults, and the span of absolute judgments, the number of separate values that can be judged without a reference scale, which is also about seven. Subsequent research showing that short-term memory depends on word length (reviewed earlier), and findings that the span of absolute judgments is also influenced by a number of variables that Miller did not take into account (Garner, 1962), meant that Miller's "magical number seven" could no longer be taken seriously.

However, Miller also noticed that short-term memory span appeared to be independent of amount of information. That is, span for digits is about the same as for letters, which is about the same as for words, even though words have much higher information value than letters, which have higher information value than digits (in the technical sense defined by information theory, Attneave, 1959). The interesting observation here is that we seem limited to processing a small number of items, irrespective of how much information they contain. This led Miller to propose the concept of a "chunk," an independent item of information of varying size (arbitrary size). The concept of chunk has not only survived but has been of great importance in cognitive psychology.

Subsequent research has tended to reduce the estimate of the number of chunks that can be processed in parallel. Broadbent (1975) analyzed the way items were grouped in recall, and found that the largest groups tended to be of three items. He argued that the findings addressed by Miller could be explained by postulating two systems, the first of which feeds information to the second, and both having a capacity of three items. The typical span of short-term serial recall could then be explained by assuming that items are divided between these systems, so the total number that could be recalled would be about six.

There is other evidence indicating that these suggestions might be at least approximately correct. Fisher (1984) examined the visual-search task and found evidence that the number of alphanumeric characters that could be processed in parallel had a mean of four for adult participants, with a range of three to five. With various spatial arrangement factors carefully controlled, Fisher found that it took the same time to process eight characters in a single frame as to process two successive frames of four characters. There were a number of converging lines of evidence indicating that up to four items of information could be processed in parallel.

Recall that Halford et al. (1988) found that the capacity of primary, or active memory, was also four or five items in adults, and two or three items in 8- to 9-year-old children. This experiment uses a methodology that is quite independent of that used by either Broadbent or Fisher, but it reaches essentially the same conclusion. We have then several very different methodologies all converging on the finding that adults can process about four items, or chunks, of information in parallel.

In a review of working-memory architecture, Schneider and Detweiler (1987) proposed several regions corresponding to functions such as visual, auditory, speech, lexical, motor processes, and so on. They also suggested that each region has a number of levels, and that there are a number of modules in each level. Given that the amount of information that can be stored in a module is very large, this means that the capacity of working memory is also very large, and far exceeds the "magical number seven" suggested by Miller (1956). Their review also led them to conclude, however, that there are general purpose structures that could process about four modules of information in parallel, consistent with the evidence outlined above.

To summarize, there are several lines of research indicating that adults process about four independent items or chunks of information in parallel. It turns out that the concept of a chunk can be linked to a dimension, which was used to quantify conceptual complexity earlier and also to a vector of activation values in a PDP system.

Chunks, Dimensions, and Vectors

There are several ways in which chunks may be compared with attributes on dimensions. A chunk is a unit of information that has a certain coherence, in the sense that its components are to a large extent indivisible. The chunk CAT cannot be decomposed into its components "C," A, "T" and remain the same chunk. Remove one of the letters from CAT and it is no longer the same chunk. Attributes on a dimension are units of information that share this same property of coherence. The attribute "red" on the color dimension is a unit of information in the sense that it cannot be decomposed and remain the same unit. Both chunks and attributes on dimensions may have fuzzy boundaries, but in both cases there are limits to the number of features that can be changed without the unit losing its identity.

Each chunk has a unique content; if a chunk has the content CAT, it cannot have an alternative content such as DOG. We can think of chunks as like slots, each of which can be filled in one and only one way, at any one time. Attributes within one dimension are similar in that they are in complementary distribution; if the color dimension has the value "red," then it cannot have another value such as "green."

The content of one chunk is independent of the content of other chunks; if the first chunk has the content CAT, the second chunk can have other values that are logically independent of the content of the first chunk. Similarly, the attributes of different dimensions are independent. If the color dimension has the value "red," the shape dimension can have values such as "square," "round," and so on, in a way that is logically independent of the values of the color dimensions.

Chunks are of arbitrary size, and their status does not depend on their information value. For example words have a much higher information content than letters, which have a higher information content than digits. This is true both intuitively and in terms of the information theory definition of information (information value, $H = \log_2 N$, where N is the number of equally likely alternatives, Attneave, 1959). Yet a word, a letter or a digit constitute one chunk. The information value of an attribute on a dimension would depend on the number of alternative values, but there are many situations where this does not appear to affect its status as a psychological unit of information. It affects absolute judgments (Garner, 1962) but it does not affect concept attainment tasks, which depend on the number of dimensions rather than the number of values on each dimension (Haygood & Bourne, 1965).

There are therefore a number of parallels between chunks and dimensions. Both are independent, coherent units of information of arbitrary size. The comparison serves to draw our attention to a paradox in the nature of chunks. Because chunks may be of arbitrary size (alphanumeric characters, words, sentences), there is no severe restriction on the amount of information that they may contain. We can increase the total amount of information processed by increasing the amount of information that is packed into each chunk (Simon, 1974). Yet, although there is little or no restriction on the total amount of information, there is a severe restriction on the number of units or chunks. The restriction is therefore in the number of separate units, rather than in the actual amount of information processed. It seems then that there is limited independence in the system, so that no matter how much information we process, it can only be divided into a small number of independent units.

Dimensions resemble chunks in that they are independent, because an attribute on any one dimension is independent of attributes on other dimensions as we have seen. A value on a dimension, like a chunk, is an independent item of information of arbitrary size. If the limiting factor is the number of independent units, it should apply to both chunks and dimensions. If we hypothesize that the limitation in the number of dimensions is like the limitation in the number of chunks, we can extrapolate from research on chunks to provide an estimate of the number of dimensions that can be processed in parallel. The best estimate of the number of independent dimensions that can be processed in parallel would be four, the integer central tendency of the empirical estimates in the last section.

An empirical prediction that follows from the hypothesis that adults process only four dimensions in parallel is that the most complex interaction that we should be able to interpret with clarity and precision is three way, that is, three independent variables and one dependent variable (Halford et al., in press). The three independent variables and the dependent variable each constitute one dimension. A three-way interaction consists of a set of mappings of the form $A, B, C \rightarrow N$ and is a four-dimensional structure (equivalent to one quaternary relation). Interpretation is equivalent to a mapping from one repesentation, such as a figure, to a mental model of the process that the interaction represents, so interpretation of a four-dimensional structure is likely to mean mapping four dimensions in parallel. Interpretation of interactions is the appropriate test because it is difficult to process the dimensions serially, because the interpretation of one dimension affects interpretation of others.

This prediction was tested by Halford et. al. (in press) who surveyed research workers in Psychology, Education, and Agriculture who were experienced in interpreting statistical interactions such as those that arise from analysis of variance. Respondents were asked what the most complex interaction they could interpret with clarity and precision was, assuming it was presented in a clear figure, and ignoring scale and nonlinearity problems. The modal response was three-way, which was also the central tendency of the responses, which ranged from two- to four-way.

These self-report data were checked in a structure-mapping experiment. Participants were shown an interaction represented as a bar graph with alphabetic labels. The bars were movable so participants could rearrange the figure as they thought appropriate. They were also given a verbal description of an isomorphic interaction, but with word labels that bore no semantic relation to the alphabetic labels on the figure. Their task was to find the correct mapping between the two forms of the interaction, that is, assign words to alphabetic labels. They were asked not to test hypotheses serially but to try to process the problem as a whole. This was monitored by recording the arrangements they made. They were also not permitted to make notes of their hypotheses, although the problem data remained in view, so it did not impose a burden on short-term memory. Success was high on three-way interactions, but extremely poor on four-way. The two studies suggest that the maximum number of dimensions that adults process in parallel is approximately four.

Our next problem is to consider why such an apparently paradoxical limitation should exist. An answer is suggested by the nature of the representations in PDP models. These consist of a pattern of activation over a large number of units, normally expressed in theories as a vector. Each vector can represent an arbitrarily large amount of information, but because the units are richly interconnected, there is a sense in which the vector represents one item. This suggests that a vector is somewhat like a chunk, in that both comprise independent items of information of arbitrary size. The limitation in the number of chunks implies a restriction on the number of independent vectors that can be represented concurrently. Halford et al. (in press) proposed that the reason for this is that there is a restriction on the number of vectors that can enter into a tensor product representation. Recall from chapter 2 that a concept of dimensionality N corresponds to a tensor product of rank $N+1$; that is, there is one vector for each dimension, plus one for the predicate (Fig. 2.8). Halford et al. (in press) proposed that as the dimensionality increases, the computational cost increases logarithmically, and it is this factor that limits the dimensionality of concepts that can be represented. This would be a "soft" limit, because exceeding the limit would not lead to catastrophic breakdown but to reduced clarity of representations with consequent increased solution times and tendency to errors.

It appears, therefore, that adults are probably limited to processing about four chunks or dimensions in parallel, because if information is represented according to a PDP architecture, to process more than four dimensions in parallel would entail a tensor product of Rank 5. This is likely to impose an excessive computational demand. The next question concerns the number of dimensions that children can process, which leads to a reformulation of the question of whether processing capacity changes with age.

Number of Dimensions Processed in Parallel by Children

A series of studies conducted by Halford (1978) and Halford and Wilson (1980) have a direct bearing on the question of the number of dimensions that children can process in parallel. The experiments were specifically designed to assess children's ability to recognize correspondences between structures of varying dimensionalities, as a function of age. In all of the experiments the level of structure mapping was manipulated while holding other aspects of the task constant. Extensive pretraining was employed to ensure that children fully understood task demands and had appropriate strategies. Tests were performed to ensure that this requirement was met.

The tasks that were used entailed first learning a structure and then mapping the prelearned structure into a new task. The new task had the same underlying structure as the one that had been learned but was based on different materials. Therefore the children had to perform a structure mapping to relate the prelearned structure to the new task. Children were taught a structure by being trained to perform a series of movements around a square array as shown in Fig. 3.18. Movement in space, of their own bodies or of toys, is a highly familiar activity to young children. The task was performed by placing a toy car at one of the locations p, q, r, s on the array. Geometric figures represented "secret signs" saying which movement should be performed with the car. The four possible movements were: stay at the same place (S), go one step clockwise (C), one step diagonally (D), or one step anticlockwise (A). The child's task was to move the car to the location indicated by the figure-sign; for example, if the car was at q, and a star (say) was presented representing D, the diagonal movement, the car should be moved to s (see table in Fig. 3.18). Children were trained by trial and error with feedback and explanation until they knew the meaning of a set of geometric figures, then a new problem was created by randomly allocating a new set of figures to the movements. Children proceeded through a series of learning-set tasks in this way until they had learned the structure.

They were then tested for ability to map this structure into another one. This was done by presenting an unknown structure that was isomorphic to the system they had learned. The unknown structure was based on a set of colored houses, and a new set of geometric figures was used to define movements from one color to another (instead of from one place to another). An example of such an unknown structure is shown in the table in Fig. 3.18. Children would be taught that (for instance) triangle meant to go from red to green, green to blue, blue to yellow, and yellow to red. The reader can obtain a "feel" for the task by trying to arrange the four colors around the array in Fig. 3.18 in such a way that they will be consistent with the table in Fig. 3.18. Of the 24 possible arrangements, 8 are consistent mappings of colors into locations; that is, the operators on the colors correspond consistently to spatial movements. The child had to arrange the houses around the array so as to make the unknown structure isomorphic to the previously learned structure. An appropriate mapping of one structure into the other is shown in Fig. 3.18.

The type of mapping required in the task can be manipulated by selecting the movements that are used. If we use only Movements S, C, and A, then it is possible to select a location for any color by considering only a single relation. For example, if we find that triangle means to go from red to green, then all we have to do is place green on the next corner clockwise or anticlockwise around the square. Continuing this strategy will result in a satisfactory mapping between the structures. This is a relational mapping.

If, however, we use Movements S, C, D then a relational mapping will not be adequate, because diagonal movements must be distinguished from clockwise and anticlockwise movements, and this can only be done by examining two relations. Suppose for example that red is at p, and triangle means to go from red to green. It is possible that green should be placed at q, or diagonally opposite at r: there is no way of deciding between these alterna-

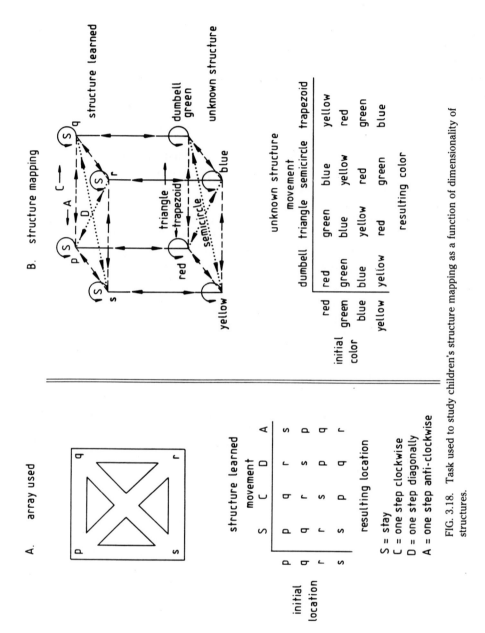

FIG. 3.18. Task used to study children's structure mapping as a function of dimensionality of structures.

tives on this information alone. If however we find that triangle means to go from red to green and from green to blue, then triangle must represent the nondiagonal movement, and green must go at q, with blue at r. This is a system mapping because it is based on two binary relations. As a further example, semicircle means to go from red to blue and from blue to red, so red and blue must be placed diagonally opposite each other. Again, this is a system mapping.

Children aged 4 to 6 years were given learning set training on this task at relational-mapping and system-mapping levels (Halford & Wilson, 1980). The criterion for success was performance after experience on a series of problems of the same type. This gave opportunity to acquire appropriate strategies and meant that early failures due to any incorrect orientation or misunderstanding of task demands would not prejudice the final outcome.

The results showed a significant age-by-levels interaction such that children over 5 years were much better able than 4-year-olds to master system mappings, whereas there was no difference for relational mappings. It seems that children under 5 years were unable to construct a system mapping but were able to construct a relational mapping. Children older than 5 years could also construct system mappings. A second experiment, using a similar logic, showed that children became able to construct multiple system mappings, which entail four dimensions processed in parallel, at age 11 years.

This research indicates that children become able to construct progressively more complex structure mappings as they grow older. Children under 5 can construct relational mappings, children older than 5 years can also construct system mappings, and children older than 11 years can also construct multiple system mappings. Given the dimensionality of these mapping tasks as defined in chapter 2, this implies that two dimensions can be processed in parallel by 3- to 4-year-olds, three dimensions at age 5 years, and four dimensions at age 11 years.

Several points should be noted about this evidence. The failure of the younger children to perform the higher level mapping tasks cannot reflect failure to understand task demands or apply task-appropriate strategies. Pretraining and pretesting ensured that both of these requirements were met, and the hypothesis that failure was due to these factors would find it very hard to explain why the children succeeded on the lower level tasks. Recall that lower and higher level tasks were closely matched and even had the same components. There seems to be strong evidence, therefore, that the results reflect ability to process given levels of structure, rather than extraneous factors. Furthermore the results reflect failure after extensive learning-set training that would have given ample opportunity to learn task demands and acquire the necessary domain knowledge. We can have considerable confidence, therefore, that the results reflect genuine age differences in capacity to process structure.

To summarize this section, it appears that a chunk can be identified with a dimension, and that similar limitations apply to both. There is evidence that the number of dimensions that can be processed in parallel reaches three at approximately age 5 years and reaches the adult level at approximately 11 years. The limit may be attributable to the computational demands of computing the tensor product of more than five vectors. It would be a soft limit, leading to increased latencies and errors, rather than to catastrophic breakdown. Performance would be reduced to chance level, or to that level that could be achieved with less complex representations, but total inability to perform would not normally be expected.

Recoding and Conceptual Chunking

It is obvious that many concepts are more complex than four dimensions, so if humans can process a maximum of four dimensions in parallel, how can we deal with more complex concepts? Two processes, conceptual chunking and segmentation, handle this problem. Conceptual chunking entails recoding a multidimensional structure as a unidimensional structure or, more generally, as a structure with fewer dimensions. This can only occur under certain conditions and is a not a universal method for reducing all processing loads.

An everyday example of a conceptual chunk would be velocity. Velocity is a three-dimensional concept, defined as velocity = distance/time ($V = s/t$). However it can be recoded as a single dimension. We commonly do this by thinking of velocity (speed) as the position of a pointer on a dial, as the rush of air in the face, blurring of close objects passing by, and so on.

Once multiple dimensions are recoded as a single dimension, that dimension occupies only one chunk, it is represented by a single vector, and it can then be combined with up to three other chunks. Velocity can now be combined again with time to give acceleration, normally defined as distance divided by time ($a = 2st^{-2}$). Acceleration can now be chunked into a single dimension, perhaps encoded as the feeling of being thrust backward as an aircraft accelerates on takeoff. Acceleration can now be combined with mass to produce the concept of force, $F = ma$, and so we can bootstrap our way up to more and more complex concepts.

Conceptual chunks are similar to mnemonic chunks in that a number of formerly separate items of information are recoded as a single item, but there is more emphasis on structure, that is, relations, functions or transformations, between elements, in conceptual chunks. The chunk corresponding to velocity does not consist merely of the concatenation of distance and time, but actually embodies the function $V = s/t$.

In the formulation of Halford et al. (in press), velocity would be represented as a Rank 4 tensor product, with vectors representing velocity (v), dis-

tance (s) and time (t), as well as a vector representing the multiplication operation. If velocity is recoded as a single vector, then acceleration can be
represented as a Rank 4 tensor product, with vectors representing acceleration (a), velocity (v), time (t), and the operation. If we now represent acceleration as a single vector, we can represent force (F) as a Rank 3 tensor product,
with vectors representing F, mass (M), a, and the operation.

At first it seems that we must be getting something for nothing when the
more complex concept, Force, is represented by a tensor product with no
more vectors than the less complex concept, velocity. Actually however there
is a cost to the more efficient representation. This is that some of the constituent structure is no longer immediately accessible. If we write force as $F =$
$2mst^{-2}$, its representation corresponds to a Rank 6 tensor product, because
all dimensions (mass, distance, and both time dimensions, as well as force
itself) are expressed as separate vectors. The effect of distance and time on
force are expressed in the representation (the partial derivatives $\partial F/\partial t$ and
$\partial F/\partial s$ are expressed). However when force is expressed as $F = ma$, the
effect of variations in distance and time (the partial derivatives mentioned
above) cannot be expressed.

It only makes sense to fold s and t into velocity, v, if the actual values
of s and t are irrelevant. For an example of a situation where the actual values
are relevant, consider footraces; 100 meters in 10 seconds is reasonably fast,
but 1,500 meters in 150 seconds, although the same velocity, is implausibly
fast. On the other hand, when someone is booked for exceeding the speed
limit, actual time and distance are irrelevant. In the latter case, but not in
the former, it is appropriate to recode the three vector representation into
one vector.

The dimensions that are relevant in a situation tend to be reflected in the
language used to describe it. In a footrace, where the distance and time are
relevant, we say a person ran 100 meters in 12 seconds. We would not say
they ran at 30 kilometers per hour. When discussing the speed of a car, we
do not say it went 2.5 kilometers in one minute, we simply say it went at
150 kilometers per hour. In the former case, two dimensions, distance and
time, are given because both are relevant. In the latter case, only one dimension, speed, is given because distance and time are irrelevant.

Thus, conceptual chunking, or recoding multiple vectors into a single vector, does not dispose of capacity limitations so much as it allows us to operate within them. Given that we can only represent concepts of up to four
dimensions in parallel, we must have ways of representing complex concepts
that do not exceed this limit. We do this by combining multiple vectors into
single vectors. However when we want access to the components of the complex concepts, we must descend to the more specific representation again.
To gain access to the components, we must sacrifice the efficiency gained
by chunking. There tends to be a trade-off between efficiency and flexibility.

Another implication is that representation of complex concepts is heavily dependent on availability of efficient codes. Because we are stretching our capacity for representations to process all the interrelations between distance, time, and mass that occur in the concept of force, we need concepts that provide efficient codes. We can only represent up to about four independent sources of variation (four degrees of freedom) in parallel, so we require codes that enable us to represent complex concepts without exceeding this limit. This is why expertise is so important to representation, because without it we are restricted to very simple systems. One characteristic of an expert, as compared with a novice, is that the expert can recognize examples of concepts on the basis of their deep structure (Chi & Ceci, 1987; Holyoak, 1991). When experts examine a situation in simple mechanics, they represent it in terms of the most efficient concepts. In the case of force, they represent it in terms of mass and acceleration. The novice either tries to represent too many dimensions (such as distance and time), because he or she does not have access to the important higher order concepts such as acceleration, or represents irrelevant dimensions.

Another limitation of conceptual chunking is that, like mnemonic chunking, it is only possible with constant mappings of components into chunks. The mnemonic chunk "CAT" is possible because "C," "A," and "T" map into the word CAT in constant fashion. In the conceptual chunk "speed," the dimensions of distance and time map into speed in constant fashion, defined by the ternary relation of division.

Chunking can produce massive gains in efficiency but at the expense of a certain amount of rigidity. While a concept is encoded as a chunk in this way, its constituent structure is less accessible, and alternative combinations cannot be generated. Hence novices, although they are less likely to see the conventional structures quickly and efficiently because they have not coded the information into efficient chunks, might, for that very reason, more readily see novel structures.

Segmentation entails decomposing structures into smaller components that can be processed serially. This usually results in a strategy, or sequence of steps, for performing the task. However, some knowledge of the task structure is required for a serial processing strategy to be organized. The process of strategy development is considered in chapter 4.

Requirements for Testing Limits to Dimensionality

The problem of testing the theory that there are limits to the number of dimensions that can be processed in parallel is complicated by the ability of humans to recode representations into fewer dimensions. However, there are principles that govern this process, and these can be used to devise appropriate tests. As we have seen, all the dimensions that are relevant to the current decision must be represented, and factors that vary independently within the current task must be represented as separate dimensions. Therefore, two factors that are currently relevant and that vary independently cannot be represented as a single conceptual chunk. Chunking also requires constant mapping over some amount of experience. Newly encountered structures, or structures that are continually varying, cannot be chunked. These principles can be used to ensure that representations of a particular level are being employed. Our work in the past has shown that it is possible to constrain participants to map particular levels of structure in parallel under certain conditions.

ARCHITECTURE OF WORKING MEMORY

The architecture of working memory has been extensively examined from a PDP perspective by Schneider and Detweiler (1987). They proposed several regions corresponding to functions such as visual, auditory, speech, lexical, motor processes, and so on. They also suggested that each region has a number of levels, and that there are number of modules in each level. They also proposed that there are general-purpose pathways linking the regions that can process about four modules (chunks) of information. Working-memory research reviewed earlier provides strong evidence that there are at least three systems, which Baddeley (1990) called the central executive, the phonological loop, and the visual short-term memory.

PDP models do not require a central executive for any specific task, because they naturally settle to a solution that best fits all constraints operating in parallel. However, it is probably essential to have some way of controlling the sequence of processes performed and of linking activities in different regions.

It is clear that working memory contains more than one system, so it is inappropriate to talk about processing resources or capacity as though there were only one. The resources for fine motor coordination or for accessing the lexicon may well be very different from resources for mental arithmetic or analogical reasoning. On the other hand, there probably has to be a system that is not specialized for content and that can serve the functions of coordinating processes occurring in different regions, and at different times, and of operating on representations in tasks such as representational redescription and analogical reasoning. I propose that there is a general-purpose capacity in this sense.

To summarize the argument so far, we have considered several concepts of capacity, including resources, short-term memory span, total processing space, primary memory, central processing space, processing speed and dimensionality of representations. The resource concept is viable, but tasks can be difficult for many reasons besides limited resources, and techniques are available for identifying resource-limited processes. Short-term memory span cannot be identified with the workspace of cognition in any straightforward way, although it is possible that STM capacity is matched to the capacity of the central processor. Span undoubtedly increases with age due to improved strategies, domain knowledge, and processing speed, which permits faster renewal of decaying traces.

The theory that total processing space is the sum of operating space and short-term storage space is incompatible with working-memory evidence that STM storage and cognitive processing entail systems that are partially distinct. Primary memory is possibly related to the cognitive workspace and seems to have a capacity of about four items, but considerably more research is needed before its status is clear. Central processing space is operationalized in a number of interesting tasks, but their status as measures of capacity requires to be established.

There is strong evidence for a global-processing-speed factor that increases with age and possibly is related to processing capacity. There is more than one capacity, but there is probably a general-purpose system that relates processes to one another, operates on representations to produce explicit knowledge, and performs analogical reasoning. This general-purpose system is also capacity limited because of the computational cost of processing more than about five vectors in parallel. This corresponds to evidence that the number of dimensions that can be processed in parallel by adults is about four and reaches three at about 5 years.

DOES PROCESSING CAPACITY CHANGE WITH AGE?

Now that the technical aspects of capacity have been examined, we are ready to address the fundamentally important question of whether processing capacity changes with age. As I point out at the beginning of the chapter, even the very convincing evidence that much of cognitive development depends on acquisition of knowledge or strategies does not tell us whether capacity remains constant or changes with age. The approach that has been commonly adopted of relegating capacity to the residual that has not been explained by other factors is inadequate, because it takes no account of measurement error and because it does not lead us to an understanding of the nature of capacity.

Evidence that capacity remains constant over age is mainly indirect. As we have seen, it consists mainly of evidence that other factors produce change. Although this undoubtedly shows that cognitive development is not entirely attributable to growth of capacity, it does not logically imply that capacity is constant. Arguments that it does are commonly made, and are often uncritically accepted, but they only cloud the issue. Some of the other evidence that capacity remains constant with age relate to noncentral processes such as the phonological loop, and tell us little about the workspace of higher cognitive processes.

On the other side of the coin, the evidence that capacity changes with age is certainly not voluminous, but it does appear to be growing. Some of the most important evidence is that evidence that shows a general-processing speed factor that changes with age. Its relation to processing capacity is as yet unclear and subject to speculation. However, the fact that processing speed predicts many high-level cognitive functions, and there are possible mechanisms by which increased capacity would lead to faster processing, mean that this is a promising line of investigation. There is also evidence that primary memory increases with age.

There is growing physiological evidence that processing capacity might increase with age. Thatcher, Walker, and Giudice (1987) reported an exponential growth function, with periodic spurts, in the development of the cerebral hemispheres. There is also an impressive series of studies by Diamond (1985, 1988, 1989) indicating that tests for understanding of the object concept in infancy might be related to maturation of the frontal lobes. Evidence that delayed response and the A-not-B task are related to maturation of the cortex has been reported by Goldman-Rakic (1987). There is also evidence that certain forms of complex learning are related to maturation of the hippocampus (Rudy, 1991). Although these studies do not yet cover a very wide range of cognitive functions, they show that the hypothesis that capacity changes has been dismissed prematurely.

The dimensionality metric for conceptual complexity, together with the PDP concept of representations, both outlined earlier, lead to a reformulation of the question. According to this view, one factor that increases with age is the dimensionality of representations. That is, the number of independent vectors that can be processed in parallel increases with age. This would not increase overall capacity, because the total amount of information that could be stored would not be affected. However, it would lead to the ability to process concepts of greater structural complexity.

Increased modularity of representations would not necessarily require more units but would require that representations be differentiated into more vectors. This is consistent with the fact that differentiation has long been known to be a basic process in development, as Werner's (1948) classical work has shown. Furthermore, Siegler (1989b) reviewed mechanisms of cognitive development and pointed out that the number of synapses grows to its maximum around the time of birth, then gradually declines, reaching adult levels at about age 7. The implications of the physiological evidence are not fully clear at present, but they constitute a promising line of investigation.

There is evidence that older children can process structures of higher dimensionality. The structure mapping studies of Halford (1978) and Halford and Wilson (1980), summarized in Fig. 3.18, showed that the dimensionality of structures that can be mapped increased with age. Numerous instances of the difficulty that young children experience with structures of high dimensionality are considered later in this book.

The consequences of the hypothesis that the dimensionality of representations increases with age is explored through the remainder of this book. Tasks for which the underlying cognitive processes are sufficiently well understood are analyzed in terms of the dimensionality of representations they require, and this can be related to typical ages of attainment and to other variables. However it is possible to extend some existing methodologies to address the capacity-change issue.

Methodology and Capacity Change

One way to approach the question of whether capacity changes with age would be to extend the easy-to-hard paradigm by including age as a variable, as shown in the path-analysis diagram in Fig. 3.19. Recall that, in accordance with the easy-to-hard paradigm, the secondary task performed jointly with the primary task, secondaryj, is a measure of capacity. If capacity to perform the criterion task changes with age, then age should predict secondaryj, which in turn should predict the criterion task; that is, in path-analysis terms, the product of paths e and c (emphasized in Fig. 3.19) should provide significant prediction. Thus path-analysis technique, applied to studies with age added as a factor to the easy-to-hard paradigm, has the potential to pro-

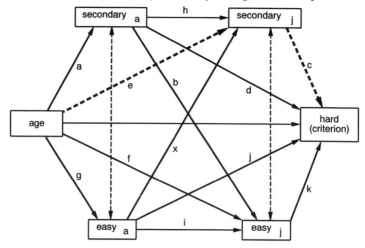

FIG. 3.19. Path analysis of easy-to-hard paradigm modified to study change in capacity with age.

vide data very relevant to the question of whether information-processing capacity changes with age. The easy-to-hard paradigm can also be extended to test a notion that has been of long-standing importance in cognitive development, the idea that two tasks are acquired at the same point in development because of a common underlying structure. The present theory predicts that two tasks that have the same level of dimensionality, if presented in a common format, should have similar levels of difficulty because of the processing loads they impose. This prediction cannot be tested using correlations because they can occur for many reasons besides common processing loads. However the prediction can be tested precisely using a double easy-to-hard paradigm.

We can illustrate this by considering two tasks that, in terms of the argument of this book, should impose equivalent processing loads. Suppose for example that we consider class inclusion, as discussed in chapter 8, and transitive inference, as discussed in chapter 7. Both of these tasks are three-dimensional and, therefore, should impose similar processing loads. We would expect a significant positive correlation between these tasks, but that does not establish that they impose the same load. We would also expect that they would be mastered at about the same time, but this might be influenced by details of the task format. How then can we test the proposition that they are acquired at the same time because of processing load?

We can extend the easy-to-hard paradigm as shown in Fig. 3.20 in order to answer this question. Recall that, if a task is capacity limited, it should be predicted by performance on a secondary task performed jointly with an easy version of the primary task. That is, if transitive inference is capacity limited, it should be predicted by performance on (say) a probe RT task performed jointly with an easier ordering task. This is essentially the logic used by Halford et al. (1986), summarized in Fig. 3.13. The predictions for the double easy-to-hard paradigm are shown by the arrows in Fig. 3.20. First, the two three-dimensional tasks should predict each other. Second, and more importantly, if class inclusion and transitive inference are capacity limited, they should be predicted by the secondary task, performed jointly with the easy versions of the primary tasks. Notice however that these predictions cross over. That is, each task should be predicted by a secondary task performed jointly with an easier version of the other task, as well as by the secondary task performed jointly with its own easy version. For example, the secondary task, performed jointly with an easier classification task, should predict performance on the transitive inference task as well as performance on the class inclusion task. As with the easy-to-hard paradigm, scores on the easy tasks and the secondary task, performed alone, would be partialled out from the predictions.

The logical structure of this paradigm is shown in Appendix 3.A.

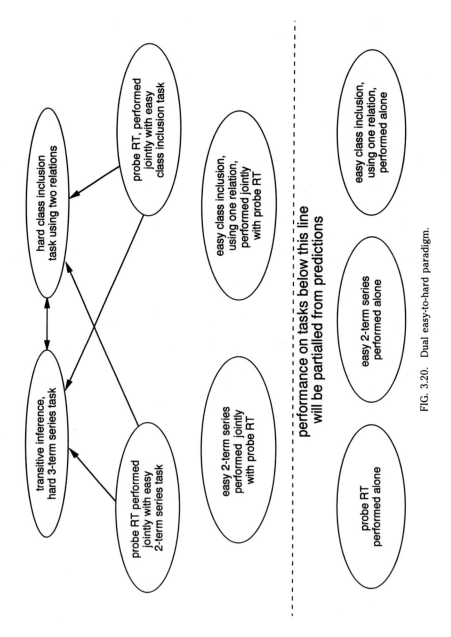

FIG. 3.20. Dual easy-to-hard paradigm.

SUMMARY AND CONCLUSIONS

Capacity is not the only factor that accounts for cognitive development, and acquisition of declarative and procedural knowledge also play a major role. Nevertheless capacity must be understood before the complete picture of cognitive development can be given. Many claims in the literature that capacity remains constant over age are based on indirect evidence and effectively relegate capacity to the residual variance after other factors are investigated. This is not satisfactory because it doesn't take into account measurement error and does not advance understanding of the capacity concept.

Several different concepts of capacity appear in the literature. The first is resource, which is a type of mental energy that can be allocated to tasks. It entails the idea that performance is a function of the resources allocated (the performance-resource function, Fig. 3.1), that tasks vary in the demand they make on resources (the slopes of the performance-resource functions vary, Fig. 3.2), and that tasks that compete for a common, limited resource will show a trade-off in performance (the performance-operating characteristic, Fig. 3.3.). Secondary tasks can be used to assess resource demands of a primary task (Fig. 3.4), although certain precautions are necessary. Interactions do not inevitably accompany competition for resources (Fig. 3.5), and interpretational difficulties with dual-task deficits can be alleviated using the easy-to-hard paradigm (Fig. 3.6). Demand for resources is not the only cause of task difficulty, and number of steps, knowledge required, availability of the correct hypothesis, and short-term memory storage load also affect solution times and errors. Consequently it is essential to know when task difficulty does reflect processing resources, and the easy-to-hard paradigm is useful for this purpose.

The conceptual-complexity metric based on the dimensionality of a concept, or the number of independent items of information required to represent it, is used to generate predictions concerning the information-processing loads of transitive inference and certain algebraic tasks. These predictions are tested using secondary-task indicators, with positive results. The concept of resources has been criticized because it includes no specification of mechanisms but, although a process theory is desirable, it complements rather than replaces a resource theory.

Short-term memory has often been regarded as the workspace of cognition, but working memory research indicates that short-term recall reflects the operation of a relatively specialized system, the phonological loop, which is at least partly independent of cognitive processes entailed in reasoning. Working-memory research also calls into question the hypothesis that total processing space is the sum of operating space and short-term storage space. Cognitive processing and short-term memory storage do not trade off in the simple manner implied by this hypothesis. Consequences derived from this hypothesis, to the effect that total processing space remains constant over age, are called into question by the same evidence.

Primary memory, or the information about which we are currently thinking, has been investigated and found to have a capacity of four to five items for adults, three to four items for children. It is possibly a component of working memory, but there is little research on the question so far.

Central processing-space (M-space) measures have been used successfully to predict cognitive tasks, but more research is required to establish that the predictions reflect capacity, rather than knowledge or other variables.

There is evidence of a general-processing-speed factor that grows with age, and is possibly related to processing capacity. One speculation is that representations might decay, and faster processing would mean more information could be maintained. Another possibility, based on PDP models, is that higher capacity might lead directly to faster processing because of greater clarity of representations.

Miller's concept of the number of chunks has been reassessed, and the evidence suggests that adults process approximately four chunks in parallel. Chunks are identified with the number of dimensions that can be processed in parallel, which are linked to the number of vectors that can be processed in a PDP system. The number of dimensions that children can process in parallel is investigated directly, and is found to be two at age 3-4, three at age 5 and four at age 11.

A PDP model of the representation of concepts is invoked to explain why human beings should be limited to processing a relatively small number of dimensions in parallel. According to the model, each dimension is represented as a vector, and the interaction of the dimensions corresponds to the tensor product of the vectors. The hypothesis is advanced that the number of dimensions that can be processed in parallel is related to the complexity of computing tensor products of more than about five vectors.

The number of dimensions that need to be processed in parallel to perform a task depends on the information that must be represented simultaneously and on the number of independently varying items of information within the immediate task. Representations can be recoded into fewer dimensions, a process called *conceptual chunking*. It leads to great gains in efficiency, but some computational possibilities are lost. One important benefit of expertise is that it permits the most appropriate and efficient representations to be created, which do not overload capacity.

There is more than one pool of processing capacity, but there is probably a central process that coordinates activities occurring in different regions, or at different times, and relates one representation to another. The available evidence suggests it can process about four independent items in parallel.

The question of whether processing capacity increases with age is reformulated in terms of the theory advanced. It is suggested that the number

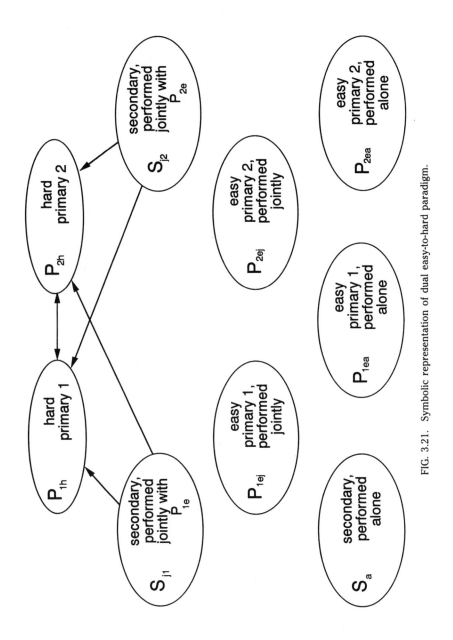

FIG. 3.21. Symbolic representation of dual easy-to-hard paradigm.

of dimensions that can be processed in parallel might increase with age, possibly due to differentiation of representations. This would not increase overall capacity but would permit more complex structures to be processed and, therefore, more complex concepts to be understood.

There is a small but growing body of evidence that certain processing capacities increase with age, although the evidence that they remain constant is mostly indirect or relates to noncentral processes. However, greater insights into the nature of capacity should enable research questions to be refined and methodologies improved. A number of extensions of the easy-to-hard paradigm are suggested as potentially useful for this purpose.

APPENDIX 3.A: SYMBOLIC REPRESENTATION

The logical structure of the double easy-to-hard paradigm, is shown in Fig. 3.21. There are two primary tasks, *P1* and *P2*, which are selected because they are hypothesized to make similar processing demands. There are easy versions of each task, *P1e* and *P2e*, and hard versions, *P1h* and *P2h*. The easy versions would be performed alone (*P1ea, P2ea*) and jointly with a secondary task (*P1ej, P2ej*). There would also be a single secondary task, that would be performed alone (*Sa*) and jointly with the easy versions of each of the primary tasks, that is, with easy *P1ej* and *P2ej*. We will call these secondary tasks *Sj1* and *Sj2*, respectively. Performance on the two primary tasks performed alone, and of the secondary task performed alone (i.e., *P1ea, P2ea,* and (*Sa*) would be partialled out from all predictions. The critical predictions are indicated by the arrows in Fig. 3.21.

One prediction is that the two hard primary tasks should predict each other. Such a prediction, if obtained with performance on the easy primary tasks and the secondary task performed alone partialled out, as indicated above, would reflect common demands for resources by the hard primary tasks. Furthermore the two secondary tasks performed jointly with the easy primary tasks, being indicators of capacity, should predict both hard primary tasks.

4

BASIC LEARNING PROCESSES IN COGNITIVE DEVELOPMENT

In chapter 2, *mental models* were defined as representations that are active while solving a particular problem and provide the workspace for inference and mental operations. A *representation* was defined as an internal structure that mirrored the structure of a segment of the environment. This implies that mental models depend on information about the environment. Not all the information relevant to a problem will be activated at any one time, but information about the world is nevertheless essential to mental models.

The use of mental models requires a store of world knowledge that can be accessed to construct representations. A major problem, therefore, is to explain how this world knowledge is acquired. The importance of world knowledge to cognitive development has been demonstrated by Carey (1985) and Chi and Ceci (1987), but the acquisition process has received surprisingly little attention in the cognitive-development literature. Therefore the first aim of this chapter is to explore processes for acquiring world knowledge. The second aim is to explore processes entailed in developing strategies and skills. These questions do not exhaust the topic of learning, because analogies can play an important part in knowledge acquisition. However, analogies constitute a set of processes that are to some extent distinct from basic learning mechanisms, so the role of analogies in learning is discussed in chapter 5.

Traditional learning theory was mainly concerned with the acquisition of stimulus–response associations (Hall, 1966; Hilgard, 1956; Kimble, 1961). This class of theories found very little application to cognitive development, which might explain why there has been so little attention to the role of learning in the area. That situation has changed in the last decade, and there are now theories that have important implications for cognitive development and that also assist with the interpretation of some interesting phenomena that were glossed over or ignored by traditional learning theory. The theories of Rescorla (1988), Holland, Holyoak, Nisbett, and Thagard (1986) and Holyoak, Koh, and Nisbett (1989) are particularly relevant here, and it is to them that we turn. All of these theories attempt to deal with the acquisition of information about the world, or declarative knowledge, so that is our first topic.

ACQUIRING DECLARATIVE KNOWLEDGE

Ways of representing declarative knowledge were considered in chapter 2. These included schemas, propositional networks, condition–action rules, contingencies, and parallel distributed processes (PDP). Two of these, condition–action rules and contingencies, are central to contemporary theories of learning in the cognitive domain. Learning has been extensively investigated within PDP, but the implications are mainly at the microstructure level, whereas cognitive development first needs some global learning principles. Therefore we focus on macrostructure processes conceptualized in terms of contingencies and condition–action rules but refer to PDP where microstructure issues arise.

Contingencies

Rescorla (1988) showed that contemporary theory requires a fundamentally new interpretation of classical conditioning. Formerly it was conceptualized in terms of a stimulus–response association, that is a conditioned stimulus acquiring the ability to elicit a response normally elicited by an unconditioned stimulus. By contrast, contemporary theory "sees conditioning as the learning that results from exposure to relations among events in the environment. Such learning is a primary means by which the organism represents the structure of its world" (Rescorla, 1988, p. 152).

Learning relations among events in the environment, or contingencies, is an important component of cognitive development, and it provides building blocks for higher level cognitive processes. Rescorla demonstrated that the principles of classical conditioning are relevant to this process.

Consistent with chapter 2, contingencies are used to refer to knowledge about relations between events that is not explicit, in the sense that it is not conscious, it is not manipulable by other cognitive processes, and it is not possible to modify it without external input. In this respect it differs from declarative rules, which have more of an explicit quality. However contingencies and condition–action rules are governed by many of the same principles, as Holyoak et al. (1989) showed.

Condition–Action Rules

As mentioned in chapter 2, declarative condition–action rules are representations because they have assertions or predictions about the environment on their action sides, instead of actions to be performed. Therefore, the question of how representations are acquired refers in a major way to the principles governing acquisition of declarative condition–action rules. Procedural condition–action rules encode actions and the circumstances in which they are to be performed. They share some of the same acquisition principles, although there are also some differences. We will consider how both kinds of rules are acquired.

The backbone of traditional learning theory was the principle of *reinforcement*, which stated that when a response is made to a stimulus, and followed by a positive outcome, such as a reward or satisfying state of affairs, that response is strengthened. The stimulus would then have increased power to elicit that response in the future. In a general sense this principle applies to the acquisition of condition–action rules, but it requires considerable refinement.

A more appropriate learning theory for our purposes was formulated by Holland, Holyoak, Nisbett, and Thagard (1986). It applies to a range of processes from elementary learning to scientific creativity. Further developments of this theory have been shown to provide a powerful model of conditioning (Holyoak, Koh, & Nisbett, 1989). The theory of Holland et al. subsumes the reinforcement principle but adds several other principles. It is based on condition–action rules, and the basic idea is that rules are activated when their conditions match the current situation, which normally includes a goal. Thus a rule must be relevant to the current goal in order to be activated. The action side of the rule has two components, a description of the expected state of affairs, and an action appropriate to that state. Thus the model blends declarative and procedural knowledge. Rules compete to represent a given situation on the basis of strength acquired through past success. Rules can be activated in parallel and can support each other. After activation the strength of rules is revised depending on the outcome. If the rule was confirmed, in the sense that the predicted events occurred, and the action succeeded, then strength is increased, otherwise it is decreased.

Holland et al. (1986) argued that their model is consistent with the work of Rescorla (1968) on secondary reinforcement. Condition–action rules that represent relations between events in the environment are sensitive to the predictive value of stimuli that are included in their condition side. This is consistent with Rescorla's finding that rats were sensitive to the predictive value of a secondary reinforcer. The basic logic of these experiments is that a signal, such as a tone, is associated with shock in the same way for all the treatment groups. The independent variable is the degree to which the shock also occurs in the absence of the tone. The tone is a better predictor of shock when the shock does not also occur in the absence of tone. Rescorla found that the effect of the tone depended on its predictive value when the tone–shock association was held constant. Holland et al. showed how these observations are highly compatible with the idea that the participants acquired rules that predict the environment. Holland et al. (1986) developed the theory into a general theory of induction that accounts for an impressive number of phenomena relating to acquisition and use of high-level concepts. Holland et al. (1986) did not distinguish between declarative and procedural rules. The condition side of their condition–action rules includes both assertions about the world (declarative) and actions (procedural). However, either type of rule can be created by simply setting one or other component to zero. The declarative–procedural distinction is useful and corresponds to some differences in experience, as we later see.

Declarative rules represent relations between events in the environment, so the learning principles that govern their acquisition must ensure that they make predictions that correspond to the environment. This means that for a declarative rule to succeed, the assertion that is contained on its action side must correspond to the state of affairs that exists after the rule has been activated. Therefore, declarative rules are strengthened when they successfully predict reality. The condition side of a declarative rule will normally include a goal, to ensure the rule is only activated when it is relevant to the person's current goals. However, a declarative rule is not strengthened solely by satisfaction of a goal. The outcome must correspond to the assertion contained in the action side of the rule, which is not a requirement for a procedural rule.

For a procedural rule to succeed, the action or procedure that it specifies when it is activated must be followed by a satisfactory outcome of some sort. In traditional learning theory terminology, it must be "reinforced."

Examples of each type of rule are shown in Fig. 4.1. For the procedural rule the goal is "find food," and the associated action is to move to a particular place where feeding has taken place previously. The outcome is to find and eat food. This outcome satisfies the goal, and so the rule is strengthened. This is essentially the same as strengthening a stimulus–response association by reinforcement, the basic principle of traditional learning theory. Notice that there is no need for the food to correspond to expectation. For example, if the person had expected carrots and had received bananas, the goal would still be satisfied, and the rule strengthened. Reinforcement does not need to correspond to expectations, it only has to satisfy goals.

In the declarative rule the action side is not an overt action or procedure, but an assertion that a particular kind of food, pies, will be found at a particular place. This rule is confirmed and strengthened if, and only if, pies are

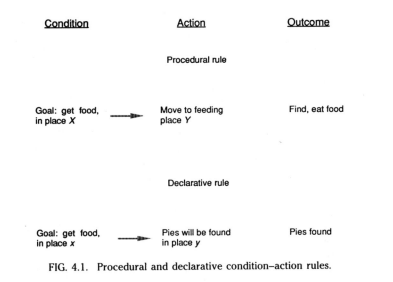

FIG. 4.1.   Procedural and declarative condition–action rules.

found. It is not confirmed if (say) caviar is found, even though caviar might have been more desirable. A declarative rule is strengthened only by an outcome that corresponds to the declarative assertion in the action side of the rule, not merely by satisfying the goal.

Readers familiar with the history of learning theory will have recognized that the procedural–declarative distinction as used here corresponds closely to the distinction between S–R (Stimulus–Response) and S–S (Stimulus–Stimulus) learning processes, which were once a controversial issue in learning (Hilgard, 1956). The difference between the two types of rules is important because with declarative rules, but not with procedural rules, the outcome must correspond to the assertion in the action side of the rule. Declarative rules have a representational function and are generally more relevant to the development of children's understanding of the world.

The ability to learn contingencies and rules that represent the environment is not exclusive to humans, and it is probably quite basic biologically. As we have seen, it is now thought to underlie classical conditioning, which is one of the most basic learning mechanisms. This means that the processes by which children acquire their stored representations of the world might not be unique but may have some features in common with those used by infrahuman animals. There is a considerable number of established phenomena in the animal learning literature that can be readily interpreted in terms of the acquisition of contingencies or declarative rules. I will examine some of this literature even though it does not appear on the face of it to concern children, because it demonstrates the validity and generality of certain basic learning principles governing acquisition of representations.

Contingencies and Declarative Rules
in Traditional Learning

There is evidence that animals learn contingencies or rules that model and predict their environment. Prokasy (1956) trained rats in an E-maze in which they received 50% reinforcement in both arms of the maze. On one side there was a stimulus that reliably predicted whether that trial would be rewarded, whereas on the other side the stimulus occurred with the same frequency but uncorrelated with reward. Retracing was not permitted, so the rats could not switch to the other side if the signal indicated they were not going to receive reward. The rats still preferred the side where the stimulus predicted reward, even though they derived no material advantage from it. Thus, the rats seemed to learn a contingency that a certain stimulus predicted a particular outcome, even though it did not help them achieve their goal of obtaining food. They were learning contingencies that we can express as follows:

Contingency 1: maze, Stimulus A → food
Contingency 2: maze, Stimulus B → no food

Such studies also suggest that there is a pervading goal to predict the environment. I would postulate that this goal is always active, but at a low level. It can be easily overridden by other, stronger goals such as obtaining food or a mate, or fleeing enemies, but it is always there, ready to influence behavior and cognition when no more urgent goals are active.

Secondary reinforcement can also be interpreted in terms of contingencies or declarative rules. Traditionally, learning theorists have interpreted secondary reinforcement as a kind of substitute reward: If no actual reward was available to maintain behaviors, it could be maintained by stimuli that had been associated with a reward. Actually, however, the literature is probably more consistent with the notion of contingency: Rescorla's work has led to a secondary reinforcer being interpreted as a stimulus that signals that a reward is coming.

There are further studies that imply that the value of a "secondary reinforcer" depends on the information it provides. Egger and Miller (1962, 1963) found that a secondary reinforcer was more effective if it was a nonredundant predictor of reward, implying that the strength of a secondary reinforcer depends to some extent on its information value. Seggie and Halford (1968) showed that in a T maze task a stimulus acquired the properties of a "secondary reinforcer" if it signalled to which side of the maze the rat would be going in a forced-choice trial, even if it was not differentially associated with reward. Thus, the fact that the stimulus predicted something about the environment was enough to promote learning.

The importance of the ability of a stimulus to predict the environment was demonstrated in another way by Halford and Halford (1969) and Holgate and

Halford (1972), who had rats press a bar that was followed by a tone. At other times the tone sounded independently of barpress and was followed by a reward. The tone failed to acquire secondary reinforcing properties. This is difficult to understand in terms of secondary reinforcement theory because the same tone that followed reward also followed the response, so it should have been associated with reward and maintained the response. However it is easy to understand in terms of the contingency hypothesis, because the stimulus is of no value in predicting reward; the tone following response does not signal that the response is going to be rewarded, because the reward is independent of the response.

Saltzman (1949) found that the degree to which a stimulus acquired secondary reinforcing properties depended on how well it discriminated between alternatives. Rats received reward in one goalbox on 25 trials, and on another 14 trials they ran to a distinctively different goalbox where they were not rewarded. Thus, one goalbox was predictive of reward where the other one predicted nonreward. Another treatment group ran to a single goalbox where they were always rewarded on 25 trials, whereas another group had 25 rewarded and 14 nonrewarded trials in the same goalbox. The positive goalbox was a better secondary reinforcer for the first group than for any of the others. The concept of contingency makes it easy to understand why this should be so. For the first group there were two contingencies of the form:

Contingency 3: maze, Goalbox 1 → reward

Contingency 4: maze, Goalbox 2 → no reward

The second group only had the first of these contingencies, whereas the third group had a contingency of the form:

Contingency 5: maze, goalbox → reward 64% of time.

Contingency 5 is a predictor of low validity, whereas Contingencies 3 and 4 together are very good predictors of the outcome of maze running, and this facilitated learning.

The predictive value of rules or contingencies has also been shown to be important in children's learning. Bryant (1982) had children compare two blocks of wood, one standing on a table and one on the floor, by two methods. The first utilized a black rod, which could be compared with both blocks and permitted children to decide which was taller of Block A and Block B by transitive inference (e.g., Block A = rod > Block B, therefore Block A > Block B). The other method was to lift the block on the floor onto the table where it could be directly compared with the other block. The experimental group was given 10 trials using both methods on the same pair of blocks, so they could see that the methods agreed. The control group had 10 trials using each method, but never on the same pair of blocks, so they could never discover the agreement. Learning was clearly superior in the group that experienced the agreement. This result is easy to understand in terms of declarative rule acquisition. Consider Rule T1;

Rule T1: Block A > rod, rod = Block B → Block A > Block B

This rule means that the transitive inference procedure predicts what is observed when the two blocks are placed side by side. The experiment provides good confirmation of the principle that children learn declarative rules that predict the environment.

The conclusion of this section is that the learning process, even in animals such as rats, normally results in rules or contingencies being learned that model or predict the environment. Furthermore, humans and other animals are sensitive to the degree to which a particular stimulus does predict the environment. Contingencies and declarative rules are learned better if they are good predictors. In the remainder of this chapter, and throughout this book, we show how learning mechanisms can account for the process of cognitive development. Our purpose here has been to show that the basic learning mechanisms that operate in cognitive development are quite consistent with evidence from a wide range of learning contexts.

Studies of Strength Reduction

The problem of how learned responses are weakened tended to be rather difficult for traditional learning theory. The basic tenet was that responses were weakened when not reinforced; that is, when the goal that gave rise to them was not satisfied. However the effects of punishments or negative reinforcers have always appeared less clearcut (Kimble, 1961).

Declarative rules and contingencies are weakened when the statements they make are not confirmed by external events. This is not necessarily the same as not satisfying the goal. The difference can be well illustrated by some classical studies in avoidance learning (Solomon, Kamin, & Wynne, 1953). Dogs were placed in a shuttle box and, after a signal, were subjected to intense shock, from which they could escape by leaping over a barrier into the other compartment of the box. The dogs soon learned to avoid the shock by leaping over the barrier when the signal appeared. Once the avoidance response was established, the shock was terminated, but this failed to extinguish the response, which actually continued with shortening latencies for hundreds of trials. This finding, which was consistent with common observations of avoidance learning, presented a paradox for traditional learning theory. The problem was to explain what reinforced and maintained the avoidance response when shock was terminated, because the animal continued to jump despite the fact that the reward, escape from shock, no longer existed.

The favored explanation was that the signal–shock sequence resulted in the signal becoming a conditioned stimulus for anxiety, and that the avoidance response was reinforced by anxiety reduction (the "two-factor" theory of avoidance learning). This explanation was not however consistent with observation, because the dogs showed no sign of anxiety on trials when they could jump, but only when they were prevented from jumping. Solomon and Wynne (1954) conceded that the anxiety-reduction hypothesis did not account for the data.

However these findings are easy to explain in terms of contingencies as follows:

Contingency A1: signal, no jump → shock

Contingency A2: signal, jump → no shock

If the experimenter terminates the shock after the animal has learned to jump, neither of these contingencies will be disconfirmed, because the new experience is consistent with the stored contingency. The animal continues to jump because not to do so risks a very painful shock, and the absence of shock after Contingency 2 is activated is quite consistent with the contingency. The contingency is not disconfirmed, in fact it is confirmed because the outcome corresponds to prediction. Therefore the contingency is strengthened, not weakened by what should, in terms of traditional learning theory, have been an extinction situation.

An important principle follows from this. It is that contingencies and declarative rules do not need to be maintained by reinforcement as traditional learning theory contended. They will be strengthened if the predictions they make are consistent with the outcome in the situation where they are activated. Rules are only weakened when they do not correspond to the outcome. In the paradigm of Solomon, Kamin, and Wynne (1953), this can best be done by preventing the dogs from jumping, because this leads to no shock, which disconfirms Contingency 1. In fact, Solomon et al. (1953) were able to extinguish the avoidance response in their dogs by placing an obstruction in the way of the dogs' jumping. When they were unable to jump, the dogs experienced an outcome that was inconsistent with Contingency 1. They also learned a new contingency:

Contingency A3: signal, no jump → no shock

Notice that Contingency 2 remains, but jumping ceases because Contingency 3 is able to compete with it successfully.

There are studies in other paradigms that indicate that declarative rules and contingencies are changed when the statements they make are disconfirmed, not when they are followed by nonreinforcement. There are two studies by Bitterman, Fedderson, and Tyler (1953) and Elam, Tyler, and Bitterman (1954) in which rats were given irregular 50% reinforcement. In the discrimination group, reinforced and nonreinforced trials terminated in distinctively different goalboxes, but for the nondiscrimination group all trials terminated in the same goalbox. In extinction, half the discrimination group ran to the originally rewarded goalbox (the "secondary reinforcement" condition), whereas the other half (the "no-secondary reinforcement" condition) ran to the originally nonrewarded goalbox. The nondiscrimination group ran to the originally rewarded goalbox in the "secondary reinforcement" condition, or to a new goalbox in the "no-secondary reinforcement" condition. Traditional learning theory would predict better performance in the secondary reinforcement conditions of both the discrimination and nondiscrimination groups. This did occur in the nondiscrimination group, but in the discrimination group the opposite result occurred; those rats that ran to the originally rewarded goalbox performed worse.

The contingencies learned by the two groups could be written as:

Discrimination group:

Contingency D1: maze, Goalbox 1 → reward 100%

Contingency D2: maze, Goalbox 2 → nonreward 100%

Nondiscrimination group:

Contingency N1: maze, goalbox → reward 50%, nonreward 50%

The extinction experience entailed entering a goalbox and receiving no reward. For the discrimination group in the secondary reinforcement condition, this meant entering a goalbox that had previously been associated with reward on 100% of trials. The extinction experience would therefore be a strong disconfirmation of Contingency D1. Therefore, rather than maintaining performance as secondary reinforcement theory would predict, the contingency would be rapidly weakened and performance would deteriorate. The nondiscrimination group in the secondary reinforcement condition would be entering a goalbox on which they had previously been rewarded 50% of the time, so the experience of nonreward would not be so discrepant from Contingency N1 that they had learned. Because the strength of the contingency would tend to be maintained, the behavior of running to the goalbox would be more persistent. The theory of learned contingencies readily explains the paradoxical results of these studies. These data also show that rats learn contingencies that include estimates of the probability of relative frequency of contingencies, something that humans also are known to acquire easily (Hasher & Zacks, 1979).

The implication for cognitive development is that learning occurs only when experience conflicts with the child's rules. Nothing is learned if the child sees no discrepancy between the outcome of a situation and the prediction made by his/her rules.

This point is quite consonant with an extensive data base of cognitive developmental training studies. Elsewhere (Halford, 1982) I have reviewed some 80 studies in which children were trained in conservation. A striking feature of these studies was that almost any procedure could achieve some degree of success, at least in some circumstances. It appeared that it was only necessary to challenge a child's existing beliefs, by providing an outcome that was inconsistent with that expected on the basis of the child's existing rules. Once this happened the child would do the rest. This implies that cognitive development is promoted by experience that is discrepant from existing rules or that existing rules do not predict. This principle is not unique to cognitive development in the child, however, but is quite consistent with basic learning mechanisms observed in infrahuman animals.

At first sight this principle might seem to contradict the study of Bryant (1982), where it was shown that it was agreement, not conflict, that facilitated children's learning. We have already discussed the fact that agreement was important in Bryant's study because it showed that one procedure could predict another. But the argument of this section implies that mild conflict, or at least experiences where existing rules fail to predict an observed outcome, is necessary for new rule acquisition. How would we reconcile this principle with Bryant's study?

The probable explanation is that all of Bryant's (1982) participants had experienced inability to predict in the pretest. Children were asked to compare the two blocks, one on the table and one on the floor. The rod was available for their use, but they were not instructed to use it. Unless they already knew the transitive inference rule (and pretest scores indicate most did not), they would have no way of knowing whether their judgments were right or not. This, then, was something that their existing knowledge did not predict.

Redundant Rules Are Not Learned

A major function of learning is to acquire contingencies and declarative rules that predict, or make informative statements about, the environment. It would be consistent with this principle if experiences that add no new information do not lead to learning. This corresponds to the well-established phenomenon of *blocking* (Kamin, 1968), which means that redundant cues do not lead to learning. Holland et al. (1986) reviewed a number of studies of this phenomenon, but it is well illustrated by a paper that predates even Kamin's observations. Bruner, Matter, and Papanek (1955) trained rats in a black–white discrimination in a multiunit T maze. Then the correct choices were arranged in a left–right pattern. After training on the combined cues, the black–white cues were deleted, and the animals were trained on the left–right alternation alone. The degree to which the combined training facilitated left–right alternation depended on how much training had been given on the original black–white discrimination. Rats who had overlearned the black–white discrimination learned little about the redundant left–right cues. In our terms this is entirely understandable, because the left–right cues had no predictive value. Everything the rats needed to know about the location of reward was already indicated by the black–white cues.

Holland et al. (1968) showed how the blocking principle explains some important findings in scientific education. Even students who have passed courses in physics and mechanics still tend to see everyday physical phenomena in Aristotelian terms that are inconsistent with what they have been taught in their formal courses. For example, instead of believing that a physical object remains in a state of uniform motion until an opposing force stops it, as they have learned in Newtonian mechanics, students tend to continue believing that objects naturally slow down unless a force maintains their motion.

The latter, Aristotelian rule, is the way things appear in everyday life. Consequently students acquire this rule and, because it appears to predict common experience, the more sophisticated and accurate Newtonian rule appears redundant. Consequently the Newtonian view is not really learned, at least not in the context of everyday observations, even though students have passed examinations on it. These observations indicate how powerful the blocking effect is. New rules are not learned unless they are clearly seen to predict something that is not predicted by existing rules.

Summary

Declarative rules and learned contingencies are representations that can be learned by principles that are general to human and infrahuman animals. Contingencies and declarative rules are strengthened when they are activated in a given situation, and the predictions they make are confirmed. If the predictions are disconfirmed, they are weakened. However, increments of strength only occur if the learned contingencies and declarative rules are nonredundant. Procedural rules and stimulus–response associations are learned in accordance with the reinforcement principle, according to which, if the responses they produce when activated lead to satisfying states of affairs, an increment of strength results.

ADDITIONAL LEARNING PRINCIPLES

There are a number of additional principles that govern the acquisition and use of contingencies and rules.

Support

Rules can operate in conjunction with other rules and can strengthen or weaken each other. This process is called support by Holland et al. (1986). It can operate in one of two ways. One is when two rules are activated simultaneously, and their actions, whether procedural or declarative, correspond. An example is provided by Rules r1 and r2:

Rule r1: if in the African bush → run for shelter

Rule r2: if you see a lion → run for shelter

Being in the African bush might arouse anxiety at any time, leading to a tendency to run, as in Rule r1, but this rule would probably be too weak to send us scuttling for shelter. Seeing a lion also provokes anxiety and makes us want to leave, but if the lion is in a lion park or zoo, we would not run. Thus, the mere presence of a lion is insufficient reason for taking to our heels, so Rule r2 would also be weak. If Rules r1 and r2 were both activated however, the support they give to each other may lead to enough strength to fire both of them, causing us to run for shelter. Thus, we run if we are in the African bush and see a lion.

Rules may also support each other if they are activated successively. Rules may be chained so that the output of one rule provides the input of another, that is, if the action side of one rule is the same as the condition side of the other rule. Where two or more rules in a chain are ultimately successful, either by satisfying a goal or by making a valid statement about the environment, they can pass strength from one to another. The last rule might pass strength back to earlier rules that have helped in the enterprise. Mechanisms by which this can be done have been specified by Holland et al. (1986, chapter 3, the "bucket brigade").

Carey (1985) showed that learning depends to a very considerable extent on what is already known. Children and adults show resistance to learning many scientific concepts simply because they lack the relevant domain-specific knowledge. Concepts do not exist in isolation but are embedded in a body of knowledge the various components of which show a degree of mutual interdependence. Therefore, in order to learn a concept one must know at least some of the concepts on which it depends.

This dependence of learning on preexisting knowledge can be partly explained by the support concept. Because rules can support each other, then rules are easier to learn in mutually consistent sets. It is also important that there should not be other rules that are inconsistent with those to be learned. People who lack knowledge of a particular domain normally do not have a vacuum in that area of their knowledge but have some rules that are actually incorrect. These rules still have practical utility in that they do predict some everyday experiences, otherwise of course they would have been weakened and would have ceased to be activated, or they would have been supplanted by stronger rules. Possession of the relevant domain-specific knowledge helps to ensure that there will be no invalid rules that conflict with acquisition of the appropriate rules.

Another reason why existing knowledge facilitates learning is that it can provide useful analogs or mental models that help predict or structure new information, as we discuss in chapter 5. Yet another reason is that it provides concepts that enable more efficient coding of the new information.

Focused Sampling

Existing rules can also facilitate the acquisition of new rules by a process that Holland et al. (1986) called focused sampling. This means that cues that have been successful predictors in the past will be given greater attention. An important implication of this is that people tend to learn clusters of mutually supportive rules. It also means that one role of prior knowledge is to direct attention to the appropriate features of a situation.

Shaping

Procedural rules may be modified through shaping by selective reinforcement. This is a very basic learning mechanism that is described in most elementary psychology texts, and it amounts to rewarding responses that conform to some criterion or that achieve a particular goal, and not rewarding others. The result is a gradual shift of behavior towards the criterion performance. Although this very basic mechanism must find application in cognitive development, it is equally clear that other mechanisms are required. Declarative rules require another process because, as we have seen, they are strengthened when the statements they make conform to reality, not simply when they are reinforced.

Building New Rules

The previous section considered the processes by which rules are strengthened or weakened under the influence of feedback from the environment. The purpose of this section is to consider mechanisms for modifying rules and producing new rules. In cognitive development a major source of new rules is the process of regularity detection. Further mechanisms include specialization, generalization, composition, and category formation.

Regularity Detection.   Much of cognitive development probably depends on scanning experience for regularities. There is so much variation in the environment that it is probably not possible to discover most of it by creating hypotheses. The most novel acquisitions are probably first made by an unconscious and automatic scanning process that is carried on concurrently with our other activities. I believe that such a process has been underemphasized in cognitive developmental theories, and we return to it a number of times througout this book.

Imagine a child who experiences many dogs that vary in size, color, location, and demeanor. This is a very complex set of experiences, but there are certain regularities that might be detected. Some dogs are more friendly than others. Also, dogs sometimes wag their tails, and sometimes they do not. There is a moderate positive correlation between tail wagging and friendliness. A child needs to discover the link between tail wagging and friendliness. Such discoveries probably often occur automatically, without conscious hypothesis testing. This discovery needs to occur before an hypothesis can even be formulated. The regularity, once detected, can provide the basis for an hypothesis and for the formation of a new rule. Therefore, we need to examine models of regularity detection.

Wallace, Klahr, and Bluff (1987) developed a self-modifying system called BAIRN, which is capable of detecting consistent sequences in its own experience. The model, which has been implemented on a computer, maintains a timeline, or episodic memory record of its experience. It periodically scans the timeline, and if it detects a sequence of events that meet certain criteria of consistency and motivational significance, then a new rule corresponding to the sequence is stored in long-term memory. To qualify as the basis for a new rule, a detected sequence must have some novelty value and not simply repeat previous experience. This is consistent with the point made earlier that new rules are only learned when they add information to that provided by old rules.

However, PDP mechanisms outlined in chapter 2 provide a natural explanation for regularity detection. Recall that stimuli are represented as patterns of activation values over a large number of units, and that learning occurs by modifying the connections between these units. Multiple experiences are stored on the same set of connections by successively making small modifications to a large number of weights. This mechanism automatically stores links between events, even if there is considerable random variation in the events. The reason is that the weights representing the links between events that co-occur with some regularity will tend to be strengthened more than links between events that only co-occur at random. Such a system naturally encodes statistical regularities. There is a gradual buildup over time of links that represent environment regularities, despite the randomness that is inherent in the environment. This process could well be the original source of many new acquisitions that are important in cognitive development.

RULE MODIFICATION PROCESSES

In this section we consider ways that existing rules can be modified.

Specialization

Specialization, often called discrimination, occurs by adding new conditions to a rule. Imagine a small child who is inclined to run away whenever he or she sees a dog. This rule could be expressed as:

Rule dog: see a dog → run for shelter

With parental encouragement and experience of friendly dogs, the child gradually learns that most dogs will not harm her, and that it is only dogs that bark and growl that should be avoided. Rule dog will then be amended by adding these conditions, yielding a new rule:

Rule angry dog: see a dog, dog barks and growls → run for shelter

This is probably not the only learning that would occur. The child would probably concurrently learn a further rule such as;

Rule friendly dog: see a dog, dog wags tail → pet dog

The result is two rules, both more specialized than rule dog, that provide for more discriminating behavior. Note, however, that rule dog is not "extinguished" as traditional learning theory would have proposed, but remains in the child's repertoire. It can serve as a default rule where neither of the rules "angry dog" or "friendly dog" matches the situation. If for example the child sees a dog that neither growls and barks, nor wags its tail, but just watches her, she may well default to rule "dog" and seek shelter.

Generalization

There are several mechanisms that can produce generalization. These are removal of conditions from rules, condition substitution, "any-of" substitution, and abduction. An example of generalization by removal of conditions from rules can be given using rule "small brown dog":

Rule "small brown dog": if you see a small, brown dog → pet dog

If the family dog is small and brown, the child might first learn to pet just this dog. As the child's experience of dogs widens, it might learn to pet dogs that are small and white, or even dogs of any size and color. The result would be the rule:

Rule "dog": if you see a dog → pet dog

The rule "small brown dog" has been generalized simply by removing some of the conditions.

Generalization by condition substitution amounts to learning a new rule with conditions that are more general. For example rule "small brown dog" could be generalized by adopting instead rule "friendly dog," where the condition "small brown" is replaced by "wags tail." The condition "wags tail" is more general than "small brown" because there are more dogs that wag their tails than there are small brown dogs. Condition substitution can come about by several rules being learned in parallel. It is possible that rule "small brown dog" and rule "friendly dog" are being acquired concurrently, but because of higher exposure to the small brown dog, that rule gains strength more rapidly initially. As experience of dogs widens, rule "friendly dog" gradually overtakes rule "small brown dog."

Any-of substitution amounts to substituting "any-of" for a set of specific instances, that is, substituting a variable for a constant. For example, a child who experiences several dogs that wag their tails might first adopt the rule "this dog wags its tail," then "that dog wags its tail" and so on, but will eventually conclude that "any dog wags its tail." This principle is similar to the concept of variable substitution in artificial intelligence, where a variable is substituted for a set of specific instances.

Holland et al. (1986) specified two factors that are important in this type of subtitution. The first is the number of instances that are required; that is, how many tail-wagging dogs must be encountered before the child decides dogs in general wag their tails. Holland et al. contended that people are sensitive to the degree of variability of particular attributes in their environment. If a particular set of objects is known to be highly variable, many instances will be required before "any-of" substitution occurs. If the objects are not very variable, few instances will be required. Consider for example the generalization that swans are white, which was held to be valid by Europeans before black swans were discovered in Australia. Such a generalization seems safe because birds of a particular species usually do not vary much in color. Ravens are almost invariably black, blue-jays are invariably blue, rarely pink or green, and so on. On the other hand a generalization such as "people in town X are friendly" is more hazardous, because people are quite variable in this respect.

A second factor is that memory must be searched for counterexamples. The generalization "swans are white" is disconfirmed immediately when a bird that is positively identified as a swan is found to be anything other than white. Although people do not systematically search the environment looking for disconfirming instances, they will not adopt a generalization if they can readily retrieve a counterexample from memory.

The last type of generalization is abduction, which amounts to creating an hypothesis to account for a new or unusual situation. Imagine a child who has long been accustomed to seeing dogs walking on four legs suddenly seeing a dog stand on its hindfeet. The child might say "dat a funny dog." This might not seem a very sophisticated hypothesis, but it does summarize the child's observations quite well; dogs normally walk on all fours, so a dog that stands on its two back feet only must be a "funny" dog. A person with more domain-specific knowledge might suggest the dog was trying to reach something above its head, or might have received special training in standing on its hindfeet, but the young child's hypothesis is quite appropriate for the knowledge he or she has. Whatever hypothesis is adopted must be consistent with available information in semantic memory and must survive further experience. A child will eventually discover that there is nothing funny about dogs that stand on their hindfeet, and that all dogs may do so on occasions, and so will abandon the "funny dog" hypothesis in favor of an hypothesis about situations that cause dogs to stand on their hindfeet.

Composition

New rules may be created by combining elements of old rules. If a child has two rules that provide moderately good prediction in a particular situation, it is sometimes possible to produce a new, more precise rule by combining the best features of the existing rules. Consider the following rules:

Rfw: dog, small, wags tail → dog is friendly

Rlf: dog, large, familiar → dog is friendly

Rfw might reflect a child's experience with one or two dogs that happen to be small, and that are also friendly, perhaps because they are owned by neighbors. However, the family might own a dog which will of course be familiar and that happens to be large, which gives rise to rule Rlf. Both rules provide moderately good prediction of friendliness in dogs, but rule Rfw would provide even better prediction:

Rfw: dog, familiar, wags tail → dog is friendly

Dogs that one is familiar with are likely to be friendly, and this is especially so if they wag their tails. Thus, a rule with higher validity has been created by combining the best features of existing rules. This process will not normally entail a conscious recombination by the child. It probably occurs continuously and automatically, and there are established system-modification mechanisms by which it can occur. Holland et al. (1986) discussed the genetic algorithm by which elements of conditions or actions can be switched from one rule to another on a random basis, not unlike the crossing over of genetic material between chromosomes. The combinations so produced may be better or worse than the parent rules that gave rise to them, but because the new rules must compete with all others, those that yield more accurate predictions can be expected to grow in strength, whereas the rest will be weakened. The end result, therefore, is statistically more accurate rules. If we descend to the more fine-grained level of analysis based on PDP mechanisms, it becomes apparent that the refinement of new rules in this way may well occur automatically. This is because connections between conditions and actions that regularly co-occur will tend to be strengthened more than those between events that do not regularly co-occur, leading to automatic selection of combinations that optimize prediction of the environment.

Both Case (1985) and Fischer (1980) postulated that composition rules are important in the transition from one cognitive level to another. Case (1985) based his primary transition mechanism on a process known as hierarchical integration, whereas Fischer (1980) based it on intercoordination. Both entail the idea that separate processes that are relevant to a particular situation become combined into a single, more powerful, rule. Siegler (1981) expressed the same kind of idea in the form of hierarchies of increasingly powerful rules, and Halford and Wilson (1980) defined several levels of representational processes such that each level integrates the lower levels.

These integrative mechanisms that have been used to explain the transition from lower to higher cognitive levels can almost certainly be explained in terms of the composition of rules. We can illustrate how more powerful rules can be created through composition using Siegler's (1981) rules for understanding the balance scale. Some of the performances by younger children are based on rules that take into account weights only. For example, they might use the rule, weight on left > weight on right → left side goes down.

Later they learn to take into account distance, which can be done by incorporating new conditions in the rules. For example, weight on left > weight on right, distances equal → left side goes down.

The second rule is more accurate and represents a higher level of conceptual development. It can be achieved by adding a new condition, which is essentially a composition mechanism. The acquisition of rules for the balance scale is examined in more detail in chapter 9.

The new rule would of course be subject to the usual tests and would grow in strength to the extent that it yielded superior predictions to its competitors. It could also undergo refinement by the usual mechanisms such as specialization (addition of further conditions where necessary) and generalization (elimination of unnecessary conditions). An important point however is that acquisition of these rules, which have often been taken to reflect transition to a new stage of cognitive development, can occur through normal learning mechanisms that are of general validity.

TRANSFER OF LEARNING

Transfer depends on two main types of processes: similarity and analogy. Transfer based on stimulus similarity was a major concern of traditional learning theory, and there is a review in the classic work of Osgood (1953). The principle is that transfer depends on stimulus similarity: The degree to which a learned association is transferred to a new situation depends on the similarity of the new stimulus to that involved in the original learning. Whether transfer is positive and beneficial, or negative and detrimental, depends on response similarity also. For example, negative transfer occurs if the new stimulus is similar to the old, but the required response is different from the old one.

The same principle applies to condition–action rules, because the likelihood of a rule being activated in a different situation depends on whether the new stimuli match the conditions in the rule. However, condition–action rules have discrete conditions, which makes it difficult to model the effect of similarity. PDP models are much better equipped to predict the effects of transfer where the new situation resembles, but is not completely the same as, the old. This is because stimuli are represented not as discrete units, but as vectors of activation values, and degree of similarity can be modeled by similarity between vectors.

In higher level cognitive processes, transfer often depends on availability of an appropriate strategy. As work to be discussed in chapter 5 has shown, strategies can be transferred to new situations that are superficially very different from the old. The main reason for this is the way rules that strategies comprise are encoded. Rules are usually based on features that remain invariant across situations. Consider, for example, a simple addition algorithm. It usually contains rules such as "add the numbers in the right column." The algorithm applies to any sum that is set out appropriately in columns, because all such sums contain a right column. The numbers that comprise the sum might vary over a wide range, but the column structure remains constant, so that the cues on which the strategy depends also remain constant. Therefore transfer based on strategies is a special case of transfer based on stimulus similarity.

Transfer based on analogies is considered extensively in chapter 5, but the important point to note here is that analogical transfer breaks this dependence on stimulus similarity. Analogies permit transfer across tasks that have common structural properties, but that may differ radically in the stimulus attributes they contain. On the other hand, the structure-mapping processes entailed in analogies can impose high processing loads, as we saw in chapter 3, and this can place restrictions on analogical transfer in certain circumstances.

CONSTRAINTS AND LEARNING

It has been argued by Keil (1981, 1990) that the learning and induction processes that underlie cognitive development require constraints that direct them along certain lines, otherwise the task of acquiring appropriate representations of the environment would be impossible. A series of papers summarizing this area of theory and associated empirical work appeared in a recent issue of *Cognitive Science* (Keil, 1990). The main grounds for the argument are that experience by itself is not adequate to lead us to the right inductions. Any experience can give rise to an unlimited number of inductions, and some constraints are necessary to limit the possible inductions so as to make the task tractable.

Some of the constraints are innate, whereas others are acquired and represent an effect of prior learning and conceptualization. For example, it is possible that we have an innate orientation to information about causes, and this facilitates learning about causal effects. Brown (1990) presented evidence that children learn causal relations about tools more readily than they learn equivalent information about colors. In another domain, Gelman and Greeno (1989) assumed implicit knowledge of counting principles that facilitate acquisition of counting. It has also been suggested by Newport (1990) that processing capacity limitations help direct attention to language. This idea is supported by Elman (1991), who found that a PDP simulation of acquisition of sequential constraints in language was more efficient if restrictions were placed on the amount of information being processed. Acquired constraints have been proposed in the form of theories by Carey (1985). The idea is that we need theories of the world to choose between the unlimited number of inductions that are possible in a particular situation.

The theoretical argument for the operation of constraints is very persuasive, in that a reasonably deep consideration of the induction problem quickly leads to the conclusion that it requires the guidance of constraints in order to succeed. The constraints operate in subtle, often pervasive ways, that have been difficult to bring under empirical scrutiny. Nevertheless, a body of interesting evidence has accumulated. It would be a reasonable conclusion that the learning principles outlined earlier need to be supplemented by constraints that reduce the complexity of the induction process.

In terms of the picture of learning processes that is being built up, constraints are likely to have three main kinds of effects. The first is that they direct attention to appropriate features of experience; for example, the fact that movement, or the connection between one object another (such as a string), is more likely to affect causal relations than, say, color. Second, constraints affect the way experience is encoded. As Spelke (1990) suggested, we have an innate tendency to organize experience into intact units or "things." Third, constraints affect our abductions, or the hypotheses we create on the basis of our inductions. Given that there is an unlimited number of ways of accounting for a particular experience, we will choose a way that accords with our "theories" of the world. The word "theory" was used by Carey (1985) by analogy with the theories of scientists, but the mental models that influence cognitive development are probably less explicit and less accessible to consciousness than scientific theories. Nevertheless, previously learned principles, implicit and imprecise though they may be, provide a necessary constraint on children's abductions.

STRATEGY SELECTION AND DEVELOPMENT

Strategy-selection mechanisms can be divided into two kinds, metacognitive and associative. With metacognitive mechanisms the participant makes strategy choices based on an understanding of the problem. With associative selection, the participant has a set of possible strategies, each of which is associated with a particular confidence level that the task can be successfully performed.

Associative Strategy Development

We begin by considering the associative mechanisms described by Siegler (1989a), Siegler and Jenkins (1989), and Siegler and Shrager (1984). This model has been applied to arithmetic, spelling, word identification in reading, and balance scale tasks. We illustrate its application to problems where children are asked to add small numbers, such as 3 + 3. A basic tenet, which has been well substantiated (Siegler, 1987), and is consistent with arguments we present in later chapters, is that people use more than one strategy for a task. The strategies are normally tried serially; if the first one fails, the second is tried, then the third, and so on.

If given a problem such as "3 + 2 = ?" the child first tries to retrieve the answer from memory. There is a distribution of answers that are associated with this problem. According to data provided by Siegler and Shrager (1984), the answer 2 might be associated with 3 + 2 with probability .09, answers 3 and 4 each with probability .11, answer 5 with probability .55, 6 with probability .07, and other answers collectively with probability .07. The correct answer is the most probable one, but it is not the only answer that can be retrieved. An interesting feature of the model is that the better the answer is known, the more peaked the distribution of associations will be; that is, the more probable the dominant, correct answer relative to the others.

When an answer is retrieved, its associative strength is compared with a confidence criterion. If it is above the criterion, the answer is given, otherwise the search of memory continues until the search-length criterion is reached. If no answer exceeds the confidence criterion before the search-length criterion is reached, the child switches to a new strategy. The next strategy tried is likely to be the "elaborated representation." This entails using fingers or images to represent the numbers, thereby adding further associations that might strengthen the association between problem and answer. This strategy is also subject to the confidence and search-length criteria. If it again fails, the child switches to a new strategy, which entails actually counting fingers to determine the answer.

This model has some interesting features that will be found relevant to strategy-selection mechanisms in other situations. First, metacognitive knowledge plays little if any role. There is no appeal to the child's understanding of number or of the counting process. The selection of strategies is based on the child's confidence that the strategy will yield the answer. Memory retrieval is tried first because, in that child's experience, it has a good record of providing answers to addition problems quickly and reasonably reliably. When it fails, the strategy with the next best record is tried, then the next best, and so on. The selection is based on the child's stored knowledge about how good the answer provided by the strategy is. If the strategy can be relied on to provide a good answer, it is retained, otherwise it is replaced.

Metacognitive Selection Mechanisms

This class of models, by contrast with associative models, are based on understanding of, or declarative knowledge about, the task. There are two main types that concern us here, those based on planning nets, and those based on domain-general processes or "weak" methods.

Planning net models have been developed by VanLehn and Brown (1980) in the domain of subtraction, by Greeno, Riley, and Gelman (1984), in the domain of counting, and by Greeno and Johnson (1985), in the domain of arithmetic word problems. In all these models, declarative knowledge is used to construct strategies applicable to particular task contexts. The idea is that people do not have strategies ready-made for every situation but that they devise strategies based on their knowledge of the relevant concept and the demands of the task.

The model of VanLehn and Brown (1980) is based on planning nets, which are directed graphs, the nodes of which represent plans for strategies, and the links of which represent inferences concerning how well each proposed strategy conforms to declarative knowledge. VanLehn and Brown expounded the planning net concept by reference to a base-1 subtraction task using Dienes blocks. For example, if the task was $8 - 5 = 3$, there would be 8 blocks on the top mat and 5 on the bottom mat. Each time a block is removed from the bottom mat, a block is also removed from the top mat. When the bottom mat is empty, the answer is the number of blocks on the top mat. The declarative knowledge required for this task is equivalent to the following points:

1. When the bottom mat is empty, the answer is the number of objects on the top mat.
2. The number of objects removed from the top mat must equal the number removed from the bottom mat.
3. A prerequisite for picking up a block is that the hand must be empty.
4. Putting down a block results in the hand being empty again.

The strategy is constructed from this knowledge, using planning heuristics, which are rules that constrain strategies to be consistent with declarative knowledge. To illustrate how planning would proceed, first the goal to empty the bottom mat is activated, then a loop is implemented to achieve this goal (an heuristic known as "hill climbing"). The loop entails testing to see if the mat is empty, and if it is not, setting the goal to remove objects from it. Then retest and iterate this procedure until the goal of an empty mat is satisfied. The goal of removing objects from the mat in turn causes the primitive action of picking up objects from the mat to be adopted. However, the adoption of this action entails Constraint 2 above, that the number of objects removed from the mat must be equal. This in turn activates the action of removing from the top mat. Thus each proposed strategy is checked against the relevant declarative knowledge and adjusted if it does not fit. In this way a strategy is devised that is consistent with the participant's knowledge of the task.

The concept is a sophisticated and powerful one. Van Lehn and Brown (1980) showed how a model of the planning process can provide much more fundamental insights into the nature of a task or concept than models based on "surface structure" or the actual procedures used. The reason is that procedures may vary considerably even though the essential concept remains the same. The procedural differences are often trivial or even irrelevant, with the result that models of specific processes may fail to capture the essence of a task. It may be preferable to adopt a model based on the underlying logic of the task. Planning-net models enable this to be done, but I would claim it is also one of the advantges of structure-mapping models, a point that I develop in detail in numerous places throughout this book.

The model of Greeno et al. (1984) is based on essentially the same philosophy as the planning net models but differs in the way it is implemented. Its starting point was the observation by Gelman and Gallistel (1978) that young children's efforts at counting, although prone to error, nevertheless reflected an implicit knowledge of the logic of counting. For example, if they counted a set of objects in a straight line beginning with the first one, then were asked to count again making the second object the "one," or even the "two," "three," and so on, they could still succeed better than chance. Since these are unconventional counting procedures, it is unlikely that they would have been learned by rote as a skill. The fact that young children were able to perform correctly indicates they understood something about the logic of counting and could devise a strategy to fit the constraints imposed.

To model this achievement Greeno et al. postulated three kinds of competence: conceptual, procedural, and utilizational. They are defined relative to one another, and the designation of any particular item of knowledge as one type of competence or the other might vary depending on how the global task is defined.

Conceptual competence is defined as action schemata that can be used in planning. The action schemata have a degree of general validity; that is, they are not schemas for specific actions but really represent understanding of the logic of a class of actions. This understanding can be applied to a variety of different actions, depending on the task demands. An example is action schema 11 (Greeno et al., 1984, p. 113), called KEEP-EQUAL-INCREASE. Its purpose is to ensure that people progress through a set of objects to be counted, and through the list of numbers 1, 2, 3 . . . n, at the same rate, so that they progress to a new number when and only when they progress to a new object in the set. The prerequisite is that the number of objects already counted must equal the numbers used; for example, if we have so far counted three objects, we must have progressed to number 3. The postrequisite is that this situation must be maintained after the process is completed. The consequence of the schema is that both the set of objects and the set of numbers must be incremented by one in each counting step; for example, as you progress to the fourth object to be counted, you also progress to the fourth number.

Procedural competence is like the planning heuristics in the model of Van-Lehn and Brown (1980). It is knowledge about how to assemble action schemata into a strategy. Since every action schema has consequences and prerequisites specified, selection of schemata can be done by means-end analysis. That is, an action schema is chosen whose consequences match the current goal. Then another action schema is chosen whose consequences match the prerequisites of the first schema, and so on.

Utilizational competence comprises ability to combine conceptual and utilizational competence with information about the task setting. A given set of action schemata could generate many different action sequences, but a sequence must be chosen that is appropriate to the specific demands of the task. Ability to do this is utilizational competence.

Greeno et al. provided specifications for a simulation model that accounts for young children's ability to count, given a variety of situational constraints. It demonstrates a plausible mechanism by which basic knowledge of number can be translated, not just into one counting strategy, but into a variety of strategies that can be adapted to the task.

Nevertheless the model raises the issue of just what kind of knowledge about number and counting children have. Gelman and Gallistel (1978) postulated that young children understand five principles of counting: cardinality, that is, the last number reached is the cardinal value of the set; one-to-one correspondence, that is, every object must be assigned a unique number, and each number used must be assigned to one and only one object; indifference to object order, that is, it makes no difference in what order objects in a set are counted; stable order of numerals, that is, the counting numerals must be used in their standard sequence; abstraction, that is, the objects to be counted need not be of the same kind.

The way conceptual competence is formulated in the Greeno et al. (1984) model implies that these principles are understood in a form that is equivalent to logical rules of general validity. Set theoretic notation is used in the formal specification of the schemata and, although being careful of course not to confuse the terms of the model with the phenomena they are intended to describe, it is still true that understanding of logical, generally valid, principles is attributed to the children.

This model appears capable of explaining the development of counting knowledge, but if the planning-nets approach is to be applied more widely to acquisition of cognitive skills, it seems desirable that a way be found to use it with mental models that are not based on universally valid logical rules. The history of cognitive psychology has shown, however, that in general logic does not make a good model for human cognitive processes. For example, prototypes make a better model of natural categories than does a set-theoretic definition of categories (Rosch, 1978), whereas heuristics such as availability and representativeness more faithfully capture the essence of human reasoning than does the predicate calculus (Kahneman & Tversky, 1973; Tversky & Kahneman, 1973). Holland et al. (1986) showed that pragmatic rules make a better model of the way people understand the world than would a purely syntactic theory. Therefore, we need a more pragmatic theory of mental models to constrain the strategy-acquisition processes in cognitive development.

Understanding Based on Specific Experience of Counting

I would like to explore briefly the possibility that acquisition of counting skills might be based on acquired knowledge. It is not that the idea of innate quantification skills is implausible. However, it would be more in keeping with a number of other models if at least some aspects of counting were constrained by acquired knowledge that might supplement innate knowledge of numerosity.

Understanding of elementary counting might be based on specific experience of counting, as shown in Fig. 4.2. Suppose a child has learned to assign numbers to objects, so there is one and only one object for each number, and the numbers are assigned in the correct order. The child has not learned counting principles but simply a skill of counting in a conventional way. Some understanding might emerge as a by-product of skill acquisition. For example, the child might know, probably implicitly, that in counting one moves from one object to the next. The child also knows that one moves from one numeral to the next, and recognizes that the relations between numerals correspond to the relations between objects. Recognizing this correspondence is similar to analogical reasoning, as Fig. 4.2 shows. If we regard the objects as the base and the numerals as the target, then counting amounts to mapping numerals into objects, just as analogy entails mapping base into target. This is a relational mapping, and it is validated by the fact that the relation "next" between objects corresponds to the relation "next" between numerals. In one type of constrained count, the second (third, fourth, etc.) object in the array is counted first. This change might be handled by a simple transformation of the mental model acquired in experience of standard counts. In the constrained count, the second (third, fourth) object is mapped into the numeral 1, then the last numeral is mapped to the first object in the array. The basic mental model has not changed. The point of this is to illustrate that the concept of elementary counting can be represented by a specific experience, and it has the structure of a series of spoken numerals connected by a succession relation. This suggestion in no way replaces the planning-nets model of Greeno et al. (1984). It should be seen as a suggestion for increasing the generality of the approach by providing alternative sources of mental models.

How does this mental model of understanding differ from that of Greeno et al. (1984)? An important difference is that the standard count structure mapping could be learned initially in a highly specific form. It need not entail knowledge of generally valid, logical principles of counting. Even a specific experience of counting can serve as a model of another counting task and can be applied to it by analogical mapping. It can be transferred to the constrained counting task with the addition of a simple transformation rule. According to this approach, understanding emerges from previously learned

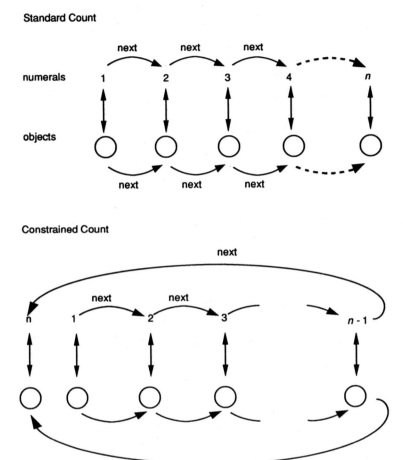

FIG. 4.2. Possible representations for standard and constrained counting.

skill. This is consistent with the skill acquisition model of Anderson (1987), to which we turn next.

Skill Acquisition Based on Domain-General Knowledge

A very carefully researched computational model of skill acquisition has been presented by Anderson (1987), based on the general cognition model known as ACT* (Anderson, 1983). Skill acquisition, according to this model, begins with declarative knowledge and uses domain-general or "weak" methods, such as analogical reasoning, means–end analysis, hill climbing, or pure forward search to build procedures for performing the task. Once learned, the procedures are compiled into production rules that can operate automatically, without activating the declarative knowledge that was used in their development. This greatly reduces the demand on resources. The load can be further reduced by a process that Anderson calls composition, in which a number of production rules are combined into a single rule. This process is similar to chunking. Once production rules are constructed, they are strengthened by associative learning mechanisms.

The declarative knowledge can take the form of instructions, properties of objects, or examples of previously experienced problem-solving procedures, which can be used as templates. Templates are used by analogical reasoning, with transformations and adjustments. Analogies sometimes lead to errors, so the analogous procedures are corrected to remove the errors.

Transfer of procedures learned in this way depends on similarity. Production rules formed by this model will transfer to new situations in which the stimuli match the condition side of the productions. It is therefore a type of "identical elements" transfer process. Transfer to situations that do not match existing productions (that do not share identical elements with the original learning situation) requires new productions to be built.

As far as I am aware this model has not been used explicitly to simulate acquisition of cognitive developmental concepts. However, a model by Halford, Smith, Maybery, Stewart, and Dickson (1991) that simulates acquisition of transitive inference strategies has quite a lot in common with Anderson's skill-acquisition theory. Therefore I summarize the model of Halford et al. in the next section.

A Simulation Model of Strategy Development

This model (Halford et al., 1991, 1992) was designed to account for the way children develop basic reasoning skills by practice within a domain, using their world knowledge. Transitivity and the closely related task of constructing ordered sets were chosen as the focus of the study because they are developmentally important landmarks, there is a large high-quality data base, and they are important to practical skills such as ordering and quantification.

Consider the transitive inference problem:

John is happier than Bill.

Tom is happier than John.

Who is happiest?

As suggested in chapter 1, the process of making the transitive inference entails integrating the premises into a single ordered set, Tom, John, Bill. The inference, Tom is happier than Bill is then easily made from the ordered set. Therefore, integrating the premises into an ordered set should be at the core of the strategy that a child develops.

The model begins with domain-general knowledge, and develops the strategies it needs for a particular domain through experience with that domain. The development of the strategies is constrained by the concept of the task. In this respect the model resembles the planning-net model of Greeno, Riley, and Gelman (1984), which showed how counting strategies were constrained by a concept of number. In our model, strategy development is constrained by a concept of order. It is therefore inherent in the model that acquisition of transitive inference strategies is based on an understanding of the task, as represented in the concept of an ordered set that a child is postulated to have. However, not all strategy development is based explicitly on understanding, and associative strategy development mechanisms are incorporated through the strengthening and weakening of strategies according to their success.

It is assumed that in order to have a psychologically realistic concept of order, a child must know (a) at least one relation, such as greater than, happier than, and so on, (b) that each element occurs once and only once, (c) that end elements have the same relation to all other elements; for example, in an ordered set {a, b, c, d}, a has the same relation to all of b, c, d, (d) that the position of an element that is not at the end is defined by its relation to elements on each side of it; for example, $b < a$, $b > c$, and (e) that the same relation exists between all pairs (this effectively provides the transitivity property of the concept of an ordered set).

All these properties can be instantiated in any ordered set of at least three elements. This has important implications, because it means that a child who knows an ordered set of at least three elements has a basis for a concept of order. A concrete instance of an ordered set can be used by analogical reasoning.

Children encounter plenty of concrete instances of ordered sets. Children of different sizes can form an ordered set, as can stackable blocks or other toys that vary in size. The three bears also form a nice ordered set of three elements; daddy, mommy, and baby bear are ordered for size and a number of other attributes. Therefore, children have plenty of experiences that provide them with the basis for a concept of order.

A child who had no strategy for transitive inference could use a known ordered set, such as three different-sized blocks, as an analog to solve the current example problem, as shown in Fig. 4.3. Tom is mapped into the largest block, John into the middle block, and Bill into the smallest. The relation "happier than" then consistently corresponds to "larger than."

A specific case of an ordered set can therefore provide a template for the correct ordering of the elements in a transitive inference task, through analogical reasoning. Participants who have no transitive inference strategies

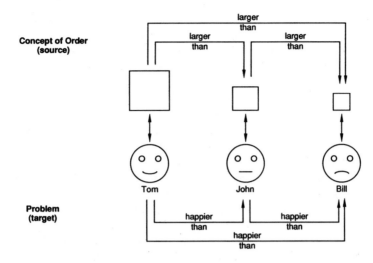

FIG. 4.3. Mental model of ordered set mapped into ordering task.

can use a concrete analog as a criterion for the development of strategies. Once the strategies exist, there is no longer any need for analogical reasoning.

Play experience with concrete instances of ordered sets provides children with the declarative knowledge they require to guide their development of transitive inference strategies. However, they also need procedural knowledge. This is mainly in the form of operators, together with their initial and final states. An example of an operator that is useful in constructing ordered sets is APPEND, which is illustrated in Fig. 4.4.

For example, given that elements ab are already in order, when the premise $b > c$ is presented, it is useful to append c onto ab, yielding abc. Physical actions, or the motor equivalent of the append operator, can be learned by play experiences. That is, children can learn that if you have a row of elements, you can add another element to the row, so it becomes the end element. Such actions form the building blocks of strategies for ordering ob-

Constructed Order	Premise	Action
a b	b > c	append
a b c		

FIG. 4.4. Append operator.

jects. In the Halford et al. (1991, 1992) model they are assumed to have been learned and stored in memory, and to be available for use by means–end analysis. That is, if the initial state and the desired final state are known, an appropriate operator can be selected by searching memory.

The model is implemented as a self-modifying production system written in PRISM II (Ohlsson & Langley, 1986). When it begins to run it has only domain-general productions that perform such actions as setting and removing goals, storing and retrieving information, comparing elements to find matches, reading premises and giving feedback. It builds productions specific to transitive inference through experience with the task. I will give an example using a sample problem as shown in Fig. 4.5. Once built, the productions construct an ordered set in working memory consistent with the mechanisms demonstrated by Foos, Smith, Sabol, and Mynatt (1976).

The first premise is $a > b$. The model checks whether there is an ordered string already in working memory, finds there is not, and adds the string ab to working memory. This can be done because the model is set up with

Constructed Order	Premise	Action
- - -	$a > b$	insert in WM
$a\,b$	$b > c$	append
$a\,b\,c$		

FIG. 4.5. Sequence of steps in N-term series task.

domain-general productions for storing information in working memory. When the premise $b > c$ is presented there is no production that has a string in working memory plus a premise, in its condition side, because the model is not equipped initially with productions for dealing with transitive inference.

This puts the model into a modification phase. First it searches for a concept appropriate to its present goal, which is ORDER OBJECTS. This causes the concept of order to be retrieved from memory. Analogical reasoning is used to determine the correct order, by mapping the premises $a > b$ and $b > c$ into an ordered set retrieved from memory, as shown in Fig. 4.6. It is recognized that the ordering abc would be consistent with the concept of order. Means-end analysis is then used to select an operator that will produce the order abc. Then a new production is built that includes the APPEND operator, as shown in Fig. 4.7. This production will match any state in which working memory contains one or more objects in a string, and the first object in the premise matches the last object in the string. On the action side, the APPEND operator will place the second object in the premise on the end of the string.

When a subsequent problem occurs that requires this production it will fire, without the effortful process of having to build it. Thus, strategies, which in this model consist of productions, can operate in relatively automatic fashion once they are acquired. Understanding is not required for problems of a type that the model has already learned to solve.

When a correct solution is obtained, positive feedback increases the strength of the productions involved in the solution. Negative feedback results in weakened productions. Productions that lead to errors are gradually weakened below threshold and cease to fire. This clears the way for construction of new productions that avoid the errors.

When the model first builds productions, some of them do lead to errors. Some of these errors occur because of the processing load imposed by system mappings, that is, mapping both premises into an analog, as in Fig. 4.3 and 4.6. This can result in a tendency to focus on the most recent premise, ignoring the implications of earlier premises. We call this the relational strategy, and it is illustrated in Fig. 4.8, using a problem form studied by Foos et al. (1976) and in our own laboratory.

The first premise, $c > d$ results in the string cd being stored in working memory. The next premise, $a > b$ contains no element that matches any element in cd. If the model is operating at a low level of cognitive effort, either because of low arousal, competition for resources, or inadequate processing capacity, then it pays attention only to the most recent premise and performs a relational mapping. That is, it maps $a > b$ into the analog of an ordered set, ignoring $c > d$. Therefore the production that is built simply inserts ab after cd, yielding the order cdab, without recognizing that the order of the pairs is indeterminate. When $b > c$ is presented, attention is

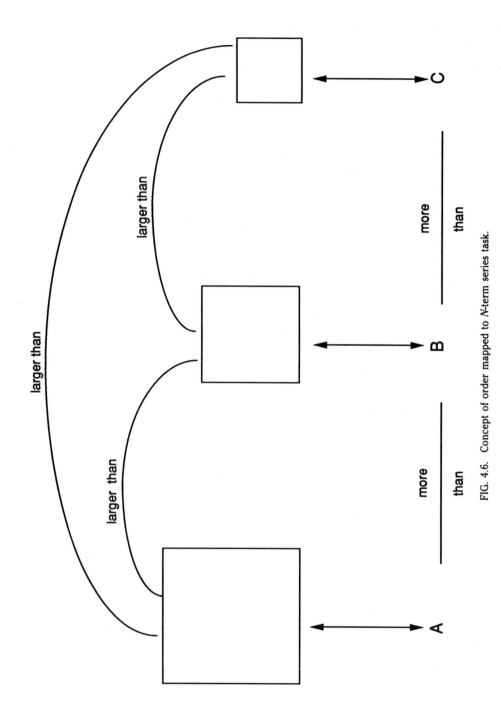

FIG. 4.6. Concept of order mapped to *N*-term series task.

Production built:

(((constructed order (<relation> <Obj *a*. . . . . . Obj *n* >))

(new premise   <Obj 1> <relation> <Obj 2>)

(match Obj 1 Obj *n*)

───────────▶

(add-to WM (perform APPEND <Obj *n* > <Obj 2>)))

Instantiation:

working-memory contents	premise	new working-memory contents
a b	*b > c*	*a b c*

FIG. 4.7. Production built by model.

again paid only to the most recent premise, resulting in a production that simply switches *b* to the front of the list, yielding the order *bcda*. Data from Foos et al.'s (1976) study, and from our own laboratory, show that this is a common error for children and for adults under high processing load.

This error leads to negative feedback, which weakens the productions involved in the incorrect solution, clearing the way for new productions to be built. The negative feedback also increases effort, which causes the most recent premise to be integrated with previous premises when a new production is being built. This leads to a production based on system mapping, which is shown in the lower half of Fig. 4.8.

Now when $a > b$ is appended to the string, a marker is inserted to indicate that the order of the pairs is indeterminate. Then when $b > c$ is presented, a production is built that switches *ab* to the front of the string, yielding *abcd*. Correct feedback strengthens this production.

The model makes these errors when it first builds strategies, but then builds new productions that provide correct solutions to problems with all permutations of premises. It also recognizes when a problem is unsolvable, because it codes indeterminacies in the ordered set in working memory.

	constructed order	premise	action
Relational Strategy	- - -	$c > d$	insert in WM
	$c\,d$	$a > b$	concatenate
	$c\,d\,a\,b$	$b > c$	delete - insert
	$b\,c\,d\,a$		
System Strategy	- - -	$c\,d$	insert in WM
	$c\,d$	$a > b$	concat indet
	$(c\,d)\wedge(a\,b)$	$b > c$	switch
	$a\,b\,c\,d$		

$\wedge$ is indeterminacy marker

FIG. 4.8.   Relational and system level strategies.

Errors can result from both processing and memory storage difficulties. The first has the consequence illustrated earlier. It occurs because mapping two premises into an ordered set imposes a high processing load, as discussed in chapter 3. This means that young children have particular difficulty considering two premises jointly, even when short-term retention problems are eliminated by memory aids (Halford, 1984; Halford & Kelly, 1984). There is, therefore, a processing deficit because the load imposed by two premises causes children, and to a lesser extent adults, to consider only the most recent premise in default, which causes the kinds of errors we have seen.

The second source of errors is forgetting part of the string. The most common error is to lose the indeterminacy marker, as Foos et al. (1976) showed. Thus, even adults who have already developed appropriate strategies make errors sometimes due to excessive short-term memory load. Children are more prone to lose information from short-term memory in this way, and this is another parameter that varies with age.

Summary of the Model

The model begins with domain-general knowledge and, by building productions, develops its own strategies for a specific domain, in this case transitive inference and ordering tasks. Previous, concrete experience is used to guide the development of strategies, by analogical reasoning. The concept of order is based on knowledge that any child could be expected to acquire. Procedural knowledge is utilized by means–end analysis.

The model blends metacognitive strategy development processes, based on understanding of the concept of order, with associative strategy development mechanisms, based on strengthening and weakening of productions. However, understanding is not required for routine application of strategies.

The model reproduces the most common errors on a selection of problem forms that includes all permutations of premises. It recognizes indeterminate problems in a way that follows naturally from its understanding of the concept of order. The model corrects its own errors by building more adequate strategies.

The model provides a "sufficiency test" for a theory that holds that reasoning skills can be acquired by an active construction process that works on knowledge gained in everyday experience. The acquisition process utilizes principles and processes that have been validated in other contexts. The same principles apply to children and adults, who differ only in a number of efficiency parameters.

The model implies that strategies are part of what develops, but these strategies are built on domain-general and domain-specific knowledge acquired through everyday experience. Furthermore the construction of strategies is modulated by information processing and memory storage parameters.

This model is similar in a number of ways to Anderson's (1987) skill-acquisition model. It uses domain-general methods, analogical reasoning and means-end analysis to build strategies based on production rules. These domain-general methods operate on domain-specific knowledge acquired through previous experience. Both models are therefore consistent with Siegler's (1989a) argument that cognitive development depends on an interaction of domain-general and domain-specific knowledge. In the case of the Halford et al. (1991, 1992) model, this is knowledge about ordered sets of objects, although the model is not restricted in principle to this domain. Both models use associative learning mechanisms to adjust the strength of strategies and skills once they are acquired.

There are also some differences. Analogies are used in a slightly different way in the Halford et al. model, because the ordered set is used as a template for the output of a strategy, whereas in Anderson's model, analogical reasoning is used to model a new procedure on a previously experienced procedure. Also, the Halford et al. model, in its present form, does not have the composition processes for chunking sets of productions into a single production. Perhaps the most important difference, however, is that in the Halford et al. model, development of strategies is constrained by some understanding of the task, whereas in Anderson's model understanding emerges as a by-product of skill acquisition, after the skill has been acquired. Understanding in the Halford et al. model takes the form of knowledge based on specific, concrete experiences, but there is still a sense in which the child has a concept of the task, whereas this does not appear to be the case in Anderson's model. Glaser (1990) distinguished models of proceduralized skill acquisition, such as Anderson's, from self-regulatory skill-acquisition models, of which he reviewed several examples. The latter models assume that people have some understanding of the task and can use it to monitor their performance, and devise appropriate corrections. The Halford et al. model is closer to Glaser's self-regulating models than to proceduralized skill-acquisition models. There is really no conflict here, because both models can be applicable in different domains. The amount of understanding required for a skill can vary from one situation to another, and this will influence the degree of self-regulation that is likely to occur.

SUMMARY AND CONCLUSIONS

Given that world knowledge is important both to understanding and to cognitive development generally, it is essential to explore basic learning mechanisms that can account for acquisition of knowledge. The work of Rescorla on classical conditioning indicates that it should now be seen as a means by which representations of relations between events in the world are acquired. It is suggested, however, that these representations are implicit, in the sense that they are probably not conscious or accessible to manipulation by other cognitive processes. The name *contingency* is given to this kind of implicit representation.

Declarative rules are representations that are more cognitively accessible, and are more likely to be recognized consciously. They can be learned by principles very similar to those that govern acquisition of contingencies. Declarative rules are strengthened by confirmation, in contrast to procedural rules, which are strengthened by a satisfying state of affairs (reinforcement). Evidence is reviewed from a number of basic learning paradigms, including secondary reinforcement, avoidance learning, punishment, and extinction, that even infrahuman animals learn contingencies, or declarative rules, that represent relations between events in the world. Furthermore both humans and infrahuman animals are sensitive to the value of cues as predictors of environmental events. Some developmental learning data is shown to be consistent with this formulation. It suggests that the learning principles that underlie cognitive development are of general validity, and apply in many other contexts as well.

Rules that are redundant, in the sense that the events they predict are already predicted by other rules, tend not to be learned, consistent with the principle of blocking. Learning occurs where relations between events are discrepant from, or disconfirm, existing rules.

Rules can be mutually supportive or inhibitory, which accounts for one component of the effect of prior knowledge on learning. If prior knowledge includes rules that support the rules to be learned, it will be facilitative. If prior knowledge is inconsistent with new information, as occurs if misconceptions have been learned, it will inhibit new acquisitions. Prior knowledge can also lead to focussed sampling, which influences the information attended to.

Acquisition of new rules is often based on detection of regularities in the environment, which may occur very naturally and automatically. PDP models of the microstructure of cognition suggest that regularity detection is a basic emergent property of the way cognitive processes function.

Development of new rules depends on specialization or discrimination, generalization, any-of substitution, abduction, and composition, all of which have been modeled in detail by contemporary learning theories. These theories appear capable in principle of accounting for the transition mechanisms proposed by cognitive developmental theories, which appear to rely primarily on composition.

Transfer of learning depends on similarity or analogy. Strategies can mediate efficient transfer if the rules they comprise are based on stimuli that are invariant across the domain of application of the strategy. Analogy mediates transfer based on structural, rather than item, similarity but can impose high processing loads in some cases.

Induction of rules from experience requires constraints to limit the number of possible inductions. Any set of experiences is consistent with an indefinitely large set of inductions, and appropriate selections cannot be made on the basis of experience alone. There is evidence of both innate and acquired constraints that increase sensitivity to particular kinds of information and thereby facilitate learning.

The development of strategies, skills, and procedural knowledge can be based on either associative processes, metacognitive processes, or both. The model of Siegler and his collaborators emphasized associative processes, whereas the planning-net models of VanLehn and Brown, or Greeno, Riley, and Gelman, are metacognitive, and propose that strategy acquisition guided by a concept of the task. The skill acquisition model of Anderson, based on the ACT* theory, is based on the domain-general methods of analogy, means–end analysis, hill climbing, and pure forward search, that operate on declarative knowledge to construct cognitive skills, modeled as production rules.

A theory of strategy development in transitive inference by Halford et al. is similar to the model of Anderson's, but it emphasizes the guiding role of task understanding, whereas in Anderon's model understanding tends to be a by-product of skill acquisition. Understanding can be based on knowledge acquired through experience, such as play. However, once strategies are developed, they can be applied to familiar situations without activating the knowledge and understanding used in their development. This model implies that strategies are part of what develops, but that strategies are built on domain-general abilities, some of which may be innate, and on domain-specific knowledge acquired through experience. Also, the construction of strategies is modulated by information processing and memory-storage factors.

5

ANALOGIES AND
STRUCTURE-MAPPING PROCESSES

It has long been recognized that analogies are of fundamental importance to human cognition (Polya, 1971; Spearman, 1923). There have also been a number of attempts to incorporate analogies into artificial intelligence (Burstein, 1983; Evans, 1968; Winston, 1982). In chapter 1, I pointed out that mental models can be based on analogies. In chapter 2, an analogy was compared with a representation, on the basis that the former is a mapping from one representation to another, whereas the latter is a mapping from representation to the environment. In this chapter I examine the role of analogies in cognitive development.

THEORY OF ANALOGY

As Gentner (1983) showed, an analogy can be defined as a mapping from one structure, the base or source, to another, the target. Normally the source is the part that is already known, whereas the target is the part that has to be inferred or discovered. A simple example is shown in Fig. 5.1A. The source comprises two elements, cat and kitten, and the relation "parent of" between them. The target comprises the elements horse and foal, with the same relation between them. There is a mapping from source to target such that cat is mapped into horse, and kitten into foal, and the relation between cat and kitten then corresponds to the relation between horse and foal.

A Complete Structure

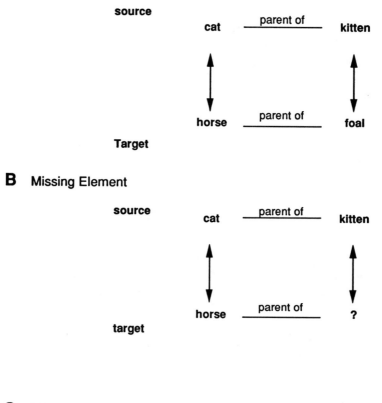

B Missing Element

C Missing Relation

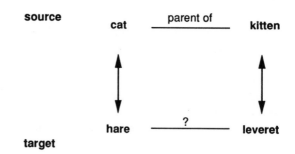

FIG. 5.1. Five types of analogical-reasoning problem.

D Missing Element and Relation

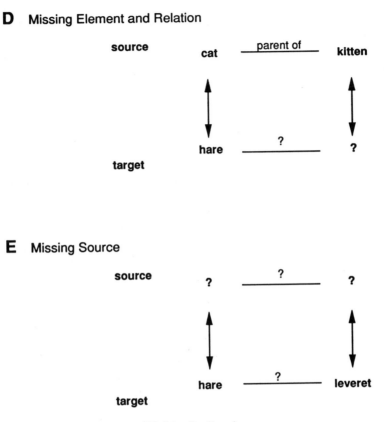

E Missing Source

FIG 5.1. Continued.

Attributes, Relations, and Systematicity

As Gentner (1983) pointed out, the goodness of an analogy depends on correspondence between relations, rather than on source and target nodes having similar attributes. The analogy in Fig. 5.1A is good because the "parent
of" relation holds between source and target nodes, but the nodes need not
have similar attributes.[1]

The analogy does not imply that a horse is similar to a cat, or that a
foal is similar to a kitten. Similarity of source nodes to target nodes is not

---

[1]Gentner (1983) defined attributes as predicates with one argument (e.g., BIG[cat]), and relations as predicates with two arguments (e.g., PARENT__OF[cat kitten]). However, relations
can have more than two arguments. Binary relations have two arguments, ternary relations
three, quaternary relations four, and so on.

logically required for an analogy to be sound. This does not mean that attributes are irrelevant to analogies, because similarity of source and target nodes might facilitate initial recognition of analogies, as we later see. It simply means that attribute similarity is not part of the definition of a good analogy.

Relations are also mapped selectively. There are many relations between source nodes that are not mapped into target nodes, and vice versa. This is best illustrated with a more complex analogy, such as the Rutherford analogy, analyzed by Gentner (1983). The analogy is between the structure of the hydrogen atom and the solar system, and the essence of Gentner's analysis is shown in Fig. 5.2. The sun is mapped into the nucleus of the atom, and the planet is mapped into the electron. The theory of planetary motion was therefore the source, and the theory of the atom was the target. Consistent with the point made earlier, attributes of the sun, such as its size, color, and temperature, are not assigned to the nucleus, nor are the attributes of planets applied to the electron. The relations between sun and planet are assigned to the target selectively. Three of the relations between sun and planet, "attracts," "more massive than," and "revolves around," are applied to the target. The relation "hotter than" between sun and planet is not assigned to the target. The important question is why.

Gentner (1983) explained the selection of relations for mapping on the systematicity principle. That is, only those relations are mapped that enter into a higher order structure. The value of the Rutherford analogy is that the system that governs planetary motion is similar to that that governs the motion of the electron around the nucleus of the atom. Therefore only those relations are mapped that form part of that system. Because the relation "sun hotter than planet" is irrelevant to the system, it is not mapped.

This example illustrates an important property of analogies and metaphors, which is that they often draw attention to subtle or abstract correspondences between things and situations. At least in the scientific field, this correspondence is usually based on structural similarity rather than on similar attributes. This gives analogies considerable power, because it means they can be used to link superficially dissimilar situations.

Types of Analogy

There does not appear to be any agreed-on taxonomy of analogies, but a number of types were identified by Halford et al. (in press). These are shown in Fig. 5.1 and will be considered in turn.

Source: solar system

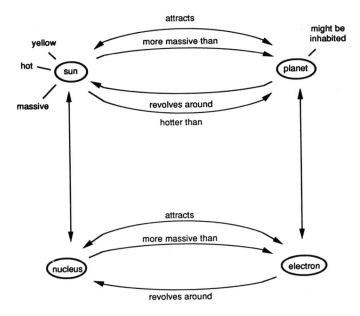

Target: hydrogen atom

FIG. 5.2. Simplified representation of the Rutherford analogy.

Complete Structure. Both source and target structures are fully represented when the problem is presented. The task consists of finding the right mapping from source to target, for example, finding that cat corresponds to horse, rather than to foal, and so on.

Missing Element. One element is missing from the target. Classical analogies of the form A:B::C:D are of this type, if the source relation is made readily apparent at presentation.

Missing Relation. The relation between target elements is missing and must be inferred. Suppose a child did not know what a leveret was and asked what the word meant. She might be told that, just as cats have kittens, hares have leverets. She then infers that since cats are parents of kittens, hares are parents of leverets. This illustrates the role of analogies in semantic development.

Missing Element and Relation. This type is similar to the one above, except that an element and a relation are both missing from the target. This type of problem would occur if a child were asked a question: If cats have kittens, what do hares have? The child knows cats are parents of kittens, so infers this relation in the target, and finds that hares are the parents of leverets. Classical analogies of the form $A:B::C:D$ are of this type, if the participant has to infer the relation between A and B. The analogies used in psychometric tests are commonly of this type

Missing Source. Suppose a child sees the words "hare" and "leveret" in the same context, but does not know what they are. The child then has to find a suitable analog. He might be told that it's like a cat and kitten. He then infers since cat is the parent of kitten, hare is the parent of leveret.

Quite a lot of problem solving entails finding a suitable analog for the problem presented. Even transitive-inference problems (such as "John is happier than Tom, Tom is happier than Bill") require the solver to find a suitable schema into which the problem can be mapped, as illustrated in Fig. 1.3. Part of the creativity of the Rutherford analogy probably consisted of recognizing that the solar system offered a suitable source.

Levels of Mapping in Analogies

The analogies in Fig. 5.1 are based on relational mappings, because they depend on a single relation, and their validity depends on similarity of source and target relations. This means they conform to the criteria for a relational mapping as defined in chapter 2. There is no systematicity in relational analogies, because there is only one relation in both source and target, so there cannot be any higher order structure. Now let us consider a more complex analogy, such as that shown in Fig. 5.3A. This analogy entails systematicity, as defined by Gentner (1983), because the relations in source and target are part of a coherent structure. The relations "John pushes Bill" and "Bill collides with Mike" form part of a causal chain, because pushing is the cause of colliding. This coherent structure is represented by the higher order relation "cause."[2]

----

[2]Following Gentner (1983), a first-order relation has objects as arguments, whereas a second-order relation has relations as arguments. Thus in this representation, "pushes" is a first-order relation because its arguments are "John" and "Bill," whereas "cause" is a second-order relation because its arguments are the relations "pushes" and "collides with." We can express a hier-

A

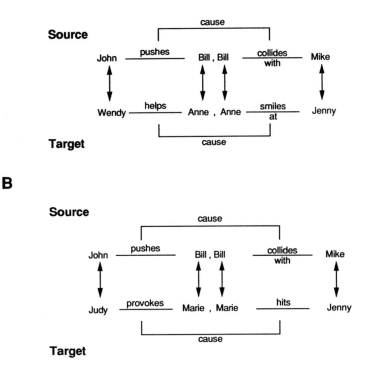

FIG. 5.3. System mapping (A) and two relational mappings (B).

Notice that the mapping does not depend on element similarity (e.g., between John and Wendy, or Bill and Anne, etc.). Furthermore, it does not depend on similarity of first order relations; it is not necessary for "pushes" to resemble "helps," or for "collides with" to resemble "smiles at." The higher order relation "cause" is similar in source and target, and this validates the analogy. Notice, however, that it could also be validated by structural correspondence. It conforms to the criteria for a system mapping given in chapter 2. It meets the consistency criterion, because each element in the source is mapped to one and only one element in the target. It also meets the correspondence criterion, because where a predicate in one structure is mapped to a predicate in the other structure, their arguments are also mapped; when "pushes" is mapped to "helps," then John (an argument of "pushes") is mapped

---

archy of predicates; {P3 [P2 (P1 (Obj))]}; that is, third-order predicates take second-order predicates as arguments, which take first-order predicates as arguments, which take objects as arguments. We enclose second-order predicates in brackets [ ], and third-order predicates in braces { }.

to Wendy (an argument of "helps"), and so on. The mapping does not meet the criteria for an element mapping because it is not based on similarity of source and target elements, nor does it meet the criteria for a relational mapping because it is not based on similarity of first-order relations. However it meets the criteria for a system mapping.

By contrast, the mapping in Fig. 5.3B does meet the criteria for a relational mapping, because "pushes" does resemble "provokes" and "collides with" does resemble "hits." Therefore Fig. 5.3B could be decomposed into two relational mappings, each validated by similarity of first-order relations; if we cover the second half of the diagram, we can see that the mapping of "John pushes Bill" into "Judy provokes Marie" has some validity because of the similarity of the relation. Similarly, if we cover the first half of the diagram, we can still see that it is appropriate that "Bill collides with Mike" maps to "Marie hits Jenny." However, if we cover half the diagram in Fig. 5.3A, the remaining half does not constitute a valid mapping; for example, we have no reason to map "John pushes Bill" into "Wendy helps Anne," if we do not take into account the rest of the diagram. This highlights the fact that more information must be represented in parallel to recognize the validity of the mapping in Fig. 5.3A because it cannot be decomposed into two lower order mappings. In general, an analogy depends on a system mapping only if it cannot be decomposed into a number of relational mappings. A computer-simulation model of relational and system mappings (Bakker & Halford, 1988) can allocate tasks to the appropriate level objectively.

Analogy, Metaphor, Similarity, and Abstraction

Gentner (1983) showed that not only analogies, but metaphors, similarities, and abstractions can be handled by structure-mapping theory. Metaphors are similar to analogies except that there tends to be more emphasis on attribute similarity. If we say that a certain acquaintance is a bear, we are probably referring to the person's size or gait, so these attributes of a bear are mapped into the person. Attributes are mapped selectively, so the metaphor does not imply that the person has four legs or is covered with fur. On the other hand there appears to be less emphasis on mapping relations from source to target in some metaphors than in analogies. In general, there is undoubtedly overlap between the natural language meanings of the terms "analogy" and "metaphor," and there are some comparisons that could be described by either term.

Literal similarity means that source and target share a large number of attributes and a large number of relations; that is, the number of attributes and relations mapped is large in comparison to the number that are not mapped (Gentner, 1983). Thus, if we say that person A is similar to person B, we probably mean they have similar height, hair color, personality or other attributes, but we may also mean they earn their livings the same way, have similar hobbies, or relate to other people the same way, which implies their relations to the environment correspond.

An abstraction is a mapping in which the source is an abstract relational structure. This means that the elements of the source have few or no attributes. The source elements may be defined mainly, or even entirely, by their relation to other source elements. An important implication of this is that in an abstraction, the emphasis is on the relational structure. This means that if children are to acquire abstractions, it is important that they learn the structure of the examples they experience. Good analogs can help here, because mapping from an example to an analog forces children to pay attention to corresponding relations in the two structures. This is particularly true if the example and analog belong to different domains, which share few attributes.

Criteria for Good Analogies

The features that make analogies useful in learning or thinking can also be expressed in structure-mapping terms. Gentner (1982) listed six features that can be used to evaluate analogies; base or source specificity, clarity, richness, systematicity, scope, and validity. We explain each of these in turn:

Source specificity is the degree to which the structure of the source is explicitly understood. For an analogy to be good, the user needs to have information about the objects and relations in the source stored in semantic memory. It will not be possible to map the source into the target, then use the source to generate inferences about the target, unless this information is available. I would add that, because structure mapping imposes a processing load, as we saw in chapters 2 and 3, the source information must be well enough known to make its retrieval effortless. Otherwise the analogy will be too difficult to use.

Clarity refers to absence of ambiguity in the mappings from source to target. High clarity means that each source node is mapped into one, and only one, target node and vice versa.

Richness is the number of predicates per node that can be mapped from source to target. It is equivalent to the density of attributes and relations that are mapped. The Rutherford analogy in Fig. 5.2 has moderately high richness because three relations are mapped from each node.

Systematicity was defined earlier and refers to the conceptual coherence of an analogy or the degree to which the relations that are mapped form a higher order structure.

Scope refers to the number of different cases, or instances, to which the analogy can be applied. For example the analogy between cat–kitten and horse–foal in Fig. 5.1 has high scope because there are unlimited examples of parent–offspring relations.

Validity (appropriateness), as used by Gentner (1982), means that the analogy leads to valid inferences. "Motherhood is a career" might be considered an invalid analogy if it were taken to imply that rewards such as pay, promotion, and retirement benefits that normally attach to certain careers also applied to motherhood. Because mothers are not normally paid in cash, are not promoted for good performance, and do not receive retirement benefits, it would not be valid to map these attributes from the source (career) into the target (motherhood).

Gentner's term *validity* is potentially confusable, in the context of this work, with the validity criteria for structure mappings given in chapter 2. The term *validity*, as used in this book, is really closer to Gentner's concept of clarity, as mentioned above. Consequently we will substitute the term *appropriateness* for Gentner's term *validity*.

Expressive analogies are distinguished, by Gentner, from explanatory analogies. The former are mostly used in literature, whereas the latter are mostly used in science. An explanatory analogy should be high in clarity, scope, and systematicity, whereas richness tends to be more important for expressive analogies. Both types need source specificity and applicability. Gentner contrasted explanatory analogies such as the Rutherford analogy with expressive analogies such as those used by Shakespeare and T. S. Eliot. The richness of allusion that is often one of the most salient attributes of a good poem tends to be accompanied by some ambiguity as to what refers to what; that is, the mappings can be ambiguous. This amounts to lack of clarity, in terms of the criteria above. It can often increase the interest of a poem, but it is frustrating and confusing in science.

PROCESS MODELS OF ANALOGIES

In this section we consider in more detail how analogies are constructed. There are several models of human analogical reasoning, some of which are based on computer simulation of the process.

Sternberg's Model

The first account of analogical reasoning processes that was actually validated empirically as a model of human reasoning was that of Sternberg (1977a, 1977b). The model was restricted to proportional analogies of the form A

is to *B* as *C* is to *D* and was validated using Sternberg's componential-analysis technique. Sternberg postulated five main cognitive processes that were required to solve such analogies;

Encoding is the process of perceiving each element and storing the relevant attributes in working memory.

Inference is the process of discovering the relation(s), or transformation(s) between *A* and *B*, for example, discovering the relation "parent of" between cat and kitten in the source of Fig. 5.1A. Notice that this is not the way the term *inference* is used in Gentner's theory or in the rest of this discussion. The process that Sternberg called inference would be part of encoding the source; that is, finding attributes and relations attached to source nodes.

Mapping links the *A* term to the *C* term; for example, in Fig. 5.1A, cat is linked to horse.

Application is the process of applying the *A–B* relation to the *C–D* pair; for example, in Fig. 5.1, the relation "parent of" between cat and kitten is applied to the term "horse," to generate the term "foal." This is similar to the inference process in Gentner's theory, and in this work.

Justification is optional and entails showing that the answer chosen makes the *C–D* relation as close as possible to the *A–B* relation.

Goswami (1992) reviewed the developmental literature relating to this model and concluded that 3- to 4-year-old children can be taught to use all the components in Sternberg's model.

The Structure-Mapping Engine (SME)

The structure-mapping process defined by Gentner (1983) has been developed into a computer-simulation model by Falkenhainer, Forbus, and Gentner (1990). The model is called the Structure-Mapping Engine, and it constructs analogical correspondences in three steps.

In the first step, elements and predicates (attributes and relations) of the source are paired off with elements and predicates of the target. The pairings are made according to "match hypothesis constructor rules," based on similarity of attributes, first-order relations, or higher order relations. For example, a relation such as "greater than" between two elements in the source might be paired with the relation "greater than" between two elements in the target. The evidence for each match is assessed based on both the item itself and its arguments. For example, the match between the relation "greater than" in source and target might be supported by evidence that their arguments have similar attributes. In general, the evidence for a match increases to the extent that it is supported by the higher order structure in which it participates.

In the second step, these matches are collected together into global matches, called Gmaps. To be included in a Gmap, a match must be accompanied by other matches that pair up all the source and target elements and relations in a consistent way. If this cannot be done, the match is discarded, thereby eliminating irrelevant or inconsistent maps. Then the Gmaps are merged. In the third step, candidate inferences about the target are computed; that is, a predicate in the source that does not appear among corresponding target elements, and is consistent with the mappings made, is selected as a candidate inference (e.g., in Fig. 5.1C, "hare is the parent of leveret" would be a candidate inference).

In the fourth step, the best global match is selected based on evidence for its individual matches, the number and relative size of the connected components (a completeness criterion), and the applicability of the candidate inferences.

Falkenhainer et al. showed that their program can "discover" the Rutherford analogy, and the analogy between heat flowing down a silver bar from hot coffee to melting ice, and water flowing from a beaker with high pressure to a vial of low pressure. This means that their model has passed the "sufficiency" test; that is, it is an adequate mechanism to discover certain important analogies.

COPYCAT

The COPYCAT model (Mitchell & Hofstadter, 1990) solves problems of the form: if *abc* changes to *abd*, to what does *ijk* change? (Answer: *ijl*) It does this by coding the source, *abc* → *abd* in terms of the transformation "replace rightmost element by its successor." However, the model has also been presented with problems such as: if *abc* changes to *abd*, to what does *xyz* change? The answer "*xya*" is not permitted, because alphabets do not "wrap around" (are not cyclic). The answer given on some trials, and which is seen as most satisfying, is "*wyz*." This entails switching or "slipping" from the concept "successor of" to the concept "predecessor of." The new rule becomes "replace the leftmost element by its predecessor." This is achieved by a system known as a *slipnet*, which adjusts representations while the analogy is being solved.

The fact that the domain of application of COPYCAT is restricted to alphabetic strings should not obscure the importance of its contribution, which lies largely in the fact that it builds it representations dynamically. This makes the important point that analogies are not merely ways of relating one structure to another but are also a means by which representations are built up and modified. Analogies are therefore centrally involved in the processes of coding and representation.

The Analogical Constraint Mapping Engine (ACME)

A parallel processing model of the structure-mapping process has been developed by Holyoak and Thagard (1989). The model is based on a number of constraints that are satisfied in parallel. These constraints are:

1. Structural constraint. This constraint embodies the uniqueness and correspondence criteria defined earlier. That is, there must be a one-to-one mapping of source elements into target elements, and if a predicate is mapped, its arguments are also mapped.
2. Semantic similarity means that source predicates are mapped into target predicates with the same or similar meanings.
3. Pragmatic centrality means that correspondences are favored if they are important to the person's goals.

There are two additional restrictions designed to limit the number of potential mappings and thereby reduce the amount of computation required. These are the type restriction (i.e., an element can only be mapped into an element, an attribute into an attribute, a relation into a relation, and so on), and the part-correspondence restriction (e.g., a goal in one task must be mapped into a goal in the other, initial states must be mapped into each other, etc.).

The basis of the model is a "cooperative algorithm," a procedure that permits the various constraints to be satisfied in parallel. This is done in a type of spreading activation model in which the constraints operate as either excitatory or inhibitory links.

This can be illustrated by referring to the mapping in Fig. 5.3B. The hypothesis that John is mapped into Judy would inhibit, and be inhibited by, the hypothesis that Bill is mapped into Judy. This inhibitory link therefore embodies the uniqueness constraint. On the other hand the hypothesis that "pushes" is mapped into "provokes" has an excitatory link to the hypothesis that John is mapped into Judy and Bill is mapped into Marie. This link therefore embodies the correspondence constraint.

The model has been found capable of recognizing the fortress-radiation convergence problems of Gick and Holyoak (1983), the Rutherford analogy analyzed by Gentner (1983), the systematicity stories used by Gentner and Toupin (1986), as well as a purely formal analogy between arithmetic addition and the union of classes. Systematicity is captured by the structural constraint, without need of a specific principle. In effect, systematicity is a special case of relational consistency.

A particularly interesting feature of the Holyoak and Thagard model is that a set of logical constraints are satisfied by a spreading activation model. The model itself contains no logical rules as such. The constraints exist purely as positive (excitatory) or negative (inhibitory) weights linking the activation of the various mapping hypotheses. Another significant feature of the ACME model is that it can construct mappings based purely on structural correspondence, without element or relational similarity at any level. The existence of similar elements, or similar first- or higher order relations facilitates mapping but is not necessary to it.

The fact that these constraints operate in parallel means the model has similarities to parallel distributed processing models discussed in chapters 2 and 3. ACME differs from PDP models in the type of representations used. ACME uses "localist" representations, in that each predicate and each argument is represented by a single node, so each representation is based on a single unit, whereas in PDP models all representations are distributed over a number of units (a vector). A PDP model of analogical reasoning is presented in the next section.

The Structured Tensor Analogical Reasoning (STAR) Model

The Structured Tensor Analogical Reasoning model (Halford, Wilson, Guo, Gayler, Wiles, & Stewart, in press) was developed with the dual aims of providing an analogical reasoning model based on PDP architectures, and one that made realistic demands on processing capacity. The reason for the first aim was the belief that because much of human reasoning is basically analogical, PDP theories would be better able to account for higher cognitive processes if they could be extended to handle analogies. The reason for the second aim was that the other models we have considered, SME, ACME, and COPYCAT, do not address the capacity limitations discussed in chapter 3. This question is of some importance in general cognition, but if analogical reasoning models are to play a significant role in cognitive development, where the question of change in processing capacity over age has central relevance, then capacity limitations had to be addressed.

The basis of the model is the representation of predicate-argument bindings outlined in chapter 2. Recall that a predicate-argument binding is represented by the tensor product of vectors representing the predicate and its arguments. For example, in Fig. 2.5 the predicate (relation) LARGER-THAN is represented by one vector, and its arguments "elephant" and "dog" are each represented by vectors. The binding of the predicate to its arguments is represented by the the tensor product of these three vectors. With a three-place predicate, such as addition, the binding is represented by the tensor product of four vectors, as shown in Fig. 2.6. Likewise, transitivity is represented by the tensor product of four vectors, as shown in Fig. 2.7.

Different levels of structure can be represented by tensor products of different rank. The structural complexity of concepts is measured by their dimensionality, defined as the number of independent units of information required for their representation. A concept of dimensionality N is represented by a tensor product of rank $N+1$, that is, with $N+1$ vectors. The tensor product formulation for representing different levels of structure in concepts is used as the basis for an analogical reasoning model—hence the Structured Tensor Analogical Reasoning model.

The essence of the analogical reasoning process in terms of this model is illustrated in Fig. 5.4, using the analogy in Fig. 5.1. The fact that cat is the

Tensor-Product Representation

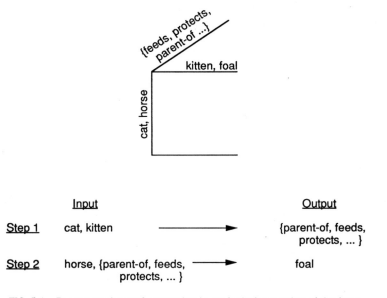

FIG. 5.4.   Representation and processing in analogical reasoning of the form
A:B::C:?

parent of kitten and that horse is the parent of foal are both represented in
a Rank-3 tensor product as shown in Fig. 5.4. The bindings for PARENT-OF(cat,
kitten) and PARENT-OF(horse, foal) are superimposed on the representation,
it being normal for representations to be superimposed in PDP models, as
discussed in chapter 2. Setting up this representation corresponds to the "encoding" step in Sternberg's (1977a, 1977b) model, discussed earlier.

The next step is to enter the arguments, cat and kitten, into the tensor
product representation. It responds with an output representing all predicates
consistent with this pair of arguments. That is, it responds with "predicate
bundle," comprising predicates such as PARENT-OF, FEEDS, PROTECTS, and
so on. The output is actually a vector equal to the sum of the vectors representing all predicates contained in the predicate bundle. This step corresponds
fairly closely to the "inference" step in Sternberg's model.

The next input comprises the predicate bundle and the argument "horse."
This corresponds to the "mapping" step in Sternberg's model. The output is
the argument "foal," which corresponds to Sternberg's application step. (As
the model currently exists, it has no equivalent of Sternberg's justification
step, but it is not logically inconsistent with the model, and is in any case
optional.) Simulation has shown that the model can solve missing-element
analogy problems in this way.

Other cases of analogy outlined in Fig. 5.1 can also be handled by STAR. Halford et al. (in press) conducted simulations of the missing source, incomplete target case, but I explain how, in principle, the model would handle the other cases.

The complete structure type of analogy is handled by first entering source arguments (e.g., cat, kitten) and obtaining a predicate bundle. Then target arguments (e.g., horse, foal) are entered, and a target predicate bundle obtained. The goodness of the match can be assessed by the similarity of source and target predicates. Mathematically, this can be done by computing the inner product of the vectors representing the target bundles,[3] as Halford et al. (in press) showed.

This approach implies that there must be a common predicate in source and target for an analogy to be formed. This is not a logical requirement for analogical mapping, because the ACME model can find matches based solely on structural correspondence, with no shared predicates. However it may be a psychological requirement. For example, Gick and Holyoak (1983) found that common coding of source and target facilitated solution. It is possible that all human analogical reasoning requires similarity at some level. If it is not at the level of elements or first-order relations, it might occur at the level of higher order relations (as in Fig. 5.3). This issue remains to be resolved by future research and model building.

The missing-relations case can be handled by entering source arguments (cat, kitten, in the example in Fig. 5.1) into the tensor-product representation and obtaining the predicate bundle corresponding to all predicates that apply to the source argument set (PARENT-OF, FEEDS, PROTECTS, etc.). Target arguments are entered into the tensor product in a separate step, and the vector representing the sum of all predicates applying to the target arguments is obtained. The inner product of vectors representing source and target predicate bundles provides a measure of the degree of match obtained. Individual relations can be identified by obtaining the inner product of the predicate bundle with vectors representing specific predicates, as Halford et al. (in press) showed.

In the missing source case, the target arguments must first be entered into the tensor product, thereby obtaining the vector representing the sum of all predicates consistent with target arguments, as in the missing-relations case. Then this vector is entered into the tensor-product representation, and the tensor product representing all possible argument sets is obtained. This set of arguments will include the target arguments as well as all other arguments in the representation consistent with the predicate. Specific arguments can be identified by obtaining the inner product of this vector with the vectors representing individual arguments. Sets of vectors representing arguments

---

[3]The inner product is roughly equivalent to a measure of correlation.

are then entered into the tensor product represention, and the vector representing the sum of all predicates consistent with the selected set of arguments is obtained. The inner product of this vector with the vector representing the source predicate is obtained, and it represents a measure of the degree of match. In this way, a source that can be mapped into target can be found. This process essentially entails using the target predicate as a retrieval cue to find possible sources.

Structural Limitations in Analogical Reasoning

The operation of the model has been illustrated using analogies based on predicates with two arguments, specifically the binary relation PARENT-OF. It can be generalized to predicates with up to four arguments. Mathematically, it can be generalized to predicates of any number of arguments, but evidence in chapter 3 indicates this is unrealistic.

A problem arises however when source and target structures with more than four arguments are involved. Some complex structures might entail many predicates and, consequently, many arguments. According to our formulation, only a limited number of vectors can be actively represented in parallel. Success will therefore depend on either coding the structure into fewer vectors or on restricting the representation at any one time to a manageable number of predicates and arguments, or some combination of these. Coding into fewer vectors is probably a component of expertise and is an aspect of conceptual chunking, discussed in chapter 2.

Analogical Reasoning and Human Memory

The STAR model of analogical reasoning is consistent with a recent mathematical model of human memory by Humphreys, Bain, and Pike (1989). According to Humphreys et al., a number of memory paradigms that were once considered to require distinct stores can utilize a single representation based on the tensor product of three vectors, as shown in Fig. 5.5. There is one vector representing each of cue, target, and context. Episodic memory is context specific, for example, "what beverage did you drink for breakfast?" The cue is "beverage," the context is "breakfast," and the target is "fruit juice," "coffee," or whatever (I will assume it to be fruit juice). The memory is represented by the tensor product of the vectors representing "beverage," "breakfast," and "fruit juice." When the vectors representing "beverage" and "breakfast" are entered into the representation, it responds with the vector representing "fruit juice." Semantic memory is context independent and is represented by the summation of all the episodic memories, superimposed on the representation. Retrieval is achieved by using as input a vector

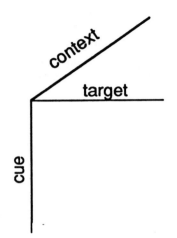

FIG. 5.5. Tensor-product representation in memory.

representing the cue, and a random vector in place of context (this has the effect of collapsing over all the different contexts). Therefore, in response to the question "name a beverage," a vector representing all of "fruit juice," "coffee," and so on, is retrieved. Individual beverages can be recognized by computing the inner product of vectors representing them with the vector retrieved.

As Wiles et al. (1992) showed, the memory model of Humphreys et al. (1989), and the STAR model of analogical reasoning by Halford et al. (in press) share many of the same processes. One implication is that analogical reasoning might be regarded as a special case of memory retrieval. To see this, recall how the cat:kitten::horse:foal analogy (in Fig. 5.1A) is solved according to the STAR model (the process is summarized in Fig. 5.4). When cat and kitten are entered as input, the relation "parent of" is obtained. This can be interpreted as using "cat" and "kitten" as cues for the retrieval of "parent of." Similarly, "horse" and "parent of" are used as retrieval cues for "foal."

It is by no means novel to suggest that human reasoning depends heavily on memory, because this point has been made by Tversky and Kahneman (1973), as mentioned in chapter 2. However, the fact that the same mechanisms can model human memory and analogical reasoning, which arguably is at the core of human inference, implies a high degree of theoretical integration. Furthermore, as we see later in this chapter, the types of representations used by the STAR model, and in the memory model of Humphreys et al. (1989), may also be important in a number of learning tasks.

Factors Affecting Analogical Reasoning

In this section we consider the factors that affect how easily analogies can be constructed and used. The main factors we consider are stimulus similarity, stimulus complexity, encoding, processing load, and domain knowledge.

Stimulus similarity is not essential to analogies because, as we have seen, we can have a valid analogy between superficially very different situations. However, stimulus similarity can affect how easily an analogy is noticed.

Participants in a study by Holyoak and Koh (1987) found it easier to recognize an analogy between two problems when the problem elements were similar, but element similarity did not affect their ability to apply the analogy once it was recognized. The target was the radiation problem; there is an inoperable tumor that can be destroyed by X-rays, but rays of sufficient intensity to destroy the tumor would damage surrounding tissue. The solution is to use several weaker rays that converge on the tumor.

Prior to attempting the X-ray problem, participants were presented with one of four stories that varied in either element (surface) or relational (structural) similarity to the target. The stories with similar elements concerned a light bulb with a broken filament that could be fused by using several weak laser beams that converged on the filament. The dissimilar stories entailed using ultrasound to break up a filament. The assumption is that lasers are more similar to X-rays than ultrasound is and that fusing a filament is more similar to destroying a tumor by X-rays than breaking up a filament by ultrasound is.

In the stories with high structural similarity, the constraint was to avoid breaking the glass with strong lasers or strong ultrasound. This directly parallels the constraint not to damage body tissue in the X-ray problem. In the low structural similarity stories, the constraint was that no single instrument of sufficient intensity was available.

After a reasonable attempt at solution had been made a hint was given, suggesting the link between the stories and the target problem. Prior to the hint, transfer was affected by both element and structural similarity. After the hint, transfer was affected by structural similarity only. The inference is that relatively superficial similarities between source and target elements facilitated recognition of the analogy but did not help to apply it once it was recognized. Structural similarity, however, assisted both recognition and application.

Often the more powerful analogies have source and target that belong to different domains, for example, the analogy between the atom and the solar system in Fig. 5.2. This makes it unlikely that the analogy can be based on similar elements in source and target, so that analogy will have to be recognized by noticing structural correspondences. This may sometimes be too difficult, especially for children. As Holland et al. (1986) pointed out, the role of a teacher, parent, or peer is then to demonstrate the possibility of an analogy to a child. This is one example of the role of pedagogy in assisting children to develop adequate mental models of the world.

The general principle that recognition of an analogy is facilitated by similarity should be interpreted to include higher order relations. The analogy in Fig. 5.3 is made more psychologically plausible by the higher order relation "cause." The fact that the same higher order relation occurred in source and target increases similarity and makes the analogy easier to recognise.

Encoding and categorization can influence the likelihood of analogy being noticed. Encodings that emphasize the relational structure of the task seem to facilitate analogical reasoning. Relational encoding seems to be promoted by experience with multiple analogs. Using the X-ray problem, Gick and Holyoak (1983) found that a verbal statement of the convergence principle, or a diagram illustrating it, was of little benefit to participants trying to find the analogy. However, when two analog stories were told, and participants were required to summarize the differences between them, verbal or visual statements of the convergence principle were more likely to emerge; for example: "Both the stories used the same concept to solve a problem, which was to use many small forces applied together to add up to one large force necessary to destroy the object" (Gick & Holyoak, 1983, p. 23). This encoding preserves the essential relational information, omitting the specific object attributes, such as whether the forces consisted of troops, lasers, or ultrasound, and whether the object to be destroyed was a tumor, a fortress, or a filament. Verbal or visual illustrations of convergence, combined with two analogs, promoted better summary statements and more discoveries of the analogy. Consistent with the findings of Gick and Holyoak (1983), Zhe Chen and Daehler (1989) found that abstract encoding of a problem solution facilitated analogical transfer by first-grade children.

It is interesting to recall the principle of multiple embodiment advanced by Dienes (1964) in his work on analogs for teaching children mathematics. Dienes argued that it was better to present children with two concrete embodiments of a mathematical relationship than one. This principle was based on pedagogical experience rather than experimentation, but it is essentially consistent with the evidence that has emerged from recent research.

Such an abstract encoding reduces the representation to a small number of conceptual chunks. The elements of the source are a small force, a large force, and an object to be destroyed. The relations are "small forces ADD-TO large force," and "large force DESTROYS object(to be destroyed)." The tumor is readily mapped into "object to be destroyed," and then it is only necessary to map weak X-ray into small force, and strong X-ray into large force. Thus, efficient coding greatly reduces the information-processing load of the task. Without such conceptual chunking, the processing load would be prodigious. On our hypothesis that even adults can process representations of no more than four independent dimensions in parallel without recoding the problem, it would exceed the capacity of child or adult. Recoded as described above, however, it can be represented in no more than four vectors.

Notice also how expertise is relevant to chunking, because it helps recognize the relevant aspects of the task. An army has many attributes, but the only relevant ones are that it is a force, and its size. Tumors also have many attributes, such as that they are painful, life-threatening, and so on. Again, however, there is really only one relevant attribute, that a tumor can be destroyed by X-rays of sufficient strength. The value of expertise is that it enables the task to be encoded in a small number of attributes and relations that capture its essential properties.

Domain Knowledge

It is clear that an analogy cannot be solved unless the person has the requisite knowledge of the appropriate domain. For example the analogy between converging small armies destroying a fortress and converging X-rays destroying a tumor cannot be recognized unless the ability of X-rays to destroy tissue is known. However, it is also clear that domain knowledge is not the only factor that governs success. Gentner and Block (1983) found no difference between science and liberal arts students in ability to interpret either scientific or general analogies. On the other hand, Novick (1988) found that experts in the domain were more likely to show positive- and less likely to show negative-analogical transfer than novices. It appears that domain knowledge is important, but it is not the only factor influencing analogical reasoning.

Goals

So far we have considered the abstract or syntactic properties of analogies, but real psychological examples of analogies are likely to be influenced also by pragmatic factors, such as goals. The fact that in the last example an X-ray was coded as a force is influenced in part by problem-solving goals. In other contexts an X-ray might not be categorized as a force but, for example, as a physical process to be explained by theory, whereas an army might be categorized as a social organization.

Stimulus Complexity

Even simple proportional analogies, of the same basic structure as those in Fig. 5.1, can be made difficult if the stimuli are complex or if more than one transformation is used. Analogies with varying numbers of elements and trans-

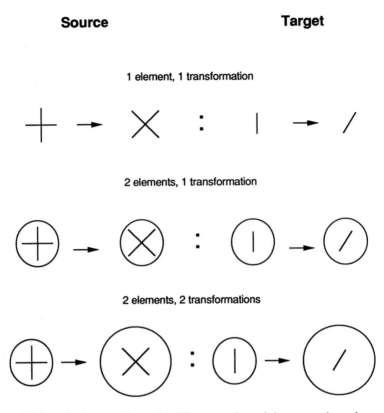

FIG. 5.6. Analogy problems with different numbers of elements and transformations.

formations are shown in Fig. 5.6. In the first case, there is one source element, a cross, and it undergoes a single transformation, rotation 45 degrees to the right. Correspondingly, there is one target element, a vertical line, which undergoes the same transformation. In the second case, there are two elements, a cross and a circle (vertical line and circle), but one transformation, rotation 45 degrees to the right. In the third case, there are two elements, and two transformations, rotation of the cross (vertical line), and enlargement of the circle.

The number of elements and transformations has been shown to affect the difficulty of analogies. Mulholland, Pellegrino, and Glaser (1980) used geometric analogies, similar to those often used in psychometric tests, and varied the number of elements from one to three and the number of transformations from one to three. Both factors affected latencies, and number of transformations also affected errors. Sternberg and Rifkin (1979) also found an effect of number of transformations on difficulty of schematic and human picture analogies.

Processing Loads

As we saw in chapter 2, higher level structure-mapping rules impose higher processing loads, and this theoretical prediction was confirmed for premise integration, in transitive inference, in chapter 3. The purpose of this section is to see how levels of structure mapping apply to the kind of analogical reasoning tasks we have been considering in this section.

First, recall from chapter 3 that short-term memory loads are not to be identified with processing loads. Information can be held passively in short-term memory for use in later problem-solving steps, but its storage does not interfere directly with concurrent processing. However, processing loads depend on the amount of information that must be processed in parallel, but they are not influenced by information that is stored passively without being processed.

The total amount of information that needs to be processed does not necessarily affect processing load, because in many tasks it is possible to decompose the task into smaller steps. The processing load at any given point in the performance will depend on the amount of information being processed at that point. For example, in Fig. 5.6, the two-element, two-transformation problem does not necessarily impose a higher load than the two-element, one-transformation problem. It is possible that the tranformations can be performed serially, in two steps: Step 1, enlarge the circle. Step 2, rotate the bar. The load is that imposed by a single step, because only one step is performed at any given time. For similar reasons, the analogy in Fig. 5.3A would impose a load appropriate to a relational mapping, because it can be processed as two successive mappings. The analogy in Fig. 5.3B cannot be decomposed in this way, and must be processed as a single system mapping.

The general form of the representation required for relational and system mappings in terms of the STAR model is shown in Fig. 5.7. If the mapping requires a binary relation (unary operator, or univariate function) and its two arguments to be processed in parallel, it can be represented by the tensor product of three vectors, as shown in Fig. 5.7A. If it requires a ternary relation (or binary operation, or bivariate function, all of which are special cases of ternary relations) and its arguments to be processed in parallel, it must be represented by the tensor product of four vectors, as shown in Fig. 5.7B.

CHILDREN'S ANALOGICAL
REASONING ABILITY

In this section I consider evidence for young children's ability to solve analogical reasoning tasks.

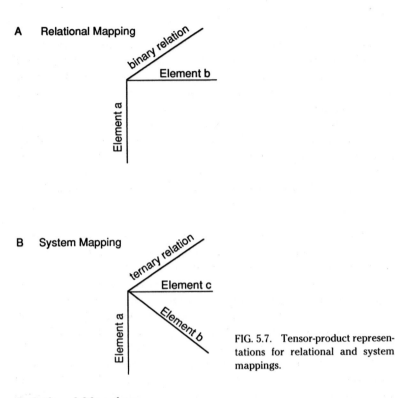

FIG. 5.7. Tensor-product representations for relational and system mappings.

Relational Mappings

Given evidence reviewed in chapter 3 that children of 3–4 years can perform relational mappings, and that many analogical reasoning tasks can be processed as relational mappings (or as a succession of such mappings), it would be expected that young children should be able to handle a large range of analogical reasoning problems. There is considerable evidence to support this prediction.

Gentner (1977b) assessed the analogical reasoning ability of 4- to 6-year-olds and college students by asking them to map body parts onto inanimate objects such as trees and mountains, that is, to say where the head, shoulders, knees, and so on, would be if they existed on a tree. The mapping from person to tree can be performed on the basis of relational similarity; knee is above feet in the source (human) and knee is above feet (roots) in the target (tree). The 4-year-olds performed as well as the older children and adults, confirming that they are capable of analogical reasoning based on relational mappings.

On the other hand, Gentner and Stuart (1984) and Gentner (1988) found that with age there was a shift from judgments based on attributes to judgments based on relations. For example, children aged 5–6 years, and 9–10 years, and adults were asked to interpret metaphors. The metaphors could be based on attribute similarity, for example, the sun is like an orange (both are round and orange); relational similarity, for example, a camera is like a tape recorder (both record events to be reexperienced later); or both, for example, a hummingbird is like a helicopter (both have stubby shapes and blurry parts, both use rapid motion in flight). Interpretations based on relationality increased with age, whereas those based on attributionality did not.

However, there is evidence in other contexts that seems to indicate that 3-year-olds can code relations and can map them from one situation to another in certain circumstances. The study by DeLoache (1987, 1989), discussed in chapter 2, showed that children approaching 3 years of age can find a toy hidden in a room after seeing its position indicated in a model or photograph. This task can be conceptualized as a mapping from model (or photograph) to the real room. The position of the toy could presumably be encoded as a single relation, for example, "behind the sofa." If performed on this basis, the task would amount to a relational mapping from "model toy behind model sofa" to "real toy behind real sofa." Furthermore, as I pointed out earlier (Halford, 1982), there is evidence in other contexts that young children can encode binary relations. Bullock and Gelman (1977) tested 2- to 4-year-old children on transfer of a set-size discrimination; for example, if they chose the larger set from a set of one and a set of two, they should also choose the larger set from a set of three and a set of four. They were able to do this before the age of 3 years.

Although it is hazardous to extrapolate from these data to analogies, the evidence does suggest that 3- to 4-year-old children can encode simple binary relations. However, this does not exclude the possibility that younger children might be more likely to adopt attributional encodings, even though relational encodings are within their reach. Whether attributes or relations are used as a basis for encoding might depend on how much of the structure is processed. If we focus on one object at a time, it seems more appropriate to encode it in terms of attributes; for example, if we focus on a cat, we might encode it as having pointed ears, fur, four legs, and so on. If we focus on two objects, it becomes more appropriate to encode it in terms of the relation between them; for example, if we focus on a cat and a kitten, relations like "parent of," "larger than," and so on, become more appropriate. As we consider larger segments of a structure, it becomes progressively more likely that relational encodings will win out over attributional encodings. For example, in the structure in Fig. 5.3A, if we consider John, Bill, and Mike, it becomes appropriate to consider the relations "pushes," "collides with," and "cause." Gentner and her colleagues (personal communication) showed by simulation that the Structure-Mapping Engine is more likely to adopt relational encodings if larger segments of structure are processed. It seems possible then that children as young as 3 years can encode (binary) relations but become progressively more likely to adopt relational than attributional encodings due to such factors as the amount of structure processed.

Systematicity

Systematicity entails recognizing that a relation enters into a coherent system of relations and, therefore, depends on recognizing a larger segment of structure. Therefore ability to utilize systematicity should increase with age. Evidence consistent with this prediction comes from a study by Gentner and Toupin (1986). Children aged 4–6 and 8–10 were read a story containing a short event sequence involving some animal characters; for example, a seagull visits a walrus, bringing a wagon. While they are playing, the cat, a friend of the walrus, returns and becomes angry because the walrus is playing with someone else.

After hearing the story the children acted it out with toy animals and props. Then they were told an analogous story involving a different set of characters, and were required to act it out.

Systematicity was manipulated by using a descriptive term (e.g., a jealous cat) and a moral (e.g., it is not a good idea to be jealous). If children are sensitive to the overall organization of the story, they should perform better when the descriptive term and moral are provided, because these specify a higher order structure to the story. Systematicity produced a significant effect only for the 8- to 10-year-olds.

On the other hand, what Gentner and Toupin called the "transparency" of the mapping affected performance at both ages. This factor was manipulated by varying the degree to which characters in the test stories resembled those in the source stories. Transparency was high when the test characters resembled the corresponding characters in the source stories, was moderate when there was little resemblance at all, and low when the test characters resembled noncorresponding source characters (i.e., when mappings were crossed). Transparency as used here is equivalent to element similarity; in high transparency conditions mappings can be made on the basis of similarity of corresponding elements in source and target. In these conditions systematicity is really unnecessary, and its effect was small, but increased as transparency decreased. However, if a task that requires systematicity can be encoded as a system mapping, then it should be possible for 5-year-olds under some conditions. There have been few studies of systematicity in children so far, but further investigation with more refined techniques would be worthwhile to test this prediction.

Analogical Transfer of Problem Solutions

There is evidence from a study by Holyoak, Junn, and Billman (1984) that children as young as 4 years can solve problems using solution to an analogous problem. Two bowls were placed on a table, one within the child's reach and containing gumballs, and one out of reach. Also provided were a walking cane, a large rectangular sheet of heavy paper, and a variety of other objects. The problem was to transfer the gumballs from the near to the far bowl without leaving the seat. One solution is to use the cane to pull the far bowl within reach. Another is to roll the paper into a tube, and roll the gumballs down it into the other bowl.

Children were told stories that entailed solving analogous problems, such as a genie who transferred jewels from one bottle to another by rolling his magic carpet into a tube, or by using his magic staff to move the distant bottle nearer. Four-year-olds could solve the problem even when the similarities between source stories and the target problem were relatively low. For example, in Experiment 3 the source story entailed Miss Piggy rolling up a carpet to transfer jewels to a safe. There are not many resemblances between a carpet and a square of cardboard, or between a bowl and a safe. This suggests that relational mappings were probably used to some degree. On the other hand, young children's solution processes were fragile and easily disrupted by such things as adding extra characters to the stories or by altering goals.

Two other studies that demonstrate young children's ability not only to recognize analogies but to use them in problem solving were reported by Crisafi and Brown (1986) and Brown, Kane, and Echols (1986). Crisafi and Brown used a task in which two separately learned motor performances had to be combined to achieve a goal. For example, the child would first learn to obtain a penny from a toy bank, and a dime from a purse. Then the penny had to be inserted into another machine to obtain a gum ball. In another version of the task the child might learn to obtain a white button from a carton and a grey button from a pan. Then the white button had to be inserted into a truck to obtain a candy bean. Crisafi and Brown demonstrated transfer between one such task and another in 2- to 4-year-olds. Transfer was facilitated by providing a hint that the problems were similar, and also by assisting children to verbalize the solution process. This task entails combining prelearned motor sequences, and the problem is that it is not clear what mental representations are required. It is virtually certain that the whole solution path does not need to be repesented, because the motor performances are known beforehand and do not need to be generated from a mental model.

The study by Brown, Kane, and Echols (1986) used a technique that was similar in some respects to that used by Holyoak, Junn, and Billman (1984). Three- to five-year-old children were told a story about a genie who needed to transfer his jewels from one bottle to another. The child was asked to find the solution, which entailed rolling up a sheet of paper and rolling the jewels down the tube, then act the solution out. Then the child was presented with two further problem situations involving a rabbit or a farmer who needed to transfer something from one place to another and where the solution again was to roll a sheet of paper and use it as a tube. It is important to notice that, in this task, as distinct from that used by Holyoak et al., the solution to all three problems entails using precisely the same object, the sheet of paper, in the same way. In the Holyoak et al. paper the genie story used a magic carpet, and the child was required to use a sheet of paper.

Successful transfer was observed by Brown et al., at least with 4- to 5-year-olds. Furthermore transfer was significantly related to children's encoding of the goal structure of the first task. On the other hand, that goal structure always entailed the common element, rolling a sheet of paper to use as a tube. The possibility exists therefore that transfer was based on recognition that a piece of paper can be rolled into a tube to transfer objects from place to place.

It is interesting to compare this task with the definition of an analogy given earlier, as a structure-preserving map from source to target. The essence of an analogy is that it is based on common relational structure in source and target, rather than on common attributes. In the Brown et al. task it appears to have been a particular attribute of an object, that it could be rolled into a tube, that was central to the task. Transfer was undoubtedly demonstrated, and it was mediated in some way by a cognitive representation. But as Brown and Kane (1988) point out, the transfer was probably based on element similarity. However Brown and Kane (1988) did show analogical transfer, independent of perceptual similarity, between different instances of concepts such as tool use, and mimicry as a means of defense. Interestingly, they used learning set training as a means of promoting transfer, which reinforces the point that learning set acquisition and analogical reasoning are related.

Evidence that children can use analogical transfer in solving more complex problems has been provided in a series of studies by Gholson and his colleagues (Gholson, Dattel, Morgan, & Eymard, 1989; Gholson, Eymard, Long, Morgan, & Leeming, 1988). They used the farmer's dilemma, the missionaries and cannibals, and the three-disk tower-of-Hanoi puzzles, together with a number of isomorphs, with children aged 4–10 years. There was a sequence of moves that was common to each type of problem, which can be illustrated with the farmer's dilemma. A farmer has to move a fox, a goose, and some corn in a wagon that will only transport one thing at a time. The problem is to move all three things without ever leaving the fox with the goose or the goose with the corn, because in either case the former would eat the latter. The solution is to take the goose first, then go back, take the fox, then take the goose back, then take the corn, then go back, then take the goose again. The structure of this task is similar to the tower-of-Hanoi puzzle, in that both involve a sequence of forward and backward moves. Excellent isomorphic transfer was shown, even by the youngest children. Gholson et al. (1989) suggested this might have been because extensive experience with the source tasks gave the children plenty of opportunity to acquire a high quality representation of the source.

Classical Analogies

There has been a long-standing view that young children cannot perform classical analogies of the form a:b::c:? In terms of the taxonomy in Fig. 5.1, these are missing element, or missing element and missing relation analogies. By contrast, problem-solving analogies of the type presented to children are closest to complete structure analogies, because both source and target are supplied and the child has to find the mapping between them. In problem-solving analogies, the child often has to recognize that an analogical mapping is possible, whereas in classical analogies it is usually made clearer that analogical reasoning is intended.

Goswami (1991) reviewed the literature relevant to the question of why classical analogies should be harder. Several possible reasons are examined, but the most likely one is found to be that classical analogies have usually been based on more abstract relations. She reviewed quite extensive literature showing that if the relations are familiar to children, even 3- to 4-year-olds perform very well on analogical reasoning tasks. The techniques that have been shown to be successful with young children can be illustrated by the study of Goswami and Brown (1990). Using pictures, they presented children analogies based on the relation "lives in," for example, "bird is to nest as dog is to doghouse." The distractors offered were "bone" (to control for association), another "dog" (to control for mere appearance) and a "cat" (to control for category match). Even 4-year-old children performed better than chance and resisted suggestions that another solution would be appropriate.

It seems to be clear, therefore, that young children can perform simple analogical reasoning if the task format and content are appropriate. This is quite consistent with the argument of this book because these analogies would be relational mappings, and on evidence that binary relations can be represented even by children as young as 2–3 years, it should be possible to obtain successful reasoning by even younger children.

CHILDREN'S USES OF ANALOGIES

Given that even young children can perform analogical reasoning, we can examine ways that this ability can be utilized. There are several different ways that analogies can be used by children:

1. As a source of hypotheses about an unfamiliar situation, or as a source of new declarative rules.
2. As a source of problem-solving operators and techniques.
3. As a mechanism of semantic development.
4. As an aid to learning.
5. As a mechanism for transfer of learning.
6. As an aid to restructuring concepts.
7. As a source of mental models.

We will consider each of these in turn.

Hypotheses and Declarative Rules

Analogies can be used to suggest hypotheses about unusual or unfamiliar situations. Inagaki and Hatano (1987) hypothesized that the reason children personify nonhuman animals and inanimate objects is that they use analogy as a way of predicting what these other objects would do in unfamiliar situations. They presented 5- to 6-year-old children with hypothetical situations about a rabbit, a tulip, and a rock; for example, what would it do if its owner left it in a shop? They found more personification for the rabbit than for the tulip, and more for the tulip than for the rock. This suggests that analogies are used as sources of hypotheses about unfamiliar situations, but these hypotheses are tested against, and constrained by, other knowledge that the child possesses.

Source of Problem-Solving Operators and Techniques

One technique advocated by Polya (1971) to facilitate problem solving was to think of a similar problem. It is possible that many novel problems are approached by using a technique, or operator, employed in an analogous problem. In the last section we examined numerous studies indicating that young children can use analogous situations as a source of problem-solving strategies. They can even handle complex, multimove sequence problems, provided they have adequate opportunity to learn the source (Gholson et al., 1989).

The use of analogies in problem solving has been analyzed by Carbonell (1981), but the process can be represented by a conventional structure-mapping diagram as shown in Fig. 5.8. The source is the problem-solving process used previously on a now-familiar problem. The elements of the structure-mapping are states and goals, and the relations are operators that effect changes from the initial state to one or more subgoals and then to the

Familiar Problem (**source**)

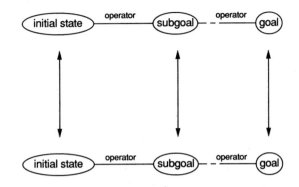

Unfamiliar Problem (**target**)

FIG. 5.8.   Structure mapping for procedural analogy.

final goal. The target is a novel problem. The use of analogies entails mapping the states, goals, and operators of the novel problem into the familiar one. For example in the hollow-tube problem used by Holyoak et al. (1984), the initial state is that the balls are in one bowl, the goal is to have them in another bowl, and the operator is to move them down a tube. Forming the tube is a subgoal, and the operator that achieves it is to roll a sheet of cardboard. The source is a similar problem solved by a genie. The initial state was that the genie's jewels were in one bottle. The goal was to have them in another bottle, the operator being to roll them down a tube made from the magic carpet. Providing the carpet was a subgoal achieved by commanding the carpet to roll itself into a tube. The mechanism of analogy construction in problem solving is probably not basically different from that in other situations. In place of elements and relations we have states, goal (states), and operators, but the structure-mapping process is essentially the same.

Mechanism of Semantic Development

A mapping process similar to that used in analogies may be important in acquiring new word meanings. Heibeck and Markman (1987) introduced unfamiliar words such as "chartreuse" to 2- to 4-year-old children by presenting them with sentences in a natural, conversational fashion. For example, the child might be told, "Do you see those two books on the chair in the corner? Could you bring me the chartreuse one, not the red one, the chartreuse one" (p. 1023). Even 2-year-olds were found to acquire new word knowledge in this way.

Sight of Books (**source**)

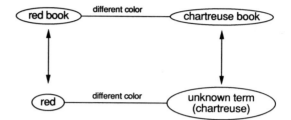

Sentence (**target**)

FIG. 5.9. Structure mapping for semantic task.

A structure mapping that might account for the basic core of this process is shown in Fig. 5.9. The source is the sight of the actual books, because they are visible and their color (as distinct from the color name) is therefore known. The sentence is the target, because it contains one unknown term. The term "red" is known, and is mapped into the visible red book. The phrase "not the red one" implies that the relation "different color" is involved. The unknown term is therefore mapped into the color attribute of the chartreuse book. This is a missing-element problem, as in Fig. 5.1B. The analogical inference is that "chartreuse" is the name of that color. If this analysis is accepted, it implies that 2-year-old children can perform relational mappings, as the current theory predicts.

Aid to Learning and Transfer

The learning process can be facilitated by using an analogical model to predict information that has to be learned. The time and effort required for learning is greatly reduced, and in some cases might amount to little more than finding a suitable model and mapping it into the material to be learned. When a model is used it is easier to learn an integrated set of material than a set of unrelated, or loosely related materials, because an integrated set can be mapped more readily into the analogical model. The reason is that coherence facilitates structure mapping.

A series of learning studies that examine the effect of mapping material into a mental model has been conducted in our laboratory (Halford, 1975; Halford, Bain, & Maybery, under review). To illustrate the task, imagine trying to learn the following set of items:

T, N → T
T, C → R

T, A → L

R, N → R

R, C → L

R, A → T

L, N → L

L, C → T

L, A → R

If we try to learn the items individually, by rote, it is quite difficult, especially if they are presented in random order, as occurs in the experiment cited above. However, if we map them into a mental model, they are very easy to learn. One way would be to use movements around an equilateral triangle as an analog, as shown in the first isomorph in Fig. 5.10. *T*, *R*, and *L* correspond to the vertices of the triangle (Top, Right, and Middle). *N*, *C*, and *A* correspond to movements, Null, Clockwise, and Anticlockwise, respectively. Once this mapping is made, all nine items can be predicted, and no further learning is required. This set of items was devoid of semantic content so as to highlight the effect of structure. However, it makes us aware just how much we depend on mental models to structure even apparently simple learning tasks. In the experiments we conducted the items were based on trigrams and geometric figures, as shown in Fig. 5.10, but they had the same cyclic structure as the example above and were based on a mathematical group, the Cyclic 3-Group. The items could be learned using a spatial mental model, or a mathematical structure such as the group of residue classes, modulo 3, as shown in Fig. 5.10. Halford (1975) found the consistent condition was very much easier to learn than the inconsistent condition (defined as in Fig. 5.10). This would be expected according to analogy theory, because the consistent task can be mapped into an analog, whereas the inconsistent task cannot. There was also an association between learning and ability to recognize a spatial analog of the task. In the incomplete condition, participants were able to predict the items they had never seen. There was also high transfer to analogs of the task (with the same structure, but different items) in the consistent condition.

This experiment illustrates some points about use of analogical models in learning.

1. An analogical model greatly facilitates learning, because once the elements and relations of the learning task are mapped into the model, much of the learned material can be predicted from the model.
2. An analogical model is most beneficial where a set of items are interrelated in a consistent way.

Consistent Condition			Inconsistent Condition			Incomplete Condition		
Stimuli		**Responses**	**Stimuli**		**Responses**	**Stimuli**		**Responses**
BEJ	✦ →	BEJ	BEJ	✦ →	BEJ	BEJ	✦ →	
BEJ	○ →	ZAS	BEJ	○ →	ZAS	BEJ	○ →	ZAS
BEJ	□ →	POB	BEJ	□ →	POB	BEJ	□ →	POB
ZAS	✦ →	ZAS	ZAS	✦ →	ZAS	ZAS	✦ →	
ZAS	○ →	POB	ZAS	○ →	BEJ	ZAS	○ →	
ZAS	□ →	BEJ	ZAS	□ →	POB	ZAS	□ →	
POB	✦ →	POB	POB	✦ →	POB	POB	✦ →	POB
POB	○ →	BEJ	POB	○ →	BEJ	POB	○ →	BEJ
POB	□ →	ZAS	POB	□ →	ZAS	POB	□ →	ZAS

Isomorphs

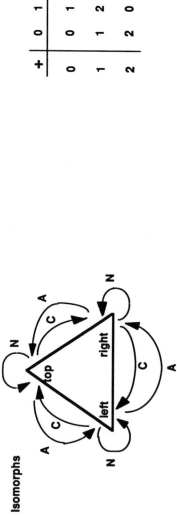

+	0	1	2
0	0	1	2
1	1	2	0
2	2	0	1

FIG. 5.10. Learning-set task based on cyclic 3-Group.

216

3. Transfer of learning can be facilitated by mapping one task into the analog, then using the analog to predict new tasks of the same kind. Notice that a series of tasks with the same structure but different items, or with items rearranged in an unpredictable manner, amount to what has traditionally been called a "learning-set" task, a point to which we will return.

Other studies showing that transfer can be based on structure mapping have been conducted by Reed (1987) and Novick (1988). Reed's technique was to ask adult participants to estimate whether the solution to one problem could be applied to another. There were four kinds of relations between problems. Equivalent problems had the same structure and the same surface properties. Similar problems had the same kind of surface properties but had different structure. Isomorphic problems had the same structure but different surface properties. Unrelated problems were different in both structure and surface properties. Sensitivity to structure would be demonstrated if equivalent problems were rated higher than similar problems, and isomorphic problems higher than unrelated problems. This sensitivity was demonstrated, but only where the structural similarities and differences were not too subtle. Thus, people do use structure for transfer, but their awareness of the structural properties of tasks is not necessarily complete. Novick (1988) found that experts were more likely than novices to recognize structural similarities between tasks, whereas novices were more likely to focus on surface features.

Aid to Restructuring Concepts

One reason analogies are important in promoting cognitive development is that they almost never fit exactly. Most analogies permit a partial mapping of source into target, which helps bring order to an unfamiliar situation and may be a source of valuable insights. However, analogs rarely fit exactly, and the source is rarely a perfect mirror of a target.

The imperfections of an analogy mean that declarative rules and predictions derived from the analogy will sometimes fail to be confirmed. This can provide a stimulus to find a more adequate mental model. Carroll and Mack (1985) contended that this is probably the most valuable aspect of analogies. Also, we saw earlier in this chapter how the COPYCAT model of analogical reasoning creates representations dynamically and will construct whole new representations to deal with discrepancies.

Changes to mental models are particularly likely to occur where the target is more complex, in some important way, than the source. The mapping from source to target must then necessarily be partial. In the beginning it will probably lead to some useful predictions, but eventually the discrepancies will become apparent, as predictions fail to be confirmed. It will be then that a press to create a more adequate model, perhaps by combining two simple models or by adding one or more new rules to the existing model, will be felt. We saw in chapter 4 how new rules, with more conditions, can be added to mental models to provide more detailed and specific representations. This is one way that cognitive development can proceed, and analogies that provide partial fits to a situation are an important stimulus to this kind of development. This role of analogies in promoting cognitive development now seems ripe for empirical investigation. Readers familiar with Piagetian cognitive developmental psychology will recognize how this mechanism captures part of Piaget's notions of assimilation and accommodation. Mapping source into target corresponds broadly to assimilation, and adjusting the source corresponds to accommodation.

As Mental Models

Analogies are useful as mental models to facilitate understanding of concepts. The use of analogies for understanding elementary computer programming has been investigated by Mayer (1976, 1979) and Chee (1987). However, a study by Gentner and Gentner (1983) provided a clear account of how analogies can be used as mental models of electricity.

There are two situations that make good sources for analogical models of electricity. One is liquid flow, and the other is teeming crowds. In the liquid flow model, the wire or conductor corresponds to a pipe, the battery to a reservoir, a resistor to a restriction in the pipe, and voltage to water pressure.

In the teeming crowd model, the wire corresponds to a path along which the crowd must pass, current corresponds to the number of people passing a given point, a resistor corresponds to a gate through which people must pass. Both models can be useful, but each has advantages when dealing with different aspects of electricity.

The liquid flow model is useful for understanding batteries, because a reservoir is a good analog of a battery. Placing two reservoirs one above the other is analogous to connecting two batteries in series because it increases the height of water in the reservoir, thereby increasing the pressure. This corresponds to the fact that connecting batteries in series increases voltage.

However, moving crowds provide a better analog for the effect of resistors in an electrical circuit. It is easy to envisage that a gate slows the rate at which people move along a path, just as a resistor reduces current in a conductor. Two gates in series further decrease flow, just as two resistors in series further decrease current. It is also easy to see that two gates in parallel increase flow of people, which corresponds to the fact that two resistors in parallel decrease resistance and increase current.

Gentner and Gentner (1983) examined the effects of both analogies on high school and college students' understanding of electricity, and found results supporting these predictions.

Neither of these models however is a completely adequate model of electricity. A sophisticated understanding of electricity needs to include a more precise account of the quantitative relationships between voltage, resistance, and current, as expressed for example in Ohm's law. Analogs such as liquid flow or teeming crowds are not a substitute for this. What then is their value?

It is probably that analogs facilitate early acquisition of an integrated conception of a concept such as electricity. Without such an analog there is a danger that the equations that express the quantitative relations between voltage, resistance, and current will be learned by rote, without a genuinely coherent conception of how electricity behaves. The result will be ability to perform the kinds of computations required in examinations, at least of the traditional variety, but with the kind of inadequate understanding that results in the persistence of naive or absurd beliefs.

Advantages and Disadvantages of Analogs in Learning

We can see that analogs can have great advantages in learning and memory tasks, because they provide a mental model from which the to-be-learned material can be generated, thereby reducing the amount of learning that is required. Mnemonics and concrete aids are also analogs, because their value derives from the fact that they reflect the structure of the material to be learned.

Mnemonics can be thought of as analogs that are mapped into the material to be remembered. For example, the method of loci (Norman, 1976), practiced by orators in ancient Greece, consisted of learning the layout of a large building such as a temple, then assigning sections of the speech to parts of the building. Such a mnemonic could be expressed as a structure mapping between a source, consisting of the locations and the spatial relations between them, and a target, consisting of sections of the speech, with the logical or temporal relations between them.

Concrete analogs have been popular in teaching mathematics, as the multitude of commercially available mathematical games attests. In fact, the construction of concrete analogs for mathematical concepts has reached great heights of ingenuity, as is evidenced in the work of Dienes (1964). The reason why analogs have proved specially attractive in mathematics education may well be that mathematics consists of integrated systems of information, and analogs are particularly useful for learning such material, as we have seen. Although we discuss children's understanding of mathematics further in chapter 8, it is worthwhile in the present context to show how structure-mapping theory can be applied to mathematical analogs so as to assess their merits and deficiencies. There are advantages of analogs as an aid to learning:

1. They reduce the amount of learning effort and serve as memory aids.
2. They can provide a means of verifying the truth of what is learned.
3. They can increase flexibility of thinking.
4. They can facilitate retrieval of information from memory.
5. They can mediate transfer between tasks and situations.
6. They can indirectly (and, perhaps, paradoxically) facilitate transition to higher levels of abstraction.

On the other hand there are some potential disadvantages, including:

1. Structure mapping imposes a processing load, as discussed in chapter 3, that can actually make it more difficult to understand a concept.
2. A poor analog can generate incorrect information.
3. If an analog is not fully integrated, and is not well mapped into the material to be learned or remembered, it can actually increase the learning or memory load.

We explain these points by first using as an example the simple mathematical analogs in Fig. 5.11. A popular way to teach simple addition facts is by using small sets of objects, as in Dienes blocks, or simply crosses on paper to represent small numbers. Figure 5.11A shows such an analog in structure-mapping format, with a set of one object mapped into the numeral 1, a set of two objects mapped into the numeral 2, and so on. The use of the same analog to represent a simple arithmetic relationship, $2 + 3 = 5$, is shown in Fig. 5.11B. Collis (1978) pointed out how this analog can be used to represent some more sophisticated mathematical notions, including addition and multiplication, commutativity, operations on ratios, and proportion. I apply structure-mapping theory to assessing this analog. First, notice that in Fig. 5.11A the mapping from sets to numerals is clear and easily verified. It is easy to recognize, by subitizing or counting, how many elements each set contains. In Fig. 5.11B, the mapping of the numerals 2, 3, 5 into their respective sets is also clear and easily verified. The relation between the two addend sets and the sum set is also clear—the sum set includes all elements of the two addend sets, which have no common elements (are disjoint). This means that the structure of the source is clear and readily accessible (high source specificity in Gentner's terms). If we arrange sets in order of increasing magnitude as shown in Fig. 5.11A, it is easy to see that each set contains one more element than its predecessor. This is one of many useful relationships that are contained in the analog and that are readily available for mapping into the target.

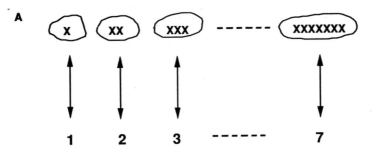

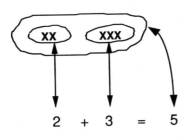

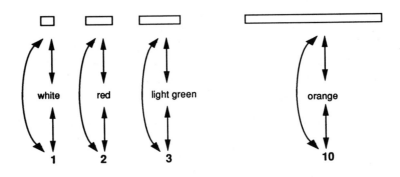

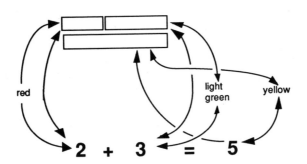

FIG. 5.11. Concrete analogs for elementary number.

Contrast this with another analog of elementary number facts, the cuisenaire rods, shown in Fig. 5.11C and 5.11D. In this case it is not so clear which rod should be mapped into each numeral. The longer rods are mapped into the larger numerals, but it is difficult to be sure precisely which numeral is represented by a rod of a given length. The rods are distinctive colors, to facilitate this differentiation, but as Fig. 5.11C shows, the colors complicate the mapping process. There is a two-stage map from rod to color to numeral. The colors are arbitrary, so the mapping from rod to color and the mapping from color to numeral must be rote learned. Learning this arbitrary double mapping greatly increases the load on the children. The relationships in the source are not as clear as in the sets analog. For example, it is not as clear that each rod represents one more unit than its predecessor.

The use of the Cuisenaire analog to represent $2 + 3 = 5$ is shown in Fig. 5.11D. Because of the two-stage mapping rod-color-numeral, which parallels the rod–numeral mapping, we can see that the structure mapping is much more complex than the corresponding mapping in Fig. 5.11B based on sets. A structure-mapping analysis therefore predicts that the sets analog would be more efficient than the colored rods analog. The sets analog also permits verification of the truth of what is learned. As Fig. 5.11B shows, the sets analog provides a concrete model verifying that $2 + 3 = 5$. Furthermore, it is a model that a child can learn to construct at any time so as to verify this relationship. The third advantage, facilitation of memory retrieval, occurs because an analog can provide an additional retrieval cue.

The sets analog illustrates how flexibility of thinking can be increased. The analog in Fig. 5.11B was constructed to show that $2 + 3 = 5$, but it can be used equally well to verify that $3 + 2 = 5$, and then that $2 + 3 = 3 + 2$ (the commutativity property), and even that $5 - 3 = 2$, and $5 - 2 = 3$. Many good analogs can be accessed in several different ways, which makes it easy to examine a concept from a number of angles.

One reason why analogs facilitate transition to higher levels of abstraction is that they promote learning of integrated structures. For example, the analog in Fig. 5.11A would facilitate the learning of numbers as an ordered set, whereas analogs such as that in Fig. 5.11B would facilitate the learning of integrated sets of relationships such as $1 + 1 = 2$, $1 + 2 = 3$, $1 + 3 = 4 \ldots 3 + 4 = 7$, $3 + 5 = 8$, and so on. Structure mappings can be best made when the source structure is well learned (the property that Gentner, 1982, called *source specificity*). When learning arithmetic using a concrete analog, the concrete material is the source and the arithmetic facts are the target. An analog that gives access to these complex relationships promotes construction of a more adequate mental model of arithmetic. When the transition is made to a higher level of abstraction, the arithmetic structure is the source, and the algebraic relationships that mirror the arithmetic are the target. A good source for learning algebra depends on having a good mental model of arithmetic relations. To the extent that concrete analogs promote such a mental model of arithmetic, they facilitate acquisition of algebra.

OTHER APPLICATIONS OF STRUCTURE MAPPING

In this section I consider cases of structure mapping that would not normally be regarded as analogies. The use of analogies is already very widespread, as we have seen, and they have even been used to facilitate reading and spelling (Goswami, 1986, 1988). Now I show how structure mapping, the basic process in analogies, is applicable to a once well-known phenomenon that at the time seemed very remote from analogical reasoning: learning sets. I also suggest that structure mapping might be involved in some kinds of humor.

Learning Sets

The learning-set paradigm consists of a series of problems that all have similar form, but in which the surface features vary from problem to problem. This was true of the tasks used in our laboratory (Halford, 1975; Halford et al., under review) discussed earlier. Learning sets were originally used to study learning and transfer in animals (Harlow, 1949), although they have also been used extensively with children (Reese, 1965). However, as I have pointed out elsewhere (Halford, 1989) the paradigm has considerable unused potential for the study of cognitive development, because there are a number of concepts that are more structurally complex than those used with animals, and that might demonstrate important age differences in children if used in a learning-set format.

Learning-set tasks represent a case of transfer based on structure mapping *par excellence* because the learning-set paradigm is designed so there is no basis for transfer between tasks other than common structure. Therefore, if there are age-related limitations in structure-mapping ability, it should be possible to study them by using learning-set tasks with different structural complexities.

Learning sets also have a number of features that are interesting in relation to a theory of understanding. First, they demonstrate how a general concept can be acquired through experience with specific instances: They are a clear case of induction. Second, they have been used successfully to discriminate between species at different phylogenetic levels, and I have argued elsewhere (Halford, 1989) that they can be used to assess capacity to transfer.

Comparative learning studies (Bitterman, 1960; Bitterman, Wodinsky, & Candland, 1958) have shown that species with no apparent differences in ability to learn individual tasks differ in ability to transfer the basis of discriminations, or in learning-set acquisition. Some of this research has utilized reversal learning set, in which a discrimination is learned, then it is reversed so the opposite alternative is rewarded, then this is reversed, and so on. Interest centers on the speed with which successive reversals are made. Monkeys, rats, and pigeons learn to make reversals more and more quickly, as shown by decreasing error rate across problems. However, fish show no improvement across problems, and turtles do so only on spatial, not on visual discrimination problems.

One implication of this is that acquisition of individual associations might impose low processing demands and therefore does not discriminate among higher and lower species. What does discriminate between species at different phylogenetic levels is the ability to extract a common principle from a series of tasks and transfer it to new tasks. This entails recognizing the common structure of a number of tasks, mapping that structure into a mental model, and then mapping the model into new tasks. This suggests that it is the ability to code a complex set of contingencies, and the consequent ability to map the code from one situation to another, that discriminates between species. It would be very valuable to know whether it discriminates between children of different ages in a similar way. Later in this section I examine literature that is relevant to this question, but because the studies were not specifically designed to address this question, they unfortunately provide no definitive answer to it.

To show how learning-set acquisition is relevant to cognitive development, we first have to analyze the basic principles. I will do this first with a very basic learning-set paradigm, simple discrimination learning set, the structure of which is shown in Fig. 5.12. The first problem consists of a triangle, response to which is rewarded, and a circle, response to which is not rewarded. Suppose this is the first problem in a series of problems. A later problem (Task

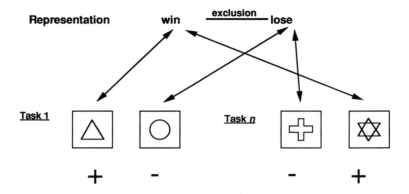

FIG. 5.12. Structure mapping for two-object discrimination learning set.

n in Fig. 5.12) might comprise a cross and a star, the latter being the positive (rewarded) stimulus.

The common structure of all these problems is a "win" stimulus, response to which is rewarded, and a "lose" stimulus, response to which is not rewarded. There is also an exclusion relation between these stimuli; the win element is not the lose element, and vice versa.

One way of viewing learning-set acquisition is to say that it consists of mapping an individual problem into a mental model, then this model, which is mapped into further problems, can be used to predict the correct response to them. The essential requirement for the mental model is that it must incorporate the structure of the task; that is, a win element, a lose element, with the exclusion relation between them. In terms of structure-mapping theory, a specific example would suffice, so that one problem can provide a mental model for the others.

Some of the responses to a new problem can be predicted because of the exclusion relation. That is, once (say) the win element on a new problem is identified, the exclusion relation implies that the other element must be the lose element, and vice versa. This gives rise to the "win-stay, lose-shift" strategy that underlies successful discrimination learning-set acquisition.

The problem is to specify how this structure mapping is acquired. It is essentially a relational mapping, because its validity depends on the fact that the relation between the win and lose elements in the learning-set representation is the same as that between the problem elements. However, there is clearly considerably more to acquiring a learning set than simply constructing a relational mapping.

It is tempting to use the "any of" substitution principle to try to explain learning-set acquisition, but the superficiality of such an explanation soon becomes apparent. Suppose we say that a particular learning set depends on the following types of rules:

ls+: triangle, reward → respond "triangle" next trial

ls−: circle, no reward → do not respond "circle" next trial

For the second problem different stimuli would be substituted for triangle and circle, leading eventually to a rule of the form:

ls+: Stimulus *x*, reward → respond "Stimulus *x*" next trial

ls−: Stimulus *y*, no reward → do not respond "Stimulus *y*" next trial

Substituting variables for specific stimuli appears to solve the problem, but really it conceals some of the most interesting aspects of the problem. Notice that the rule format that we have provided really contains the structure of the problem. That is, by providing two rules, one with a rewarded

stimulus and one with a nonrewarded stimulus, we have effectively provided the very structure that the participant in the task must discover! This is
a caveat against using variable ("any-of") substitution without carefully considering whether it is justified. How then is the structure discovered?

It seems reasonable to expect that the process would depend on recognizing that the most relevant property of a stimulus is the fact that it was rewarded on the previous trial. The first positive stimulus has many attributes;
it is a triangle, it has a certain size, hue, brightness, orientation, and so on.
A great many rules could predict the correct response to the first problem.
For example the rule; size $x \rightarrow$ respond, triangle $\rightarrow$ respond, and so on. These
invalid rules become eliminated by successive problems. This elimination
process was recognized in an early theory of learning set acquisition, error
factor theory (Harlow, 1949). The only rule that will survive is:

"Stimulus x" rewarded previous trial $\rightarrow$ respond "Stimulus x"

This is recognizable as the ls+ rule mentioned above, but we have said
more about its acquisition. This is still not sufficient, however, because simply identifying the relevant property of the stimulus does permit the correct
response to be predicted. It is also necessary to discover that the relevant
property of the other stimulus is that it was not rewarded on the previous
trial. This leads to the rule:

"Stimulus y" not rewarded previous trial $\rightarrow$ do not respond "Stimulus y"

These acquisitions constitute the learning-set rule mentioned earlier. It is
still necessary however to recognize the relation between these two rules.
That is, it must be recognized that there is an exclusion relation between
rewarded and nonrewarded stimuli on any trial. This permits the prediction
that, if one stimulus is rewarded on the first trial of a new problem, the other
stimulus will not be rewarded, and vice versa. The two rules, ls+ and ls−,
in effect constitute the discrimination learning-set concept.

Learning-set acquisition also depends on ability to apply the concept, once
learned, to a new problem. Given a new problem, such as problem n in Fig.
5.12, one stimulus must be mapped into the win element and one into the
lose element. This mapping is equivalent to seeing the correspondence between the discrimination learning-set concept and the new problem. Without
seeing this correspondence, it is not possible to predict the correct response
on the next trial of the problem.

Learning-set acquisition therefore entails recognition of correspondence
between the structure of a mental model and the structure of the current
task. This depends on structure mapping, which, as we have seen, imposes
a processing load. I suggest that this load may be the reason why interproblem

learning discriminates between species and between children of different ages, when acquisition of individual problems does not. According to the arguments in chapters 2 and 3, the load should depend on the dimensionality (structural complexity) of the tasks used. This prediction has been tested with positive results by Halford and Wilson (1980), as discussed in chapter 3. It has also been tested in the context of multiple classification (Halford, 1980), as is discussed in chapter 8. However, there are some other tasks that vary in structural complexity that have the potential to shed light on this question.

LEARNING SETS AND TASK COMPLEXITY

There are a number of learning tasks that have a relatively complex structure and are known to cause difficulty for young children. These are oddity, conditional discrimination, negative patterning, and transverse-pattern discrimination. The first two of these have been reviewed elsewhere (Halford, 1982), whereas the last two were the subject of a recent investigation by Rudy (1991). The tasks are summarized in Fig. 5.13.

Oddity

In *simple-oddity* discrimination the child has to choose the single object that is different from the others; for example, in a set with two triangles and a circle, the circle is odd. In *dimension-abstracted oddity* the stimuli vary in at least two dimensions, only one of which defines an odd stimulus. For example, in a set of one green circle, two blue triangles, and a blue square, the green circle is odd. The odd object is defined by color, because there is only one green object, and all the rest are blue. Shape does not define an odd object, because there are two circles, one triangle, and a square.

The structure of simple oddity is based on a single relation, that of difference; the odd object is different from all the others. The participant does not need to process the fact that the other objects are all the same, because this is guaranteed by the stimulus sets presented; the remaining stimuli are always the same.

The structure of dimension-abstracted oddity is defined by two relations, difference and similarity. The odd object is different from all the others, and it is necessary to establish that they are the same as each other. This is not guaranteed by the procedure, because it is not true in the other dimension. In the example above, the green circle is odd because it is different in color from the others, which are all the same color (blue). However circle is not odd because, although it is different in shape from the others, they are not the same as each other (two are triangles and one is a square).

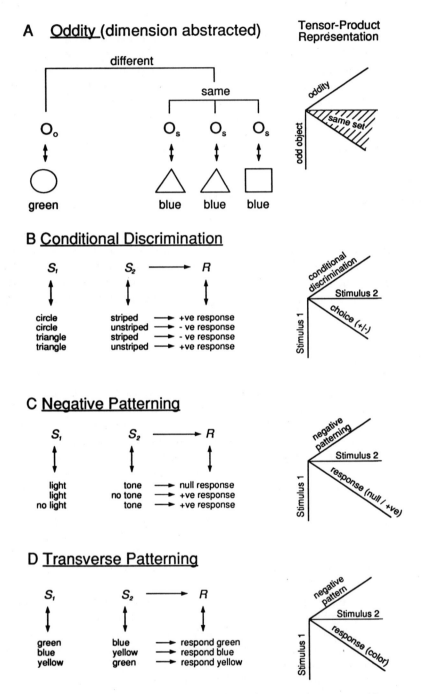

A **Oddity** (dimension abstracted)

Tensor-Product Representation

different

same

O_o

O_s O_s O_s

green

blue blue blue

oddity

odd object

same set

B **Conditional Discrimination**

S_1 S_2 ⟶ R

circle	striped	⟶ +ve response
circle	unstriped	⟶ - ve response
triangle	striped	⟶ - ve response
triangle	unstriped	⟶ +ve response

conditional discrimination

Stimulus 2

choice (+/-)

Stimulus 1

C **Negative Patterning**

S_1 S_2 ⟶ R

light	tone	⟶ null response
light	no tone	⟶ +ve response
no light	tone	⟶ +ve response

negative patterning

Stimulus 2

response (null / +ve)

Stimulus 1

D **Transverse Patterning**

S_1 S_2 ⟶ R

green	blue	⟶ respond green
blue	yellow	⟶ respond blue
yellow	green	⟶ respond yellow

negative pattern

Stimulus 2

response (color)

Stimulus 1

FIG. 5.13. Four tasks with structure mapping and tensor-product representation.

Based on the principle enunciated in chapter 2 that the complexity of a representation depends on the number of dimensions that vary independently within a task, dimension-abstracted oddity is more complex than simple oddity. The latter is defined by a binary relation (difference), whereas the former is defined by two relations (difference and similarity). Accordingly, dimension-abstracted oddity has the more complex structure. Because simple oddity is based on a single binary relation, it is essentially two-dimensional and can in principle be represented by a tensor product of Rank 3. Dimension-abstracted oddity is based on two binary relations and is equivalent to a ternary relation, so it is three-dimensional and needs to be represented by a Rank-4 tensor product.

A number of studies have reported considerable difficulty in teaching children oddity, and this is especially true of dimension-abstracted oddity (Halford, 1982). However, Soraci, Dencker, Baumeister, & Bryant (1991) reported success in teaching simple oddity to 3- to 4-year-olds using bimodal stimuli. A tone was used to signal whether the shape stimuli were odd or the same. A recent (unpublished) study in our laboratory showed that appropriate verbal instruction greatly increased success with 3- to 4-year-olds and 5- to 6-year-olds, on both simple and dimension-abstracted oddity, and good learning set transfer was also obtained. However, there was evidence that the younger children did not perform the task on the same basis as the older children.

The structural aspects of oddity have not been analyzed because research on the topic has been oriented to animal discrimination learning concepts. However, although recognizing that much research is still needed on the structure of the oddity concept, it appears that in principle it could be based on structure mapping, as with analogies. A preliminary structure-mapping analysis is shown in Fig. 5.13A.

I will assume first that the participant has some kind of schema that represents the essential relationships in the dimension-abstracted oddity task. The schema might consist simply of a previously learned task of this kind. The content of the schema does not matter, provided the structure of the task is represented. The essential features of the schema are:

1. An object that is different from all the others (the "odd" object).

2. A set of objects that are all the same as each other, although different from the odd object (the "same set"). In dimension-abstracted oddity, the "same set" cannot be represented as a single chunk, because variation within the set is possible. In our reference example (shown in Fig. 5.13A), elements of the "same set" differ in shape. Because the relation between elements in the same set is one of the things that can vary, it must be represented as a binary relation, and therefore two dimensions are allocated to it.

The task can be performed by mapping a particular problem into the schema. The problem is solved if the relations in the schema (equivalent to the source in analogies) correspond to the relations in the target (equivalent to the target in analogies).

A tensor-product representation, consistent with that used in the STAR model of analogical reasoning, is shown in Fig. 5.13A. It consists of a Rank-4 tensor-product, with four vectors, one representing the oddity concept (equivalent of the predicate vector in the STAR model), one representing the "odd object," and two vectors representing the "same set," together with the relation between them. With simple oddity the relation between elements in the "same set" does not vary, and it can be chunked into a single vector. According to this analysis, dimension-abstracted oddity is a three-dimensional concept, and simple oddity is a two-dimensional concept.

Conditional Discrimination

The conditional-discrimination task has two stimulus dimensions that interact so that they reverse each other's effects. For example, Gollin (1966) used either a circle or a triangle on either a striped or an unstriped background. On a striped background, the triangle is positive, but on an unstriped background, it is negative. Similarly for the circle (see Fig. 5.13B). This task, like oddity, has been found difficult for young children (see review by Halford, 1982).

A structure-mapping analysis is shown in Fig. 5.13B. The schema comprises a representation of two stimuli, which jointly determine the response. Individual items are mapped into this schema. As the tensor-product diagram shows, the task is three-dimensional, as with dimension-abstracted oddity.

Negative Patterning

In a negative patterning task there are two stimuli, and the participant is expected to respond to either, but not to both (the task is identical to the "exclusive OR" in logic). The form of the task is $A+$, $B+$, $AB-$. For example, the participants respond to either a light or a tone, but not to both together. This task is very similar to conditional discrimination, in that the response is determined jointly by two stimulus dimensions. As the tensor-product diagram in Fig. 5.13C shows, it too is three-dimensional. Rudy (in press) presented evidence that this task is dependent on maturity of the hippocampus in rats.

Transverse Patterning

The form of this task is $A+/B-$, $B+/C-$, $C+/A-$. An example is shown in Fig. 5.13D. When green and blue stimuli are presented, choose the green (green$+$/blue$-$). When blue and yellow are presented, choose the blue

(blue + /yellow −). When yellow and green are presented, choose yellow (yellow + /green −). Rudy (in press) showed that this task also depended on maturity of the hippocampus in rats, and that it was not performed until age 55 months by children. This despite the fact that they could perform a control task of the form $A + /B−$, $C + /D−$, $E + /F−$. This constitutes yet more evidence for physiological maturation of capacity to process structurally complex concepts. As the structure-mapping diagram in Fig. 5.13D shows, this task also is three-dimensional.

Nondecomposable Three-Dimensional Concepts

An interesting feature of oddity, conditional discrimination, negative patterning, and transverse patterning is that all depend on relations between elements, rather than on elements themselves. With the exception of simple oddity, all are ternary relations and are three-dimensional. Furthermore, there is evidence that they depend on a certain degree of maturity of the central nervous system, although much more evidence is needed on this question.

Conditional discrimination, negative patterning, and tranverse patterning are also interesting in that they are not decomposable into lower level concepts. At the level of single stimulus dimensions they are ambiguous, because each stimulus is associated equally with two contradictory outcomes. For example, in negative patterning stimulus A is associated with both positive and negative outcomes. The same is true for stimulus B. In all these tasks, the outcome is determined by an interaction of the stimuli.

It is interesting to compare the representations needed for these concepts with the tensor-product representations used in the memory model of Humphreys et al. (1989) shown in Fig. 5.5. In the memory model there is an association between a cue and a target that is modified by context. Context and cue interact to determine the target item. The representation required for the relational learning tasks is similar except that an additional vector is required to represent the concept. An important similarity, however, is that all depend on the interaction of two or more stimulus dimensions. As we later see, this idea of interaction between separate dimensions of a task is very important in many cognitive performances.

Chunking of Relational Concepts

It is possible of course to chunk the vectors representing the two stimuli into a single vector. For example, in the conditional discrimination task in Fig. 5.13B, the stimuli "circle" and "striped" could be combined into a single vector representing the *configuration* "striped circle." However, the stimuli will not then retain their identity in other combinations. Their compositionality (Fodor & Pylyshyn, 1988) will be lost. Suppose, for example, that we introduced a square and a cross on striped or unstriped backgrounds. We would expect that participants who understood the conditional discrimination principle would recognize that if a square were positive on a striped background, it would be negative on an unstriped background. The problem would be that there would be no respresentation of striped/unstriped. It would be necessary to learn new configurations, "striped square," and "unstriped square." Each new combination would have to be learned separately, and the ability to generate solutions from the conditional-discrimination principle would be lost.

It is interesting to note that a similar problem emerged in memory models. Using the representation in Fig. 5.5., Humphreys et al. (1989) pointed out that the effect of context cannot be handled by combining cue and context in one vector, because the three-way combinations of cue, context, and target cannot then be computed. Thus, the tasks we have considered in this section, and the memory model of Humphreys et al. (1989), again illustrate that chunking can sometimes lead to loss of computational power. Whether two dimensions of a task can be chunked or not depends on whether it is necessary to process variations in both dimensions. If variations occur in each dimension independently of the other, and if it is necessary to process both sources of variation, then the dimensions cannot be represented as a single chunk.

Humor

In this section we briefly consider the work of Maybery and his collaborators (Maybery & Aitken, personal communication, 1988; Heng, 1990) showing how structure mapping can be used to analyze children's jokes. A sample joke is, "What did the big chimney say to the little chimney?"[4] The structure-mapping analysis is shown in Fig. 5.14. The incongruity occurs because it is normally the purpose of chimneys to smoke, but the joke implies that the larger chimney, being older, is entitled to deny the smaller chimney permission to smoke. This is by analogy with the adult–child relationship in which adults' senior status and larger size entitles them to deny permission to children to smoke. The resolution of the incongruity in the joke is achieved by mapping relations between large and small chimneys and smoking into the relations between adult, child, and smoking.

Although there is as yet little data to define the type of mental model used in this joke, it appears to be a system mapping. The essence of it is the second-order relation, roughly equivalent to entitlement, between seniority and permission. If this analysis is correct, then this joke requires a system mapping,

---

[4]Answer: "You're too young to smoke."

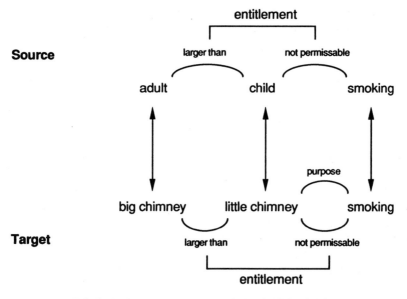

FIG. 5.14.   Structure-mapping analysis of children's joke.

and data discussed in chapter 3 indicate that it should be understood at 5 years of age.

Children's ability to understand the jokes was investigated by asking them to choose between original jokes and matched control stories with the resolution removed; for example, "What did the big window say to the little window?" "You're too young to smoke." Understanding is indicated by preference for the joke rather than for the control story. Maybery and Aitken found that when 5-year-olds were primed to both meanings of the double-meaning word (e.g., the two meanings of smoke), they showed understanding of the jokes, consistent with the structure-mapping analysis. Converging evidence was provided by the finding that recall for the jokes was superior to recall of control stories, indicating that children were sensitive to the story structure.

SUMMARY AND CONCLUSIONS

Much human reasoning is basically analogical, and analogies can also be used as an aid to learning and transfer. An analogy is a structure-preserving map from a source, or sources, to a target. Attributes are not normally mapped, and relations are mapped selectively, those relations that enter into a coherent structure being more likely to be mapped (the principle of systematicity). Analogies can be classified according to the information supplied to the problem solver. In complete structure analogies, source and target are complete, and it is only necessary to find the right mapping between them. Then there are analogies with a missing element, a missing relation, or both, and there are analogies with the source missing. In these cases the correct mapping must be found and used to supply the missing information.

Most common analogies correspond to either relational or system mappings, though some complex cases may correspond to multiple-system mappings. The level of mapping depends on the minimum information required to establish the validity of the mapping, rather than on the total information in the structures of source or target. If an analogy with many relations in source and target can be decomposed into a series of mappings each based on a single relation, it is a relational mapping. Only if two relations must be considered jointly does the analogy entail a system mapping.

Analogies are distinguished from metaphors, which are based more on attributes. A literal similarity is based on common attributes. An abstraction is a mapping based on an abstract representation of the source. Criteria for good analogies include source specificity (knowledge of the source), clarity of the mapping, richness, systematicity, and the validity or appropriateness of the analog.

The process models examined include that of Sternberg, plus the Structure-Mapping Engine, COPYCAT, the Analogical Constraint Mapping Engine, and the Structured Tensor Analogical Reasoning model. The last model is based on parallel distributed processing architecture and makes processing demands consistent with capacity limitations outlined in chapter 3. It proposes that the most complex source and target structures that can be mapped in parallel are those with four dimensions of stimuli. Structures more complex than this must be either decomposed and the segments processed serially, or some dimensions must be chunked into a single dimension. Effective chunking requires that the important attributes be recognized, and this is a component of expertise. The STAR model shares basic mechanisms with a contemporary mathematical model of human memory and integrates analogical reasoning with memory processes.

Factors affecting analogical reasoning include stimulus similarity, encoding and categorization, domain knowledge, goals, stimulus complexity, and processing loads.

Most analogies that children are asked to perform entail relational mappings. There is extensive evidence that children can perform simple problem-solving analogies from the age of 3, and can transfer multistep problem solutions to problem isomorphs from age 4, provided they have adequate opportunity to acquire a good source representation. Children as young as 2–3 years can encode relations and transfer them to isomorphic tasks and can also handle spatial analogies based on a single relation. Traditional findings that young children cannot perform classical analogies of the form $A:B::C:?$ are mostly attributed to use of excessively complex or unfamiliar relations. There does seem to be a shift from reliance on attributes to reliance on relations with age, but it probably reflects the way the task is coded rather than ability to represent relations per se. There is evidence that relational encodings tend to result from processing larger amounts of structure.

Children can use analogies as a source of hypotheses about an unfamiliar situation, as a source of problem-solving operators and techniques, as a mechanism of semantic development, as an aid to learning and transfer, as an aid to restructuring concepts, and as a source of mental models. Analogs aid learning because they enable the material to be predicted and thereby reduce the amount of learning effort, they serve as memory aids, and they can provide a means of verifying the truth of what is learned. They can increase flexibility of thinking, can facilitate retrieval of information from memory, and can mediate transfer between tasks and situations. They can also indirectly (and, perhaps, paradoxically) facilitate transition to higher levels of abstraction. Some potential disadvantages of analogies in learning are that they can impose a processing load, and a poor analog can generate incorrect information.

It is argued that structure mapping does not only occur in analogies but also mediates what has traditionally been called interproblem transfer in learning sets, and may possibly be involved in humor. The possible representations entailed in some relational concepts, oddity, conditional discrimination, negative patterning, and transverse patterning are analyzed. These concepts are known to be difficult for young children, and there is recent evidence that at least some of them depend on maturity of the nervous system. It is argued that they depend on the ability to represent more than one stimulus dimension in parallel, that the tasks cannot be decomposed, and that the representations cannot be chunked into fewer dimensions without losing the ability to generate solutions from the principle.

PART

III

THEORY

6

How Understanding Develops: A Cognitive Developmental Theory

The purpose of this chapter is to draw together the arguments in chapters 1 to 5, and to present the main theoretical tenets of this book. The resulting theory will then be applied to a number of specific problem domains in chapters 7 to 9.

The book is concerned with defining and explaining children's mental models, skills, and strategies, rather than with categorizing them as having, or not having, a particular concept. Any concept can be understood in a number of different ways, and this understanding corresponds to different kinds of mental models. I believe it is more useful to characterize children's understanding in this way than to engage in potentially endless debate about whether the concept is really understood or not. It is not that there is no room for debate, and in later chapters I examine a number of issues concerned with children's understanding of concepts. However, the debates are more likely to be fruitful if that understanding is defined in terms of detailed mental models and strategies, than if it is simply categorized in all-or-none fashion.

UNDERSTANDING

In this section I draw together various aspects of the topic of understanding from previous chapters.

Role of Understanding

It is reasonable to ask why we should study understanding rather than, say, describe children's skills and strategies. It might be asked what understanding adds. The answer is that understanding is the source of a lot of skills and strategies. In some contexts strategies can be learned by shaping, and in other contexts strategies can be taught, with little or no understanding on the part of the child. However, it is impossible to equip a child with all the skills and strategies he or she might need in dealing with the complexity of the world. The child must have the ability to construct his or her own strategies as the need arises. In some contexts this process depends on, or at the very least is aided by, an understanding of the task. An example is the acquisition of transitive-inference strategies discussed in chapter 4. There the child uses declarative knowledge of ordered sets and procedural knowledge about operators that can be applied to ordered sets, as the building blocks of strategies for N-term series, or transitive-inference tasks.

The development of these strategies has a degree of autonomy, in that the child actively constructs the strategy, tests, and modifies it through experience with the task. It is not that social influences cannot facilitate strategy acquisition. Adults and peers can draw attention to relevant aspects of the task, help children encode task features efficiently, maintain motivation, and provide feedback. However, adults cannot program the strategy into the child, the way one feeds a program into a computer. The child has skill-acquisition processes that construct the strategy from the knowledge available, making use of whatever environmental supports are provided.

Even if it were possible to program skills into children, they would still need to modify the skills to deal with changed circumstances, or to recover losses due to forgetting. Understanding is necessary for the modification, adaptation, and maintenance of skills as conditions of performance change.

It is not that understanding inevitably accompanies all skilled performance. Once skills have been acquired, they may be applied to familiar tasks automatically, without understanding, and therefore without the processing loads that understanding imposes. This is a prerequisite of efficient performance in many situations. Furthermore, skills can be acquired with minimal understanding in some contexts, such as acquisition of computer programming commands. Understanding then tends to follow skill acquisition, rather than precede it. However, the understanding that follows from strategy acquisition tends to facilitate acquisition of further skills and guides the modification of skills for changed circumstances.

Properties of Understanding

As explained in chapter 3, understanding entails having a mental model that represents the structure of the concept or phenomenon. A mental model is a representation that is active while solving a particular problem, it provides a workspace for mental operations, it is general in the sense that it can be transferred from one situation to another, it can generate predictions about the world, it can be used to organize informaton, and it can guide the development of skills and strategies.

Representations are not "pictures in the head," and there need be no resemblance between a cognitive representation and any aspect of the world it represents. The validity of representations is defined by two properties, consistency and correspondence.

Consistency means that a given cognitive process must always represent the same environmental input. This means that mappings from representation to the environment must be unique, in the sense that each representation is mapped into one and only one feature of the environment, and vice versa. As noted in chapter 2, there was some disagreement on this point. Holland et al. (1986) argued for a many-to-one mapping from the environment to representations, thereby creating a categorization function. However, Grossberg (1980) argued that there must be a feedback process that ensured that each cognitive representation was mapped to only one environmental input. I argued that at the microstructural level, mappings are unique, and the categorization function is handled by averaging overinputs. As noted in chapter 2, this can occur automatically in PDP representations.

Correspondence means that relations (more generally, predicates) in the representation must correspond to relations in the segment of the environment represented. Technically, it means that if a relation (predicate) in a representation is mapped into a relation (predicate) in the world, the arguments of the representation relation (predicate) must be mapped into the arguments of the world relation (predicate). For example, in Fig. 5.3A, when the relation "pushes" is mapped into the relation "helps," the arguments of "pushes," John and Bill, are mapped to the arguments of "helps," Wendy and Anne.

The two properties of consistency and correspondence provide objective criteria for representations, which means they can be handled mathematically, and by simulation. This removes any suggestion of homunculi looking at pictures in the head. Consistency and correspondence are soft constraints, but they tend to ensure that the structure of representations corresponds to the segment of the world they represent.

Representations correspond to segments of the world, but the particular part of the world that is represented is a segment of a person's environment. Therefore, representations are mapped into segments of the environment. It need not be part of the person's direct environment. Any aspect of the world with which the person interacts is part of that person's environment. To a novelist, fantasies about life, even extraterrestrial life, might be part of his environment, whereas to a mathematician, certain mathematical concepts and symbols are part of her environment.

Mental models are not purely syntactic, they also include semantic information. They are frequently content-specific representations and may consist of specific examples, or of prototypical examples, rather than logical principles. For example, a child's, or even an adult's, mental model of an ordered set is more likely to consist of a representative example than a formal mathematical definition. One way that mental models differ from psycho-logic is that they contain more semantic information.

Mental models depend on domain knowledge, although they are not always drawn from the same domain as the problem to which they are applied. They are often based on an analogy from another domain. Nevertheless, specific content knowledge of the current situation or of an analogous situation is normally entailed in the construction of mental models. The domain knowledge can be declarative (knowing that), or procedural (knowing how). It has been found necessary to distinguish the two kinds of knowledge in cognitive psychology (Anderson, 1983), and they also have different consequences in basic learning paradigms, as discussed in chapter 4.

Declarative knowledge comprises a set of stored representations of the world that can be implicit or explicit. Implicit representations are typically unconscious, are not accessible to strategic cognitive operations, and cannot be modified without external input. Explicit representations are cognitively accessible and can be modified without external input, by the operation of strategic cognitive processes (e.g., changing hypotheses). Explicit representations are more likely to be accessible to consciousness, but the data on this question are not clear enough at the present time to make this a criterion of explicit knowledge. There is probably some knowledge that can be influenced by cognitive processes but that is not conscious. Explicit knowledge can often be represented verbally, but again this is a correlated rather than a defining attribute of explicitness. Especially when dealing with young children, it is not clear that they could give a verbal account of all knowledge that was explicit in the sense of being cognitively accessible. The three criteria, cognitively accessible, consciously accessible, and verbally stateable, are related, but it is not clear at the present time that the relationship is close enough for all three to be defining criteria of explicit knowledge. The most important criterion for our purposes is that explicit representations can be operated on by strategic cognitive processes, so they can be related to other representations, can be organized into structures or systems, and can be used to guide the development of strategies and skills.

Procedural knowledge comprises a set of actions to be performed, together with the conditions for performing them, and the predicted outcomes for each performance. Procedural knowledge is well modeled by production rules, which are a type of condition–action rule. Both take the form of condition–action pairs.

Although Anderson (1983) represented declarative knowledge as propositional networks, Holland et al. (1986) showed that it can be represented by condition–action rules. For this to be done, the action side of condition–action rules must include an assertion, or message, about the world. I have given the name "declarative rule" to condition–action rules that are representations, and the name "procedural rule" to condition–action rules that specify actions to be performed.

Where knowledge of relations between states of the world is implicit, it is represented by contingencies. Where it is explicit, it is represented by rules. As discussed in chapter 2, condition–action rules can incorporate variables. On the other hand, contingencies represent the equivalent of constants. They represent content-specific information in the form of sets of instances. They do not necessarily represent a single instance, because they can represent prototypes or characteristics common to a number of instances. However, the information is always content specific to some exent, and contingencies do not represent variables. This indicates another basis for the implicit and explicit distinction: Implicit knowledge is content-specific, whereas explicit knowledge includes variables.

The importance of knowledge to understanding, and to cognitive development generally, means that the processes by which that knowledge is acquired have a central role. This means that it is necessary to examine learning and induction processes.

LEARNING

I have identified two kinds of learning that are important to cognitive development. The first type comprises the basic learning and induction processes by which information about the world is acquired and the raw material of mental models is stored. The second type comprises mechanisms for building cognitive skills and strategies.

Basic Learning Processes

It is a major tenet of this book that much of cognitive development can be attributed to learning processes that are of general validity, in the sense that they also occur in other contexts. These processes, outlined in chapter 4, are part of the normal process of adaptation to the environment, and many of them are to be observed in other animals as well as ourselves. These learning processes are the basic mechanism by which information about the environment becomes stored in the nervous system, and they are the raw material of which mental models are composed.

According to interpretations by Rescorla (1988) and Holland et al. (1986), classical conditioning is a means by which humans and other animals acquire representations of the world. Classical conditioning leads to stored representations of environmental contingencies, such as:

bell → food

Other phenomena from traditional studies of learning, such as secondary reinforcement, have been reinterpreted in a similar way (Halford & Halford, 1969; Holgate & Halford, 1972; Seggie & Halford, 1968). A secondary reinforcer is a stimulus that signals that reward is coming. It entails learning a contingency of the form:

signal → reward

In chaper 4, I outlined a number of studies that originated in traditional learning psychology that are consistent with this interpretation of learning. According to this new interpretation, basic learning processes lead not just to stimulus–response associations but to stored representations of contingencies between states of the world. These contingencies take the form:

Contingency: signal → expected state

They are, therefore, one means by which much declarative knowledge of the world is acquired.

Stored contingencies are evoked when a stimulus pattern occurs that matches the signal component of the contingency. For example, if an animal in a salivary conditioning experiment has been given trials comprising a bell followed by food, presentation of the bell activates this contingency and leads to a representation of the expected state, food.

However, stored contingencies are not accessible in the absence of a stimulus pattern that matches the signal. For example, it would not be possible to retrieve the contingency by strategically searching memory. Contingencies are implicit knowledge, and they require an eliciting stimulus for their activation. They are not accessible to strategic cognitive processes.

Where declarative knowledge is explicit, in the sense that it is accessible to strategic cognitive processes, it is represented in the form of declarative condition–action rules. These take the form:

Rule: condition → prediction

A number of examples are discussed in chapter 4. It is necessary to distinguish between contingencies and condition–action rules in order to incorporate the implicit–explicit distinction into the theory of learning.

When procedural knowledge is implicit, it takes the form of stimulus–response associations. Where it is explicit, it takes the form of procedural condition–action rules. These take the form:

Rule: condition → action

The same basic learning principles apply to contingencies and to rules. They differ primarily in that rules, being explicit knowledge, are more connected to other representations. The basic learning principles are:

1. Contingencies, and declarative condition–action rules, that correctly predict states of the world are strengthened; those that make incorrect predictions are weakened.

2. Stimulus–response associations, and procedural condition–action rules, are strengthened if they lead to a satisfying state of affairs, or reinforcement, even if the specific state is not the one predicted.

3. Redundant contingencies, stimulus–response associations, and condition–action rules are not learned. The learner is sensitive to the information value of a signal, and if it predicts a state that is already predicted by another signal, no learning occurs. Similarly, if a response or action is already associated with a stimulus or condition, associations to redundant stimuli tend not to be learned. In such cases the new contingency, stimulus–response association, or rule is said to be blocked.

Additional principles are that rules can support or inhibit each other, signals that have been successful predictors in the past are more likely to be sampled (focused sampling), generalization occurs by removing conditions from rules, discrimination occurs by adding conditions to rules, and new rules can be created by composing features of old rules (composition).

Implicit and Explicit Knowledge

Implicit knowledge, based on contingencies and stimulus–response associations, can be well modeled by parallel distributed processing (PDP) architectures (which represent events by sets of activation values of vectors over a number of neural units). PDP mechanisms also provide natural explanations for prototype formation (by averaging across vectors representing instances of a category), regularity detection (because associations between regularly co-occurring vectors tend to be strengthened), discrimination, and generalization (because stimulus similarity is reflected in overlap between vectors). They also have the interesting properties of graceful degradation (continued functioning, but with less clarity and efficiency when part of a representation is lost) and graceful saturation (continued functioning, with reduced clarity and efficiency when capacity limitations are exceeded, i.e., when too much information is represented in a vector). The last characteristic is important because it suggests a soft capacity limitation.

However, although PDP models offer exciting technical bases for many important phenomena and provide microstructural accounts of learning mechanisms, they have not yet been elaborated so as to specify the psychological principles that govern this learning. They contain no equivalent of the learning principles formulated above with respect to condition–action rules and contingencies. One problem with PDP models is that they are too powerful and have not yet been sufficiently constrained by psychological data to make good models of some cognitive processes.

It is also not yet clear how explicit knowledge can be represented in PDP architectures. As the work of Clark and Karmiloff-Smith (in press), discussed in chapter 2 showed, explicit knowledge will probably require "second-order" PDP architectures, which include an extra level that operates on the first-order representations. No such model appears to exist at present, but progress is being made towards modeling higher cognitive processes such as language, production rules, and analogies in PDP architectures, as discussed in chapters 2 and 5. At present, PDP architectures make good models for many aspects of the microstructure of cognition, but it is not yet practicable to model the whole of cognitive development in this way.

PDP architectures can accommodate variables, at least in some situations. As we saw in chapter 2, following Smolensky (1990), variable-constant bindings can be handled by the tensor product of two vectors, one representing the variable and one representing the constant. However, this representation is much more complex than the representation of content-specific information contained in contingencies. Examination of PDP representations shows that the representation of variables is very different from the representation of content-specific information. It illustrates once again the value of the insights provided by microstructure models.

Explicitation

At this time there is a paucity of models of the process by which implicit knowledge is converted to explicit knowledge. As discussed in chapter 2, Karmiloff-Smith (1986, 1990) described the process in terms of representational redescription but did not provide an explicit account of the mechanism. Although much work remains to be done on the question, it does seem that the implicit–explicit transition corresponds in part to induction. Holland et al. (1986) modeled induction as the acquisition of condition–action rules that represent the environment. If we accept that condition–action rules correspond to explicit knowledge, this implies that induction leads to explicit knowledge. Although this inference rests on a number of assumptions, it is worthwhile to consider its implications.

It is possible that the first step in converting implicit knowledge to explicit knowledge is *abduction*, that is, setting up a hypothesis to define a recognized contingency. Consider, for example, a child who learns that a dog that wags its tail is friendly. The child has presumably had a number of experiences in which the sight of a dog wagging its tail has been followed by a number of friendly behaviors. The contingency between tail wagging and friendliness would probably be learned automatically. It would be implicit and can be well modeled by PDP architectures. Tail wagging would be represented by a vector, and friendly behaviors by another vector, and the weight matrix that represents the asssociation between the vectors would be adjusted each time the experience occurs to strengthen the association. Because the most typical tail-wagging stimuli would become most strongly associated with the most typical friendliness stimuli, there would be a tendency for prototypical tail wagging to become associated with prototypical friendliness. This process would occur automatically, probably without the child's awareness. Theoretically, it constitutes a basic instance of a PDP pattern associator, and it contains no real mysteries.

Once the tail wagging → friendliness contingency has been learned, I postulate that the child is able to reflect on it. This is a strong assumption, because it entails the child having cognitive access to an association that he or she has learned. Once the child reflects on, or examines, the contingency that has been learned, he or she creates a hypothesis. This is the process of abduction, and it need not necessarily be verbal. That is, it does not necessarily depend on the child having words with which to express the contingency. It does imply however that the child creates a new representation, possibly in propositional form. Abduction therefore entails creating a representation of a representation; the new representation is a recoding of the learned contingency between tail wagging and friendliness.

This new representation is the beginning of the explicitation process. It amounts to a weak condition–action rule of the form:

Rule friendly dog: dog, wags tail → dog is friendly

If this rule makes predictions that correspond to the environment, it will be strengthened. If its strength rises above threshold, it will become part of the child's accessible dog knowledge.

The process of explicitation begins by reflecting on a learned contingency, then a hypothesis is created that defines the contingency, thereby recoding it into a new representation. The abduction process is probably guided by constraints that reduce the search space for hypotheses that define the regularity.

The second major assumption in the proposals I make about explicitation is that this new representation is part of a system of representations. A likely candidate here would be a propositional network. This means that the new representation will be linked to other representations, such as other instances of friendliness. The child will then be able to access the representation through other cognitive activities, without environmental input. For example, if the child is trying to think of friendly things, she will probably retrieve tail-wagging dogs as an instance. Insofar as the representation is implicit, it will only be activated by a stimulus pattern that corresponds to the representation of tail-wagging dogs. That is, in a contingency, the representation of friendly dog is activated only by a stimulus pattern that corresponds to the signal component of the contingency.

Because explicit knowledge needs to be connected to a network of other representations, it is probable that most new knowledge obtained through recognition of regularities in the environment is first acquired in the form of contingencies. It is then recoded into new representations that connect it to networks of other representations. Another aspect of this recoding is that variable representations can be adopted, and then a binding of variable-to-constants is established. This means that explicit knowledge, in the form of rules, comprises a very different kind of representation from a contingency, even when the same environmental relationships are being represented. Nevertheless, the same basic learning mechanisms apply, because rules are subject to strengthening and weakening according to the validity of the predictions they make and are subject to blocking and other learning processes.

Contingencies, a form of implicit knowledge, are therefore the foundation of much world knowledge. However, they are converted into explicit rules by the process of abduction, which leads to a new representation based on the learned contingency. The new representation must survive the testing process to which all rules are subjected.

Social input would probably help the child verbalize the rule. However, there are at least two reasons for thinking that explicitation does not depend entirely on social input. First, the social input would have to be related to an existing representation to be meaningful. If a child had not at least partly learned the contingency between tail wagging and friendliness in dogs, it is unlikely that verbal instruction would be effective. Second, the sheer vastness of the world knowledge that a child must acquire precludes all of it being supplied by social input. It is most unreasonable to assume that the child knows only what we are aware of it knowing. It is much more reasonable to assume that the child learns a multitude of contingencies, most of which are also known to us, but of which we are not consciously aware. Both children and adults have a lot of implicit knowledge, much of which is probably acquired automatically without any pedagogical input. If this seems unreasonable, then reflect that before Piagetian psychology became known, most people were not aware that a child needed to understand transitivity. Yet by the age of about 7–8 years most children acquired this concept, without either they or their elders being aware that they were acquiring it. It is true of course that we can facilitate acquisition of those concepts of which we are aware, but there are too many concepts for all to be taught, so children must have processes for developing concepts on their own.

Strategy and Skill Acquisition

The development of strategies depends on both associative and metacognitive processes, as discussed in chapter 4. According to the self-regulating strategy-acquisition models, the metacognitive aspect depends on a concept of the task, which constrains or guides the development of strategies. In the model of counting development by Greeno et al. (1984), the task concept is coded in the form of universally valid logical rules, which are probably partly innate. In the model of transitive inference strategy development by Halford et al. (1991), the task concept is based on concrete experience of ordered sets. Both these models, and that of Anderson (1983), propose that declarative knowledge guides the acquisition of procedural knowledge. However, Anderson's model is not self-regulatory in the sense of Glaser's (1990) in that it does not specify that strategy development depends on a concept of the task. In this model understanding is a by-product of strategy development, rather than something intrinsic to it.

It seems reasonable that both self-regulatory and non-self-regulatory strategy-acquisition processes should occur, but in different circumstances. Anderson's model gives a very good account of computer programming, especially as acquired through the LISP-Tutor, a computer-aided instruction program. There are presumably many other situations where skills are acquired without need for real understanding; for example, learning to kick a ball. However, it is unlikely that strategy acquisition is never based on, or at least aided by, understanding. There are some tasks, including counting and transitivity, where a concept of the task has been shown to guide children's strategy development.

Strategy development depends on the domain-general methods, analogy, means–end analysis, hill climbing, and pure forward search. These are basic forms of cognitive equipment that most people are assumed to have. They operate on declarative knowledge, in the context of experience with a task, to produce domain-specific strategies, as discussed in chapter 4.

Once strategies are constructed, they are subject to the same basic learning processes that apply to procedural rules, as discussed earlier. Strategies can be applied without understanding and without the metacognitive processes used in their formation. These processes become operative only if a strategy must be relearned or adapted to changed circumstances.

Transfer of Learning

There are essentially two kinds of transfer discussed in chapter 4. The first is influenced primarily by stimulus similarity, and extent of transfer depends on the degree of similarity between eliciting stimuli in training and transfer tasks. As mentioned in chapter 4, this factor is tacitly acknowledged in design of strategies, which are often designed so eliciting stimuli will be as constant as possible from one task to another. An addition algorithm, for example, might contain an instruction such as "add the digits in the rightmost column." The conventions for performing addition are such that every sum contains a rightmost column, so this stimulus is constant across problems. Similarly for stimuli such as "next column to the left," "carry digit," and so on.

The other kind of transfer is based on analogical mapping and is independent of similarity of individual stimuli. Analogical mapping can be used to transfer problem-solving procedures from one task to another. The analogy is normally based on some kind of structural similarity between task structures.

Learning-set tasks exemplify transfer based on structure mapping par excellence, because they entail extracting the structure common to a number of specific tasks and transferring it to a new task. The various learning-set tasks have nothing in common except their structure, so learning-set acquisition is a pure case of structure-based transfer. Ability to extract the structure that is common to a number of tasks that have nothing in common except their structure provides a very important mechanism of generalization.

Learning set is really a form of induction. First it entails learning the association between stimuli and reward. Those features of the stimuli that are most consistently rewarded will become most strongly associated. In simple two-object discrimination learning set, the fact that a stimulus was rewarded on the previous trial is the feature that is most consistently associated with reward. Then a mental model is created that entails the essential features of the stimuli, together with the relational structure of the task. In two-object discrimination learning there is an exclusion relation between the stimuli, because if one is rewarded the other is not, and vice versa. Transfer to new problems can be effected by mapping the problem into the mental model, which can be used to predict appropriate responses.

Research showing that learning-set acquisition discriminates among animals of different phylogenetic levels might reflect evolution of structure-mapping ability. Learning sets with more complex structures have also been shown to discriminate between children at different ages, as discussed in chapter 3.

NATURAL REASONING PROCESSES

Basic learning processes are the means by which a vast store of world knowledge is acquired. Many reasoning processes draw directly on this knowledge. As a number of investigators have shown (Henle, 1962; Tversky & Kahneman, 1973, 1983), much human reasoning depends on memory retrieval. For example, the decision as to whether a letter occurs more often in the first or third position in a word is often made by retrieving instances of each from memory and comparing frequencies of each type. The decision as to whether a person is a feminist bank teller is made, not by application of abstract probability rules, but by retrieving the prototype of a feminist bank teller, then testing to see whether the description of the person is representative of the prototype. Thus, many reasoning problems are undertaken by retrieval of content knowledge.

Problems can also be solved by applying rules; and as we have seen, basic learning processes lead naturally to the acquisition of rules. It seems reasonable to expect that we learn a rather vast assemblage of rules that reflect the regularities of our environment and are very important to our ability to adapt to the environment. Most natural problem-solving processes are an extension of this process.

However, information learned in this way, vast and useful as it is, has one restriction. This is that it can only be evoked by stimuli that match the signal in the contingency or the condition in the condition–action rule. In the latter case the information is accessible to cognitive processes under strategic control, which greatly increases flexibility. The information can be accessed by using cognitive processes to generate a stimulus that matches the condition side of the rule, so access is under cognitive rather than environmental control. However, a stimulus that matches the condition side of the rule must still be produced. Transfer still depends, as noted in chapter 4, on stimulus similarity of some sort. However, analogical mapping overcomes this limitation because it gives access to knowledge on a basis other than literal similarity.

Analogical Mapping

Following Gentner's (1983) theory, an analogy is a structure-preserving map from a source (or base) to a target. Attributes are not normally mapped, and relations are mapped selectively, those that enter into a coherent overall structure being more likely to be mapped (the principle of systematicity). Because analogies tend to be independent of attributes, they are a form of abstraction. They also relate one representation to another and might be involved in the process of explicitation. Abduction, or creating a hypothesis to define a regularity, might be facilitated by comparing two representations of the regularity, and this process is closely akin to analogy. Evidence reviewed in chapter 5 showed that coding of a structure was facilitated if two instances of it were experienced.

An analogy is similar to a representation in that both are mappings from one structure to another, and the validity of both types of mappings depends on the uniqueness and correspondence criteria defined earlier. However, an analogy is a mapping from one representation to another, whereas a representation is a mapping from a cognitive structure to a segment of the environment.

Levels of Mapping

Four levels of structure mapping were defined in chapter 2 and are summarized in Fig. 2.8. These are element, relational, system, and multiple-system mappings. They increase in abstractness, in that the higher level mappings are less dependent on similarity. Element mappings depend on element similarity, prior learning, or convention. Relational mappings depend on similarity of first-order relations (i.e., relations that have objects as arguments). System mappings and multiple-system mappings theoretically can be validated by structural correspondence, independent of any form of similarity. Alternatively, they can be validated by similarity of higher order relations, that is, relations that have lower order relations as arguments. The increasing abstractness of the higher level mappings is obtained at the cost of increased processing load.

The four levels of structure mapping also differ in the complexity of the structures being mapped. Element mappings map unidimensional structures based on a single element. Relational mappings map two-dimensional structures based on binary relations, unary operators, or univariate functions. These are all structures defined as sets of ordered pairs. System mappings map structures that are three-dimensional and are based on ternary relations, binary operations, or bivariate functions. These are all structures defined on sets of ordered triples. Multiple-system mappings map structures that are four-dimensional and are based on quaternary relations, compositions of binary operations, or trivariate functions. These are all structures defined as sets of ordered 4-tuples.

The level of mapping does not depend on the total amount of structure in a mapping but on the amount of structure that must be used in a single step to validate the mapping. Some analogies based on many relations can still be decomposed into a series of relational mappings that are performed successively, as discussed in chapter 5 with respect to the mapping in Fig. 5.3B.

Empirical work on structure mappings so far suggests that relational mappings can be made by young children, at least by the age of 3–4 years. This is consistent with studies of analogical reasoning by preschoolers, which show they can cope if the relations are familiar and the format is suitable. There is evidence that children as young as 2 can represent binary relations, implying that they would be capable of representations based on Rank-3 tensor products. According to the STAR model of Halford et al. (in press) this means that analogical reasoning based on relational mappings should be possible at age 2.

There are several computational models of analogy, SME, COPYCAT, ACME, and STAR, all of which are discussed in chapter 5. These models provide confirmation that analogical reasoning processes do work as they are claimed to work and are therefore important to cognitive developmental theory. They provide a "sufficiency test" for some important processes underlying cognitive development. One of these models, COYCAT (Mitchell & Hofstadter, 1990) shows how representations can be created dynamically during analogical reasoning. STAR (Halford et al., in press), suggests that analogical reasoning may be a special case of memory retrieval. Another, ACME (Holyoak & Thagard, 1989), demonstrates that analogies can be based on pure structural correspondence, and can also be performed by parallel constraint satisfaction processes. Finally SME (Falkenhainer et al., 1990) demonstrates the sufficiency of the structure-mapping process.

Analogical mapping has several roles in cognitive development. It is a major component of inference and, together with memory retrieval discussed above, it probably accounts for a major part of natural human reasoning. Where inferences cannot be made by retrieval of content knowledge or rules, they tend to be made by mapping the problem into a schema, which is used as a source. This was illustrated with transitive inference in chapter 1. Analogy also facilitates learning by enabling material to be mapped into a mental model, which permits unknown information to be predicted, thereby reducing the amount of learning required. This was discussed in chapter 5. It is a major component of strategy and skill development, as discussed in chapter 4, and it is important in those cases of transfer that are not based on literal similarity, as discussed in chapter 5.

TASK COMPLEXITY AND PROCESSING CAPACITY

Having surveyed some basic mechanisms in cognitive development, we now examine factors that are known to influence task difficulty. We also consider whether capacity accounts for age differences in performance.

Task Demands

As noted in chapter 3, tasks can be difficult for many reasons, most of which do not affect demand for processing resources. These include lack of domain knowledge, availability of the correct hypothesis, and short-term memory load. Information that has to be held for short periods, for use in later problem-solving steps, imposes a load on short-term memory but does not constitute a processing load per se. Processing load is influenced only by information that currently influences cognitive processes.

Processing load does affect ability to understand concepts, and it also influences ability to translate understanding into strategies. Some processing loads are extrinsic, in the sense that they are imposed by features that are not inherent to the material, such as poor presentation. Intrinsic processing loads, however, are related to task complexity. The most appropriate metric for this is based on dimensionality, that is, the number of independent items of information required to represent the task. Tasks can be allocated to equivalence classes on the basis of the number of dimensions that are required to represent them. This is illustrated in Fig. 6.1. Figure 6.1 shows the structure of transitivity and class inclusion tasks. Transitivity consists of three relations, aRb, bRc, and aRc. Class inclusion consists of a superordinate class, B, which has two subclasses, A and A,' such that A and A' are included in B (e.g., apples and pears included in fruit). In class inclusion, R_1 corresponds to "included in," and R_2 corresponds to "complement of." The two tasks are very different in surface form but, as Fig. 6.1 shows, they have similar underlying structures. Both consist of three elements linked by three binary relations. The elements and relations are different, yet they have a common structure that is captured by the fact that both are ternary relations; that is, each is a structure with three arguments. Both are three-dimensional concepts. Other cognitive tasks can be allocated to equivalence classes based on one, two, three, or four dimensions. This dimensionality influences intrinsic processing load.

Task Complexity and Representations

The intrinsic processing load imposed by a task depends on the number of dimensions that must be used to represent the concept. This is determined by two principles, both of which were explained in chapter 3: (a) Only aspects of the task that constrain current cognitive processes must be actively represented, and (b) aspects that vary independently of each other within the current task must be represented by separate dimensions. Where aspects of a task are constant, or all vary together, they can be coded as a single dimension.

This means that the processing load imposed by a task can be assessed only by analyzing the processes involved in the task. Furthermore, where a task consists of a series of steps, as most higher cognitive processes do, the load may vary from one step to another. The intrinsic difficulty level of the task corresponds to the highest processing load imposed.

Assessment of the total amount of processing entailed in the task is not sufficient to specify processing load, because not all the information will normally be processed in parallel. Most complex tasks are divided into segments. Processing is parallel within each segment, but the segments are processed serially. To assess the task load, it is necessary to know the maximum amount of information that is processed in parallel in any one segment.

This might be disappointing to those who want to predict performance on the basis of a single processing load parameter. However, such predictions are not realistic because they fail to take into account the fact that in most cognitive tasks processing is partly serial and partly parallel. Because

Transitivity

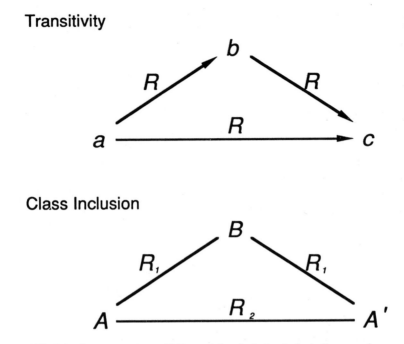

Class Inclusion

FIG. 6.1. Structures of transitivity and class-inclusion tasks in the same format. From Halford (1992). Reprinted by permission of Karger AG, Basel, Switzerland.

there are limits to the amount of information that can be processed in parallel, as shown in chapter 3, tasks are segmented into components that are performed serially. The number of serially processed segments does not affect processing load unless the business of keeping track of segments or organizing activities imposes a load.

Chunks, Dimensions, and Vectors

As argued in chapter 3, a chunk and an attribute on a dimension are both independent units of information of arbitrary size. I also suggested that a vector in a PDP architecture is capable of representing one dimension. It follows that the complexity of a concept, as measured by its dimensionality, corresponds to the number of chunks of information processed in parallel and to the number of vectors required in a PDP representation. Processes based on representations of more than one dimension entail computing the tensor product of the vectors corresponding to the dimensions. Each dimension must be represented as a separate vector in the tensor product, otherwise there are some combinations that cannot be computed, as explained in chapters 3 and 5. Processes based on multivector representations are computationally costly, which gives a natural basis for capacity limitations, to which we turn next.

Capacity Limitations

Objections are sometimes raised to the whole concept of capacity limitations because they are seen as pessimistic and as preempting attempts to improve children's performance. I would argue however that it is unscientific to entertain such value judgments, and that in any case we are most likely to enhance children's performance if we have penetrating, realistic models of the processes and factors involved. There is plenty of evidence that both adults and children have capacity limitations, but this does not prevent them from achieving remarkable successes. Much of the excitement of the field lies in discovering how this is done.

It is also argued that the evidence points strongly to capacity being constant from infancy to adulthood. However, as I argued in chapter 3, these claims are usually based on indirect evidence, such as findings that strategies or familiarity are important. Although I recognize the significance of these findings, they do not show that capacity remains constant. It is undoubtedly true that much of the improvement in recall, for example, is due to improved strategies, or better coding based on greater familiarity. This does not logically exclude increases in capacity, however. As we saw in chapter 3 there is a modest, but solid and growing body of evidence that some kinds of capacity do increase with age.

It is also common to argue that children only fail tasks due to tests that are inappropriate because of misleading demands, requirements for domain knowledge that the child does not have, and so on. A lot of these claims are well substantiated, but this argument becomes circular unless something is done to define a valid test. Otherwise we can get into the situation where validity is defined in terms of results. Suppose we have (say) 20 tests, 19 of which give negative results, and one gives positive results, and we say the one test yielding positive results is the valid one. Unless there are sound, objective reasons for accepting this one test and rejecting all the others, the argument is clearly circular. In effect, a valid test has been defined as one that gives positive results. Add to this the fact that researchers, and (I believe) many journals, have a bias to publish positive results, and the field is in danger of giving a seriously misleading picture of children's performance.

The bias towards positive results can also mean that atypical results are taken as typical. Many demonstrations of understanding of concepts by very young children occur only in very restricted circumstances. Quite often they turn out to be artifacts, as I have pointed out elsewhere (Halford, 1989), but even when they are sound, it is necessary to establish that they are reasonably robust and representative. At the very least, something should be done to specify the range of conditions under which success is achieved and the factors that govern it. As I pointed out in chapter 1, we need to define the mental models children have, rather than categorize children as having or not having a particular concept.

Capacity and Age

With these impediments to studying the concept of capacity removed, I consider again the question of whether capacity increases with age. Several lines of evidence were presented in chapter 3 that suggested that capacity does increase with age. First, there is physiological evidence that certain cognitive performances are related to maturation of parts of the nervous system. Second, there is evidence that the capacity of primary memory increased from 8–9 years to adulthood. Third, there is evidence that structure mapping with three-dimensional structures was very difficult for children below 5 years, despite extensive training and thorough familiarity with task procedures and demands. Finally, there is evidence of a global-processing-speed factor that increases with age and is consistent with a change in capacity.

Controversy will no doubt continue on this issue, but in chapter 3 I made two further proposals that are relevant to the debate. One was that extensions of the easy-to-hard paradigm could be used to assess changes in capacity over age. Another was that the question could be reformulated. In particular, I proposed that representations might become more differentiated with age, so more dimensions could be represented in parallel. This would not increase overall capacity, but it would increase the rank of the tensor products that can be computed, as these are defined in chapters 2 and 3. This would mean that more complex structures, of higher dimensionality as defined in the complexity metric in chapter 3, could be represented.

Evidence for capacity limitations all comes from cognitive tasks that require explicit representations of some kind. However, there is really no evidence that implicit learning is capacity limited. The work of Reber (1989) showed that humans have prodigious capacity for implicit learning of quite complex relationships, but many of these acquisitions are probably rather restricted in that they are evoked only by situations that resemble the original stimuli. The limitation in the number of dimensions of cognitive representations discussed in chapter 3 applies to explicit representations, which are accessible to strategic cognitive processes as discussed earlier.

Evidence available suggests that children can process one-dimensional structures at least by 1 year, two-dimensional structures by 2 years, three dimensional structures by 4½–5 years, and four-dimensional structures by 11 years. The advantage of the dimensionality metric is that it enables capacity to be related directly to processing demands of tasks.

Capacity Overload

Where a concept has a dimensionality greater than the child's capacity, there are three possibilities:

1. The task might be decomposed into smaller segments that can be processed serially. This is not always possible because, as noted in earlier chapters, some tasks cannot be decomposed in this way. For example, conditional discrimination, negative patterning, and transverse patterning tasks, all discussed in chapter 5, cannot be decomposed.

2. The representation can be chunked, or recoded into fewer vectors. This reduces the dimensionality of the representation and thereby reduces the processing load. This is not always possible without loss. For example, if it is done with conditional discrimination, negative patterning, and transverse-patterning tasks, then interproblem transfer potential is lost, as explained in chapter 5.

3. The participant can default to a lower level concept. An example would be in transitivity and serial-order tasks, where instead of considering two relations, one relation only is considered, as discussed in chapter 4. In many situations, including transitivity, this leads to partially correct performance. If the nature of the default is known, it is possible to predict the types of errors that result, as illustrated with transitivity in chapter 4.

Recall that processing capacity is defined in terms of the number of vectors that can be processed in parallel in a PDP representation. The graceful saturation property of PDP representations means that this will be a soft limit. When the number of vectors is too great, no catastrophic breakdown of performance occurs. Instead there is a loss of clarity in the representation, which leads to increased solution times and greater susceptibility to error. It also causes solutions to be adopted that are consistent with a proper subset of the dimensions; that is, with some of them but not all of them. Thus, the default to a representation of lower dimensionality will tend to occur automatically through graceful saturation.

What of the claim that children can be taught any performance, given enough of the right kind of training? To some extent, it is true. For example, I do not doubt that a 2- to 3-year-old child could be taught some simple transitive inference strategies that would lead to correct solutions to a set of transitive inference problems in a given context. I am quite confident that I could, in fact, devise such a strategy and teach it successfully. The strategy would, however, be learned with only partial understanding. That in itself is not a fault because, as we have seen, we all use many strategies without fully understanding why they work. It would mean, however, that the child would have limited ability to adapt the strategy to new contexts. The child would not be able to generate logically equivalent strategies even for isomorphs of the original training tasks. Furthermore, the child would not be able to use the transitivity concept as the basis for further conceptual development. I consider the last two points in more detail.

If the aim of training is to teach the child an algorithm that is needed for a particular performance, there is really nothing wrong with this situation. After all, we all learn many things that we do not understand. I once recall learning an algorithm that enabled me to find square roots. It is probably an anachronism now that pocket calculators compute square roots without effort or error, but at the time it was quite serviceable, even though I do not recall understanding how it worked, nor was I ever particularly interested in the question. The sole value of the algorithm was that it enabled me to perform a necessary task in a standardized format. To take another example, I use this word processor with little or no understanding of how it works. This skill is useful for practical purposes. I could not use this skill to devise another word processor, but that is not my trade. Where a strategy or skill is an end in itself, and where it can be performed in standardized situations, there is little loss in learning the strategy without understanding.

The situation is quite different, however, when a concept must be used as the foundation for other concepts, or as a component in a body of knowledge. Transitivity is such a concept. It is not only, or even primarily, used to solve transitive inference tests in a laboratory. It is the basis of a great many other concepts, some of which are the foundations of a whole domain of knowledge. Transitivity is entailed in understanding an ordered set, which is fundamental to understanding ordinal scales, such as positions in a race, and it is also fundamental to understanding quantification beyond the level of a nominal scale. With transitivity and serial order tasks, learning an algorithm, without understanding, to solve laboratory puzzles, simply does not do the job. It is really irrelevant to the whole purpose of understanding transitivity. It produces data dubiously demonstrating that the child "has transitivity," whatever that means, but it does little to provide a child with a mental model that can be used as a foundation stone for a body of knowledge that is of fundamental importance in even a moderately technological society.

Therefore when the complexity of a concept exceeds a child's capacity, we do not find a brick wall. There are ways of enabling tasks related to the concept to be performed, but with limitations. Whether these limitations matter depends on the purpose of performing the task. If the purpose is to provide the child with a foundation on which to build a body of conceptual knowledge, the limitations may well be significant. If the purpose is to provide the child with a strategy that performs a specific task in standardized circumstances, the limitations probably will not matter.

Another possibility is that understanding can be partial. When a child defaults to a representation of lower dimensionality than that entailed in the concept, some partial understanding can still occur. For example, an ordered set can be processed as a succession of ordered pairs; for example, that a is followed by b, which is followed by c, and so on. With such a representation there will be no recognition of transitivity, because the separate binary relations are never composed into the ternary relation. To see this, examine the structure of the transitivity concept in Fig. 6.1. Imagine looking at this figure through a small window that permits only one relation to be viewed at a time. The interesting thing about this situation is that everything can be seen; one can see aRb, bRc, and aRc *separately*. The problem is that the view is fragmented. Unless the successive views are integrated into a composite representation, the overall structure is never seen. This is essentially the position of a child who defaults to a two-dimensional representation while dealing with a three-dimensional concept. Everything is represented, but the representation is fragmented. The result is that the higher-order relationships in the structure cannot be computed. For example, it is not possible to compute the relationship between aRb, bRc, and aRc.

An analogy might help here. Imagine that an experimenter performed an experiment with a three-factor design, then applied a two-way analysis of variance, first to factors A and B, then to B and C, then to A and C. This is very poor research technique, but that is not our point. What is important in the present context is that most of the conclusions would be (at least approximately) correct. That is, the experimenter would draw correct conclusions about all main effects and two-way interactions. Only the three-way interaction would be ignored. If another researcher subsequently replicated the experiment, with a proper three-way analysis, s/he might discover a telltale three-way interaction that falsified the earlier interpretation of some of the results. But if the three-way interaction were never examined, no one would ever realize the restricted nature of the conclusions based on two-way analyses.

I suggest this is a good analog of the performance of a hypothetical child, or adult, who performs a task entailing a three-dimensional concept using two-dimensional representations. Most of the performance will probably not be detectably different from that of a person using a three-dimensional representation. Only the telltale three-way relations will reveal the difference. When viewed this way, much of the controversy in the cognitive development literature about children's understanding becomes more explicable. A lot of evidence of apparent success in complex tasks by young children could have been generated by children who defaulted to lower dimensionality representations. This would not lead to catastrophic failure, but on the contrary, would produce success on many components of the tasks. Only those telltale tests that require children to recognize relations of high dimensionality would discriminate the children using adequate representations from the others.

This theory can be used to reassess some of the issues that have occurred in the cognitive-development literature. The problem in the past has been that issues have been defined in categorical terms. That is, the question has been whether the child understands the concept or not. Therefore any demonstration of successful performance is accepted as demonstrating understanding. There has been insufficient recognition that understanding is not all-or-none, and successful performances can occur without understanding. The result has been that many claimed successes, even when valid, apply only to very restricted circumstances. Evidence of failure has been similarly overinterpreted, because failure in one task has often been treated as though it implied a complete lack of understanding. A more complete and realistic picture requires that on the one hand, partial understanding should be recognized, and on the other hand, that ability to generalize and adapt performances to new contexts should be investigated.

Chunking, Segmentation, and Expertise

As explained in chapter 2, conceptual chunking entails recoding a representation into fewer vectors. Typically, a concept is recoded into a single vector. This produces massive gains in efficiency, because it means that the remaining capacity can be used to represent other concepts. Since adults can represent four vectors in parallel, this means that three more vectors can be represented. The cost is that computational possibilities within the structure are lost.

To illustrate, recall the concept of a nuclear family, comprising parents and children, discussed in chapter 3. This could be represented as a three-dimensional structure, isomorphic to the class inclusion concept represented in Fig. 6.1. In place of the superordinate class B, we have "family," in place of the first subordinate, A, we have "parents," and in place of the second subordinate class, A', we have children. Relation R_1 corresponds to "included in," whereas R_2 corresponds to "parent–child relationship." This represents the internal structure of the family. It is a ternary relation, is three-dimensional, and would be represented as a Rank 4 tensor product.

However we can also chunk the concept of family into a single dimension. This is more efficient in that it uses less representational capacity. It also enables us to represent other concepts, such as a second family, community, neighborhoods, and so on. In this case we represent the external structure of the family. However, in doing this, we have lost the internal structure. We can no longer represent the relation between parents and children, or the relation of children to family. For example, we could no longer compute the way family size would be affected by adding two more children.

One implication of this argument is that while a representation is chunked into one dimension, we cannot compute relations within the internal structure of the concept. However, we gain the ability to compute relations in the external structure of the concept, because we can use the capacity that is freed up by the chunking process to represent other concepts. Second, the idea that we represent only a limited number of dimensions in parallel means that we must constantly shift from one level of representation to another. It implies that we keep creating temporary representations, each based on up to four dimensions, to provide a workspace for the current cognitive process. Remember that we are talking here about limitations that apply to both adults and children. The same principles apply at all ages, but the evidence in chapter 3 indicates that the number of dimensions that can be represented in parallel increases with age.

The second way that we maintain processing load within our capacity is by segmenting tasks into components, each of which entails no more than the number of dimensions that can be represented in parallel, and which are performed serially. This entails using a strategy that connects the components into a coherent, goal-directed sequence. Development of a strategy based on understanding requires ability to represent the concept, as shown in chapter 4 with respect to transitivity. Therefore, strategy development based on understanding depends on sufficient processing capacity being available. Strategies can be learned without understanding, by learning individual steps, together with cues indicating when each step is to be performed. In this case there is limited ability to adapt the strategy to changed circumstances. However strategies are learned, they typically increase efficiency by reducing the processing at any given time.

Strategies are a major component of expertise. However, understanding is probably an underrated aspect of expertise. Holyoak (1991) recently argued that expertise is more adaptable than previous treatments of the topic might have indicated. I would suggest that expertise is not just a collection of strategies and skills, analogous to the software of a computer installation. Expertise entails the ability to develop new strategies and to adapt old strategies to changed circumstances. It is more dynamic than is often suggested.

Another major component is ability to code concepts in an efficient way. Efficient conceptual chunking requires not only that concepts be recoded into fewer dimensions, but that the chunks be chosen so that they represent the important aspects of the task. Experts know which are the "powerful" dimensions in a concept, the dimensions that carve the concept at its joints. Experts perceive large, meaningful patterns in a domain and represent problems at a deeper level than novices (Chi, Glaser, & Farr, 1988). Furthermore the superior memory often noted in experts is probably due to coding more information into a chunk (Miller, 1956; Simon, 1974).

COMPARISON WITH OTHER THEORIES

In this section I contrast this theory with related theories in cognition and cognitive development.

Piagetian Theory of Thought Operations

The theory in this book does not postulate stages in the sense that Piaget did. It holds that most cognitive skills are learned, and learning without understanding is not specifically constrained with respect to age. However, I do postulate that understanding, from which many cognitive strategies are generated, depends on representation of concepts, and that the dimensionality of representations increases with age. As noted earlier, this implies a soft limit and does not imply sudden or simultaneous acquisition of all concepts at a particular level. However, when ability to add a new dimension to a representation emerges, children will acquire ability to operate on a new class of concepts.

As I have pointed out elsewhere (Halford, 1989, 1992), young children have persistent, and largely unexplained, difficulties with some concepts that I have identified as entailing representations of high dimensionality. Transitivity and class inclusion are two examples. It is possible that the factor of dimensionality of representations can provide an alternate explanation for many of the phenomena that Piaget explained in terms of stages. The explanation that I have proposed in this book is based on research in cognitive psychology and cognitive science in the last few decades, and it utilizes information that was simply not available when Piaget was writing on this topic. I now explore the ability of the present theory to account for the phenomena that Piaget attributed to stages.

One-dimensional concepts correspond approximately to Piaget's preoperational thought, in that both comprise representations of elementary categories without representation of relational information. Two-dimensional concepts bear a similarly approximate correspondence to Piaget's intuitive stage, in that both entail representing one relation at-a-time. The theories agree that in this stage there is difficulty in tasks that require relations to be integrated, such as transitivity, seriation, and inclusion.

Piaget distinguished between the preoperational and concrete operational stages on the basis that the former is based on function logic, whereas the latter is based on groupings. A function is said not to be reversible (Piaget, Grize, Szeminska, & Vinh Bang, 1968/1977), whereas an operation is. These two structures are not distinguished mathematically in this fashion, and Piaget's emphasis on reversibility is somewhat idiosyncratic.[1]

The concrete operational stage was based on a set of "groupings" (*groupement*), of which Baldwin (1967) gave a clear explanation. The central idea of the grouping (Piaget, 1957) is a set of elements with a composition operation, and it was pointed out by Sheppard (1978) that the *groupoid*, that is, a set with a single binary operation, is the closest mathematical concept to Piaget's notion of grouping.

Leaving aside the idiosyncrasies of Piaget's theorizing, the distinction between functions and operations contains the idea that operations are more complex structures mathematically than functions, or relations. This question was discussed in chapter 2 and in Appendix 2B. Functions (strictly, univariate functions), relations (strictly, binary relations), and unary operators are of equivalent complexity, and are less complex than binary operations and bivariate functions. We will refer to univariate functions, binary relations, and unary operators as "relational level" structures. They have a common type of structure based on ordered pairs. For example, if weight is a function of height, then for every height, there will be a corresponding weight, so the function may be thought of as the set of pairs {($h1, w1$), ($h2, w2$) . . . (hn, wn)}. Binary relations such as "larger than" also consist of ordered pairs such that the first member of the pair is larger than the second. A unary operator such as "inverse" corresponds to a set of ordered pairs such that one member of a pair is the inverse of the other. These are all two-dimensional structures and are involved in relational mappings.

Binary operations are more complex structures and consist of ordered triples. The formal definition was given in Appendix 2B, but an example would be the operation of addition, which consists of all ordered triples of the form {(2, 1, 3) . . . (3, 5, 8) . . .}, such that the third element is the sum of the first two. Structures at this level are 3-dimensional and are involved in system mappings.

As we saw in chapter 3, there is evidence that three-dimensional concepts are first represented at 4½–5 years of age. This level of concept has the same structural complexity as the groupoid, which underlies Piaget's concept of concrete operations. Thus the present theory implies that many of the concepts that Piaget regarded as concrete operational cause difficulty for young children because they entail three-dimensional representations.

Formal operational structures (Piaget, 1950) were based on the 16 binary

---

[1]Both functions and operations may be either reversible or irreversible, and reversibility is not inherent in the definition of either. A function is a set of ordered pairs (*a, b*) that associates with every element *a* in Set A an element *b* in Set B (formally: A function from a Set A to a Set B is a Set f of ordered pairs (*a, b*) (where *a*εA, *b*εB) such that for each element *a* of A there is precisely one *b*εB such that ((*a, b*)εf). A binary operation is a set of mappings of the form, A × A → A (formally: A binary operation * on a Set A is a function from the Set A × A of ordered pairs of A into A, *:A × A → A).

operations of symbolic logic, the INRC group, and a lattice. The basis of formal operational structures has been lucidly explained by Baldwin (1967) and Ginsburg and Opper (1969). The binary operations are really binary connectives of logic; that is, they really represent the 16 possible truth tables for two binary variables. Examples would be conjunction, $A \cap B$, and disjunction, $A \cup B$. The set of conceptual rules considered by Haygood and Bourne (1965) has the same formal basis as the 16 binary operations of propositional logic in Piaget's system.

The four elements of the INRC group are transformations of these operations. I is an identity element, equivalent to a null transformation. N is the negation operation, formally equivalent to de Morgan's theorem; for example, $N(A \cup B) = \bar{A} \cap \bar{B}$. The reciprocal is a different type of negation; for example, $R(A \cup B) = \bar{A} \cup \bar{B}$. The correlate is obtained by substituting conjunction for disjunction and vice versa: for example, $C(A \cup B) = A \cap B$ (the correlate is actually a composition of the negation and the reciprocal (i.e., $N * R = C$). The INRC group (mathematically, the Klein group) is a composition of these elements, as shown in Table 6.1. Thus whereas the essence of concrete operational structures is the idea of a composition operation on a set of elements, formal operations are a composition of the operations themselves. Therefore, a structure formed at the concrete operational level becomes integrated into a higher level structure at the formal operational level.

Piagetian theory of formal operations again has some idiosyncracies, but the basic idea is that formal operations are compositions of binary operations. That is, each element of the INRC group is a composition of 2 of the 16 binary operations. As pointed out in chapter 2, and earlier in this chapter, four-dimensional representations can handle compositions of binary operations. Therefore I propose that the reason for the difficulty that children younger than about 11 years have been observed to have with formal operational concepts is that they entail four-dimensional representations.

The present theory has another similarity to Piaget's in that it entails an active construction of cognitive strategies, albeit with the stimulation from interaction with the environment. This is reminiscent of a common situation in cognitive psychology where concepts to which Piaget attached great importance but that were not favored by mainstream psychology in his day, such as schema, have found a prominent place in contemporary cognition (Halford, 1989).

The present theory is like Piaget's in that it gives a prominent role to structure. The complexity of concepts, and the processing loads they impose, is defined in terms of the structural complexity of the concepts. Furthermore, analogical mapping, which is so important to many cognitive processes, depends on structure. However, structures in the present theory originate through learning, whereas in Piaget's theory they did not. On the other hand, the learning theories I have found appropriate in this context are very different

TABLE 6.1
The INRC Group

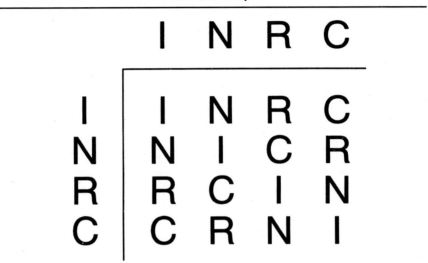

	I	N	R	C
I	I	N	R	C
N	N	I	C	R
R	R	C	I	N
C	C	R	N	I

from the learning theories that existed in Piaget's day. I suspect that if Piaget were writing on cognitive development now he would find the learning and induction theory of Holland et al. (1986) quite congenial.

The structures that are entailed in the present theory are representations of structures in the environment. Therefore, cognition is very much environmentally determined, and, in that respect, the present theory is also quite consistent with the work of Anderson (1990), who argued that many properties of cognitive processes reflect properties of the world. This emphasis on cognitive representations as reflections of environmental structures seems to be a major difference between the present theory and that of Piaget.

On the other hand the present theory forges an unexpected link between Piaget's theory and PDP models. It implies that as children acquire the capacity to represent an additional dimension in a tensor product (as shown in Fig. 2.8), they become capable of a higher level of reasoning. To put it in rather simplistic terms, ability to add a dimension to representations enables a shift to a new stage. Thus the developments of PDP models undertaken by Halford et al. (in press) in the STAR model provide an unexpected vindication of a concept that was at the core of Piagetian theory.

Chapman

A number of papers by Chapman (1987, 1989, 1990) present neo-Piagetian analyses of cognitive development that make an interesting comparison with the present theory. Chapman (1987) postulated representational schemes, which appear to be representational units that have a certain integrity and are independent of other repesentations. There is a possible identification between Chapman's representational schemes and my concept of dimensions in representation, in that one schema might correspond to one dimension. The concepts have different origins, Chapman's schemes being much more tightly identified with Piagetian theory, whereas my dimensions are more closely related to information-processing approaches, and to PDP theory. What Chapman (1987) called an operational schema corresponds approximately to my idea of the tensor product of vectors, because both have the function of coordinating representations to permit inferences. Again, however, the origins of the concepts are quite different. Nevertheless, the fact that analyses with such different starting points can converge on basically consistent solutions is encouraging in itself. The common aim seems to have been to define the representational basis for human decision making, and the commonalities in the proposed models suggest that some basic properties of human representations might have been identified.

Chapman postulated that attentional capacity determines the number of schemes that can be coordinated. At the first preoperational stage, only one representational schema can be considered. This is consistent with my theory that at 1 year, which is approximately the age of onset of Piaget's preconceptual stage (the first preoperational stage), children can represent one dimension. However, Chapman proposed that one schema can represent a class or a relation, whereas in my theory representation of a relation requires two dimensions. At the second substage, Chapman postulated two schemes, which can represent a functional relation. This is consistent with the argument of Halford and Wilson (1980) that 2-year-olds can represent binary relations and univariate functions (functions of the form "A is a function of B"). At the concrete operational stage Chapman postulated children can represent an operational schema of the form $(X \circ Y = Z)$. This is consistent with the Halford and Wilson (1980) claim that 5-year-olds can represent binary operations, and with the present claim that three-dimensional representations are possible at this age. Chapman postulated that at the second concrete operational substage, children can represent an operational scheme with an additional variable, such as $(W \circ X \circ Y = Z)$. This again is consistent with Halford and Wilson's claim that 11-year-old children can represent compositions of binary operations, and with the present theory that they can represent four dimensions.

There is therefore considerable correspondence between the present theory and that of Chapman, and they appear to have developed in parallel through the 1980s. However, Chapman's theory is based on Piagetian schemes, and in that respect it is similar to that of Pascual-Leone (1970, 1984), which was discussed in chapter 3 and elsewhere (Halford, 1982, 1987). My theory, by contrast, has been based on a mathematical theory of representations and, more recently, on the way information is represented in PDP models of the microstructure of cognition. There is much more than a difference in terminology here. The two theories relate to quite different areas of literature, but more importantly, when you probe beyond surface characteristics, they have quite different properties. For example, in my theory the reasons for capacity limitations, and the manner in which they would change over age, derive from properties of parallel-distributed-processing representations, which are certainly not involved in Chapman's theory. My reason for preferring the information processing and PDP basis for the theory of representations is that it enables cognitive development theory to draw on the contributions of cognitive psychology and cognitive science, which provide great conceptual power. It also provides the opportunity to check and develop arguments through mathematical analysis and computer simulation, which ultimately takes us well beyond intuition.

Case

Case's (1985) theory of processing space was discussed in chapter 3, where I presented evidence that conflicts with his claim that total processing space is the sum of operating space and short-term storage space. This should not detract, however, from the importance of Case's suggestion that processing efficiency is the main factor that increases with age. This insight constitutes one of the most significant contributions to cognitive development in the last two decades.

However, this idea, which was first enunciated more than 10 years ago (Case, 1978, 1980), needs updating and further development. As I pointed out elsewhere (Halford, 1987), the identification of processing efficiency with processing speed is too simple and causes a number of difficulties. For example, it conflicts with the usual relation between processing speed and performance. According to the performance-resource function, discussed in chapter 3, performance is positively related to resources; that is, speed is an *increasing* function of resources (see Fig. 3.1). However, according to Case's formulation, speed is inversely related to resources, because faster performance means more efficiency, which utilizes fewer resources.

The problem here is that speed and efficiency need to be measured independently, but Case does not seem to have provided a way of doing this. In this book, I define processing efficiency in terms of operations such as conceptual chunking and segmentation, which reduce the number of dimensions of representations that need to be processed in parallel. This means processing efficiency is defined independently of speed. Speed can then be expressed as a function of efficiency; specifically, speed is a function of conceptual chunking, skills, and strategies.

As pointed out elsewhere (Halford 1987), the present theory is the only one that quantifies the complexity of the major classes of structures. Pascual-Leone (1970) assessed processing loads but did not define structures. Case (1985) defined four major levels of structure, the sensorimotor, relational, dimensional, and vectorial. Loads are assessed as $OPx + s$, where OPx is an unspecified parameter corresponding to one of the levels mentioned above, and s refers to the load imposed by the substages. The value of s increases from 0 to 3 as children progress through the substages within each of the major levels. However, a point that often seems to be overlooked is that there is no quantification of the load imposed by the major levels in Case's theory. As pointed out elsewhere (Halford, 1987), I am in basic agreement with the levels because the relational, dimensional, and vectorial levels can be derived from levels 1, 2, and 3, respectively defined by Halford and Wilson (1980). However, the dimensionality metric used here is unique in giving a quantitative value to the load imposed by these levels of representation.

There are further differences with respect to the complexity metric used. As discussed in chapter 3, Case used a goal-hierarchy metric, whereas I use a dimensionality metric. Another feature of Case's formulation that distinguishes it from the one offered here is that the load imposed by a task depends on the stage of development at which it is performed. A task that imposes a load of $3s$ units at the end of the relational stage imposes a load of $0s$ units at the beginning of the dimensional stage. This means the theory really contains no metric for task complexity. Another difference, as explained in chapter 3, is that I consider it is necessary to use techniques that establish that tasks are capacity related or capacity limited.

Case (1992) defined central conceptual structures, which apply to both quantitative and social thought. They appear to be similar in some respects to pragmatic-reasoning schemas (Cheng & Holyoak, 1985), which will be discussed in more detail in chapter 7. This provides another point of contact between our theories, but at a very general level. Furthermore I believe it is necessary to explain how such schemas can be acquired, as discussed in chapter 4, and the actual processes by which they are used, as discussed in chapters 5 and 7. This point highlights another difference, which is that the present theory deals with process models of various aspects of cognitive development, and is less a "stage" theory than Case's formulation. For example, the present theory has no equivalent of Case's substages, the progressive acquisition of concepts being attributed to learning, induction, and skill-acquisition processes.

Fischer (1980) proposed a skill-acquisition theory of cognitive development that I discussed in detail elsewhere (Halford, 1980, 1987). Commonalities between Fischer's theory and mine include the idea of a succession of levels and the concern with the acquisition of skills and strategies. However, my theory is much more oriented to information processing and is based more on formal models than is Fischer's. Also, in my theory, strategies are derived from, but are definitely distinct from, representations of concepts, whereas in Fischer's theory, skills and representations appear to be much more closely identified.

Fuzzy Trace Theory

Brainerd and Reyna (in press) argued that representations in reasoning problems are not based on verbatim representations of premise information but on extraction of the "gist." This is common ground because, as noted in chapter 2, I emphasized recoding processes, and the process models I proposed entail various transformations of the input. Parallel-distributed-processing models entail representations that are fuzzy, in that items are coded as vectors of features. However, PDP models have many other properties besides fuzziness, as discussed in chapter 2.

Dynamic-Systems Model

Van Geert (1991) proposed a dynamic-systems model of cognitive and language growth that entails learning under capacity limitations. The model includes a mathematical account of growth in dynamic systems, without detailed psychological process interpretations of the dynamics (Van Geert, 1991, p. 45). The theory therefore provides less process detail than the present model, but is nevertheless consistent with the present approach in its basic tenets. Van Geert did not adopt a specific view on questions such as the growth of capacity with age, but nevertheless derived some interesting predictions. For example, Van Geert showed (1991, pp. 40–41) that an increase in capacity can lead to stepwise growth, but only for processes (variables) that are close to their upper limit. In the context of the present theory, this would mean that acquisition of concepts would be affected by ability to use representations of higher dimensionality only if expertise in those concepts was already close to the maximum possible with the earlier, lower dimensionality representations. This emphasizes the continual interaction of learning and capacity in cognitive development.

Social Processes in Cognitive Development

A number of psychologists have emphasized the importance of the social environment in cognitive development, particularly with respect to higher functions and more abstract concepts. For example, Sigel (1981, 1982, 1984) has shown the importance of parents' and teachers' "distancing" behaviors, which help a child break space and time barriers in their conceptualization.

Vygotsky (1962) was an early leader in this field, arguing that while children are naturally active in their environments and play an active role in their cognitive development, the social environment makes an important and even indispensable contribution. The cross-cultural literature also shows how variations in the cultural and social environment affect the types of concepts that children acquire (Dasen, 1984; Dasen & Jahoda, 1986).

The present theory places the emphasis on the interaction between processing capacity on the one hand, and learning, induction, and strategy-development processes on the other. The social environment per se will not change processing capacity, except insofar as an enriched and stimulating environment can promote physiological growth. However, the social environment has a massive effect on learning and induction. It does this through directing children's attention, maintaining motivation, providing feedback, and, perhaps most important of all, providing efficient ways of coding and representing objects and events. I have noted a number of times in this book how important efficient codes are to problem solving because of the limited number of independent dimensions that can be processed in parallel. Many of these codes are culturally derived, because it is beyond the scope of any individual to develop them, as Carey (1985) pointed out so eloquently.

On the other hand, social processes do not change the basic learning and reasoning mechanisms as such. For example, they do not change the basic processes by which information about the environment comes to be stored in memory, as outlined in chapter 4, nor do they change basic analogical reasoning mechanisms as described in chapter 5. In other words, they do not change the basic cognitive equipment that is "wired in" to the child. They do, however, change the environment in which these processes operate and can thereby have a massive influence on their effectiveness. For example, they can make analogical reasoning much easier by enabling the child to code the relevant relation (Goswami, 1992). Therefore, social processes have a fundamentally important influence on the environment in which learning and induction processes operate, and thereby influence the effectiveness of the reasoning processes that result.

ANALYSIS OF STRUCTURE-MAPPING LEVELS

Many of the predictions from this theory depend on the dimensionality of representations entailed in tasks, and it is therefore necessary to have ways of establishing this. Complete rigor in this respect will ultimately depend on computational models, such as the simulation models of Bakker and Halford (1988) and Halford et al. (1991, 1992, in press). One advantage I would claim for the present theory is that key processes are defined in such a way that they can be readily translated into simulation models. However, we are some way from having a computational model of every cognitive-developmental task, and it is therefore necessary to provide some guidelines for assessing the dimensionality of representations and the level of structure mappings. These can serve in a practical role, with simulation providing the final "court of appeal."

As explained in chapter 2 and earlier in this chapter, the complexity of a representation is determined by the number of dimensions that must be used to represent the concept. This is based on two principles, as noted earlier in this chapter. The first is that only aspects of the task that constrain current cognitive processes must be actively represented, and aspects that vary independently of each other within the current task must be represented by separate dimensions. Where aspects of a task are constant, or all vary together, they can be coded as a single dimension.

Levels of structure mapping are related to dimensionality of representation, as noted in chapter 5. Representations with one, two, three, or four dimensions are entailed in element, relational, system, and multiple-system mappings, respectively. To establish the level of a structure mapping and the dimensionality of the corresponding representation, four main criteria must be met.

First, the representation or mental model that participants use for the task must be known to the theorist. In this book I have adopted transitivity as a prototypical case, not only because it entails many of the properties of reasoning tasks in general, but because the mental model that is typically used for transitive inference is well established. This was necessary because predictions based on structure-mapping theory can be made only to the extent that we can confidently diagnose or infer the mental model that is being used.

Second, we must ensure that the mappings have not been prelearned. If the mappings from Structure 1 to Structure 2 are already known, structure-mapping processes do not need to be used, and the corresponding processing loads will not occur. To illustrate this, imagine a transitive-inference task of this form: An elephant is bigger than a dog, a dog is bigger than a mouse; which is biggest, an elephant or a mouse? According to the theory we considered in chapter 1, which I examine further in chapter 7, a transitive inference entails mapping the premise elements into ordinal positions in an array. This is done using the premise information, and the mapping process imposes a processing load, as we saw in chapter 3. However, in the present example, none of this is necessary, because we already know that an elephant is bigger than a mouse. Therefore the processing load that normally occurs in the premise integration phase of transitive inference would not occur here.

This means that structure-mapping predictions should be tested on tasks where the mappings are not already known to participants. The cases considered in earlier chapters were all drawn from familiar domains; for example, they involved relations such as "happier than," "taller than," and so on. However, the problem elements were assigned to slots in premises arbitrarily, so prior knowledge could be used to circumvent the mapping processes that were intended to be used. The general principle is that familiar domains may be used, but the assignment of elements and relations in one structure to elements and relations in the other structure must not be known beforehand.

The third requirement is that chunking must be avoided, because it would reduce the dimensionality of representations and thereby reduce processing loads. Chunking can be obviated by requiring participants to generate a new structure that is isomorphic to an existing one. This happens in transitive inference, where the premise elements and relations must be organized into a new structure, an ordered set. Other ordered sets are known, but the particular ordered set corresponding to the elements and relations in the problem must not be known beforehand. It must be generated from the premise information in the problem. This ensures that the structure has to be represented as an appropriate number of dimensions and cannot be chunked. The general principle is that if the elements and relations of the problem have not been previously mapped into the required structure, that structure cannot already exist as a chunk. For example, given the problem Tom is smarter than John, Mark is smarter than Tom, if we already know that Mark, Tom, John are ordered for smartness in this way, this constitutes a single chunk, which occupies one vector and one module. If the task presents us with entirely new information about these three people, we must construct the ordered set, Mark, Tom, John. No chunk can exist until the set is constructed, and the construction process entails a three-dimensional representation and a Rank 4 tensor product, such as that shown in Fig. 3.8.

The general principle here is that processing demands are imposed by tasks that require variables to be processed. Recall from chapter 2 that the tensor product representation for predicates and arguments, derived from the STAR model (Halford et al., in press), is designed to treat predicates and arguments as variables. If a predicate and a set of arguments are constants, they can be treated as one vector, and the tensor product representation is unnecessary.

Fourth, the level of structure mapping required should be assessed by considering the minimum information necessary to recognize the correspondence between two structures. For example, if it is possible to establish the correspondence by considering only one relation at a time, then the task is a relational mapping. However, if two or more binary relations have to be considered jointly, it is a system mapping. In chapter 3 we showed that premise integration is a system mapping because it is not possible to unambiguously map problem elements to representation elements without considering two relations in a mapping decision.

Notice that it is the information in each mapping decision that determines the level of mapping, not the total number of relations in the situation. For example, in a transitive inference task, it would be possible to use a string of premises such as $1 < 2, 2 < 3, 3 < 4, 4 < 5$, and so on. Clearly, there are more than two relations here, but it is still only a system mapping. The reason is that the mapping can be made by considering the relations in pairs. From $1 < 2$ and $2 < 3$ we can infer the order is 1, 2, 3. The set $\{1, 2, 3\}$ then becomes a chunk, and it can be combined with $3 < 4$ to infer the order 1, 2, 3, 4, and so on. Thus any set can be ordered by considering pairs of relations, so an ordering task is always a system mapping.

Whether relations should be considered jointly or separately depends on whether they interact. Relations within an ordered set interact. In a problem such as "Bill is taller than Tom" and "Bill is shorter than Jack," the first premise only assigns Bill to ordinal Position 1 or 2 (i.e., it eliminates Position 3). We need the second premise as well to show that Bill is in Position 2. This shows that the premises interact, in that one premises alters the impliction of the other. This means they must be considered jointly, and cannot be considered independently.

A similar situation obtains in the balance scale task, considered in chapter 9. There weight and distance from the fulcrum interact, because each modifies the effect of the other. Greater distance from the fulcrum increases the effect of weight, and vice versa. This means the two factors must be considered jointly, which in turn constrains the level of structure mapping required.

SUMMARY POSTULATES

The theory can be summarized in the following postulates, which are intended to be interpreted in the light of the discussion in preceding chapters. The postulates are numbered according to the chapter in which the primary justification is to be found.

Postulate 1.0. Cognitive development depends on the interaction of learning and induction processes with growth in the capacity to represent concepts.

Postulate 2.0. Information is represented in the form of mental models that tend to be content-specific. A mental model comprises the representation that is currently active.

Postulate 2.1. Learned contingencies and stimulus–response associations entail implicit knowledge, which is not accessible to strategic cognitive processes.

Postulate 2.2. Acquisition of explicit knowledge entails creation of new representations (representational redescription), which are connected to other cognitive representations and are accessible to strategic cognitive processes.

Postulate 2.3. Aspects of a task that constrain a particular decision or computation can be represented in parallel. Aspects that vary independently within the current situation must be represented by separate dimensions.

Postulate 2.4. The number of dimensions required to represent a concept is a measure of the structural complexity of the concept.

Postulate 2.5. In parallel-distributed-processing representations each dimension is represented by a separate vector. Where tensor products of vectors are used to represent predicate-argument bindings, a concept of dimensionality N will be represented by a tensor product of rank $N+1$, due to the need for a vector representing the predicate. Where the predicate is constant, the tensor product representation of a concept of dimensionality N will be rank N.

Postulate 2.6. The representations used in PDP architectures provide for automatic averaging, prototype formation, generalization, discrimination, and regularity detection, all of which are important to cognitive development. (Although the issue is unsettled at the time of writing, it appears that there is no essential incompatibility between representations based on PDP and those based on condition–action rules. They are different levels of description.)

Postulate 3.0. The dimensionality of concepts that can be represented increases with age: One-dimensional concepts are represented at 1 year, two-dimensional concepts at 2 years, three-dimensional concepts at 3 years, and four-dimensional concepts at 11 years (approximate median ages of attainment). The maximum dimensionality of concepts that adults can represent is normally four (range three-to-five).

Postulate 3.1. Representations of higher dimensionality impose higher processing loads.

Postulate 3.2. Concepts of higher dimensionality may be recoded into fewer dimensions (conceptual chunking). This reduces the processing load, but some relations between dimensions of the concept will no longer be represented unless a return is made to the unchunked representation, which will also increase the processing load.

Postulate 3.3. Conceptual chunking requires experience with a constant mapping of components into chunks.

Postulate 3.4. Concepts of higher dimensionality can be segmented into components that are processed serially. Strategies are normally required for such processing.

Postulate 3.5. Adoption of more efficient codes, which represent the essential structure of concepts in fewer dimensions (conceptual chunking), is one of the major attainments both of cognitive development and expertise.

Postulate 4.0. Cognitive development depends on knowledge acquisition, which depends on: (a) basic learning and induction processes that enable the child to acquire a store of contingencies and declarative condition–action rules that represent aspects of the environment, and (b) acquisition of procedural condition–action rules and strategies.

Postulate 4.1. Learned contingencies and declarative condition–action rules are both strengthened when they make predictions that are confirmed and are weakened when they make predictions that are disconfirmed.

Postulate 4.2. Learned contingencies and declarative rules are more likely to be learned when the predictions they make are informative and nonredundant. Where another stimulus in the same situation elicits a learned contingency or rule that predicts an event, acquisition of a new rule predicting that same event will be blocked.

Postulate 4.3. Stimulus–response associations and procedural condition–action rules are strengthened when the responses they produce are rewarded or "reinforced."

Postulate 4.4. Knowledge stored as learned contingencies, stimulus–response associations, and condition–action rules can be modified by processes that include generalization, discrimination, recomposition, and recoding.

Postulate 4.5. A concept of the task can be used to guide the development of strategies (strategy acquisition based on understanding).

Postulate 4.6. A concept of the task can be represented in a content-specific form, based on experience, that can be used by structure mapping (analogy).

Postulate 4.7. Strategies and procedural condition–action rules can be learned by associative processes, without understanding, but transfer will be a function of literal similarity between original learning and transfer situations.

Postulate 4.8. Social processes assist children to adopt efficient codes, provide feedback, direct attention to relevant aspects of tasks or situations, and maintain motivation.

Postulate 4.9. Active experience is required for conceptual development. Concepts are not acquired solely by instruction. Social input must be related to a child's own representations to be useful.

Postulate 4.10. Condition–action rules can be activated in parallel and can be mutually supportive or inhibitory, thereby providing for coherence.

Postulate 4.11. Material to be learned can be mapped into a mental model or analog, which permits information to be predicted, thereby saving learning effort.

Postulate 5.0. Analogical reasoning entails mapping a base or source structure into a target structure. Both structures are cognitive representations (as defined in chapter 2).

Postulate 5.1. Structure mapping imposes a processing load that depends on the dimensionality of the representation required (as defined in chapter 2). Element mappings require one-dimensional representations, relational mappings require two-dimensional representations, system mappings require three-dimensional representations, and multiple-system mappings require four-dimensional representations.

PART

IV

DOMAIN-SPECIFIC PROCESSES AND CONCEPTS

7

INFERENCES AND HYPOTHESIS TESTING

This chapter is concerned with the question of how children develop the ability to make inferences. Because induction was discussed in chapters 4 and 6, the primary focus is on deductive inferences, which are divided into relational and categorical. However, abduction and hypothesis testing are considered because these were not discussed earlier. Relational deductive inferences include transitive inferences and linear ordering problems. These are sometimes called N-term series or linear syllogism problems, but this label does not cover all possibilities, because there are nonlinear problems such as $a > b, a > c$, therefore a is biggest, that do not form series or linear structures. Transitivity has been used as a reference task throughout this work, but the processes of transitive inference will now be considered in more detail. Categorical deductive inferences include inferences based on category memberships, such as All A are B, all B are C, therefore all A are C.

We begin with transitivity because it is probably the most widely researched topic in the area. Then we examine other kinds of deductive inference, and finally we consider inductive inferences and hypothesis testing.

TRANSITIVITY

An example of a transitive inference is: if $a > b$, and $b > c$, then $a > c$. Transitivity has a precise mathematical definition,[1] but the way it is understood psychologically may be different from the mathematical concept of

---

[1]A relation R defined on a set S is transitive if aRb and aRc imply aRc for every a,b,c in S.

transitivity. The best course therefore is to consider both the mathematical and psychological concepts of transitivity.

To relax the mathematical definition slightly, transitivity means that if R is a transitive relation, and if R exists between a and b, and also between b and c, then the relation R will exist between a and c; that is, $a R b$ and $b R c$ implies $a R c$. Examples of transitive relations include those concerned with size, weight, distance, and measurable properties generally. On the other hand "lover of" is nontransitive; if a is the lover of b, and b is the lover of c, it is unlikely that a is the lover of c.[2]

The psychological significance of transitivity rests firstly on the fact that it is part of the definition of the psychologically important concept of serial order. Mathematically, an ordered set is one on which an asymmetric, transitive, binary relation is defined. For example, if we take the ordered set (a, b, c, d), where a is the biggest and d is the smallest, then it will be true that $a > b, b > c, c > d$, but also $a > c, a > d, b > d$. The relation "bigger than" is asymmetric (because $a > b$ implies $b > a$ cannot be true) and transitive.

The concept of order is important in many situations. Understanding the numbering of houses on a street depends on understanding order, as does understanding positions in a race, and a multitude of everyday concepts. Order is also important to all but the most primitive concepts of quantification. Only the lowest level of scale, the nominal scale, does not depend on order. An ordinal scale clearly entails a concept of order; an interval scale entails the concept of order, plus a definition of the distance between the elements, and an addition operation. A ratio scale entails everything that is entailed in the interval scale, plus a zero point, and a multiplication operation. Thus, understanding of quantification beyond the nominal scale entails a concept of order, which in turns entails transitivity.

Another reason why transitivity is important is that it exemplifies a class of tasks that require symbolically represented information to be integrated mentally. Transitive inferences require premise relations to be integrated symbolically, and a test of transitivity must entail this to be considered valid. Suppose, for example, that participants are shown three sticks, a, b, c, such that a is the longest and c is the shortest, and the three sticks are obviously different in length. They are first shown that $a > b$, then $b > c$. They are then asked whether a is more than or less than c (a ? c), with a and c visible. It will be obvious from inspection of the sticks that $a > c$. Because the answer can be generated perceptually, this is not an adequate test of transitive inference. We can only accept the task as requiring transitive inference if we can be confident that two relations, $a > b, b > c$, were represented internally, then integrated mentally. The participant must not be permitted to examine the

---

[2]A relation is nontransitive if aRb and bRc imply aRc for some, but not all a,b,c. A relation is intransitive if aRb and bRc does not imply aRc for any a,b,c.

three sticks and compare *a* and *c* perceptually. The problem must be solved by mental representation and integration to be considered a test of transitive inference.

Mental integration is a basic aspect of thought that virtually always entails integration of formerly separate items of information into some new synthesis. One of the reasons transitivity is an attractive topic to study is that it entails mental integration in a task that is simple enough to be readily analyzed, both theoretically and empirically. Transitivity also entails a number of other processes such as encoding and manipulation of premises.

Both transitivity and serial-order (sometimes called seriation) tasks belong to the class of *N*-term series tasks. In this class of tasks participants are presented with premises specifying the relation between pairs of elements, then they are asked to specify the order of the elements or a subset of them. Alternatively, they are asked to nominate the element that has the most, or the least, of the relevant attribute. For example, if the size relation is used, they are asked to nominate the largest, or the smallest, element.

Mechanisms of Transitive Inference

The numerous competing models of transitive inference were integrated by Sternberg (1980a, 1980b) into a "mixed model" that has proved capable of accounting for very high proportions of the variance in solution times. A brief outline of the Sternberg model is given in Fig. 7.1. First the premises are read and encoded into linguistic deep-structural base strings; for example, the premise "Bill is not as tall as Mike" becomes "Bill is tall +; Mike is tall." Then the premises are each encoded separately into imaginal arrays, Bill–Mike and John–Mike. The arrays might be top–bottom or left–right according to individual preferences, but the former is chosen in Fig. 7.1. Because the first premise contains a negative, the first array is inverted, so Bill–Mike becomes Mike–Bill. The two separate arrays are then integrated into a single three-term array, John–Mike–Bill. Then the term required by the question, in this case the tallest person, is located and the response is made. Sternberg's model integrates linguistic processes first defined by Clark (1969) and imaginal processes defined by DeSoto, London, and Handel (1965), and Huttenlocher (1968). It also takes into account earlier contributions such as the operational model of Hunter (1957). It can account for all three-term series problems to which the answer is determinate, and recently incorporated additional processing steps to account for people's ability to recognize when a problem is indeterminate; for example, Bill is shorter than Tom, Tom is taller than Mike, who is shortest? It has also been shown that the same processes can account for *N*-term series reasoning by children down to about 8 years of age (Sternberg, 1980b).

However the Sternberg model does not account for *N*-term series problems with more than three elements, nor does it account for other variations such

1. Read problem, e.g., Bill is not as tall as Mike,

    Mike is shorter than John.

    Who is tallest?

2. Encode premises, yielding linguistic deep-structural base strings:

    Bill is tall +

    Mike is tall

    Mike is short +

    John is short

3. Map the terms into the imaginal arrays:

    Bill

    Mike

    John

    Mike

4. Process the negatives in the premises:

    Mike

    Bill

    John

    Mike

5. Integrate the arrays:

    John

    Mike

    Bill

6. Locate response required by the question (tallest term) and respond.

FIG. 7.1. Sequence of steps in Sternberg's mixed model of transitive inference.

as the use of nonadjacent relations (e.g., $a > b$, $b > c$, $a > c$) that occur in some ordering tasks.

A set of processes that can be used to arrange four or more elements in order has been defined by Foos, Smith, Sabol, and Mynatt (1976). They can be applied to problems of the form $a > b$, $b > c$, $c > d$ . . . , and so on, or to permutations of these premises. The five processes are all concerned with integrating premise elements into an ordered set that is held in short-term memory. They are summarized in Table 7.1. The model assumes that as premises are processed, the resulting elements are stored as an ordered string in short-term memory. When the next premise is presented, a match is sought between the elements of the new premise and the elements already stored in short-term memory. For example, after the premise $a > b$ is processed, the elements ab would be stored in short-term memory. Then when premise $b > c$ is presented, the matching element, b, is located, and c is added to the string, yielding abc.

There are two processes for finding a match: M1 and M2. M1 is used when a term is added to the end of the string in short-term memory, whereas M2 is used when a term is added to the front of the string. The other processes in the Foos et al. model are N, for no match, D1, for double match where the order of elements in the string does not need to be changed, and D2 for double match where the order does need to be changed. We illustrate these processes by considering problem forms 2–6.

In problem form 2, elements ab are first stored in short-term memory,

TABLE 7.1
Processes Used to Construct Linear Orders According to Model
by Foos et al. (1976)

Problem Form	Premises	Process after Second Premise	Process after Third Premise
1	ab, bc, cd	M1	M1
2	ab, cd, bc	N	D1
3	bc, ab, cd	M2	M1
4	bc, cd, ab	M1	M2
5	cd, ab, bc	N	D2
6	cd, bc, ab	M2	M2
7	ab, bc, ac	M1	D1'
8	ab, ac, bc	I1	R1
9	bc, ab, ac	M2	D1'
10	bc, ac, ab	I2	R2
11	ac, ab, bc	I1	R1
12	ac, bc, ab	I2	R2

The processes are match (M), no match (N), and double match (D). The numeral 1 means the order already stored is retained, 2 means it is reversed. The premises are shown without a relation between terms, e.g., $a > b$ is shown simply as ab.

then when *cd* is presented, no match between the premise and the stored string can be found. Consequently, the string *ab*cd* is stored, the marker * indicating that the order of *bc* is unknown. This is process *N*, for no match. Then when *bc* is presented, a double match (D1) is found because both *b* and *c* are in the stored string. In this case the original order of the stored string is retained, but the marker is removed, yielding the order *abcd*.

In problem form 3, *bc* is stored first, then when *ab* is presented, the matching element *b* is found, and the string *abc* is constructed. This is process M2 because an element is added to the front of the string. When *cd* is presented, process M1 finds the match and constructs the string *abcd*. Cases 4 and 6 operate according to the same processes as those that occur in Cases 1–3, but Case 5 entails process D2. The string *cd* is stored first, but no match is found with *ab* (process *N*), so the string *cd*ab* is stored. When *bc* is presented, there is a double match, because both *b* and *c* occur in the stored string. However, this time the order of the stored elements must be reversed (process D2) yielding *abcd*.

The processes vary reliably in difficulty; double matches (D_1 and D_2) are harder than single matches (M_1 and M_2). Matches that require change of order or addition of elements to the front of the string (M2 and D2) are harder than processes that do not (M1 and D1). Double-match processes impose higher loads on short-term memory, because two premises plus a marker, five elements in all, must be stored, whereas after a single match a set of only three elements must be stored. The elements are sometimes stored in short-term memory as visual images, and sometimes as strings that are rehearsed.

This model supplements the Sternberg model in that it shows how strings of indefinite length could be constructed, because the five processes could be iterated over any number of premises. However, it still does not deal with ordering tasks that include nonadjacent relations, such as $a > c$, $c > d$, $b > d$, and so on. These are important in any model of ordering processes that wants to be ecologically valid because relations between nonadjacent elements do occur in real-life ordering tasks. Suppose for example that we want to rank order students according to grade. If we know that Bill's grade is better than Tom's (Bill > Tom), we cannot conclude that Bill and Tom are adjacent. There may be other relations Bill > Jenny, Jenny > Tom, so that the true order may be Bill, Jenny, Tom. When a relation is first presented, we do not know whether it is between adjacent elements or not; in the above example, we do not know at first whether Bill is adjacent to Tom, or whether other students come in between. The existence of nonadjacent relations considerably complicates the ordering process, and any psychological theory of ordering that takes no account of this cannot be considered ecologically valid.

A difficulty that arises when nonadjacent premises occur is that the order of two of the elements can be indeterminate. For example, the premises

$a > b$, $a > c$ imply that a is first, but the order of b and c is indeterminate. If $a > b$ is an adjacent relation, the order will be abc, if $a > b$ is a nonadjacent relation, the order will be acb. This indeterminacy can only be resolved by the bc relation.

A set of additional processes that can take account of nonadjacent relations was defined by Maybery, Halford, Bain, and Kelly (unpublished manuscript) and are shown in the lower half of Table 7.1. Process I1 occurs in cases such as ab, ac, where the first element matches, but the order of the remaining elements is indeterminate. A second indeterminate case, I2 occurs with premises bc, ac, where c must be last but the order of the first two elements is unknown. These indeterminacies are resolved by processes R1 and R2 for I1 and I2 respectively.

Each of these processes can be modelled effectively in a computer program, and successful simulations of ordering tasks using these processes have been run in our laboratory. Two difficulties arise however. The first is that we seem to have a proliferation of specialized processes, each capable of dealing with one specific situation. This makes for a rather cumbersome and implausible model of N-term series reasoning. The proliferation of processes makes the model difficult to handle, and it is implausible because it seems unlikely that people develop a specific process for handling every conceivable ordering task, especially given that the number of such tasks is unlimited. The second problem, which is related to the first, is that it is unclear whether all these processes belong to a single strategy, or whether multiple strategies are involved. The implication is that it is unlikely that we can account for N-term series reasoning by defining specific processes and strategies. What is needed is some way that a person can devise, or construct, a solution process that is appropriate to each task as it is presented. Strategy-development mechanisms were discussed in chapter 4 for both transitive inference and counting.

Acquisition of Transitivity

It was argued in chapter 4 that the strategies used in transitive inference can be acquired through processes that are applicable to a wide range of cognitive skills. I outlined the model of Halford et al. (1991), which simulates development of transitive inference strategies. This model shares some basic philosophical notions with Anderson (1987), Greeno et al. (1984), Greeno and Johnson (1985), and VanLehn and Brown (1980), and Siegler and Shrager (1984), as discussed in chapter 4. The model has both metacognitive and associative strategy selection mechanisms. It assumes that if skills exist to perform a particular task, they are used, and if not, they are developed. Existing skills are strengthened when successful, and weakened when they produce errors. Associative mechanisms operate as a first resort, using existing skills. If these fail, metacognitive mechanisms are invoked to develop new skills.

The model does not postulate strategies in the sense of an indivisible set of activities that always occur in the same way. It is based on a large collection of specific skills, each of which is used for performing a given activity. These skills are modeled as production rules. In effect, each production rule can be thought of as a specific skill. However production rules and, by implication, skills do not always occur in the same combination. A child, or an adult, might have one of many subsets of these skills at any one time. However we can continue to use the word "strategy" for convenience, provided it is recognized that the composition of skills a given strategy entails can change from time to time. Strategies are therefore dynamic, rather than static. In effect, a strategy is an approximation to a variable set of skills.

Overall the solution processes developed by the model correspond fairly closely to the theories of Sternberg (1980a, 1980b) and Foos, Smith, Sabol, and Mynatt (1976), in that the main process is the assembly of problem elements in an ordered set. The development of skills is constrained by the concept of order, which is acquired through experience (such as play with blocks that form series) and can be instantiated as an ordered set of at least three elements. Analogical mapping is used to test the correspondence between an order produced in a problem and the concept of order. Operators are learned by manipulative experience and are stored in long-term memory, together with initial and final states, so they can be used in means–end analysis.

Now let us consider an example of strategy development in N-term series reasoning. A major acquisition is a strategy for integrating premises, because this is a source of difficulty for 3- to 4-year-olds (Halford, 1984; Halford & Kelly, 1984). Very young children, and older children under high-load conditions, tend to treat each premise pair independently. Given the premises $c > d, a > b$, they are inclined to simply give the order $cdab$, without any recognition that the order of da, or bc, is unknown. Baylor and Gascon (1974) also observed this kind of behavior in children's initial weight-seriation strategies.

The 3- to 4-year-olds tested by Halford (1984) were unable to integrate premises even though they had extensive training in task demands, were given brief training on the specific premises of each problem, had a memory aid that ensured premise retention, and had the problem presented to them in very small steps. Five- to six-year-olds succeeded in these conditions, but the same failure to integrate appeared in the performance of older children under the much more demanding conditions of the Baylor and Gascon study, in which children had to develop their own strategies. This implies that ability to integrate premises under optimal conditions is present at age 5 but may not be employed in more demanding conditions. Thus there is no "stage" of integration. It does not appear suddenly or in all-or-none fashion. Its first appearance at approximately age 5 years is due to the high processing load that it imposes, but that load also affects the performance of older children and adults.

Consider now a child who has the processing capacity to integrate premises, but is not doing so in some particular task. Suppose the child is given the sequence of premises $c > d$, $a > b$, $b > c$, under optimal conditions, where premise retention is assured, and each premise can be processed in sequence. The child first constructs the order *cd*, then *cdab*, then when $b > c$ is presented, *b* is shifted to the front of the string, yielding *bcda*. We have observed children doing this in our laboratory without making any effort to retrieve or check the $a > b$ premise. How does the child discover the inadequacy of this strategy?

There first needs to be some feedback that reduces the child's confidence in the strategy that has been used. Although the strategy is above the child's confidence criterion, it will be applied without metacognitive processing to assess its validity. Metacognitive processes are invoked only when confidence falls below the criterion, as discussed in chapter 4. When this happens, the ordering obtained by the strategy is compared with the concept of order, using the type of structure-mapping processes illustrated in Fig. 7.2. If the strategy conforms to the concept of order it is applied, otherwise it is repaired or, if this is not possible, replaced with another strategy. The confidence that the new strategy will solve the problem is then assessed, and the cycle repeated. Let us return to our example of the child who has produced the order *bcda* from the premises $c > d$, $a > b$, $b > c$. Suppose the child has received feedback that indicates that the order is incorrect. The feedback might come from an external source, such as a parent, teacher, or sibling who says the solution is wrong. Alternatively, it might be internal and come from inspecting the ordered set created. If, for example, the child is trying to assemble four blocks differing in height, he or she might have been expecting something resembling a staircase. The resulting staircase does not ascend uniformly but has a disappointing roller-coaster quality about it. Any of these experiences constitutes feedback that can reduce the child's confidence in the strategy used. It then becomes more likely that on a subsequent attempt at the task the child will examine the strategy by mapping its output into the concept of order.

The structure mapping will show not only that the ordering is incorrect but also what is missing. The problem lies with one relation that is not mapped into the concept of order in a way that is consistent with the other mappings. In Fig. 7.3 it is the relation "less smart than." Recognition of this discrepancy sets up a subgoal to change that relation. This, in turn, results in the subgoal to find out the missing relation between Mike and Tom. Alternatively, in the example with the premises $c > d$, $a > b$, $b > c$ leading to the order *bcda*, it leads to the subgoal of finding the relation between *a* and *b*. The proce-

Representational Array

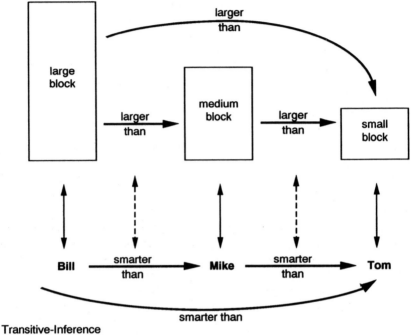

Transitive-Inference
Problem

premises: Bill is Smarter than Tom

Tom is smarter than Mike

inference: Bill is smarter than Mike

FIG. 7.2.   Valid mapping of transitive-inference problem into an ordered set
learned through experience.

dure for finding or retrieving the missing relation can then be incorporated
into the strategy. Thus, a strategy that has failed to integrate premises begins to do so.

Acquisition of the ability to integrate premises corresponds to transition
from preoperational to concrete operational reasoning in Piagetian theory,
because premise integration is the essence of transitive inference, which was
regarded by Piaget as a concrete operational concept. This acquisition has

Representational Array

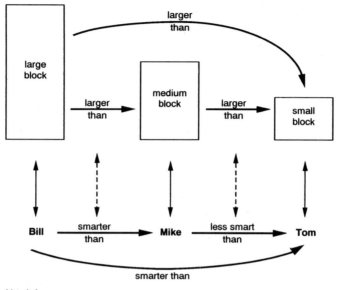

Transitive-Inference
Problem

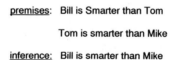

premises: Bill is Smarter than Tom

Tom is smarter than Mike

inference: Bill is smarter than Mike

FIG. 7.3. Invalid mapping of transitive inference problem into an ordered set learned through experience.

occurred through normal learning processes that are applicable to a multitude of other tasks. The important point that is again illustrated here is that cognitive development does not require specific learning or "transition" mechanisms. Normal learning processes are sufficient, if we understand how they work.

The fact that transitive inferences are validated by system mapping means that their validity is ultimately dependent on experience. To see why this is true, consider the structure mapping in Fig. 7.4. Here the inference "John kicks Peter, Peter kicks Terry, therefore John kicks Terry" is mapped into the ordered array top–middle–bottom. This is a valid system mapping, but the inference is incorrect because "kicks" is not a transitive relation.

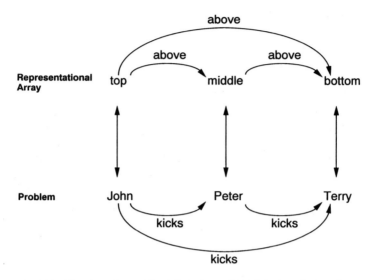

FIG. 7.4.　Mapping of transitive-inference problem into top–down schema.

Nothing about the system mapping indicates why "kicks" should not be transitive. It can only be learned by experience, because it is a fact rather than a logical principle. It is an item of world knowledge.

It would be predicted, therefore, that transitive inferences are likely to be overgeneralized. This prediction is confirmed by Kuczaj and Donaldson (1982), who found that 5- to 9-year-old children tended to apply transitive inferences to relations like kick, like, and love. They reasoned that if the boy loves the girl, and the girl loves the dog, the boy loves the dog. It was not until around the age of 10 years that appropriate discriminations between transitive and nontransitive relations were made.

Children's Understanding of Transitivity

The traditional Piagetian view (Piaget, 1947/1950) was that transitivity is not understood until late in childhood, but many of the tests used made demands that went well beyond transitive inference. In one of the tests (Piaget, Inhelder, & Szeminska, 1960) children are shown one tower of blocks on a table and another on the floor, with a rod that can be be used to measure the blocks. The idea is that if, for example, tower A is taller than the rod, which is taller than tower B, then tower A is taller than tower B. Although this task entails transitive inference, it contains a flaw that was once common in tests of conceptual competence. That is, it assumed that the strategy that the experimenter had in mind when devising the test would be self-evident to participants, who would automatically attempt to use it, and the resulting performance could therefore be accepted as reflecting ability to use that strategy. The fallacy is that the test requires not only the ability to make a transitive inference, but the metacognitive knowledge that the measurement procedure is appropriate.

Braine (1959) attempted to overcome what were thought to be the negative biases of transitive inference tests by developing a nonverbal assessment of transitivity, but this was criticized by Smedslund (1963). The ensuing controversy was reviewed by Miller (1976), who concluded that it did not resolve the issue of when children understand transitivity.

A more momentous development occurred when Bryant and Trabasso (1971) put forward their technique for assessing transitivity, which is based on the premise that children's failure is due to an inability to remember the premises. To prevent children from forgetting the premises, they were taught relations between color-coded sticks, $a > b, b > c, c > d, d > e$. Then they were tested on all possible pairs, $a ? b, a ? c, \ldots a ? e, b ? c, \ldots d ? e$. The crucial pair is $b ? d$, because $b > d$ has not been learned but must be inferred. Also, false positives occurring by labeling one stick "large" and the other "small" are eliminated because both b and d should carry both labels. The result was that 3- and 4-year-old children made above chance correct responses on the $b ? d$ pair. This seemed to provide a striking disconfirmation of the Piagetian view that transitivity is not acquired until late in childhood.

There are several reviews of the literature arising from this paradigm (Breslow, 1981; Halford, 1982, chapter 6; Halford, 1989; Thayer & Collyer, 1978; Trabasso, 1975, 1977). We only sketch the developments that have been crucially important to the picture as we currently understand it.

A series of experiments (Riley, 1976; Riley & Trabasso, 1974; Trabasso, 1975, 1977) showed that people perform this task by assembling the elements into an ordered array, probably in the form of an image. Once the ordered array is constructed, any two elements can be compared by accessing the array.

As we saw earlier, transitivity and serial-order tasks are linked by the fact that transitivity is a defining property of an ordered set. The research by Riley and Trabasso shows they are psychologically linked, because transitive-inference tasks are typically performed by arranging the task elements in order. This means that ordering tasks and transitivity may not differ in the underlying processes; both entail using relational premise information to arrange elements in order. In transitive-inference tasks participants are asked to nominate the element that has the most, or the least, of the relevant attribute (e.g., which is largest?). In ordering tasks, they are asked to state the order of the set of elements, or a subset of them (e.g., which is larger, b or d?).

Another implication of the work by Riley and Trabasso is that the real test of transitivity occurs not in the test phase, as was originally intended, but in the training phase. Recall that children were taught the premises $a > b, b > c, c > d, d > e$, and that they learned these premises by assembling the elements into the ordered array, a, b, c, d, e. This is the effortful part of the task, because once the array is constructed, the comparisons in the test phase can easily be made by just accessing the array. Notice also that assembling the elements into an ordered array entails transitivity in some way, because transitivity is a defining property of an ordered set.

This means that we must examine the training phase to see whether it constitutes an unbiased test of transitivity. It was pointed out by Kallio (1982), Halford (1992), and Halford and Kelly (1984) that there were two features of the training procedure that unduly aided the children and inflated their performances. The first was that the premises were presented in serial order; for example children would first be taught $a > b$, then $b > c$, and so on. The second is that children who failed to learn the premises were eliminated, and the elimination rates were quite high in some studies. This would have seemed reasonable when learning the premises was regarded simply as a means of equipping the children for the test phase. When it was realized that learning the premises really constituted the test, these procedures ceased to be legitimate. However, Halford and Kelly (1984) and Kallio (1982) showed that serial-order cues during training helped children construct the ordered array. When preschool children were tested with these factors eliminated, they failed to perform at better-than-chance level.

There are two main classes of explanation for the difficulties that young children have with transitive inference. One is that they encode the premises in absolute, rather than relational terms (Siegler, 1989b). For example, given the premise (as in Fig. 7.2) that "Bill is smarter than Tom," they code Bill as "smart" and Tom as "not smart." This leads to conflict when the premise "Tom is smarter than Mike" is presented, because Tom is now coded as "smart," which conflicts with the earlier coding. Notice, however, that relational coding does not completely remove this conflict. If we code both premises in relational terms, "smarter than," rather than "smart," we still have the problem that in the first premise Tom is "less smart," whereas in the second premise Tom is "smarter." This conflict can only be removed by integrating the premises into an ordered set of three, Bill, Tom, Mike. There may be a tendency, however, for both children and, to a lesser extent, adults to encode premises in absolute terms. A probable reason is that absolute encoding imposes a smaller processing load, because it entails a one-dimensional representation. The predicate SMART(Bill) is one place, whereas the predicate SMARTER-THAN(Bill, Tom) is two place. The first is one dimensional, whereas the latter is two dimensional.

Nevertheless, the way the problem is encoded is clearly important. Relational encoding will facilitate mapping the premises into a suitable analogy, such as that in Fig. 7.2, and thereby contribute to the development of appropriate problem-solving skills. Given that the process of analogical reasoning tends to change the way base and target are encoded (Mitchell & Hofstadter, 1990), it is likely that relational encoding is adopted in the course of attempting to map the problem into a suitable analog.

The other explanation is that preschool children have difficulty integrating premises in N-term series tasks. Integrating premises into an ordered triple requires a three-dimensional representation. In structure-mapping terms, as we saw in chapter 3, it is a system mapping and it requires both premises to be considered jointly. This has been shown by Maybery et al. (1986) to impose a high processing load for adults. We will now examine evidence about how this processing load affects the performance of young children.

Perner and Mansbridge (1983) required children to learn pairs with a common term ($a > b, b > c, c > d$) or an equal number of pairs without a common term ($a > b, c > d, e > f$). Seven-, 8-, and 10-year-olds found the pairs without a common term easier to learn. This would be expected if the pairs are learned without integrating them. The reason is that if pairs like $a > b, b > c$ are learned separately, without integrating them into the ordered set abc, the common term tends to be encoded in a way that produces conflict; b is encoded as "small" in the $a > b$ pair, but as "large" in the $b > c$ pair. This problem does not arise in the pairs without a common term, because each element is encoded in only one way.

On the other hand, Perner and Mansbridge found that pairs with a common term were easier for the 12-year-olds and adults to learn. If pairs are integrated into an ordered array, $abcd$, they would actually be easier to remember, because only four elements must be retained. Perner and Mansbridge found an age-by-conditions interaction of the form; pairs with a common term were easier over age 12, and harder below that age.

This experiment illustrates an interesting point about integrating; the process of integrating items of information can be cognitively effortful, but once achieved it reduces the processing load and eliminates conflict. The older children and adults were apparently able to integrate relatively easily, with the result that the items were easier to remember. Evidently the gain in ease of retention outweighed the effort of integration. The younger children, however, were either unable to integrate the pairs, or the effort of doing so outweighed the benefits to recall. Another interesting feature of this study was that performance on pairs with a common term correlated with age and intelligence test scores, but performance on pairs without a common term did not. This suggests that the processing load imposed by premise integration may be related to intelligence.

Halford and Kelly (1984) also contrasted pairs with and without a common term, using younger children. They found that preschool children aged 3–4 years showed zero-order performance on pairs with a common term, although they learned pairs without a common term. By age 5 this difference disappeared. This suggests that the difficulty of integrating pairs may be too great for children under 5 years of age.

It is interesting to relate these tasks to the conditional discrimination, negative patterning, and transverse patterning tasks discussed in chapter 4. On the surface they are very different tasks, but there is an important underlying similarity. The task of learning $a > b, b > c, c > d, d > e$ can be represented in the following way; given a, b say "a large," given b, c say "b large," and so on. This can be written as; $a, b \rightarrow a; b, c \rightarrow b; c, d \rightarrow c;$ $d, e \rightarrow d$. Compare this with the transverse patterning task in Fig. 5.13; green, blue $\rightarrow$ green; blue, yellow $\rightarrow$ blue; yellow, green $\rightarrow$ yellow. The common feature of the tasks is that the correct response cannot be based on a single cue; for example, "a" is equally associated with two responses, as also is green, and so on. Recall that the work of Rudy (in press), discussed in chapter 5, showed that tasks that have this property are difficult for children under 5 years. Furthermore, Rudy presented evidence that this ability was a function of physiological development. As discussed in chapter 5, transverse patterning, negative patterning, and conditional discrimination, are all three-dimensional concepts. Transitivity, specifically the process of integrating premises into an ordered triple, is also a three-dimensional concept, as explained in chapters 2 and 3. These superficially very different concepts have two things in common. They are based on three-dimensional representations, and they are very difficult for children under about 5 years of age.

The hypothesis that 4-year-olds cannot integrate premises was confirmed in a more direct way by Halford (1984). Children in the adjacent-only condition were given brief training on premise sets such as $a > b, b > c, c > d, d > e$, and $e > f$. Each peg was of a different color. In the adjacent-and-nonadjacent condition they received the premises $a > b, b > c, c > d,$ $d > e, b > d$. Thus the same number of premises were used, but $e > f$ was replaced by the nonadjacent premise, $b > d$. A memory aid, consisting of pairs of pegs whose colors matched those of the items to be ordered, was provided to ensure premise retention.

Children were given tests for ordering of the elements b, c, d, in which they never had to order more than two elements at a time. For example, they would be asked to place bc in order, then add d. The number of relations they had to consider to obtain the correct order was manipulated, holding other factors constant. For example, in the adjacent-only condition, ordering bd requires two relations to be considered, $b > c, c > d$, whereas in the adjacent-and-nonadjacent condition only one relation, $b > d$, must be considered.

It was consistently found that 3- and 4-year-old children performed no better than chance where two relations had to be integrated in a single decision, although they performed without error when the same task could be performed using only one relation at a time. They could also interpret two relations in successive decisions, as when they had to place *bc* in order, then add *d*. On the other hand 5- to 6-year-old children succeeded on all tasks. These results support those of Halford and Kelly (1984) and Kallio (1982) in showing that premise integration is a source of difficulty for children below the age of 5 years.

More recent evidence suggests, however, that 4-year-olds can make transitive inferences under certain conditions. Pears and Bryant (1990) presented premises in the form of pairs of colored blocks one above the other, for example, Block A above B, Block B above C, C above D, and D above E. Children were required to build a tower with another set of blocks of the same color as the premise blocks, with a top–down order A, B, C, D, E consistent with the premises. Before building the tower, they were asked inferential questions, such as whether Block B would be above or below Block D. This procedure elegantly tests the ability to make transitive inferences based on spatial position (e.g., B above C, C above D, therefore B above D), and 4-year-olds performed significantly above chance in two experiments.

Pears and Bryant acknowledged that the task might be performed by manipulating images of the premises. For example, given that B is above C and C above D in the pairs of blocks that are currently visible, it is possible to imagine pair B–C sitting on top of pair C–D, and it would then be apparent that in a tower B would be above D. Pears and Bryant claimed however that this is a legitimate way to make a transitive inference. I agree that it is a legitimate transitive inference for this task, but it does not follow that children who can make that inference could make transitive inferences in other contexts. If we wished to adopt a categorical approach to cognitive development, we could certainly categorize 4-year-olds as "having" transitivity on the basis of this evidence. A more important question is whether the processes that succeed here would generalize to other tasks.

We still have the problem of explaining why children find other transitive inference tasks difficult. In this respect it is instructive to compare Pears and Bryant's procedure with that of Halford (1984). Both used color-coded premises, both obviated the need for retention of premises in memory, and both used tasks that were appropriate for young children. However, my task had premises coded in the form of colored pegs in a board. Children were asked to arrange tubes, that contained sticks of different lengths and whose colors matched those of the pegs, in an order consistent with the pairs of pegs on the board. Pears and Bryant suggested that the difficulties children in my study experienced may have been because it was hard for them to translate spatial position into length.

Actually, however, this cannot be true in its entirety, because my data showed that even 3-year-olds could order the tubes without error consistent with the pegboard, provided the ordering task was constructed so they could process the premises serially. Therefore, they were undoubtedly able to translate the pegboard information into the task of ordering the tubes. What they could not do is make this translation by processing two premises jointly. When they had to order tubes using information from two premises in a single decision, 3- to 4-year-olds failed. Therefore, the comparison of my study with that of Pears and Bryant suggests that 3- to 4-year-olds had trouble mapping from one representation to another when this mapping depended on two premises (that collectively expressed two relations). Furthermore, their failure on this task is consistent with difficulties encountered in numerous other tasks, as we have seen.

This hypothesis has recently been tested in our laboratory (Andrews & Halford, 1988). We used the tower of five blocks employed by Pears and Bryant (1990) and an isomorphic sticks task that required children to order sticks from left to right. However, to avoid the terms left–right, left was defined as closer to a stuffed toy frog. We also employed two mapping tasks, in which children had to use pairs of blocks to determine the order of sticks, or vice versa. The inference task based on mapping requires children to map two premises jointly, whereas the corresponding construction task can be performed by processing the premises one at a time. If Pears and Bryant's demonstration of transitive inference is valid, then by Postulates 3.0 and 5.1, and from the argument above, it would be predicted that children under 5 years would succeed on all tasks except the inference question based on mapping, because this is a system mapping and entails mapping two relations jointly.

Pears and Bryant's finding of above-chance transitive inference in 3- to 4-year-olds was replicated for the blocks task but not for the sticks task, which suggests it is not very robust. The prediction that 3- to 4-year-olds would fail on the inference task based on mapping was confirmed, even though they succeeded on all construction tasks, showing that they could map one relation from blocks to sticks or vice versa. Despite the great ingenuity shown by Pears and Bryant in devising a transitive inference task that is eminently suitable for young children, we still find severe limits to their ability to process two relations.

Other Tasks Requiring Integration of Relational Premises

It is interesting to note that there are other tasks besides transitivity that require relational premises to be integrated. We devised one such task to assess the cognitive development of Aboriginal Australian children (Boulton-Lewis, Neill, & Halford, 1987). Our reasoning was that premise integration is a major landmark in cognitive development because it marks the ability to acquire system concepts, and it is difficult because of the processing loads it imposes, as discussed in the next section. However, standard transitive-inference tasks might be inappropriate for children in another culture. Accordingly, we wanted a task that required relational premise information to be integrated, but that was appropriate to the Aboriginal Australian culture.

It is known that kinship systems are central to Aboriginal Australian culture, so it was decided to build a new premise-integration task within the kinship domain. The central idea is that one kinship relation (such as sister of) can be integrated with another kinship relation (such as mother of), yielding a further relation (such as aunt of). That is, if Mary is Wendy's sister, and Wendy is Peter's mother, then Mary is Peter's Aunt. This requires integration of two binary relations in a way that closely parallels their integration in transitive inference. To make the task suitable for children, they were shown a picture of a hypothetical family, each person was given a name, and the relations between persons was explained (e.g., Mary is Wendy's sister, Wendy is Peter's mother, etc., but names and relationship terms appropriate to the participants were used). The child was then asked questions that required inferences to be made by integrating premises. For example, what relation is Mary to Peter? It was found that Aboriginal Australian children made such inferences at approximately the same age as Anglo Australian children made transitive inferences.

Processing Load Effects

The present theory predicts that transitivity will be difficult for young children for reasons that are somewhat different than those offered by Piagetian theory. My argument is that transitivity is a three-dimensional concept that, at the parallel distributed processing (PDP) level of analysis, requires a Rank 4 tensor product, as shown in Fig. 3.8 and discussed in chapter 3. Children who cannot construct this representation could learn restricted strategies for coping with transitive inference. For example, they could acquire strategies that do not integrate premises. These strategies give correct answers on some problems but lead to errors on others. Children who cannot represent transitivity adequately would be unable to develop strategies that were applicable to a wide range of situations. They would not be able to use the concept as the basis for the development of other concepts.

Chapman and Lindenberger (1989) argued that transitive inference also imposes high demands on attentional capacity. They suggested that three relational variables ($X \rightarrow Y$, $Y \rightarrow Z$, and $X \rightarrow Z$) must be assigned values simultaneously. There are both similarities and differences between this analysis and my own. Their reference to relational variables that must be assigned values suggests the problem is partly one of variable binding. In our analogical reasoning model (Halford et al., in press), the tensor-product representation was adopted partly to provide a way of handling predicate-argument binding in a PDP representation. Chapman and Lindenberger did not base their argument on PDP representation, however, so that the similarities between their position and mine have occurred independently. Also, my theory does not contain relational variables, at least not as they use the term. Another difference is that I do not think it is necessary to process all relations, *XY*, *YZ*, and *XZ* simultaneously. Only two relations, *XY* and *YZ*, need be processed concurrently. The third can be inferred or "read off" from the representation. This reflects a general difference between our approaches, because I do not think processing-load analyses should be based on the structure of the entire task. The reason is that the whole task is not normally processed in parallel. A process model is required so that the amount of information that needs to be processed in parallel can be determined. Inspection of the task can provide very misleading analyses of processing loads.

Direct confirmation that the difficulties young children experience with transitive inference are due to capacity limitations was provided by Halford, Maybery, and Bain (1986), as discussed in chapter 3. The easy-to-hard paradigm (Hunt & Lansman, 1982) was used, with an easy task that required only one premise to be considered, and a hard task that required premises to be integrated. Recall that the easy-to-hard paradigm assesses capacity limitations by using a secondary task performed concurrently with the easy primary task. To the extent that the hard primary task is capacity limited, it should be predicted by the secondary task, used as a measure of capacity left spare by the easy primary task. Performance on the easy primary task and secondary task performed alone is partialled out. Using this paradigm, Halford et al. (1986) showed that capacity limitations were a factor in the transitive inferences of 3- to 6-year-old children.

Another type of evidence that working-memory limitations affect children's transitive inferences has been provided by Oakhill (1984). The 8- to 9-year-old children were given transitive inference tasks such as "John is not as good as Bill, Bill is not as good as Fred, Who is best?" In the memory-aid condition they were given three cards containing the three names mentioned in the premises and two labels, "best" and "worst." They could use these to provide an external representation of the order of elements so the premises would not need to be integrated mentally. Note that this is a working-memory aid, because it allows the elements to be manipulated and rearranged, rather than just stored. It produced a considerable gain in performance, suggesting that transitive-inference tasks impose a sizeable load on working memory.

Summary of Transitive Inference

The psychological significance of transitivity is that it is a prototypical inference task and is crucial to the concept of an ordered set, which has many real-life applications, and is a component of understanding quantification. Process models agree that transitive inferences typically entail arranging premises as an ordered set. The origin of transitive inference strategies has been modeled by computer simulation. It has been shown that strategies can be developed from a concept of order, instantiated as an ordered set of at least three elements that is induced from ordinary life experience. This concept of order is used by analogy, which entails a system mapping, which imposes a high processing load. This load can lead to strategies that do not integrate premises. The process of strategy development entails the same processes in children and adults, but younger children are more susceptible to high processing loads.

The question of when children understand transitive inference has been contentious. Studies that claim success with 3- to 4-year-olds have been found to give undue assistance in ordering, to have eliminated participants who might not have understood the concept, or to be applicable only in very restricted contexts. The evidence is quite consistent with the argument in chapter 3 that transitivity is a three-dimensional concept that imposes a high processing load. This load can be reduced by an efficient strategy but development of the strategy and ability to generalize it to new situations will be impaired if children lack the capacity to represent the concept properly. Ability to process analogies based on transitivity will require a three-dimensional representation, based on a Rank 4 tensor product, as shown in Fig. 3.8. Children who cannot use such a representation will not be able to use an ordered set as an analog to guide the development of strategies.

CATEGORICAL AND CONDITIONAL SYLLOGISMS

Transitive inferences are linear syllogisms but in this section we will consider categorical and conditional syllogisms.

An example of a categorical syllogism is the inference:

All men are mortal

Socrates is a man

Socrates is mortal

"All men are mortal" is the major premise, and "Socrates is a man" is the minor premise. The line drawn below the minor premise is the "inference line," which separates the premises from the conclusion, "Socrates is a man."

Another example of a categorical syllogism is:

All B are C

All A are B

All A are C

In both cases the major premise describes a relation between two sets of items (the set of men and the set of mortal things; Set B and Set C). The second premise describes a relation between an item and a set of objects (Socrates and the set of men) or between two sets (Set A and Set B). The conclusion also describes a relation between an item and a set, or a relation between two sets.

Conditional syllogisms have a premise of the form "If A then B." The second premise asserts the truth or falsity of either the antecedent (A) or consequent (B), whereas the conclusion affirms or negates the other term (Sternberg, Guyote, & Turner, 1980). For example:

If A then B

A

B

This syllogism represents the argument form known as *modus ponens.* Another example:

If A then B

not B

----

not A

This exemplifies the argument form *modus tollens.*

There are also two fallacies, known as denial of the antecedent (if A then B, not A, therefore not B) and affirmation of the consequent (if A then B, B, therefore A).

A longstanding question has been whether human deductions are actually based on logical rules. In the last century it was generally assumed that human thought was inherently logical, so that the British mathematician and logician George Boole (1854/1951) entitled his book *An Investigation of the Laws of Thought, on Which are Founded the Mathematical Theories of Logic and Probabilities.* Unlike Boole, Piaget (1947/1950, 1957) did not regard logic as defining the laws of thought, nor did he believe that logic per se explained psychological phenomena. Explanations were to be found in more biological processes, but logic was a human creation that represented a kind of idealization of thought. Piaget attempted to model human thought and its development in children by a series of "psycho-logics" that became progressively more complete and "equilibrated" as the child progressed.

An early indication that human thought might be based on extra-logical processes came from the work of Henle (1962). Syllogisms embedded in short narratives were presented to psychology graduate students, and they were asked to evaluate their logical validity. Henle found that the evaluations were not based on the logical structure of the arguments, but on whether the participants agreed with the premises. They tended to reject premises with which they disagreed, and to import other premises that they regarded as reasonable.

A study by Luria (1976) that was carried out in 1931–1932, but not published until much later, found that some Russian peasants did not accept the logical nature of tasks that were presented to them. For example, if told that in a certain place to the north, all the bears were white, and that a person saw a bear at that place, they would decline to predict what color the bear would be, claiming they had no knowledge of bears in that location. These participants seemed unprepared to make predictions that went beyond their own experience. In Sigel's (1981) terms, they had not learned "distancing" strategies. That is, they had not learned to go beyond the here and now.

However, it has been shown that children's dependence on empirical knowledge can be overcome. Even children as young as 4 years will accept premises that violate their empirical knowledge if they are presented as make believe (Hawkins, Pea, Glick & Scribner, 1984) if they relate to a remote situation, such as another planet, if they are based on play, or if they are accompanied by visual imagery (Dias & Harris, 1988, 1990; English, in press).

There is nothing to suggest that human reasoning is inherently illogical, but it does appear that we do not have an innate, or automatic, appreciation of logical rules. It appears that people must learn to use logical rules and that they do not naturally use them in everyday life. As Shaklee (1979) pointed out, the work of Tversky and Kahneman (1973) shows that human decision making depends on such factors as availability of information in memory and the degree to which a particular item is representative of a category. These "natural" reasoning processes are decidedly nonlogical in the sense that they depend on mechanisms that do not correspond to logical deduction. They are not illogical because, as Henle (1962) and Luria (1976) pointed out, all the incorrect responses could be explained by failure to accept the (to us) logical character of the task demands, and there was no compelling evidence of reasoning that contradicted logical rules. Natural reasoning might be described as independent of, rather than opposed to, logic.

Attempts have been made to understand human inferences by studying how the binary connectives implication (A implies B, $A \rightarrow B$) conjunction (A and B, $A \cap B$) and disjunction (A or B, $A \cup B$) are understood (Byrnes & Overton, 1988; Evans, 1972; Overton, Byrnes, & O'Brien, 1985; Peel, 1967; Rumain, Connell, & Braine, 1983; Staudenmayer, 1975; Sternberg, 1979; Wason & Johnson-Laird, 1972). It is clear from these studies that connectives like implication are not naturally understood the way they are defined by logicians. For example, the conditional, A implies B ($A \rightarrow B$) is often understood as the biconditional, A implies B, and B implies A ($A \longleftrightarrow B$).

This explains why there is a tendency to accept the fallacies denial of the antecedent and affirmation of the consequent. Consider the reasoning:

A ⟷ B
not A
----
not B

and;

A ⟷ B
B

A

These argument forms are valid, but the same arguments are not valid if the conditional A → B is substituted for the biconditional A ⟷ B. These arguments that logicians regard as fallacious are appropriate if the form "if A then B" is taken to mean A ⟷ B, instead of A → B. Another finding is that disjunction is sometimes interpreted as the "inclusive OR" and sometimes as the "exclusive OR." These studies have been reviewed in more detail elsewhere (Evans, 1982; Halford, 1982), but their import for our present argument is that there is no direct or simple correspondence between human reasoning and the connectives of standard logic.

The way people process natural language expressions like "if" seems to reflect world knowledge. The world abounds in situations where "if" means "if and only if." For example; "if you have a driver's licence, you can drive a car" means if and only if. In other contexts "if" does not mean "if and only if"; "if it is raining, there are clouds," does not mean "if and only if," because clouds can occur without rain. In chapters 4 and 6 I argued that people naturally acquire a store of contingencies and rules that represent their world. The way they interpret expressions such as "if" and "or" seems to reflect this world knowledge, rather than automatic reference to any specific set of logical rules.

Recognition that formal logic does not make a good model of natural reasoning has led several theorists to propose alternative ways of describing human inference. Perhaps the first major undertaking of this kind was that by Osherson (1974b, 1975, 1976), who proposed and tested a deduction model that attempted to capture the properties of natural deductions. Braine (1978) incorporated many of the features of Osherson's model into a theory of "inference rule schemata." The schema for dealing with "if A then B" was based simply on the idea of an inference line. That is, the meaning of "if A then B" was equivalent to asserting that if A is true, B may be concluded, and would be written:

A

B

What this really asserts is that if a person accepts the statement "if A then B" as valid, and if A is true, then B may be concluded. Unlike the conditional in standard logic, "if then" is not based on a truth table, but has the status of a rule that sanctions certain conclusions. Some deductions that are valid in standard logic, such as *modus tollens*, could be made from the natural interpretation of "if then" the way Braine has defined it.

It is easy to restate such an inference-rule schema as a condition–action rule of the type outlined in chapters 1 and 4. The condition side of the rule is "A is true" (or "A occurs"), and the action side is "B is true" (or "B occurs"). Acquisition of this rule would permit the conclusion "B is true" whenever the condition "A is true" is met. The format of condition–action rules can be adapted to handle inference schemata.

The formulations by Osherson and Braine imply that inferences are equivalent to rules that sanction a conclusion, given certain premises. In our terms these rules are equivalent to condition–action rules, in which the condition is the premises, and the action is the conclusion that can be made. We will consider this idea in more detail after reviewing theories of the inference process.

Inference Processes

One attempt to explain how people make transitive inferences is the transitive-chain theory of syllogistic reasoning (Guyote & Sternberg, 1981; Sternberg, Guyote, & Turner, 1980; see also the discussion of this model by Johnson-Laird, 1983). The way premises are represented in the model is illustrated in Fig. 7.5, with Euler circles shown for comparison. The premise "All A are B" has two possible representations, one in which A is a proper subset of B,[3] and in one in which A is equivalent to B. Each set is partitioned into two complementary subsets, so A is partitioned into a1 and a2, and B is partitioned into b1 and b2. The expression a1 → B signifies that a partition of A is included in B. The two expressions a1 → B and a2 → B mean that all of A is included in B. However, the expressions b1 → A and b2 → −A mean

---

[3]A proper subset of a Set S does not include all members of S.

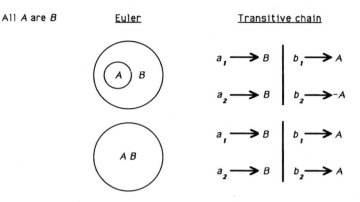

FIG. 7.5. Euler and transitive-chain representation of categorical syllogism.

that part of B is included in A, but another part of B is included in not A.

The most distinctive feature of the theory is that it uses rules similar to transitivity for combining representations. One such rule is the match rule, which states;

$$xi \rightarrow Y \text{ and } yj \rightarrow Z ==> xi \rightarrow Z$$

This rule means that where x is a subset of Y, and y is a subset of Z, then x may be a subset of Z. By applying the transitive-chain rules to all the possible representations for the premises, all the possible conclusions can be derived. The combination procedure is complex, but the theory has two interesting features. First, it takes an important step towards an integrated theory of deductive reasoning by linking categorical syllogisms to linear syllogisms and transitive inference. Second, it suggests a natural process by which people could represent and combine categorical premises. A premise such as "All A are B" can be represented by recognizing that any example of A will be included in B (hence both partitions of A are included in B, as in Fig. 7.5.), but there may be some examples of B that will not be included in A (hence b1 → A, b2 → −A, in Fig. 7.5). The theory really means that people think of the various interpretations of the premises then combine these interpretations. Major sources of error are in failure to consider all the possible representations of the premises and inability to find an appropriate description for the combined representations.

Johnson-Laird's Mental Models

Johnson-Laird (1983) proposed a mental models theory of deductive reasoning, and Johnson-Laird and Byrne (1991) extended the approach and added new supporting data. The theory proposes three steps: (a) Construct a mental model of the first premise; (b) add the information in the second premise to the mental model of the first premise, taking into account the different ways in which this can be done; and (c) frame a conclusion to express the relation, if any, between the "end" terms that holds in all models of the premises.

These processes are illustrated in Fig. 7.6. The premise "All cognitionalists are psychologists" is represented by showing examples of cognitionalists that are psychologists (expressed as cognitionalist = psychologist), and no cognitionalists that are not psychologists. The possibility that there may be psychologists that are not cognitionalists is indicated by showing some psychologists in parentheses that are not paired with cognitionalists. The premise "All psychologists are scientists" is represented by showing a scientist for each psychologist, and also a scientist that might not be a psychologist. Because this model is the only one that validly represents these premises, the conclusion "All cognitionalists are scientists" can be read off from the mental model. This conclusion fulfills steps 3 by linking the end terms, cognitionalist and scientist, in a way that is consistent with the model.

Other deductions require more than one model to express all the valid interpretations of the premises, as shown in the remainder of Fig. 7.6. The mental model for the premise "No children are adults" consists of placing children and adults on opposite sides of a "fence" so that no child is paired with an adult. The premise "Some adults are scientists" is represented as explained for the previous example. Model 1 would then appear to justify the conclusion "No children are scientists."

Actually, however, there are two further models that are consistent with the premises. The second premise does not rule out the possibility that there are some scientists that are not adults. Model 2 indicates that some children might be scientists, and Model 3 indicates that all of them might be. Johnson-Laird (1983) claimed that with his system, three models are sufficient to represent all possibilities in two premises.

The third step is to frame a conclusion that expresses the relation between children and scientists. The conclusion "Some scientists are not children" is consistent with all three models. Were there no conclusion that was consistent with all three models, the decision "can't tell" would be justified.

A common source of error is to accept the first model that is consistent with the premises and to not search exhaustively for all possible models. Johnson-Laird (1983) presented evidence that the difficulty of syllogistic reasoning is a function of the number of models that must be constructed. Problems that require three models are harder than those that require two, which in turn are harder than those that require one.

Johnson-Laird made another point about the difficulty of syllogisms that is similar to the point made in chapter 3 and earlier in this chapter, about the difficulty of N-term series reasoning. This is that the need to hold one premise representation in store, while integrating the second premise with it, is a major source of difficulty. Just how difficult this is depends on another factor, the figure of the syllogism. A problem of the form "All A are B, All B are C" (A-B, B-C figure) is easier to integrate than B-A, C-B, which is easier than A-B, C-B. The reason is that there is less strain on working memory if the new premise can be integrated directly with the old without having to invert or otherwise transform any of the premises. These factors are reminiscent of those that affect the difficulty of N-term series reasoning, discussed earlier. The number of models required for a problem probably also contributes to the working-memory load, but procedural knowledge (how to generate the different models) will also affect difficulty of reasoning.

All the deductive-inference models that we have considered so far in this chapter have a feature in common: They all depend on procedures that are domain independent; that is, they apply to all problems irrespective of the particular domain of discourse from which they are drawn. An alternative view is that reasoning depends primarily on domain-specific knowledge. That

All cognitionalists are psychologists

cognitionalist = psychologist

cognitionalist = psychologist

cognitionalist = psychologist

(psychologist)

(psychologist)

All psychologists are scientists

cognitionalist = psychologist   = scientist

cognitionalist = psychologist   = scientist

cognitionalist = psychologist   = scientist

(psychologist) = (scientist)

(psychologist) = (scientist)

= (scientist)

Conclusion: All cognitionalists are scientists.

FIG. 7.6.   Mental model for syllogistic reasoning problem, based on theory of Johnson-Laird (1983).

No children are adults.

child
child
child

---

        adult
        adult
        adult

Some adults are scientists.

Model 1

child
child
child

---

      adult = scientist
      adult = scientist
     (adult)   (scientist)

Model 2

child
child
child   = scientist

---

      adult = scientist
      adult = scientist
     (adult)

Model 3

child   = scientist
child   = scientist
child   = scientist

---

      adult = scientist
      adult = scientist
     (adult)

Conclusion: Some scientists are not children.

FIG. 7.6 Continued

is, children learn to reason within a particular domain by acquiring knowledge of that domain. See Glaser (1984) for a review of research on this problem. This approach is most relevant to tasks in which there is a large domain-knowledge component, considered in detail in chapter 9.

PRAGMATIC REASONING SCHEMAS

A "middle-of-the-road" theory has been proposed by Cheng and Holyoak (1985) and Cheng, Holyoak, Nisbett, and Oliver (1986). According to this theory people use "pragmatic-reasoning schemas," which are abstract-knowledge structures derived from ordinary life experiences. They apply across several domains, but they are not devoid of semantic content and are not universally valid like logical inference rules.

An example of a pragmatic-reasoning schema is permission, a concept that abounds in everyday life but that has a structure that is very similar to the concept of implication. The concept of permission means that you can perform action A if and only if permission P is obtained; A if and only if P, or A implies P. The structure of the permission schema is shown in Table 7.2. A symbolic version of the permission schema A → P (A implies P) is also shown to facilitate comparison with the truth table for implication. It can be seen that the permission schema is isomorphic to the concept of implication. Cheng et al. (1986) applied the concept of permission schemas to Wason's (1966) selection task, illustrated in Fig. 7.7. In the standard form, there are four cards, each of which has a letter on one side and a number on the other, and participants are given the hypothetical rule: If there is an A on one side of a card, there is a 4 on the other side. Participants must determine which cards must be turned over to test the validity of this rule. The correct solution is A and 7, because if there is something other than a 4 opposite the A, or if there is an A opposite the 7, the rule is falsified. Few participants arrive at the correct solution, however, the most common choice being A and 4. Turning over 4 is unnecessary because the rule does not imply that

TABLE 7.2
The Structure of the Permission Schema

Permission Schema		Action→Permission	Permission schema (Symbolic) $A{\to}P$			Implication A	P	$A{\to}P$
Action	permission	allowed	A	P	+	1	1	1
Action	no permission	not allowed	A	$\bar{P}$	−	1	0	0
No action	permission	allowed	$\bar{A}$	P	+	0	1	1
No action	no permission	allowed	$\bar{A}$	$\bar{P}$	+	0	0	1

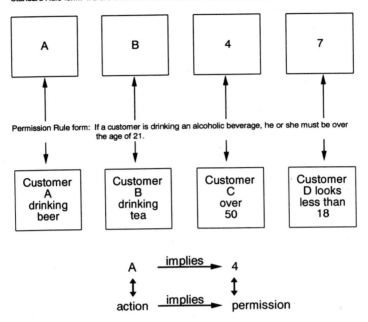

Standard Rule form: If there is an A on one side, there is a 4 on the other side.

Permission Rule form: If a customer is drinking an alcoholic beverage, he or she must be over the age of 21.

FIG. 7.7. Mapping of selection problem into schema induced from life experience.

there should be an A opposite the 4. In fact, this represents the fallacy of affirmation of the consequent: misinterpreting A implies 4 to mean 4 implies A. There are several reviews of research on this task (Cheng & Holyoak, 1985; Evans, 1982; Johnson-Laird, 1983; Halford, 1982). Cheng et al. (1986) presented four versions of this problem. The permission version, which is also shown in Fig. 7.7, entailed a rule such as; If a customer is drinking an alcoholic beverage, then he or she must be over 21. Participants were then given four cases: Customer A is drinking a beer, Customer B is drinking tea, Customer C is certainly over 50, Customer D looks less than 18. As Fig. 7.7 shows, the permission version can be mapped into the standard version.

The permission version was contrasted with three other versions: the standard or arbitrary version; a converse bias version, "If a washing label has "silk" on one side, then it has "dry clean only" on the other side"; and a biconditional version, "If a card has a circle on one side, then it has the word "red" on the other, and conversely, if it has the word "red" on one side, then it has a circle on the other.

Participants made more appropriate choices on the permission version of the problem, consistent with the hypothesis that the permission schema is a natural means of solving the problem. On the other hand participants who were given training in the conditional rule (A implies B) showed improved performance only if they were trained to apply the rule to examples of the four-card problem. A second experiment in which college students were given training on propositional logic, including *modus ponens* and *modus tollens*, showed very little improvement on the four-card problem. This implies that even participants who possess the abstract-logical rules have difficulty applying them to this problem, which suggests that natural-solution processes for this task are not based on abstract-logical rules.

Another pragmatic schema is obligation; that is, a situation A incurs the necessity of performing action B (A → B). In their Experiment 3, Cheng et al. (1986) showed that teaching rules for mapping the obligation schema onto the four-card problem improved performance, even in the arbitrary versions of the problem. This suggests that arbitrary or abstract problems may be solved by mapping them into a familiar schema such as obligation or permission.

This provides important support for the hypothesis that abstract reasoning can be performed by mapping the problem into specific, familiar examples that are isomorphic to it. Table 7.2 shows that the truth table for implication (the conditional rule) is isomorphic to the permission schema. Figure 7.7 shows how the standard form of the problem, based on the conditional rule, can be mapped into the version based on a permission rule. This implies that people can perform the selection task by mapping it into a familiar, real-life schema with which it is isomorphic. We can generalize this point by saying that an abstract-reasoning task can be performed by mapping it into any familiar schema with which it is isomorphic. Permission and obligation are merely two examples of such situations. To illustrate how people might use familiar situations in this way, suppose an intelligent person, untutored in logic, was asked to decide the validity of the following inference; *a* implies *b*, not *a*, therefore not *b*. Being untrained in logic, the person will not immediately recognize that this is an example of the fallacy of denial of the antecedent. How might a person decide the question?

An effective strategy would be to find a familiar situation that is isomorphic to the problem. Different individuals could choose different schemas, but a suitable schema would be the observation; rain implies clouds. It is not true that if there is no rain, there are no clouds. This situation can be mapped into the abstract reasoning problem as shown in Fig. 7.8. The contingency between rain and clouds is used as a mental model for the abstract-inference task. Because the mental model is known not to hold, the inference is that the logical deduction that is mapped into it is invalid. Several important points follow from this discussion. The first is that natural reasoning, even when directed to more abstract problems, can be performed by mapping the reasoning problem into a familiar schema with which it is isomorphic. It is probably more common to reason this way than by applying logical rules, which are normally only available to those who have received training in logic and are experienced in applying it.

Mental Model (**source**)

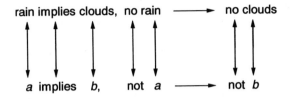

Problem (**target**)

FIG. 7.8.   Mapping of logical inference into schema induced from life experience.

The second point is that structure mapping plays an important role in deductive reasoning, because it permits abstract, arbitrary, or novel problems to be solved by mapping them into familiar schemas with which they are isomorphic. Structure mapping therefore plays a similar role in categorical and relational syllogisms. Recall that N-term series problems are solved by mapping the premises into the positions of an ordered array such as left–right or top–bottom, as discussed in earlier. Here too, a familiar schema is applied to the solution of a new problem by structure mapping. Thus structure mapping removes some of the need for abstract-logical rules in the context of natural or "everyday" reasoning.

The third point is that the difficulty of making the structure mapping will be a major component of the difficulty of reasoning. Cheng and Holyoak showed that people naturally possess the permission schema but have difficulty applying it to some problems. Anything that makes the mapping of the schema into the problem easier facilitates reasoning.

The concepts of implication and permission are binary operations, and are therefore three dimensional (notice that the assignments in Table 7.2 are sets of ordered 3-tuples). Thus a structure mapping of the type exemplified above is a system mapping. It follows therefore that inferences of this type should be within the capacity of children from a median age of 5 years.

PRAGMATIC REASONING SCHEMAS AND MENTAL MODELS

There are both similarities and differences between pragmatic-reasoning schemas as defined by Cheng and Holyoak (1985) and Johnson-Laird's (1983) theory of mental models. Both entail representations that have a relatively specific semantic content. However, according to Johnson-Laird's (1983) theory, mental models are constructed so as to represent the possible ways of combining the premises. A new model is produced for each problem, at least the first time it is encountered. According to the theory of Cheng and Holyoak

(1985), an existing concept or schema, induced from previous experience, is used to represent the problem. Thus, the essential difference appears to be that pragmatic-reasoning schemas are induced from previous experience, whereas mental models as defined by Johnson-Laird are constructed to fit specific tasks.

Light, Girotto, & Legrenzi (1990) suggested that pragmatic reasoning schemas should be defined "as clusters of context-sensitive rules relating to goals and actions" (p. 372). However, I see no reason to restrict the theory to schemas that relate to goals and actions. The important insight that we have obtained from the work of Johnson-Laird (1983) and Cheng and Holyoak (1985) is that deductive inferences are typically made by mapping problems into schemas or mental models that are familiar, or that they can be readily constructed by the person, and have a relatively specific semantic content. Theories based on this conception of reasoning can be expected to undergo further elaboration, as has already occurred (Johnson-Laird & Byrne, 1991). For example, Manktelow and Over (1990) suggested that performance on the Wason selection task can be better explained by mental models that take into account costs and benefits (utilities). Although I agree that the concept of pragmatic-reasoning schemas could benefit from further development, I see no reason why utilities should be incompatible with it.

In chapter 2 we defined mental models as representations that are active while solving a particular problem and provide the workspace for inference and mental operations. Schemas are really used to structure these representations. For example, in the four-card problem, permission was used to structure the representation of the problem, whereas in transitivity, an ordered set was used for the same purpose. Schemas are therefore a kind of "template" used by analogy to structure the representation of a particular problem.

Part of the problem of inference making then will be to find a mental model for the inference that needs to be made. This implies that inferences will be easier when an appropriate model is readily available, but will tend to be difficult otherwise. Difficulties will also arise when the model that people habitually use is inappropriate.

A mental model that people seem likely to use in many inference situations is prediction; that is, A predicts B. As pointed out in chapter 4, people learn declarative rules that provide predictors of the environment; dogs with raised hackles bite, summer days are hot, rain makes the ground wet, and so on. We all know a myriad of predictor rules of this kind, and they are constantly used as we interact with our environment. Given that declarative predictor rules pervade all our cognitive activity, it seems likely that they would be used as mental models for inferences.

The use of predictor schemas as mental models could help explain the typically observed pattern of behavior in the four-card problem, discussed earlier. The rule "If there is an A on one side of the card, there is a 4 on the other side" could be interpreted not as the logical rule "A implies 4," but as the predictor rule "A predicts 4." If this rule were used, the four-card problem would be interpreted as asking whether A is a reliable predictor of 4. It would then be appropriate to turn over A to see whether the predicted 4 does occur. It would also be appropriate to turn over the 4 to see whether it was predicted by an A. This is the commonest pattern of response for children and adults (O'Brien & Overton, 1982).

The predictor rule "A predicts B" is closer to the biconditional (A implies B and B implies A) than to the conditional (A implies B). They can both be represented by the same truth table, as shown in Table 7.3. Another way of putting this is to say that the biconditional interpretation makes A a better predictor of B than the conditional interpretation. The reason is that under the biconditional, there are no occurrences of B without A, and A and B are in effect perfectly correlated. Under the conditional, B occurs whenever A occurs, but B can also occur in the absence of A. The correlation is therefore less than perfect. Therefore, if the natural language interpretation of "if then" is interpreted in terms of a prediction schema, this would result in a pattern of inferences that is closer to the biconditional than to the conditional. This could account for the tendency to turn over the card containing a 4 in the Wason selection task (Fig. 7.7).

It remains to explain why, when performing the Wason selection task (Fig. 7.7), people do not characteristically turn over the 7. It is clear that the 7 would test the predictive reliability of the rule "if A then 4," because if there is an A opposite the 7, the rule that A predicts 4 is falsified. Why then is the 7 not turned over?

A possible reason that would follow from the argument above is that we all know a myriad of predictor rules, and it would be maladaptive and impossibly burdensome to seek disconfirming evidence of them. To revert to the most banal examples of predictor rules; dogs with raised hackles bite, rain makes the ground wet. Yet we do not normally look for cases where dogs bite without having raised hackles, or where the ground is wet without rain having occurred. As Tschirgi (1980) pointed out, we test hypotheses in

TABLE 7.3
The Truth Table for the Predictor Rule "A Predicts B"

A	B	A implies B and B implies A		"A predicts B"
		A	B	
1	1	1		1
1	0	0		0
0	1	0		0
0	0	1		1

a "sensible" fashion. When things turn out all right, we do not seek causes or look for falsifying evidence of our hypotheses. We only seek to test our hypotheses when things turn out badly. Therefore, the general tendency to seek confirmatory evidence (Evans, 1989) might not be as maladaptive as it seems. As Anderson (1990) pointed out, the cognitive activities that seem anomalous on the surface might turn out to be very adaptive when considered in terms of their role in organism–environment interaction.

Mental models will tend to be changed when the predictions they make are not confirmed. Wason (1964), O'Brien and Overton (1982), and Overton et al. (1985) showed that reasoning errors can be corrected by self-contradiction, and this effect can be interpreted in terms of the present theory. The procedure entails giving participants a rule such as "If a worker is x years of age or older, then that person will receive at least $350 each week." They are then given a series of exemplars such as "person 15, $100 per week; person 70, $400 per week," and asked to state what conclusion, if any, can be drawn, about the age represented by x. According to the implication rule interpretation of "if then," if a person age 15 receives $100, then x must represent an age greater than 15. The reason is that a person receiving less than $350 must be below the age represented by x. However, nothing can be concluded from examplars like "age 70, $400" because a person could be below the age represented by x and still receive at least $350.

However, people tend to think that a person receiving $350 must be at or above the age represented by x; that is, they interpret "if then" as the biconditional or, in terms of our current argument, as a predictor rule. This leads to the fallacy of inferring that if, for example, a person aged 60 receives $600, the age represented by x must be at most 60.

When the exemplar "age 65, $200 per week" is encountered, this contradicts the fallacious inference, because it implies that x must represent an age greater than 65. Wason (1964) showed that adults abandoned this fallacy after encountering this type of contradiction, and O'Brien and Overton (1982) obtained a similar result with 18-year-olds, but not with 10- and 14-year-olds.

The predictor-rule interpretation implies that age predicts wage; if the person is age x or over, they receive at least $350; if under age x, they receive less than $350. This rule leads to the false prediction, based on the exemplars above, that x must represent an age of at least 65. When this prediction is falsified, the predictor rule model of "if then" is abandoned, and most participants adopt the conditional rule.

According to this theory, the difficulty with the four-card problem is that the mental model that is most naturally adopted, based on the prediction schema, is inappropriate, given the way the task is defined. A more appropriate schema, in the sense that it is structurally closer to the truth-functional definition of material implication, is the permission schema. Cheng et al.'s

(1986) finding that permission versions of the four-card problem were easier suggests that the permission format made the appropriate, permission schema, more available, and made participants less dependent on the prediction schema.

It remains to explain why the prediction schema is not weakened by disconfirmation and replaced with a more appropriate schema such as permission. The reason is that the prediction schema serves very well most of the time. Statements of the form "if A then B" can be appropriately interpreted as predicting that if A occurs, B occurs; if a dog's hackles are raised, it will bite; if it is raining, the ground will be wet. If someone tells me, "if you work hard, you will be promoted," then I develop expectations that if I work hard promotion will occur, if I do not work hard, promotion will not occur. Thus in many contexts the natural meaning of "if A then B" takes the form of a prediction of B, given A. Use of this schema leads to confirmation a high proportion of the time. There are "conversational implicatures" (Grice, 1975; Rumain, Connell, & Braine, 1983) that tend to support the "if and only if" interpretation of "if then," and thereby maintain the interpretation.

The standard logic interpretation of "if then" in terms of the conditional does not correspond well with experience of the world. For a brief discussion of this point, see Cheng et al. (1986). One problem is that the conditional "if A then B" is formally identical to "not A or B." Thus the statement "if the sky is green, the sea contains water" corresponds to "either the sky is not green, or the sea contains water," and is therefore a true statement! The value of the material conditional lies in its role within a formal deductive system, but it is not a good format for predictive rules about the world.

CHILDREN'S DEDUCTIVE INFERENCES

There is evidence that deductive inferences can be made by quite young children. Positive results have been obtained with first- to fourth-grade children (Kuhn, 1977), with 6- to 8-year-olds (Hill, reported by Suppes, 1965) and even with 5-year-olds (Somerville, Hadkinson, & Greenberg, 1979). The studies by Hill and by Somerville et al. were noted earlier (Halford, 1982) as being particularly well controlled. Hill et al. presented premises of the form:

If that boy is John's brother, then he is 10 years old

That boy is not 10 years old.

Is he John's brother?

A baseline was employed with the form:

If that boy is not 10 years old, is he John's brother?

The baseline item does not permit a deductive inference and controls for noninferential responding based on response bias, retrieval of information about John from memory, and guessing. Somerville et al. (1979) presented problems of the form:

The boy is playing in the house.

The girl is playing in the garden.

The dog is playing with the boy.

The cat is playing with the girl.

The boy drew a picture of the cat.

The girl drew a picture of the dog.

Who is playing in the house? (the dog)

The premises about the cat provide a distractor, and the premise "the girl drew a picture of the cat" controls for inferences based on association. Children were also taught the premises to ensure they could be retrieved. The content of the problems used by both Hill and Somerville et al. is familiar to young children, being concerned with variables such as age, brotherhood, and location. However, false positives based on retrieval from semantic memory are avoided, because the truth value of each conclusion could not be known without the premises. For example, children of that age know about brotherhood, but no child knows whether the hypothetical boy is John's brother or not.

There have been a number of studies of preschool children's ability to mentally combine prelearned behavior segments (Crisafi & Brown, 1986; Halliday, 1977; Hewson, 1978; Kendler & Kendler, 1956). For example Halliday (1977) trained 4-year-old children to press one panel to obtain a square and another to obtain a triangle. They then learned to insert the square (triangle) into a hole to obtain candy. They were then tested for ability to obtain candy by first pressing the appropriate panel to obtain the square, then inserting the square to obtain the candy. This calls for two previously learned behaviors to be combined mentally. A basically similar task was used by Crisafi and Brown (1986) to study analogical transfer in young children, as discussed in chapter 5. Piaget (1953) also demonstrated that children in the 6th sensorimotor substage (i.e., children aged 1½–2 years) could mentally combine previously acquired sensorimotor schemata to solve a problem.

Piaget contended that this was essentially a sensorimotor performance that did not require the operations of thought. In terms of the current theory, these performances can be executed without a mental model because the relevant behaviors have been prelearned. To account for such performances, intelligent though they undoubtedly are, it is only necessary to postulate that the children have the ability to search for an operator that will achieve a subgoal; that is, when the task is to obtain candy, and the means of obtaining the candy (a square) is not available, then the subgoal of obtaining the square can be set and the operator for achieving it executed. This only requires a subgoal to be set and a means of achieving it to be retrieved from memory. There is no need to postulate a mental model that represents all the relations in the situation.

Availability of an appropriate mental model has been shown to affect children's reasoning in other contexts. Piper (1985) found that Grade 6 children made more correct inferences than Grade 12 children when the context was based on a space-exploration fantasy, but made less inferences in more realistic situations. It appeared that familiarity with space stories, presumably through television, made it easy to construct a mental model of the premises. Thompson and Myers (1985) found that more inferences were made from stories based on physical than on psychological causes, even though the structure of the inferences was the same. The 4-year-old children were considerably worse than the 7-year-olds on psychological-cause stories, but the difference was much smaller on physical-cause stories. It seems that four-year-olds have trouble constructing mental models based on psychological causes, but most of them could construct mental models based on physical-cause situations (although it should be noted that 13% of 4-year-olds had to be eliminated for failure in a warmup task that involved inferences).

The applicability of pragmatic reasoning schemas to children's reasoning has been demonstrated in a study by Light et al. (1990), who found that 12-year-olds took account of pragmatic factors, such as the type of rule and the motives of the violator, in selection and evaluation tasks. It has been shown that 6- to 8-year-old children can perform a reduced form of the Wason selection task if it is presented in a way that enables them to use a familiar pragmatic reasoning schema. Light, Blaye, Gilly, and Girotto (1989) taught children a prohibition rule, that trucks must not be in the center of the city, and found improved performance on an arbitrary rule, "all triangles must be in the center." It seems therefore that children can use pragmatic reasoning schemas, at least by the age of 6 years.

LOGICAL NECESSITY

There are two main ways of recognizing the logical validity of an argument. One is to know which argument forms are valid. For example *modus ponens* (A implies B, A, therefore B) is a valid argument form, irrespective of content. The argument aRb, bRc, therefore aRc is valid provided R is a transitive relation, as in a > b, b > c, therefore a > c.

However, our discussion of the mechanisms of inference making indicates that it does not depend on domain-independent rules of this kind, but on the use of mental models. With this technique logical validity must be assessed by taking two steps: The first is to construct a mental model that represents the premises, and the second is to check that there are no mental models that represent the premises adequately but that would lead to denial of the argument.

Consider for example the argument discussed earlier in relation to Johnson-Laird's theory: No children are adults, some adults are scientists, therefore no children are scientists. As Fig. 7.6 shows, the first mental model suggests that this is a valid argument. We know it is not, because there are two alternative models that also represent the premises adequately but deny the argument. That is, Model 2 shows that the premises can be represented in a way that includes the possibility of some children being scientists. Model 3 allows the possibility of all children being scientists. According to this view, validity can be assessed by checking whether an argument follows from every model that represents the premises.

As Johnson-Laird pointed out, it is difficult to check that all possible models (within a given format, such as that in Fig. 7.6) are consistent with the conclusion. If validity entails checking all possible models, we would expect it to be difficult. There is considerable evidence that recognizing the logical validity of an argument is more difficult and develops later than ability to make inferences, as I have pointed out elsewhere (Halford, 1982). We have seen that even 5- to 7-year-old children can make elementary inferences. They have much more difficulty in evaluating the logical validity of that conclusion; that is, deciding whether it necessarily follows.

Osherson and Markman (1975) found that 7-year-olds could not distinguish contradictions and tautologies from empirical statements, suggesting they were not sensitive to the logical form of an argument. Staudenmayer and Bourne (1977) found that Grade 3 children were almost totally unable to evaluate argument forms based on the conditional, even after extensive training. Similar conclusions were reached by Kuhn (1977) and Shapiro and O'Brien (1970).

Moshman and Franks (1986) tested children's ability to recognize the validity of arguments based on transitivity, categorical syllogisms, disjunction of propositions (e.g., either bears fly or birds fly, bears do not fly, therefore birds fly) and conjunction (cars have motors, trucks have motors, therefore cars and trucks have motors). Several techniques were used to assess understanding of validity, including sorting arguments into valid and invalid classes (with alternative sortings available, based on empirical truth or content), labelling arguments as valid or invalid, or sorting them into valid and invalid piles. Brief training in the concept of validity was also given. Consistent with previous research, above-chance success was not observed until 11–12 years of age.

An exception to these findings occurs in a study by Tunmer, Nesdale, and Pratt (1983). These authors presented 5- to 7-year-old children with stories that were consistent or inconsistent, either implicitly or explicitly. An example, with variations shown in parentheses, is; "Cars won't go if they don't have petrol in the tank (Mrs. Smith has a car that she uses for shopping). Mrs. Smith's car didn't have any petrol at all. She had to walk to the shop to get some bread (She drove her car to the shop to get some bread)" (Tunmer et al., 1983, p. 101).

The explicit, consistent version, is the one with the sentences in parentheses omitted. In the implicit version, the first premise, "Cars won't go if they don't have petrol in the tank," was replaced with the irrelevant sentence in parentheses, "Mrs. Smith has a car that she uses for shopping." In the inconsistent version, the inference, "She had to walk to the shop to get some bread," was replaced by the sentence in parentheses, "She drove her car to the shop to get some bread."

The article claims to assess understanding of logical consistency by asking children whether each story was sensible or not. Even 5-year-olds performed above chance, and the authors therefore concluded that children of this age can understand logical consistency if they are tested on familiar materials. The flaw in this argument is that it fails to make the distinction between domain familiarity and knowledge of the truth value of specific items. It is perfectly reasonable to use familiar domains, such as cars and shopping. It is not legitimate, however, to use items that can be answered from prior knowledge. The fact that cars will not go if they have no petrol is a fact that can be retrieved from semantic memory, and it in no way reflects understanding of logical consistency.

A more appropriate type of item would be; "Mr. Jones will not buy a car if it is not red. This car is not red. Mr. Jones is going to buy this car." Here the domain is familiar. However, one cannot decide on information retrieved from memory whether Mr. Jones will buy a red car. That can only be decided by comprehending the premises and integrating them into a mental model. The study by Tunmer et al. (1983) does not require this and, therefore, is not relevant to children's ability to understand logical consistency.

Children's ability to distinguish logical from illogical syllogisms was investigated by Markovits, Schleifer, and Fortier (1989). They used syllogisms adapted from a study by Hawkins, Pea, Glick, and Scribner (1984) that had shown successful reasoning in preschool children. Logical syllogisms were connected in a way that permitted inference: A-B, B-C. Illogical syllogisms were not connected: A-B, C-D. Consistent with previous studies, they found that 6-year-olds made inferences, but discrimination between logical and illogical syllogisms increased with age, being slight at age 6 but very consistent at age 11 years. English (in press) found evidence for implicit recognition of the distinction.

There is evidence that recognition of indeterminacy might be difficult because of the complexity of the task rather than because of linguistic factors.

Falmagne, Mawby, and Pea (1989) gave second- and third-grade children a task in which they were first given a proposition about cards in a box; for example, all the cards have big circles. Two kinds of probe sentences were used, one involving the copula *is* (e.g., there is a red circle), the other involving the modal term (e.g., there can be a red circle; there has to be a red circle). The form of the probe did not influence difficulty. Difficulty was also found to persist when indeterminacy was indicated by true or false responses, rather than by "can't tell." However, difficulty was reduced when the probe referred to a single object; for example, "I am looking at a card, is it a red circle?" (Falmagne et al., 1989, p. 161). Their explanation is that a simpler representation, and a simpler executive process, can be used with the single-object task. Children might represent the proposition "all the cards have big circles" in terms of size, with "default" values for other attributes, color and number. When the probe consists of the proposition that a card contains a red circle, the indeterminacy can be recognized directly by comparing a representation of the probe with the representation of the original proposition. However, probes that require more explicit decisions (Are there any red circles, are they all red circles?) require more elaborate representations (that there are both red and nonred circles), as well as an executive process for comparing the probe representation with aspects of the proposition representation. Falmagne et al.'s very ingenious study seems to have been the first to demonstrate empirically the importance of structural complexity in judgments of indeterminacy.

Excluding the flawed study by Tunmer et al., the evidence indicates that recognition of logical necessity is more difficult than making an inference. Understanding of necessity appears to develop by about 11–12 years of age. The representations and strategies entailed in assessing logical validity are only beginning to be understood. Johnson-Laird (1983) suggested that recognition of validity depends on checking all possible representations. The proposals of Falmagne et al. (1989) are essentially consistent with this, because they suggest that assessment of determinacy requires a rather complete representation. The task can be simplified if it is restructured in a way that permits a simpler representation and a simpler strategy. Both proposals implicate the complexity of the representation as a factor in the assessment of determinacy.

The representation used will depend on the particular task, but there is one general factor in judgments of logical validity that will affect the complexity of the task. This is that assessment of validity entails an additional dimension on the representation. When an inference is generated, by whatever process, recognition of validity entails assessing whether the inference would always be true, sometimes be true, or never be true. This always/sometimes/never dimension is additional to whatever dimensions were entailed in the representation from which the inference was generated. This extra dimension corresponds to the switch from one representation to another. It is a dimension of representations. For example, in Fig. 7.6 it corresponds to the switch from Model 1 to Model 2, or from Model 2 to Model 3. To assess the complexity of logical validity more precisely we must first investigate the nature of the representations used in more detail, and there has been insufficient empirical study of this to constrain detailed modeling. However, the principle that representation of validity entails a dimension that is additional to the representations entailed in making the inference should be taken into account in development of models in this area.

Induction was considered in chapters 4 and 6, and will not be discussed again here. However, there has been a series of studies that have been interpreted as demonstrating induction in young children, although they appear to be more relevant to categorical deduction. We consider them here briefly.

CHILDREN'S CATEGORICAL INFERENCES

There is evidence that young children can use categories to constrain their inferences (S. A. Gelman & Markman, 1987; S. A. Gelman, 1988). Gelman and Markman showed children an object, such as a cat, and told them a new fact about it, such as that it can see in the dark. They were then asked whether this fact applied to another member of the same category with similar appearance, another member of the same category with different appearance (a different-colored cat), a member of a different category with similar appearance (a skunk), and a member of a different category with different appearance (a dinosaur). Three- to four-year-old children were sensitive to category membership and recognized that the newly learned facts were more likely to generalize to members of the same category than to members of other categories.

The use of category labels increased discrimination between categories. S. A. Gelman (1988) used a similar methodology with preschool and second-grade children (aged 4 years and 7–8 years, respectively). She taught children new facts, such as that a rabbit eats alfalfa, to ensure that generalization could not have been based on prior knowledge. She also varied the generalizability of the facts. For example, the fact that a rabbit eats alfalfa generalizes to all rabbits, whereas the fact that a particular rabbit is cold does not. Finally, she varied the level of the categories, reasoning that there would be more generalization with basic-level categories (e.g., rabbits), where there is high similarity between the instances, than with superordinate categories (e.g., animals), where there is less similarity. Children of both ages were sensitive to category membership, to the level of the category, and to the generalizability inherent in the property, showing less generalization for incidental properties, such as being cold. These studies indicate that young children have a good knowledge of the distribution of properties over categories and can use this knowledge to infer how a property will be shared. They know that if one rabbit eats alfalfa, other rabbits are likely to do so, because rabbits tend to be similar in what they eat. On the other hand, being cold is a property of an individual rabbit rather than of a category, and there is no reason to infer that other rabbits will be cold.

It has also been shown that children learn different rules in different domains. For example, Komatsu and Galotti (1986) showed that 6-, 8-, and 10-year-old children recognize that social conventions can change but that physical and logical rules are unlikely to change. This suggests that when children acquire inductive rules, they also learn something about the constancy of the rules in that particular domain. Physical rules, such as that pencils fall when dropped, tend to be more immutable than social rules, such as the convention that dogs should be called "dogs," and children do appear to recognize this.

These studies show that young children can use categories to constrain inferences but that they do not address the question of how the inductions are made. Presumably the child has a representation of the contingencies between attributes, for example, that being a particular kind of animal influences the kinds of things that are eaten. The mechanisms discussed in chapter 4 would seem to be relevant to these acquisitions but, surprisingly perhaps, there does not appear to have been investigation of the induction processes that led to the knowledge base used in these tasks.

Empirical evidence concerning the induction process can be obtained from matrix- and letter-completion tasks of the kind that have been commonly used in psychometric tests. Consider, for example, the sequence used by Ferrara, Brown, and Campione (1986): PZUFQZVF___ __ __ __ (correct answer RZWF). To solve this problem we must first detect the regularity, then define a rule that expresses the regularity, and then apply this rule so as to continue the sequence.

Some insights into how the rule is discovered are provided by a sequence of hints that Ferrara used successfully to teach 8- to 11-year-old children to solve such problems. The sequence of hints for the problem above (Ferrara et al., 1986, Appendix) was this:

1. "Is this problem like any other you've seen before?" If so: "How did you solve the other problem?"
2. "Read the letters in the problem out loud. Did you hear a pattern in the letters?"
3. "Are any of the letters written more than once in the problem? Which ones? Does that give you any ideas about how to continue the pattern?"
4. "How many other letters are there between the two Zs? And how many other letters are there between the two Fs? Does that give you any ideas about how to complete the pattern?"

5. "Are the letters in the problem next to each other in the alphabet? Which ones? Does that help you to solve the problem?"
6. "How many other letters are there between the P and the Q in the problem? And how many other letters are there between the U and the V? Does that give you any ideas about the answer?"
7. "Point to the P and the Q in the alphabet, and to the U and the V. Does that help at all?"

Next the experimenter placed a transparency over the problem, that showed a bee flying from the P to the Q, then a sequence of other transparencies showing animals moving from one letter to the next in the sequence.

This sequence of hints highlights the information that the problem solver needs to process in order to discover the regularities in the problem. The first hint suggests use of analogy: Is this problem like any you have seen? Other hints sensitize the child to the regularities in the material and help the child find the right hypotheses to encode the regularities. Ferrara et al. found that younger children required more hints to solve the problems than did older children, and average-IQ children required more hints than high-IQ children. These differences were more pronounced in transfer tasks. These results suggest that ability to make inductive inferences is a component of intelligence and that this ability is one of the things that develop as children mature. One thing to note, however, is that this procedure seems to promote explicit induction, in which the child is aware of the rules being acquired. However, as Reber (1989) showed, humans have great power for implicit induction, that is, finding regularities in material without explicit recognition of the rules acquired. The processes discussed in chapter 4 are more relevant to this type of process.

INDUCTION AND MENTAL MODELS

Inductive inferences can never be validated, but they can be disconfirmed (Popper, 1959). A generalization (based on the universal quantifier) can never be confirmed, because the possibility of an exception, or negative instance, cannot be eliminated. The generalization "all swans are white" seemed quite solid in Europe, but it was disconfirmed when explorers entered the Swan River in Western Australia and saw black swans for the first time.

Accordingly, inductive inferences always have the status of hypotheses that are subject to disconfirmation. It is critical to the validity of inductive inferences that we have some way of testing them. As we saw in chapter 4, there are natural mechanisms that cause inductively learned rules to be strengthened when their predictions are confirmed and weakened when they are disconfirmed. However, these mechanisms rely on confirmations and disconfirmations occurring through interaction with the environment, and the strength of rules is normally changed in small increments. These mechanisms are problematic and slow. There are, however, more explicit, if more specialized, hypothesis-testing mechanisms.

Assessing Hypothesis Testing

Inhelder and Piaget (1955/1958) observed children's attempts to test hypotheses on a variety of scientific phenomena, such as the pendulum and the balance scale, and concluded that hypothesis testing was not observed until the formal operational stage, in adolescence. Their conclusions were not supported, however, by Bynum, Thomas, and Weitz (1972). A more objective technique for assessing hypothesis testing was developed by Levine (1966) and subsequently applied to children (Cantor & Spiker, 1978; Gholson, Levine, & Phillips, 1972; Kemler, 1978; Parrill-Burnstein, 1978; Spiker & Cantor, 1979; Tumblin, Gholson, Rosenthal, & Kelley, 1979). This research was reviewed by Halford (1982) and by Gholson (1980), who also extended the data and analysis.

Levine's technique is summarized in Fig. 7.9. (reproduced from Halford, 1982, Fig. 9.2). A pair of stimuli are presented on each trial, and each stimulus comprises values of four attributes: shape (X or T), size (large or small), color (black or white), and position (left or right). The participant chooses a stimulus from each pair and is told (on feedback trials, i.e., Trials 1, 6, 11, 16) whether the choice is correct or not. The participant's hypothesis is diagnosed from the pattern of choices over the four blank (nonfeedback) trials between each pair of feedback trials. The participant must find out which of the eight attributes is always correct for that problem. In the example shown in Fig. 7.9, the first hypothesis, black, is abandoned after negative feedback on Trial 6. It is replaced by the hypothesis right, which is also abandoned, after negative feedback on Trial 11. The next hypothesis, "X," is supported after positive feedback on Trial 11, and is in fact the correct hypothesis. More details of the procedure are given by Levine 1966, and Halford (1982, pp. 262–264).

MENTAL MODELS AND HYPOTHESIS TESTING

Our next concern is to define the type of reasoning required to test hypotheses. Because an hypothesis can only be disconfirmed, testing it amounts to seeing whether a hypothesis is disconfirmed or not. We will consider the testing process in more detail, using the the example in Fig. 7.9. The critical trials are summarized in Fig. 7.10. The first hypothesis is that color is relevant, and that black is positive. On Trial 1 this was associated with positive feedback, because the choice of the large black X on the right was pronounced

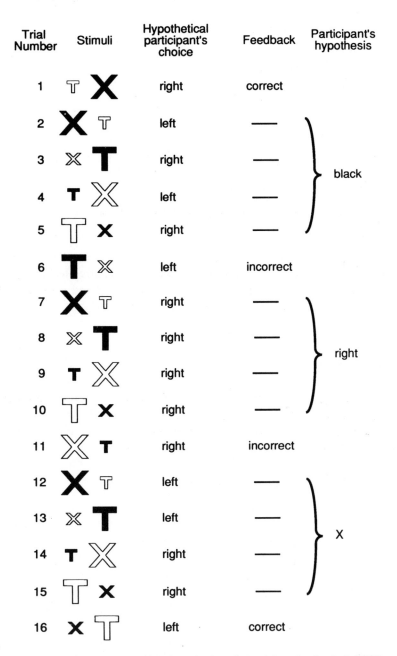

Trial Number	Stimuli	Hypothetical participant's choice	Feedback	Participant's hypothesis
1	T X	right	correct	
2	X T	left	—	
3	X T	right	—	
4	T X	left	—	black
5	T X	right	—	
6	T X	left	incorrect	
7	X T	right	—	
8	X T	right	—	
9	T X	right	—	right
10	T X	right	—	
11	X T	right	incorrect	
12	X T	left	—	
13	X T	left	—	
14	T X	right	—	X
15	T X	right	—	
16	X T	left	correct	

FIG. 7.9. Sequence of trials in hypothesis-testing task based on Levine's (1966) blank-trials technique. Reproduced from Halford (1982), Fig. 9.2.

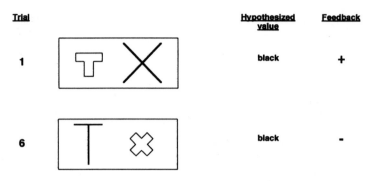

FIG. 7.10.   Disconfirming evidence of hypothesis that black is positive, occurring over two feedback trials in a hypothesis-testing task.

"correct." The critical test of the hypothesis "black" comes on Trial 6, where the choice of the large black T on the left results in negative feedback. This disconfirms the hypothesis, with the result that it was abandoned on subsequent trials. The information that disconfirms the hypothesis is as follows:

black → correct

black → incorrect

From this we know that the hypothesis "black" is invalidated. Importantly, we also know that "white" is invalidated. How we do we know this?

We know it because we expected to find that the correct value of the relevant attribute would be associated with positive feedback, and the incorrect attribute with negative feedback. That is, we have a mental model of the task in which there is one relevant dimension, the correct value of which is always associated with positive feedback, and the incorrect value with negative feedback, as shown in Fig. 7.11, Case 1. The obtained sequence in which black is associated with both positive and negative feedback cannot be mapped into the mental model of the task consistently. The inconsistency is that black is mapped into both the correct and the incorrect value. The other way a hypothesis can be disconfirmed in this task is shown in Case 2 in Fig. 7.11. Here the hypotheses "black" and "white" have both been associated with positive feedback. This also is inconsistent with the mental model (because the two +s in the experience are mapped into a + and a − in the mental model). Case 3 is, however, consistent because all mappings are unique; black is mapped into the correct relevant attribute, white into the incorrect relevant attribute, + is mapped to + and − to −.

The structure mappings in Fig. 7.11 are system-level mappings, because each depends on two (binary) relations. They would require three-dimensional

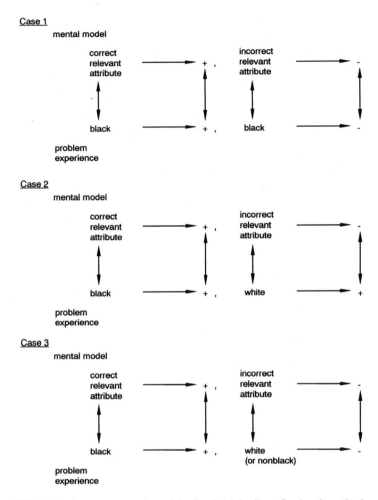

FIG. 7.11. Structure mapping of feedback trials disconfirming hypothesis "black" into mental model for unidimensional hypothesis-testing task (Levine, 1966).

representations, and they should be difficult for children below 5 years of age, but should be quite possible from 5 years onwards.

There is, however, a simpler way to test hypotheses in this task, as shown in Fig. 7.12. Here the mental model simply entails the expectation that the correct attribute will lead to positive feedback. Nothing is expected about the incorrect attribute. Disconfirmation occurs simply because the expected positive feedback does not occur. Hypothesis testing using this mental model only entails using relational mappings, with two-dimensional representations, and should be possible for children as young as 2–3 years. There does not appear to be any study reporting hypothesis testing with such young children, but a structural-complexity analysis suggests that research to date might have underestimated young children's abilities in this area. These two mental models correspond to two hypothesis-testing strategies that have been observed with children (Gholson et al., 1972). The more complex model in Fig. 7.11 corresponds to dimension checking, in which each dimension (color, shape, size, position) is sampled in turn. When one attribute leads to disconfirmation, the dimension is abandoned, because it is recognized that the other attribute cannot be correct either. For example, having found that black is incorrect, there is no point in trying white. This inference depends on the fact that both positive and negative values of the dimension are integrated in the same mental model, as in Fig. 7.11.

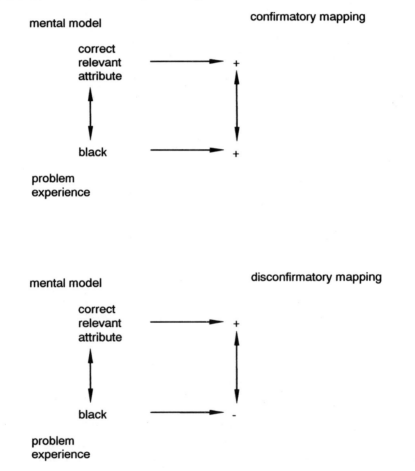

FIG. 7.12. Structure mappings associated with hypothesis-testing strategy in blank-trials task.

The less complex model corresponds to the strategy of hypothesis checking, in which both attributes of a dimension might be tried independently of each other. For example, having found that "black" leads to disconfirmation, the child might try "white" as the next hypothesis. Young children have been found to use this strategy (Gholson et al., 1972). This occurs because, as shown in Fig. 7.12, only one value of the dimension occurs in the mental model, so no inference can be made about the other value.

Because the dimension-checking strategy (Fig. 7.12) requires only two-dimensional representations, it should not cause difficulties for children from the age of 2 years, whereas dimension-checking strategies (Fig. 7.11) that require three-dimensional representations will cause difficulties until about 5 years of age. Cantor and Spiker (1978, 1984), Kemler (1978), Parrill-Burnstein (1978), and Tumblin, Gholson, Rosenthal, and Kelley (1979) showed that strategies equivalent to hypothesis checking could be taught to children as young as 5 years, and I have summarized this research elsewhere (Halford, 1982). The present theory predicts that the mental model for this strategy could be acquired even earlier. If other sources of difficulty were removed, by using the minimum number of dimensions that are logically required (one relevant and one irrelevant), and by making sure the procedure was completely appropriate for very young children, success should be possible as young as 2 years.

MULTIDIMENSIONAL HYPOTHESIS TESTING

Hypothesis testing in Levine's blank-trials paradigm always entailed only one relevant dimension, and this fact was communicated to participants through explanation or training. This is a major difference from the tasks used by Inhelder and Piaget (1958), where more than one dimension was often relevant. For example in the balance scale, four dimensions, weight and distance on the left and weight and distance on the right, were relevant, as discussed in chapter 9. Even where one dimension was relevant, as in the pendulum problem, participants did not know this until after they had solved the problem. In fact, solving the problem included showing that the length of the string was the only relevant dimension, and that other factors such as weight and the force with which the pendulum was set swinging were irrelevant.

It would be highly desirable to diagnose multidimensional hypotheses using a technique that preserved the objectivity of Levine's blank-trials method. Levine's procedure was extended to deal with multidimensional hypotheses by Halford, Cross, and Maybery (1984). The task entails conceptual-rule identification, after the model of Haygood and Bourne (1965). The procedure is illustrated in Fig. 7.13 (reproduced from Halford, Cross, & Maybery, 1984, Fig. 1). The participant is told which are the relevant attributes, in this case small and square, and is asked to find the correct conceptual rule from the eight alternatives, conjunction, inclusive disjunction, conditional, biconditional, alternate denial, joint denial, exclusion, and exclusive disjunction. We trace through a sample set of trials, using Fig. 7.13. The stimuli vary over three dimensions: shape (triangle, octagon, square), size (small, medium, large), and shading (blank, crossed, striped). The rule-identification paradigm (Haygood & Bourne, 1965) is used, so the relevant attributes, small and square, are told to participants in advance, and their task is to identify which one of the eight conceptual rules is relevant.

On Trial 1, the stimulus is a small, crossed square; the participant responds "yes" and receives feedback that the response is correct. Trials 2–6 are blank

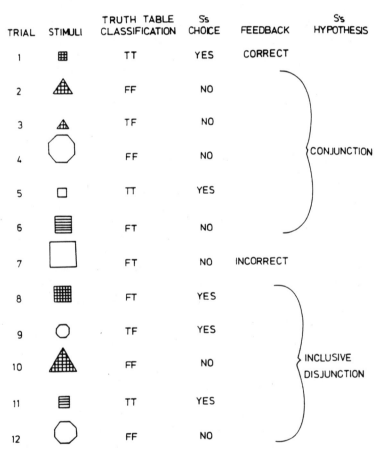

FIG. 7.13. Sequence of trials in rule-identification task with multidimensional hypotheses. From Halford, Cross, and Maybery (1984), Fig. 1.

trials, and the pattern of choices over these trials causes us to diagnose that the participant is using conjunction as the first hypothesis. (Notice that the only "yes" response is on Trial 5, where the stimulus is small and square). Now we want to consider the mental models that are entailed in recognizing when a hypothesis is disconfirmed.

On Trial 7 the stimulus is large and square, and the participant responds "no," consistent with the hypothesis. The feedback is that this is incorrect, and five more blank trials follow. This time the hypothesis is diagnosed as inclusive disjunction, because all stimuli that are small, or square, or both, are responded to with "yes," whereas those that are neither small nor square are responded to with "no." Notice that the participant has changed hypothesis following negative feedback on Trial 7. This example illustrates the technique that Halford et al. (1984) used to diagnose the hypotheses that people used in a rule-identification task.

In the example in Fig. 7.13 the participant's first hypothesis is conjunction of small and square. This is disconfirmed on Trial 7, when large and square is found to be correct. The mental model that the person has of this task includes the knowledge, acquired through extensive instructions, that there are two relevant dimensions. Under the hypothesis that the rule is conjunction, it would be expected that when the correct values of both dimensions occur, this should be a positive instance. (Under inclusive disjunction, an instance is positive when the correct value of either or both relevant dimensions occur.) The mental model for conjunction is shown in Fig. 7.14, where it is mapped into the hypothesis "small and square." The three types of disconfirming cases that can occur are shown in Fig. 7.15. The first case, just considered, is where small and square is positive, and large and square is also positive. In this case the correct conceptual rule cannot be the conjunction of small and square. This is the type of disconfirmation that occurs in Fig. 7.13. On Trial 1, small square is a positive instance (the participant chooses it and is told it is correct). However, on Trial 7, large square is also positive (the participant rejects it and is told that is incorrect). Therefore small square

Mental Model

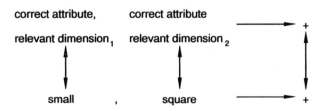

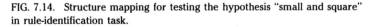

FIG. 7.14. Structure mapping for testing the hypothesis "small and square" in rule-identification task.

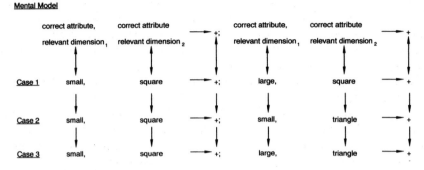

FIG. 7.15.　Three structure mappings that disconfirm the hypothesis "small and square."

and large square are both positive instances of the concept, so the concept cannot be conjunction of small and square. The second case is where small square and small triangle are both positive; that is, the second relevant dimension is changed. The third case is where small square and large triangle are both positive; that is, both the first and second dimensions are changed. In either of these cases the concept cannot be conjunction of large and square.

The structure mappings required to detect that the hypothesis is disconfirmed are multiple system mappings, because each structure mapping is a composition of two ternary relations, such as (small, square, +). Accordingly, it would be predicted that testing hypotheses of this type would be very difficult before about 11 years of age. The same prediction holds for testing hypotheses based on the other seven conceptual rules, and the argument is shown in Appendix 7.A.

Predictions can also be made for attribute identification in two-dimensional concept-attainment tasks. That is, where the procedure is similar to that shown in Fig. 7.13, but the participant is told which conceptual rule is relevant and must discover the relevant attributes. These predictions also are derived in Appendix 7.A.

One implication of this section is that hypothesis-testing tasks cover a wide range of complexities of mental models. Some require very simple mental models and should be attainable by 2- to 3-year-old children, but there are others that should produce difficulty for children under 11 years. The two ends of this distribution remain to be explored empirically. However, it is valuable to make predictions for which there are as yet no data, because they cannot be *ad hoc*. The derivation of these predictions is too complex to have been influenced much by one's intuitions as to what children can do. Because they are made in advance of any relevant data, they represent a good test of the power of the theory.

SUMMARY AND CONCLUSIONS

When humans make inferences they do not typically invoke formal rules from logic or mathematics but use mental models to represent the premises. The mental models might be constructed specifically for the task, or schemas induced from experience might be used as a kind of "template" to structure the representation. Both schemas and mental models contain relatively specific semantic information and are normally used by analogy. The mapping of a mental model into a problem imposes a processing load that depends on the dimensionality of the representation. However, the load can be reduced by strategies that segment the task into smaller steps that are performed serially.

A computational model of transitive inference was presented in which strategies are developed under the guidance of a concept of order that compromises a representation of an ordered set of at least three elements. The concept of order is not based on abstract principles but is induced from ordinary life experience. It is used by analogy to guide the processes in the strategy, which entail organizing premise elements in order. Procedural knowledge, also acquired through experience, is used by means–end analysis. The development of an adequate strategy, which integrates premises, depends on sufficient processing capacity to represent the three-dimensional structure entailed in the concept of order. Inadequate capacity, or failure to allocate sufficient resources to the task due to low effort or competing demands, results in strategies that treat premises separately, without integration. These strategies give correct answers to some problems, but there are important classes of problems to which they produce errors. Children without the capacity to represent three-dimensional concepts could be taught transitive-inference strategies but would have restricted ability to generalize the strategies; they would not be able to use transitivity as the foundation for other conceptual developments, such as those in the area of quantification.

Given evidence that children under about 5 years typically cannot represent three-dimensional concepts, it follows that they will have only a limited comprehension of transitivity. This prediction has been countered by widespread and cogent claims in the literature that children as young as 3 do understand transitivity. This literature is assessed and it is argued that 3- to 4-year-olds make transitive inferences only under very restricted conditions, where lower level representations can be used. This is consistent with the argument in chapter 6, where it was pointed out that tasks that exceed processing capacity do not lead to catastrophic breakdown but to default to a representation of lower dimensionality.

Inferences based on categorical and conditional syllogisms also typically employ mental models, some of which are based on schemas induced from experience, such as pragmatic reasoning schemas. It is hypothesized that some of the common errors found in Wason's selection task (four-card problem) can be attributed to use of schemas such as prediction that do not conform to the truth functional definition of "if then." Children appear to be able to make simple, logical inferences at least from age 5, but understanding of logical necessity entails more complex representations and typically develops at around 11 years.

Three different levels of mental model were found to be entailed in hypothesis testing, ranging from two-dimensional for hypothesis checking, three-dimensional for dimension checking, and four-dimensional for rule identification. Because hypothesis checking entails only two-dimensional representations it should be possible at least by age 2 years, implying that empirical studies to date have probably underestimated abilities of young children in this area. This illustrates that structural complexity analyses, coupled with capacity theory, have the potential to predict as yet unobserved abilities, and it is a fallacy to give them such pejorative value labels as "pessimistic" or "deficit models."

APPENDIX 7.A: HYPOTHESIS-TESTING PREDICTIONS

To test hypotheses, participants must search for negative evidence. In order to evaluate evidence, they must compare trial outcomes with a representation of the concept. Suppose, for example, that a participant is testing hypotheses in an attribute-identification paradigm involving an affirmation concept. One value of a relevant dimension is associated with a positive outcome ($r \rightarrow +$) and the others are associated with a negative outcome ($\bar{r} \rightarrow -$). That is, the truth table for affirmation can be expressed as the associations $r \rightarrow +$, $\bar{r} \rightarrow -$ (one value of the relevant dimension is positive, the complementary values are negative). The pattern of associations that can occur between values of relevant dimensions and outcomes in each of the five concept types is shown in Table 7.4. These can be obtained from the truth table and amount to converting truth table definitions of conceptual rules to a more psychologically meaningful form. To illustrate how the associations are specified, notice that for conjunction, a positive outcome occurs with r_1 and r_2 (in row 1 of the truth table), but r_1 also occurs with a negative outcome in row 2, and r_2 occurs with a negative outcome in row 3. However $\bar{r}$ occurs only with negative outcomes (in row 2 for r_2, row 3 for r_1, and row 4 for both r_1 and r_2). Therefore the three associations that occur between a value of a relevant dimension and a trial outcome are $r. \rightarrow +$, $r. \rightarrow -$, and $\bar{r} \rightarrow -$, as shown in Table 7.4 (r occurs with both positive and negative outcomes, and $\bar{r}$ occurs only with a negative outcome).

In conjunction and disjunction the associations are the same for r_1 and r_2, but in the conditional rule a different set of associations occurs for r_1 and

r_2. In the biconditional rule r_1, $\bar{r}_1$, r_2 and $\bar{r}_2$ are all associated with both $+$ and $-$. To obtain nontautological associations, the two relevant dimensions must be considered jointly, as shown in Table 7.4.

The process of checking whether a set of trials is consistent with a dimension being relevant can be represented as a structure mapping, examples of which are shown in Fig. 7.16. A pair of trials such as red $\rightarrow$ +, blue $\rightarrow$ −, is consistent with the representation of the affirmation concept, and a consistent structure mapping can be constructed. A pair of trials such as red $\rightarrow$ +, red $\rightarrow$ −, cannot be reconciled with the hypothesis that color is relevant nor mapped into the associations that occur in affirmation in a way that produces a consistent structure mapping. A pair of trials in which two different attributes are associated with the same outcome is also inconsistent with the dimension being relevant, and this is shown in Case 3 of Fig. 7.16.

Testing an hypothesis that a dimension is relevant corresponds to a structure mapping. Testing which dimensions are relevant in affirmation concepts requires system mappings. The strategies dimension checking and focusing require the relevance of dimensions to be checked (Gholson, Levine, & Phillips, 1972) so they require system mappings. Hypothesis checking entails testing individual attributes, not dimensions, and only requires relational mappings.

TABLE 7.4
Truth Tables for the 5 Conceptual Rules (Basic Concept Types)

Relevant Dimensions		Affirmation (r_1 relevant)	Conjunction	Disjunction	Conditional	Biconditional
r_1	r_2	+	+	+	+	+
r_1	$\bar{r}_2$	+	−	+	−	−
$\bar{r}_1$	r_2	−	−	+	+	−
$\bar{r}_1$	$\bar{r}_2$	−	−	−	+	+
Associations		$r \rightarrow +$ $\bar{r} \rightarrow -$	$r. \rightarrow +$ $r. \rightarrow -$ $\bar{r}. \rightarrow -$	$r. \rightarrow +$ $\bar{r}. \rightarrow +$ $\bar{r}. \rightarrow -$	$r_1 \rightarrow +$ $r_1 \rightarrow -$ $\bar{r}_1 \rightarrow +$ $r_2 \rightarrow +$ $\bar{r}_2 \rightarrow +$ $\bar{r}_2 \rightarrow -$	$r_1, r_2 \rightarrow +$ $\bar{r}_1, r_2 \rightarrow -$ $r_1, \bar{r}_2 \rightarrow -$ $\bar{r}_1, \bar{r}_2 \rightarrow +$

The binary numbers 1 and 0, which are conventionally used, are replaced by values of the relevant dimensions r, $\bar{r}$, and by the positive and negative outcomes $+$, $-$, for convenience in exposition.

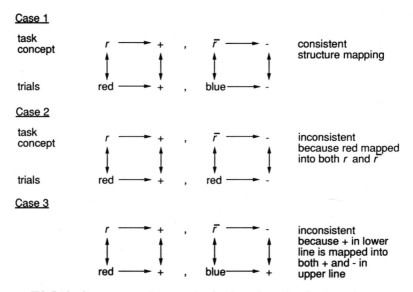

FIG. 7.16. Structure mappings associated with attribute-identification task, testing hypothesis that color is relevant.

The associations entailed in the other four conceptual rules are shown in Table 7.4. The structure mappings for each of these cases are shown in Table 7.5. Where a set of trials are consistent with that dimension being relevant for that conceptual rule, it is possible to produce a consistent structure mapping. In other cases it is not. The inconsistent structures for affirmation, conjunction, disjunction, and the conditional are all system mappings. This implies that hypothesis testing in the attribute-identification paradigm for these concepts requires strategies based on system mappings and therefore should begin to emerge at 5 years.

The predictions for rule identification are summarized in Table 7.6. The rule associations are taken from the truth tables (Table 7.4). The left column of Table 7.6 shows all the combinations of stimuli that can occur. Pairs of relevant attributes, a. and b. are associated with outcomes + and −. Any structure mapping with just one such association must be consistent because each stimulus, a. and b., occurs only once and can therefore be mapped into only one of r or r. Inconsistent mappings cannot occur and hypotheses cannot be falsified with one such occurrence. Therefore pairs of occurrences are shown in the left column of Table 7.6. There are three types of cases: where both occurrences are assigned to +; where one is assigned to + and one to −; and where both are assigned to −. These three cases are crossed with cases where the value of a is changed from first to second occurrence, where the value of b is changed, or both are changed.

The internal cells of the Table 7.6 show which structure mappings are con-

TABLE 7.5
Structure Mapping for Attribute Identification Hypotheses.
The Vertical Bijective Arrows Have Been Omitted.

Associations	Consistent Structure Mappings	Inconsistent Structure Mappings
Affirmation $r \to x$ $\bar{r} \to \bar{x}$	$r \to x$ / $a_1 \to x$; $r \to x$ / $a_2 \to x$ plus the patterns shown for affirmation	$r \to x,\ r \to x$ / $a_1 \to x,\ a_2 \to x$; $\bar{r} \to \bar{x},\ \bar{r} \to \bar{x}$ / $a_1 \to \bar{x},\ a_2 \to \bar{x}$; $r \to x,\ \bar{r} \to \bar{x}$ / $a_1 \to x,\ a_1 \to \bar{x}$; $r \to x,\ \bar{r} \to \bar{x}$ / $a_2 \to x,\ a_2 \to \bar{x}$
Conjunction	$r \to x$ / $a_1 \to x$; $r \to x$ / $a_2 \to x$ plus the patterns shown for affirmation	$r \to x,\ r \to x$ / $a_1 \to x,\ a_2 \to x$; $\bar{r} \to \bar{x},\ r \to \bar{x}$ / $a_1 \to \bar{x},\ a_2 \to \bar{x}$; $r \to x,\ r \to x$ / $a_1 \to x,\ a_1 \to x$; $r \to x,\ r \to x$ / $a_2 \to x,\ a_2 \to x$
Disjunction $r. \to x$ $r, \to x$ $\bar{r}, \to x$ $\bar{r}, \to \bar{x}$	$\bar{r} \to x$ / $a_1 \to x$; $\bar{r} \to x$ / $a_2 \to x$ plus the patterns shown for affirmation	$\bar{r} \to \bar{x},\ \bar{r} \to \bar{x}$ / $a_1 \to \bar{x},\ a_2 \to \bar{x}$; $\bar{r} \to \bar{x},\ \bar{r} \to \bar{x}$ / $a_1 \to \bar{x_1}\ a_2 \to \bar{x}$; $\bar{r} \to \bar{x},\ \bar{r} \to \bar{x}$ / $a_1 \to \bar{x},\ a_2 \to \bar{x}$; $\bar{r} \to \bar{x},\ \bar{r} \to \bar{x}$ / $a_1 \to \bar{x},\ b_2 \to \bar{x}$
Conditional $r_1 \to x$ $r_2 \to x$ $r_1 \to \bar{x}$ $\bar{r}_2 \to x$ $\bar{r}_1 \to x$ $\bar{r}_2 \to \bar{x}$	$r_1 \to x$ / $a_1 \to x$; $r_2 \to x$ / $a_2 \to x$ $r_1 \to \bar{x}$ / $a_1 \to \bar{x}$; $\bar{r}_2 \to x$ / $a_2 \to x$ $\bar{r}_1 \to x$ / $a_1 \to x$; $\bar{r}_2 \to \bar{x}$ / $a_2 \to \bar{x}$	$r_1 \to x,\ r_1 \to x$ / $a_1 \to x,\ a_2 \to x$; $r_2 \to \bar{x},\ r_2 \to \bar{x}$ / $a_1 \to \bar{x},\ a_2 \to \bar{x}$; $r_1 \to \bar{x},\ r_1 \to \bar{x}$ / $a_1 \to \bar{x},\ b_2 \to \bar{x}$; $r_2 \to \bar{x},\ r_2 \to \bar{x}$ / $b_1 \to \bar{x},\ b_2 \to \bar{x}$
Biconditional $r_1 r_2 \to x$ $\bar{r}_1 r_2 \to \bar{x}$ $r_1 \bar{r}_2 \to \bar{x}$ $\bar{r}_1 \bar{r}_2 \to x$	$r_1, r_2 \to x$ / $a_1 b_2 \to x$ $r_1 \bar{r}_2 \to \bar{x}$ / $a_1 b_1 \to \bar{x}$ ………… $\bar{r}_1 \bar{r}_2 \to \bar{x}$ / $a_2 b_2 \to x$	$r_1 r_2 \to x,\ r_1 r_2 \to x$ / $a_1 b_1 \to x,\ a_1 b_2 \to x$; $r_1 r_2 \to x,\ \bar{r}_1 \bar{r}_2 \to x$ / $a_1 b_1 \to x,\ a_1 b_2 \to x$; $\bar{r}_1 \bar{r}_2 \to x,\ \bar{r}_1 \bar{r}_2 \to x$ / $a_1 b_1 \to x,\ a_1 b_2 \to x$; $\bar{r}_1 r_2 \to \bar{x}, \bar{r}_1 r_2 \to$; $a_1 b_1 \to \bar{x},\ a_1 b_2 \to$; $r_1 \bar{r}_2 \to \bar{x},\ \bar{r}_1 r_2 \to \bar{x}$ / $a_1 b_1 \to \bar{x},\ a_1 b_1 \to x$

335

TABLE 7.6
Summary of Structure Mappings for Rule Identification Hypotheses

		Conjunction Rule Associations	Disjunction Rule Associations	Conditional Rule Associations	Biconditional Rule Associations
		1. $r_1r_2 \to x$	1. $r_1r_2 \to x$	1. $r_1r_2 \to x$	1. $r_1r_2 \to x$
The possible pairs of stimulus-outcome associations		2. $r_1\bar{r}_2 \to \bar{x}$	2. $r_1\bar{r}_2 \to x$	2. $r_1\bar{r}_2 \to \bar{x}$	2. $r_1\bar{r}_2 \to \bar{x}$
		3. $\bar{r}_1r_2 \to \bar{x}$	3. $\bar{r}_1r_2 \to x$	3. $\bar{r}_1r_2 \to x$	3. $\bar{r}_1\bar{r}_2 \to \bar{x}$
		4. $\bar{r}_1\bar{r}_2 \to \bar{x}$	4. $\bar{r}_1\bar{r}_2 \to \bar{x}$	4. $\bar{r}_1\bar{r}_2 \to x$	4. $\bar{r}_1\bar{r}_2 \to x$
A value changes	$a_1b_1 \to +$ $a_2b_1 \to +$	inconsistent	1 & 3 consistent	1 & 3 consistent	inconsistent
	$a_1b_1 \to +$ $a_2b_1 \to -$	1 & 3 consistent	2 & 4 consistent	2 & 4 consistent	1 & 3, 2 & 4 consistent
	$a_1b_1 \to -$ $a_2b_1 \to -$	2 & 4 consistent	inconsistent	inconsistent	inconsistent
B value changes	$a_1b_1 \to +$ $a_1b_2 \to +$	inconsistent	1 & 2 consistent	3 & 4 consistent	inconsistent
	$a_1b_1 \to +$ $a_1b_2 \to -$	1 & 2 consistent	3 & 4 consistent	1 & 2 consistent	1 & 2, 3 & 4 consistent
	$a_1b_1 \to -$ $a_1b_2 \to -$	3 & 4 consistent	inconsistent	inconsistent	inconsistent
A & B change	$a_1b_1 \to +$ $a_2b_2 \to +$	inconsistent	2 & 3 consistent	1 & 4 consistent	1 & 4 consistent
	$a_1b_1 \to +$ $a_2b_2 \to +$	1 & 4 consistent	1 & 4 consistent	2 & 3 consistent	inconsistent
	$a_1b_1 \to -$ $a_2b_2 \to -$	2 & 3 consistent	inconsistent	inconsistent	2 & 3 consistent
		inconsistent if anything changes & the outcome remains positive	inconsistent if anything changes & the outcome remains negative		

sistent. Consider, for example, the fourth case: The combination $a_1b_1 \rightarrow +$, $a_1b_2 \rightarrow +$, will produce an inconsistent structure mapping with every combination of the four rule associations for conjunction. Therefore the rule cannot be conjunction. On the other hand, this combination will form a consistent structure mapping with the first and second associations of the disjunction rule, and therefore the hypothesis that the rule is disjunction cannot be rejected.

An intuitive understanding of this can be gained by substituting red for a_1 and triangle and circle for b_1 and b_2 respectively. The combination $a_1b_1 \rightarrow +$, $a_1b_2 \rightarrow +$ then becomes red triangle is positive, red circle is positive. Given that these are relevant attributes, we know that the rule cannot be conjunction, because if the concept is "red triangle," red circle cannot be positive, and vice versa.

In this case two associations of the form $a.b. \rightarrow +/-$, $a.b. \rightarrow +/-$ must be used to reject an hypothesis. The task therefore requires two bivariate functions to be mapped and so a multiple-system mapping is required.

8

CLASSIFICATION, QUANTIFICATION, AND CONSERVATION

This chapter is concerned with two related topics: classification and quantification. At some level, classification is a prerequisite for quantification because objects have to be grouped into equivalence classes before they can be assigned quantitative labels in a consistent way. The lowest level of quantitative scale, the nominal scale, is really equivalent to classification. Therefore we will consider classification first, then proceed to quantification.

CLASSIFICATION

There is now substantial evidence that natural categories are not based initially on defining attributes but are built around prototypes (Rosch, 1973; Rosch, 1978). A prototype is the central tendency of a category, is the most typical instance, and is the instance that shares the most attributes with other members of the same category and fewest attributes with members of other categories. For example, in the category corresponding to most people's understanding of the word *bird*, a robin or a finch might be prototypical because they share most of the attributes of birds, with respect to size, shape, colors, nesting site, and general behavior.

It is well established that we have powerful mechanisms for extracting prototypes from sets of variable stimuli. Franks and Bransford (1971) and Posner and Keele (1968) presented adults with sets of stimuli that varied around a prototype in such a way that the prototype was the central tendency of the stimuli in the set. In the acquisition phase the prototype was not shown. In the recognition phase the prototype was shown, together with a set of new stimuli not shown in the acquisition phase. The prototype received the highest recognition score, and scores generally decreased as a function of distance from the prototype. The implication is that people were able to construct the prototype from rather brief inspection of stimuli that varied around it. Furthermore, there is evidence that infants can extract prototypes from sets of varied stimuli (Sherman, 1985).

As noted in chapter 2, distributed memory representations have the property that they detect prototypes automatically (Rumelhart & McClelland, 1986). Each stimulus is represented as a pattern of activation over a large set of neural units. The patterns are stored by adjusting the weights of the connections between units, and different patterns are superimposed on the same set of weights. Recognition occurs by matching the features of the probe stimulus with the features in the stored representations. Because the prototype is the stimulus that shares the most features with others in the set, it is most readily recognized.

It has been suggested that the first concepts to be learned tend to basic-level categories (Rosch, Mervis, Gray, Johnson, & Boyes-Braem, 1976). A basic-level category is the highest level of category that shares perceptible attributes with other members of the category and does not share these attributes with members of other categories. For example "chair" is a basic-level category, and chairs share features such as legs, a seat, and a back. The subordinate categories of chair are lounge chairs, office chairs, dining chairs, and so on, and the superordinate category is furniture. Unlike chairs, all items of furniture do not have common perceptible features, though they might share functional attributes.

However, the claim that basic-level categories are learned first has been challenged by Mandler (1989). Infants of 1–2 years of age were presented with objects, and their grouping arrangements noted. Fewer infants differentiated basic-level categories within the same superordinate category (dogs vs. horses) than in different superordinate categories (dogs vs. cars). Furthermore, superordinate-level categories (animals vs. vehicles) were better differentiated than basic-level categories within the same superordinate-level category (dogs vs. horses or cars vs. trucks). There are, however, a number of complications that are inherent in this issue. First, superordinate-level categories, or basic-level categories in different superordinate-level categories, are probably more perceptually differentiated than basic-level categories within the same superordinate category. It is true, as Mandler suggested (1989, p. 133) that within-class similarity of a basic-level category (e.g., dogs) remains the same whether it is contrasted with cars or horses. However, dogs and horses are less differentiated perceptually than dogs and cars. A second problem is that hierarchical classifications are difficult to analyze in terms of conventional multifactor experimental designs, because basic-level and superordinate-level categories are not inherently independent and cannot be crossed in experimental design. The reason is that superordinate-level categories, by definition, contain basic-level categories. For example, the contrast of animals versus vehicles is also a contrast of dogs and horses versus cars and trucks. That is, contrasts of superordinate categories necessarily entail contrasts of basic-level categories, which might contribute to the differentiation. It is still possible, therefore, that basic-level categories might be more significant first classifications than Mandler's data suggest.

Early Classification Ability

The tendency to create groups of similar objects has been observed even in infancy. Sugarman (1982) gave infants sets of eight objects, divided into two subsets of four (e.g., four sailor dolls and four boats). She found that even 12-month-olds tended to create single groupings (three or four boats), and two groups (boats and dolls) were commonly created by 2 years of age. However, it was not until approximately 3 years that children processed both groups simultaneously, by placing first a boat, then a doll, then another boat, and so on. Younger children tended to make one grouping first, then turn to the other one.

There is abundant evidence that preschool children can classify by a single criterion, such as shape, color, or size (Campbell, Donaldson, & Young, 1976; Denney & Acito, 1974; Kofsky, 1966; L. B. Smith, 1983; Zimmerman, 1974). On the other hand, there has been some controversy as to when children can perform multiple classification or understand the concept of class inclusion.

Multiple Classification

Two types of multiple-classification tasks have traditionally been used. One entails free sorting of objects that vary over two or more dimensions such as shape, color, or size. The instructions are often rather open-ended and consist simply of telling the child to put together things that are alike (Inhelder & Piaget, 1964). In these circumstances performance might often underestimate children's capabilities. On the other hand, as I have pointed out elsewhere (Halford, 1982), it is important when assessing multiple classification to ensure that adequate baselines are used not only for chance but also for single-criterion classification. Children who are using only one criterion will be successful some of the time, probably above chance in most tasks, and baselines for such performances should be established. The other traditional multiple-classification task is matrix completion, which consists of partly completing a matrix in which (say) the rows vary in color and the columns vary in shape, then asking the child to complete the matrix.

There are numerous studies indicating that children first make multiple classifications between 5 and 8 years (Blasingame & McManis, 1977; Caruso & Resnick, 1972; Jacobs & Vandevenfer, 1971; Mackay, Fraser, & Ross, 1970; McLaughlin & Brinley, 1973; Parker, Sperr, & Rieff, 1972; Smedslund, 1964). There are a number of studies showing high success rates by children under 5 years on single criterion classification but low success rates on multiple classification (Denny, 1972; Kofsky, 1966; Kuhn, 1972; Overton & Brodzinsky, 1972; Overton & Jordan, 1971; Parker, Rieff, & Sperr, 1971).

An important issue when children fail a task is whether the failure represents some basic inability or simply reflects lack of knowledge. This question can be answered in part by ensuring that children have the requisite

One Attribute

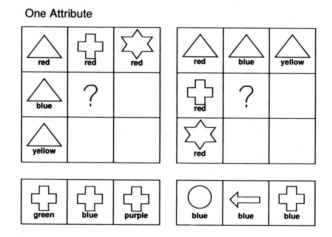

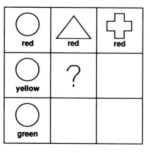

Two Attribute

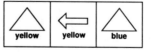

FIG. 8.1.   Modified matrix-completion tasks. From Halford (1980). Reprinted by permission of Elsevier Science Publishers B.V., North Holland.

knowledge of the task. This was done in a learning-set study of multiple classification (Halford, 1980), using the type of problems shown in Fig. 8.1. A matrix was presented with five elements, comprising one row and one column, in place, and children aged 3, 4, 5, or 6 years were asked to fill one square at a time. They were also given three choices to fill each square. There were two main conditions. In the one-attribute condition it was necessary to consider only shape or color, but not both. In the first example given in Fig. 8.1 all the choice elements are crosses, and it is only necessary to choose the right color. In the other one-attribute example all the choice elements are blue, and it is only necesary to choose the right shape. In the two-attribute task the choice elements vary in shape and color, both of which must be considered to make a correct choice. The one-attribute tasks are really single-criterion classification, because only one criterion, shape or color, has to be considered in any one task, whereas the two-attribute task is a multiple-classification task. Therefore the experiment contrasts single- and multiple-criterion classification within the same situation, and with other factors controlled.

The children were given extensive training in performing the task. First, they were given feedback for each choice they made. For example, in the two-attribute task in Fig. 8.1, if the blue triangle was chosen, the experimenter discussed the choice with the child, whose attention was drawn to the fact that it was the same shape as the figure above it, but not the same color as the figure beside it. The child was then asked to make a further choice, and the procedure repeated until the correct element was chosen. Then the next square was indicated for filling, three new choice cards were provided, and the procedure was repeated. Filling the four squares in this way constituted one trial. The next trial began by removing the four elements from the squares filled by the child, then repeating the procedure. A problem was complete when the child could fill all four squares without error. The next problem was begun by setting a new matrix and repeating the procedure. This was continued for 16 problems, or until all four cells of a new problem could be filled without error on the first trial.

All children learned every problem; that is, all were able to choose the correct element to fill each vacant square after training. Furthermore, all children succeeded in reaching the learning set criterion for the one-attribute task. That is, they all reached the point where they could choose the correct elements to fill all four cells of a new one-attribute problem. However, only children with mental age over 5 years reached the learning set criterion for the two-attribute task. Most of the younger children made no interproblem progress on the two-attribute task.

Several points can be made from these observations. The first is that it is essential to ensure that the required knowledge is available to children before assessing their capabilities. Many children who failed on early problems succeeded on later problems, indicating that their early failure reflected inadequate knowledge of some kind. Perhaps they did not fully understand the task demands, perhaps they were unfamiliar with the matrix format or with the concept of classifying by shape and color, or perhaps they lacked relevant strategies or metacognitive skills. The procedure did not differentiate between different types of knowledge, but to the extent that children improved their performance as a result of training, knowledge of some kind is implicated.

The second point, however, is that knowledge was not the whole story. Most of the younger children, although they succeeded in all aspects of the one-attribute task and mastered all the two-attribute tasks after training specifically on each task, never got to the point where they could correctly fill the cells of a two-attribute matrix when it was first presented. Thus the factor that differentiated children according to age was ability to transfer the principle of the two-attribute task.

It might be argued that this ability might still be attributed to knowledge. Carey (1990) provided a rather dramatic demonstration of the importance of knowledge reorganization to the problem solving of even sophisticated adults. It might seem reasonable to suggest that this factor is so powerful that it can never be eliminated as an explanation for age differences in performance. Another possibility is that older children might have a strategy for processing first one dimension, then the other, and finally combining the two. For example, in the two-attribute task in Fig. 8.1, they might first decide that the middle square should be filled by a triangle, then that it has to be yellow, then respond "yellow triangle."

I certainly would not want to deny the enormous importance of knowledge reorganization and strategies in cognitive development. However, there is grave danger in using these concepts as blanket explanations for all age differences. If all age effects for which there is no apparent explanation are simply attributed to "knowledge reorganization" or "strategies," then theories based on these concepts become untestable. To make them testable, it is necessary to specify the type of knowledge reorganization, or strategy, that would explain the age differences. Experiments can then be performed to see whether the ages differ in these particular knowledge structures or strategies. If they do not, the theory is falsified. Without such specification, however, the theory cannot be falsified, and it has a spurious aura of power as a result.

A further point is that knowledge and capacity explanations are not mutually exclusive, because acquisition of knowledge does not logically exclude growth of capacity. Furthermore, they are not even independent. Recall from chapter 5 that strategies based on understanding are developed from a concept of the task. For strategies to be developed in this way the child must be able to represent the task structure, and this imposes processing loads that depend on the dimensionality of the concept. Therefore, the fact that older children have strategies that younger children lack does not logically eliminate age differences in capacity. Where children of a given age persistently fail to acquire adequate strategies, despite mastery of every component of the task, there are good reasons for entertaining the hypothesis that they lack the capacity to represent the task structure.

The failure of the younger children is difficult to attribute to inability to understand task demands, because all children learned individual problems in both one- and two-attribute conditions. Odom and Cunningham (1980) suggested that the development of classification might depend on more dimensions becoming salient, and their data indicate that unidimensional and multidimensional classification is a function of salience. It is difficult to see how salience could account for these results, because children coped readily enough with either dimension alone. It is the ability to integrate two dimensions, or two attributes, that created problems. Odom and Cunningham also found that 4-year-olds failed to perform better than chance on the two-dimensional problems.

These data provide tight constraints on attempts to explain age differences in this task. Why should children fail to transfer the principle of the two-attribute task when they can master individual two-attribute tasks and can both learn and transfer one-attribute tasks?

First we must consider what is entailed in performing the matrix-completion task. Just matching a stimulus to others in the same row or same column is not sufficient to constrain the correct solution. For example in the two-attribute task in Fig. 8.1 we could fill the center square with a red circle, because red matches the color of the figure above and shape of the figure to the left, but this would not be the correct solution. In order to solve the problem one must notice which attribute changes in each dimension. Shape changes across the columns, so as we move from the left to the center column circle is transformed to triangle. Color changes down the rows, from red to yellow to green. Therefore the mental model that is needed is one that coordinates changes in rows and columns. The basics of such a model are shown in Fig. 8.2. Now let us try to trace the performance of a child participating in the two-attribute matrix-completion task. On the first problem she finds that the center square should be filled by a yellow triangle. There are several hypotheses that might be adopted to account for this. These are that the item should be:

yellow

triangle

yellow and triangle

same color as the item to the left

same shape as the item above

Two-attribute Task

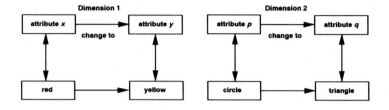

Problem

One-attribute Task

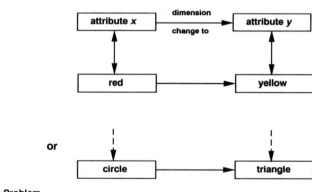

Problem

FIG. 8.2. Mental models required for matrix-completion tasks.

same color as the item to the left, and same shape as the item above

change shape from Column 1 to Column 2

change color from Row 1 to Row 2

change shape from Column 1 to Column 2, and change color from Row 1 to Row 2

change attribute x to attribute y from Column 1 to Column 2

change attribute p to attribute q from Row 1 to Row 2

Any of these hypotheses would fit this problem. Suppose, however, that the next problem learned had the same layout as the first one-attribute matrix in Fig. 8.1 (the same matrices can be used for one-attribute and two-attribute problems, because only the choice cards differ). The hypotheses that would be viable for this problem, taken alone, are:

blue

cross

blue and cross

same shape as the item above

same color as the item to the left

same shape as the item above

same color as the item to the left and same shape as the item above

All six hypotheses are viable for any one problem. However, two problems eliminate the specific hypotheses, such as yellow, blue, cross, or triangle. All the same-color and same-shape hypotheses remain viable. Single-attribute hypotheses would be eliminated where a solution based on one attribute is attempted and found to be incorrect. For example a participant whose hypothesis for the two-attribute matrix in Fig. 8.2 was "same color as item on the left" might put a yellow arrow in the center square, and the resulting negative feedback would disconfirm this hypothesis. The only hypothesis that would survive a series of two-attribute problems would be:

change attribute x attribute y from Column 1 to Column 2

change attribute p to attribute q from Row 1 to Row 2

All other hypotheses would be weakened because they would predict answers that would fail to be confirmed. The surviving hypothesis is the mental model of matrix completion that the child acquires from learning-set training. Transfer to new problems is achieved by mapping the elements of a new problem into the mental model. That is, an attribute must be found that changes from one value to another in each dimension. The structure mapping required is shown in Fig. 8.2. For the two-attribute task, there are two changes, equivalent to two binary relations, that must be mapped from model to problem, and so a system mapping is required. For the one-attribute task, only one relation must be mapped, so a relational mapping is required. The type of neural-net structure required to represent the multiple-classification concept is shown in Fig. 8.3. It is necessary to represent a change from one attribute (the input attribute) to another (the output attribute) on the same dimension. Because this must be done for more than one dimension, the dimension must be represented. Finally, the task must be represented, to dis-

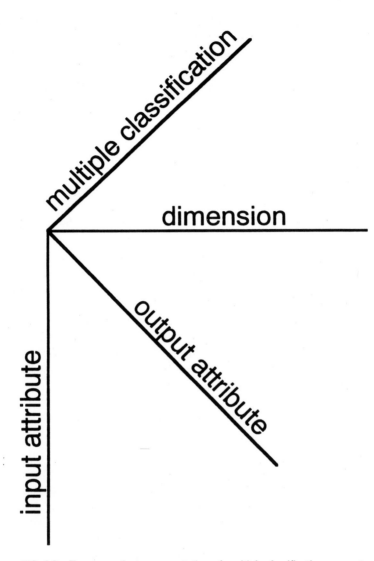

FIG. 8.3.   Tensor-product representation of multiple-classification concept.

tinguish it from other tasks. In terms of the dimensionality metric in chapter 3, the task is three-dimensional, and the neural-net representation is based on a Rank 4 tensor product. The single criterion classification task can be represented by collapsing over the dimension vector in Fig. 8.3, thereby reducing it from a Rank 4 to a Rank 3 tensor product. A child who could not represent a three-dimensional concept (with a Rank 4 tensor product), but who could represent a two-dimensional concept (with a Rank 3 tensor product) would have no difficulty with single-criterion tasks, but would not progress to multiple-classification tasks.

Hierarchical Classification

The most commonly investigated hierarchical classification task is class inclusion; for example, the idea that apples and pears are included in fruit. However, inclusions can be combined to form hierarchies; apples and pears are included in fruit, fruit and meat are included in food, and so on. Understanding inclusion is commonly assessed by asking children to compare the superordinate set with one of the subsets; for example, are there more apples or more fruit?

Piaget (1950) claimed that children did not understand inclusion until they reached the concrete operations stage at 7–8 years, but Winer (1980) reviewed the literature and concluded that the age of acquisition was even later. I also examined the literature to determine the earliest age at which class inclusion had been validly demonstrated by any study and found there was no solid evidence that it was understood before approximately 5 years (Halford, 1982). Some of the more crucial studies are considered in detail later in this section.

Major research efforts have been made to try and explain why young children make errors on the inclusion problem. Piaget's explanation was that children lacked grouping I, additive composition of classes, until they reached the age of 7–8 years, but there is little evidence that these groupings exist or that they could explain children's reasoning ability (Osherson, 1974a; Sheppard, 1978). Consequently several alternative models have been proposed.

Klahr and Wallace (1976), Trabasso, Isen, Dolecki, McLanahan, Riley, and Tucker (1978) and Wilkinson (1976) all proposed that the problem is at least partly in the way sets are quantified. Suppose, for example, that the child is shown 10 houses, 7 of which are white and 3 are red. Answering the question, "Are there more houses or white houses?" depends on quantifying the houses (10), quantifying the white houses (7), and because $10 > 7$, saying there are more houses. The difficulty occurs because children know that objects must not be counted twice, so the seven white houses are not counted as houses; that is because they have been counted as part of the subset, they are not counted as part of the superordinate set. The result is that when houses are quantified, only the nonwhite houses are counted, which results in number of white houses = 7, number of houses = 3, therefore there are more white houses.

There are doubts, however, as to the appropriateness of these quantification models, as I pointed out in detail elsewhere (Halford, 1982). First, it is somewhat implausible to suggest the task is always performed by counting. For example, I know there are more children than boys, even though I cannot count all the children and boys in the world. We know there are more children than boys because of the relationships between the sets. Because boys are included in children, and there are children who are not boys (i.e., boys is a proper subset of children), it follows logically that there are necessarily more children than boys. The quantification models of inclusion reasoning do not capture this logic, and they do not explain why we know that, for example, there must be more children than boys, without knowing the actual number of elements in any of the sets. There is also data that casts doubt on the quantification explanation (Dean, Chabaud, & Bridges, 1981), as I discussed elsewhere (Halford, 1982). Furthermore, Brainerd and Kingma (1985) found that class-inclusion reasoning was independent of recall of set numerosities, suggesting that inferences were not based on set quantification.

A major alternative explanation has been that children do not recognize that the inclusion question refers to the superordinate set. For example, given 10 houses, 7 white and 3 red, when asked "more houses or more white houses?" they do not recognize that "more houses" refers to the superordinate set, "all houses" (Youssef & Guardo, 1972; Kalil, Youssef, & Lerner, 1974; Shipley, 1979; Winer, 1974).

The basic idea here is that even adults might respond to an inclusive comparison (superordinate vs. subset) as an exclusive or distributive comparison (subset vs. subset). Imagine, for example, that you are asked whether there are more dogs or more animals in your neighbourhood. Because this is an unusual form of question, you might well assume that the questioner meant "more dogs or more other kinds of animals (such as cats)." If you happened to live in a neighbourhood with lots of dogs, you might well answer "more dogs." The questioner would probably need to tell you that she really meant animals including dogs; that is, that a superordinate–subordinate comparison was intended. Brainerd and Kaszor (1974) did find that children who answered inclusion questions incorrectly were able to recall the question correctly, but accurate recall is not really evidence against the misinterpretation hypothesis.

Markman and Seibert (1976) proposed that collective terms such as "family," "bunch" and "pile" would make it clearer that the superordinate class was meant (e.g., "the white houses or the whole pile of houses"). They found improved performance when collective terms were used. However, Dean, Chabaud, and Bridges (1981) suggested that the large number connotation of collective terms might have biased children towards the set with most elements.

A related hypothesis is that children interpret the inclusion question as requiring a second modifier for the superordinate set (Grieve & Garton, 1981). The question "more white houses or more houses" is interpreted as though a modifier had been intended for both sets, and becomes "more white houses or more red houses?" Grieve and Garton presented children with two superordinate sets, each with two subsets. For example; four horses, three black and one white, and four cows, two black and two white. They found that children answered symmetric questions (black horses vs. black cows; black horses vs. white horses) better than asymmetric questions (horses vs. black cows; horses vs. black horses). The asymmetric questions lack a modifier for the superordinate class, which evidently causes children to interpret it as though a modifier were present (white horses vs. black horses).

The symmetric–asymmetric manipulation is, however, confounded with a level-of-hierarchy factor. All the symmetric questions refer to sets at the same level of the hierarchy. Both sets might be at the superordinate level (horses vs. cows), or both at the subordinate level (black horses vs. white horses; black horses vs. black cows), but either way, both sets are at the same level. All the asymmetric questions refer to sets at different levels of the hierarchy. For example "horses versus black cows" and "horses versus black horses" contrast a superordinate set with a subordinate set, or with a set at a lower level of the hierarchy.

Halford and Leitch (1989) obviated this problem by designing a hierarchy in which comparisons between levels could be either symmetric or asymmetric. For example they presented 27 horses, 15 small and 12 large, and the small horses consisted of 9 black and 6 white. They asked both asymmetric inclusion questions (horses vs. small horses) and symmetric inclusion questions (small horses vs. black horses). They found inclusion questions to be consistently more difficult than other questions, irrespective of whether they were symmetric or asymmetric. Halford and Leitch also contrasted minor-subset with major-subset comparisons. On the misinterpretation hypothesis, minor subset comparisons (more horses or more large horses?) are more likely to be answered correctly than major subset comparisons (more horses or more small horses?) because in the former cases the superordinate "horses" is reinterpreted as the larger subset "small horses" and in the latter it is reinterpreted as the smaller subset "large horses." They found that minor-subset questions were answered more accurately than major subset questions at all ages, consistent with the misinterpretation hypothesis. However, this factor was modified by an age $\times$ asymmetric–symmetric $\times$ major–minor subset interaction. For the 6- and 8-year-olds only, the tendency to perform better with minor subsets was more pronounced with the symmetric items. This suggests that the tendency to misinterpret the inclusion question as a subset comparison is greater with symmetric questions, contrary to Grieve and Garton (1981). Furthermore, this factor had more influence on children over 5 years, suggesting that it was not the cause of the age effect.

Therefore, although linguistic factors might sometimes result in the superordinate/subordinate question being misinterpreted as a subordinate/subordinate question, this is not the whole explanation for the errors that occur, and it certainly does not explain why young children have such persistent difficulties with this task. The evidence shows that the inclusion concept per se is a cause of difficulty, expecially for young children, and we still have to explain why this is so.

Another explanation is that young children fail because the task is unfamiliar to them. According to this hypothesis the problem can be overcome by adapting the task so young children can relate to it more readily. Siegel, McCabe, Brand, and Matthews (1978) showed 3- to 4-year-old children three smarties and two jelly beans and asked whether they would rather eat the smarties or the candy. Performance was significantly improved relative to the standard form of the question. However, this presents a binary choice, and a chance baseline would be 50%. Yet most of the results that were reported as positive were at or below this level. For example, the authors reported, "For the 4-year-olds, significantly more children were likely to pass the eat-candy task than the more-candy task, 50% versus 26%" (Siegel et al., 1978, p. 690). Because none of the performances was shown to be above baseline, these data cannot be accepted as demonstrating knowledge of class inclusion.

McGarrigle, Grieve, and Hughes (1978) used a number of techniques to improve the class-inclusion performance of young children. For example, in their Experiments 1 and 2 they obtained more correct answers when an adjective was used to emphasize that the question referred to the superordinate set (more black cows or more sleeping cows, where black and white cows were included in sleeping cows). However, the highest proportion correct was .52, and because the questions presented a binary choice, this is not significantly above a chance baseline.

The most interesting and most widely cited data presented by McGarrigle et al. come from their Experiments 4 and 5. They used an array with four red steps to a chair and two further white steps to a table. A teddy bear was placed at the end of the array, and comprehension of inclusion was assessed in Experiment 4 by asking, "Are there more (red) steps to go to the chair or more steps to go to the table?" Both forms of the question were asked, in counterbalanced order, after which the children were asked, "Is it further to go to the chair or further to go to the table?" Then the first two questions were asked again in the same way as before. The procedure in Experiment 5 was similar except that all the steps were white, and the child was asked, "Are there more (white) steps to go to the chair or more steps to go to the table?"

Of the eight questions designed to measure inclusion in these two experiments, four produced results that were significantly better than chance in children aged 3–5 years (by my calculation, because McGarrigle et al. did not consider chance). However, three of the four questions showing positive results were asked after the question "Is it further to go to the chair or further to go to the table?" This question could have encouraged the children to interpret the task as a comparison of two distances.

All the questions that McGarrigle et al. intended as class-inclusion tests can be answered by comparing the distance to the chair with the distance to the table. Furthermore, most of the positive results were obtained after this encoding had been encouraged by asking a distance question. Therefore, it cannot be concluded that children's performance on these tasks demonstrates understanding of class inclusion.

A study by L. Smith (1979) showed that 4- to 7-year-old children could answer questions about inclusion hierarchies. The questions were either inclusion questions ("Are all dogs animals? Are all animals dogs?") or class inference questions, ("A pug is a kind of dog. Does a pug have to be an animal?") Younger children performed better when they were not asked questions involving the quantifier "some" ("Are some animals dogs?"). Nevertheless, even when this factor was removed, the questions remained difficult for the 4-year-olds. It should also be noted that the 4-year-olds came from middle- and upper-middle-class suburbs. Because performance is a function of individual as well as developmental differences, children who are above average would be expected to succeed earlier. These data do not necessarily contradict findings that the task is normally difficult for children under 5 years.

The processes involved in this task may well be different from those in the normal class-inclusion test. There is nothing wrong with that, of course, but it is important not to lump together tasks that entail different underlying processes, because that can only result in fallacies and confusions. I argue that class inclusion is difficult because it entails mapping the problem into a schema that requires a three-dimensional representation, whereas it is doubtful that this is required in the task used by Smith. Because people already know that dogs are animals, once a pug is linked to a dog, it is a matter of network search to recognize that a pug is an animal. Therefore it appears that class inclusion requires structure mapping, whereas in Smith's task the answer can be retrieved from semantic memory. Although the paper by L. Smith is a very interesting exploration of children's semantic knowledge about inclusion hierarchies, more information about processes is needed before we can decide whether it has implications for children's understanding of class inclusion as usually conceived.

Hodkin (1987) performed an elegant analysis of the proportion of responses made by inclusion logic, by subclass comparison, and by guessing, in 4-, 6- and 8-year-old children. She asked children questions comparing the superordinate with the larger subclass, and questions comparing the superordinate with the smaller subclass. Because the only way to be wrong on the superordinate-smaller subclass comparison is by guessing, the errors on this task can be used to estimate the proportion of guessed responses. With guessing partialled out, the only way to be correct on the superordinate-larger subclass comparison is by applying inclusion logic, so the proportion using inclusion logic can be estimated. Responses to the superordinate-smaller subordinate comparison can be right by guessing, by inclusion logic, or by subclass comparison. Because the first two have been estimated, the third can be estimated. She found that nonverbal procedures increased the number of correct responses, as conventionally defined, but that this was due to a higher rate of guessing. There was no evidence that 4-year-olds used inclusion logic.

We still have the problem, therefore, that children under 5 years have difficulty with class inclusion, and existing theories do not appear to provide an adequate explanation. In the next section I propose a new model of class-inclusion reasoning, and I suggest that it explains why class inclusion should be difficult and is consistent with some important contemporary theories of deductive inference.

Processes in Class Inclusion Reasoning

Unlike transitivity, discussed in chapter 7, where there have been a number of successful process models, the processes entailed in class inclusion have remained largely mysterious. Set-quantifications theories, as discussed in the last section, are relevant to some aspects of the task, but they cannot capture the essence of inclusion logic, because we know the superordinate has more members than a subclass without knowing how many members are in either set. Furthermore, Campbell (1991) showed that class inclusion does not have set quantification as a prerequisite.

Rabinowitz, Howe, and Lawrence (1989) proposed a model based on the assembly of a number of subskills (such as interpretation of the question). The subskills impose a load on working memory, as also does their assembly into a solution procedure. As the skills become more automatic the load diminishes. I agree that skills are developed, but I believe their development depends on a concept of the task, so it is necessary to determine what this concept is. Brainerd and Reyna (1990b) proposed that class inclusion depends on the cardinal ordering principle (Russell, 1903), which states that the more inclusive set is necessarily the more numerous. This principle comes closer to capturing the essence of class-inclusion logic than previous proposals, but it does not appear to be a plausible mental model. It is an abstract logico-mathematical concept, and, as we saw in chapter 7, there is little evidence that human reasoning is based on concepts of that kind. Furthermore, it is quite unclear how young children would acquire this principle, because even most adults have not heard of it. Children are very unlikely to have been taught the principle explicitly, and it is hard to see how they would induce an implicit knowledge of it from life experience. I propose that class-inclusion reasoning is based on a schema induced from experience in a similar manner to the pragmatic-reasoning schemas discussed in chapter 7.

We can define inclusion reasoning as the inference that if nonempty sets A and A′ are included in B (i.e., each of A and A′ are proper subsets of B), then B > A and B > A′. I propose that the inference is made by mapping the problem into a familiar, real-life schema that has been acquired through experience. The appropriate relation is then retrieved from the schema and applied to the problem using the mapping rules. First we will consider the properties that an inclusion schema needs to have, then we will consider how it can be used to make the inclusion inference.

The inclusion schema is really defined by the relations between the component sets, as shown in Fig. 8.4A. An inclusion schema must comprise the idea that there is a superordinate set, with two or more (nonempty) subsets.

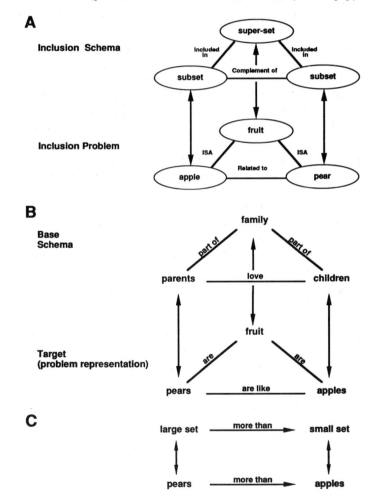

FIG. 8.4. Structure mappings for inclusion concept.

The person need not explicitly represent the fact that one set is a superordinate and the others are subordinates. Any schema that is isomorphic to the class-inclusion schema in Fig. 8.4A would theoretically be adequate. In addition to this logical requirement, a schema must be known to the child, and it must be possible to retrieve the relevant relations from it.

An example of a real-life schema that might be used for inclusion is the family, because it comprises the subsets of parents and children, as shown in Fig. 8.4B. It is a schema that is well known to young children, and the small set size makes it easy to retrieve the relevant relations. For example, if there are two parents and one child, the number of members in the family (three) is within the subitizing range, and even young children should be able to recognize that the family set (three) contains more members than the set of parents (two) or child(ren) (one).

Another possible schema for inclusion would be a path divided into two parts, as in the experiment of McGarrigle et al. (1978) discussed earlier. Their task entailed four steps to a chair and a further two steps to a table, so steps-to-chair are included in steps-to-table. There are difficulties in using this task as a test of inclusion reasoning, as I pointed out earlier, because it is possible that it could be performed by length comparison. An interesting point, that gives considerable insight into the implications of structure mapping theory is that it can serve as a schema for inclusion, even though it is not itself a valid test of inclusion. The reason is that it is isomorphic to the inclusion concept. Recall from chapter 2 that a mental model need only be structurally isomorphic to the task, and it does not need to share other properties of the task. Therefore the divided-path task can serve as a mental model for inclusion, although it is not an inclusion task itself.

For inclusion reasoning to be carried out using the divided-path task as a schema, the inclusive set (fruit in Fig. 8.4) would be mapped into the total path, and the subsets (apples, pears in Fig. 8.4) would be mapped into the path components. For example, apples could be mapped into the path component from the teddy to the chair, and pears could be mapped into the path component from the chair to the table. Another plausible schema would be the *part–whole schema*, which occurs in many situations, including arithmetic word problems, to be discussed later, and might well be induced from life experience.

The inclusion schema is used as a mental model by mapping the problem into it as shown in Fig. 8.4. Then the relation "superset greater than subset" can be retrieved from the model. It is applied to the problem using the mapping rules; because fruit is mapped into the superset, and apples is mapped into a subset, and superset is more than subset, it follows that fruit is more than apples.

The mapping of the fruit-versus-apples problem into a mental model of inclusion permits the inference that fruit is more than apples to be drawn.

Notice that the size relation between fruit and apples is difficult to obtain otherwise, because we do not know how many pieces of fruit, or how many apples, exist. On the other hand we do know that a whole path is more than part of that path or, more generally, that the whole of any object is more than a part of that object. This relation can be obtained by inspection of the object or by inspection of an image of the object. A small child is also more likely to know that his family contains more members than the set of his parents because the number of members is small enough to be recognized directly, by subitizing. These familiar situations, in which the relevant relation can be readily retrieved, can be used as mental models of unfamiliar problems, or problems in which the appropriate relation is less obvious.

If we accept that inclusion inferences are made by mapping the problem into a pragmatic-reasoning schema in this way, we are led to a new explanation for the difficulty of the concept. The difficulty occurs because a system mapping is required, and this imposes a high processing load, as we saw in chapters 2 and 3. The problem is to decide which set should be mapped into the superordinate and which into the subordinate components of the mental model. This can only be decided by examining the relations between sets, because no set is inherently a superordinate or subordinate. For example "fruit" is a superordinate when compared with apples and pears, as in Fig. 8.4, but is a subordinate when compared with meat and food, because fruit and meat are both food. We only know a set is a subordinate or a superordinate when we examine its relations to other sets.

To qualify as a superordinate, a set must have at least two nonempty subsets. That is, we know fruit is the superordinate in Fig. 8.4 because it has subsets of apples, pears, and other specific fruits. To qualify as a subset, a set must be part of a superordinate set, and there must be at least one other subset of that superordinate. That is, we can only identify super- and subordinates by examining at least two relations to other sets in each case. Because identification of super- and subordinates depends on compositions of relations, it is a system mapping, as defined in chapters 2 and 3.

The class-inclusion concept is a ternary relation, because it is a relation between a superordinate and two subsets (superordinate, subset$_1$, subset$_2$), and is a three-dimensional concept. The type of neural-net representation required is shown in Fig. 8.5. It is a Rank 4 tensor product with vectors representing the superordinate and each of the subsets, with, of course, a vector representing the inclusion concept. Notice that superordinates with more than two subsets can still be handled by this representation because the subsets can always be partititioned into one subset and its complement. For example, if fruit consists of apples, bananas, pears, and oranges, we can still take apples as one set, and bananas, pears and oranges as the complement. Alternatively, we can take apples and bananas as a set, with pears and oranges as the complement. The important thing is that the relations

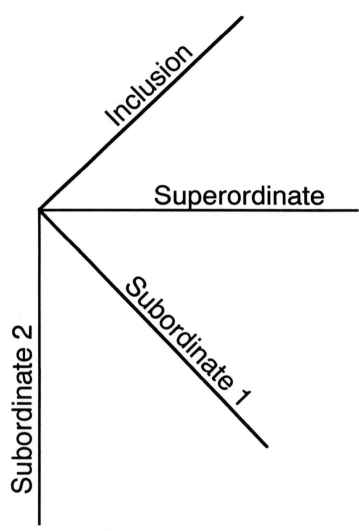

FIG. 8.5. Tensor-product representation for inclusion concept.

of inclusion and complementation must be represented, because these are the essence of the concept, and this can be done using the structure in Fig. 8.5. What would happen if a child could not represent the three-dimensional inclusion concept? According to the argument in chapter 6, he or she would probably default to a lower dimensional representation, with a binary rather than a ternary relation. What ternary relation would this be? There is an obvious candidate—the size relation between two of the sets. Furthermore the larger the size difference, the more salient would be the representation of this relation, and the more likely it would be to be chosen. The type of mapping that would be entailed is shown in Fig. 8.4C. It is well recognized that children often err by comparing two sets, but we may have been mistaken in assuming that this was the *cause* of the failure. It seems more likely that it is a *default reaction*, caused by inability to represent all dimensions of the problem in parallel.

Notice that, according to this formulation, the difficulty of inclusion reasoning arises from the task of identifying superordinate and subordinate sets. Recall that this has been a recurring theme in other explanations for the difficulty of inclusion. The models of Klahr and Wallace (1976), Trabasso et al. (1978), and Wilkinson (1976) proposed that children quantify the second subset rather than the superordinate set, because they misapply counting rules. Other explanations have been based on linguistic factors. One, as discussed earlier, was that people interpret the inclusion question as a subclass comparison because it is more normal to interpret such questions that way. Another linguistic explanation was that children assume there is a missing modifier and therefore adopt the modifier that refers to the smaller subset (Grieve & Garton, 1981). All these explanations have one important feature in common: They all suggest that the process of identifying superordinate and subsets is difficult, though the reasons they give for this vary. The present formulation agrees that identification of superordinate and subsets is the major source of difficulty, but for a different reason. The reason is the structural complexity of the inclusion concept, arising from the fact that it is based on relations between three sets.

Figure 8.5 specifies the type of representation required for inclusion, in PDP architecture. As with transitivity, discussed in chapters 4 and 7, problem solving skills can be developed under the guidance of a concept of the task. There does not appear to be a comprehensive model of how this is done, but there are a number of studies that provide important clues. The work of Rabinowitz et al. (1989), discussed earlier, addresses the assembly of subskills, though there is no guidance from a concept of the task, as there is with the transitive-inference model discussed in chapter 7. Thornton (1982) showed that classification strategies continue to develop between ages 5 and 10. If we accept evidence that children can represent inclusion and also multiple classification by age 5, this implies that considerable work must be done to assemble flexible, broadly applicable strategies. Furthermore, this strategy development is probably guided by linguistic cues, with superordinate sets being indicated by nouns, and subordinates by adjective-noun combinations (Waxman, 1990).

Testing the Structure-Mapping Hypothesis

The only theory that seems to explain why class inclusion is so difficult, especially for young children, is that it entails representing three dimensions in parallel. That is, the structural complexity that is inherent in the problem is the primary cause of the difficulty. If a child cannot represent the three-dimensional inclusion concept, he would not be able to map a problem into an appropriate schema. If the process of mapping sets into superordinate and subordinate nodes of the inclusion schema is the major source of difficulty in inclusion reasoning, this same difficulty should be observed in a problem that is an isomorph of inclusion, because an isomorph would have the same structure, without necessarily sharing other properties of the inclusion task. A test of this hypothesis was made by Leitch (1989) and Halford and Leitch (1989).

The mininum case of an inclusion hierarchy would consist of two elements that have at least one attribute in common and at least one on which they differ. For example, a red triangle and a red square are an inclusion hierarchy, because both are red, but one is triangular and the other square. Thus, triangle and square are included in red. The experimental technique of Halford and Leitch utilized minimal inclusion hierarchies of this kind. They can be mapped into the inclusion schema as shown in Fig. 8.6. To obviate the difficulties caused by the unusual linguistic form of the inclusion question as discussed earlier, a different task was devised. Children were shown two dolls, called Sally and John, and told that they like to have toys that are a bit the same and a bit different. The child was asked to help the experimenter find a present for Sally and John, one they would like. The children were shown a series of pairs that were of three kinds, inclusive, identical, or disjoint, as shown in Fig. 8.6. They were asked whether Sally and John would like each pair and to give a reason. Then feedback was given, pointing out the shared and/or disjoint features of each pair, and discussing whether they were suitable for Sally and John.

Children aged 3–6 years received four problems each comprising one trial of each type. To allow for the possibility that children might fail the task because of lack of knowledge, the learning curve over the four blocks was examined. There was a significant blocks-by-age interaction; the 6-year-olds improved, and their performance was virtually perfect on the fourth block. The 4-year-olds, by contrast, showed no improvement, and their performance never exceeded chance. This task had none of the linguistic properties of the inclusion question, but it did require children to map a set of objects into a schema consisting of one common attribute and two distinct attributes, and that is therefore isomorphic to the inclusion schema. Children less than 5 years old had considerable difficulty doing this, which supports the hypothesis that the difficulty young children have with the inclusion schema is at least partly due to the complexity of mapping the problem elements into the schema.

According to structure-mapping theory, the difficulty should be at least partly caused by the processing loads imposed by system mapping. This was tested by Halford and Leitch (1989) using the easy-to-hard paradigm described in chapter 4. Children aged 3–8 years performed an easy and a hard classifi-

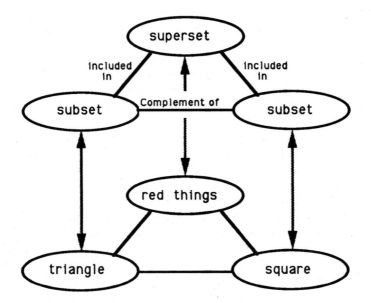

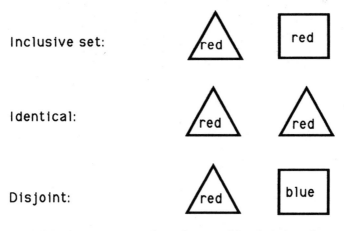

FIG. 8.6. Class-inclusion analog task, mapped into inclusion schema.

cation, and a secondary task was used to assess processing capacity. The hard task was similar to the one used in the previous experiment and required children to recognize a pair of stimuli that formed a minimal inclusion hierarchy, such as two red objects, one square and one triangular. The easy task required children to recognize whether stimuli were the same (both same color or both same shape) or were different (two different colors or two different shapes). The secondary task was probe reaction time, and consisted of a tone to which children had to respond by blowing a puff of air into a microphone as quickly as possible.

According to easy-to-hard theory (Hunt & Lansman, 1982), if the inclusion task is capacity limited, performance on it should be predicted by performance when the easy classification task and the secondary task are performed together. The reason is that the secondary task indicates the processing capacity that is left spare when performing the easy classification task. This measure should predict the hard classification task, if it is capacity limited. Performance on the easy classification task and the secondary task, when performed alone, is partialled out to remove any variance due to task similarities. Positive evidence of capacity limitation was obtained; that is, performance on the easy classification task performed jointly with the secondary task predicted performance on the inclusion isomorph task, with performance on the two predictors performed separately partialled out.

The inclusion isomorph task, although it contained none of the linguistic difficulties associated with the traditional inclusion question, continued to be difficult for children under 5 years. However, all the children readily discriminated between pairs that were the same or pairs that were different. The fact that they could do this shows they could cope with the task format and rules out most explanations in terms of task variables. However, the processing load imposed by the system mapping entailed in the inclusion task was simply too great for the younger children.

Comparison of Classification with Categorical Inferences

In chapter 7, we examined studies by Gelman and Markman (1987) and Gelman (1988) that showed that even 3- to 4-year-old children could make inferences based on category membership, largely independently of appearance. For example, if told that a cat could see in the dark, they inferred that another cat could do likewise, but that a skunk that resembled a cat would not do so. We need to consider how this task differs from the classification tasks we have considered in this chapter and why the latter pose difficulties not posed by the former.

The inference tasks used by Gelman test children's knowledge of the distribution of properties within and between categories and of constraints between properties. For example, a property such as seeing in the dark will be shared by other objects in the same category, but it will not spread to other categories. On the other hand, a property such as being cold is not shared even within categories. Then there are constraints between categories, so that if objects have the property of being living things, they will also have certain other properties, such as having a particular internal substance. Knowledge of these constraints was also tested in Gelman's work.

We need to consider the type of processes that could produce these inferences. Parallel-distributed storage processes would automatically provide information about the distribution of properties and of constraints between properties. Each property would be represented as a pattern of activation, and different patterns would be superimposed on the same set of connection weights. This would mean that the distribution of a set of properties over a set of exemplars of a category would be represented automatically as a direct result of the distributed storage system. Constraints between properties would be coded by the connection weights between patterns and would also be coded automatically. This can all be done using one or two vectors, and the high-dimensional representations used for multiple classification and class inclusion are not required.

The distribution of properties, and constraints between properties, would be represented in memory as a result of experience and could be retrieved directly. These tasks, therefore, do not require inferences based on mapping the task into a mental model, as is required for multiple classification or inclusion. It is the process of mapping into a mental model that imposes the processing load, and this explains why these tasks are difficult for young children, whereas inferences about the distribution of properties or constraints between properties are not difficult.

Summary of Classification

Categories can be formed in infancy, but classification by two criteria is more difficult. Multiple classification is possible earlier than Piaget's theory predicted but remains very difficult for children under 5 years because of the three-dimensional representation required for this concept. Class inclusion is also possible earlier than Piaget predicted; it is within the capacity of 5-year-olds, but it is very difficult below this age. A number of methodological improvements have eliminated false negatives and false positives from earlier tests, resulting in earlier attainment of both concepts, but some of the earliest claimed successes, such as class inclusion by 3-year-olds, are found to be flawed.

Multiple classification and class inclusion are both three-dimensional concepts that require to be represented by Rank 4 tensor products, as shown in Fig. 8.3 and 8.5. Representation of the concept can guide development of skills and strategies, but there are no comprehensive models of this process for classification so far. There is evidence that performance with concepts of the structural complexity of class inclusion is capacity limited. Where children lack the capacity to represent the structure of inclusion, they default to lower dimensional representations based on comparison of two sets. However, this should not be confused with the cause of class inclusion failure. Young children can make inductive inferences about categories before they make class inclusion inferences because the former require representations of lower dimensionality.

QUANTIFICATION

There appear to be three ideas that are basic to the concept of quantity. These are the idea of classification, the idea of order, and the idea of composition. Classification is important because quantities must be sorted into equivalence classes of equal magnitude. For example, all sets of two objects must be sorted into the equivalence class denoted by the cardinal number 2. Order is important because quantities have to be rank ordered with respect to magnitude. Composition is important because all quantities, except perhaps those of zero or unit magnitude, are composed of smaller quantities added together.

These properties are reflected in measurement scales. A nominal scale is equivalent to classification, with the classes designated by numbers. For example, if we divide people into male and female, and assign the value 0 to males and 1 to females, we have a nominal scale. An ordinal scale is clearly based on rank ordering so that, for example, positions in a race constitute an ordinal scale. The concept of order, as discussed in chapter 7, is relevant here. An interval scale has the additional properties that distances between scale values are specified, and the values are additive. The Celsius or Fahrenheit temperature scales are interval because temperatures are additive (20 degrees + 10 degrees = 30 degrees), but 0 degrees is not a true zero, and multiplication has no meaning (100 degrees is not twice as hot as 50 degrees). A ratio scale has a true zero point, and both addition and multiplication are defined. The Kelvin temperature scale is a ratio scale because it has a true zero (equivalent to -273 degrees celsius), and because multiplication is meaningful (100 degrees Kelvin is twice as hot as 50 degrees Kelvin).

There is no suggestion that children develop an understanding of quantification by learning the formal properties of measurement scales. Such an idea would run counter to everything I have said about the development of mental models. When discussing transitivity in chapter 7, I suggested that children acquire a concept of order by developing a prototype of an ordered set, rather than by learning the formal mathematical definition of an ordered set. In chapter 7, it was suggested that inferences are made not by reference to binary connectives of standard logic but by real-life schemas such as permission, obligation, and prediction. In a similar way, consideration of measurement scales helps us to define what needs to be understood to develop a concept of quantity but does not of itself tell us what mental models of quantity will be like.

Nevertheless it seems reasonable to expect that a mental model of quantity would entail the concepts of classification, order, and composition in some form. We would expect that children should be able to classify things according to magnitude or numerosity, that they would be able to rank order the resulting classes, and that they would have some idea that quantities are composed of other quantities added together. We have already explored the first two ideas, and it is clear that children can form classes from infancy and they have a concept of order from middle childhood.

They also have a partial concept of order, in the sense that they can at least order individual pairs, from 2–3 years of age. As discussed in chapter 6, Bullock and Gelman (1977) showed that children understand the idea that one small set is larger than another. They trained 2- to 4-year-olds to discriminate between one and two toy animals. The children were able to transfer the discrimination to sets of three versus four animals, showing that they recognized the magnitude relation between the sets. This entails representing a single binary relation, and it is a relational mapping. Children of this age have difficulty integrating relations so as to construct ordered sets of three or more items for the reasons given in chapters 3 and 7, but they can order elements in pairs.

Children also understand something of composition, at least from middle childhood. Bearison (1969) taught 5- to 6-year-olds conservation of liquids by demonstrating that a quantity was composed of a lot of smaller quantities added together, so children of this age must be capable of recognizing the additivity of quantity.

Development of anything more than a primitive concept of quantity requires a concept of number, because numbers, or quantitative labels of some sort, are required to measure quantities and bring order to the concept of quantity. In the next section, therefore, we will consider the child's concept of number.

Number

The mathematical concept of a number system comprises five properties:

1. There must be an addition operation
2. There must be a multiplication operation
3. Both operations must be commutative; that is, $a + b = b + a$; $a \times b = b \times a$.

4. Both operations must be associative; that is, $a + (b + c) = (a + b) + c$; $a \times (b \times c) = (a \times b) \times c$.
5. Multiplication is distributive with respect to addition; that is, $a(b + c) = ab + ac$.

This implies that a proper understanding of number must go considerably beyond the ideas of classification, order, and composition that are entailed in quantity. The concept of number entails the properties of the addition and multiplication operations and the ability to relate the operations to one another, as specified in the distributive law. As we later see, these properties of number have proven to be crucial to children's understanding of mathematics.

As with quantity, we cannot accept the mathematical definition of number as a specification of the way people normally understand it, because virtually no children and very few adults can utilize the formal definition. We must therefore ask what kind of mental models are used for number.

Mental Models of Number. A possible mental model for elementary number would be as shown in Fig. 8.7. Resnick (1983a) proposed that a preschool child's mental model of number takes the form of a number line, in which numbers correspond to positions in a string, with each number linked to its successor by the "next" relation. There is some evidence that mental models of small numbers may have essentially this form. Sekuler and Mierkiewicz (1977) found that latencies for comparing two numbers between 1 and 9 were inversely related to the difference between them. That is, the shortest latencies were for the most separated pairs, like 1 and 9, whereas the longest latencies were for the closest pairs, like 1 and 2, or 7 and 8. Furthermore, basically the same linear function fitted the data at all ages from kindergarten to adult, though the slope was steeper for younger children. These data would be consistent with a mental model consisting of an image of the numbers arranged in a line. Siegler and Robinson (1982) found that even 3-year-olds had some knowledge of the order of numbers. When asked to classify numbers as "big," "little," or "medium," the numbers they classified as little were smaller than those they classified as medium, which were smaller than those they classified as big. However, increased differentiation occurred with age.

Two multidimensional scaling studies also found small numbers were consistently ordered. Siegler and Robinson (1982) scaled similarity estimates of small numbers, using errors in comparisons as data. The idea is that the more similar the representations of two numbers, the more errors young children will make in comparing them. The scale values did reflect the rank ordering of the numbers, with numbers that were closer together in the rank order having more similar scale values. However, the best solution was two-

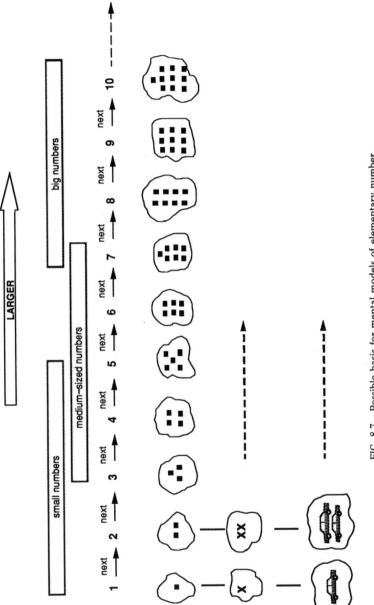

FIG. 8.7. Possible basis for mental models of elementary number.

dimensional rather than linear, and the numbers tended to form clusters, with 1, 2, 3 forming one cluster, 4, 5 another, and 6, 7, 8, 9 another.

Miller and Gelman (1983) scaled similarity judgments of kindergarten, third- and sixth-grade children, and adults on the numbers 0–9. They also found two-dimensional solutions, but with the numbers consistently ordered at all ages. The only exception was in the kindergarten children, where 0 fell outside the rank order based on magnitude. They also found that the numbers tended to fall into magnitude clusters, and the solutions for older children and adults tended to reflect other properties such as odd–even, and multiplicative relations, so that 2, 4, 8 tended to fall into one cluster.

It seems then that even 3- to 4-year-old children can not only recite the order of the number names but have some idea of relations between the magnitudes the numbers represent. That is, they can not only recite "one, two, three, . . ." but actually realize that "three" represents a larger magnitude, or larger set, than "two," and so on for other pairs.

Another important feature of number is cardinality, that is, the idea that all sets with the same number of elements have the same cardinal value. This idea is shown in Fig. 8.7, where each number is associated with examples of sets with the appropriate number of elements. Thus the number 2 is associated with two dots, two crosses, two cars, and so forth, signifying that the number 2 represents the equivalence class of all sets containing two elements. Piaget (1941/1952) contended that the conception of number depended on coordination of ordination and cardination. This idea is incorporated in Fig. 8.7, because the sets are grouped according to their cardinal value, and the cardinal values are rank ordered, so sets with one member precede sets of two members, which precede sets of three members, and so on.

The next question concerns the type of mental model that provides the foundation for an elementary understanding of number operations. Collis (1978) showed that children can be taught number operations very efficiently using the type of models shown in Fig. 8.8. For addition, they are taught to create two disjoint sets, count the number of elements in each set, then count the total number of elements in the two sets combined. Resnick (1983a) also suggested that young children might first learn addition by counting through first one set then the other. This model corresponds to the set-theoretic definition of addition, in which $n(A) + n(B) = n(A \cup B)$, where A and B are disjoint sets. A number of years ago a "New Mathematics" program was used in schools, based on the principle of teaching arithmetic by teaching the formal set-theoretic justifications, the idea being that children would thereby understand the operations they were learning to perform. The approach of Collis differs from the New Mathematics technique in at least two ways, however. First, the children do not need to learn the formal definitions for Collis' technique. For example, they do not need to know the formal concept of union, or the definition of disjoint sets. What they need to

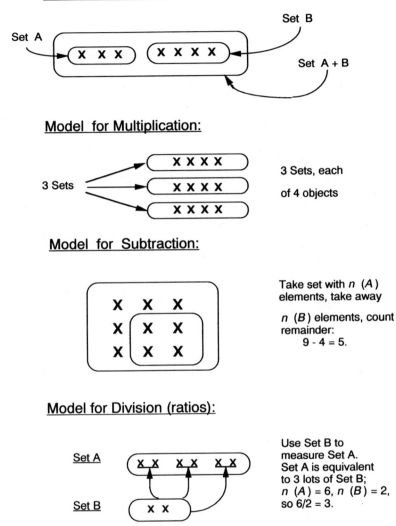

Model for Addition:

Model for Multiplication:

Model for Subtraction:

Model for Division (ratios):

FIG. 8.8. Possible mental models for arithmetic operations, based on set analogs.

know is how to construct the models, that is, how to draw a set representing the augend, another representing the addend, how to count through both sets, and so on (Collis, 1978). Second, they are taught how to map the model to the mathematical concept. The New Mathematics program tended to assume that if children knew the abstract definition of an operation, they would be able to perform that operation. By contrast, with Collis' technique, children are taught how to construct the model and how to use it to validate their arithmetic operations. For example, given the sum 2 + 4 = ?, children know how to construct a set of two crosses, a (separate) set of four crosses, then count right through to determine the answer. The operation, the model for understanding it, and the procedure for mapping one into the other are all taught together.

The same technique can be used to model some basic properties of arithmetic operations, as illustrated in Fig. 8.9. Commutativity of addition, and

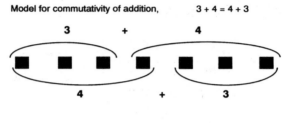

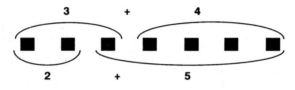

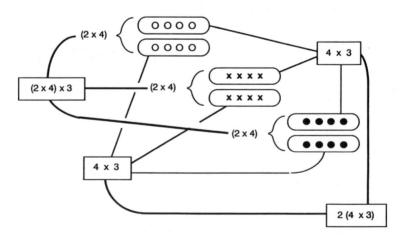

FIG. 8.9.   Possible mental models for properties of arithmetic operations, based on set analogs.

alternative compositions for a number, are modeled by dividing the same set two ways. Associativity of multiplication is also illustrated, using six sets combined in two ways. To model $(2 \times 4) \times 3$, sets of four items are combined, then this is repeated three times. To model $2 \times (4 \times 3)$, three sets of four objects are combined, then this combination is repeated twice (Collis, 1978).

Enumeration Processes.   No one would be able to develop their concept of number very far without enumeration processes, because it would not be possible to assign numerical values to sets, nor to explore size relations between sets, and many of the complex relationships between numbers would be inaccessible. Klahr and Wallace (1976) proposed three enumeration processes: subitizing, or estimation of small sets by direct inspection; counting; and estimation, which is the approximate enumeration of large sets by inspection (e.g., crowd estimation). Gelman and Gallistel (1978) contended that subitizing is really a primitive form of counting, but they agreed with Klahr and Wallace that it can be used by children as young as three.

Counting is clearly the most important enumeration process, and it is to it that most research has been devoted. Counting entails the following processes:

1. Select the first object to be counted.
2. Apply the first number tag (number name) to that object.
3. Move to the next object.
4. Apply the next number tag to that object.
5. Iterate steps 3 and 4 until all objects have been counted.
6. Adopt the last number tag used as the cardinal value of the set.

Gelman and Gallistel (1978) proposed that counting entails the following principles:

1. One-to-one: there is one and only one number tag for each object.
2. Stable order: the number tags are used in a fixed order (1, 2, 3, . . . , etc.).
3. Cardinal number: this means that the last number tag used is the cardinal value of the set.
4. Abstraction: attributes of objects other than their set membership are irrelevant. This means you can count any objects, irrespective of the features they may have.
5. Order irrelevance: the count is the same irrespective of the order in which objects are counted.

Gelman and Gallistel contended that even 2- to 3-year-old children had implicit knowledge of these counting principles. For example, although their knowledge of the English number tags was defective, they tended to use the right number of tags and to use their tags in the same order, consistent with the one-to-one and stable order principles. For example a child shown a two-item array might go "two, five," and for a three-item array might go "two, five, nine."

Gelman and Gallistel contended that, if counting is simply a skill, children should not be able to perform appropriately in novel situations where they would not have acquired the skill. On the other hand, if children understand the principles of counting, they should be able to adapt their procedures to novel situations. The constrained-counting task was used to assess this issue. Children were asked to count an array of five objects, making the second item the "one," so that the normal left-to-right order could not be used. If the child understood the one-to-one principle, he or she should still attempt to apply one and only one number tag to each item. Five-year-olds did this almost perfectly.

A study by Gelman and Meck (1983) suggested that although 3-year-olds had difficulty with the constrained-counting task, they still might have have a basic understanding of the counting principles. Therefore, instead of having the children count, they allowed them to watch a puppet count, and the children had to decide whether its counting was correct or not. The puppet performed in three ways: correct counting, incorrect counting (such as counting an object twice, or missing one), and unconventional but correct counts, such as starting in the middle, proceeding to the end, then counting the items at the beginning. Three- and 4-year-olds generally recognized correct counts and errors and mostly realized that unconventional counts were still correct. On the other hand, Briars and Siegler (1984) found that 3-year-olds mostly did not recognize that the unconventional counts were correct, although they found evidence that 5-year-olds did understand counting. Becker (1989) presented evidence that 4-year-olds use number words to denote whether sets are in one-to-one correspondence. It seems clear that some kind of understanding underlies children's counting, even though there may be doubt as to when and how that understanding is acquired.

The processes by which understanding of counting principles guides the counting process has been modeled in two computer simulation studies, one by VanLehn and Brown (1980) and one by Greeno, Riley, and Gelman (1984), both of which were discussed in chapter 3. The model of Greeno et al. subsumed many of the principles of VanLehn and Brown's model; it has been developed further and models more closely the counting process as it is used by children.

According to this model, children have an implicit knowledge of counting principles that are generally valid. The knowledge is implicit in the same way that knowledge of the grammar of a language is implicit. It is known in the sense that it provides a constraint on action, even if it is not conscious, cannot be verbalized, and permits legitimate procedures to be recognized. Just as our knowledge of grammar permits us to recognize legitimate sentences of our language, even though they may never have heard them before, knowledge of counting principles permits children to recognize legitimate counting procedures (Gelman & Greeno, 1989).

There is another parallel between understanding of grammar and understanding of counting. This is that just as grammar is generative, in the sense that knowledge of grammar permits us to produce an infinite variety of new sentences, understanding of counting principles permits us to generate an indefinitely large set of counting procedures. It is this generative property that permits children to adapt their counting strategies to unusual tasks, such as the constrained-counting task of Gelman and Meck (1983) discussed earlier.

There is also a suggestion that these principles may arise from innate constraints. For example Gelman (1982) cited evidence that primitive tribes invent their own enumeration systems based on body parts, so each finger counts as a numeral, the wrist as another, the forearm as another, and so on. Starkey, Spelke, and Gelman (1991) argued that number is a natural domain of cognition, based on principles such as one-to-one correspondence that are innate. Cooper (1984) presented evidence, based on habituation–dishabituation studies, that infants can discriminate the number of objects in a set in certain conditions. For example, they can discriminate "more than" and "less than" relations between small sets. Note that this supports the point made in chapters 6 and 7 that recognition of simple relations develops quite early, so failures in tasks such as transitivity are unlikely to be due to inability to recognize relations. From a functionalist viewpoint, it seems reasonable to expect that there may be biologically based enumeration processes, because they would have survival value. It would be useful to be able to discriminate the number of pursuing predators, the number of one's own species in a group, the number of available food sources, and so forth. As discussed in chapter 4, the model of Greeno et al. (1984) proposes that children's counting skills are guided by implicit understanding of abstract counting principles. However, as I suggested in chapter 4, it is more likely that mental models of counting are based on specific counting experiences that are used by analogy. Nevertheless, there is agreement that some understanding of number and counting is present very early in childhood, the dispute being about the form of the representation.

Concrete Models in Mathematics

So far we have considered the most basic concepts of number, such as order and the number line, counting, and operations on small sets. By middle childhood, however, children's knowledge advances beyond these topics in two ways. First, they are required to develop skill in certain algorithms for addition, subtraction, multiplication, and division of numbers containing more than one digit. Second, they need to develop understanding of some basic numerical concepts such as place value, commutativity, associativity, and the distributive law. These acquisitions are interdependent to some extent, because children's understanding of general properties of number influences the procedures they use.

In this section, I examine mental models children can use for certain number operations and consider the relevant psychological processes. The aim is not to suggest teaching techniques but to conduct an analysis of psychological processes. Development of pedagogy from an analysis such as this requires further applied research that is beyond the scope of this book. I believe that considerable damage can be done by translating concepts directly from cognition or cognitive development into classroom practice without developing the intervening theory or conducting the requisite applied research. In this case I believe considerable additional work is required to translate this analysis into teaching techniques.

A frequent finding from research on children's mathematics is that their errors are not random but are often due to invented procedures. That is, when children forget the rules they have been taught, they often invent a *malrule* that meets some of the superficial constraints of the situation (Payne & Squibb, 1990; Resnick, 1983a; Resnick & Omanson, 1987).

Examples of such invented strategies are shown in Fig. 8.10. In the first case, the child has evidently forgotten or mislearned the procedure required for subtracting 9 from 2 so has subtracted 2 from 9, and also 4 from 8 (the smaller-from-larger malrule). In the second case, the child attempts some regrouping of the minuend, so as to subtract 7 from 2, but does not know the correct procedure when there is a 0 present, so borrows from the 100s column instead (the borrow-across-zero malrule). In the third case, the child again does not know the procedure and subtracts the 0 from the 5 instead (the $0 - N = N$ malrule). These malrules have certainly not been taught, so they must have been invented so as to repair incomplete algorithms (Brown & VanLehn, 1982; VanLehn, 1990). The repair has been constrained by superficial syntactic criteria such as having one and only one number in each column, having only one decrement in each column, and so on. However, the invented procedures take no account of the principles on which the correct algorithms are based. The smaller-from-larger and $0 - N = N$ malrules overlook the meaning of the conventional notation that calls for the bottom number to be subtracted from the top number. The borrow-across-zero malrule fails to conserve the minuend, because 100 is borrowed from the 100s column but only 10 is added to the units column, so 602 effectively becomes 512. Thus the malrules are being constrained by superficial syntactic criteria without adequate concern for the semantic referents. The problem is either that the children do not understand the procedures they are using, or that

Smaller-from-larger

$$\begin{array}{r} 5\,4\,2 \\ -\,3\,8\,9 \\ \hline 2\,4\,7 \end{array}$$

Borrow-across-zero

$$\begin{array}{r} {}^{5}\!\!\not6\,0_{1}2 \\ -\,3\,2\,7 \\ \hline 2\,2\,5 \end{array}$$

$0 - N = N$

$$\begin{array}{r} 7\,0\,9 \\ -\,3\,5\,2 \\ \hline 4\,5\,7 \end{array}$$

FIG. 8.10.   Malrules in subtraction. From Resnick (1982). Reproduced by permission of L. B. Resnick and Lawrence Erlbaum Associates.

they cannot apply that understanding to the task perhaps because of the processing load that would be imposed.

Resnick and Omanson (1987) suggested that children may have some knowledge of, and mental models for, place value but have difficulty in relating this declarative knowledge to subtraction procedures. They worked with second- and third-grade children who knew how to represent place value using Dienes blocks and coins. The basic idea of these representations is shown in Fig. 8.11. Units are represented by small square blocks, tens are represented by blocks that are as long as 10 units blocks, and hundreds are represented by square blocks equal in area to 10 tens blocks (Fig. 8.9A). The area rela-

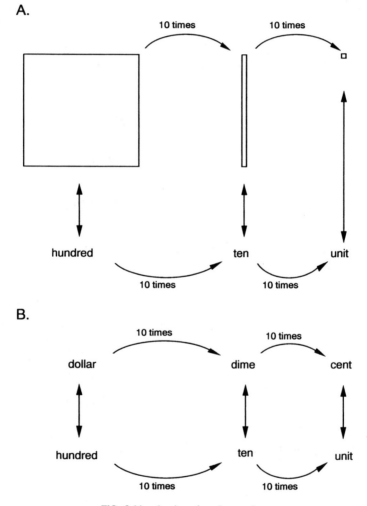

FIG. 8.11. Analogs for place value.

tions between the blocks reflect the magnitude relations between quantities represented. With an alternate coin representation, a dollar represents 100, a dime 10, and a cent 1 unit. Resnick and Omanson found that the children could write numerals to represent numbers, correctly using the place-value notation, and could construct valid representations using the concrete analogs, Dienes blocks, or coins. They could also validly represent recompositions, such as changing 34 from 3 tens and 4 units to 2 tens and 14 units. However, they were not able to relate this understanding to the regrouping procedures in addition and subtraction. Furthermore, an attempt to train the children to map their concrete representations into the arithmetic procedures was not particularly successful. We can begin to understand why children would have difficulty mapping these concrete representations into regrouping procedures, and why relatively brief mapping training might not remedy the problem, if we define the mappings involved more completely.

Figure 8.12 shows the structure mapping for a simple trade operation, where 324 is changed to 200 plus 110 plus 14 (as would occur if, for example, 179 were subtracted from 324). In the concrete representation, 324 is represented as 3 hundreds blocks, 2 tens blocks, and 4 units blocks. The first point to notice about this mental model is that it really entails a two-stage vertical mapping. The 3 hundreds blocks are mapped into the 3 digit in the hundreds column in accordance with the place-value notation. However they must also be mapped into a cognitive representation of the quantity 300, which in turn has to be mapped into the notation. That is, we have mappings from concrete analog, to cognitive representation of quantity, to notation. Moving horizontally we have a quantity-conserving change in which the original representation is replaced by 2 hundreds blocks, 11 tens blocks, and 14 units blocks. In classroom practice this might be done in a number of steps, but the important point is that in order to appreciate the value of the concrete representation, the child must recognize that this is a quantity-conserving change. This is not easy to see because we have to sum 300 + 20 + 4 and recognize that it is equal to 200 + 110 + 14.

On the right-hand side we again have a two-stage mapping from concrete analog to quantity to place-value notation. The value of the concrete analog is lost unless it is realized that there is a quantity-conserving change at all three levels. All in all, this is a very complex structure mapping, but it is only part of the mapping that is required to understand the borrowing procedure in subtraction, as we soon see.

The way Dienes blocks can be used as a concrete analog to help children understand subtraction is shown in Fig. 8.13, which has been reproduced from Resnick (1982). To subtract 139 from 300, one first trades 1 hundreds block for 10 tens blocks, then 1 tens block is traded for 10 units blocks, and the equivalent changes are made to the place-value notation. Then 1 hundreds block, 9 units blocks, and 3 tens blocks are removed, leaving 1 hundreds block,

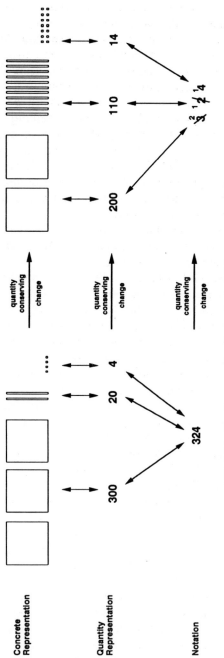

FIG. 8.12. Structure mapping for concrete aid in regrouping task.

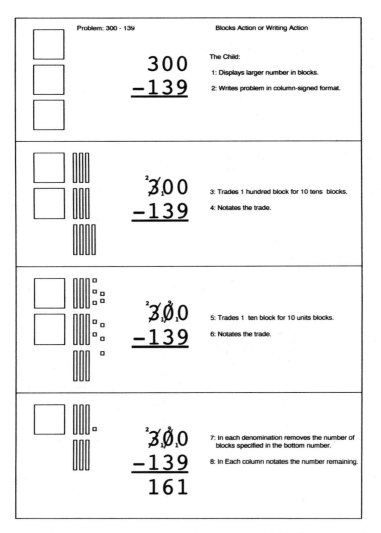

FIG. 8.13.   Concrete analog for subtraction. From Resnick (1982). Reproduced
by permission of L. B. Resnick and Lawrence Erlbaum Associates.

6 tens blocks, and 1 unit block, giving the answer 161. This figure illustrates
the technique but does not display the actual mappings required. The structure mapping required to show how 324 minus 179 can be understood in
terms of a concrete analog is shown in Fig. 8.14. The regrouping procedure
is illustrated in the left side of the figure, as in Fig. 8.12. The number to be
subtracted, 179, is shown as a concrete analog, as quantities 100 plus 70 plus
9, and in place-value notation, 179. The resulting quantity, 145, is shown in
the same way. Note that the structure-mapping diagram is designed to show

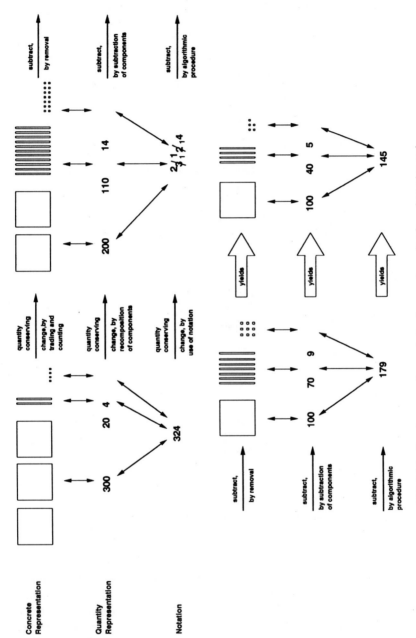

FIG. 8.14.   Structure-mapping analysis of concrete analog for subtraction task.

relations between elements of the representation, corresponding relations between the things represented, and the mapping from one to the other. It is not designed to show the sequence of steps in the subtraction procedure. Consequently, the regrouping procedure is shown to the left of subtraction, but this is not intended to convey that one occurs before the other. Structure mapping is a way of analyzing the relations that are inherent in the structure of a concept and revealing their complexity. That is, it shows the structure of a concept. It can guide the development of, but is not a substitute for, a process model.

To realize how the concrete analog justifies the subtraction procedure the child must recognize several sets of relationships:

1. The vertical mappings from each concrete display to the quantity represented, and then to the place-value notation.

2. There is a quantity-conserving change at all three levels from the initial representation, 324, to the representation with regrouping, 200 plus 110 plus 14.

3. The subtraction process yields the same relationships at all three levels. For example, at the top level, when we remove a hundreds block from a set of two hundreds blocks, the result is one hundreds block. Similarly, at the next level, when we subtract 100 from 200, the result is 100. Similarly again, at the lowest level, subtracting a 1 in the hundreds column from a 2 in the hundreds column yields a 1 in the hundreds column. Thus the same relationships obtain at each of the three levels. This is also true for tens and units. It is the fact that the same set of relations hold at all three levels that provides the justification for the arithmetic procedure. The problem is that children will not recognize the justification unless they can see this complex set of relationships. If the justification is not understood, the concrete analogs may be worse than useless, because they are extra things to learn, take time to manipulate, and cause distraction.

Taken over all, there is a very complex set of relationships. It is really a composite of many lower level mappings. It entails more information than an adult could process in parallel if the theory of capacity outlined in chapter 3 is correct. Therefore even an adult could only process the whole mapping in parallel if it were chunked into fewer dimensions. This could be done by making trading into a chunk. This would mean the transformation of 3 hundreds, 2 tens, and 4 units into 2 hundreds, 11 tens, and 14 units would be coded as a single, quantity-conserving step. Its complexity would be that of a binary relation, that is, a relation between two equal quantities. Subtraction, or the removal of 1 hundred, 7 tens, and 9 units, would be another chunk. It is equivalent to one binary relation (a ternary relation), because it entails three entities, the minuend, the subtrahend, and the difference. Borrowing is a binary relation and is two dimensional, whereas subtracting is a ternary relation and is three dimensional. These two concepts could not both be represented in parallel, but this is not necessary because they can be performed and represented serially. If done this way, the highest processing load would be equivalent to one three-dimensional concept. Other chunks required are that of a number composed of hundreds, tens, and units, and the concept of place value, which entails the relation of power between successive columns (column 1 comprises 10^0, column 2 comprises 10^1, and column 3 comprises 10^2).

Each of these chunks would have to be prelearned. For example, children must be skilled in recognizing the mapping of block displays into numbers, they must know that trading entails a quantity-conserving transformation, and so on. This is a book about cognitive development, rather than pedagogy per se, and I do not want to preempt consideration of the complex issues concerning the best way to teach such things. I want to show how complexity analysis provides insight into the reasons why tasks can be difficult and how these difficulties can be overcome. To use the analogs effectively, components of the task must be chunked, implying that considerable expertise on the part of the child is necessary before analogs become beneficial. The importance of expertise in analog use has been reinforced by Hatano, Amaiwa, and Shimizu (1987) in the context of abacus use.

Some further insights can be obtained by assessing the structure mapping in Fig. 8.14 according to the criteria for a good explanatory analogy devised by Gentner (1982) and summarized in chapter 5. The first of these is base specificity, which corresponds to the degree to which the structure of the base is understood. In Fig. 8.14 this means that the structure of the block analog must be well understood, including the size relations between the blocks (the fact that a hundreds block is 10 times a tens block, which is 10 times a unit block). This entails learning the chunks for number, regrouping, and subtracting as they are represented in the blocks.

Resnick and Omanson (1987) found that children who had facility with the verbal quantity labels profited more from mapping training. This is quite consistent with the structure-mapping analysis, because children who had learned the chunks would be better able to apply verbal labels to them and would be better able to represent the mapping from analog to number.

The structure mapping rates quite well according to Gentner's next criterion, clarity, which means that there are no ambiguous mappings. It also rates well according to richness, because of the large number of mappings that are made, and according to scope, because of the many applications of the analogy.

The structure mapping rates very highly in systematicity, because the many relations between elements at the same level do provide a coherent overall structure. This is both a strength and a weakness, however. The value of the analogy lies mainly in the complex set of relationships that are represented, but this also makes it very complex and difficult to recognize. An important point is that children need to recognize not only the vertical mappings between elements at the different levels but also the corresponding relations between levels. That is, it is not sufficient to know the mappings from 3 hundreds blocks to the quantity 300 and then to the 3 in the hundreds column, plus the other vertical mappings of this type. It is also necessary to realize that, for example, the quantity-conserving change between the two block arrangements is mirrored in a quantity-conserving change between the quantities represented at the next level, and that this in turn is mirrored in a quantity-conserving change at the notation level. The training procedure used by Resnick and Omanson might have been more successful in teaching the vertical mappings and might not have taught children to recognize the corresponding relations at the different levels.

Lampert (1986) also developed an ingenious teaching technique for problems involving the operations of addition and multiplication (see also commentary by Gelman, 1986, and Greeno, 1986). Examples of her techniques are shown in structure-mapping format in Fig. 8.15. Children are encouraged to find several ways of making up $1, using two different kinds of coins. (Solutions are 5 dimes plus 10 nickels, 8 dimes and 4 nickels, etc.). This technique really uses a familiar domain, coins, as an analogical base for teaching the properties of addition and multiplication. Figure 8.15A shows how 6 dimes plus 8 nickels can be used as a base to teach the mathematical equation $(6 \times 10) + (8 \times 5) = 100$. Another of Lampert's techniques is shown as a structure mapping in Fig. 8.15B. Children were shown four butterflies in each of 10 jars, then a further two jars also containing four butterflies each. This illustrates the distributive law, $(4 \times 10) + (4 \times 2) = 4(10 + 2)$. Much of the

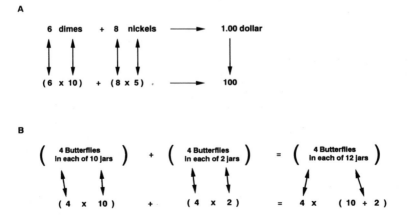

FIG. 8.15. Concrete analogs for arithmetic tasks.

value of Lampert's technique lies in the fact that it constitutes a good explanatory analogy according to Gentner's (1982) criteria discussed earlier. There is high base specificity, because coins and the relationships between them are very well known, even by young children, who usually learn early that a dollar is worth 10 dimes, and a dime is worth 10 cents, and so on. The examples are also constructed to provide high clarity (unambiguous mappings), systematicity is provided by the higher order rules such as the distributive rule, and the analogy has high scope.

Concrete aids can be effective in mathematics education, especially if skillfully used, as a recent review by Sowell (1989) made clear. However, their benefits are by no means automatic, and they can even be a hindrance if used inappropriately. Concrete aids are technically analogs, and analysis in terms of structure-mapping theory and the theory of complexity provides useful insights into the psychological processes entailed in using these aids.

Because concrete aids are analogs, analysis in terms of analogy theory indicates how they can be used more effectively. Where concrete aids are used effectively, they provide the basis for a mental model of an arithmetic task, such as subtraction. This mental model can guide the development of skills and strategies, just as mental models of counting guide the development of counting skills, or a concept of order guides the development of transitive inference strategies, as discussed in chapters 4 and 7. The strategy-selection models of Siegler (Siegler, 1988; Siegler & Shrager, 1984) were discussed in chapter 4. These models emphasize the role of associative processes, whereas the counting model of Greeno et al. emphasizes metacognitive processes, and the transitive inference model of Halford et al. integrates both processes. In the present context, the important point is that effective mental models are important in developing strategies and in monitoring their application. A child with a good mental model of an arithmetic task such as subtraction will be more likely to understand why some malrules are inadmissible.

Arithmetic Word Problems

Because arithmetic word problems (e.g., Joe had eight marbles, then he gave some marbles to Tom. Now Joe has three marbles. How many marbles did he give to Tom?) relate to real-life situations, it seems intuitively clear that they should be easy to solve. Actually, however, they are notoriously difficult. Part of the problem has been traced to misunderstanding the language used in the problems (Cummins, Kintsch, Reussler, & Weimer, 1988). However, it has also been suggested that difficulty is experienced in mapping the problem into an appropriate schema. Kintsch and Greeno (1985) and Greeno and Johnson (1985) identified three basic types of problems, which are summarized in Fig. 8.16. With *change* problems there is a start set (Joe had three

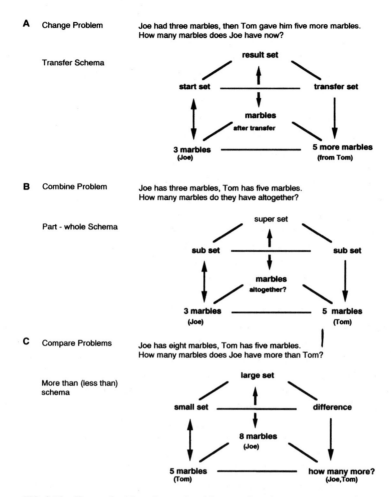

A Change Problem   Joe had three marbles, then Tom gave him five more marbles.
                          How many marbles does Joe have now?

      Transfer Schema

                                    result set

                         start set ——————— transfer set

                                    marbles
                                  after transfer

                         3 marbles ——————— 5 more marbles
                           (Joe)   (from Tom)

B Combine Problem   Joe has three marbles, Tom has five marbles.
                          How many marbles do they have altogether?

      Part - whole Schema

                                    super set

                         sub set ——————— sub set

                                    marbles
                                  altogether?

                         3 marbles ——————— 5 marbles
                           (Joe)   (Tom)

C Compare Problems   Joe has eight marbles, Tom has five marbles.
                          How many marbles does Joe have more than Tom?

      More than (less than)
      schema   large set

                         small set ——————— difference

                                    8 marbles
                                     (Joe)

                         5 marbles ——————— how many more?
                           (Tom)   (Joe,Tom)

FIG. 8.16. Types of arithmetic word problems analyzed as structure mappings.

marbles), a transfer set consisting of items added to or subtracted from the
start set (Then Tom give him five more marbles), and a result set (How many
marbles does Joe have now?). For *combine* problems, there are two subsets
(Joe has three marbles, Tom has five marbles) and a superset (How many
marbles do they have altogether?), which is the sum of the subsets. For *compare* problems, there is a large set (Joe has eight marbles), a small set (Tom
has five marbles), and a difference set (How many more marbles does Joe
have than Tom?).

Arithmetic word problems share with class inclusion the property that they
entail identifying sets. For example, given the problem in Fig. 8.16A, we need
to recognize that three marbles is the start set, five marbles is the transfer

set, and the result set is the sum of these, eight marbles. As shown in Fig. 8.16, it is really a type of structure-mapping process in which elements of the problem text are mapped into slots in the scheme.

According to Kintsch and Greeno's model, the identification of the sets is achieved using linguistic cues in the problem wording. First, a simple language parser extracts propositions from the problem sentences. For example, the first sentence in the combine problem, "Joe has three marbles," yields the propositions; $x1$ = Joe (Joe is assigned a slot), P3 = THREE(MARBLES) (there are 3 marbles), and HAVE($x1$, P3), (Joe has three marbles). The second proposition triggers representation of a set containing three marbles. Linguistic cues are used to identify the sets. For example, the HAVE-ALTOGETHER proposition cues the third set to be assigned the role of superset. This in turn causes the first two sets to be assigned the role of subsets. Then a calculational strategy is triggered to compute the value of the superset. The model is an extension of the text-processing model of van Dijk and Kintsch (1983), and in general it works by arranging the text propositions into a coherent framework, comprising three sets together with the relations between them.

The Kintsch and Greeno model depends heavily on linguistic processes to interpret the problem sentences and assign the sets to the relevant schema. It is possible, however, to solve arithmetic word problems in a way that is less dependent on linguistic processes. Greeno and Johnson (1985) proposed two alternative processes. One is schema based and entails mapping the sets into a schema, as shown in Fig. 8.16. The other is based more heavily on propositions and does not entail constructing a schema as such. Although any model must of course account for text-comprehension processes that extract meaning from the sentences that compose the problem, there can be variations in the amount of reliance placed on linguistic cues. Structure-mapping theory is most directly applicable to schema-based procedures.

The generic schema for arithmetic word problems consists of two parts and a whole, shown in Fig. 8.17A. Resnick (1983a) also suggested the part–whole schema, shown in Fig. 8.17B, as the basis for understanding arithmetic word problems. Notice that the part–whole schema is structurally similar to the inclusion schema in Fig. 8.4A discussed earlier. It is a system mapping and should impose processing loads similar to other system-mapping tasks such as transitive inference and inclusion. The processing loads occur because of the need to map the sets into the slots of the relevant schema. The problem is similar to that of identifying the superordinate set and subsets in the inclusion schema. In both cases, the difficulty arises because the sets are identified by their relations to other sets. This point was made with respect to class inclusion earlier. With arithmetic word problems, we cannot decide from the first sentence whether the designated set is a subset or superset. For example, in the change problem in Fig. 8.16A, "Joe had three marbles"

A

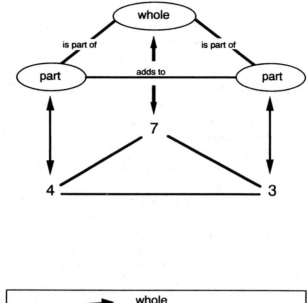

B

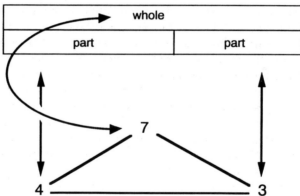

FIG. 8.17.   Mappings of arithmetic word problems into part–whole schema.

designates a subset, but in Fig. 8.16B "Joe has eight marbles" designates a
superset. Even two sets are not necessarily sufficient to correctly identify the
roles of the sets. Consider, for example, the sentences "Joe has five marbles"
and "Tom has three marbles." Five marbles could be a subset or superset
depending on the third sentence. If the third sentence is "How many more
marbles does Joe have than Tom?" then five marbles is the superset. If,
however, the third sentence is "How many marbles do they have altogether?"
then five marbles is a subset and eight is a superset. As with inclusion

problems, the sets can only be identified with certainty when the whole structure, of three sets and the relations between them, is known.

There is substantial evidence that linguistic factors are responsible for much of the difficulty of arithmetic word problems. Cummins et al. (1988) found that abstract or ambiguous language contributed to errors, and that error patterns were better predicted by a linguistic comprehension model than by a model of logical set relations. De Corte, Verschaffel, and De Win (1985) and Carpenter, Hiebert, and Moser (1981) showed that wording that clarified the semantic relations between given and unknown quantities facilitated performance by year 1 and year 2 children. Hudson (1983) found that young children performed poorly on this problem: "There are five birds and three worms. How many more birds are there than worms?" However, there was a dramatic improvement when the last sentence was changed to: "How many birds won't get a worm?"

The problem is that linguistic comprehension and structure-mapping processes are difficult to separate. The language will inevitably be hard to comprehend if the set relations to which it refers cannot be adequately represented. Some of the manipulations that appear to apply only to language might facilitate mapping of problem sets into the schema, by providing cues as to which set is the whole and which are parts.

Alternatively, experimental manipulations might actually influence representation of set relations. For example, the study by Hudson (1983), discussed immediately above, could well induce a simpler set schema. The original version of the problem tends to induce a part–whole schema, with five birds as the whole, whereas three worms and the difference between worms and birds (two) are the parts. The changed wording tends to induce a comparison of two sets; the birds set (five) is compared with the worms set (three). This is a simpler schema than the part–whole schema. Recall the default to a set-comparison schema in inclusion, and notice that the change introduced by Hudson (1983) appears to be analogous to the simplification that occurs by default in the inclusion task.

The complexity of set relations in arithmetic word problems appears to be a factor in the difficulty of this class of problems and constitutes part of the reason why these intuitively easy tasks are notoriously difficult. This difficulty is at least partly analogous to the difficulty of class inclusion. The tasks entail different domain knowledge, in that class inclusion does not require the number expertise or the arithmetic operations that are entailed in arithmetic word problems. However, despite the domain shift, there is an underlying structural similarity. Thus the situation is similar to the one we experienced with transitivity and class inclusion, where two superficially dissimilar problems from different domains were found to share common underlying structural complexities.

Algebra

In this section I consider possible bases for children's understanding of algebra. For the pure mathematician the justification for algebraic rules and manipulations lies in the properties of mathematical groups, rings, and fields, but few algebra students ever come to understand mathematics at this level. Earlier in this chapter, and in chapter 4, I suggested that the understanding of number is based on sets, and understanding of arithmetic is based on set operations. Now I consider the similarities and differences between arithmetic and algebra in this respect.

Arithmetic deals with constants, whereas algebra deals with constants and variables. A major component of making the shift to algebra, therefore, is to acquire an understanding of variables. However, understanding of variables poses a number of special problems. Viewed from a PDP perspective, representation of constants is a natural process, because a vector of activation values represents content-specific information, as discussed in chapter 2. Representation of variables is much more computationally demanding. Smolensky (1990) proposed that variable–constant bindings can be represented by the tensor product of two vectors, one representing the variable and one representing the constant (see Fig. 2.4). This is a much more complex representation than that which is needed for constants, which suggests that thinking in terms of variables might impose high processing loads.

Children's understanding of algebra is also influenced by factors that are inherent in the way variables are defined. Bahr (in preparation) distinguished five ways in which constants can be defined:

1. *Ecological reference*, that is, by reference to some commonly observed feature. For example, "5" might be defined by reference to the fingers of one hand.
2. *Cardinal reference*, which means that a constant is defined by reference to sets of equal cardinality, as suggested in chapter 4.
3. *Ordinal reference*, as when a number is typically used to refer to a particular position, for example, Saturday is the seventh day of the week.
4. *Number system reference*, where a number is defined by its role in the number system. For example, 0 and 1 are the additive and multiplicative identities.
5. *Expression reference*, where a number is defined by reference to an expression, for example, $8 = 3 + 5$ defines 8 as the sum of 3 and 5; $i = \sqrt{-1}$, and so forth.

A constant may be defined in all five ways, but they are not all applicable to variables, and some of them are not applicable in the same way. A variable cannot be defined with respect to a commonly occurring number, such as the fingers of the hand, but there are naturally occurring variables, such as speed or tree height. However, the mapping of the variable into the corresponding observations is much less obvious than in the case of many constants.

Variables cannot in general be defined with respect to cardinal or ordinal reference, because they have no fixed values. They can be defined by number-system reference; for example, we can define variable a as the sum of variables b and c ($a = b + c$). This type of definition entails understanding of the number system. They can also be defined by expression reference, that is, a variable is commonly defined by its relation to other terms in the expression, for example, velocity equals distance over time ($v = s/t$). Again, however, ability to process the expressions is essential to understanding.

Given that variables cannot normally be defined by reference to sets, their understanding requires knowledge of the structure of the number system. That is, understanding of variables and of algebra needs to be based on understanding of arithmetic. Therefore I will argue that algebra is understood by analogy with arithmetic. Whereas sets provided the base for understanding arithmetic, arithmetic provides the base for understanding algebra. This is consistent with the point made by Resnick (1987) that most children justify algebraic rules by using arithmetic examples. For example they would justify the distributive law by calculating the type of example shown in Fig. 8.18A. This justification is a structure mapping. The base, or known structure, in this case is the arithmetic example, and the target is the algebraic rule. Thus, the justification is really a form of analogical reasoning. It is a straightforward case of a multiple-system mapping.

Nevertheless malrules, or inappropriately invented rules, occur, as Resnick (1987) pointed out in a review of the literature. These are generated by first creating a prototype rule, then generating new rules that match the prototype and provide apparent justification. The type of prototype used is illustrated in Fig. 8.18B, and the rules generated from it are exemplified in Fig. 8.18C. The fact that the malrules are not justified could be recognized by comparing them with appropriate arithmetic examples, as the structure mapping in Fig. 8.18D shows.

Whereas the base that was used to justify arithmetic rules was normally a concrete analog, as illustrated in Figs. 8.7, 8.8, 8.9, 8.11, 8.12, 8.13, 8.14, and 8.15 (see also Fig. 5.11), in algebra the base may be concrete or it may be a known arithmetic relationship. The example in Fig. 8.18 illustrates the use of an arithmetic relationship to justify an algebraic rule. However, concrete analogs have also been used to justify algebraic rules to children. Bruner and Kenney (1965), following an approach advocated by Dienes (1964), showed how concrete analogs can be used to justify quadratic expressions such as $(x + 2)^2 = x^2 + 4x + 4$. Two possible concrete analogs for this ex-

A

source   3 (5 + 2) = (3 x 5) + (3 x 2)

↕ ↕ ↕   ↕ ↕   ↕ ↕

target   *a* (*b* + *c*) = (*a* x *b*) + (*a* x *c*)

B

Prototype

$$a \square (b \triangle c) = (a \square b) \triangle (a \square c)$$

C

Malrules generated from prototype

$$a + (b \times c) = (a + b) \times (a + c)$$

$$\sqrt{b + c} = \sqrt{b} + \sqrt{c}$$

D

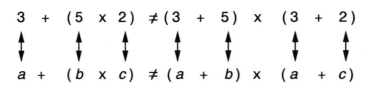

3 + (5 x 2) ≠ (3 + 5) x (3 + 2)

↕ ↕ ↕   ↕ ↕   ↕ ↕

a + (*b* x *c*) ≠ (*a* + *b*) x (*a* + *c*)

FIG. 8.18. Representations of the distributive law. Figures 8.18B and 8.18C are adapted from L. B. Resnick (1987). Reproduced by permission of L. B. Resnick and Lawrence Erlbaum Associates.

pression are shown in Fig. 8.19. In Fig. 8.19A a square is drawn on a line of length $x + 2$, and the square is divided into areas representing x^2, $4x$, and 4. The same identity can be represented by weights on a balance beam, as shown in Fig. 8.19B.

  The use of two analogs illustrates the principle of multiple embodiment (Dienes, 1964), which means that two analogs promote better learning than

A

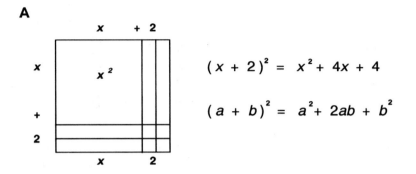

$$(x + 2)^2 = x^2 + 4x + 4$$

$$(a + b)^2 = a^2 + 2ab + b^2$$

B

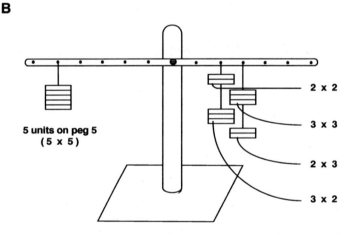

FIG. 8.19. Concrete aids for quadratic used by Bruner and Kenney (1965). Figure 8.19A is adapted from Bruner and Kenney (1965). Reproduced by permission of J. S. Bruner and Chicago University Press.

one. This is consistent with the point made by Gick and Holyoak (1983), discussed in chapter 5. The reason for this can be explained by structure-mapping theory. In essence, the argument is very similar to the reasoning in chapter 5 where we explained why learning-set training enabled children to extract the most general principle from a series of problems. Irrelevant or partially valid principles may be consistent with one problem but are gradually filtered out as they are found to be inconsistent with subsequent problems. For example, the fact that the blocks analog in Fig. 8.19A consists of a number of areas added together is irrelevant to the principle that is illustrated. The second analog (Fig. 8.19B) does not consist of areas, so this irrelevant feature is eliminated. The inadequate rules are disconfirmed because they provide incorrect predictions on some of the problems.

So far we have examined a number of concrete analogs for algebraic rules, but I would now like to examine how arithmetic knowledge can be used to provide an analogy for understanding of an algebraic rule, the distributive law. We trace through a possible sequence of steps that might be entailed in acquiring the distributive law through structure mapping, as outlined by Halford and Boulton-Lewis (1992). Some hypothetical steps are shown in Fig. 8.20. In Fig. 8.20A, we represent the child's knowledge that $3(2 + 1) = 9$. This knowledge must be acquired through calculation, and the child must learn to interpret and manipulate parentheses and operation symbols in arithmetic expressions. There is, therefore, procedural knowledge that must be acquired. Our concern here, however, is primarily to express the conceptual knowledge that underlies the procedural knowledge. We can express this conceptual knowledge that $3(2 + 1) = 9$ corresponds to $3 \times 3 = 9$, that is, process the operation in parentheses, which yields 3, then process the operation represented by the numeral that precedes the parentheses. This knowledge that $3(2 + 1) = 9$ corresponds to $3 \times 3 = 9$ can, like other structural correspondences, be represented as a structure mapping, as shown in Fig. 8.20A. Note that, once again, structure mapping is a conceptual tool for analyzing structural correspondences and does not represent a process model as such.

The next step is for the child to recognize that $(3 \times 2) + (3 \times 1) = 9$ corresponds to $6 + 3 = 9$. This is represented as a structure mapping in Fig. 8.20B. This is essentially similar to the process in Fig. 8.20A. It is a major step from there, however, to recognize that $3(2 + 1) = (3 \times 2) + (3 \times 1)$. Understanding this depends on recognizing that it corresponds to $3 \times 3 = 6 + 3$, which is shown as a structure mapping in Fig. 8.20C. The child already knows that $3 \times 3 = 9 = 6 + 3$, because of previous experiences of the kind shown in Fig. 8.20A and 8.20B. Therefore the known relationship $3 \times 3 = 6 + 3$ can serve as a mental model that enables the child to understand $3(2 + 1) = (3 \times 2) + (3 \times 1)$. For this understanding to occur, the child must recognize the structural correspondence between the kinds of expressions, as shown in Fig. 8.20C.

The next step is probably to acquire further examples of this correspondence. Another example is shown in Fig. 8.20D. Furthermore Fig. 8.20E expresses the correspondence between a new example and the original example. The idea here is that a child might adopt one prototypical example and compare it with other examples, recognizing the correspondence between the prototype and numerous other examples. The prototype then becomes a kind of template for the general rule. A further example of this process is shown in Figure 8.20F.

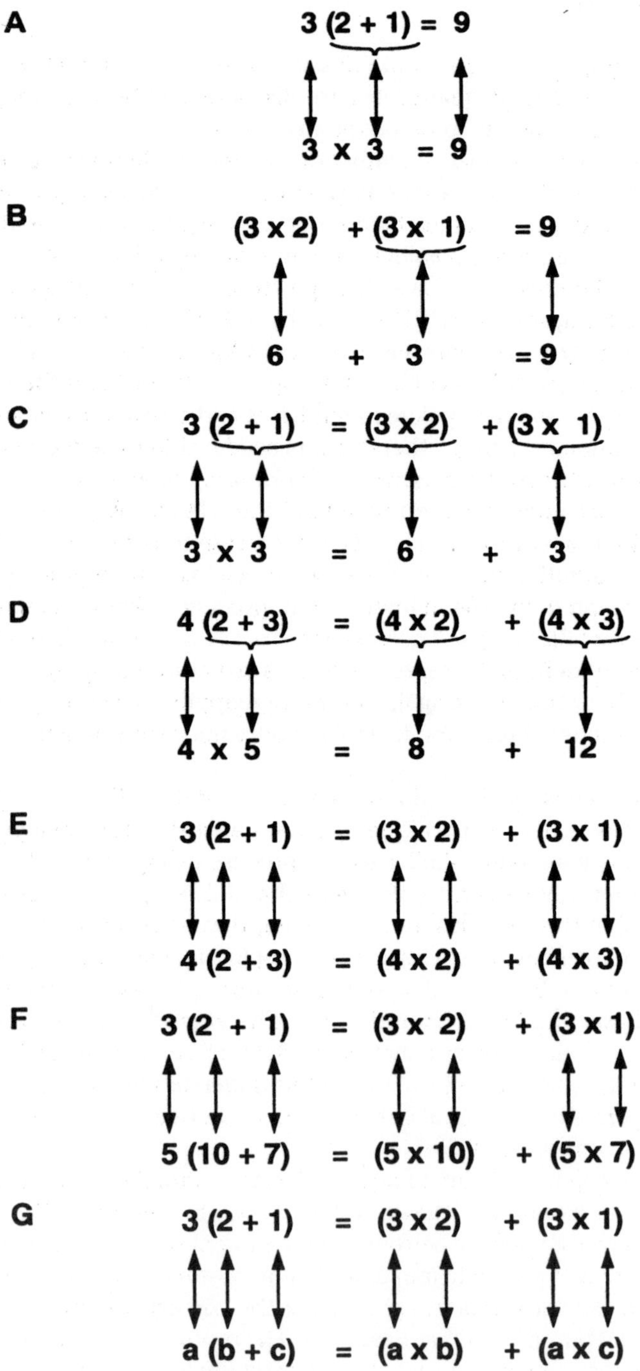

A $3\,(2 + 1) = 9$

$3 \times 3 = 9$

B $(3 \times 2) + (3 \times 1) = 9$

$6 + 3 = 9$

C $3\,(2 + 1) = (3 \times 2) + (3 \times 1)$

$3 \times 3 = 6 + 3$

D $4\,(2 + 3) = (4 \times 2) + (4 \times 3)$

$4 \times 5 = 8 + 12$

E $3\,(2 + 1) = (3 \times 2) + (3 \times 1)$

$4\,(2 + 3) = (4 \times 2) + (4 \times 3)$

F $3\,(2 + 1) = (3 \times 2) + (3 \times 1)$

$5\,(10 + 7) = (5 \times 10) + (5 \times 7)$

G $3\,(2 + 1) = (3 \times 2) + (3 \times 1)$

$a\,(b + c) = (a \times b) + (a \times c)$

FIG. 8.20. Structure-mapping analysis for understanding of distributive law.

The final step occurs when the child recognizes the correspondence between the prototype arithmetic example and the general rule. An additional process is required here, because the child must know that letters can be used to represent unknown numbers. This fact would normally be taught in other ways, such as showing children how to draw a container representing an unknown number of objects, then teaching them how to write a letter to represent the unknown number of objects. Assuming the child has already learned to represent unknown numbers by letters, the step in Fig. 8.20G can be taken once the correspondence between the algebraic law and the arithmetic example is recognized.

The fact that letters can represent unknown numbers is a component of the domain knowledge that is required to learn the algebraic law, but it does not explain how the algebraic rule is understood. The point that I want to illustrate through this extended example is that understanding depends on recognition of the correspondence between the algebraic rule and one or more reference examples. Structure-mapping analyses of this correspondence shows that it depends on a series of multiple-system mappings. I do want to emphasize that I am NOT advocating that children be taught to make structure-mapping diagrams, which would only be a useless burden for them. Structure mappings are a conceptual tool for the cognitive theorist, and we are not trying to make children into cognitive theorists. I want to illustrate the types of analogical correspondences that are probably needed for children to use their arithmetic knowledge as a base for understanding an algebraic law.

I would like to leave this section by noting a paradox. This is that if understanding of algebra depends on understanding of arithmetic, and if understanding of arithmetic is promoted by appropriate experience with concrete analogs such as sets, then experience with concrete materials ultimately promotes algebra. Thus, concrete experience ultimately facilitates acquisition of an abstraction. This is quite understandable, however, once we realize that acquisition of arithmetic and algebra depends on having mental models of the relational structure in these domains. To the extent that concrete analogs promote representation of this relational structure, they promote acquisition of abstractions.

Elementary Calculus

Algebraic examples are sometimes used to teach the basic ideas of differential calculus, as illustrated in Fig. 8.21. After teaching students the idea of a limit, they are given a series of arithmetic examples involving x plus an increment delta x, and y plus delta y, as shown in the table in Fig. 8.21. They then are shown how to calculate $y + \Delta y$, Δy, and $\Delta y/\Delta x$, and finally shown what $\Delta y/\Delta x$ becomes as Δx tends to zero. Although I do not want to specifi-

Algebraic examples (source)

$$y = x^2 \qquad x = 2, \ y = 4$$

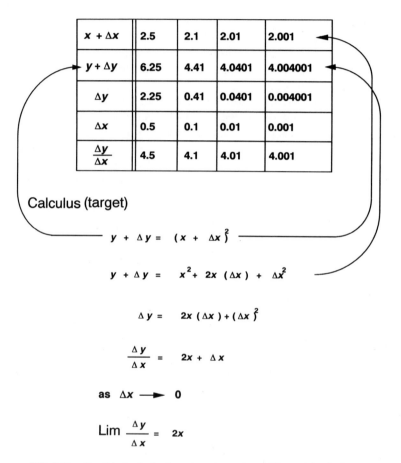

$x + \Delta x$	2.5	2.1	2.01	2.001
$y + \Delta y$	6.25	4.41	4.0401	4.004001
Δy	2.25	0.41	0.0401	0.004001
Δx	0.5	0.1	0.01	0.001
$\dfrac{\Delta y}{\Delta x}$	4.5	4.1	4.01	4.001

Calculus (target)

$$y + \Delta y = (x + \Delta x)^2$$

$$y + \Delta y = x^2 + 2x(\Delta x) + \Delta x^2$$

$$\Delta y = 2x(\Delta x) + (\Delta x)^2$$

$$\frac{\Delta y}{\Delta x} = 2x + \Delta x$$

$$\text{as } \Delta x \longrightarrow 0$$

$$\text{Lim} \ \frac{\Delta y}{\Delta x} = 2x$$

FIG. 8.21. Possible basis for learning elementary differential calculus.

cally advocate this method of teaching calculus, it does illustrate that algebraic examples can be used as a base for teaching differential calculus by analogy. Children learn to understand calculus by mapping it into algebraic examples that they already understand. Not all the vertical mappings have been shown in Fig. 8.21, because it would make the diagram too complex if they were all drawn in. However, all the terms in the calculus expressions have analogs in the algebraic examples. As with other forms of analogical learning, when teaching calculus by using algebraic examples as a base it is essential to ensure that the base relationships are well known and understood. The child will construct his or her understanding of calculus by mapping the relations between the algebraic terms into his or her model of the calculus. For this to happen the relationships between terms in the base must be well known (Gentner's principle of base specificity).

Learning Mathematics

At one time there would have been considerable debate between Piagetians who advocated that learning should be based on understanding, and learning theorists who averred that it depends on strengthening the right associations. Little of this debate remains, and Resnick (1987) noted that dissension has been replaced by consensus: "We are in the midst of a major convergence of psychological theories. Functionalists and structuralists, learning theorists and developmental psychologists, information processing psychologists and Piagetians are finding common ground in today's research on cognition" (Resnick, 1987, p. 19).

There is common ground that mathematical concepts are acquired by actively constructing mathematical rules, based on the materials provided. We saw earlier how children invented their own subtraction rules, and how they invented their own malrules in place of the distributive law. We have also seen how even quite young children can adapt to the constrained-counting task, using their understanding of the principles of counting. As Resnick (1983a) pointed out, children construct their understanding of mathematical concepts, they do not simply mirror what they are taught.

It is clear, therefore, that understanding plays a highly significant role in the development of mathematical thinking, although this does not deny that associative-strategy selection mechanisms operate as well, nor does it imply that nothing is learned without understanding, as explained in chapter 6. As we saw with N-term series reasoning, strategies can be selected on the basis of past associations with success or failure, without metacognitive mechanisms operating at every step. As discussed earlier, Siegler (1988) showed how associative-strategy selection mechanisms can account for a considerable amount of mathematical activity. There is really no need for a controversy between advocates of cognitive and associative theories here. As I argued in chapers 4 and 7, associative mechanisms will be used where they are adequate, but where new strategies are required, metacognitive mechanisms take over.

Associative-strategy selection mechanisms work by choosing the most dominant strategy in a particular situation. A confidence rating is given for that strategy, and if it is below criterion, a new strategy is chosen. If no strategy is above the confidence criterion, either the criterion must be lowered or a new strategy must be constructed. Thus new strategies are developed where no existing strategy is judged to be adequate. This is consistent with the examples we have considered in this chapter, where malrules were constructed in situations where children could not retrieve the correct rule.

In many cases where children invent malrules they actually know the correct principles (Resnick, 1987). The problem is that they cannot apply these principles to constrain their strategies. The result is that they construct strategies that are inconsistent with the principles they know. Part of the reason for this is that the structure mappings from mental model to strategy are often immensely complex, as the examples illustrated in Figs. 8.14, 8.19, and 8.20 illustrate. There is little chance that children could construct these mappings for themselves. Consequently, children must learn appropriate chunks so they can code the relevant structures efficiently.

One factor that has frequently been overlooked is that the mapping of mental models onto problems imposes a processing load. We saw in chapter 3 that adults who were solving transitive-inference problems showed evidence of processing load effects at the point where they had to map the premises into an integrated representation. This occurred even after extensive experience with the particular type of problem used. The problem for children might often be that they know the relevant principles but cannot cope with the processing load associated with applying those principles to the problem. A child who knows place value might still borrow across zero, as in Fig. 8.10, trading 100 for 10, and thereby failing to conserve the quantity in the minuend. The problem is that the child lacks the capacity to map the principles into the problem, because he or she cannot code it efficiently.

Recognition of the role of understanding in mathematics learning has led to changing conceptions of instruction. The role of instruction has become to provide materials on which learners' constructive processes can operate (Resnick, 1987). Another role of instruction, however, is to provide experiences that will confirm or disconfirm mental models that children construct. As a corollary of this, instruction must provide a means of selecting more appropriate rules. To develop these ideas, we need to return to the theory of learning outlined in chapter 4.

Mental models may be regarded as collections of declarative rules. These rules are strengthened when they make nonredundant assertions that correspond to environmental events and are weakened when they make assertions that are disconfirmed. For mental models to be developed, therefore, children must have experiences that discriminate between valid and invalid mental models. If experience is too restricted, invalid models can adequately predict the observed events and, therefore, will fail to be eliminated.

Consider the mental model for addition in Fig. 8.8, based on the work of Collis (1978). Children can learn that if they construct a set of three objects and another set of four objects, then count right through both sets, they will obtain the answer "seven objects." However, any one experience of this type can be encoded in several ways, and a child's first rules for this situation might not be appropriate. A child might conceivably formulate a rule that applied only to crosses, or whatever other object was used in the examples. The child might adopt the rule "four crosses plus three crosses gives seven crosses." When the same child sees four apples in one set and three more in another, the child might fail to predict that there will be seven apples altogether. The rule he or she has formulated says nothing about apples.

When a parent or sibling asks the child to count the apples, and the child finds there are seven, he or she might formulate the rule "three apples plus four apples gives seven apples." The child now has two rules, one for crosses and one for apples. The same child might then construct several similarly specific rules for a number of other situations. As Saxe, Guberman, and Gearhart (1987) showed, mothers play a lot of games with their children involving number. The child might first formulate a specific rule for each of several situations encountered in the course of such games. Then, by induction, as discussed in chapter 4, the child replaces these specific rules with a much more general one, $3 + 4 = 7$. This rule will survive and displace the others because it is much more effective in predicting what happens. It can predict the outcome of the process of creating a set of three and a set of four, then counting through both sets, irrespective of what objects are contained in the sets.

Even in this (to us) extremely simple situation, a fairly wide variety of experiences are necessary to enable the child to construct the right rule. Of course parents, siblings, and teachers can help a lot by suggesting appropriate rules. The instructor might say to the child "there you see, 4 plus 3 gives 7." This assistance is useful because it makes an appropriate rule available, and therefore assists the induction process.

The child will not learn simply because he is told it, however. For the rule to become part of the child's mental model, he must have experiences in which the rule makes valid predictions. Information provided by instruction helps, but it is not the whole learning process.

Once the child has learned a general rule for 3 plus 4 equals 7, the child still has a long way to go to understand the basis of simple addition. He or she has to formulate a rule for other set sizes, then a rule that predicts what happens when we create any two disjoint sets and count through both of them. Then and only then will the child have a rule that provides a valid mental model of addition. Then and only then will the child have a rudimentary understanding of addition.

This is not to say that all learning must be "discovery" learning. If a child had to discover through free exploration the complex set of relationships that underlie even elementary arithmetic, it might take several lifetimes. Clearly, instructors are required to provide the necessary experiences, to help the child construct appropriate models of experience, and to develop skills. As discussed in chapter 6, social processes are vital to direct children's attention to appropriate features of a situation, maintain motivation, provide feedback, and to supply efficient ways of coding and representing concepts. However, for the rules to be learned, the child must find that they predict the experiences. Learning is not all discovery, but it is more than simply being told. Telling can help supply rules, but learning depends on experiences in which those rules are found to make valid assertions about the environment.

Important as understanding is, it is not the whole of learning mathematics. Another important aspect is to learn the relevant associations. As Siegler (1987, 1988) showed, it is necessary to have the appropriate associations between elements. The elements "3 + 5 = " must be associated with "8," and there must be a peaked distribution of associations, so there are no "wrong" answers that strongly compete with the right answer. As the distribution becomes more peaked, retrieval becomes more automatic and imposes a lower processing load.

The associations need not be divorced from understanding. The declarative rules that constitute understanding should provide support for the procedural rules that associate a particular response with a particular stimulus.

A second aspect is that the children must be taught how to translate understanding into performance. In some very simple situations, such as the constrained-counting task, they appear to be able to do this, although one might speculate that even here they have had considerable practice at relating their understanding to action. However in more complex situations, such as subtraction algorithms, the mapping relationships are of a complexity that is well beyond the ability of children to discover. In general, the process of relating understanding to performance is very complex, as the planning net of models of VanLehn and Brown (1980) and Greeno et al. (1984), discussed in chapter 4, make clear. Children need instruction to translate declarative knowledge into complex skills.

Rules are never learned in isolation. Children will always have prelearned rules that they can apply to a particular situation. If those rules are inappropriate, they will conflict with the rules to be learned. If they are appropriate, they will support the rules to be learned. If the child already has a partially valid mental model, he or she will have a good chance of predicting the material to be learned. Both of these factors can enormously facilitate the learning process.

A striking example of the way prior knowledge can be used in the acquisition of new knowledge is revealed in studies of the way the Oksapmin children of New Guinea acquire arithmetic operations (Saxe, 1985). The Oksapmin have a counting system based on body parts, with 1 for the right thumb, 2, 3, 4, 5 for the fingers, 6 for the wrist, and so on across the body, so the right shoulder is 10, the nose 14, left shoulder 16, left little finger 27, and so on. When faced with the task of adding two numbers, Oksapmin people would use a "counting on" strategy based on this system. For example, to add 6

+ 8, they would count to the wrist (6), then continue naming further body parts. The traditional Oksapmin people kept no systematic record of the number of new body parts added. The result was that they really only reached a rather global estimate of the sum. However, those Oksapmin who had experience in dealing with money developed a systematic way of keeping track of the augend in addition. To add 6 + 8, they would count to the wrist (6), then continue naming body parts with the names of parts denoting 1 to 8. Thus right forearm, normally 7, would be called 1, the right elbow (normally 8) would be called 2, and so on to the nose (normally 14), which would be called 8. The correct answer, 14, could then be given.

This example illustrates three points. First, it clearly shows how a new concept, addition, was acquired by utilizing a preexisting concept, numeration by body parts, as an analog. The augend and addend are mapped into the body-part representation of numbers. Second, it shows the creative ingenuity that people use to construct mathematical techniques. The strategy of counting by naming body parts, not with their usual names, but with the parts denoting 1, 2, and so on, provides a valid means of keeping track of how far one has counted. It clearly illustrates how people invent techniques based on their own conception of the task. Third, it shows how experience with problems will eliminate invalid techniques, so only valid ones survive. Those Oksapmin people who had little contact with money had little experience with addition problems. They would therefore suffer few disconfirmations of the predictions made by their rules. In the problem 6 + 8, if they globally counted from 6 they might produce the answer 12, or 15, but they probably would not find out that it is incorrect. Thus the crude procedure that they invented would not be disconfirmed. However, in a transaction involving money, two people who counted globally would arrive at different answers, which would lead to disputes, which would have the effect of disconfirming at least one of the answers obtained. A more valid way of generating the answer would then have to be found.

The importance of environmental confirmations and disconfirmations is also illustrated by studies of mathematical techniques used by child street vendors (Saxe, 1991). Brazilian children with little formal schooling, but who earned their living selling candy in the streets, had accurate techniques for performing complex tasks such as adding large numbers and comparing ratios. To add 37 + 24 they would add 30 + 20 and 7 + 4, and obtain 50 + 10 + 1, and finally 61. The child vendors needed to compare ratios to decide whether, for instance, it was better to sell 1 box of candy for Cr 200 or 7 for Cr 1,000.

Although the vendors had inferior knowledge of the standard orthography, they had a representation of number based on the money bills that they used in trading. Thus they could identify money bills with their numbers occluded, and they performed computations by composing bill values. They appeared to have learned a number of valid ratio comparisons that were useful in their work. The vendors were typically superior to nonvendors in these activities, although they generally had less schooling.

These findings illustrate the role of experience in selectively confirming valid rules and disconfirming invalid rules. Invalid rules would lead to highly salient disconfirmations, because the errors they caused would tend to reduce profits. Children who had received little schooling had invented their own rules, and experience had ensured that only valid rules had survived.

Summary of Quantification

Quantification depends on the ideas of classification, order, and composition. Classification is required so sets of equal magnitude can be grouped into equivalence classes, thereby providing a basis for the concept of cardinality. The concept of order depends on integrating asymmetric binary relations and is related to acquisition of transitivity. Concepts of composition appear to be understood by young children and form the basis for arithmetic operations of addition and multiplication, which in turn are essential to the concept of number. Mental models of number appear to incorporate the idea of order, often in the form of a number line or similar analog. Enumeration processes include subitizing, estimation, and counting, the last of which appears to be based on some fundamental ideas of number that are likely to be partly innate.

Arithmetic is understood using concrete set analogs as the base for mental models, which in turn guide the development of skills. Concrete analogs, however, can impose high processing loads because of the complexities of the structures represented. The load can be reduced by learning to recode the structures as smaller numbers of chunks, and by developing strategies for processing segments of the structures serially. Arithmetic word problems cause difficulties that are partly attributable to the complexity of the structures that must be mapped into schemas. The difficulties are analogous to those that occur in class inclusion tasks.

Algebra is understood using arithmetic as a base. This implies that the degree to which the structure of the number system, and arithmetic operations, are understood will be a significant factor in the ability to learn algebra. Calculus is understood using algebra as a base.

CONSERVATION

One of the most persistently troublesome problems in cognitive development has been to explain how children learn conservation, that is, that a quantity remains the same when simply moved or rearranged. I have reviewed the literature on this problem elsewhere (Halford, 1982, 1989). The origin of this knowledge turns out to be surprisingly difficult to explain.

Consider, for example, a quantity of liquid in a short, wide container. Suppose it is poured, in full view of a child, into a taller and narrower container. Traditionally, the problem of conservation has centered on why children of less than 5–6 years generally do not know that the quantity remains the same when simply poured from one vessel to another, without anything being added or subtracted (Gelman, 1969). Actually, however, it might be just as reasonable to ask how older children and adults do know this. That is, instead of trying to explain young children's failures, perhaps we should try and explain our own successes. This, too, turns out to be harder than expected.

When we witness the above demonstration, how do we know quantity is conserved? The traditional Piagetian explanation is that conservation depends on concrete operations, which are reversible, and which are not acquired until approximately 7–8 years. The reversibility of concrete-operational thought means that the apparent change is accompanied, in thought, by its own reversal, and so the quantity is seen as remaining the same. One problem with this argument is that reversibility does not necessarily entail conservation. As Berlyne (1965) pointed out, stretching a rubber band is reversible, but the length of the band is not a constant, so there is really no conservation.

In the conservation situation, both conserving and nonconserving judgments are reversible. Suppose, for example, that we see liquid poured from a short, wide vessel into a tall, narrow one. There is really nothing inconsistent about saying that the quantity increases then decreases again. Thus, a reversible nonconservation judgment is perfectly possible. We do not believe that quantity increases then decreases when transferred in this way, but the basis of this belief is not consistency within this situation. It must have some broader basis, going beyond the immediate situation.

An alternative explanation is that we acquire conservation by learning to attend to the relevant dimension (Gelman, 1969). For example, when liquid is poured into a taller and narrower vessel, the height of the column of liquid increases, but this is not a relevant dimension. Quantity is the relevant dimension, and it remains constant. There are, however, two problems with this explanation. First, as I pointed out elsewhere (Halford, 1970), height is not irrelevant to quantity of liquids in a vessel. An increase in quantity is quite frequently accompanied by an increase in height. In general, quantity is constrained by height acting jointly with other dimensions such as breadth. The second problem is that this explanation begs the question of the origin of this knowledge. How do children come to understand the quantity dimension, what does this understanding amount to, and how do children know that quantity remains constant on this dimension?

A third explanation is that we learn to conserve by discovering the compensating changes in the two dimensions. For example, we learn that the increase in height is compensated by a decrease in breadth. A logical difficulty is that we would need to perform a precise calculation to know that the compensations are exact, and there is no evidence that most people perform the calculations. With cylindrical containers, the increase in height is much greater than the decrease in breadth, and it certainly is not obvious that the effects of these changes are equal and opposite. Empirical work generally does not support the argument that understanding of compensation is a necessary and sufficient condition for conservation, although compensation does appear to support conservation (Halford, 1982, chapter 8).

A fourth explanation is that conservation is acquired by quantifying the material before and after the transformation (Klahr & Wallace, 1976). For example, with discontinuous quantity, such as a set of beads, the child counts or subitizes the beads, then they are rearranged, then the child counts or subitizes them again. He or she finds that the quantity is always the same after the transformation and therefore adopts the rule that the transformation leaves quantity unchanged. This rule is adopted because it achieves economy in cognitive processing, because it eliminates the need for the second quantification operation.

This theory has considerable plausibility for small sets, but it is not clear how it explains conservation of sets too large to be quantified accurately, nor how it accounts for conservation of continuous quantities such as liquids. To know that the amount of liquid in a tall, narrow container is the same as it was in the short, wide container before pouring, a child would need to measure the height and breadth of both columns of liquid, and apply the formula $V = \pi R^2 H$ to show that the volumes are in fact equal. It is doubtful whether even most adults have ever done this.

A fifth possible explanation would be that children learn the rule that just pouring liquid, or rearranging discontinuous quantities, leaves the amount unchanged. This rule appears to explain how people make conservation judgments, but on closer examination the explanation turns out to be circular. We need to explain the origin of the rule, but the justification for the rule depends on our knowledge that quantities are conserved, which presents us with the original problem all over again.

There have been a large number of experimental attempts to train children to conserve (see reviews by Beilin, 1978; Field, 1987; Halford, 1982). A wide range of training techniques have been used, but the outcome does not appear to favor any one teaching method. Any technique works at least sometimes, and no technique consistently succeeds with all children in a sample. Thus, training studies have failed to isolate a single process underlying conservation acquisition. The result has been that for a considerable time the theory of conservation has been at an impasse, with many proposals, but no fully substantiated explanations. However, a recent project by Simon,

Newell, and Klahr (1991) provided, for the first time, a computational (computer simulation) model of conservation.

The Q-SOAR Model of Conservation Acquisition

This model by T. Simon et al. (1991) takes as its starting point the theory of Klahr and Wallace (1976), mentioned in the last section, that children learn that quantity is conserved by quantifying the sets and finding that there is the same number before and after the transformation. The model is based on the SOAR architecture (Newell, 1990), which accounts for a wide variety of cognitive processes. It specifically simulates acquisition of conservation in a study by Gelman (1982), in which 3- and 4-year-old children counted two rows each of four turtles, then one row was transformed, and they were asked to say again whether they were the same or different, on the basis of counting.

SOAR is based on a number of problem spaces, in which operators are applied to states to attain goals. For example, if the goal is to to quantify a set of turtles, the QUANT-C, or quantify by counting, operator is used. If no decision can be made, an impasse occurs, and a shift is made to a new problem space to find a solution to the problem. For example, in a conservation problem the DETERMINE-RESPONSE operator is tried in the conservation space. If this fails the RESPOND space is selected, and it contains the operators measure, compare, and recall. If Measurement is selected, this in turn leads to the QUANT-C operator, then to the COMPARE operator. The effect is to count the two rows of turtles and decide whether they are the same. After Q-SOAR has solved a problem it learns a new production (basically similar to the production-system models discussed in chapter 4, but somewhat more powerful), which can be applied in future. New acquisitions of this kind in SOAR are called chunks, but the meaning is not quite the same as the way the term chunk is used in the memory literature, nor is it the same as the conceptual chunks that have been discussed in this book. In SOAR, a chunk is a new production, in effect a new rule or procedure, whereas in chapter 3 a chunk was defined as an independent item of information of arbitrary size related to a dimension and a vector in a PDP representation.

The Q-SOAR model learns the conservation rule by counting the objects in two rows before and after the transformation and finding that they are equal. Having found this, it retains the formation in the form of new chunks that can be applied to future problems in a rule-like way. That is, after experience corresponding to that of the children in Gelman's (1982) study, the Q-SOAR program adopted the conservation rule, thereby simulating the children's learning. It also simulated the performance of the control condition after the corresponding experience. Thus, the model provides a very precise and sophisticated account of conservation acquisition for small sets of objects, and it can be expected to show some degree of generalization, though it does not deal with continuous quantities. One of many interesting features of the model is that it predicts that learning speed is influenced by the goal-versus-encoding interaction; that is, that learning depends on coding a situation in a way that is appropriate to the current goal. For instance, if the goal is to measure quantity, the situation must be encoded in terms of quantity-relevant features such as length and density of material. This, once again, highlights the importance of encoding to cognitive development.

Learning that a particular transformation leaves quantity unchanged by quantifying the quantity before and after the transformation is an important aspect of conservation, but our analysis earlier indicated that it also depends on wider aspects of the concept of quantity. That is, we adults conserve because conservation is consistent with out concept of quantity. I will explore this explanation in the next section.

Conservation and the Concept of Quantity

The literature on conservation suggests that there is no single basis for acquiring conservation, but that many factors contribute to conservation understanding. It seems likely that the conservation rule is supported by a child's entire understanding of quantity. That is, when we see liquid poured from a short, wide vessel to a tall, narrow one, to say it is now more would conflict with everything we know about quantity. Therefore the entire concept of quantity that each of us understands conflicts with nonconservation and supports conservation. How does the concept of quantity support the conservation rule in this way?

First we need to consider what the concept of quantity is. We cannot define it exhaustively, because it probably has components that have not yet been recognized, but we can certainly identify some of its constituents. First, quantity consists of the idea of composition, that is, the idea that any quantity is composed of a number of units added together. Second, quantity entails the idea of order, so that quantities can be rank ordered with respect to magnitude. Third, it entails the idea that quantity can be assessed by subitizing, counting, and measurement operations.

The concept of quantity consists of a large number of declarative rules. This explanation is only made possible by the postulate, discussed in chapter 2, that rules can be activated in parallel, and that concurrently activated rules can be mutually supportive. Some of the rules that would be relevant to conservation are shown in Fig. 8.22.

The Nonconservation rule is expressed as "move quantity → quantity changed." This means that if you move a quantity, such as by pouring it to a different vessel or by rearranging a set of elements, the quantity becomes

Rules Relating to Conservation

FIG. 8.22. Rules relating to conservation.

changed. The Conservation rule contradicts this: "move quantity → quantity unchanged." The remaining rules are supportive rules.

Rule Compensation expresses the observation that if you change one dimension, without adding or subtracting anything, then an opposite change will occur in another dimension. This rule can be confirmed by direct observation, because it is possible to see that as (say) height increases, breadth decreases. The rule does not say these changes are equal in magnitude or effect, nor does it say that they imply invariance of quantity. The compensation rule is simply the observable fact that, with nothing added or removed, a change in one dimension will always result in a change in another dimension.

Reversibility is the observable rule that if you move a quantity, then move it back, without doing anything else to it, you will have the same quantity again. Again this rule does not, of itself, imply quantity is maintained. It simply expresses an empirically observable fact. In that sense it is closer to what Piaget would have called "renversibilité" (translated as revertibility).

The Rank rule predicts that if you move a quantity, the rank order of that quantity relative to other quantities remains unchanged. This is by contrast with a rule that might hold that if you move a quantity it becomes more than another quantity that was formerly more than or equal to it, or that it becomes less than a quantity that was former less than or equal to it. The idea of this rule is that it predicts that the rank order of quantities remains unchanged when you only move them, without adding or removing anything. This rule cannot be observed directly like the Compensation and Reversibility rules. However, children might be able to learn that when they move quantities, they do not have to reassess the rank ordering of those quantities.

Rule Requantify is essentially the rule proposed by Klahr and Wallace (1976) as the basis for conservation, and modeled by Simon et al. (1991) as discussed in the last section. It says that if you have a particular quantity Qx, then move it, you still have Qx. This rule can be learned for situations where the child can perform the relevant quantification processes. As Klahr and Wallace (1976) showed, it would be learned first for sets that are within the subitizing range (up to three elements). Once children learn to count, the rule could be extended to sets that are within the child's counting range. The rule could also be learned for continuous quantities where it is clear that they remain constant, as where a liquid is poured from one container to another one of identical shape. The problem has been, however, as Simon et al. (1991) acknowledged, that the rule cannot be learned directly for all situations. For example, it is hard to see how it could be learned in the standard liquid conservation situation, where the child has no way of quantifying the pre- and post-move quantities.

This problem has always seemed rather intractable until PDP models showed that the central tendency of a set of experiences can be computed automatically by superimposing the representations on the same vector, as discussed in chapter 2. The quantities resulting from a transformation might be misleading on some occasions, but their central tendency would tend towards conservation. To see this, imagine a cylindrical container of liquid 3 inches high and 3 inches in diameter. Suppose it is poured into a much taller and narrower vessel, in which case it will appear to be more. If, however, it is poured into a much shorter and wider vessel, it will appear to be less. If we average these two effects, one more, one less, they tend towards a "same" judgment. That is, although the individual experiences suggest nonconservation, their central tendency suggests conservation. It is possible, therefore, that requantification based on the central tendency of multiple post-transformation judgments would promote conservation rather than nonconservation, even for discontinous quantities.

Rule Add implies that if you add, you will have more quantity. Rule Subtract implies that if you subtract, you will have less quantity. Both these rules can be learned by direct observation in a great many situations.

Rule Composition says that a quantity can be decomposed into units that are added together. Increase says that if you increase a quantity, you will have more units, and Decrease says that if you decrease quantity you will remove units. These rules are conceptual rather than empirical, and they probably cannot be learned by direct observation. As we have seen, they are integral to even elementary concepts of number and are probably learned in that context and applied to discontinuous quantities by analogy.

Conservation Based on Multiple Supportive Rules

The essence of my argument is that conservation is acquired because the Conservation rule receives support from all the other rules, whereas the Nonconservation rule receives support from none of them. Conservation and Nonconservation rules both receive confirmation from direct experience, depending on the particular situation. The Conservation rule will be confirmed when the child is capable of quantifying before and after the move. This occurs when sets are small or when a continuous quantity is moved from one vessel to an identical one. The Nonconservation rule receives support when the quantity appears to be different after the move. If liquid is poured from a short, wide vessel to a tall, narrow one, there are salient cues indicating that it is more. This confirms the Nonconservation rule, at least for isolated experiences. One prediction that follows from this analysis is that young children should not have just one sort of rule. They should have both Conservation and Nonconservation rules, because both are confirmed by experience. Consistent with Bryant (1972), this implies that young children experience conflict between conservation and nonconservation.

Where the Conservation rule wins out is in the support that it receives from other quantity-relevant rules. The Conservation rule is more consistent with the other rules than is the Nonconservation rule. The Conservation rule predicts that if you move a quantity so that one dimension changes, then because the quantity remains constant, there must be an opposing change in the other dimension. Thus, the Conservation rule predicts the Compensation rule (see Halford, 1970, or Klahr & Wallace, 1976, for a discussion of this point). The Nonconservation rule makes no clear prediction here. If quantity changes when moved, then a change in one dimension may or may not be accompanied by a change in the other dimension. To use our example, if we pour liquid from a short, wide container to a tall, narrow container, the height increases. But if quantity also increases, there is no special need for breadth to decrease. It could stay the same, or even increase. Thus the Nonconservation rule makes no clear prediction, whereas the Conservation rule predicts that breadth must decrease.

A similar situation obtains with Reversibility. The Conservation rule predicts that because quantity remains constant when moved, if you move it back again it must be the same. The Nonconservation rule is consistent with it being the same, but does not make this prediction as clearly.

The Requantify rule, wherever it applies, certainly supports Conservation, because quantity will be found to be at least approximately the same after it is moved. Although requantification might not be possible in some situations, the rule might still be activated and add support to the Conservation rule.

The Add and Subtract rules support the Conservation rule by making it more informative. As discussed in chapter 4, rules tend to be enhanced if they increase discrimination between situations. Given that we know that Add results in more quantity and Subtract in less, the Conservation rule, which holds that Move (without adding of subtracting) leaves quantity unchanged, provides a sharp discrimination between the three types of situations. This should increase the likelihood of the Conservation rule being learned. Consistent with this, Wallach and Sprott (1964) and Halford and Fullerton (1970) showed that children would acquire conservation if required to discriminate between actions that merely rearranged a set of objects and actions that added or removed objects.

Rules Increase and Decrease imply that units are added or removed. The Conservation rule implies no units are added, whereas the Nonconservation rule implies units are added or removed when quantity is moved. Here again, the Conservation rule provides the sharper discrimination, because it implies that units are never added or removed when quantity is moved, whereas they are when Add or Subtract are applied.

According to this analysis, no one type of experience leads to, or supports, acquisition of conservation. It is truly a reflection of our whole concept of quantity. It is therefore heavily dependent on prior knowledge of quantity, and the theory predicts that conservation acquisition will be a function of children's knowledge about quantity and number. That is not to say, however, that conservation could necessarily be acquired at any age if children were taught enough about number and quantity. Some quantification concepts, such as the concept of order, impose certain processing loads. As we saw in chapter 7, the concept of order entails integrating relations, and there is evidence that children lack the processing capacity to do this until a median age of approximately 5 years.

Young children can be taught conservation rules in restricted situations, as the study by Gelman (1982) demonstrated. There have been a considerable number of studies that are consistent with this interpretation (see Halford, 1982, 1989a, 1989b, for reviews). However, where conservation develops out of a broadly applicable concept of quantity, including the concepts of classification, order, and composition, as discussed earlier, it is unlikely to develop before a median age of approximately 5 years. There is a complex empirical literature on this question, which I have considered in detail elsewhere (Halford, 1982, 1989a, 1989b; Halford & Boyle, 1985), and I think it is a fair summary that there is no solid evidence of broadly based conservation or quantity knowledge before approximately 5 years. Children younger than this undoubtedly know a lot about quantity; for example they are fully capable of recognizing size relations between sets and continuous quantities, and they grasp elementary counting, and so forth, as I have already discussed. However, there is no evidence that they have the kind of integrated conception of quantity that would enable them to spontaneously arrive at the inference that some transformations consistently leave quantities conserved, despite appearances.

Another prediction from the present theory would be that conservation would be most readily acquired in conditions where the Conservation rule receives the most direct support. This occurs with small sets, because children can quantify them accurately, and there are no major, visible changes of dimensions, such as where vessels change shape radically. If liquid is poured from one vessel to an identical one, the cues provide no support for the Nonconservation rule. Consequently, it is more likely that the Conservation rule will be dominant. Both of these predictions are consistent with empirical data (Bruner, Olver, & Greenfield, 1966; Siegler, 1981).

SUMMARY AND CONCLUSIONS

Classification ability is present at least in rudimentary form in infancy, but ability to represent hierarchies of classes and ability to classify by two criteria, as in matrix completion tasks, do not appear to be present until approximately 5 years. The many explanations for young children's failures, especially on class inclusion tasks, although they have accounted for part of the problem, have not fully explained observed age effects. It is argued that class inclusion and matrix completion depend on three-dimensional representations, which have consistently been found to cause difficulty for children under 5 years of age.

The process of class-inclusion reasoning is postulated to depend on mapping the problem into a schema induced from life experience, consistent with the processes suggested in chapter 7 to underlie transitive inference and the Wason selection task. The complexity of the structures to be mapped, based on three-dimensional representations, is suggested to be a cause of difficulty.

A similar factor is suggested to be responsible for much of the difficulty observed for arithmetic word problems. Where children are unable to represent the required three-dimensional structure, they default to lower dimensional structures, which results in set comparisons. However the tendency to compare two subsets in class-inclusion tasks is a consequence of a default resulting from excessive representational load, and should not be confused with the cause of failure.

Children's concept of number is based on classification, order, and composition. Early mental models are shown to entail ordering of numbers, together with groupings of like numbers. Young children also grasp the idea that quantities are composed of other quantities added together. Early understanding of arithmetical addition and multiplication can be based on experience with small sets, used as analogs. Children show early understanding of basic enumeration processes including subitizing, estimation, and counting, the last of which probably has a basis that is partly innate. Understanding of complex algorithms such as those used in subtraction can be faciliated by concrete analogs, but complexity analysis shows the mapping from analog to concept entails high processing loads in many cases. This must be reduced by conceptual chunking and by segmenting the mapping process into components that are processed serially.

Whereas sets provide analogs for arithmetic operations, arithmetic operations and concrete experience with numbers provide an analogical base for understanding algebra. Therefore algebra acquisition will depend on the degree to which the structure of arithemetic operations are understood.

Conservation acquisition does not depend on any one rule or experience but arises from the entire conception of quantity. This can be represented as a set of mutually supportive rules. The relatively late spontaneous acquisition of conservation may be attributable not to the task itself but to the complexity of some quantity concepts, especially the concept of order, which provides the basis for conservation.

9

SCIENTIFIC CONCEPTS

In this chapter we consider the way children understand a number of scientific concepts. We begin with the balance scale because of the longstanding interest in it, and because there is plenty of high-quality research to constrain theories of mental models for this task. We then consider a number of kinematics problems, with special focus on the way children understand the relations between time, speed, and distance, their concept of motion, and the differentiation between speed and acceleration. Then as an example of a complex kinematics problem, we consider the Rutherford analogy between the structure of the atom and the structure of the solar system. We consider the appearance–reality distinction because it is basic to scientific thought. The themes of knowledge organization and structural complexity, together with their interaction, are present throughout the chapter.

BALANCE SCALE

The type of balance scale that has been commonly used to study children's understanding of mechanical equilibrium is shown in Fig. 9.1. There are a number of equally spaced pegs on each side, on which weights can be placed, and a pair of chocks that can be placed underneath the beam to hold it level. This is so weights can be placed on the balance and children asked to judge what will happen when the chocks are removed. The beam will balance when the product of weight and distance on the left equals the product of weight and distance on the right. That is:

$$W_L \times D_L = W_R \times D_R$$

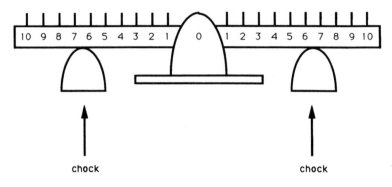

FIG. 9.1.   Balance scale.

Siegler (1976, 1981) used the rule assessment technique, discussed in chapter 6. He placed weights on each side of the balance, with chocks in place, and asked children to judge whether the beam would balance or whether the left or right side would go down.

With Siegler's Rule I, children's judgments about the balance beam depended solely on weight, irrespective of distance. If the weights were equal the beam balanced, otherwise the side with the heavier weight went down. With Rule II, distance was considered, but only if the weights were equal. Rule III entailed considering both weight and distance but provided no way of resolving the case where the greater weight was on one side but the greater distance on the other. Rule IV took account of both weight and distance, cases of conflict being handled by the cross-products rule.

As with other response pattern analyses, discussed in chapter 6, the rule being used could be diagnosed from the pattern of judgments made over the six problem types. Children using any of the four rules would make correct predictions on balance problems, those using Rules II and III would do so on the first four and three problem types respectively, whereas only participants using Rule IV would succeed on conflict-distance and conflict-balance problems.

Siegler (1976, 1981) found that most 5-year-olds used Rule I, most 8- to 10-year-olds used either Rule II or Rule III, whereas most 12- to 14-year-olds and adults used Rule III. Rule IV was rarely used even by adults. Siegler (1981) found that most 3-year-olds used no diagnosable rule. Attempts to induce more mature responding by training on the conflict problems were more successful with 8- than with 5-year-olds (Siegler, 1976). The reason turned out to be that 5-year-olds did not encode distance. When taught to encode distance, they showed similar benefit from training to the 8-year-olds.

Surber and Gzesh (1984) presented an analysis of the balance scale based on information-integration theory, discussed in chapter 2. Children aged 5–13 years and adults were presented with a balance scale on which one adult, equal in weight to three children, was placed on one side, and one or more children on the other side. They were asked to perform one of three tasks: judge the correct adult distance as a function of number of children and their distance from the fulcrum; judge child distance as a function of adult distance and number of children; judge number of children as a function of adult and child distance. For all three tasks the correct multiplicative rule would be revealed in the judgments by an interaction in the form of a diverging fan between the two factors. For example, adult distance would increase as a function of both child distance and number of children, with a supra-additive interaction (each factor increasing the effect of the other) resulting in diverging curves.

Not even adults gave consistent evidence of using the correct multiplicative rule, a result that is consistent with Siegler's findings. However, the results for 5-year-olds contrasted with Siegler's, in that they tended to base judgments on distance rather than weight. Their judgments of adult distance varied as a function of child distance, but not number of children (weight). Similarly, their judgments of child distance were a function of adult distance, but not number of children. Their judgments of number of children were actually related positively, that is, in the wrong direction, to children's distance, although this effect was due to a subset of the age sample.

The modal strategy observed by Surber and Gzesh appeared to be based on the idea of compensation, originally observed by Inhelder and Piaget (1955/1958). That is, a change in one dimension must be accompanied by a compensating change in the other dimension if balance is to be maintained. For example, if you increase the distance of the adult from the fulcrum, you must increase the number of children on the other side, or their distance from the fulcrum, or both. Sometimes the two factors were combined multiplicatively, sometimes additively. Additive information-integration rules have been observed in other tasks such as area judgment (see Anderson, 1980, for a review).

At first sight the findings of Surber and Gzesh (1984) appear to be in conflict with those of Siegler. Whereas Siegler found 5-year-olds focused on weight, Surber and Gzesh found they concentrated on distance. Whereas Siegler found that most children over 5 years and adults used Rule II or III, Surber and Gzesh found them to use compensation rules. The differing findings can almost certainly be attributed to the very different methodologies, as Surber and Gzesh explained, but on closer analysis the differences are not as great as they appear. Actually considerable common ground can be found between these two studies.

Siegler found that 5-year-olds based their judgments on weight; Surber and Gzesh found they were based on distance. The common feature here is that only one dimension was used by 5-year-olds, at least prior to the extensive training used by Siegler (1976), a point to which we will return. The second area of common ground is that in Siegler's Rules II and III and in Surber and Gzesh's compensation rules, weight and distance are processed by noticing differences, such as that weight on the left is greater than weight on the right. Furthermore, the dimensions are processed separately, there being no attempt to combine weight and distance by, for example, a multiplicative rule.

Consider, for example, a child viewing a problem in which four weights are placed on Peg 1 on the left, and two weights on Peg 2 on the right. Using Siegler's Rule III, the child will notice that the weights are unequal, then notice that the distances are unequal, but will not be able to combine these two pieces of information to obtain the correct answer, that the beam will balance. The child using a compensation rule will notice that there is more weight on the left, so distance must be increased on the right. The common feature is that weight and distance differences are noticed separately, then an attempt is made to determine how they compensate for each other.

Siegler's model is presented in the form of a binary decision tree, but the sequential decisions that are thereby implied do not appear to be intrinsic to the model. I have recast it in a form that is more suitable for structure-mapping analysis. Figure 9.2 contains a set of rules that express all the different compensations that occur in the balance. Siegler's Rule II is equivalent to rules 1–4 plus 7, whereas Rule III is equivalent to all nine rules. Thus, Siegler's Rules II and III are quite consistent with the compensation rules. This argument implies that the very different methodologies of Surber and Gzesh and Siegler have yielded results that are in basic agreement in this respect.

The next task is to try to define the mental models that might be applied to the balance scale. I would like to suggest that a primitive way of thinking about the balance is in terms of a downward force or "push" on each side. If the downward push is the same on both sides, then the beam balances, otherwise the side with the greater push goes down. This is consistent with the findings of McCloskey (1983) that naive concepts of motion entailed the idea of impetus. An object moves because an impetus to motion is imparted to it, and the impetus gradually dissipates and must be renewed to maintain motion. Downward "push" is an intuitive physical notion, like impetus.

Several different levels of mental model are shown as structure mappings in Fig. 9.3. At the element-mapping level, a weight is identified as supplying a downward push, signified by mapping the mental model, Push, into weight. This is equivalent to a person thinking of the weight as a downward push. A person operating at this level would think of only one weight and not be concerned about the other side of the balance. Metz (1987a, 1987b) found that the most primitive level of thinking about the balance entailed considering the weight on one side only. At the relational-mapping level, the mental model consists of a downward push on each side, together with the relation between them. The push on Side 1 can be more than, equal to, or less than the push on Side 2. The difference between weights, or the difference be-

1. $W_L = W_R$ and $D_L = D_R$ ⟶ balance

2. $W_L = W_R$ and $D_L > D_R$ ⟶ left down

3. $W_L = W_R$ and $D_L < D_R$ ⟶ right down

4. $W_L > W_R$ and $D_L = D_R$ ⟶ left down

5. $W_L > W_R$ and $D_L > D_R$ ⟶ left down

6. $W_L > W_R$ and $D_L < D_R$ ⟶ uncertain

7. $W_L < W_R$ and $D_L = D_R$ ⟶ right down

8. $W_L < W_R$ and $D_L > D_R$ ⟶ uncertain

9. $W_L < W_R$ and $D_L < D_R$ ⟶ right down

Siegler Rule II : 1, 2, 3, 4, 7

Siegler Rule III : 1 - 9

FIG. 9.2. Concept of balance scale in condition–action rule format.

tween distances, can be mapped into this model. Notice that there are two types of mapping that can be performed equally validly with this model. Either the weights or the distances on the two sides can be mapped into the model, but weight and distance cannot both be mapped. This is consistent with the findings that 5-year-old children can base their judgments on either weight or distance, but not both. The preference for one or the other cannot be based on structural simplicity, because their complexities are equal. When the procedure does not emphasize distance, there will probably be a preference for weight because a weight rule receives more confirmation from everyday ex-

A Element mapping

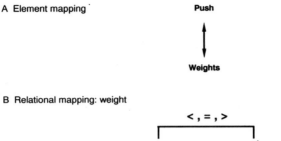

B Relational mapping: weight

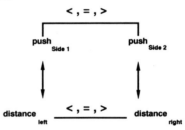

C Relational Mapping: distance

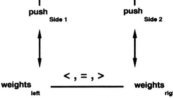

FIG. 9.3. Structure-mapping analysis of balance-scale concept.

perience. Everyone lifts objects and knows that a heavy weight exerts more downward push (or pull). However, the rule that greater distance exerts more downward push requires special conditions for its confirmation.

The system-mapping level expresses the compensation rules, or Siegler's Rules II and III. In this case the mental model includes two kinds of push, called a and b so as not to impose any special characteristics on them by assumption. Weights can be mapped into one kind of push, distance into the other. The difference between weights is represented, as is also the difference between distances. The combination of these can be either negative, zero, or positive. For instance, if the weight on Side 1 is less than the weight on Side 2, and if distance on Side 1 is less than or equal to the distance on Side 2, then the combination is negative, and Side 2 will go down. In certain cases the distances cancel each other out, and the result will be zero, and the beam will balance.

The major difference between relational- and system-mapping models is that both weight and distance can be mapped into system models. Differen-

D System mapping

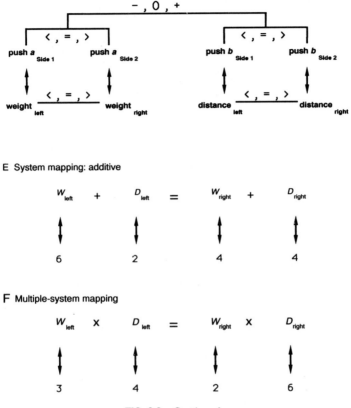

E System mapping: additive

F Multiple-system mapping

FIG. 9.3. Continued.

tiation of weight and distance probably becomes possible when they can be mapped together. It is probable that they would only be differentiated when they were seen as having distinct consequences. Prior to that they would be seen as simply two ways of varying the push; you can increase push by increasing weight, or by moving the weight further out from the fulcrum. Representation of both weight and distance in the same mental model would be conducive to differentiating them, so as to avoid conflict.

A more sophisticated mental model would entail mapping the problem elements into a multiplicative formula and abandoning the downward push model of the balance. There also appears to be a transitional phase, in which an additive rule is used. Surber and Gzesh (1984) found evidence suggesting that the additive formula might be an intermediate step between compensation rules and the multiplicative formula. An additive rule is really a system mapping because the weight and distance factors can be processed separately, because they do not interact. Therefore two separate representations can be used that are processed serially. That is, the effect of weight does not alter the effect of distance, or vice versa, with an additive rule. With a multiplicative rule, however, the factors do interact and must be considered jointly. This implies that the multiplicative rule must be at a higher level. It comprises two binary operations that must be considered jointly, so it is a multiple-system mapping.

PREDICTIONS

Given the data in chapter 3 about the ages at which children can make each level of structure mapping, it would be predicted that the most primitive concept of balance could be understood by 1-year-olds, that the weight or distance rules taken separately would be within the grasp of 2-year-olds, that the compensation rules could be learned by 5-year-olds, and that the correct multiplicative balance rule could be acquired by 10- to 11-year-olds. These predictions are clearly much more optimistic than empirical studies of the balance scale to date. Why then is performance so much poorer than the predictions suggest it should be?

A clue is obtained from the fact that Siegler successfully trained 5-year-olds to use both weight and distance. This is equivalent to using at least some of the compensation rules, and means that these children performed system mappings on this task. This of course is precisely what the theory predicts should have been possible, although this particular proposition has the status of a postdiction at this time. The important point, however, is that performance was greatly improved by training, and performance after training corresponded very closely to what structure-mapping theory predicts. This indicates that most initial performances on the balance scale may be a reflection of lack of knowledge rather than lack of processing capacity. That is, most people are performing below their optimal level on this task, and performances could be greatly improved. Structure-mapping theory suggests some levels of performance that could be achieved by training.

We can make several new predictions about the levels of performance that should be possible. One is that Siegler's training experiment would have been less successful in teaching compensation rules to children below 5 years (unless children of above-average ability were used). Perhaps the most significant prediction is that children younger than 5 years should be able to use either a weight or a distance rule but not both in the same context. This could be tested by a training procedure in which children were shown variable weights always placed at the same distance. The effect of weight would of course be much clearer if the "noise" produced by variations in distance were removed. Different weight values would also need to be made quite distinctive. Quite young children should then learn to predict that the side with the greater weight would go down, and the beam would balance when the weights were equal.

Similar training could be conducted with another group of children using equal weights placed at varying distances. They would then learn that behavior of the beam depended on distance from the fulcrum. Children under 5 years should find it difficult to take account of both weight and distance, however.

Another procedure that should work would be to train a group of young children on weight, then with clear contextual cues differentiating the two situations, on distance. They should be able to learn both rules in their respective contexts. Attempts to combine both rules should, however, cause difficulty before a median age of 5 years.

It should even be possible to teach weight rules to 2-year-olds if the weights are made clearly different. According to structure-mapping theory, 2-year-olds should be able to make relational mappings. Because weight rules, or distance rules, require only relational mappings, 2-year-olds should be capable of learning to apply these rules, provided that the task makes no other demands for which they lack the knowledge. As we saw in chapter 8, their number knowledge would not permit them to count more than small sets of weights, so it would be necessary to use no more than one to three weights on each side. An alternative would be to use single weights of clearly different size. Similarly with distance rules, the distances would need to be clearly different on the two sides. As we see later in this chapter, 2-year-olds cannot understand distance in the context of motion, but they should be capable of learning to recognize which of two lines is the longer, if the differences are made clear enough.

The structure-mapping predictions about the ability of 2- to 5-year-olds to understand weight and distance rules clearly differentiate it from Case's theory. Case (1985) argued that children would not be able to predict which side of a balance would go down by comparing weights until Substage 0 of the dimensional stage, at 3.5 to 5 years (see Case, 1985, pp. 101–102). The present theory predicts that this should be possible at 2 years. Case predicted that children would not be able to decide which side of a balance would go down by counting the weights on each side until Substage 1 of the dimensional stage, at 5–7 years (Case, 1985, pp. 103–104). Again, the present theory predicts that if the sets of weights are kept within the counting range of the children, children younger than 5 should be able to perform this task.

The present theory also predicts that 2-year-olds should be able to learn a distance rule if they are given a sufficiently "cleaned up" set of experiences with varying distances. Case (1985), however, predicted that the distance rule should not be understood until the dimensional stage, beginning usually at 5 years, because distance, like weight, is a dimension.

The present theory attributes more to knowledge than does Case's formulation. Information-processing capacity sets limits to the levels of structure mappings that can be constructed, but within the levels progress is a function of knowledge and skill. The predictions about the weight and distance rules are a clear example of this. Case attributed the progression from Substage 0 to Substage 1 of the dimensional stage to an increase in processing efficiency, which reduces operating space required, leaving one more unit of short-term storage space. By contrast, structure-mapping theory attributes the equivalent progression, from comparing weights by inspection to comparison by counting, to acquisition of counting skills. This is a knowledge-based acquisition, rather than a change in processing capacity.

It should also be possible to teach 10- to 11-year-olds to use the correct multiplicative rule. Here again structure-mapping theory appears to differ from Case's formulation (Case, 1985, pp. 108–113). Case predicted that 11- to 13-year-olds would perform the task by comparing ratios, so with two weights on Peg 2 and four on Peg 1, they would note that there were twice as many weights on one side and the distance was twice as great on the other. The present theory does not dispute that this strategy could be used by children of this age, and I agree that this is one of the intermediate steps that could occur in development of the balance concept. Structure-mapping theory does predict, however, that this is not the only way that 11-year-olds could perform the task. The balance formula, in Fig. 9.3F, permits several different ways of performing the task, including comparing weight ratio to distance ratio, as postulated by Case, but also by comparing products of weight and distance on the two sides. According to the present theory, only lack of knowledge would prevent 11-year-olds from using any of these procedures.

One problem is to differentiate the cross-products rule from the compensation rule, because they produce similar performances in many situations. For example with four weights on Peg 2, versus two weights on Peg 4, weight is greater on the left, but distance is greater on the right, so the compensation rule correctly predicts that the beam will balance. The solution is to use the type of problems devised by Buntine (1987), with, for example, four weights on Peg 2 versus three on Peg 3. Here the compensation rule predicts incorrectly that the beam will balance. Another suitable problem for this purpose is shown in Fig. 9.3F.

ACQUISITION PROCESSES

In this section I outline how the balance beam concept would be expected to be learned under the theory outlined in this book. In the next section two computational models of the process are considered.

According to the present theory, the acquisition process is a function of both processing capacity and learning. The preceding section makes predictions based on the processing demands of the various balance-scale rules. However, knowledge will also be an important factor, as two examples we have already seen demonstrate.

First, children's quantification skills determine the kinds of differences between weights and distances they can process. A child who could only subitize but not count would recognize that three weights are more than one weight, but not that 10 weights are more than 9 weights. Also, a child who does not encode distance, perhaps because he or she has not realized that it is important to the balance scale, would not succeed on problems requiring this factor to be considered. This is not attributable to processing limitations because, as we have seen, a distance rule by itself is no more complex than a weight rule taken by itself. The relevance of distance is likely to be seen later because the environment provides less experience with situations where distance increases "downward push."

The initial understanding of the balance scale by a person of any age who has not encountered it before is likely to be based on analogy with other situations experienced in real life. Everyone has experienced situations where the weight of an object makes it push something down: a weight pushing down the hand, a cat depressing the surface of a cushion, and so on. Everyone has such notions available, but the problem for the novice is to work out how they apply to the balance scale.

I propose that a novice proceeds by trying to construct a mental model that matches the processes that are observed in the balance. These processes may already be partly known, they may be learned through explanation or demonstration by the experimenter, or they may be discovered by rudimentary experiments by the persons themselves. However the processes are observed, the essential problem is still the same: to construct a mental model that mirrors these processes.

The sophistication of the mental model will depend on two things: processing capacity and knowledge. Consider two extreme cases. On the one hand, an intelligent adult with reasonable mathematical knowledge, who also knows that "downward push" is influenced by both weight and distance from the fulcrum, might begin by hypothesizing that the weight and distance should be combined by addition or multiplication and compared with the sum or product of the weight and distance on the other side. This performance reflects reasonably extensive knowledge, because even though the person knows nothing about the balance scale per se, he or she has plenty of other knowledge that can be applied to it. This person also has ample processing capacity to recognize the correspondence between the combined effects of weight and distance and the behavior of the scale. Such a person would quickly recognize that if you increase the distance you can maintain balance by decreasing the weight, or increasing the weight or distance on the other side (compensation) and, having mathematical knowledge, would try to find a way of combining these effects.

At the other extreme, consider a 1-year-old, who can represent only one-dimensional concepts, can only recognize correspondences based on element similarity, and has little mathematical knowledge. The only hypothesis available will be that the weight pushes the beam down. The child might pick up one of the weights, notice that it resembles other things that he or she has lifted that seem to push the hand down, and conclude that it does the same to the balance. This is equivalent to mapping the weight on the balance scale into the concept of "downward push," on the basis of similarity. This knowledge might seem primitive to us, but it is not useless. It comprises the beginnings of an understanding of the problem.

Progress from this point will be a function of two things: experience and processing capacity. An early stimulus to development is likely to be when the infant notices that his or her prediction about the behavior of the balance fails to be confirmed. The infant might place a weight on the balance expecting it to go down, but instead of going down it actually goes up, because he or she has placed the weight on the other side of the fulcrum. This probably will not result in an immediate insightful restructuring, as proposed by Gestalt psychologists (Wertheimer, 1945), nor a transition to the next "stage" of development, as proposed by Piagetians. All it will probably do is weaken the rule that the weight makes the balance go down. It will probably take several more experiences of this kind before the factor, side of the balance, enters the rule. The new rule will be something like "weight makes balance go down, unless it is on the other side." Putting this transition in the form of condition–action rules, we have:

Rule 1. weight $\rightarrow$ balance goes down

Rule 2. weight on side x $\rightarrow$ side x goes down

Thus a new condition has been inserted, and the action side has been refined. This rule will in turn be disconfirmed when a weight is placed on Side 1, but it fails to go down because a heavier weight has been placed on Side 2. A number of experiences of this type will lead to the rule:

Rule 3. heavier weight on side x $\rightarrow$ side x goes down

Ability to formulate this rule and apply it to examples of the balance will require sufficient processing capacity for relational mappings. Thus we see how experience and processing capacity will interact. Case (1985) traced progressive development from very primitive to more sophisticated rules on the balance scale. Although there are some parallels between his account and mine, I make several predictions that are more optimistic than Case's, as we have seen. The two theories differ further in the factors that are responsible for acquisition. Case postulated, as noted above, that progression is due to increased short-term storage space. I postulate that progress is due to learning, with processing capacity being a limiting factor only insofar as it determines the dimensionality of representations and, thereby, the level of structure mapping that is possible. However, there is considerable progress within each level of structure mapping, and that is due to learning rather than processing capacity. A further difference is that, as noted in chapter 3, processing capacity is a different construct from short-term storage space.

Several further developments are possible once the weight rule is formulated. One is refinement. Instead of just recognizing that one weight is more than, equal to, or less than another, these cases could be further differentiated into "much more than," "more than," . . . "much less than." It might then be noticed that if weight on the left is "much more" than weight on the right, the left side will go down "hard," and so forth. Another possibility is that the weight rule will be disconfirmed when it is found that the side with the heavier weight sometimes does not go down. By the same process of disconfirmation, formulation of exceptions, and finally formulation of a new rule, as discussed in chapter 4 and illustrated earlier, this will eventually lead to a rule that takes account of distance. It is necessary of course that distance be encoded so it can be incorporated in the new rule. The next rule might be:

Rule 4. distance equal, heavier weight → side goes down

By this process, the various rules in Fig. 9.2 can eventually be formulated. Again, however, we note that this will depend on processing capacity being adequate for system mappings.

The system-mapping rules will also prove to be unsatisfactory when they fail to predict what happens in the case where weight is greater on one side but distance is greater on the other side. This might be partly overcome by resorting to the more refined comparisons based on "much greater than," and so on, discussed above. If we can say weight on the left is "much greater than" weight on the right, but distance on the right is only "greater than" distance on the left, then we can predict the left side will go down. This means that one difference is being judged larger than another difference, which introduces a primitive type of interval information into the task, and from here it is but a short step to the additive combination rule that is specified in Fig. 9.3E. Thus progression within system mapping stages may well depend on refinement of comparisons, leading to an additive rule. When this too is disconfirmed, it will tend to be replaced by the multiplicative rule, but only provided the child has the processing capacity to map multiple-system level rules into problems.

Notice that it does not matter very much in what sequence the developments within a level occur. It matters little whether a child who has formulated a weight rule next differentiates comparisons into more steps, or whether his next step is to integrate distance into the rule. Sooner or later both of these steps will probably be required, but the order of their acquisition is not important. Thus there is a certain amount of equifinality here.

COMPUTATIONAL MODELS

A parallel-distributed processing (PDP) model of the way the balance beam concept is learned has been presented in different forms by McClelland (1991) and by Jenkins (1989). I present the essential ideas that are common to both versions of the model. The model comprises three layers of units. The lowest layer represents weight and distance values on each side. The top level represents the output, one unit signifying right side down, one unit left side down. If these units are activated to an equal extent (within specified limits), the response "balance" is obtained. In between there are what are called "hidden units" (so called because they are not connected directly to either input or output). Two of the hidden units are activated by connections to the weight input units, and two are activated by connections to the distance input units. The hidden units in turn activate the output units. The system learns the principle of the balance by adjusting the weights of the connections between the three layers of units. On each trial the activation of the output units is compared with the correct activation, and the weights are adjusted to reduce the discrepancy. Back propagation is then used to adjust the activations of the hidden units.

The system was subjected to a large number of trials in which weight varied more frequently than distance. This effectively simulates the predominance of weight over distance experiences in the environment. The system was found to progress through Siegler's (1976, 1981) four rules, discussed earlier. However, a large number of trials were required for the system to learn the balance-beam rules in this way.

This model has two points in common with the account of the balance scale given above. First, there is recognition of the role of learning, and second, I share the assumption that a bias towards weight is environmentally induced. The major difference is that in the McClelland-Jenkins theory in its present form, the model has no role for analogical reasoning or mapping of the problem into a mental model. One consequence of this is that it can only learn the principle of the balance over a large number of trials. However, I think it is likely that a person who had no specific knowledge of the balance could acquire the principle in very few trials, or even in one trial, by mapping it into another concept that was analogous to it. That is consistent with the acquisition process that I have outlined.

An analogical reasoning model of the balance scale could be based on the type of representation shown in Fig. 9.4. The mental model is the formula

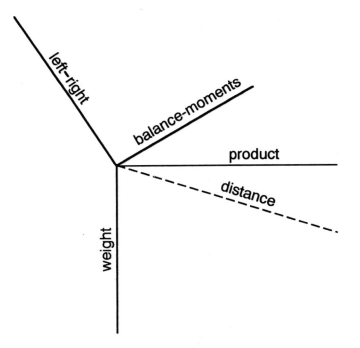

FIG. 9.4. Tensor-product representation of balance-scale concept.

$A \times B = C \times D$; that is, an equality of two products. This is an idea that should be familiar to most reasonably well-educated people from middle childhood on. Additional knowledge required would be how to code the balance in terms of weight and distance from the fulcrum, as discussed earlier. A person who had all this knowledge might still employ quite primitive reasoning about the balance scale because of failure to realize that the equality of two products was an appropriate mental model. However, a few minutes of explanation should suffice to indicate the appropriateness of the model. The person could then map the problem into the model with W_L mapped into A, D_L mapped into B, W_R mapped into C, and D_R mapped into D. Computations could then be performed using the $A \times B = C \times D$ formula, then mapped back to the balance scale. This type of analogical reasoning can be performed in accordance with the STAR model (Halford et al., in press), as outlined in chapter 5. The representation in Fig. 9.4 is basically appropriate for this purpose. The problem, coded as the variables W_L, D_L, W_R, and D_R, constitutes the target, and the formula $A \times B = C \times D$ is the base. Use of this mental model would greatly reduce the need for learning, because it predicts many of the relationships that have to be learned, consistent with the processes discussed in chapter 4. In effect, mapping the balance-scale problem into this mental model takes advantage of past learning in other contexts. The use of analogical reasoning in this way supplements the model of McClelland and Jenkins, discussed earlier, by showing how learning could be greatly accelerated, but this new proposal still utilizes the PDP architecture.

This particular mental model is based on the multiplicative rule, shown in Fig. 9.3F. It requires a four-dimensional representation, and the analogical reasoning entails a multiple-system mapping. This would impose a processing load that would tend to cause difficulties for children under about 11 years of age. Note, however, that children over a median age of 11 years and adults should be able to employ this reasoning, yet empirical work to date shows they rarely employ the multiplicative rule. Therefore this model predicts that there is scope for improved performance by these participants, using analogical reasoning with the mental model proposed here.

MECHANICS

In this section we consider how people understand and solve problems in mechanics. These problems depend on the concepts of mass, weight, distance, time, speed, velocity, acceleration, friction, force, gravity, inertia, energy, work, density, and volume. These concepts differ from those we have discussed in most of the preceding sections of this book in a number of important ways.

First, most of the research is not explicitly developmental, in the sense that the age variable is not manipulated. Most of the studies had the purpose of applying cognitive science to the improvement of scientific and technological education. Therefore they are more concerned with the factors that differentiate novices from experts than with age per se. Nevertheless, they have important implications for cognitive development, because they provide striking illustrations of the role of knowledge in cognitive performance, and because they give us the opportunity to analyze some complex tasks.

Second, the knowledge and skills required for these tasks cannot be acquired by natural interaction with the everyday environment. In this respect they contrast with most, if not all, of the tasks we considered earlier. Concepts like transitivity, conservation, classification, and deductive and inductive inferences can be at least partly learned by the child through normal interaction with the environment and without explicit instruction. It should even be possible to learn the basic principles of the balance scale through observation and experimentation, if there is sufficient exposure. By contrast, understanding of the motion of falling bodies, orbital motion of planets, or circular motion could not possibly be obtained by personal observation, without formal instruction. The reason is that it depends on concepts whose definitions have been developed by the culture over a long time, through the efforts of many of our most able individuals, and no single person could rediscover very much of this knowledge unaided, or in a cultural vacuum. As Carey pointed out (Carey, 1985, 1986; Wiser & Carey, 1983), many of the concepts that people are expected to use in these tasks took considerable periods of the history of science to develop. A person cannot perform adequately without access to this cultural knowledge base.

A third difference is that most of the tasks we consider here are too complex to be represented by a single concept or schema. They contrast with many of the tasks considered in earlier chapters in this respect. For example, a transitive inference can be made by mapping the problem elements into a single representation consisting of an ordered set, and the balance scale can be understood by mapping it into a single formula. With many of the tasks to be considered in this section, more than one formula is required, so representation has to proceed in a number of steps. This means that more than one structure mapping is required, and this process is an important development of the theory of structure mappings.

Partly as a result of the esoteric nature of the knowledge required, misconceptions about mechanics phenomena abound. We recall from chapter 1 that most people have an impetus theory of motion (McCloskey, 1983) that has parallels with medieval and Aristotelian theories of motion. Here are some of the common misconceptions (Champagne, Klopfer, & Anderson, 1979):

1. A force must be applied to an object to keep it moving. When the force is removed, objects gradually lose their stored momentum and slow down.
2. Acceleration is identical to speed, or alternatively, acceleration is the initiation of motion.
3. Heavy objects fall faster than lighter objects.

Although each of these notions is fundamentally incorrect in terms of Newtonian mechanics, all of them tend to be maintained by environmental confirmation. Due to the ubiquity of friction, an object only moves with constant velocity as long as a the force moving it is maintained. If we are pushing an object along, when we stop pushing, the object slows down and eventually stops, unless another force such as gravity keeps it moving. To understand this situation properly it is necessary to recognize that friction, or other factors such as air or water resistance, are always operating in our environment, and the force is required to overcome them. Without friction or drag, no force would be required to maintain motion. This principle cannot be observed directly without special procedures. It can be observed in a thought experiment, where we imagine the effect of removing friction. The problem is that to do this we have to consider at least three concepts: force, motion, and friction. The correct principle cannot be understood if any of these is missing.

The notion that acceleration is identical to velocity (often confused with speed) is difficult to disconfirm in everyday experience, because the human eye is insensitive to acceleration (Champagne et al., 1979). To overcome this limitation requires some complex observations. Velocity is distance travelled in a particular direction, divided by time, but acceleration is a change of velocity over time. Even if we ignore the directional component of velocity, and just think of speed, the differentiation of speed and acceleration remains quite complex. We must obtain (at least) two observations of speed, each of which implies dividing distance by time. Then we must subtract the first speed from the second, and divide by the time difference between the two observations of speed. This definition of acceleration ($A = dt^{-2}$, where A = acceleration, d = distance, and t = time) entails a four-dimensional representation, but it also requires a set of observations that would need to be carefully set up and that do not occur naturally.

The notion that heavy objects fall faster than light objects may be due to the common experience, mentioned earlier, that heavy objects exert more downward pull (or push) than light objects. In principle, disconfirmation of the notion only requires that one release two objects of different weight and observe their rate of fall. This can be done by releasing them simultaneously and observing whether they reach the ground together or whether the heavier one hits the ground first. In practice, however, few people ever perform this experiment, and even if they do they might not have confidence in the results. They might suspect that the heavier object was really faster than the light object but the difference was too small to notice, and so on.

These misconceptions do not exist in isolation but form part of a consistent belief structure. For example, Champagne, Klopfer, Solomon, and Cahn (1980) reported cases of students who believe that velocity remains constant when force is constant, yet believe that objects accelerate in free fall. They justify this belief by stating that gravity becomes greater as one approaches the center of the earth, and this in turn is justified by pointing out that there is no gravity in outer space. The principle is partly correct, in that gravitational attraction is reduced as the distance between the bodies increases, but over a fall of a few feet the difference is of zero order and certainly not sufficient to explain the observed increase in velocity.

Also, Champagne, Gunstone, and Klopfer (1984) mentioned that some students justify their belief that heavy objects fall faster by referring to Galileo's experiment showing that a coin falls faster than a feather in air. They misremember the point of the experiment, which is that air resistance exerts more force on the feather. The true implication of Galileo's experiment was that without air resistance the feather and coin would fall at equal speeds.

These two examples illustrate the point discussed in chapter 4 that prior knowledge exerts a strong influence on acquisition of new knowledge. Everyone has very extensive experience of objects in motion and in free fall. Everyone has developed a belief structure, or set of rules, that predicts these everyday phenomena sufficiently accurately for discrepances not to be apparent to casual, unsystematic observation. New knowledge tends to be assimilated into this belief structure and becomes distorted in the process. This greatly adds to the difficulty of learning mechanics. On the other hand, prior knowledge is not the only factor that contributes to this difficulty; conceptual complexity is undoubtedly a factor, as our example with the differentiation of velocity and acceleration illustrated.

Complexity is also a factor in failure to understand that heavy objects do not fall faster than light objects. People's perception that heavy objects have more downward pull than light objects is basically consistent with the value of force due to gravity, F_G, which is determined by this equation:

$$F_G = Gm_e m_f / D^2 \tag{1}$$

where G = gravitation constant
  m_e is the mass of the earth
  m_f is the mass of the falling body
  D is the distance between the centers of mass of the earth and the falling body.
Clearly, the force *is* greater for falling bodies with larger mass. The reason the larger mass does not result in faster fall is that the mass to which it is applied is also larger, so the acceleration is the same. To see this, recall the formula $F = ma$, where a is acceleration. Substituting in (1) we have:

$$m_f a = Gm_e m_f / D^2$$

The mass of the falling body occurs on both sides of the equation, so it cancels out, and acceleration is independent of the mass of the falling body. The correspondence between this formula and the appropriate set of observations (or thought experiments) constitutes a complex mapping.

There are other, simpler ways to gain a partial understanding of the problem. For example, one could, as Galileo did, imagine the free fall of a 20-pound cannon ball compared with a 10-pound cannon ball. Naive theory says the 20-pound ball falls faster. Now think of the 20-pound ball as divided into two 10-pound balls. They should each fall more slowly, at a rate appropriate to a 10-pound ball. Now what if we connect the two 10-pound balls by a gossamer thread, making them one ball again? The implausibility of the notion that this should make them fall faster provides a *reductio ad absurdum* for the hypothesis that rate of fall depends on mass. This way of understanding the problem is structurally simpler, but it does not provide a full account of the relevant relationships between mass, force, distance, and acceleration.

THE NOVICE–EXPERT SHIFT

The examination of scientific reasoning makes us acutely aware of the role of domain knowledge in cognitive processing because of the obvious need for specialized knowledge when dealing with these problems. Although the importance of domain-general and domain-specific knowledge is self-evident, we must raise the question of its importance relative to other factors. For example, can we explain cognitive development purely in terms of knowledge acquisition, so that concepts like capacity become redundant?

One theorist who emphasized the overwhelming importance of domain knowledge is Carey (1985; Wiser & Carey, 1983). Carey gave numerous examples of the way domain knowledge underlies the development of children's reasoning. The essence of her argument is that much of cognitive development consists of conceptual changes, many of which show parallels to the conceptual developments that occurred in the history of science. According to this view, cognitive development has little to do with growth of memory or processing capacity, but has to do with conceptual change. Carey outlined four components of conceptual change: representation of new relations among concepts, creation of new schemata, changed solution to old problems, and fundamental changes in core concepts. This theory implies that what we call here conceptual complexity really reflects the extent of the conceptual development process that is required. Thus, a simple concept is one that can be understood by a novice or naive person, whereas a complex concept requires considerable expertise to be understood.

To illustrate this point, we consider the distinction between heat and temperature, which, as Wiser and Carey (1983) pointed out, took some decades of the history of science to develop. To see the distinction, imagine combining two vessels containing different amounts of water at different temperatures. If we take 50 ml of water at 100 degrees Celsius, and 100 ml at 60 degrees Celsius and combine them, a naive person might think that the resulting temperature would be obtained by simply adding the component temperatures, that is, it would be 160 degrees. This is not due to inherently faulty reasoning but to inadequate knowledge of the way temperature and heat are defined. Temperatures are simply not additive in that way. Heat, on the other hand, is additive and is defined as the product of mass, specific heat, and temperature. To perform the calculation we first need to convert the temperatures to Kelvin, by adding 273 degrees. The first lot of water contains $50 \times 373 = 18{,}650$ calories (the specific heat of water is 1), and the second contains $100 \times 333 = 33{,}300$ calories, so the combined water will contain 51,950 calories. It has a volume of 150 ml, therefore 150 grams, so the temperature will be $51{,}950/150 = 346$ degrees Kelvin, or 73 degrees Celsius. The difficulty of this problem arises not from the complexity of the reasoning per se, but simply from the requirement of knowing the relationships between heat, mass, volume, and temperature. If these relationships are known, the problem is simple. Its complexity reflects mainly the conceptual sophistication required to plan the path to solution.

The argument of the present book is that knowledge and conceptual sophistication are important, but that other factors are also important. Chapter 4 was devoted to learning mechanisms that can account for acquisition of a knowledge base and to ability to construct appropriate mental models for complex tasks. However, I have also suggested in chapter 3 that processing capacity will set limits to the number of dimensions that can be processed in parallel. These two factors, learning and processing capacity, are considered in relation to each problem. Therefore, there is no disagreement with theorists such as Carey on the importance of knowledge, provided it is not interpreted as excluding other factors. There is also agreement that representation of concepts is of supreme importance. I would like to develop this argument further by returning to the mechanics problems considered earlier.

REPRESENTATION AND THE NOVICE–EXPERT SHIFT

When problem solving has such a sizeable component of knowledge, it is to be expected that there will be a considerable difference between experts and novices. However, there are also differences between these two groups in the way they represent the problem (Chi, Feltovich, & Glaser, 1981; Chi, Glaser, & Rees, 1982; Larkin, 1983). For example, Larkin (1983) described how novices represent problems in terms of familiar objects, then proceed to envision events in temporal sequence; Event 1 occurs, then Event 2, and so on. The expert, on the other hand, adopts what is called a "Physical Representation" based on concepts such as force, energy, acceleration, and so on.

We illustrate the novice and expert approaches by reference to the problem in Fig. 9.5 (reproduced from Larkin, 1983, Fig. 5.3). The problem is this: What horizontal force F must be applied to the large cart in Fig. 9.5 so that the smaller carts will not move relative to the large cart (neglecting friction)?

The novice begins with statements such as "if you accelerated it at a certain speed, the wind would push on $m1$ so $m2$ wouldn't fall" (Larkin, 1983, p. 81). Notice the confusion of acceleration and velocity, shown by the statement about accelerating it at a certain speed. Notice also the appeal to the familiar relationship between speed, wind, and pushing. This solution attempt appears to be based on an analogy with the everyday experience that if you move fast, there is a wind force that tends to push you back. The expert's approach is to apply two physical schemas to the problem. In one schema, the solution is to accelerate the three carts to the right, thereby supplying a pseudoforce on Cart $m1$ to balance the tension in the string caused by the

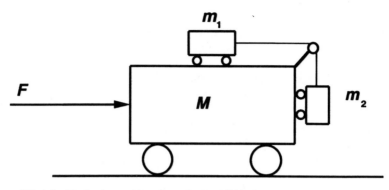

FIG. 9.5. Mechanics problem. From Larkin (1983). Reproduced by permission of J. H. Larkin and Lawrence Erlbaum Associates.

weight of Cart $m2$. Schema two focuses on the force that needs to be applied to all three carts.

As Larkin noted, this is a complex problem that requires coordination of more than one schema. One way to solve the problem is to reason that the force applied to Cart $m1$ must equal the tension in the string, which is equal to $m2\ g$. The acceleration this force will impart to Cart $m1$ can be calculated from the formula $F = ma$, where F is force, m = mass, and a = acceleration. Therefore we have:

$$m2\ g = m1\ a$$

which gives a value for acceleration, $a = m2\ g\ /\ m1$.

The acceleration of $m1$ must be the same as the acceleration of the whole structure if $m1$ does not move relative to M. The required force is obtained by applying the formula $F = ma$, using the value of a obtained above, and this time the value of m is the sum of the masses of all three carts. Therefore the expression for F is:

$$F = (M + m1 + m2)\ (m2\ g\ /\ m1)$$

We have really applied two schemas here. The first is that we use acceleration of $m1$ to apply a (pseudo) force to it opposing the tension in the string. In the second schema, we apply the formula $F = ma$ to calculate the force that will be required to accelerate the set of three carts by the required amount.

Several kinds of knowledge would be required to solve this moderately difficult problem. First, we need to know that the force tending to move Cart $m1$ can be neutralized by accelerating the cart. Second, we need to know how to obtain a precise value for this force. Third, we need to know how to to use the formula $F = ma$ to calculate the force required to provide the desired acceleration. Fourth, we need to know how to relate these items of information. As Larkin noted, and as we illustrated earlier, the problem solution depends on coordinating two schemas. In this case the coordination depends on the fact that whatever is done to one of the carts must be done to all three, so as to prevent them moving relative to one another. Therefore the mass of all three carts must be taken into account when calculating the force required.

How are these schemas applied? Larkin supplied an analysis of expert problem solving in which each schema has a number of slots that are filled with instantiations from the problem elements. For example, in the schema $F = ma$, the variable m is instantiated (filled) with the total mass of the three carts, and the variable a is instantiated with the acceleration required to be applied to Cart $m1$ to balance the tension in the string.

It is difficult, however, to understand just how an expert recognizes that this set of formulae will model the phenomena in question. They are undoubtedly helped by the interconnectedness of their knowledge. For example, Champagne, Klopfer, Solomon, and Cahn (1980) showed that experts tend to have rich semantic networks in which all the key concepts of mechanics are connected together. Novices on the other hand tend to put things into clusters that do not really make their interrelations clear. For example, inertia, momentum, speed, velocity, acceleration, and impulse are clustered together because they all have to do with moving objects.

Another clue is obtained from the fact that novices tend to use means–end analysis, whereas experts use a forward-chaining strategy (Sweller, Mawer, & Ward, 1983). Experts tend to start with the givens and select a formula that permits them to derive a value that can be used in the next step, and so on until the goal is achieved. Novices tend to choose a formula that gives them the desired quantity, then set subgoals to obtain the values required for this formula. For example, for the problem in Fig. 9.5, novices would start with the formula for force in the whole system, then seek an expression that will give the value of acceleration.

This suggests that experts somehow know what chain of formulas will be required, an hypothesis that is supported by the fact that their protocols usually indicate little time was required to find the appropriate schemas. Chi et al. (1982) suggested that experts store "chunks" of equations. However, the problem still exists of explaining how an expert knows which chunks or group of equations will mirror the structure of a particular phenomenon. I would like to explore this question in relation to the problem in Fig. 9.5.

If the whole problem were to be represented in parallel, with a separate dimension for each variable, it would be a very complex representation indeed, and on the basis of the capacity limitations outlined in chapter 3, I would say that no adult could process such a representation. This implies that segmentation and chunking must be involved. That is, the task must be decomposed into components that can be processed serially, and some variables must be combined into chunks.

Segmentation has been suggested already, when I pointed out that a value for acceleration would be obtained first, then this would be used to obtain a value for force. This divides the problem into two major steps, but these steps would also probably be subdivided into a number of smaller components.

Conceptual chunking would occur by combining variables. For example, the downward force acting on $m2$, which (as noted above) equals $m2\ g$, has been expressed in terms of two variables ($m2$ and g). However, it could be represented as a single variable, the "downward force on $m2$, F_{m2}. This is an example of low-level conceptual chunking. Another chunk would be the acceleration pseudoforce on $m1$, $m1\ a$, which can also be expressed as a single variable. In both cases three-dimensional concepts have been recoded as single dimensions. Another case of chunking occurs when all three masses are combined into a single mass, equal to $M + m1 + m2$. These chunks combine several component dimensions into single dimensions, thereby reducing the complexity of the representation required and, thus, the processing load.

However, these chunks are not sufficient in themselves, because they give a fragmented, somewhat incoherent representation of the problem. Some "overarching" chunks are required as well. An appropriate chunk would be the "balance of forces." That is, the problem really entails balancing an acceleration pseudoforce against a gravitational force. An expert would tend to recognize very quickly that the problem can be represented in some way such as this. An expert, therefore, would represent it first as an overarching chunk, then decompose that chunk into its constituents, realizing that the gravitation force will be composed of the product of mass and gravitation, hence the representation as $m2\ g$, mentioned earlier. The acceleration pseudoforce will be composed of mass and acceleration, hence $m1\ a$, as mentioned earlier. The acceleration force must be sufficient to balance the gravitation force, hence $m1\ a = m2\ g$, as mentioned earlier. In short, the expert knows how to represent the problem efficiently, with minimum processing load. This is accomplished by representing two or more variables as a single variable (conceptual chunking) and by processing these chunks serially (segmentation) under the guidance of an overarching chunk. Thus, solving the problem means moving from one representation to another in a coherent, organized way. Acquisition of expertise is partly a matter of acquiring these chunks and also of learning higher order chunks that express the relations between the lower order chunks.

Children's scientific knowledge has been observed to undergo some changes that parallel the novice–expert shift. Chi and Ceci (1987) noted that the associations between children's concepts tend to be weaker, more idiosyncratic, more perceptual in character, and less structured. In a study of children's dinosaur knowledge, Chi and Koeske (1983) found that older children had concept representations that included increased number of attributes, more connections between attributes, and greater strength of association between attributes. This cohesion of knowledge undoubtedly becomes more important as more difficult problems are encountered that require multiple schemas to be applied.

The attainment of expert knowledge is partly a matter of acquiring appropriate chunks. This entails a learning process, one of learning the associations between components and chunks, for example, learning that force = mass × acceleration. This means learning to express force in terms of the ternary relation between force, mass, and acceleration. Extensive experience with the mapping of components into chunks is required. However, children also need to learn the "external structure" of chunks, or how they relate to one another. This entails taking chunks as components and mapping them into further chunks, thereby creating the higher order chunks that give the overarching concepts discussed earlier. All this requires experience with situations that instantiate constant mappings of components into chunks. The result is representations that are much more efficient and that allow complex problems to be processed without excessive processing loads. We see another example of this when we consider the Rutherford analogy between the atom and the solar system.

THE CONCEPT OF TIME

As well as being able to form high-level connections between concepts, reasoning in mechanics requires that the basic constituent concepts of time, speed, and distance and the relations between them be understood. Friedman (1978) reviewed the development of time concepts in children and concluded that appreciation of experiential time, that is, the ability to perceive succession and duration, is well developed in young children. However, logical time, the notion that an event is correlated with a unique position on a temporal continuum, and conventional time, the ability to use cultural symbols such as clocks for time, develop in middle childhood.

Siegler and Richards (1979) applied the rule-assessment technique to a modified version of the task used by Piaget to study the developmental priority of time and speed. Two trains ran on separate tracks, and the time, speed, distance, end point, end time, beginning point, and beginning time of each train were varied. The problems were devised so that three types of rules for each of time, distance, and speed, would yield unique patterns of responses and would therefore be diagnosable. According to Rule I, judgments would be based solely on stopping point. That is, the train that ended at the furthest point would be judged to have traveled furthest, fastest, and for the longest time. According to Rule II, stopping times would be considered only if the stopping points were the same. According to Rule III, all factors would be considered appropriately.

Five-year-olds tended to use Rule I exclusively, that is, they based their judgments of distance, speed, and time on the stopping point. Eight- and 11-year-olds tended to use Rule III for speed and distance but used lower level rules for time, and appeared to have difficulty discriminating time and distance. The procedure of this study might have imposed a high processing load, because time had to be judged by monitoring the time that elapsed from start to stop. This would have to be done concurrently with noticing speed and distance from start to stop. The task would have been further complicated by the fact that time, speed, and distance had to be judged for two trains concurrently. If these concurrent performances overloaded the younger children, they might have had to fall back on the stopping point because, as Wilkening (1981) pointed out, this would be the only information available at the end of a trial.

Wilkening (Wilkening 1980, 1981; Wilkening, Levin, & Druyan, 1987) used information-integration theory to investigate the relations between time, speed, and distance. Children were shown a turtle, guinea pig, or cat representing different speeds, running for different distances or durations. Given two variables, they were asked to judge the third. With this procedure the animal provided a cue to help children recall the speed of running. Also, only one animal ran on any one trial, so there was less information to be processed. It was found that even 5-year-olds could combine time and speed multiplicatively to judge distance, but there was an eye-movement strategy that simplified the task. That is, children would move their eyes along the track at appropriate speed for the duration of the run, thereby ensuring that a reasonably accurate estimate of distance was computed automatically. When combining distance and speed to estimate time, 5-year-olds used both dimensions, but with an additive rule. However, when asked to judge speed, given distance and time, 5-year-olds considered only distance and ignored time. The probable reason for this is that time information is not visibly present in this task but must be retrieved from memory. Five-year-olds might have found recall imposed too high a processing load when they were trying to perform the task of integrating two variables. Nevertheless, Wilkening et al. (1987) showed that when time was the only factor to be considered, 5-year-olds could make accurate judgments of duration and could additively combine two durations.

It would appear to be a reasonable summary that a basic understanding of time, speed, and distance is present from 5 years of age and that combinations of these variables can be made if memory demands are minimal. However, there may be a tendency to recognize direct relationships before indirect. Acredolo, Adams, and Schmid (1984) found evidence that first-grade children tend to use a "more-is-more" rule, believing that if something travels for a longer time, it also travels faster. The inverse relationship between time and speed appeared to be a source of difficulty.

THE RUTHERFORD ANALOGY

Gentner's (1983) analysis of the Rutherford analogy between the structure
of the hydrogen atom and the solar system was discussed in chapter 5. The
basis of the analogy is that an electron orbits the nucleus of the atom in the
same way as a planet orbits the sun. As shown in Fig. 9.6, orbital motion
of planets and electrons depends on a balance between forces. On the one
hand, there is the gravitational attraction between the planet and the sun,
and an electrostatic attraction between the electron and the nucleus. Opposing

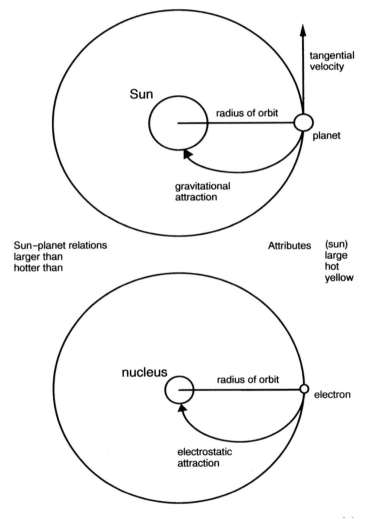

FIG. 9.6. Representation of the Rutherford analogy between structure of the
solar system and structure of the atom.

this force is the inertial tendency for the orbiting body to move at a tangent to the orbit. Gravitational or electrostatic attraction tend to hold the orbiting body in orbit and prevent it moving further away from the sun or nucleus.

As Gentner (1983) pointed out, the analogy entails selectively mapping certain relations between the sun and planet into relations between nucleus and electron. The relation "orbits around" between planet and sun is mapped into the corresponding relation between electron and nucleus. Similarly, the relation "larger than" between sun and planet is mapped into the corresponding relation between nucleus and electron. These relations are mapped because they meet the systematicity criterion, in that they enter into a coherent higher order structure.

The relations involved in orbital motion can be expressed in the following way. The gravitational attraction, A, is given by the formula:

$$A = GM_p M_s / R^2$$

where G is the gravitation constant, M_p and M_s are the masses of planet and sun respectively, and R is the radius of orbit. This gravitational force causes the planet to accelerate, described by:

$$M_p V^2 / R$$

where V is the orbital velocity of the planet. Because mass times acceleration equals the applied force on the planet, we can equate these two expressions, so we have:

$$GM_p M_s / R^2 = M_p V^2 / R$$

The essence of the analogy is that a corresponding set of relations exists in the atom. That is, electrostatic attraction equals mass times acceleration, expressed by the formula:

$$kq_n q_e / R^2 = m_e V^2 / R$$

where q_n and q_e are the electrostatic charges on nucleus and electron respectively. This formula defines the balance of forces in the atom in a way that parallels the balance of forces in the solar system. The analogy entails mapping the terms that define planetary motion into those that define the orbital motion of the electron around the nucleus. The full set of terms is shown as a semantic network in Fig. 9.7.

This is clearly a very complex mapping because each structure is defined by a complex set of relations, which are expressed in the equations above and in Fig. 9.7. The task that Rutherford had to perform was probably considerably more complex still because the account given above has been simplified in various ways. However, even in the form presented here, it is clearly a complex mapping. My purpose is to explore ways of simplifying it, using the concept of conceptual chunking, defined in chapters 2 and 3.

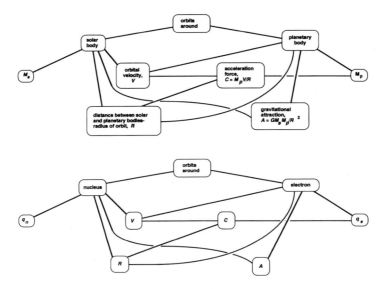

FIG. 9.7.   Representation of the Rutherford analogy.

CODING THE RUTHERFORD ANALOGY

As with the problem in Fig. 9.5, discussed earlier, if the entire Rutherford analogy were to be represented in parallel, without chunking (i.e., with a separate vector to represent every predicate and argument), the representation would be much too complex for even adults to process in parallel. Therefore, segmentation and conceptual chunking must be involved. As with other problems discussed in this book, one role of expertise is to enable more efficient coding of concepts, so they represent the significant aspects of the relevant structure without overloading processing capacity. Considerable work needs to be done to find out just how people of various levels of expertise would encode the Rutherford analogy, but we can identify some chunks that would be logical and appropriate.

The basic idea of the analogy can be expressed as the first alternative in Fig. 9.8. In this representation there are two nodes, one representing the solar body and one representing the planetary body, with the relation "orbits around" between them. The analogy can be constructed by mapping "solar body" into nucleus, "planetary body" into electron, and recognizing that the "orbits around" relation also exists in the electron. This would be a relational mapping, as defined in chapter 2, and would impose quite a low processing load. It could even be represented as a visual image, as shown in the second alternative in Fig. 9.8.

However, anything more than a very elementary mapping would require chunks expressing other relations, such as that between the attraction force and gravity, masses of the bodies, and radius of orbit. There also has to be a higher order chunk representing the causal relation between gravitational attraction, acceleration forces, and orbital motion.

An alternative chunk for orbital motion is shown in the third alternative in Fig. 9.8. This time the concept of orbital motion is represented in terms of a balance of forces, rather than in terms of the "orbits around" relation. Again, however, there would need to be chunks representing gravitational attraction and the acceleration forces. Once it was recognized that the balance of forces in the solar system could be mapped into the corresponding structure in the atom, the remaining chunks could also be mapped. This would be a serial process, and the validity of the initial mapping would depend on the remaining chunks being mapped in a way that was consistent. The details of this process have been addressed in a number of computational models of anlogical reasoning (Bakker & Halford, 1988; Falkenhainer et al., 1990; Halford et al., in press; Holyoak & Thagard, 1989).

APPEARANCE–REALITY AND CONCEPT OF MIND

In this section we consider the problem of how children understand the difference between the way something appears and the way it really is, and the related topic, the concept of mind. These topics may seem somewhat removed from the mechanics problems that we have taken as prototypical of scientific reasoning in the rest of this chapter, but the appearance–reality distinction is basic to any rational understanding of the world, and therefore it seems appropriate to consider it in the chapter on scientific thinking. Research on the concept of mind is closely related to work on appearance–reality, because it is concerned with inferences children make about their own or another person's mental model of real and unreal situations. There has been

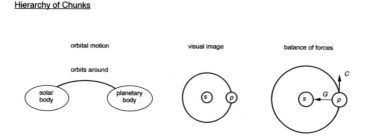

FIG. 9.8. Conceptual chunks from the Rutherford analogy.

a very high level of activity in this field in recent years, and there are already a number of reviews and theoretical treatments (Astington & Gopnik, 1991; Astington, Harris, & Olson, 1988; Flavell, 1986; Leslie, 1987; Wellman, 1990; Wellman & Gelman, 1992).

Given the complexity and rapid development of this field it would not be appropriate to present an alternative theory here. To present and substantiate such a theory would require a book in its own right. However, I propose to address three considerations that do not appear to have been taken up in previous work but that follow from the argument of this book.

The role of analogies in developing a concept of mind. I propose that when we attribute a mental state to someone else, this is at least partly by analogy with a mental state we would experience in similar situations.

The role of complexity in children's understanding of a number of situations. I suggest that some of the variations in performance that have been observed between different tasks reflect in part the complexity of the mental representations those tasks require. As in the rest of this book, I am not suggesting that complexity is the only relevant factor but that it does have a role that has not been recognized previously.

The role of learned contingencies and rules. In chapter 4, I argued that much of cognitive development is attributable to representations of environmental rules and contingencies acquired through basic learning mechanisms. Here I suggest that these rules and contingencies could form part of the basis of children's concept of mind. If one wants to adopt the view that the concept of mind is a kind of "theory," as proposed by Wellman (1990), then learned rules and contingencies could form the building blocks of such a theory.

EMPIRICAL OBSERVATIONS

In this section I consider some typical empirical phenomena that a theory of appearance–reality and concept of mind should be expected to explain. In a typical appearance–reality task (Flavell, Green, & Flavell, 1986), a small white fish is shown to a child and then covered by a blue filter, so it appears blue. The child is asked how the fish looks to his or her eyes right now (appearance question) and what color the fish is really and truly (reality question).

In the perspective-taking task the situation is similar except that the same object is shown to two people simultaneously. One has an unobstructed view, while the other views it through a blue filter. The child may fill either of these roles; that is, the child may view the object directly, with the other person viewing it through the filter, or the reverse. The child is asked how the object appears from each perspective, that is, how it appears when viewed directly and through the filter. This task is structurally similar to, and is highly correlated with, the appearance–reality task. The main difference is that whereas in the appearance–reality task the same person views the object in different ways at different times, in perspective taking two different people observe the object simultaneously.

The false-belief paradigm (Wimmer & Perner, 1983) is also related to the other two. Person1 (Bill) hides a chocolate in a box, and goes away. Then Person2 (Tom), unbeknownst to Person1, removes the chocolate and places it in a basket. The child's task is to predict where Person1 will look for the chocolate when he or she returns. The false-photograph task (Zaitchik, 1990) is structurally similar to the false-belief task and appears to be mastered at approximately the same time. Children are shown how to use a Polaroid camera, then they take a photograph of an object in Location A. While the photograph is developing, the object is moved to Location B. The child then has to predict where the object will be in the photograph.

Three-year-olds have been found to have considerable difficulty with these tasks, although all the tasks are performed readily enough by the age of 5–6 years. It has proved surprisingly difficult to overcome the failures of 3-year-olds on some of these tasks. For example, objects with familiar color, such as milk, have been used in appearance–reality tasks (Flavell et al., 1986). To obviate possible difficulties with the form of the question, two cutout pieces were used, one the same color as the (real) object, the other the same color as the object's appearance (Flavell, Green, Wahl, & Flavell, 1987). The child was asked to choose the appropriate cutout to show the real or apparent color of the object. Children have been trained in the task (Flavell et al., 1986, 1987), and the task has been tried on children of a different culture (Flavell, Zhang, Zou, Dong, & Qi, 1983). It has been found, however, that 3-year-olds consistently have difficulty with the task.

Despite this, children of this age have no difficulty deciding when they or another person is able to see or hear an object. For example, if a drum was placed behind a barrier, 3-year-olds knew that they could not see it but an experimenter on the other side of the barrier could. Also, children of this age had no difficulty with a control task in which they were required to identify a number of separate objects, some of which were not visible. For example they knew that a bird was visible in front of a wall but an elephant was invisible behind the wall (Flavell, Green, & Flavell, 1990). This is an important control, and shows that failures in the appearance–reality task were not due to memory load or to inability to cope with the overall task format.

Three-year-olds apparently can also take account of concealed attributes of objects. Siegal and Share (1990) showed children a drink containing a cockroach, then they removed the cockroach and asked whether the drink was good. They also showed children moldy bread, then covered it with spread, and asked whether it was good to eat. Even three-year-olds showed above-chance recognition that the contaminated food and beverages should not be consumed.

Three-year-olds have little difficulty recognizing different preferences that people may have. For example they readily understand that one person may think a cookie is "yummy," whereas another person thinks it's "yukky" (Flavell, 1988). Furthermore they readily understand the pretend–real distinction. Flavell, Flavell, and Green (1987) tested 3-year-olds on matched appearance–reality and pretend–real tasks. An example of an appearance–reality task was a stone that was painted to look like a fake egg. Children were encouraged to examine and feel the object to ensure they knew it was really a stone, although it looked like an egg. In a typical pretend–real task the experimenter took a curved straw and pretended it was a telephone by acting out a fake phone conversation. Three-year-olds were much more successful on all of the pretend–real tasks than on the appearance–reality tasks. This is a rather striking result when the similarities between the tasks are considered. Both entail taking the same object and contrasting its real nature with a false nature, the latter being a pretence or a distorted appearance. One problem then is to explain why pretend–real should be so much easier than appearance–reality.

FACTORS THAT INFLUENCE CHILDREN'S INTERPRETATIONS

There are a number of factors that might influence children's judgments in the situations we have reviewed. One is world knowledge. Children need to realize that appearance of objects can change from time to time or from place to place, or can be altered by such processes as viewing through colored glass or filters, or by painting. They also need to realize that objects' appearance changes depending on the angle from which they are viewed. Some of this knowledge is more accessible and therefore likely to be acquired earlier than other knowledge. For example, children have abundant opportunity in infancy to find that appearance of objects changes when perspective changes, because this can be observed as an infant is carried around. Much harder to acquire would be the knowledge that color of objects can be changed by viewing them through colored glass or filters, because there is less opportunity to observe this. The knowledge that color can be changed by painting falls in between, because it is unlikely to be acquired in infancy but is a common experience for young children who use paint sets. However the knowledge that an object can be made to look like a different object, as distinct from merely changing its color, is probably harder to acquire.

The knowledge that people's preferences differ is probably easy to learn because people, including children, constantly express preferences, either

verbally or by choosing one object and rejecting another. Wellman and Woolley (1990) showed that children understand desire before they understand
belief. In one of their experiments scenarios were acted out with a doll character who wanted to find (say) a rabbit and who finds the either the rabbit,
an alternate animal such as a dog, or nothing. Even 2-year-olds recognized
that the doll was more likely to be happy if it found what it wanted. In Experiment 2 they contrasted desire with belief in comparable tasks. In their
"not own desire" task they gave the doll two options, such as swimming or
playing with a dog. The child was asked his/her own preference, told that
the doll preferred the other option, and then asked to predict the doll's choice.
This ensured the prediction was based on the child's representation of the
doll's choice, not on the child's own choice. The "not own belief" task was
designed to parallel the desire task. The child was shown two locations, such
as a porch and a garage, and told the doll wants a dog, which is in one of
the locations. The child is asked where he or she thinks the dog is, and is
told the doll thinks it is in the other location. Then the child is asked to predict
where the doll will search for the dog. This procedure helps to ensure that
the child's prediction is based on his or her representation of the doll's belief,
not on the child's own belief. Three-year-olds performed better on the desire
task (93% correct) than on the belief task (73%).

Understanding of desire probably develops earlier than understanding of
belief because the child experiences more evidence of desire. People constantly express desires verbally and nonverbally by showing emotion and
selecting from alternatives. Perner (1988) made a similar point about intention and knowledge. Intention tends to be a better predictor of people's behavior than knowledge. If we want to predict where someone will go, we
need to know their desires or intentions. For example, if we know someone
wants a drink, we can predict they will go to a cafe, bar, or similar place.
We do not normally need to enquire about their knowledge, because the relevant knowledge is usually commonly available; most people know you can
get a drink at a bar. Therefore it is more important to find out whether someone wants a drink than to find out whether they know where to go for a
drink. Because the relevant knowledge can often be taken for granted, desire
and intention tend to be more important predictors. Given the principle in
chapter 4 that children tend to learn rules that are good predictors of the
environment, knowledge of the effect of desire and intention on behavior
is likely to be acquired earlier. Knowledge that contaminated food should
not be eaten is also likely to be acquired early, and this was probably a factor in the ability of 3-year-olds tested by Siegal and Share (1990) to deal with
concealed contaminants.

It seems very likely that the knowledge factor influences children's performance on all these tests. On the other hand, it would be most implausible
to suggest that it is the only factor. There have been many variations in each

task, and each variant requires a different kind of knowledge, yet the age of attainment of the tasks is not radically altered. Furthermore, some tasks remain difficult although the knowledge they require seems very elementary. For example, the perspective-taking task is as difficult as appearance–reality, although the knowledge required for the former should be acquired much earlier. Then there are differences in difficulty between tasks that do not seem to correspond to differences in knowledge availability. Why should the connections task be easier than perspective taking? The data are complex and new research is being conducted at a rapid rate, but the picture at the time of writing suggests that the total pattern of differences would be difficult to explain solely on the basis of the knowledge hypothesis.

Linguistic factors might also affect the difficulty of these tasks. Siegal and Beattie (1991) reasoned that when children are asked to predict where a person will look for an object in the false-belief task they might interpret the question as asking where the person would look in order to find the object. Applying their logic to the example of the false-belief task we used earlier, if Bill hides the chocolate in a box, and it is moved in his absence to a basket, the child might interpret the question "where will Bill look for the chocolate?" to mean "where will Bill look in order to find the chocolate?"

Siegal and Beattie used false-belief tasks similar to those of Wellman and Bartsch (1988). The child is told, for example; "Sam wants to find his puppy. Sam's puppy is really in the kitchen. Sam thinks his puppy is in the bathroom. Where will Sam look for his puppy? Where is it really?" They modified the question to "Where will Sam look first for his puppy?" Three- to four-year-olds were much more successful on this form of the question. They also tended to answer correctly when this form of question was used for a person who had a correct belief as to the location of the object, showing that their success in the false-belief task was not due to a generalized tendency to switch their answer from the one they would normally give. On the other hand, no comparisons are made with chance baselines, and the only case where the data are reported completely enough to make this calculation proves not to be significantly better than chance: In Experiment 2, 10 out of 12 children are correct on the false-belief "look first" question, which is not significant (chi square = 3.2 with one degree of freedom). Another question is whether this result would generalize to other forms of the false-belief task, such as that used by Wimmer and Perner (1983). It is possible that Wimmer and Perner's task is more difficult because the child sees an actual situation and has to construct her own mental model of it, whereas in Siegal and Beattie's task the situation is described to the child. I return to this issue later when we consider the mental models required by the false-belief task.

This exemplifies a general problem that arises when we treat two tasks as equivalent because they carry the same label, without considering whether the processes they entail are the same. The Wimmer and Perner (1983) task, and the Wellman and Bartsch (1988) task can both be labeled appropriately enough as "false belief" tasks, but the fact that they both carry the same labels by no means implies that they entail the same processes. They are very different procedurally and are likely to be very different at the process level also. It is therefore not justified to assume that improvements that have been achieved in one task will necessarily occur in the other.

It seems clear that linguistic difficulties cannot be the only factor that affects children's performance on the false-belief task, because it is hard to see how they would account for young children's performance on the false-photograph task. The possible misinterpretation of the question that might occur in false belief does not apply when the children are asked to say where the object will be in the photograph. The tasks are quite different in their linguistic aspects, but closely related structurally, so the common difficulties that they present would seem to suggest that a structural factor is likely to be involved in some way. We explore the possibility of such a structural explanation in a later section.

Another factor is the type of inference that is required. We can illustrate this with the false-belief task discussed above. Bill hides a chocolate in a box and goes away. Tom shifts the chocolate to a basket. The child has to predict where Bill and Tom think the chocolate will be. The child is being asked to make the inference that because Tom has seen the chocolate moved to the basket, he will search for it there. However, because Bill did not see the chocolate moved, he thinks it is in the box. That is, the child is being asked to interpret a causal factor that can produce two different representations of a situation. The child is not being asked to interpret the situation per se, but two people's representations of a situation, together with the factor that causes these representations to be different.

On the other hand, the false-belief task used by Siegal and Beattie (1991) does not require a child to interpret the causal factor that might produce two different representations. The child is told that an object (Sam's puppy) is in one location and a person (Sam) believes it is in another. The child does not have to consider why Sam thinks it is in one place when it is really in another. However, the child does have to relate the fact that the puppy is in one place to Sam's belief that it is in another. Therefore the child has to link two representations of the situation.

A similar type of inference has to be made in appearance–reality tasks. In the example given earlier, a child is expected to infer that because a person views a (white) fish at one time through a blue filter it appears blue, but because they view it at another time without the filter, it appears white. Again, the child is required to interpret a causal factor that produces a switch from one representation of a situation to another. This time the child is being asked to understand her own representations. She is expected to realize that at one time she has a representation of a blue fish, because she is viewing it through the blue filter. At other times, when the filter is not present, the child will have a representation of the fish as white. The way an object really and truly is corresponds to the way we represent it under normal circumstances, or to the way we represent it most of the time, without interfering factors.

A similar inference is also required in the perspective-taking task. One person views the white fish directly, and so represents it as white. The other person views the fish through a blue filter, and so represents it as blue. The child is being asked to infer the type of representation each person has, depending on how they are viewing the object.

Let us now consider the type of inferences required in pretend–real, preference, and connections tasks. In pretend–real tasks, the child does not have to consider the cause of the switch from one representation to another. In one situation, the child has to represent an object as what it really is, a straw in the example above. In the other situation, the child has to represent the same object as something that she pretends it to be, a telephone in our example. This implies that the child must be able to construct two alternative representations of the straw and must also recognize that the pretend representation does not correspond to reality, a point to which we will return. However, the child does not need to recognize the cause of the difference between these representations. The two representations are independent of each other, in the sense that at one time the child represents a situation one way, at another time another way, but the child is not asked to account for the difference or to predict the effect of any causal factor that might influence the type of representation adopted.

The preference task imposes similar demands. The child is not asked to consider any reason why one person thinks a cookie is "yummy," whereas another person thinks it's "yukky." The child must construct two separate representations, one of a person who thinks an object is nice and another of a person who thinks it is not nice. The child does not have to interpret any causal factor that would enable him to predict that a person will like or dislike the object. Thus the child is not asked to integrate these two representations into a single schema. It appears the child can treat liking and disliking as two separate events.

The connections task entails a display in which a person can see one object (bird in the example earlier) but cannot see another object (elephant) because it is hidden behind a wall. For the child to judge that the person can see the bird, it is only necessary to view the relation between the person and the bird. That is, the child can perceive that the person has an unobstructed view of the bird. For the child to decide that the person cannot see the elephant, she need only perceive the relation between the person and the elephant. Merely looking at the display is enough to recognize that the person's view of the elephant is obstructed. These two judgments can be made independently of one another. When examining the person's view of the elephant, one does not need to bother about their view of the bird, or vice versa. Because the display is physically present, each part of it can be viewed separately, and the child can switch from one part to another at will. It is not necessary for the child to have a representation of the whole situation at any one time. A representation of the relevant part is sufficient.

The inferences required are very simple. One entails reasoning that if a person has an unobstructed view of an object they can see it, whereas the other entails recognizing that if they have an obstructed view of an object, they cannot see it. Notice that the actual cause of the difference does not need to be processed. Because the whole scene is clearly visible, and the only question at issue is whether a person can see a particular object or not, the child only has to inspect the relevant part of the scene. The decision can be made without actually taking into account the cause. In this respect the situation is quite different from the false-belief, appearance–reality, and perspective-taking tasks.

In the Wimmer and Perner (1983) false-belief task the whole situation is not simultaneously visible. Recall that the child saw Bill hide the chocolate in a box then leave, and Tom shifted the chocolate to a basket. Then the child is asked to say where Bill and Tom think the chocolate is. At this point all that is visible is the basket, the box, Tom, and Bill. The other relevant information relates to past events: Bill hid the chocolate in the box, but he was not present when Tom shifted it to the basket. The child must retrieve this information from memory, but it is not simply a matter of recall, and it would be a mistake to see the difficulty of the problem solely in terms of memory load. The child not only has to retrieve the relevant information, but to assemble it into a coherent representation. It is possible that construction of the representation is a source of difficulty in the false-belief task, and in the next section we consider what that representation must be.

In the appearance–reality task more of the situation is visible when the child makes his judgment, and this should facilitate construction of a coherent representation. The child views a (white) fish through a blue filter, and is asked how it appears now. The relevant information to answer this question can be perceived relatively directly. However, the child is also asked what color the object is really and truly, which is equivalent to asking how it will appear when the filter is removed. The relevant information must be retrieved from memory, and an appropriate representation must be constructed. Furthermore, and this may be hardest part of the task, the second representation must be integrated with the first to create a coherent representation of the overall situation. This is necessary because the child must be able to mentally switch from appearance to reality (and back again), which means she must integrate both situations into a common representation.

In the perspective-taking task the whole situation is visible, but in other respects it is very similar to the appearance–reality task. One person views the fish through a blue filter and sees it as blue. The second person sees the fish without the blue filter and sees it as white. The child is asked to do more than recognize that the second person can see the object. The child must predict how the person sees the object, that is, what color. Given that the child must also predict how the first person sees the object, she needs a way of distinguishing the two views. In the connections task this can be done by visually switching from one part of the situation to another, but in the perspective-taking task the child is asked to infer how each person sees the object. As in the connections task, the object and both observers are visible. However, the effect of the filter on the observer is not directly observable. The child must reason that the object appears blue from one perspective because it is viewed through a blue filter but appears white from the other perspective because it is viewed without the filter. To reason this way, both perspectives must be included in an integrated representation.

The inferences required in appearance–reality, perspective-taking, and false-belief tasks are probably more complex than in the connections task for other reasons as well, as Perner (1988) pointed out. The reason is that young children probably have heuristics for judging whether someone can see something, but they are less likely to have reliable heuristics for deciding whether someone knows something. They are likely to know that if someone has an unobstructed view of something, then they can see it. This prediction is highly reliable and likely to be learned early. In this respect seeing is rather like desiring or feeling, in that it can be predicted reliably from clearly visible indictors. However, a knowledge state is harder to predict. All of us see and hear things that we do not know, either because we forget them, because they conflict with other knowledge and beliefs that we possess, or because we do not believe the speaker, and so on. Thus a simple heuristic such as "viewing means seeing" is not adequate to predict knowledge. A more elaborate mental model is required.

MENTAL MODELS THEORIES

In this section I consider theories of children's mental models of the tasks in the last section.

Flavell (e.g., 1986; Flavell, Green, & Flavell, 1990) postulated that young children cannot handle two ways of representing an object. Consequently, they tend to encode the object consistently in terms of the way it is, or consistently in terms of the way it appears. They are cognizant of a person's connections to things, so they know that a person may see or hear a particular object, and that these cognitive connections between the person and the object may change over time, and that connections may be independent of each other. However, they do not understand that the same object can be represented in our minds in more than one way, so they do not understand that we can represent the way it is and also the way it appears.

Leslie (1987) argued that pretense, like belief and other mental states, entails a decoupling of the cognitive representation from reality. He argued that this decoupling is achieved because pretend representations are not representations of reality but representations of representations; that is, they are metarepresentations. They are like representations of mental states, because pretense shares some linguistic properties (such as referential opacity[1]) with mental states. Pretense entails representations that include the knowledge that the representation is false and does not represent reality. This enables pretense to be decoupled from reality so the child will not believe the truth of what he pretends. Leslie argued that this ability to distinguish pretense from reality is present in the second year, but that it takes a further 2 years to understand false belief, because of the complexity of the situation.

Perner (1988) disagreed with Leslie's claim that pretense entails metarepresentation, because he considered that metarepresentation entails more than knowing that a particular representation is false. Perner considered that metarepresentation entails a mental model of the representation process.

The concept of metarepresentation can be clarified by a metaphor. A photograph is a representation of some slice of reality. A diagram or description of how the photograph was taken would be a metarepresentation. That is, a metarepresentation entails representing the relation between a representation and reality. Perner argued that a child does not need metarepresentations to know that pretense does not represent reality. Children only need to be able to compare the pretense representation with reality. The metaphor can help again here. Suppose you hold a photograph that incorrectly depicts a scene up in front of the scene. By comparing one with the other, you can see that the photograph does not validly represent the scene. You do not need a mental model of the photographic process to decide this. You may have no idea why the photograph misrepresents the scene or how a false photograph was taken, you simply know that the photograph is not right for that scene. Thus, you have evaluated the representation, but you have not used a metarepresentation to do so. In a similar way, we can know that a pretend action does not correspond to reality without understanding the relations between the action and reality, that is, without metacognitive knowledge. Just as it is possible to see that a photograph does not correctly represent reality by comparing the photograph with reality, it should be possible to recognize that a pretense does not correctly represent reality by comparing the pretense representation with reality.

---

[1] Referential opacity refers to the fact that normal reference relations do not apply with mental-state terms (Leslie, 1987; Quine, 1961).

TOWARD AN ANALOGICAL REASONING MODEL OF THE CONCEPT OF MIND

The concept of mind entails recognizing a correspondence between one's own mental model of a situation and the mental model of another person. In this respect it resembles an analogy, which is a correspondence between one mental model and another, as we noted in chapter 2. In this section I want to explore the similarities between the concept of mind and analogies and then to develop the argument for an analogical reasoning account of the concept of mind.

Let us first consider a very simple situation, such as a child watching someone who is looking at a bird. The child has a mental model of this situation that corresponds to the real situation, as shown in Fig. 9.9. The child also has a mental model of the other person's mental model that corresponds both to the real situation and to the child's own mental models, as shown in Fig. 9.9. The child's concept of the other person's mental model is a mapping from the child's own mental model of the situation, to the child's mental model of the other person's mental model. This mapping is shown by the heavy arrows in Fig. 9.9. In this respect it is quite similar to the mapping from one mental model to another that occurs in analogies, as shown in chapter 2, Fig. 2.2. In effect the child's own mental model of the situation functions as the base, and the child's mental model of the other person's mental model functions as the target.

It becomes possible to ask whether other properties of analogies can be applied to the concept of mind. The mapping from base to target in analo-

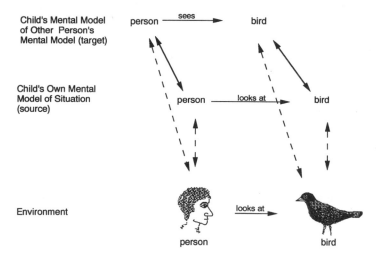

FIG. 9.9. Structure-mapping analysis of a child's concept of a person seeing an object.

gies depends on factors such as similarity and systematicity, as discussed in chapter 5. It is not known whether this is true for the concept of mind. The mapping from the child's own to the other person's mental model probably also depends on social cues that indicate whether the other person is aware of the situation or not. It is possible that autistic children may have difficulty with the false-belief task, not because of the lack of metarepresentational skills as proposed by Leslie (1987), but because they have difficulty inferring the mental state of another person. Leekam and Perner (1990) showed that autistic children perform much better on the false-photograph task than on the false-belief task, even though they are structurally similar, as noted earlier, and would not differ in their requirement for metarepresentational skills. The false-belief task, however, requires a child to form a mental model of another person's mental model, whereas the false-photograph task requires the child to form a mental model of an inanimate representation, a photograph. Their greater facility with the latter might reflect difficulties in making inferences about another person's mental state.

Now I would like to bring into focus some principles from structure-mapping theory developed in earlier chapters that are relevant to this topic. The first is that the processing load imposed by a structure-mapping task depends on the amount of information that must be processed in a single decision in order to determine the correct mapping. It does not depend on the total amount of information in the structure, because the mapping can sometimes be segmented and each component of it processed separately. Where this can be done, it is the amount that has to be processed in the segments that determines processing load.

The second principle is that when an inference has to be made in a single decision, the whole representation on which that inference is based must be processed jointly. To illustrate, recall our discussion of the processing load imposed by transitive inference in chapter 3. Given the premises (for example) $a > b$, $b > c$, therefore $a > c$, the inference $a > c$ must be based on both premises, $a > b$ and $b > c$. Therefore the premises must be processed jointly. We will apply this principle to working out the likely load imposed by tasks considered in this section.

The third principle is that when a decision can be made on the basis of information contained in the environment, only that segment of the environment need be represented. To return to the transitive-inference task, suppose it was presented so that it was perceptually obvious that $a > c$. In that case the decision that $a > c$ can be made by representing only a and c. There is no need to represent $a > b$ and $b > c$. Consequently the processing load is much less. This principle also will be applied to working out the likely load imposed by tasks in this section.

A sketch for an analogical reasoning account of the Wimmer and Perner (1983) false-belief task is shown in Fig. 9.10. Consider the situation where

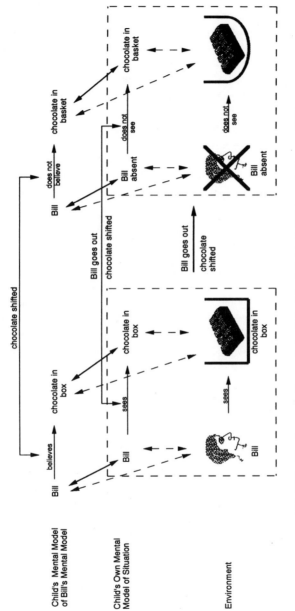

FIG. 9.10. Structure-mapping analysis of the false-belief task (Wimmer & Perner, 1983).

a person, Bill, is viewing a chocolate in a box. The child's mental model of this situation represents Bill seeing the chocolate in the box. The chocolate is now shifted to the basket, in Bill's absence. The child's mental model of the new situation represents Bill not seeing the chocolate in the basket. These two representations, taken separately, do not differ in any important respect from the one in Fig. 9.9. The important difference is that they are connected together by Bill going out and the chocolate being shifted from the box to the basket. An adequate mental model of the situation depends on representing both situations and the link between them in a single mental model. The combined mental model represents the fact that Bill has seen the chocolate in the box but not in the basket.

The false-belief task requires the child to construct a mental model of the fact that Bill believes the chocolate is in the box and does not believe the chocolate is in the basket. The justification for this is the mapping between the child's own mental model of the situation and the child's mental model of Bill's belief state. As with Fig. 9.9, the child's conception of Bill's belief state is really an analog of the child's own representation of the situation.

Each of these mental models is a complex structure. Each comprises, at the least, a representation of Bill seeing the chocolate in the box, Bill not seeing the chocolate in the basket, and the link between them. Insofar as it comprises a set of (binary) relations, it is a system mapping, as defined in chapter 2. We have seen that constructing analogies based on system mapping imposes high processing loads (see chapter 3) and is especially difficult for children below 5 years of age. This is consistent with the difficulty that young children have with the task, even allowing for the other factors mentioned earlier.

One implication of the analogical-reasoning account of the concept of mind is that children's representation of another person's mental state will be a function of their own representation of the situation. If they are unable to represent the relevant relations in the situation, then their concept of another person's representation of that situation will have to be inadequate. This is because their own representation of the situation is the base, and their representation of the other person's concept is the target. Because structure mapping depends on an adequate representation of the base, their own representaion of the situation is crucial.

Another implication is that structural complexity is a factor in the difficulty of concept-of-mind tasks. If this is so similar difficulties should be experienced with structurally similar tasks, even if they are different in other respects. In order to explore this question the mental model for the false-photograph task is shown in Fig. 9.11. The situation is that used by Leekam and Perner (1990), in which a doll is photographed in a red dress and, while the photograph is being developed, the dress is changed to a green one. The child's own mental model represents the fact that the camera was aimed at the doll

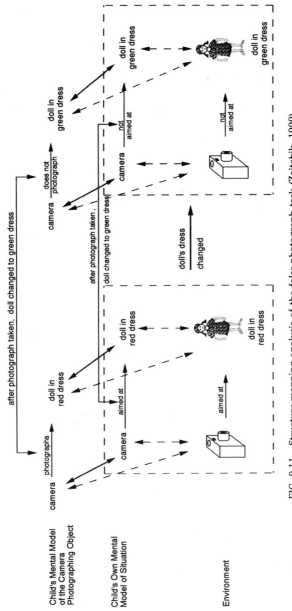

FIG. 9.11. Structure-mapping analysis of the false-photograph task (Zaitchik, 1990).

in a red dress, after which the dress was changed to green, and the camera was not aimed at the doll in the green dress. The child's representation of the photographic situation corresponds to his representation of the sequence that occurred. The structural similarity to the false-belief task is quite close.

The type of mental model that is required for appearance–reality and perspective-taking tasks is shown in Fig. 9.12. As noted previously, the two tasks are very similar, differing mainly in that appearance–reality entails the same person representing the object at two different times, whereas perspective-taking entails two different people viewing the object at one time. Apart from this the representations required are essentially the same and can be shown in one figure.

As with false belief, there are two mental models that are linked together through a causal factor. One mental model represents the object as it is. The other mental model represents the way the object appears when viewed through the filter. The causal factor that links the models is the presence or absence of the filter.

The main difference from the false-belief and false-photograph tasks is that in the former the child is developing a mental model of someone else's mental model, whereas in the false-photograph task the child is developing a mental model of a sequence of photographic events. In the appearance–reality task the child is developing a mental model of the way her own mental model switches depending on whether the object is viewed directly or through a filter. This amounts to a type of reflection on her own mental model and is not unlike Piaget's (1947/1950) concept of reflective abstraction. In the perspective-taking task the child develops a mental model of two other people's mental models, one viewing the object directly, the other through the filter.

These mental models are metacognitive in the sense that we defined above. That is, all entail some factor that causes one model to be selected rather than another. Second, all are system mappings, in that they require two relations to be integrated into a coherent representation. The individual relations are what a person sees, or believes, about an object. These separate relations are integrated into a mental model that represents the two different ways of representing the object.

The type of mental models required for the connections task are shown in Fig. 9.13. One mental model represents the observer seeing the bird, whereas the other mental model represents the observer not seeing the elephant. Notice that, by contrast with the mental models for false belief, false photograph, appearance–reality, and perspective taking in Figs. 9.10 to 9.12, there is no connection between the two mental models. Each model separately reflects a segment of the environment, but they are not integrated into an overall coherent representation because, as explained above, this is not necessary for the connections task.

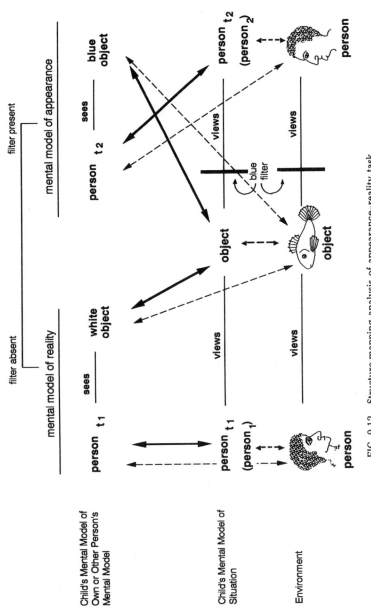

FIG. 9.12. Structure-mapping analysis of appearance–reality task.

460

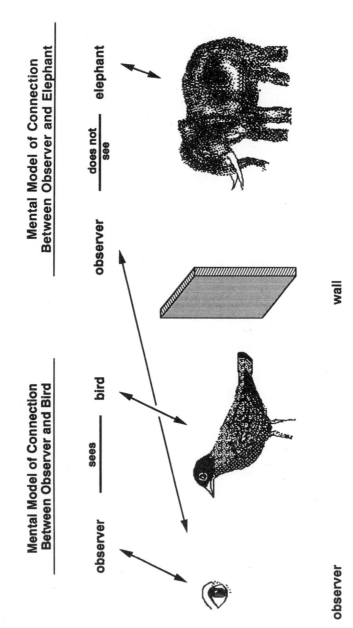

FIG. 9.13. Structure-mapping analysis of connections task.

Applying the principles mentioned earlier, those tasks that entail inferences based on the whole situation jointly require the whole situation to be represented. The appearance–reality, perspective-taking, and false-belief tasks require an inference that the other person's mental model will depend on the way an object is viewed or on what the person knows about it. This inference is based on the two possible ways of representing the object, together with the link between them. The internal representations must be inferred because they cannot be perceived directly from the environment. Therefore the information in the entire representation, as shown in Figs. 9.10 to 9.12, must be processed jointly when making a decision. Given that each representation entails two relations, together with a link between them, all of which must be processed jointly, these tasks require system mappings.

By contrast, the inference entailed in the connections task only requires the child to perceive the physical situation that is actually present; the observer is looking at a bird, and therefore it can be inferred that the observer can see the bird. The rest of the situation does not need to be processed to make this inference. Similarly, the observer is not looking at an elephant, so it can be inferred that the observer does not see the elephant. This inference can be based directly on a representation of the perceived situation, and no inference is required from other situations; that is, one can know that the observer does not see the elephant without any reference to the fact that the observer sees a bird. Each mental model consists of two relations that can be processed independently, it comprises two relational mappings, rather than one system mapping. This distinction was developed in detail in chapter 3. Therefore these tasks should impose lower processing loads than false belief, appearance–reality, and perspective taking.

The mental model for the preference task is similar and is shown in Fig. 9.14. One person has a liking relation to the cookie, and the other person

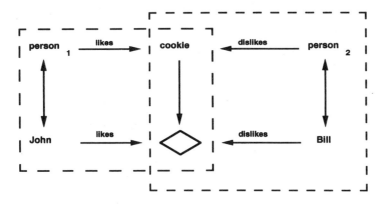

FIG. 9.14. Structure-mapping analysis of a child's concept of someone liking or disliking a cookie.

has a disliking relation. The important thing is that each relation can be validated separately. That is, we can verify that John likes the cookie, without knowing that Bill dislikes it, and vice versa. As the dotted frames show, each representation is a unit, separate from the other one. Therefore this task also entails two relational mappings rather than a single system mapping.

The contamination task of Siegal and Share (1990) only requires one relation to be represented. The child need only remember that the food or drink contains a contaminant. The child is not asked to represent two different relations between a person and an object, as in the appearance–reality, false-belief, and perspective-taking tasks shown in Figs. 9.10 to 9.12. The child is not asked to say both how an object appears and how it really is. The study does not require children to represent two alternate person–object relations, nor does it require them to integrate these relations into a coherent representation.

Siegal and Share, following Siegal, Waters, and Dinwiddy (1988), claimed that tasks with multiple questions underestimate children's abilities. However, it is not consistently true that young children fail where multiple questions are asked. Halford and Boyle (1985) found that 3- to 4-year-olds performed at very high levels in a control task with multiple questions. That task made low cognitive demands. Those failures that are apparently due to children changing their minds when multiple questions are used may simply reflect high processing demands. Also, the logic of response-pattern analysis (which includes rule assessment) discussed in chapter 6 depends entirely on multiple-question techniques. Given the importance of these analyses, the argument that multiple-question probes inevitably provide misleading data is hard to sustain.

The use of single versus multiple questions is not theory-neutral, and in some circumstances the number of questions asked might fundamentally change the cognitive processes entailed in the task. Appearance–reality might be an example of this, and we can use Siegal and Share's (1990) study to illustrate how the single-question version of the task might require simpler processes than multiple-question tasks. If we just ask children whether food is good to eat, this may only require them to retrieve a single, salient fact about the food. If, however, we ask them if the food looks good to eat, and if it is really good to eat, and require correct responses to both questions, we require them to represent two different relations between themselves and the object, and to select the appropriate representation for each question. Because the multiple-question task entails inferences about both relations to the object (i.e., it entails reasoning that the bread is bad to eat because it is moldy, but looks good because it is covered with spread), processing demands are much greater than if we ask only one question. Therefore the argument that data based on two questions underestimate children's understanding needs to be accompanied by an analysis of what processes are being assessed; otherwise it may be misleading.

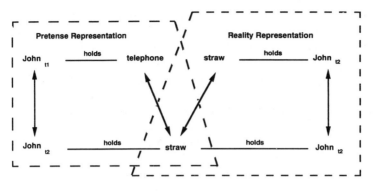

FIG. 9.15. Structure-mapping analysis of pretend–real situation.

The mental model for pretense is shown in Fig. 9.15. In the reality representation, John is correctly represented as holding a straw. In the pretense representation, John is represented as holding a telephone. Again, each representation can be validated independently. The representation of John holding a straw can be validated by a relational mapping, because it corresponds to the fact that John is actually holding a straw. The pretense representation can be seen to be invalid, because John is represented as holding a telephone, but he is in fact holding a straw. Therefore the mental model does not correspond to the environment. Notice that the pretense representation does not need to be compared to the reality representation, but only to the environment. Thus pretense may consist of two relational mappings, which is consistent with the fact that it is acquired early. Notice also that it is not a metarepresentation, because there is no need for a causal factor linking the two representations. The child knows the pretense representation is invalid because it does not correspond to reality. However, instead of weakening the representation, as occurs in standard learning situations, the representation is given a tag that indicates it is a pretense, with the result that it will not be used to predict the environment except in situations that are tagged as pretense.

This formulation has points in common with other theories, as well as some differences. In agreement with Flavell's formulation, the present theory holds that children younger than about 5 years cannot integrate multiple representations of a situation. They can process two representations separately, but they cannot integrate them into a single coherent representation that puts what *is* in relation to what appears or is believed, nor can they represent the relation between two models that arise from different perspectives. However, they have no difficulty representing each of a succession of situations separately, where each representation is independently validated by comparison with the environment.

This formulation agrees more closely with Perner than with Leslie in that it holds that metarepresentations do not develop for these tasks until approximately 5 years. It also implies, consistent with Perner, that metarepresentations are not necessary for pretense. Leslie is right in saying that pretense must be quarantined so it does not distort a child's concept of the world, but that quarantine can come about through detecting the mismatch between the pretend mental models and the environment to which they relate. Models that do not match are either weakened, as in the learning mechanisms discussed in chapter 4, or quarantined, so they will not give the child a misleading concept of the world. Notice that this reverses the cause–effect relations in Leslie's model. Leslie argued that the child knows pretense does not represent reality because it is quarantined. I argue that it is quarantined because the child knows it does not represent reality. On the other hand, I agree with Leslie that the complexity of false belief is a factor in its relatively late acquisition.

I also agree with those researchers who show that there is a sizeable knowledge component underlying these tasks. Wellman and Woolley showed that children understand desires before beliefs, and I agree with Perner that intention is probably better understood than knowledge. Furthermore, I believe these differences can be explained by basic learning mechanisms of the kind explored in chapter 4. However, I do not believe that knowledge is sufficient to explain all the differences between the tasks. The situation is similar with respect to language comprehension, which is a factor that influences difficulty, but cannot explain all the observations in the literature.

One factor that is unique to the present formulation is the processing load imposed by the construction of representations. Because false-belief, appearance–reality, and perspective-taking probably require system mappings, but the connections task, pretend–real, and preference are more likely to require relational mappings, the former impose a processing load that causes difficulty for most children below about 5 years. That is why these tasks are characteristically acquired at this age and why they tend to be relatively resistant to attempts to overcome the limitation, either by training or by more compatible test techniques. The problem is therefore quite similar to that in transitive inference or class inclusion, in that some of the concepts have a degree of structural complexity inherent in them, for the reasons I have explained in this section. Therefore the processing load that is the cause of their difficulty cannot be reduced without changing the fundamental logic of the tasks, at which point they would arguably cease to be the tasks they now are.

LEARNED CONTINGENCIES AND RULES

In chapter 4, I argued that there are basic learning mechanisms that enable children to acquire stored representations of contingencies and rules in their world. These processes apply to experience with other people as much as to experience with physical phenomena. Therefore they should be effective in acquiring knowledge about how people choose and experience things in their world. That is, they should help a child to acquire a concept of mind.

Wellman (1990) argued that a child develops a theory of mind, that is, that they develop a set of understandings in which mind is a central construct. Among his reasons for arguing this way are that children understand the basic ontological distinction between mind and the world; they understand the nature of beliefs and desires, the difference between them, and their interaction to cause action. I have no objection in principle to the idea that children's concept of mind constitutes a theory. I regard the concept of a theory as a useful analogy to the way children understand the mind. However, like most analogies its fit is less than perfect. One problem is that a theory is normally understood as explicit knowledge, whereas Wellman and other writers (e.g., Astington & Gopnik, 1991) agreed that much of the concept of mind is implicit. Another problem is that theories are normally expected to be testable, and it is even urged that we seek disconfirming evidence of them. But as we have seen, people tend not to do that. Rules and learned contingencies are weakened when they fail to predict environmental events, as we saw in chapter 4, but people do not actively seek disconfirmation, for reasons that were discussed in chapter 7. A further problem is that theories are usually thought to entail some recognition of the relation between theory and data, whereas children are often unaware of this, as Kuhn (1989) pointed out.

An account of the concept of mind based on stored contingencies and condition–action rules, as outlined in chapters 2 and 4, seems capable in principle of capturing everything that is subsumed under the concept of a theory, but it is also linked to defined learning mechanisms, it takes account of the implicit nature of much knowledge, it is modular in the sense that it comprises a lot of separate rules or contingencies, and it is much more specific than the idea of a theory, which often seems too general to be useful. As I mentioned earlier, it is impractical to present a complete account of the concept of mind here, but I will present some illustrative examples of rules or contingencies that such an account might contain.

R1: person X chooses object Y → person X prefers object Y

R2: person X looking at object Y → person X sees object Y

R3: person X sees object Y moved from A to B → person X believes object Y to be at B.

We could go on adding more examples, but the point is to show what kind of rules would be required. Each of these rules will of course be imprecise to a degree, but this points to the utility of another concept discussed in chapter 2, the default hierarchy of Holland et al. (1986). That is, we can make a hierarchy of increasingly specific rules. Rules that are more specific have more conditions and are given priority. In any situation, the rule with the most conditions that match is the one selected. Less specific rules are activated when more specific ones do not match, but the predictions that result are less reliable. An example of a default hierarchy would be:

R4: person X looking at object Y, person X interested in object $Y \rightarrow$ person X sees object Y

R4 is more specific, and more accurate, than R2. However, R4 would not match if a child were unaware of the interest state of person X. In this case R2 would match, resulting in less accurate prediction.

IMPLICATIONS OF THE CURRENT THEORY FOR CONCEPT OF MIND

The present theory proposes that the building blocks of the concept of mind are learned rules and contingencies that represent aspects of situations involving the cognitive activities of other people. These rules and contingencies are acquired as a result of experience with specific situations and are not part of a global theory. Nevertheless they do provide coherence, because of the principle that rules can be activated in parallel and can be mutually supportive or inhibitory, as discussed in chapters 2 and 4.

It is also argued that there are similarities between analogies and children's concept of mind, because both entail a mapping from one representation to another. In an analogy, the mapping is usually from one representation of the environment to another representation of the environment, as shown in Fig. 2.2. In the concept of mind, the mapping is from the child's representation of the environment to his or her representation of the other person's representation of the environment. However, some of the same logic applies to analogies and to the concept of mind.

One implication of this common logic is that structural complexity should be studied explicitly in concept-of-mind situations. This requires two types of manipulations. The first entails varying complexity while holding other factors constant, in the way that has been done for transitivity, as described in chapter 3 and for classification as described in chapter 8. Although appearance–reality, perspective-taking, and false-belief appear to be structurally more complex than connections, pretense, and preference, as the foregoing analysis indicates, these tasks differ in other ways as well. There does not appear to be any research that systematically varies structural complexity, while holding other factors constant, in this context. Until such research is conducted, we cannot be certain exactly how structural complexity affects performance. There are strong indications that it is a factor, as the foregoing analysis indicates.

The second type of manipulation entails holding structural complexity constant while varying other factors. This has been done in a few instances, and the study by Leekam and Perner (1990) is a good example. The false-belief task and false-photograph task are structurally similar, at least in the versions used by Leekam and Perner, as Figs. 9.10 and 9.11 show. They have similar difficulty levels for normal children, but false belief is harder for autistic children. This shows that structural complexity is not the only factor that affects performance and that ability to draw inferences about another person's mental state may also be relevant.

The structure-mapping analysis of appearance–reality, perspective-taking, and false belief, indicates that tasks requiring children to understand the relation between two representations of a situation tend to have higher structural complexity than those that can be performed by considering only one aspect of it, such as pretense, preference, and connections. Accordingly, they are predicted to impose higher processing loads. If the structure of these tasks could be varied while holding other factors constant, then the predictions concerning processing loads could be tested using the methods in chapter 3.

Another implication of the structure-mapping analysis of appearance–reality is that the tendency for children who cannot comprehend the task to give all appearance or all reality answers might be a default strategy. That is, unable to represent both the person–appearance and the person–reality relations, children might opt for just one. Where they give a mixture of responses, as found by Flavell et al. (1990), reversals should be approximately as frequent as correct pairs of reponses; that is, they should give an appearance answer to the reality question, and vice versa, about as often as they give the correct answer to both questions. The reason is that they should have difficulty mapping the two situations into the mental model.

SUMMARY AND CONCLUSIONS

The balance scale is represented as a set of condition–action rules that capture that knowledge found to be followed in previous empirical research. Six different levels of mental model of the balance scale are defined, based on element mappings, relational mapping–weight, relational mapping–distance, system mapping (weight and distance), system mapping–additive rule, and multiple-system mapping, based on the multiplicative rule. It is argued that mental models increase in complexity according to the level of mapping required, but mappings at the same level have equal structural complexity. Therefore mental models based on weight or distance but not both are equally complex, and both entail relational mappings. A preference for one or the other reflects greater environmental support.

Complexity analysis suggests that understanding of the balance scale should develop earlier than previous research and theories indicate. Mental models based on the idea of a single downward push (element mappings) should be possible at 1 year. Mental models based on either weight or distance but not both at once (relational mappings) should be possible at 2 years, whereas the coordination of weight and distance (system mappings) should be possible at 5 years. The potential for use of the multiplicative rule (multiple-system mapping) should be greater at age 11 years than observed previously. A proposed computational model, based on a PDP analogical reasoning mechanism, suggests it should be possible to promote understanding of the balance scale by inducing use of the multiplicative rule as a mental model.

Incorrect rules about mechanics tend to be maintained because they correspond to everyday experience, whereas disconfirmation requires special observations. However, the complexity of the relations involved is also found to cause difficulties. The novice–expert shift is argued to be related to the way concepts are encoded, experts using codes that represent the important structures of phenomena without overloading processing capacity. Problems in mechanics are often too complex to be represented in their entirety in parallel. Consequently, conceptual chunking and segmentation must be used. The representation of the Rutherford analogy between the atom and the solar system is also found to depend on conceptual chunking and segmentation. Basic understanding of time, speed, and distance, essential components of mechanics, appears to be present from age 5, but difficulties can still be experienced in representing relations between variables.

The concept of mind is analyzed, and it is suggested that three factors that have not been considered previously are important. These are acquisition of stored contingencies and condition–action rules, analogical reasoning, and structural complexity. It is suggested that much of a child's theory of the mind could consist of contingencies and condition–action rules learned through experience. The process of forming a representation of a person's state of mind is similar to analogical reasoning in that it entails mapping from our own representation of a situation to our representation of another person's representation. Some of the variation in difficulty that has been observed between different tasks is attributable to the complexity of the representations required by the inferences that must be made.

CONCLUSIONS

10

CONCLUDING COMMENTS

In this chapter, I try to provide an overview of the argument presented in chapters 1-9. Much of the motivation for this book was my belief that cognitive developmental theory needs to take account of the new conceptions of human cognition that have emerged from cognitive psychology and cognitive science in the last two decades. As a result of research in these fields we have fundamentally new conceptions of learning and induction, cognitive skills and strategies, capacity to process information, the nature of representations, and natural reasoning processes. When we examine cognitive development in the light of these new conceptions, many of the formerly dominant issues tend to be modified or even to disappear.

An example of the way new conceptions have redefined issues in cognitive development is that the stage question, which has driven much research, can be examined in quite a different way. It is no longer a matter of whether cognitive development inexorably proceeds through a fixed sequence of stages, independent of experience, as Piagetians have sometimes been interpreted as saying on the one hand, or whether it depends on knowledge acquisition and restructuring, on the other. From the new perspective, cognitive development undoubtedly depends on knowledge acquisition and conceptual restructuring, but we have a new conception of processing capacity that can account for observations formerly attributed to stages. Thus it is not knowledge versus stages, nor is it knowledge versus capacity, but a matter of how these factors interact. In this chapter I briefly examine the implications of these new conceptions for cognitive development, beginning with learning.

LEARNING

This is probably the first theory of cognitive development that gives a major role to learning and induction mechanisms. The importance of knowledge and conceptual reorganization has been emphasized in a number of recent theories, but the actual mechanisms by which knowledge is acquired have not been addressed. However, examination of the learning literature shows that both humans and infrahuman animals have mechanisms that enable them to learn the regularities and contingencies in the environment. Because of the huge store of information that a child must acquire about the world, such learning must be important to cognitive development.

Much of the information acquired in this way is implicit. We are normally unaware that we know it, and it is not accessible to strategic cognitive processes. It cannot be modified without some kind of external input. It nevertheless constitutes a very important and useful body of knowledge. Research on implicit learning has shown that some very complex relationships can be learned, without apparent effort, in this way. Thus, implicit learning appears to be largely free of the processing-load effects that are a feature of reasoning processes. It is important to recognize that a child's mentors are also unaware of most of the information that is acquired in this way. In the past we have tended to assume that cognitive development depends on acquisitions that we organize or facilitate for the child. However the world is too complex for other people to provide all the information a child needs. We should not underestimate the power of the mechanisms the child has for obtaining information without direct assistance.

This in no way denies the importance of social factors. Cross-cultural studies, as well as studies of impoverished versus enriched environments, leave no doubt as to the importance of social and cultural factors. I have not treated this aspect at length because I believe it has already received ample attention in the literature. I have been concerned to point out that social and cultural factors operate through learning and induction mechanisms that exist within the child, and these mechanisms must be understood if we are ever to obtain a comprehensive picture of cognitive development. The child is not simply a repository of socially and culturally provided information, like a file cabinet. The child actively selects, observes, codes, stores, interprets, and, where it is inconsistent with experience, rejects, information about the world. My aim in chapter 4 was to show how contemporary models of learning can provide at least a basic understanding of how this happens.

Implicit knowledge must be made explicit before it becomes accessible to strategic cognitive processes. Exactly how this happens is, as yet, only partially understood. Annette Karmiloff-Smith's concept of representational redescription provides some important cues. I have added the speculation that abduction, or providing an hypothesis to account for learned contingencies or stimulus–response associations, might be an important factor. It also must be recoded so it becomes accessible to connected knowledge structures such as propositional networks. Both my theory and Karmiloff-Smith's imply that the child must reflect on implicit information to make it explicit.

Procedural knowledge, cognitive skills, and strategies also have to be learned. There are well-developed models showing that they can be acquired through associative learning mechanisms that entail little or no understanding. Because of the high costs, in terms of processing load, of processes that entail understanding, it is likely that most procedural knowledge is acquired in this way. However, acquisitions based on understanding are also important for a number of reasons. The first is that they confer on the child a degree of autonomy, because the child can devise strategies that suit the child's goals and his or her concept of the task. Second, strategies learned with understanding can be transferred, modified, and extended to deal with changing circumstances and demands. There are also well-developed models of strategy development under the guidance of task understanding, leaving no doubt that such a process is technically viable.

CAPACITY AND COMPLEXITY

I have given a very extensive treatment of capacity because I believe it to be one of the least understood concepts in cognitive development. At least in the last two decades capacity has had "bad press," being branded with such pejorative descriptions as "pessimistic," "deficit oriented," "a panacea" (with its overtone of sarcasm), and a number of others. Theories that deny the importance of capacity, by contrast, are said to be "optimistic," "achievement oriented," or even "refreshing." However I do not believe that scientific issues can be handled by attaching pejorative labels to those theories that do not tell us what we want to hear. In short, we should not allow our desire to accelerate cognitive development to cloud our scientific judgment. Capacity is certainly not the only thing that develops, but it is a topic that must be taken into account in any comprehensive theory of cognitive development.

The last three decades of research in cognitive development have provided a very rich account of factors that affect children's cognitive activities. This has occurred in three main areas. First, refinements in assessment techniques have shown that many supposed failures were attributable not to inadequate capacity but to linguistic processes, task demands, motivation, misleading cues, or misinterpretation of responses. Much progress has been made in elimination of false negatives from the assessment of cognitive concepts. However it should be remembered that false positives have also been eliminated from a lot of assessments. In fact, some of the most famous studies purporting to demonstrate early conceptual mastery have been false positives. It would be a fair summary to say that children do appear to understand many concepts earlier than had been proposed by Piaget, but that there still seem to be ages below which certain concepts cause persistent difficulties of a kind that have only been partially explained by alternate theories. If these concepts are mastered at all, it is only in very restricted circumstances.

Second, training studies have shown that concept mastery can be promoted by special procedures. Again, it does not appear that all barriers can be swept aside just by devising a good training procedure, but significant training effects have undoubtedly been observed. Third, it has been shown that domain knowledge, conceptual organization, and strategies, or procedural knowledge, play a very large part in children's cognitive performance. One of our major achievements in the field has been to show that knowledge and strategies account for much of what develops.

Refined assessments, training, and knowledge all show that failures that might once have been attributed to inadequate capacity are often amenable to other explanations. However it has not been shown that all failures can be explained in this way. To this it might be argued that further improvements to assessment techniques, or extensions of knowledge theories, will handle these problems. This is simply a promissory note, however. If offered without specification as to how such accounts will be provided it constitutes an untestable claim. If knowledge theorists want to claim that their theories explain a particular phenomenon, they must demonstrate the validity of their claim. No theory should be given a privileged position in this respect. The present reality is that strenuous efforts by the best experimenters have failed to remove the difficulties that young children experience with certain concepts.

It is this situation that motivates a thorough analysis of capacity and complexity. One thing I want to emphasize is that capacity limitations are not restricted to children. The theory I have put forward accounts for adult and child limitations in terms of precisely the same principles. The limitations only differ quantitatively. I hope this helps to make it clearer that capacity is not a "pessimistic" concept. Adults perform some rather stupendous cognitive feats despite limitations in capacity to process information. Understanding those limitations does not block such performances but actually helps promote them. The same is true in cognitive development.

Understanding of capacity limitations helps us to specify the kinds of processes that people use in solving problems. For example, production-rule models can be made more realistic if we know how many conditions can be matched in each rule. PDP models of analogies have been found to depend on only four dimensions being processed in parallel, which in turn constrains the way information must be encoded. In short, understanding capacity is essential to understanding processes entailed in cognition and cognitive development.

I have provided a principled basis both for capacity limitations and for the way they develop. These proposals are based on empirical evidence in the literature (including, but by no means restricted to, that which originated in our own laboratory) and on a computational model. The model is based on PDP architecture and proposes that there is a limit to the number of independent vectors that can enter into a representational structure. This does not limit the total amount of information, because each vector can store an arbitrarily large amount of information. However it does limit the number of independent items, or chunks, that can enter into any one computation or decision. It also limits the orders of interaction, or levels of structure, that can be represented.

Capacity limitations are "soft" in the sense that they do not lead to catastrophic breakdowns. When a task exceeds available capacity, it can often be recoded into fewer chunks, although this leads to loss of ability to represent certain sources of variation. In effect it reduces the orders of interaction that are represented. Conceptual chunking is not always possible, either because all dimensions of the representation might represent aspects that vary independently in the current task, so they cannot be combined into fewer dimensions, or because the mapping of components into chunks has not been learned. Alternatively, the task can be segmented into steps that are performed serially. Again, however, this is not always possible, because the required strategies might not have been learned, or because the child cannot represent the structure of the concept and therefore cannot devise an appropriate strategy. If neither conceptual chunking nor segmentation are possible, default can be made to a representation of lower dimensionality. This normally leads to partially correct performance. Where the processes entailed in a task are well known, it is usually possible to predict the type of errors that will result from defaulting to lower dimensional representations. A number of such defaults are well known in the literature, but they have usually been mistaken for causes of failure, when the real cause is inability to represent all dimensions of the concept.

This formulation, which applies to adults and children, leads to a reformulation of the question as to whether capacity changes with age. It suggests that representations become more differentiated with age, so more vectors can be represented in parallel. This would not increase the overall capacity, but it would increase children's ability to process structure. It would permit children to handle those tasks that depend on several independently varying aspects that cannot be chunked into single aspects and, at least with the sophistication available to a child, cannot be segmented into steps that are processed serially. Many of the limitations that Piaget attributed to stages can be accounted for in this way.

Accompanying this proposal about the nature and development of processing capacity is a metric for conceptual complexity based on the number of independent aspects of a task that need to be represented in parallel. As I have been at pains to point out, tasks can be difficult for many reasons, but structural complexity has been shown to be a factor in some tasks that have provided persistent difficulties for children. Before this claim be dismissed as pessimistic and unacceptable, let me say that children's difficulties can be better surmounted if the reasons for them are understood. If children cannot represent more than a certain number of dimensions simultaneously, it is no use pretending that they can on the basis of some unshakeable belief that there cannot be any limitations to what children can do. The view that there must be no limitations is very pervasive in cognitive development although, ironically, limitations have never been denied in adults. It is quite alright for adults to be capacity limited, but apparently it is not permitted for children. The way I have defined capacity limitations as a function of age leaves abundant scope for improving performance. The nature of the task can be varied to minimize the amount of information that must be processed in parallel, or children can be taught strategies that segment the task into smaller, less demanding steps.

The assessment of dimensionality depends on manipulating the representations that are used for a particular task. This entails controlling processes that reduce the complexity of representations, including chunking and segmentation, as discussed in chapter 6. As some of the experiments discussed in chapter 3 illustrate, representations can be manipulated by careful experimental design. Such procedures can be checked using the techniques outlined in chapter 2 for assessing cognitive processes used in tasks. Thus we now have the empirical techniques to go well beyond intuitive assessment of processing loads. Perhaps most important of all, the fact that the present theory has been formulated in such a way that postulated processes can be simulated in an architecture that provides a principled way of dealing with capacity limitations ultimately provides assurance that structural complexity of concepts, as defined by dimensionality of representations, can be assessed objectively.

It should also be remembered that complexity analysis has shown that children's capabilities have probably been underestimated by research in a number of areas, including analogical reasoning, the balance scale, and hypothesis testing. As far as I know, this is the only theory that has predicted improvements to performance before they were observed. Other theories have predicted (or postdicted) performances that correspond to observation. Unfortunately these theories have a number of difficulties, probably the most important of which is that they are inconsistent with working-memory research. However, most improvements to performance have been methodology driven rather than theory driven. The many improvements to performance that have been reported in the literature have arisen from improved techniques of assessment, or from training. No previous theory appears to have predicted what children can do, in terms of complexity, ahead of observation. A good complexity analysis, combined with a principled account of processing capacity and its development, can point to new achievements for young children. So much for the dismissal of capacity theory as pessimistic!

Have I presented a stage theory? It depends on what is meant by stages. It is clear that precisely the same processes operate at all ages, at least from infancy. On the other hand, children become capable of representing concepts of higher dimensionality with age. Each additional dimension that can be processed in parallel opens up a new class of concepts that can be understood and about which a child can reason. As I have already mentioned, I believe this explains many of the phenomena that Piaget attributed to stages. On the other hand again, I propose that acquisition is gradual and experience driven. Physiological changes provide enabling mechanisms, but the concepts we have examined develop primarily through experience. Therefore I do not categorize children as "having" or "not having" a particular concept, but advocate tracing the successive acquisitions that occur as the concept develops. It follows of course that sudden, simultaneous acquisition of all concepts in a domain is not to be expected.

Perhaps the most striking implication of the theory is the correspondence between Piagetian stages and the dimensionality of representations as represented in PDP models. As growth in processing capacity permits each new dimension to be added to a representation, a new level of concepts becomes accessible, and there is more than a coincidental correspondence between these conceptual levels and the structures that Piaget postulated to underlie his stages (see chapter 6). There is an unexpectedly direct mapping from the rank of a tensor-product representation (e.g., in Fig. 2.8) to the "stages of thought" as defined by Piaget. Interestingly, this correspondence could not have been known before the recent development of PDP models of higher cognitive processes. Developments in this field open the way for fundamental rethinking of the concept of stage in cognitive development.

REASONING PROCESSES

Theories of cognition and cognitive development over the past several decades have had persistent difficulties in accounting for human reasoning in terms of logical rules and principles. This is true irrespective of whether they have adopted rules that are known to and sanctioned by logicians or have defined special psycho-logics. The picture that has emerged has been more consistent with the idea that human reasoning depends largely on memory retrieval. For example, Kahneman and Tversky's work suggested that availability of information in memory, or the degree to which a particular input is representative of a prototype stored in memory, is a more potent factor in reasoning than logical rules. In other contexts, rules and strategies, both of which are also stored in, and retrieved from, memory, have been highly successful in accounting for a huge array of cognitive phenomena. I do not want to challenge the main findings of this area of research. I have focused on the processes by which information comes to be stored in memory, that is, learning and induction processes, and the mechanisms by which strategies are developed.

The other innovation has been the emphasis on the role of structure-mapping processes, which include learning set acquisition and analogical reasoning. Though much of human reasoning can be attributed to memory retrieval, including rules and strategies, we do not have information in memory for every situation. An organism that is genuinely intelligent and adaptive must have the capability to generate new problem-solving strategies as it interacts with its environment. I have tried to show that analogies play a very important role in this process. They permit genuinely novel situations to be represented, by mapping them into structurally similar, but superficially different representations from other contexts. Furthermore, as the models I discussed in chapter 4 show, analogies play an important role in the development of strategies.

Analogies and, more generally, structure-mapping processes impose a processing load that depends on the dimensionality of the structures being mapped. Therefore, processing-capacity limitations, which affect the dimensionality of concepts that can be represented, set limits to the complexity of analogies that can be constructed. This in no way denies that even very young children have a natural facility with simple analogies. In fact, the present theory predicts that children should be capable of analogies based on relational mappings earlier than empirical studies have so far suggested. Furthermore, the ubiquity of analogies in young children only supports my claim that they are one of the most basic reasoning mechanisms. However, tasks that require concepts of high dimensionality to be mapped will impose high processing loads that are predicted to exceed the capacity of young children. This follows from the Structured Tensor Analogical Reasoning (STAR) model of analogical reasoning, discussed in chapter 5. Structure mapping is entailed in understanding a concept, because not only is it involved in learning sets and analogies, but it is presumably involved whenever a child must access the structure of a concept. Therefore limitations to analogical reasoning will set limits on concepts that children can understand.

Children can learn to deal with many tasks without understanding. There is nothing wrong with this, and in fact we all do it in a great many situations. For example, most of us do not understand how a word processor or a car work, but we can use them with varying degrees of skill. Therefore, limits to understanding do not set limits to performance in this sense. However they do set limits to the conceptual developments that are based on a particular concept. In this context we need to ask, not only whether children can perform a particular task, but whether they understand the concept on which the task is based. For example, a 3-year-old can be taught to use a simple strategy for performing at least a restricted type of transitive inference. But does the 3-year-old understand the concept of order on which the transitive inference is based? How representative is that performance of the 3-year-old's competence on ordering tasks in general? Can the 3-year-old use the concept of order as the basis for further conceptual developments; for example in domains such as quantification and number? There are plenty of ways to get around capacity limitations, but we need to examine what is achieved when we categorize children as having concepts at younger and younger ages. We need to ask precisely what the child understands in that domain, how that understanding was attained, and what will be entailed in further acquisitions.

All this illustrates the need to define the processes and mental models that are entailed in children's cognitive performances. This leads both to more precise predictions and to increased opportunities for promoting improved performance. We should not categorize children as understanding a concept in an all-or-none fashion, especially on the basis of success in a very restricted set of tests. We should ask what the children understand in that test, how they generate the responses that are observed, and how that performance would generalize to other tests of the same kind. We now possess ample empirical and theoretical tools to deal with such questions scientifically.

REFERENCES

Acredolo, C., Adams, A., & Schmid, J. (1984). On the understanding of the relationships between speed, duration, and distance. *Child Development, 55,* 2151–2159.

Acredolo, L. P. (1979). Laboratory versus home: The effect of environment on the 9-month-old infant's choice of spatial reference system. *Developmental Psychology, 15,* 666–667.

Allport, D. A. (1980a). Attention and performance. In G. Claxton (Ed.), *Cognitive psychology* (pp. 112–153). London: Routledge & Kegan Paul.

Allport, D. A. (1980b). Patterns and actions: Cognitive mechanisms are content-specific. In G. Claxton (Ed.), *Cognitive psychology* (pp. 26–64). London: Routledge & Kegan Paul.

Allport, F. H. (1955). *Theories of perception and the concept of structure.* New York: Wiley.

Anderson, J. A. (1973). A theory for the recognition of items from short memorized lists. *Psychological Review, 80,* 417–438.

Anderson, J. R. (1978). Arguments concerning representations for mental imagery. *Psychological Review, 85,* 249–277.

Anderson, J. R. (1979). Further arguments concerning representations for mental imagery: A response to Hayes-Roth and Pylyshyn. *Psychological Review, 86,* 395–406.

Anderson, J. R. (1983). *The architecture of cognition.* Cambridge, MA: Harvard University Press.

Anderson, J. R. (1984). Spreading activation. In J. R. Anderson & S. M. Kosslyn (Eds.), *Tutorials in learning and memory: Essays in honor of Gordon Bower* (pp. 61–90). San Francisco: W. H. Freeman.

Anderson, J. R. (1987). Skill acquisition: Compilation of weak-method problem solutions. *Psychological Review, 94,* 192–210.

Anderson, J. R. (1990). *The adaptive character of thought.* Hillsdale, NJ: Lawrence Erlbaum Associates.

Anderson, M. (1988). Inspection time, information processing and the development of intelligence. *British Journal of Developmental Psychology, 6*(1), 43–57.

Anderson, N. H. (1980). Information integration theory in developmental psychology. In F. Wilkening, J. Becker, & T. Trabasso (Eds.), *Information integration in children* (pp. 1–45). Hillsdale, NJ: Lawrence Erlbaum Associates.

Anderson, N. H., & Cuneo, D. O. (1978). The height + width rule in children's judgements of quantity. *Journal of Experimental Psychology: General, 107,* 335–378.

Andrews, G., & Halford, G. S. (1988). *Levels of mapping and young children's ability to make transitive inference.* Unpublished manuscript, University of Queensland, Brisbane, Australia.

Astington, J. W., & Gopnik, A. (1991). Theoretical explanations of children's understanding of the mind. *British Journal of Developmental Psychology, 9,* 7–31.

Astington, J. W., Harris, P. L., & Olson, D. R. (Eds.). (1988). *Developing theories of mind.* New York: Cambridge University Press.

Atkinson, R. C., & Shiffrin, R. M. (1968). Human memory: A proposed system and its control processes. In K. W. Spence & J. T. Spence (Eds.), *The psychology of learning and motivation: Advances in research and theory* (Vol. 2, pp. 89–195). New York: Academic Press.

Attneave, F. (1959). *Applications of information theory to psychology: A summary of basic concepts, methods and results.* New York: Henry Holt & Company.

Baddeley, A. D. (1986). *Working memory.* Oxford: Clarendon Press.

Baddeley, A. D. (1990). *Human memory: Theory and practice.* Needham Heights, MA: Allyn & Bacon.

Baddeley, A. D., Grant, S., Wight, E., & Thomson, N. (1975). Imagery and visual working memory. In P. M. A. Rabbit & S. Dornic (Eds.), *Attention and performance V* (pp. 205–217). London: Academic Press.

Baddeley, A., & Hitch, G. (1974). Working memory. In G. H. Bower (Ed.), *The psychology of learning and motivation: Advances in research and theory* (pp. 47–89). New York: Academic Press.

Baddeley, A. D., & Lieberman, K. (1980). Spatial working memory. In R. S. Nickerson (Ed.), *Attention and performance VIII* (pp. 521–539). Hillsdale, NJ: Lawrence Erlbaum Associates.

Baddeley, A. D., Thomson, N., & Buchanan, M. (1975). Word length and the structure of short-term memory. *Journal of Verbal Learning and Verbal Behavior, 14,* 575–589.

Bahr, M. P. (in preparation). *The understanding of algebra.* Unpublished doctoral dissertation, University of Queensland, Brisbane, Australia.

Baillargeon, R. (1986). Representing the existence and the location of hidden objects: Object permanence in 6- and 8-month-old infants. *Cognition, 23,* 21–41.

Baillargeon, R. (1987a). Object permanence in 3½- and 4½-month-old infants. *Developmental Psychology, 23,* 655–664.

Baillargeon, R. (1987b). Young infants' reasoning about the physical and spatial properties of a hidden object. *Cognitive Development, 2,* 179–200.

Baillargeon, R., & Graber, M. (1987). Where's the rabbit? 5.5-month-old infants' representation of a hidden object. *Cognitive Development, 2,* 375–392.

Baillargeon, R., Spelke, E. S., & Wasserman, S. (1985). Object permanence in five-month-old infants. *Cognition, 20,* 191–208.

Bain, J. D., Halford, G. S., Wilson, W. H., Maybery, M. T., & Kelly, M. E. (in preparation). *Concept of capacity in cognitive psychology.* Unpublished manuscript, University of Queensland, Brisbane, Australia.

Bakker, P. E., & Halford, G. S. (1988). *A basic computational theory of structure-mapping in analogy and transitive inference* (Unpublished Tech. Rep. No. 88/1). Centre for Human Information Processing and Problem Solving, University of Queensland, Brisbane, Australia.

Baldwin, A. L. (1967). *Theories of child development.* New York: Wiley.

Bartlett, F. C. (1932). *Remembering: A study in experimental and social psychology.* Cambridge: Cambridge University Press.

Baylor, G. W., & Gascon, J. (1974). An information processing theory of aspects of the development of weight seriation in children. *Cognitive Psychology, 6,* 1–40.

Bearison, D. J. (1969). Role of measurement operations in the acquisition of conservation. *Developmental Psychology, 1,* 653–660.

Becker, J. (1989). Preschoolers' use of number words to denote one-to-one correspondence. *Child Development, 60*(5), 1147–1157.

Beilin, H. (1978). Inducing conservation through training. In G. Steiner, *Psychology of the twentieth century: Piaget and beyond.* Zurich: Kindler.

Bell, T. S., & Kee, D. W. (1984). Individual differences in cognitive synthesis: An M-capacity approach. *Contemporary Educational Psychology, 9,* 323–332.

Berlyne, D. E. (1965). *Structure and direction in thinking.* New York: Wiley.

Best, J. B. (1989). *Cognitive psychology* (2nd ed.). St. Paul, MN: West Publishing Company.

Bitterman, M. E. (1960). Toward a comparative psychology of learning. *American Psychologist, 15,* 704–712.

Bitterman, M. E., Fedderson, W. E., & Tyler, D. W. (1953). Secondary reinforcement and the discrimination hypothesis. *American Journal of Psychology, 66,* 456–464.

Bitterman, M. E., Wodinsky, J., & Candland, D. K. (1958). Some comparative psychology. *American Journal of Psychology, 71,* 94–110.

Blasingame, M., & McManis, S. D. (1977). Classification, relative thinking and transitivity performance by retarded individuals. *American Journal of Mental Deficiency, 82,* 91–94.

Bobrow, D. G., & Norman, D. A. (1975). Some principles of memory schemata. In D. G. Bobrow & A. Collins (Eds.), *Representation and understanding: Studies in cognitive science* (pp. 131–149). New York: Academic Press.

Boole, G. (1951). *An investigation of the laws of thought, on which are founded the mathematical theories of logic and probabilities.* New York: Dover Publications. (Original work published 1854)

Boulton-Lewis, G. M., Neill, H., & Halford, G. S. (1985, August). *Levels of information processing capacity and cultural knowledge in a group of aboriginal Australian children.* Paper presented at the National Seminar for Teaching Mathematics to Aboriginal Children, Alice Springs, Australia.

Boulton-Lewis, G. M., Neill, H., & Halford, G. S. (1987). Information processing and mathematical knowledge in Aboriginal Australian children. *Australian Aboriginal Studies, 2,* 63–65.

Braine, M. D. S. (1959). The ontogeny of certain logical operations: Piaget's formulation examined by nonverbal methods. *Psychological Monographs, 73(5, Whole No. 475).*

Braine, M. D. S. (1978). On the relation between the natural logic of reasoning and standard logic. *Psychological Review, 85,* 1–21.

Brainerd, C. J., & Kaszor, P. (1974). An analysis of two proposed sources of children's class inclusion errors. *Developmental Psychology, 10,* 633–643.

Brainerd, C. J., & Kingma, J. (1984). Do children have to remember to reason: A fuzzy-trace theory of transitivity development. *Developmental Review, 4,* 311–377.

Brainerd, C. J., & Kingma, J. (1985). On the independence of short-term memory and working memory in cognitive development. *Cognitive Psychology, 17,* 210–247.

Brainerd, C. J., & Reyna, V. F. (1989). Output-interference theory of dual-task deficits in memory development. *Journal of Experimental Child Psychology, 47*(1), 1–18.

Brainerd, C. J., & Reyna, V. F. (1990). Inclusion illusions: Fuzzy-trace theory and perceptual salience effects in cognitive development. *Developmental Review, 10,* 365–403.

Brainerd, C. J., & Reyna, V. F. (in press). The memory independence effect: What do the data show? What do the theories claim? *Developmental Review.*

Brannelly, S., Tehan, G., & Humphreys, M. S. (1989). Retrieval plus scanning: Does it occur? *Memory and Cognition, 17*(6), 712–722.

Bremner, J. G. (1978). Spatial errors made by infants: Inadequate spatial cues or evidence of egocentrism. *British Journal of Psychology, 69,* 77–84.

Breslow, L. (1981). Reevaluation of the literature on the development of transitive inferences. *Psychological Bulletin, 89,* 325–351.

Briars, D., & Siegler, R. S. (1984). A featural analysis of preschoolers' counting knowledge. *Developmental Psychology, 20,* 607–618.

Broadbent, D. E. (1958). *Perception and communication.* London: Pergamon.

Broadbent, D. E. (1975). The magic number seven after fifteen years. In A. Kennedy & A. Wilkes (Eds.), *Studies in long term memory* (pp. 3–18). London: Wiley.

Brooks, L. (1978). Nonanalytic concept formation and memory for instances. In E. Rosch & B. B. Lloyd (Eds.), *Cognition and categorization* (pp. 169–211). Hillsdale, NJ: Lawrence Erlbaum Associates.

Brown, A. L. (1990). Domain-specific principles affect learning and transfer in children. *Cognitive Science, 14*(1), 107–133.

Brown, A. L., & Kane, M. J. (1988). Preschool children can learn to transfer: learning to learn and learning from example. *Cognitive Psychology, 20*, 493–523.

Brown, A. L., Kane, M. J., & Echols, C. H. (1986). Young children's mental models determine analogical transfer across problems with a common goal structure. *Cognitive Development, 1*, 103–121.

Brown, J. S., & VanLehn, K. (1982). Towards a generative theory of "bugs." In T. P. Carpenter, J. M. Moser, & T. A. Romberg (Eds.), *Addition and subtraction: A cognitive perspective* (pp. 117–135). Hillsdale, NJ: Lawrence Erlbaum Associates.

Bruner, J. S. (1957). Going beyond the information given. In *Contemporary approaches to cognition* (pp. 41–69). Cambridge, MA: Harvard University Press.

Bruner, J. S., & Kenney, H. J. (1965). Representation and mathematics learning. In Society for Research in Child Development, *Cognitive development in children: Five Monographs* (pp. 485–494). Chicago: Chicago University Press.

Bruner, J. S., Matter, J., & Papanek, M. L. (1955). Breadth of learning as a function of drive level and mechanization. *Psychological Review, 62*, 1–10.

Bruner, J. S., Olver, R. R., & Greenfield, P. M. (1966). *Studies in cognitive growth.* New York: Wiley.

Bruner, J. S., & Postman, L. (1948). Symbolic value as an organizing factor in perception. *Journal of Social Psychology, 27*, 203–208.

Bryant, P. E. (1972). The understanding of invariance by very young children. *Canadian Journal of Psychology, 26*, 78–96.

Bryant, P. E. (1974). *Perception and understanding in young children: An experimental approach.* New York: Basic Books.

Bryant, P. E. (1982). The role of conflict and of agreement between intellectual strategies in children's ideas about measurement. *British Journal of Psychology, 73*, 243–251.

Bryant, P. E., & Trabasso, T. (1971). Transitive inferences and memory in young children. *Nature, 232*, 456–458.

Bugelski, B. R. (1964). *The psychology of learning applied to teaching.* Indianapolis: Bobbs-Merrill.

Bullock, M., & Gelman, R. (1977). Numerical reasoning in young children: The ordering principle. *Child Development, 48*, 427–434.

Buntine, S. I. (1987). *The use of compensation rules: A reexamination of Siegler's rule assessment approach to the balance scale task.* Unpublished manuscript, University of Queensland, Brisbane, Australia.

Burstein, M. H. (1983). Concept formation by incremental analogical reasoning and debugging. In R. S. Michalski (Ed.), *Proceedings of the International Machine Learning Workshop* (pp. 19–25). Urbana-Champaign, IL: University of Illinois, Department of Computer Science.

Bynum, T. W., Thomas, J. A., & Weitz, L. J. (1972). Truth-functional logic in formal operational thinking: Inhelder and Piaget's evidence. *Developmental Psychology, 7*, 129–132.

Byrnes, J. P., & Overton, W. F. (1988). Reasoning about logical connectives: A developmental analysis. *Journal of Experimental Child Psychology, 46*(2), 194–218.

Campbell, R. (1991, April). *Shifts in the development of natural kind categories.* Paper presented at the biennial meeting of the Society for Research in Child Development, Seattle, WA.

Campbell, R., Donaldson, M., & Young, B. (1976). Constraints on classificatory skills in young children. *British Journal of Psychology, 67*, 89–100.

Cantor, J. H., & Spiker, C. C. (1978). The problem-solving strategies of kindergarten and first-grade children during discrimination learning. *Journal of Experimental Child Psychology, 26*, 341–358.

Cantor, J. H., & Spiker, C. C. (1984). Evidence for long-term planning in children's hypothesis testing. *Bulletin of the Psychonomic Society, 22*, 493–496.

Carbonell, J. G. (1981). Counter-planning: A strategy-based model of adversary planning in real-world situations. *Artificial Intelligence, 16*(3), 295–329.

Carey, S. (1985). *Conceptual change in childhood.* Cambridge, MA: MIT Press.

Carey, S. (1986). Are children fundamentally different kinds of thinkers and learners than adults? In S. Chipman, J. W. Segal, & R. Glaser (Eds.), *Thinking and learning skills: Current research and open questions* (pp. 485–517). Hillsdale, NJ: Lawrence Erlbaum Associates.

Carey, S. (1990). Cognitive development. In D. N. Osherson & E. E. Smith (Eds.), *An invitation to cognitive science: Vol. 3. Thinking* (pp. 147–172). Cambridge, MA: MIT Press.

Carpenter, T. P., Hiebert, J., & Moser, J. M. (1981). The effect of problem structure and first graders' initial solution processes for simple addition and subtraction problems. *Journal for Research in Mathematics Education, 12*, 29–39.

Carroll, J. M., & Mack, R. L. (1985). Metaphor, computing systems, and active learning. *International Journal of Man-Machine Studies, 22*, 39–57.

Caruso, J. L., & Resnick, L. B. (1972). Task structure and transfer in children's learning of double classification skills. *Child Development, 43*, 1297–1308.

Case, R. (1978). Intellectual development from birth to adulthood: A neo-Piagetian interpretation. In R. S. Siegler (Ed.), *Children's thinking: What develops* (pp. 37–81). Hillsdale, NJ: Lawrence Erlbaum Associates.

Case, R. (1980). The underlying mechanism of intellectual development. In J. R. Kirby & J. B. Biggs (Eds.), *Cognitive development and instruction* (pp. 5–37). New York: Academic Press.

Case, R. (1985). *Intellectual development: Birth to adulthood.* New York: Academic Press.

Case, R. (1992). The mind and its modules: Toward a multi-level view of the development of human intelligence. In R. Case (Ed.), *The mind's staircase: Exploring the conceptual underpinnings of children's thought and knowledge.* Hillsdale, NJ: Lawrence Erlbaum Associates.

Case, R., Kurland, M., & Daneman, M. (1979, March). *Operational efficiency and the growth of M-space.* Paper presented at the biennial meeting of the Society for Research in Child Development, San Francisco, CA.

Case, R., Kurland, M., & Goldberg, J. (1982). Operational efficiency and the growth of short-term memory span. *Journal of Experimental Child Psychology, 33*, 386–404.

Champagne, A. B., Gunstone, R. F., & Klopfer, L. E. (1984). Instructional consequences of students' knowledge about physical phenomena. In A. L. Pines & L. H. T. West (Eds.), *Cognitive structure and conceptual change.* New York: Academic Press.

Champagne, A. B., Klopfer, L. E., & Anderson, J. H. (1979). *Factors influencing the learning of classical mechanics.* Unpublished manuscript, University of Pittsburgh, Learning Research and Development Center, Pittsburgh, PA.

Champagne, A. B., Klopfer, L. E., Solomon, C. A., & Cahn, A. D. (1980). *Interactions of students' knowledge with their comprehension and design of science experiments.* Unpublished manuscript, University of Pittsburgh, Learning Research and Development Center, Pittsburgh, PA.

Chapman, M. (1987). Piaget, attentional capacity, and the functional limitations of formal structure. *Advances in Child Development and Behaviour, 20*, 289–334.

Chapman, M. (1989). Resources versus response competition: A false disjunction? *Journal of Experimental Child Psychology, 47*(1), 39–41.

Chapman, M. (1990). Cognitive development and the growth of capacity: Issues in neoPiagetian theory. In J. T. Enns (Ed.), *The development of attention: Research and theory* (pp. 263–287). Amsterdam: North Holland.

Chapman, M., & Lindenberger, U. (1989). Concrete operations and attentional capacity. *Journal of Experimental Child Psychology, 47*, 236–258.

Chee, Y. S. (1987). *Effect of structure of analogy and spreading activation on learning computer programming.* Unpublished doctoral thesis, University of Queensland, Brisbane, Australia.

Cheng, P. W., & Holyoak, K. J. (1985). Pragmatic reasoning schemas. *Cognitive Psychology, 17*, 391–416.

Cheng, P. W., Holyoak, K. J., Nisbett, R. E., & Oliver, L. M. (1986). Pragmatic versus syntactic approaches to training deductive reasoning. *Cognitive Psychology, 18*(3), 293–328.

Chi, M. T. H. (1976). Short-term memory limitations in children: Capacity or processing deficits? *Memory and Cognition, 4*, 559–572.

Chi, M. T. H. (1978). Knowledge structures and memory development. In R. S. Siegler (Ed.), *Children's thinking: What develops* (pp. 73–96). Hillsdale, NJ: Lawrence Erlbaum Associates.

Chi, M. T. H., & Ceci, S. J. (1987). Content knowledge: Its role, representation and restructuring in memory development. *Advances in Child Development and Behaviour, 20*, 91–142.

Chi, M. T. H., Feltovich, P. J., & Glaser, R. (1981). Categorization and representation of physics problems by experts and novices. *Cognitive Science, 5*, 121–152.

Chi, M. T. H., Glaser, R., & Farr, M. J. (Eds.). (1988). *The nature of expertise.* Hillsdale, NJ: Lawrence Erlbaum Associates.

Chi, M. T. H., Glaser, R., & Rees, E. (1982). Expertise in problem solving. In R. Sternberg (Ed.), *Advances in the psychology of human intelligence* (Vol. 1, pp. 7–75). Hillsdale, NJ: Lawrence Erlbaum Associates.

Chi, M. T. H., & Koeske, R. D. (1983). Network representation of a child's dinosaur knowledge. *Developmental Psychology, 19*(1), 29–39.

Clark, A., & Karmiloff-Smith, A. (in press). The cognizer's innards: A psychological and philosophical perspective. *Mind and Language.*

Clark, H. H. (1969). The influence of language in solving three term series problems. *Journal of Experimental Psychology, 82*, 205–215.

Clark, H. H., & Clark, E. V. (1977). *Psychology and language.* New York: Harcourt Brace Jovanovich.

Collins, A., & Gentner, D. (1987). How people construct mental models. In N. Quinn & D. Holland (Eds.), *Cultural models in language and thought* (pp. 243–265). Cambridge, UK: Cambridge University Press.

Collis, K. F. (1978). Implications of the Piagetian model for mathematics teaching. In J. A. Keats, K. F. Collis, & G. S. Halford (Eds.), *Cognitive development: Research based on a Neo-Piagetian approach* (pp. 249–283). London: Wiley.

Coombs, C. H., Dawes, R. M., & Tversky, A. (1970). *Mathematical psychology: An elementary introduction.* Englewood Cliffs, NJ: Prentice-Hall.

Cooper, R. G. (1984). Early number development: Discovering number space with addition and subtraction. In C. Sophian (Ed.), *Origins of cognitive skills* (pp. 157–192). Hillsdale, NJ: Lawrence Erlbaum Associates.

Crisafi, M. A., & Brown, A. L. (1986). Analogical transfer in very young children: Combining two separately learned solutions to reach a goal. *Child Development, 57*(4), 953–968.

Cummins, D. D., Kintsch, W., Reussler, K., & Weimer, R. (1988). The role of understanding in solving word problems. *Cognitive Psychology, 20*(4), 405–438.

Dasen, P. R. (1984). The cross-cultural study of intelligence: Piaget and the Baoule. In P. S. Fry (Ed.), *Changing conceptions of intelligence and intellectual functioning: Current theory and research* (pp. 107–134). Amsterdam: North-Holland.

Dasen, P. R., & Jahoda, G. (Eds.). (1986). Cross-cultural human development. [Special Issue]. *International Journal of Behavioural Development, 9*(4).

Dean, A. L., Chabaud, S., & Bridges, E. (1981). Classes, collections and distinctive features: Alternative strategies for solving inclusion problems. *Cognitive Psychology, 13*(1), 84–112.

De Corte, E., Verschaffel, L., & De Win, L. (1985). Influence of rewording verbal problems on children's problem representations and solutions. *Journal of Educational Psychology, 77*, 460–470.

DeLoache, J. S. (1987). Rapid change in the symbolic functioning of very young children. *Science, 238*, 1556–1557.

DeLoache, J. S. (1989). Young children's understanding of the correspondence between a scale model and a larger space. *Child Development, 4,* 121–139.

Dempster, F. N. (1981). Memory span: Sources of individual and developmental differences. *Psychological Bulletin, 89,* 63–100.

Denney, N. C., & Acito, M. A. (1974). Classification training in two and three-year-old children. *Journal of Experimental Child Psychology, 7,* 37–48.

Denny, N. W. (1972). Free classification in pre-school children. *Child Development, 43,* 1161–1170.

DeSoto, C. B., London, M., & Handel, S. (1965). Social reasoning and spatial paralogic. *Journal of Personality and Social Psychology, 2,* 513–521.

Diamond, A. (1985). Development of the ability to use recall to guide action, as indicated by infants' performance on AB̄. *Child Development, 56*(4), 868–883.

Diamond, A. (1988). Abilities and neural mechanisms underlying AB̄ performance. *Child Development, 59,* 523–527.

Diamond, A. (1989). Development as progressive inhibitory control of action: Retrieval of a contiguous object. *Cognitive Development, 4,* 223–249.

Dias, M. G., & Harris, P. L. (1988). The effect of make-believe play on deductive reasoning. *British Journal of Developmental Psychology, 6*(3), 207–221.

Dias, M. G., & Harris, P. L. (1990). The influence of the imagination on reasoning by young children. *British Journal of Developmental Psychology, 8*(4), 305–318.

Dienes, Z. P. (1964). *Mathematics in the primary school.* Melbourne: Macmillan.

Dijk, T. A. van, & Kintsch, W. (1983). *Strategies of discourse comprehension.* New York: Academic Press.

Duncan, J. (1980). The demonstration of capacity limitation. *Cognitive Psychology, 12,* 75–96.

Egan, D. E., & Greeno, J. G. (1974). Theory of rule induction: Knowledge acquired in concept learning, serial pattern learning, and problem solving. In L. W. Gregg (Ed.), *Knowledge and cognition* (pp. 43–103). Hillsdale, NJ: Lawrence Erlbaum Associates.

Egger, M. D., & Miller, N. E. (1962). Secondary reinforcement in rats as a function of information value and reliability of the stimulus. *Journal of Experimental Psychology, 64,* 97–104.

Egger, M. D., & Miller, N. E. (1963). When is a reward reinforcing? An experimental study of the information hypothesis. *Journal of Comparative and Physiological Psychology, 56,* 132–137.

Elam, C. B., Tyler, D. W., & Bitterman, M. E. (1954). A further study of secondary reinforcement and the discrimination hypothesis. *Journal of Comparative and Physiological Psychology, 47,* 381–384.

Elman, J. L. (1989). *Representation and structure in connectionist models* (Unpublished Tech. Rep. No. 8903), Center for Research in Language, University of California, San Diego.

Elman, J. L. (1991, April). *Incremental learning and the projection problem: The importance of starting small.* Paper presented at the Society for Research in Child Development biennial meeting, Seattle, WA.

English, L. D. (in press). Evidence for deductive reasoning: Implicit versus explicit recognition of syllogistic structure. *British Journal of Developmental Psychology.*

Ericsson, K. A., & Simon, H. A. (1984). *Protocol analysis: Verbal reports as data.* Cambridge, MA: MIT Press.

Evans, J. St. B. T. (1972). Interpretation and matching bias in a reasoning task. *Quarterly Journal of Experimental Psychology, 24,* 193–199.

Evans, J. St. B. T. (1982). *The psychology of deductive reasoning.* London: Routledge & Kegan Paul.

Evans, J. St. B. T. (1989). *Bias in human reasoning: Causes and consequences.* Hillsdale, NJ: Lawrence Erlbaum Associates.

Evans, T. G. (1968). A program for the solution of geometric analogy intelligence test questions. In M. Minsky (Ed.), *Semantic information processing* (pp. 271–353). Cambridge, MA: MIT Press.

Falkenhainer, B., Forbus, K. D., & Gentner, D. (1990). The structure-mapping engine: Algorithm and examples. *Artificial Intelligence, 41,* 1–63.

Falmagne, R. J., Mawby, R. A., & Pea, R. D. (1989). Linguistic and logical factors in recognition of indeterminacy. *Cognitive Development, 4*(2), 141–176.

Ferrara, R. A., Brown, A. L., Campione, J. C. (1986). Children's learning and transfer of inductive reasoning rules: Studies of proximal development. *Child Development, 57,* 1087–1099.

Field, D. (1987). A review of preschool conservation training: An analysis of analyses. *Developmental Review, 7,* 210–251.

Fischer, K. W. (1980). A theory of cognitive development: The control and construction of hierarchies of skills. *Psychological Review, 87,* 477–531.

Fischer, K. W. (1987). Relations between brain and cognitive development. *Child Development, 58,* 623–632.

Fisher, D. L. (1984). Central capacity limits in consistent mapping, visual search tasks: Four channels or more? *Cognitive Psychology, 16*(4), 449–484.

Fisk, A. D., Derrick, W. L., & Schneider, W. (1986). A methodological assessment and evaluation of dual-task paradigms. *Current Psychological Research and Reviews, 5,* 315–327.

Flavell, J. H. (1986). The development of children's knowledge about the appearance-reality distinction. *American Psychologist, 41,* 418–425.

Flavell, J. H. (1988). The development of children's knowledge about the mind: From cognitive connections to mental representations. In J. W. Astington, P. L. Harris, & D. R. Olson (Eds.), *Developing theories of the mind.* New York: Cambridge University Press.

Flavell, J. H., & Green, F. L. (1987). *Development of knowledge about mental representations.* Unpublished manuscript, Stanford University, Stanford, CA.

Flavell, J. H., Green, F. L., & Flavell, E. R. (1986). Development of knowledge about the appearance-reality distinction. *Monographs of the Society for Research in Child Development, 51,* 1–89.

Flavell, J. H., Green, F. L., & Flavell, E. R. (1990). Developmental changes in young children's knowledge about the mind. *Cognitive Development, 5*(1), 1–27.

Flavell, J. H., Green, F. L., Wahl, K. E., & Flavell, E. R. (1987). The effects of question clarification and memory aids on young children's performance on appearance-reality tasks. *Cognitive Development, 2,* 127–144.

Flavell, J. H., Flavell, E. R., & Green, F. L. (1987). *Young children's knowledge about the apparent-real and pretend-real distinctions.* Unpublished manuscript, Stanford University, Stanford, CA.

Flavell, J. H., & Wellman, H. M. (1977). Metamemory. In R. V. Kail & J. W. Hagen (Eds.), *Memory in cognitive development* (pp. 3–33). Hillsdale, NJ: Lawrence Erlbaum Associates.

Flavell, J. H., Zhang, X-D., Zou, H., Dong, Q., & Qi, S. (1983). A comparison between the development of the appearance-reality distinction in the People's Republic of China and the United States. *Cognitive Psychology, 15,* 459–466.

Fodor, J. A. (1975). *The language of thought.* New York: Thomas Y. Crowell Company.

Fodor, J. A., & Pylyshyn, Z. W. (1988). Connectionism and cognitive architecture: A critical analysis. *Cognition, 28,* 3–71.

Foos, P. W., Smith, K. H., Sabol, M. A., & Mynatt, B. T. (1976). Constructive processes in simple linear order problems. *Journal of Experimental Psychology: Human Learning and Memory, 2,* 759–766.

Franks, J. J., & Bransford, J. D. (1971). Abstraction of visual patterns. *Journal of Experimental Psychology, 90,* 65–74.

Friedman, W. J. (1978). Development of time concepts in children. In H. W. Reese & L. P. Lipsitt (Eds.), *Advances in child development and behavior* (Vol. 12, pp. 267–298). New York: Academic Press.

Garner, W. R. (1962). *Uncertainty and structure as psychological concepts.* New York: Wiley.

Gelman, R. (1969). Conservation acquisition: A problem of learning to attend to relevant attributes. *Journal of Experimental Child Psychology, 7,* 167–187.

Gelman, R. (1982). Accessing one-to-one correspondence: Still another paper about conservation. *British Journal of Psychology, 73,* 209–220.

Gelman, R. (1986). Toward an understanding-based theory of mathematics learning and instruction, or, in praise of Lampert on teaching multiplication. *Cognition and Instruction, 3,* 349–355.

Gelman, R. (1990). Structural constraints on cognitive development: Introduction to a special issue of Cognitive Science. *Cognitive Science, 14*, 3–9.

Gelman, R., & Gallistel, C. R. (1978). *The child's understanding of number.* Cambridge, MA: Harvard University Press.

Gelman, R., & Greeno, J. G. (1989). On the nature of competence: Principles for understanding in a domain. In L. B. Resnick (Ed.), *Knowing, learning and instruction: Essays in honor of Robert Glaser* (pp. 125–186). Hillsdale, NJ: Lawrence Erlbaum Associates.

Gelman, R., & Meck, E. (1983). Preschoolers' counting: Principles before skill. *Cognition, 13*, 343–359.

Gelman, S. A. (1988). The development of induction within natural kind and artifact categories. *Cognitive Psychology, 20*(1), 65–95.

Gelman, S. A., & Markman, E. M. (1987). Young children's inductions from natural kinds: The role of categories and appearances. *Child Development, 58*(6), 1532–1541.

Gentner, D. (1977). If a tree had a knee, where would it be? Children's performance on simple spatial metaphors. *Papers and Reports on Child Language Development, 13*, 157–164.

Gentner, D. (1982). Are scientific analogies metaphors? In D. S. Miall (Ed.), *Metaphor: Problems and perspectives* (pp. 106–132). Brighton, England: Harvester Press.

Gentner, D. (1983). Structure-mapping: A theoretical framework for analogy. *Cognitive Science, 7*, 155–170.

Gentner, D. (1988). Metaphor as structure mapping: The relational shift. *Child Development, 59*(1), 47–59.

Gentner, D., & Block, J. (1983). *Analogical development and novice-expert shift* (Unpublished Tech. Rep. BBN No. 5478). Cambridge, MA.

Gentner, D., & Gentner, D. R. (1983). Flowing waters or teeming crowds: Mental models of electricity. In D. Gentner & A. L. Stevens (Eds.), *Mental models* (pp. 99–129). Hillsdale, NJ: Lawrence Erlbaum Associates.

Gentner, D., & Stevens, A. L. (1983). *Mental models.* Hillsdale, NJ: Lawrence Erlbaum Associates.

Gentner, D., & Stuart, P. (1984). *Metaphor as structure-mapping: What develops.* Unpublished manuscript, University of Illinois, Center for the Study of Reading, Champaign, IL.

Gentner, D., & Toupin, C. (1986). Systematicity and surface similarity in the development of analogy. *Cognitive Science, 10*, 277–300.

Gholson, B. (1980). *The cognitive-developmental basis of human learning: Studies in hypothesis testing.* New York: Academic Press.

Gholson, B., Dattel, A. R., Morgan, D., & Eymard, L. A. (1989). Problem solving, recall, and mapping relations in isomorphic transfer and non-isomorphic transfer among preschoolers and elementary school children. *Child Development, 60*(5), 1172–1187.

Gholson, B., Eymard, L. A., Long, D., Morgan, D., & Leeming, F. C. (1988). Problem solving, recall, isomorphic transfer, and nonisomorphic transfer among third-grade and fourth-grade children. *Child Development, 3*, 37–53.

Gholson, B., Levine, M., & Phillips, S. (1972). Hypotheses, strategies, and stereotypes in discrimination learning. *Journal of Experimental Child Psychology, 13*, 423–446.

Gick, M. L., & Holyoak, K. J. (1983). Schema induction and analogical transfer. *Cognitive Psychology, 15*, 1–38.

Ginsburg, H., & Opper, S. (1969). *Piaget's theory of intellectual development: An introduction.* Englewood Cliffs, NJ: Prentice Hall.

Glaser, R. (1984). Education and thinking: The role of knowledge. *American Psychologist, 39*, 93–104.

Glaser, R. (1990). The re-emergence of learning theory within instructional research. *American Psychologist, 45*(1), 29–39.

Glaser, R., & Bassock, M. (1989). Learning theory and the study of instruction. *Annual Review of Psychology, 40*, 631–666.

Goldman-Rakic, P. S. (1987). Development of cortical circuitry and cognitive function. *Child Development, 58,* 601–622.

Gollin, E. S. (1966). Solution of conditional discrimination problems by young children. *Journal of Comparative and Physiological Psychology, 62,* 454–456.

Gomez-Toussaint, N. A. (1976). Mental processing capacity, anticipatory and retroactive abilities, and development of concrete operational structures. *Canadian Journal of Behavioral Sciences, 8,* 363–374.

Goswami, U. (1986). Children's use of analogy in learning to read: A developmental study. *Journal of Experimental Child Psychology, 42,* 73–83.

Goswami, U. (1988). Children's use of analogy in learning to spell. *British Journal of Developmental Psychology, 6,* 21–33.

Goswami, U. (1991). Analogical reasoning: What develops? *Child Development, 62*(1), 1–22.

Goswami, U. (1992). *Analogical reasoning in children.* Hillsdale, NJ: Lawrence Erlbaum Associates.

Goswami, U., & Brown, A. L. (1990). Melting chocolate and melting snowmen: Analogical reasoning and causal relations. *Cognition, 35*(1), 69–95.

Greeno, J. G. (1986). Collaborative teaching and making sense of symbols: Comment on Lampert's "Knowing, doing, and teaching multiplication." *Cognition and Instruction, 3,* 343–347.

Greeno, J. G., & Johnson, W. (1984). *Competence for solving and understanding problems.* Paper presented at the International Congress of Psychology, Acapulco.

Greeno, J. G., Riley, M. S., & Gelman, R. (1984). Conceptual competence and children's counting. *Cognitive Psychology, 16,* 94–143.

Grice, H. P. (1975). Logic and conversation. In P. Cole & J. L. Morgan (Eds.), *Syntax and semantics: Vol. 3. Speech acts* (pp. 41–53). New York: Academic Press.

Grieve, R., & Garton, A. (1981). On the young child's comparison of sets. *Journal of Experimental Child Psychology, 32,* 443–458.

Grossberg, S. (1980). How does a brain build a cognitive code? *Psychological Review, 87,* 1–51.

Guttentag, R. E. (1989). Dual-task research and the development of memory. *Journal of Experimental Child Psychology, 47*(1), 26–31.

Guyote, M. J., & Sternberg, R. J. (1981). A transitive-chain theory of syllogistic reasoning. *Cognitive Psychology, 13,* 461–525.

Haake, R. J., & Somerville, S. C. (1985). Development of logical search skills in infancy. *Developmental Psychology, 21,* 176–186.

Hale, S. (1990). A global development trend in cognitive processing speed. *Child Development, 61*(3), 653–663.

Halford, G. S. (1970). A theory of the acquisition of conservation. *Psychological Review, 77,* 302–316.

Halford, G. S. (1975). Effect of structure on learning and transfer: A possible link between learning and thinking. *Australian Journal of Psychology, 27,* 237–250.

Halford, G. S. (1978). Cognitive development stages emerging from levels of learning. *International Journal of Behavioural Development, 1,* 341–354.

Halford, G. S. (1980). A learning set approach to multiple classification: Evidence for a theory of cognitive levels. *International Journal of Behavioural Development, 3,* 409–422.

Halford, G. S. (1982). *The development of thought.* Hillsdale, NJ: Lawrence Erlbaum Associates.

Halford, G. S. (1984). Can young children integrate premises in transitivity and serial order tasks? *Cognitive Psychology, 16,* 65–93.

Halford, G. S. (1987). A structure-mapping approach to cognitive development. *International Journal of Psychology, 22,* 609–642.

Halford, G. S. (1989a). Reflections on 25 years of Piagetian cognitive developmental psychology, 1963–1988. *Human Development, 32,* 325–357.

Halford, G. S. (1989b). Reply. *Human Development, 32,* 383–387.

Halford, G. S. (1992). Analogical reasoning and conceptual complexity in cognitive development. *Human Development, 35*(4), 193–217.

Halford, G. S., Bain, J. D., & Maybery, M. T. (1984a). Does a concurrent memory load interfere with reasoning? *Current Psychological Research and Reviews, 3,* 14–23.

Halford, G. S., Bain, J. D., & Maybery, M. T. (1984b). Working memory and representational processes: Implications for cognitive development. In H. Bouma & D. G. Bouwhuis (Eds.), *Attention and performance X* (pp. 459–470). Hillsdale, NJ: Lawrence Erlbaum Associates.

Halford, G. S., Bain, J. D., & Maybery, M. T. (under review). *A structure-mapping account of human learning and set acquisition: Studies with complex structures.* Unpublished manuscript, University of Queensland, Brisbane, Australia.

Halford, G. S., & Boulton-Lewis, G. M. (in press). Value and limitations of analogs in mathematics teaching. In A. Demetriou, A. Efkliades, & M. Shayer (Eds.), *The modern theories of cognitive development go to school.* London: Routledge.

Halford, G. S., & Boyle, F. M. (1985). Do young children understand conservation of number? *Child Development, 56,* 165–176.

Halford, G. S., Cross, G. W., & Maybery, M. T. (1984). Hypothesis testing in conceptual rule identification. *American Journal of Psychology, 97,* 419–439.

Halford, G. S., & Fullerton, T. (1970). A discrimination task which induces conservation of number. *Child Development, 41,* 205–213.

Halford, G. S., & Halford, J. M. (1969). Secondary reinforcement: Signal or reward? A preliminary investigation. *Australian Journal of Psychology, 21*(2), 145–147.

Halford, G. S., & Kelly, M. E. (1984). On the basis of early transitivity judgements. *Journal of Experimental Child Psychology, 38,* 42–63.

Halford, G. S., & Leitch, E. (1989). Processing load constraints: A structure-mapping approach. In M. A. Luszcz & T. Nettelbeck (Eds.), *Psychological development: Perspectives across the life-span* (pp. 151–159). Amsterdam: North-Holland.

Halford, G. S., & MacDonald, C. (1977). Children's pattern construction as a function of age and complexity. *Child Development, 48,* 1096–1100.

Halford, G. S., Maybery, M. T., & Bain, J. D. (1986). Capacity limitations in children's reasoning: A dual task approach. *Child Development, 57,* 616–627.

Halford, G. S., Maybery, M. T., & Bain, J. D. (1988). Set-size effects in primary memory: An age-related capacity limitation? *Memory and Cognition, 16*(5), 480–487.

Halford, G. S., Smith, S. B., Maybery, M. T., Stewart, J. E. M., & Dickson, J. C. (1991, April). *A computer simulation model of acquisition of transitive inference.* Paper presented at the biennial meeting of the Society for Research in Child Development, Seattle, WA.

Halford, G. S., & Wilson, W. H. (1980). A category theory approach to cognitive development. *Cognitive Psychology, 12,* 356–411.

Halford, G. S., Wilson, W. H., Bain, J. D., Maybery, M. T., & Kelly, M. E. (in preparation). *Concept of capacity in cognitive psychology.* Unpublished manuscript, University of Queensland, Brisbane, Australia.

Halford, G. S., Wilson, W. H., Guo, J., Gayler, R. W., Wiles, J., & Stewart, J. E. M. (in press). Connectionist implications for processing capacity limitations in analogies. In K. J. Holyoak & J. Barnden (Eds.), *Advances in connnectionist and neural computation theory, Vol. 2: Analogical connections.* Norwood, NJ: Ablex.

Hall, J. F. (1966). *The psychology of learning.* Philadelphia: Lippincott.

Halliday, M. S. (1977). Behavioral inference in young children. *Journal of Experimental Child Psychology, 23,* 378–390.

Harlow, H. F. (1949). The formation of learning sets. *Psychological Review, 42,* 51–65.

Hasher, L., & Zacks, R. T. (1979). Automatic and effortful processes in memory. *Journal of Experimental Psychology: General, 108,* 356–388.

Hatano, G., Amaiwa, S., & Shimizu, K. (1987). Formation of a mental abacus for computation and its use as a memory device for digits: A developmental study. *Developmental Psychology, 23,* 832–838.

Hawkins, J., Pea, R. D., Glick, J., & Scribner, S. (1984). "Merds that laugh don't like mushrooms": Evidence for deductive reasoning by preschoolers. *Developmental Psychology, 20*, 584–594.

Hayes, N. A., & Broadbent, D. E. (1988). Two modes of learning for interactive tasks. *Cognition, 28*, 249–276.

Haygood, R. C., & Bourne, L. E., Jr. (1965). Attribute and rule learning aspects of conceptual behavior. *Psychological Review, 72*, 175–195.

Heibeck, T. H., & Markman, E. M. (1987). Word learning in children: An examination of fast mapping. *Child Development, 58*(4), 1021–1034.

Heng, W. (1990). *Children's understanding of lexical ambiguity in riddles.* Unpublished honors thesis, University of Western Australia, Perth.

Henle, M. (1962). On the relation between logic and thinking. *Psychological Review, 69*, 366–378.

Hewson, S. (1978). Inferential problem solving in young children. *Developmental Psychology, 14*, 93–98.

Hilgard, E. R. (1956). *Theories of learning* (2nd ed.). New York: Appleton-Century-Crofts.

Hitch, G. J. (1978). The role of short-term working memory in mental arithmetic. *Cognitive Psychology, 10*, 302–323.

Hodkin, B. (1987). Performance model analysis in class inclusion: An illustration with two language conditions. *Developmental Psychology, 23*, 683–689.

Holgate, R., & Halford, G. S. (1972). Secondary reinforcement: Signal or substitute reward? A further study. *Australian Journal of Psychology, 24*(2), 235–240.

Holland, J. H., Holyoak, K. J., Nisbett, R. E., & Thagard, P. R. (1986). *Induction: Processes of inference, learning and discovery.* Cambridge, MA: Bradford Books/MIT Press.

Holyoak, K. J. (1991). Symbolic connectionism: Towards third-generation theories of expertise. In K. A. Ericsson & J. Smith (Eds.), *Toward a general theory of expertise: Prospects and limits.* Cambridge, UK: Cambridge University Press.

Holyoak, K. J., Junn, E. N., & Billman, D. O. (1984). Development of analogical problem-solving skill. *Child Development, 55*, 2042–2055.

Holyoak, K. J., & Koh, K. (1987). Surface and structural similarity in analogical transfer. *Memory and Cognition, 15*, 332–340.

Holyoak, K. J., Koh, K., & Nisbett, R. E. (1989). A theory of conditioning: Inductive learning within rule-based hierarchies. *Psychological Review, 96*(2), 315–340.

Holyoak, K. J., & Thagard, P. (1989). Analogical mapping by constraint satisfactions. *Cognitive Science, 13*(3), 295–355.

Hoving, K. L., Spencer, T., Robb, K. Y., & Schulte, D. (1978). Developmental changes in visual information processing. In P. A. Ornstein (Ed.), *Memory development in children* (pp. 21–67). Hillsdale, NJ: Lawrence Erlbaum Associates.

Howe, M. L., & Rabinowitz, F. M. (1989). On the uninterpretability of dual-task performance. *Journal of Experimental Child Psychology, 47*(1), 32–38.

Howe, M. L., & Rabinowitz, F. M. (1990). Resource panacea? Or just another day in the developmental forest. *Developmental Review, 10*, 125–154.

Hudson, T. (1983). Correspondences and numerical differences between disjoint sets. *Child Development, 54*(1), 84–90.

Humphrey, G. (1951). *Thinking: An introduction to its experimental psychology.* London: Methuen.

Humphreys, M. S., Bain, J. D., & Pike, R. (1989). Different ways to cue a coherent memory system: A theory for episodic, semantic and procedural tasks. *Psychological Review, 96*(2), 208–233.

Humphreys, M. S., Lynch, M. J., Revelle, W., & Hall, J. W. (1983). Individual differences in short-term memory. In R. F. Dillon & R. R. Schmeck (Eds.), *Individual differences in cognition* (pp. 35–64). New York: Academic Press.

Hunt, E., & Lansman, M. (1982). Individual differences in attention. In R. J. Sternberg (Ed.), *Advances in the psychology of human intelligence* (Vol. 1, pp. 207–254). Hillsdale, NJ: Lawrence Erlbaum Associates.

Hunter, I. M. L. (1957). The solving of three term series problems. *British Journal of Psychology, 48,* 286–298.

Huttenlocher, J. (1968). Constructing spatial images: A strategy in reasoning. *Psychological Review, 75,* 487–504.

Inagaki, K., & Hatano, G. (1987). Young children's spontaneous personification as analogy. *Child Development, 58*(4), 1013–1020.

Inhelder, B., & Piaget, J. (1958). *The growth of logical thinking from childhood to adolescence* (A. Parsons, Trans.). London: Routledge & Kegan Paul. (Original work published 1955)

Inhelder, B., & Piaget, J. (1964). *The early growth of logic in the child.* London: Routledge & Kegan Paul.

Jacobs, P. I., & Vandevenfer, M. (1971). The learning and transfer of double-classification skills: A replication and extension. *Journal of Experimental Child Psychology, 12,* 240–257.

James, W. (1890). *Principles of psychology.* New York: Holt, Rinehart & Winston.

Janvier, C. (1987). Translation processes in mathematics education. In C. Janvier (Ed.), *Problems of representation in the teaching and learning of mathematics* (pp. 27–32). Hillsdale, NJ: Lawrence Erlbaum Associates.

Jenkins, E. A. (1989). Knowledge restructuring and cognitive development: A parallel distributed processing approach. In M. A. Luszcz & T. Nettelbeck (Eds.), *Psychological development: Perspectives across the life-span* (pp. 205–216). Amsterdam: North-Holland.

Johnson-Laird, P. N. (1983). *Mental models.* Cambridge: Cambridge University Press.

Johnson-Laird, P. N., & Byrne, R. M. J. (1991). *Deduction.* Hillsdale, NJ: Lawrence Erlbaum Associates.

Jordan, M. I. (1986). An introduction to linear algebra in parallel distributed processing. In D. E. Rumelhart & J. L. McClelland (Eds.), *Parallel distributed processing: Vol. 1. Foundations* (pp. 365–422). Cambridge, MA: MIT Press.

Kahneman, D. (1973). *Attention and effort.* Englewood Cliffs, NJ: Prentice-Hall.

Kahneman, D., & Tversky, A. (1973). On the psychology of prediction. *Psychological Review, 80*(4), 237–251.

Kail, R. (1979). *The development of memory in children.* San Francisco: Freeman.

Kail, R. (1986). Sources of age differences in speed of processing. *Child Development, 57,* 969–987.

Kail, R. (1988). Developmental functions for speeds of cognitive processes. *Journal of Experimental Child Psychology, 45,* 339–364.

Kail, R. (1990). More evidence for a common, central constraint on speed of processing. In J. T. Enns (Ed.), *The development of attention: Research and theory* (pp. 159–173). Amsterdam: North Holland.

Kail, R. (1991). Processing time declines exponentially during childhood and adolescence. *Developmental Psychology, 27*(2), 259–266.

Kalil, K., Youssef, Z., & Lerner, R. M. (1974). Class-inclusion failure: Cognitive deficit or misleading reference? *Child Development, 45,* 1122–1125.

Kallio, K. D. (1982). Developmental change on a five-term transitive inference. *Journal of Experimental Child Psychology, 33,* 142–164.

Kamin, L. J. (1968). Attention-like processes in classical conditioning. In W. F. Prokasy (Ed.), *Classical conditioning: A symposium* (pp. 118–147). New York: Appleton.

Kaput, J. J. (1987). Representation systems and mathematics. In C. Janvier (Ed.), *Problems of representation in the teaching and learning of mathematics* (pp. 19–26). Hillsdale, NJ: Lawrence Erlbaum Associates.

Karmiloff-Smith, A. (1986). From meta-processes to conscious access: Evidence from children's metalinguistic and repair data. *Cognition, 23,* 95–147.

Karmiloff-Smith, A. (1987, April). *Beyond modularity: A developmental perspective on human consciousness.* Paper presented at the annual meeting of the British Psychological Society, Sussex.

Karmiloff-Smith, A. (1990). Constraints on representational change: Evidence from children's drawing. *Cognition, 34*(1), 57–83.

Keating, M. B., McKenzie, B. E., & Day, R. H. (1986). Spatial localization in infancy: Position constancy in a square and circular room with and without a landmark. *Child Development, 57,* 115–124.

Keil, F. C. (1981). Constraints on knowledge and cognitive development. *Psychological Review, 88,* 197–227.

Keil, F. C. (1990). Constraints on constraints: Surveying the epigenetic landscape. *Cognitive Science, 14*(1), 135–168.

Kemler, D. G. (1978). Patterns of hypothesis testing in children's discriminative learning: A study of the development of problem-solving strategies. *Developmental Psychology, 14*(6), 653–673.

Kendler, H. H., & Kendler, T. S. (1956). Inferential behavior in pre-school children. *Journal of Experimental Psychology, 51,* 311–314.

Kimball, J. (1973). Seven principles of surface structure parsing in natural language. *Cognition, 2,* 15–47.

Kimble, G. A. (1961). *Hilgard and Marquis' conditioning and learning* (2nd ed.). New York: Appleton Century Crofts.

Kintsch, W., & Greeno, J. G. (1985). Understanding and solving word arithmetic problems. *Psychological Review, 92*(1) 109–129.

Klahr, D. (1984). Transition processes in quantitative development. In R. J. Sternberg (Ed.), *Mechanisms of cognitive development* (pp. 101–139). New York: Freeman.

Klahr, D., & Wallace, J. G. (1976). *Cognitive development: An information processing view.* Hillsdale, NJ: Lawrence Erlbaum Associates.

Klapp, S. T., Marshburn, E. A., & Lester, P. T. (1983). Short-term memory does not involve the "working memory" of information processing: The demise of a common assumption. *Journal of Experimental Psychology: General, 112,* 240–264.

Kofsky, E. A. (1966). A scalogram study of classificatory development. *Child Development, 37,* 191–204.

Komatsu, L. K., & Galotti, K. M. (1986). Children's reasoning about social, physical and logical regularities: A look at two worlds. *Child Development, 57*(2), 413–420.

Kosslyn, S. M. (1981). The medium and the message in mental imagery: A theory. *Psychological Review, 88,* 46–66.

Kuczaj, S. A., & Donaldson, S. A. (1982). If the boy loves the girl and the girl loves the dog, does the boy love the dog? The overgeneralization of verbal transitive inference skills. *Journal of Psycholinguistic Research, 11,* 197.

Kuhn, D. (1972). Mechanisms of change in the development of cognitive structures. *Child Development, 43,* 833–844.

Kuhn, D. (1977). Conditional reasoning in children. *Developmental Psychology, 13,* 342–353.

Kuhn, D. (1989). Children and adults as intuitive scientists. *Psychological Review, 96*(4), 674–689.

Kuhn, D. (1990). *Developmental perspectives on teaching and learning thinking skills.* New York: Karger.

Lampert, M. (1986). Knowing, doing, and teaching multiplication. *Cognition and Instruction, 3,* 305–342.

Larkin, J. H. (1983). The role of problem representation in physics. In D. Gentner & A. L. Stevens (Eds.), *Mental models* (pp. 75–98). Hillsdale, NJ: Lawrence Erlbaum Associates.

LeCompte, G. K., & Gratch, G. (1972). Violation of a rule as a method of diagnosing infants' levels of object concept. *Child Development, 43,* 385–396.

Leekam, S., & Perner, J. (1990). *Does the autistic child have a metarepresentational deficit?* Unpublished manuscript, Sussex University, Laboratory of Experimental Psychology.

Leeuwenberg, E. L. L. (1969). Quantitative specification of information in sequential patterns. *Psychological Review, 76,* 216–220.

Leitch, E. (1989). *The process of development of class-inclusion reasoning in young children.* Unpublished doctoral dissertation, University of Queensland, Brisbane, Australia.

Leslie, A. M. (1987). Pretense and representation: The origins of "theory of mind." *Psychological Review, 94,* 412–426.

Levine, M. (1966). Hypothesis behaviour by humans during discrimination learning. *Journal of Experimental Psychology, 71,* 331–338.

Liebert, R. M., & Wicks-Nelson, R. (1981). *Developmental psychology.* Englewood Cliffs, NJ: Prentice-Hall.

Light, P., Blaye, A., Gilly, M., & Girotto, V. (1989). Pragmatic schemas and logical reasoning in 6- to 8-year-old children. *Cognitive Development, 4,* 49–64.

Light, P., Girotto, V., & Legrenzi, P. (1990). Children's reasoning on conditional promises and permissions. *Cognitive Development, 5,* 369–383.

Logan, G. D. (1979). On the use of a concurrent memory load to measure attention and automaticity. *Journal of Experimental Psychology: Human Perception and Performance, 5,* 189–207.

Luria, A. R. (1976). *Cognitive development: Its cultural and social foundations.* Cambridge, MA: Harvard University Press.

Mackay, C. K., Fraser, J., & Ross, I. (1970). Matrices, 3 by 3: Classification and seriation. *Child Development, 41,* 787–797.

Maclane, S. (1971). *Categories for the working mathematician.* New York: Springer-Verlag.

Mandler, J. M. (1988). How to build a baby: On the development of an accessible representational system. *Child Development, 3*(2), 113–136.

Mandler, J. M. (1989). Categorization in infancy and early childhood. In M. A. Luszcz & T. Nettelbeck (Eds.), *Psychological development: Perspectives across the life-span* (pp. 127–139). Amsterdam: North-Holland.

Manis, F. R., Keating, D. P., & Morrison, F. J. (1980). Developmental differences in the allocation of processing capacity. *Journal of Experimental Child Psychology, 29,* 156–169.

Manktelow, K. I., & Over, D. E. (1990). *Inference and understanding: A philosophical and psychological perspective.* New York: Routledge.

Markman, E. M., & Seibert, J. (1976). Classes and collections: Internal organization and resulting holistic properties. *Cognitive Psychology, 8,* 561–577.

Markovits, H., Schleifer, M., & Fortier, L. (1989). Development of elementary deductive reasoning in young children. *Developmental Psychology, 25*(5), 787–793.

Maybery, M. T. (1987). *Information processing models of transitive inference.* Unpublished doctoral dissertation, University of Queensland, Brisbane, Australia.

Maybery, M. T., Bain, J. D., & Halford, G. S. (1986). Information processing demands of transitive inference. *Journal of Experimental Psychology: Learning, Memory and Cognition, 12,* 600–613.

Maybery, M. T., Halford, G. S., Bain, J. D., & Kelly, M. E. (unpublished manuscript). *Children's construction of series.* Unpublished manuscript, University of Queensland, Brisbane, Australia.

Mayer, R. E. (1976). Some conditions of meaningful learning for computer programming: Advance organizers and subject control of frame order. *Journal of Educational Psychology, 68,* 143–150.

Mayer, R. E. (1979). A psychology of learning BASIC. *Communications of the Association for Computing Machinery, 22,* 589–593.

McClelland, J. L. (1991, April). *Connectionist models of developmental change.* Paper presented at the biennial meeting of the Society for Research in Child Development, Seattle, WA.

McClelland, J. L., & Rumelhart, D. E. (1986). *Parallel distibuted processing: Explorations in the microstructure of cognition: Vol. 2. Psychological and biological models.* Boston, MA: MIT Press.

McCloskey, M. (1983). Naive theories of motion. In D. Gentner & A. L. Stevens (Eds.), *Mental models* (pp. 299–324). Hillsdale, NJ: Lawrence Erlbaum Associates.

McGarrigle, J., Grieve, R., & Hughes, M. (1978). Interpreting inclusion: A contribution to the study of the child's cognitive and linguistic development. *Journal of Experimental Child Psychology, 26,* 528–550.

McKenzie, B. E., Day, R. H., & Ihsen, E. (1984). Localization of events in space: Young infants are not always egocentric. *British Journal of Developmental Psychology, 2,* 1–10.

McLaughlin, G. H. (1963). Psycho-logic: A possible alternative to Piaget's formulation. *British Journal of Educational Psychology, 33,* 61–67.

McLaughlin, L. J., & Brinley, J. F. (1973). Age and observational learning of a multiple-classification task. *Developmental Psychology, 9,* 9–15.

McLeod, P. (1977). A dual-task response modality effect: Support for multiprocessor models of attention. *Quarterly Journal of Experimental Psychology, 29,* 651–667.

McNicol, D., & Stewart, G. W. (1980). Reaction time and the study of memory. In A. T. Welford (Ed.), *Reaction times* (pp. 253–307). London: Academic Press.

Metz, K. E. (1987a). *Developing representation of elements and actions: Preschooler's strategies on the pan balance.* Unpublished manuscript, Carnegie-Mellon University, Pittsburgh, PA.

Metz, K. E. (1987b). *Development of children's knowledge of the balance beam: An analysis of representation and strategy.* Unpublished manuscript, Carnegie-Mellon University, Pittsburgh, PA.

Michener, E. R. (1978). Understanding understanding mathematics. *Cognitive Science, 2,* 361–383.

Miller, G. A. (1956). The magical number seven, plus or minus two: Some limits on our capacity for processing information. *Psychological Review, 63,* 81–97.

Miller, K., & Gelman, R. (1983). The child's representation of number: A multidimensional scaling analysis. *Child Development, 54,* 1470–1479.

Miller, S. A. (1976). Nonverbal assessment of Piagetian concepts. *Psychological Bulletin, 83,* 405–430.

Minsky, M. (1975). A framework for representing knowledge. In P. H. Winston (Ed.), *The psychology of computer vision* (pp. 211–277). New York: McGraw-Hill.

Mitchell, M., & Hofstadter, D. R. (1990). The emergence of understanding in a computer model of concepts and analogy-making. *Physica D, 42*(1–3), 322–334.

Moray, N. (1959). Attention in dichotic listening: Affective cues and the influence of instructions. *Quarterly Journal of Experimental Psychology, 11,* 56–60.

Moray, N. (1967). Where is capacity limited? A survey and model. *Acta Psychologica, 27,* 84–92.

Moshman, D., & Franks, B. A. (1986). Development of the concept of inferential validity. *Child Development, 57,* 153–165.

Mulholland, T. M., Pellegrino, J. W., & Glaser, R. (1980). Components of geometric analogy solution. *Cognitive Psychology, 12,* 252–284.

Murdock, B. B., Jr. (1982). A theory for the storage and retrieval of item and associative information. *Psychological Review, 89*(6), 609–626.

Murdock, B. B., Jr. (1983). A distributed memory model for serial-order information. *Psychological Review, 90,* 316–338.

Navon, D. (1984). Resources: A theoretical soup stone? *Psychological Review, 91,* 216–234.

Navon, D., & Gopher, D. (1979). On the economy of the human processing system. *Psychological Review, 86,* 214–255.

Nettelbeck, T. (1987). Inspection time and intelligence. In P. A. Vernon (Ed.), *Speed of information processing and intelligence* (pp. 295–346). Norwood, NJ: Ablex.

Newell, A. (1990). *Unified theories of cognition.* Cambridge, MA: Harvard University Press.

Newell, A., & Simon, H. A. (1972). *Human problem solving.* New York: Prentice-Hall.

Newport, E. L. (1990). Maturational constraints on language learning. *Cognitive Science, 14*(1), 11–28.

Norman, D. A. (1976). *Memory and attention: An introduction to human information processing* (2nd ed.). New York: Wiley.

Norman, D. A. (1986). Reflections on cognition and parallel distributed processing. In J. L. McClelland & D. E. Rumelhart (Eds.), *Parallel distributed processing: Vol. 2. Psychological and biological models* (pp. 531–546). Cambridge, MA: MIT Press.

Norman, D. A., & Bobrow, D. G. (1975). On data-limited and resource-limited processes. *Cognitive Psychology, 7,* 44–64.

Novick, L. R. (1988). Analogical transfer, problem similarity, and expertise. *Journal of Experimental Psychology: Learning, Memory, and Cognition, 14*(3), 510–520.

Oakhill, J. (1984). Why children have difficulty reasoning with three-term series problems. *British Journal of Developmental Psychology, 2,* 223–230.

O'Brien, D. P., & Overton, W. F. (1982). Conditional reasoning and the competence-performance issue: A developmental analysis of a training task. *Journal of Experimental Child Psychology, 34,* 274–290.

Odom, R. D., & Cunningham, J. G. (1980). Integrating and disintegrating information: The role of perception and conception in the development of problem solving. In F. Wilkening, J. Becker, & T. Trabasso (Eds.), *Information integration by children* (pp. 169–181). Hillsdale, NJ: Lawrence Erlbaum Associates.

Ohlsson, S., & Langley, P. (1986). *PRISM tutorial and manual.* Irvine, CA: University of California.

Olson, D. R. (1970). *Cognitive development.* New York: Academic Press.

Osgood, C. E. (1953). *Method and theory in experimental psychology.* New York: Oxford University Press.

Osherson, D. N. (1974a). *Logical abilities in children: Vol. I. Organization of length and class concept: Empirical consequences of a Piagetian formalism.* Potomac, MD: Lawrence Erlbaum Associates.

Osherson, D. N. (1974b). *Logical abilities in children: Vol. II. Logical inference: Underlying operations.* Potomac, MD: Lawrence Erlbaum Associates.

Osherson, D. N. (1975). *Logical abilities in children: Vol. III. Reasoning in adolescence: Deductive inferences.* Hillsdale, NJ: Lawrence Erlbaum Associates.

Osherson, D. N. (1976). *Logical abilities in children: Vol. IV. Reasoning and concepts.* Hillsdale, NJ: Lawrence Erlbaum Associates.

Osherson, D. N., & Markman, E. (1975). Language and the ability to evaluate contradictions and tautologies. *Cognition, 3*(3), 213–216.

Overton, W., Byrnes, J. P., & O'Brien, D. P. (1985). Developmental and individual differences in conditional reasoning: The role of contradiction training and cognitive style. *Developmental Psychology, 21,* 692–701.

Overton, W. F., & Brodzinsky, D. (1972). Perceptual and logical factors in the development of multiplicative classification. *Developmental Psychology, 6,* 104–109.

Overton, W. F., & Jordan, R. (1971). Stimulus preference and multiplicative classification in children. *Developmental Psychology, 5,* 505–510.

Paivio, A. (1971). *Imagery and verbal processes.* New York: Holt, Rinehart & Winston.

Palmer, S. E. (1978). Fundamental aspects of cognitive representation. In E. Rosch & B. B. Lloyd (Eds.), *Cognition and categorization* (pp. 259–303). Hillsdale, NJ: Lawrence Erlbaum Associates.

Parker, R. K., Rieff, M. L., & Sperr, S. H. (1971). Teaching multiple classification to young children. *Child Development, 42,* 1779–1789.

Parker, R. K., Sperr, S. H., & Rieff, M. L. (1972). Multiple classification: A training approach. *Developmental Psychology, 7,* 188–194.

Parrill-Burnstein, M. (1978). Teaching kindergarten children to solve problems: An information-processing approach. *Child Development, 49,* 700–706.

Pascual-Leone, J. A. (1970). A mathematical model for the transition rule in Piaget's developmental stages. *Acta Psychologica, 32,* 301–345.

Pascual-Leone, J. (1984). Attention, dialectic and mental effort: Towards an organismic theory of life stages. In M. L. Commons, F. A. Richards, & C. Armon (Eds.), *Beyond formal operations* (pp. 182–215). New York: Plenum.

Payne, S. J., & Squibb, H. R. (1990). Algebra mal-rules and cognitive accounts of error. *Cognitive Science, 14,* 445–481.

Pears, R., & Bryant, P. (1990). Transitive inferences by young children about spatial position. *British Journal of Psychology, 81*(4), 497–510.

Peel, E. A. (1967). A method for investigating children's understanding of certain logical connectives used in binary propositional thinking. *British Journal of Mathematical and Statistical Psychology, 20*, 81–92.

Perner, J. (1988). Developing semantics for theories of mind: From propositional attitudes to mental representation. In J. W. Astington, P. L. Harris, & D. R. Olson (Eds.), *Developing theories of mind* (pp. 141–172). New York: Cambridge University Press.

Perner, J., & Mansbridge, D. G. (1983). Developmental differences in encoding length series. *Child Development, 54*, 710–719.

Piaget, J. (1950). *The psychology of intelligence* (M. Piercy & D. E. Berlyne, Trans.). London: Routledge & Kegan Paul. (Original work published 1947)

Piaget, J. (1952). *The child's conception of number* (C. Gattegno & F. M. Hodgson, Trans.). London: Routledge & Kegan Paul. (Original work published 1941)

Piaget, J. (1953). *The origin of intelligence in the child*. London: Routledge & Kegan Paul.

Piaget, J. (1957). *Logic and psychology*. New York: Basic Books.

Piaget, J., Grize, J. B., Szeminska, A., & Vinh Bang (1977). *Epistemology and psychology of functions* (A. Sunier, Trans.). Boston: Dordrecht-Holland. (Original work published 1968)

Piaget, J., Inhelder, B., & Szeminska, A. (1960). *The child's conception of geometry*. London: Routledge & Kegan Paul.

Pike, R., Dalgleish, L., & Wright, J. (1977). A multiple-observations model for response latency and the latencies of correct and incorrect responses in recognition memory. *Memory and Cognition, 5*(5), 580–589.

Pinker, S., & Mehler, J. (Eds.). (1988). Connectionism and symbol systems [Special issue]. *Cognition, 28*.

Piper, D. (1985). Syllogistic reasoning in varied narrative contexts: Aspects of logical and linguistic development. *Journal of Psycholinguistic Research, 14*, 19–43.

Polya, G. (1971). *How to solve it: A new aspect of mathematical method* (2nd ed.). Princeton, NJ: Princeton University Press.

Popper, K. (1959). *The logic of scientific discovery*. London: Hutchinson.

Posner, M. I., & Boies, S. J. (1971). Components of attention. *Psychological Review, 78*, 391–408.

Posner, M. I., & Keele, S. W. (1968). On the genesis of abstract ideas. *Journal of Experimental Psychology, 77*, 353–363.

Prokasy, W. F. (1956). The acquisition of observing responses in the absence of differential external reinforcement. *Journal of Comparative and Physiological Psychology, 49*, 131–136.

Pylyshyn, Z. W. (1973). What the mind's eye tells the mind's brain: A critique of mental imagery. *Psychological Bulletin, 80*, 1–24.

Pylyshyn, Z. W. (1981). The imagery debate: Analogue media versus tacit knowledge. *Psychological Review, 88*, 16–45.

Pylyshyn, Z. W. (1984). *Computation and cognition: Toward a foundation for cognitive science*. Cambridge, MA: MIT Press.

Quine, W. V. (1961). *From a logical point of view: Nine logicophilosophical essays* (2nd rev. ed.). Cambridge, MA: Harvard University Press.

Rabinowitz, F. M., Howe, M. L., & Lawrence, J. A. (1989). Class inclusion and working memory. *Journal of Experimental Child Psychology, 48*(3), 379–409.

Ramsay, D. S., & Campos, J. J. (1978). The onset of representation and entry into stage 6 of object permanence development. *Developmental Psychology, 14*, 79–86.

Reber, A. S. (1989). More thoughts on the unconscious: Reply to Brody and to Lewicki and Hill. *Journal of Experimental Psychology: General, 118*(3), 242–244.

Reed, S. K. (1987). A structure-mapping model for word problems. *Journal of Experimental Psychology: Learning, Memory and Cognition, 13*, 124–139.

Reese, H. W. (1963). Discrimination learning set in children. In L. P. Lipsitt & C. C. Spiker (Eds.), *Advances in child development and behavior* (pp. 115–145). New York: Academic Press.

Reese, H. W. (1965). Discrimination learning set and perceptual set in young children. *Child Development, 36*, 153–161.

Rescorla, R. A. (1968). Probability of shock in the presence and absence of CS in fear conditioning. *Journal of Comparative and Physiological Psychology, 66*(1), 1–5.

Rescorla, R. A. (1988). Pavlovian conditioning: It's not what you think it is. *American Psychologist, 43*(3), 151–160.

Resnick, L. B. (1982). Syntax and semantics in learning to subtract. In T. P. Carpenter, J. M. Moser, & T. A. Romberg (Eds.), *Addition and subtraction: A cognitive perspective* (pp. 136–155). Hillsdale, NJ: Lawrence Erlbaum Associates.

Resnick, L. B. (1983a). A developmental theory of number understanding. In H. P. Ginsburg (Ed.), *The development of mathematical thinking* (pp. 109–151). New York: Academic Press.

Resnick, L. B. (1983b). Mathematics and science learning: A new conception. *Science, 220*, 477–478.

Resnick, L. B. (1987). Constructing knowledge in school. In L. S. Liben (Ed.), *Development and learning: Conflict or congruence* (pp. 19–50). Hillsdale, NJ: Lawrence Erlbaum Associates.

Resnick, L. B., & Omanson, S. F. (1987). Learning to understand arithmetic. In R. Glaser (Ed.), *Advances in instructional psychology* (Vol. 3, pp. 41–95). Hillsdale, NJ: Lawrence Erlbaum Associates.

Restle, F. (1970). Theory of serial pattern learning: Structural trees. *Psychological Review, 77*, 481–495.

Riley, C. A. (1976). The representation of comparative relations and the transitive inference task. *Journal of Experimental Child Psychology, 22*, 1–22.

Riley, C. A., & Trabasso, T. (1974). Comparatives, logical structures and encoding in a transitive inference task. *Journal of Experimental Child Psychology, 17*, 187–203.

Rips, L. J. (1986). Mental muddles. In M. Brand & R. Harnish (Eds.), *The representation of knowledge and belief* (pp. 258–286). Tucson, AZ: University of Arizona Press.

Rock, I. (1985). Perception and knowledge. *Acta Psychologica, 59*, 3–22.

Romberg, T. A., & Collis, K. F. (1980). *The assessment of children's m-space* (Unpublished Tech. Rep. No. 540). Wisconsin Research and Development Center for Individualized Schooling.

Rosch, E. (1973). On the internal structure of perceptual and semantic categories. In T. E. Moore (Ed.), *Cognitive development and the acquisition of language* (pp. 111–144). New York: Academic Press.

Rosch, E. (1978). Principles of categorization. In E. Rosch & B. B. Lloyd (Eds.), *Cognition and categorization* (pp. 27–48). Hillsdale, NJ: Lawrence Erlbaum Associates.

Rosch, E., Mervis, C. B., Gray, W. D., Johnson, M. D., & Boyes-Braem, P. (1976). Basic objects in natural categories. *Cognitive Psychology, 8*(3), 382–439.

Rouse, W. B., & Morris, N. M. (1986). On looking into the black box: Prospects and limits in the search for mental models. *Psychological Bulletin, 100*(3), 349–363.

Rudy, J. W. (1991). Elemental and configural associations, the hippocampus and development. *Developmental Psychobiology, 24*(4), 221–236.

Rumain, B., Connell, J., & Braine, M. D. (1983). Conversational comprehension processes are responsible for reasoning fallacies in children as well as adults: If is not the biconditional. *Developmental Psychology, 19*(4), 471–481.

Rumelhart, D. E., & McClelland, J. L. (Eds.). (1986). *Parallel distibuted processing: Explorations in the microstructure of cognition: Vol. 1. Foundations.* Cambridge, MA: Bradford Books/MIT Press.

Rumelhart, D. E., & Ortony, A. (1977). The representation of knowledge in memory. In R. C. Anderson, R. J. Spiro, & W. E. Montague (Eds.), *Schooling and the acquisition of knowledge* (pp. 99–135). Hillsdale, NJ: Lawrence Erlbaum Associates.

Rumelhart, D. E., Smolensky, P., McClelland, J. L., & Hinton, G. E. (1986). Schemata and sequential thought processes in PDP models. In J. L. McClelland & D. E. Rumelhart (Eds.), *Parallel distributed processing: Explorations in the microstructure of cognition: Vol. 2. Psychological and biological models* (pp. 7–57). Cambridge, MA: MIT Press.

Russell, B. (1903). *The principles of mathematics.* Cambridge: Cambridge University Press.

Sachs, J. S. (1967). Recognition memory for syntactic and semantic aspects of connected discourse. *Perception and Psychophysics, 2,* 437–442.

Saltzman, I. J. (1949). Maze learning in the absence of primary reinforcement: A study of secondary reinforcement. *Journal of Comparative and Physiological Psychology, 42,* 161–173.

Saxe, G. B. (1985). Effects of schooling on arithmetic understanding: Studies with Oksapmin children in Papua New Guinea. *Journal of Educational Psychology, 77,* 503–513.

Saxe, G. B. (1991). *Culture and cognitive development: Studies in mathematical understanding.* Hillsdale, NJ: Lawrence Erlbaum Associates.

Saxe, G. B., Guberman, S. R., & Gearhart, M. (1987). Social processes in early number development. *Monographs of the Society for Research in Child Development, 52*(2, Serial No. 216).

Scandura, J. M. (1970). Role of rules in behavior: Toward an operational definition of what (rule) is learned. *Psychological Review, 77,* 516–533.

Schank, R. C., & Abelson, R. P. (1977). *Scripts, plans, goals and understanding.* Hillsdale, NJ: Lawrence Erlbaum Associates.

Schneider, W., & Detweiler, M. (1987). A connectionist/control architecture for working memory. *The Psychology of Learning and Motivation, 21,* 53–119.

Schneider, W., & Pressley, M. (1989). *Memory development between 2 and 20.* New York: Springer Verlag.

Schweickert, R., & Boruff, B. (1986). Short-term memory capacity: Magic number or magic spell? *Journal of Experimental Psychology: Learning, Memory and Cognition, 12,* 419–425.

Seggie, J. L., & Halford, G. S. (1968). The secondary reinforcing properties of a stimulus not associated with reward. *Australian Journal of Psychology, 20*(3), 185–190.

Sejnowski, T. J., & Rosenberg, C. R. (1986). *NETtalk: A parallel network that learns to read aloud* (Unpublished Tech. Rep. JHU/EECS-86/01). Johns Hopkins University.

Sekuler, R., & Mierkiewicz, D. (1977). Children's judgements of numerical inequality. *Child Development, 48,* 630–633.

Shaklee, H. (1979). Bounded rationality and cognitive development: Upper limits on growth? *Cognitive Psychology, 11,* 327–345.

Shapiro, B. J., & O'Brien, T. C. (1970). Logical thinking in children ages six through thirteen. *Child Development, 41,* 823–829.

Shastri, L. (1988). A connectionist approach to knowledge representation and limited inference. *Cognitive Science, 12*(3), 331–392.

Sheppard, J. L. (1978). A structural analysis of concrete operations. In J. A. Keats, K. F. Collis, & G. S. Halford, *Cognitive development: Research based on a neo-Piagetian approach.* London: Wiley.

Sherman, T. (1985). Categorization skills in infants. *Child Development, 56,* 1561–1573.

Shipley, E. F. (1979). The class-inclusion task: Question form and distributive comparisons. *Journal of Psycholinguistic Research, 8,* 301–331.

Siegel, L. S., McCabe, A. E., Brand, J., & Matthews, J. (1978). Evidence for the understanding of class inclusion in preschool children: Linguistic factors and training effects. *Child Development, 49,* 688–693.

Siegal, M., & Beattie, K. (1991). Where to look first for children's knowledge of false beliefs. *Cognition, 38*(1), 1–12.

Siegal, M., & Share, D. L. (1990). Contamination sensitivity in young children. *Developmental Psychology, 26*(3), 455–458.

Siegal, M., Share, D. L., & Robinson, J. (1989). *Appearance-reality knowledge in young children.* Unpublished manuscript, University of Queensland, Department of Psychology.

Siegal, M., Waters, L. J., & Dinwiddy, L. S. (1988). Misleading children: Causal attributions for inconsistency under repeated questioning. *Journal of Experimental Child Psychology, 45,* 438–456.

Siegler, R. S. (1976). Three aspects of cognitive development. *Cognitive Psychology, 8*, 481–520.

Siegler, R. S. (1981). Developmental sequences within and between concepts. *Monographs of the Society for Research in Child Development, 46*, 1–84.

Siegler, R. S. (1987). Some general conclusions about children's strategy choice procedures. *International Journal of Psychology, 22*, 729–749.

Siegler, R. S. (1988). Individual differences in strategy choices: Good students, not-so-good students, and perfectionists. *Child Development, 59*(4), 833–851.

Siegler, R. S. (1989a). How domain-general and domain-specific knowledge interact to produce strategy choices. *Merrill-Palmer Quarterly, 35*(1), 1–26.

Siegler, R. S. (1989b). Mechanisms of cognitive development. *Annual Review of Psychology, 40*, 353–379.

Siegler, R. S., & Jenkins, E. A. (1989). *How children discover new strategies*. Hillsdale, NJ: Lawrence Erlbaum Associates.

Siegler, R. S., & Richards, D. D. (1979). Development of time, speed, and distance concepts. *Developmental Psychology, 15*, 288–298.

Siegler, R. S., & Robinson, M. (1982). The development of numerical understanding. In H. W. Reese & L. P. Lipsitt (Eds.), *Advances in child development and behavior* (Vol. 16, pp. 241–312). London: Academic Press.

Siegler, R. S., & Shrager, J. (1984). Strategy choices in addition and subtraction: How do children know what to do? In C. Sophian (Ed.), *Origins of cognitive skills* (pp. 229–293). Hillsdale, NJ: Lawrence Erlbaum Associates.

Sigel, I. E. (1981). Social experience in the development of representational thought: Distancing theory. In I. E. Sigel, D. M. Brodzinsky, & R. M. Golinkoff (Eds.), *New directions in Piagetian theory and practice* (pp. 203–217). Hillsdale, NJ: Lawrence Erlbaum Associates.

Sigel, I. E. (1982). The relationship between parental distancing strategies and the child's cognitive behaviour. In L. M. Laosa & I. E. Sigel (Eds.), *Families as learning environments for children* (pp. 47–86). New York: Plenum.

Sigel, I. E. (1984). Distancing theory: Its implications for the development of representational thought. In W. E. Fthenakis (Ed.), *Tendenzen der Frühpädagogik*. Düsseldorf: Schwann.

Simon, H. A. (1972). Complexity and the representation of patterned sequences of symbols. *Psychological Review, 79*, 369–382.

Simon, H. A. (1974). How big is a chunk? *Science, 183*, 482–488.

Simon, H. A., & Hayes, J. R. (1976). The understanding process: Problem isomorphs. *Cognitive Psychology, 8*, 165–190.

Simon, T., Newell, A., & Klahr, D. (1991). A computational account of children's learning about number conservation. In D. Fisher & M. Pazzani (Eds.), *Concept formation: Knowledge and experience in unsupervised learning* (pp. 423–462). San Mateo, CA: Morgan Kaufmann.

Slobin, D. I. (1972). Some questions about language development. In P. C. Dodwell (Ed.), *New horizons in psychology* (pp. 197–215). Harmondsworth, England: Penguin.

Smedslund, J. (1963). The development of concrete transitivity of length in children. *Child Development, 34*, 389–405.

Smedslund, J. (1964). Concrete reasoning: A study of intellectual development. *Monographs of the Society for Research in Child Development, 129*, Serial No. 93, Issue No. 2.

Smith, C. L. (1979). Children's understanding of natural language hierarchies. *Journal of Experimental Child Psychology, 27*, 437–458.

Smith, L. B. (1983). Development of classification: The use of similarity and dimensional relations. *Journal of Experimental Child Psychology, 36*, 150–178.

Smolensky, P. (1988). On the proper treatment of connectionism. *Behavioral and Brain Sciences, 11*(1), 1–74.

Smolensky, P. (1990). Tensor product variable binding and the representation of symbolic structures in connectionist systems. *Artificial Intelligence, 46*(1–2), 159–216.

Solomon, R. I., Kamin, L. J., & Wynne, L. C. (1953). Traumatic avoidance learning: The outcomes of several extinction procedures with dogs. *Journal of Abnormal and Social Psychology, 48*, 291–302.

Solomon, R. I., & Wynne, L. C. (1954). Traumatic avoidance learning: The principles of anxiety conservation and partial irreversibility. *Psychological Review, 61*, 353–385.

Somerville, S. C., Hadkinson, B. A., & Greenberg, C. (1979). Two levels of inferential behaviour in young children. *Child Development, 50*, 119–131.

Somerville, S. C., & Wellman, H. M. (1979). The development of understanding as an indirect memory strategy. *Journal of Experimental Child Psychology, 27*, 71–86.

Soraci, S. A., Dencker, C. W., Baumeister, A. A., & Bryant, J. T. (1991). Generalized oddity performance in preschool children: A bimodal training procedure. *Journal of Experimental Child Psychology, 51*, 280–295.

Sowell, E. J. (1989). Effects of manipulative materials in mathematics instruction. *Journal for Research in Mathematics Education, 20*(5), 498–505.

Spearman, C. E. (1923). *The nature of intelligence and the principles of cognition.* London: MacMillan.

Spelke, E. S. (1990). Principles of object perception. *Cognitive Science, 14*(1), 29–56.

Spiker, C. C., & Cantor, J. H. (1979). Factors affecting hypothesis testing in kindergarten children. *Journal of Experimental Child Psychology, 28*, 230–248.

Standing, L., Bond, B., Smith, P., & Isely, C. (1980). Is the immediate memory span determined by subvocalization rate? *British Journal of Psychology, 71*, 525–539.

Starkey, P., Spelke, E. S., & Gelman, R. (1991). Toward a comparative psychology of number. *Cognition, 39*, 171–172.

Staudenmayer, H. (1975). Understanding conditional reasoning with meaningful propositions. In R. J. Falmagne, *Reasoning: Representation and process* (pp. 55–79). Hillsdale, NJ: Lawrence Erlbaum Associates.

Staudenmayer, H., & Bourne, L. E. (1977). Learning to interpret conditional sentences: A developmental study. *Developmental Psychology, 13*, 616–623.

Sternberg, R. J. (1977a). Component processes in analogical reasoning. *Psychological Review, 31*, 356–378.

Sternberg, R. J. (1977b). *Intelligence, information processing and analogical reasoning: A componential analysis of intelligence.* Hillsdale, NJ: Lawrence Erlbaum Associates.

Sternberg, R. J. (1979). Developmental patterns in the encoding and combination of logical connectives. *Journal of Experimental Child Psychology, 28*, 469–498.

Sternberg, R. J. (1980a). The development of linear syllogistic reasoning. *Journal of Experimental Child Psychology, 29*, 340–356.

Sternberg, R. J. (1980b). Representation and process in linear syllogistic reasoning. *Journal of Experimental Psychology: General, 109*, 119–159.

Sternberg, R. J., Guyote, M. J., & Turner, M. E. (1980). Deductive reasoning. In R. E. Snow, P. Federico, & W. E. Montague (Eds.), *Aptitude, learning, and instruction: Cognitive process analysis of aptitude* (Vol. 1, pp. 219–245). Hillsdale, NJ: Lawrence Erlbaum Associates.

Sternberg, R. J., & Rifkin, B. (1979). The development of analogical reasoning. *Journal of Experimental Child Psychology, 27*, 195–232.

Sternberg, S. (1975). Memory scanning: New findings and current controversies. *Quarterly Journal of Experimental Psychology, 27*, 1–32.

Stigler, J. W., Nusbaum, H. C., & Chalip, L. (1988). Developmental changes in speed of processing: Central limiting mechanism of skill transfer? *Child Development, 59*(4), 1144–1153.

Stillings, N. A., Feinstein, M. H., Garfield, J. L., Rissland, E. L., Rosenbaum, D. A., Weisler, S., & Baker-Ward, L. (1987). *Cognitive science: An introduction.* Cambridge, MA: MIT Press.

Stroop, J. R. (1935). Studies of interference in serial verbal reactions. *Journal of Experimental Child Psychology, 18*, 643–662.

Sugarman, S. (1982). Developmental change in early representational intelligence: Evidence from spatial classification strategies and related verbal expressions. *Cognitive Psychology, 14,* 410–449.

Suppes, P. (1965). On the behavioural foundations of mathematical concepts. *Monographs of the Society for Research in Child Development, 30,* 60–96.

Suppes, P., & Zinnes, J. L. (1963). Basic measurement theory. In R. D. Luce, R. R. Bush, & E. Galanter (Eds.), *Handbook of mathematical psychology* (pp. 1–76). New York: Wiley.

Surber, C. F., & Gzesh, S. M. (1984). Reversible operations in the balance scale task. *Journal of Experimental Child Psychology, 38,* 254–274.

Sweller, J., Mawer, R. F., & Ward, M. R. (1983). Development of expertise in mathematical problem solving. *Journal of Experimental Psychology: General, 112,* 639–661.

Thatcher, R. W., Walker, R. A., & Giudice, S. (1987). Human cerebral hemispheres develop at different rates and ages. *Science, 236,* 1110–1113.

Thayer, E. S., & Collyer, C. E. (1978). The development of transitive inference: A review of recent approaches. *Psychological Bulletin, 85,* 1327–1343.

Thompson, J. G., & Myers, N. A. (1985). Inferences and recall at ages four and seven. *Child Development, 56*(5), 1134–1144.

Thornton, S. (1982). Challenging "early competence": A process oriented analysis of children's classifying. *Cognitive Science, 6,* 77–100.

Touretzky, D. S., & Hinton, G. E. (1988). A distributed connectionist production system. *Cognitive Science, 12,* 423–466.

Trabasso, T. (1975). Representation, memory, and reasoning: How do we make transitive inferences? In A. D. Pick (Ed.), *Minnesota symposia on child psychology* (Vol. 9, pp. 135–172). Minneapolis: University of Minnesota Press.

Trabasso, T. (1977). The role of memory as a system in making transitive inferences. In R. V. Kail, Jr. & J. W. Hagen (Eds.), *Perspectives on the development of memory and cognition* (pp. 333–366). Hillsdale, NJ: Lawrence Erlbaum Associates.

Trabasso, T., Isen, A. M., Dolecki, P., McLanahan, A. G., Riley, C. A., & Tucker, T. (1978). How do children solve class-inclusion problems? In R. Siegler (Ed.), *Children's thinking: What develops* (pp. 151–180). Hillsdale, NJ: Lawrence Erlbaum Associates.

Trabasso, T., Riley, C. A., & Wilson, E. G. (1975). The representation of linear order and spatial strategies in reasoning: A developmental study. In R. J. Falmagne (Ed.), *Reasoning: Representation and process in children and adults* (pp. 201–229). Hillsdale, NJ: Lawrence Erlbaum Associates.

Treisman, A. M. (1964). Selective attention in man. *British Medical Bulletin, 20,* 12–16.

Tschirgi, J. E. (1980). Sensible reasoning: A hypothesis about hypotheses. *Child Development, 51,* 1–10.

Tumblin, A., Gholson, B., Rosenthal, T. L., & Kelley, J. E. (1979). The effects of gestural demonstration, verbal narration, and their combination on the acquisition of hypothesis-testing behavior by first grade children. *Child Development, 50*(1), 254–256.

Tunmer, W. E., Nesdale, A. R., & Pratt, C. (1983). The development of young children's awareness of logical inconsistencies. *Journal of Experimental Child Psychology, 36,* 97–108.

Tversky, A., & Kahneman, D. (1973). Availability: A heuristic for judging frequency and probability. *Cognitive Psychology, 5,* 207–232.

Tversky, A., & Kahneman, D. (1983). Extensional versus intuitive reasoning: The conjunction fallacy in probability judgement. *Psychological Review, 90*(4), 292–315.

Van Geert, P. (1991). A dynamic systems model of cognitive and language growth. *Psychological Review, 98*(1), 3–53.

VanLehn, K. (1990). *Mind bugs: The origins of procedural misconceptions.* Cambridge, MA: MIT Press.

VanLehn, K., & Brown, J. S. (1980). Planning nets: A representation for formalizing analogies and semantic models of procedural skills. In R. E. Snow, P. A. Federico, & W. E. Montague (Eds.), *Aptitude learning and instruction. Vol. 2. Cognitive process analyses of learning and problem solving* (pp. 95–137). Hillsdale, NJ: Lawrence Erlbaum Associates.

Vernon, P. A. (Ed.). (1987). *Speed of information-processing and intelligence.* Norwood, NJ: Ablex.

Vygotsky, L. S. (1962). *Thought and language* (E. Hanfmann & G. Vakai, Trans.). Cambridge, MA: MIT Press. (Original work published 1934)

Wallace, I., Klahr, D., & Bluff, K. (1987). A self-modifying system model of cognitive development. In D. Klahr, P. Langley, & R. Neches (Eds.), *Production system models of learning and development* (pp. 359–435). Cambridge, MA: MIT Press.

Wallach, L., & Sprott, R. L. (1964). Inducing number conservation in children. *Child Development, 35,* 1057–1071.

Wason, P. C. (1964). The effect of self-contradiction on fallacious reasoning. *Quarterly Journal of Experimental Psychology, 16,* 30–34.

Wason, P. C. (1966). Reasoning. In B. M. Foss (Ed.), *New horizons in psychology* (pp. 135–151). Harmondsworth, Middlesex: Penguin.

Wason, P. C., & Johnson-Laird, P. N. (1972). *Psychology of reasoning: Structures and content.* London: Batsford.

Waxman, S. R. (1990). Linguistic biases and the establishment of conceptual hierarchies: Evidence from preschool children. *Cognitive Development, 5,* 123–150.

Wellman, H. M. (1990). *The child's theory of mind.* Cambridge, MA: MIT Press.

Wellman, H. M., & Bartsch, K. (1988). Young children's reasoning about beliefs. *Cognition, 31,* 239–277.

Wellman, H. M., Cross, D., & Bartsch, K. (1986). Infant search and object permanence: A meta-analysis of the A-not-B error. *Monographs of the Society for Research in Child Development, 51.*

Wellman, H. M., & Gelman, S. A. (in press). Cognitive development: Foundational theories of core domains. *Annual Review of Psychology, 43.*

Wellman, H. M., & Woolley, J. D. (1990). From simple desires to ordinary beliefs: The early development of everyday psychology. *Cognition, 35,* 245–275.

Werner, H. (1948). *Comparative psychology of mental development* (rev. ed.). Chicago: Follet.

Wertheimer, M. (1945). *Productive thinking.* New York: Harper.

Whorf, B. (1956). *Language, thought and reality.* Cambridge, MA: MIT Press.

Wickens, C. D. (1974). Temporal limits of human information processing. *Psychological Bulletin, 81,* 739–755.

Wickens, D. D., Moody, M. J., & Dow, R. (1981). The nature and timing of the retrieval process and of interference effects. *Journal of Experimental Psychology: General, 110,* 1–20.

Wickens, D. D., Moody, M. J., & Vidulich, M. (1985). Retrieval time as a function of memory set size, type of probes, and interference in recognition memory. *Journal of Experimental Psychology, 11,* 154–164.

Wiles, J., Halford, G. S., Stewart, J. E. M., Humphreys, M. S., Bain, J. D., & Wilson, W. H. (1992). *Tensor models: A creative basis for memory retrieval and analogical mapping* (Unpublished Tech. Rep. No. 218). University of Queensland, Key Centre for Software Technology, Brisbane, Australia.

Wilkening, F. (1979). Combining of stimulus dimensions in children's and adult's judgement of area: An information integration analysis. *Developmental Psychology, 15,* 25–33.

Wilkening, F. (1980). Development of dimensional integration in children's perceptual judgement: Experiments with area, volume and velocity. In F. Wilkening, J. Becker, & T. Trabasso (Eds.), *Information integration in children* (pp. 47–69). Hillsdale, NJ: Lawrence Erlbaum Associates.

Wilkening, F. (1981). Integrating velocity, time and distance information: A developmental study. *Cognitive Psychology, 13,* 231–247.

Wilkening, F., Levin, I., & Druyan, S. (1987). Children's counting strategies for time quantification and integration. *Developmental Psychology, 23,* 823–831.

Wilkinson, A. (1976). Counting strategies and semantic analyses as applied to class inclusion. *Cognitive Psychology, 8,* 64–85.

Wimmer, H., & Perner, J. (1983). Beliefs about beliefs: Representation and constraining function of wrong beliefs in young children's understanding of deception. *Cognition, 13,* 103–128.

Winer, G. A. (1974). An analysis of verbal facilitation of class-inclusion reasoning. *Child Development, 45*, 224–227.

Winer, G. A. (1980). Class-inclusion reasoning in children: A review of the empirical literature. *Child Development, 51*, 309–328.

Winston, P. H. (1982). Learning new principles from precedents and exercises. *Artificial Intelligence, 19*, 321–350.

Wiser, M., & Carey, S. (1983). When heat and temperature were one. In D. Gentner & A. L. Stevens (Eds.), *Mental models* (pp. 267–297). Hillsdale, NJ: Lawrence Erlbaum Associates.

Youssef, Z. I., & Guardo, C. J. (1972). The additive composition of classes: The role of perceptual cues. *Journal of Genetic Psychology, 121*(2), 197–205.

Zaitchik, D. (1990). When representations conflict with reality: The preschooler's problem with false beliefs and "false" photographs. *Cognition, 35*, 41–68.

Zhe Chen, & Daehler, M. W. (1989). Positive and negative transfer in analogical problem solving by 6-year-old children. *Child Development, 4*, 327–344.

Zimmerman, B. J. (1974). Modification of young children's grouping strategies: The effects of modelling, verbalization, incentives and age. *Child Development, 45*, 1032–1041.

Author Index

Subject Index

A

Algebra, 19, 74, 114, 150, 233, 234, 399, 400, 401, 404, 406, 407, 408, 413, 423

Analogy, 9, 11–14, 17–20, 24, 26, 28, 34, 35, 38, 40, 41, 43, 44, 45, 56, 61–63, 69–70, 81–82, 85, 96, 98, 99, 131, 144, 145, 154, 167, 173, 174, 175, 180, 181, 182, 183, 184, 186, 190, 192, 194–196, 197–234, 240–241, 243–246, 251, 255, 258, 259–262, 269, 271, 274, 280, 285, 286, 295, 301, 302, 306, 308, 321, 325, 332, 342, 384, 388, 390, 392–395, 399, 401–404, 406, 407, 412, 413, 420, 423, 424, 434, 437, 438, 439, 444, 448, 449, 450, 451, 452, 454, 463–465, 467, 476, 477, 479

abstraction and, 11, 38, 41, 53, 56, 60, 71, 74, 131, 179, 197, 201, 202, 213, 214, 231, 233, 238–241, 245, 246, 259, 260, 261, 279, 317, 319, 320, 342, 365, 380, 382, 384, 399, 406, 469

advantages and disadvantages, 4, 41, 48, 159, 229, 230, 231, 233, 246, 266, 280, 438

classical, 198, 199, 222, 245

concrete analogs, 14, 182, 183, 190, 230, 233, 234, 388, 390, 392, 401, 404, 406, 413, 423

criteria for, 40, 202, 245, 260, 393, 394

appropriateness, 13, 214, 216, 222, 245, 406, 452

clarity, 203, 245, 395

richness, 202, 203, 245

scope, 203, 393, 395, 439

source specificity, 202, 203, 231, 233, 245

systematicity, 195, 199, 203, 206, 245, 395

validity, 199, 203, 245, 260

expressive, 203

factors affecting, 19, 211, 214, 245

categorization, 213, 245

complexity, 26, 28, 214, 245, 395, 423, 479

domain knowledge, 214, 245

encoding, 213, 245, 301, 302

goals, 214, 224, 245

processing loads, 28, 174, 192, 245, 246, 308, 413, 423, 467

stimulus similarity, 173, 212, 245, 254, 258, 260

in children, 19, 20, 26, 28, 202, 213, 216–223, 230, 243, 245, 246, 308, 325, 388, 393, 401, 406, 467, 476, 477

in learning, 19, 28, 154, 167, 173, 192, 202, 221, 225, 226, 228, 230, 231, 233, 234, 244, 246, 262, 286, 402, 407